Exam 70-622: *Configuring Microsoft Exchange Server 2010*

OBJECTIVE	CHAPTER	LESSON
1. INSTALLING AND CONFIGURING EXCHANGE SERVERS		
1.1 Prepare the infrastructure for Exchange.	1	1
1.2 Install Exchange prerequisites.	1	2
1.3 Install Exchange roles.	1	3
1.4 Create and configure databases.	2	1
1.5 Create and configure address lists.	2	2
2. CONFIGURING EXCHANGE RECIPIENTS AND PUBLIC FOLDERS		
2.1 Create and configure mailboxes.	3	1
2.2 Configure RBAC.	6	1
2.3 Create and configure resource mailboxes and shared mailboxes.	3	2
2.4 Create and configure recipients and distribution groups.	4	1
2.5 Create and configure public folders.	4	2
3. CONFIGURING CLIENT ACCESS		
3.1 Configure POP, IMAP, and Microsoft ActiveSync.	5	1
3.2 Configure Outlook Anywhere and RPC Client Access.	5	2
3.3 Configure federated sharing.	6	2
3.4 Configure Outlook Web App (OWA).	5	3
4. CONFIGURING MESSAGE TRANSPORT		
4.1 Create and configure transport rules.	7	1
4.2 Configure hub transport.	8	1
4.3 Configure Edge transport.	8	2
4.4 Configure message routing.	7	2
5. MONITORING AND REPORTING		
5.1 Monitor databases.	9	1
5.2 Monitor mail flow.	9	2
5.3 Monitor connectivity.	9	3
5.4 Generate reports.	10	1
5.5 Configure logging.	10	2
6. IMPLEMENTING HIGH AVAILABILITY AND RECOVERY		
6.1 Create and configure the Database Availability Group (DAG).	13	1
6.2 Perform backup and restore of data.	14	1
6.3 Configure public folders for high availability.	13	2
6.4 Configure high availability for non-mailbox servers.	13	3
6.5 Back up and recover server roles.	14	2
7. CONFIGURING MESSAGE COMPLIANCE AND SECURITY		
7.1 Configure records management.	11	1
7.2 Configure compliance.	11	2
7.3 Configure message integrity.	12	1
7.4 Configure anti-virus and anti-spam.	12	2

D1344855

Exam Objectives   The exam objectives listed here are current as of this book's publication date. Exam objectives are subject to change at any time without prior notice and at Microsoft's sole discretion. Please visit the Microsoft Learning Web site for the most current listing of exam objectives: http://www.microsoft.com/learning/en/us/ Exam.aspx?ID=70-662.

MCTS Self-Paced Training Kit (Exam 70-662): Configuring Microsoft Exchange Server 2010

Orin Thomas
Ian McLean

PUBLISHED BY
Microsoft Press
A Division of Microsoft Corporation
One Microsoft Way
Redmond, Washington 98052-6399

Library of Congress Control Number: 2010934186

Printed and bound in the United States of America.

Microsoft Press books are available through booksellers and distributors worldwide. For further information about international editions, contact your local Microsoft Corporation office or contact Microsoft Press International directly at fax (425) 936-7329. Visit our Web site at www.microsoft.com/mspress. Send comments to tkinput@microsoft.com.

Microsoft and the trademarks listed at http://www.microsoft.com/about/legal/en/us/IntellectualProperty/Trademarks/EN-US.aspx are trademarks of the Microsoft group of companies. All other marks are property of their respective owners.

The example companies, organizations, products, domain names, e-mail addresses, logos, people, places, and events depicted herein are fictitious. No association with any real company, organization, product, domain name, e-mail address, logo, person, place, or event is intended or should be inferred.

This book expresses the author's views and opinions. The information contained in this book is provided without any express, statutory, or implied warranties. Neither the authors, Microsoft Corporation, nor its resellers, or distributors will be held liable for any damages caused or alleged to be caused either directly or indirectly by this book.

Acquisitions Editors: Ken Jones and Devon Musgrave
Developmental Editors: Laura Sackerman and Devon Musgrave
Project Editor: Carol Vu
Editorial Production: Ashley Schneider, S4Carlisle Publishing Services
Technical Reviewer: Bob Dean; Technical Review services provided by Content Master, a member of CM Group, Ltd.
Cover: Tom Draper Design

Body Part No. X17-13468

For my grandmother, Joanie Thomas (1927–2010), who passed away during the writing of this book.

—O<small>RIN</small> T<small>HOMAS</small>

This book is dedicated to my parents, Robert and Isabella McLean, on their sixty-fifth wedding anniversary.

—I<small>AN</small> M<small>C</small>L<small>EAN</small>

Contents at a Glance

Contents

Chapter 3   Exchange Mailboxes   93

Chapter 7   Routing and Transport Rules   271

Chapter 9   Monitoring Exchange Server 2010   385

Chapter 11 Managing Records and Compliance 541

Acknowledgments

Writing a book is always a team effort, and we have the advantage of an excellent team working hard behind the scenes and, unlike the authors, never seeing their names on the front cover. We are grateful to our acquisitions editors—Ken Jones, who arranged the contract, and Devon Musgrave, who took over from Ken at a critical point—and to our developmental editors, Laura Sackerman and (again) Devon Musgrave, who guided us through the initial stages.

Possibly the key person in the entire team is the project editor, who holds the whole team together. We had not worked with Carol Vu previously, and it was a pleasure to do so. Carol was understanding and helpful when problems arose, but she also kept a firm hand on the schedule. We were also pleased that Bob Dean was available as our technical reviewer and was there to point out any slips we made and to question our assumptions.

Adherence to standards of layout and literacy is vital to the quality of a book and to the reader experience. We are grateful for the considerable contribution made by our copy editor, Bruce Owens.

Few creatures are as antisocial as an author in midbook, and we are both lucky to have understanding and supportive wives. This book must have been particularly stressful to Oksana, who had to cope both with moving house and with a young child, and to Anne, who had problems with her health. Nevertheless, neither wavered in their support. So, many thanks Oksana and Anne, you are an essential and valued part of the team.

Introduction

This training kit is designed for IT professionals who are responsible for managing the Exchange Server 2010 messaging system in enterprise environments. To make best use of this training kit, you should have at least one year of experience configuring and managing Exchange Server 2010 in an organizational environment.

By using this training kit, you will learn how to do the following:

- Install and configure Exchange Server 2010
- Configure Exchange Recipients and Public Folders
- Configure Client Access
- Configure Message Transport
- Monitor and troubleshoot Exchange Server 2010
- Implement High Availability and Recovery
- Configure Message Compliance and Security

Lab Setup Instructions

The exercises in this training kit require a minimum of four servers or virtual machines running Windows Server 2008 R2 Enterprise edition. Instructions for configuring all computers used for the practice labs are provided in the appendix. You need access to either the full or an evaluation version of Exchange Server 2010 to be able to perform the practice exercises in this book.

All computers must be connected to the same network. We recommend that you use an isolated network that is not part of your production network to do the practice exercises. To minimize the time and expense of configuring physical computers, we recommend you use virtual machines. Your virtual machine software must support 64-bit guests.

Hardware Requirements

You can complete almost all practice exercises in this book using virtual machines rather than real hardware. The minimum and recommended hardware requirements for Exchange Server 2010 are listed in Table I-1.

TABLE I-1 Exchange Server 2010 Minimum Hardware Requirements

HARDWARE COMPONENT	REQUIREMENTS
Processor	X64 architecture–based computer with either Intel 64 architecture or AMD processor that supports AMD64 platform
RAM	4 GB (though possible to perform labs on virtual machines with 2 GB RAM)
Disk Space	1.2 GB on the volume where Exchange is installed
Graphics Adapter	800 x 600 pixels or higher

If you intend to implement all virtual machines on the same computer (recommended), a higher specification will enhance your user experience. In particular a computer with 8 GB RAM and 100 GB available disk space can host all the virtual machines specified for all the practice exercises in this book if each virtual machine is configured with 2 GB of RAM. No single lab exercise in this book requires more than three computers to be active at any one time.

Using the CD

The companion CD included with this training kit contains the following:

- **Practice tests**   You can reinforce your understanding of how to configure and manage Exchange Server 2010 by using electronic practice tests you customize to meet your needs from the pool of Lesson Review questions in this book. Or you can practice for the 70-662 certification exam by using tests created from a pool of 200 realistic exam questions, which give you many practice exams to ensure that you are prepared.

- **An eBook**   An electronic version of this book is included for when you do not want to carry the printed book with you. The eBook can be viewed as a Portable Document Format (PDF) in Adobe Acrobat or Adobe Reader or in XMS Paper Specification (XPS).

> **Digital Content for Digital Book Readers:** If you bought a digital-only edition of this book, you can enjoy select content from the print edition's companion CD.
> Visit **http://go.microsoft.com/fwlink/?Linkid=199442** to get your downloadable content. This content is always up-to-date and available to all readers.

How to Install the Practice Tests

To install the practice test software from the companion CD to your hard disk, do the following:

1. Insert the companion CD into your CD drive and accept the license agreement. A CD menu appears.

2. Click Practice Tests and follow the instructions on the screen.

How to Use the Practice Tests

To start the practice test software, follow these steps:

1. Click Start, click All Programs, and then select Microsoft Press Training Kit Exam Prep. A window appears that shows all the Microsoft Press training kit exam prep suites installed on your computer.

2. Double-click the lesson review or practice test you want to use.

Lesson Review Options

When you start a lesson review, the Custom Mode dialog box appears so that you can configure your test. You can click OK to accept the defaults, or you can customize the number of questions you want, how the practice test software works, which exam objectives you want the questions to relate to, and whether you want your lesson review to be timed. If you are retaking a test, you can select whether you want to see all the questions again or only the questions you missed or did not answer.

After you click OK, your lesson review starts.

- To take the test, answer the questions and use the Next and Previous buttons to move from question to question.

- After you answer an individual question, if you want to see which answers are correct—along with an explanation of each correct answer—click Explanation.

- If you prefer to wait until the end of the test to see how you did, answer all the questions and then click Score Test. You will see a summary of the exam objectives you chose and the percentage of questions you got right overall and per objective. You can print a copy of your test, review your answers, or retake the test.

Practice Test Options

When you start a practice test, you choose whether to take the test in Certification Mode, Study Mode, or Custom Mode:

- **Certification Mode**   Closely resembles the experience of taking a certification exam. The test has a set number of questions. It is timed, and you cannot pause and restart the timer.
- **Study Mode**   Creates an untimed test during which you can review the correct answers and the explanations after you answer each question.
- **Custom Mode**   Gives you full control over the test options so that you can customize them as you like.

In all modes, the user interface when you are taking the test is basically the same but with different options enabled or disabled, depending on the mode. The main options are discussed in the previous section, "Lesson Review Options."

When you review your answer to an individual practice test question, a "References" section is provided that lists where in the training kit you can find the information that relates to that question and provides links to other sources of information. After you click Test Results to score your entire practice test, you can click the Learning Plan tab to see a list of references for every objective.

How to Uninstall the Practice Tests

To uninstall the practice test software for a training kit, use the Program And Features option in Windows Control Panel.

Microsoft Certified Professional Program

The Microsoft certifications provide the best method to prove your command of current Microsoft products and technologies. The exams and corresponding certifications are developed to validate your mastery of critical competencies as you design and develop—or implement and support—solutions with Microsoft products and technologies. Computer professionals who become Microsoft certified are recognized as experts and are sought after industry-wide. Certification brings a variety of benefits to the individual and to employers and organizations.

> **MORE INFO**   **ALL THE MICROSOFT CERTIFICATIONS**
>
> For a full list of Microsoft certifications, go to *http://www.microsoft.com/learning/mcp/default.asp*.

Errata and Book Support

We've made every effort to ensure the accuracy of this book and its companion content. If you do find an error, please report it on our Microsoft Press site at Oreilly.com:

1. Go to *http://microsoftpress.oreilly.com*.
2. In the **Search** box, enter the book's ISBN or title.
3. Select your book from the search results.
4. On your book's catalog page, under the cover image, you'll see a list of links.
5. Click **View/Submit Errata**.

You'll find additional information and services for your book on its catalog page. If you need additional support, please e-mail Microsoft Press Book Support at *tkinput@microsoft.com*.

Please note that product support for Microsoft software is not offered through the addresses above.

We Want to Hear from You

At Microsoft Press, your satisfaction is our top priority, and your feedback our most valuable asset. Please tell us what you think of this book at:

http://www.microsoft.com/learning/booksurvey

The survey is short, and we read *every one* of your comments and ideas. Thanks in advance for your input!

Stay in Touch

Let's keep the conversation going! We're on Twitter: *http://twitter.com/MicrosoftPress*

Preparing for the Exam

Microsoft certification exams are a great way to build your resume and let the world know about your level of expertise. Certification exams validate your on-the-job experience and product knowledge. Although there is no substitute for on-the-job experience, preparation through study and hands-on practice can help you prepare for the exam. We recommend that you augment your exam preparation plan by using a combination of available study materials and courses. For example, you might use the Training Kit and another study guide for your "at home" preparation, and take a Microsoft Official Curriculum course for the classroom experience. Choose the combination that you think works best for you.

Installing Exchange Server 2010

It is impossible to understate the importance of getting the deployment of Exchange Server 2010 right. The decisions that you make during deployment are decisions that your organization is going to have to live with for a long time. This is because while Exchange Server 2010 is relatively straightforward to deploy, if you make a problematic deployment decision, you may have to spend a significant amount of time implementing work-arounds for that initial misjudgment. There is an old saying—measure twice, cut once—which suggests that you should check and recheck your plans before implementing them in the real world. This counts doubly for the deployment of Exchange Server 2010.

While the Exchange Server 2010 setup routine stops you from installing Exchange if it detects a blocking issue, the checks that the routine performs are not infallible. As an Exchange Server 2010 administrator, you should be cognizant of the settings you should configure to prepare for an Exchange Server deployment, and you should not just rely on the operating system installation routine to perform the check for you. In this chapter, you will learn the steps you need to take to configure a network environment and a server host for the deployment of Exchange Server 2010. You will learn what you need to do to prepare an environment that already has an Exchange deployment, and you will learn how to install Exchange Server 2010.

Exam objectives in this chapter:

- Prepare the infrastructure for Exchange.
- Install Exchange prerequisites.
- Install Exchange Roles.

Lessons in this chapter:

Before You Begin

In order to complete the exercises in the practice sessions in this chapter, you need to have done the following:

- Have access to an evaluation edition of Windows Server 2008 R2 or later.
- Have access to an evaluation edition of Exchange Server 2010.
- Install Windows Server 2008 R2 on two separate computers. Ensure that the default Administrator account on each of these computers is configured with the password *Pa$$w0rd*.
- Have access to the x64 installation file for the 2007 Office System Converter: Microsoft Filter Pack.

> **MORE INFO** **OFFICE SYSTEM CONVERTER: MICROSOFT FILTER PACK**
>
> You can download the 2007 Office System Converter: Microsoft Filter Pack from the Microsoft download center at *http://www.microsoft.com/downloads/en/default.aspx*.

Lesson 1: Configure the Environment for Exchange Server 2010

Active Directory must be suitably prepared before it is possible to introduce Exchange Server 2010 or upgrade an existing Exchange deployment. If Active Directory Domain Services is not suitably prepared, it will not be possible to install Exchange Server 2010. In this lesson, you will learn what steps you need to take to prepare Active Directory and an existing Exchange environment for the deployment of Exchange Server 2010.

> **After this lesson, you will be able to:**
> - Prepare the Active Directory environment for the introduction of Exchange Server 2010.
> - Prepare an existing Exchange deployment for Exchange Server 2010.
>
> **Estimated lesson time: 40 minutes**

Preparing a New Environment for Exchange 2010

The first step preparing to deploy Exchange Server 2010 is ensuring that the domain and forest are set to the appropriate functional level. To introduce Exchange Server 2010 to an Active Directory environment, the forest must be configured at the Windows Server 2003 functional level or higher. The functional level that you can configure for a domain is dependent on the operating system deployed on each domain controller in that domain. A Windows Server 2003 functional level domain requires domain controllers running the Windows Server 2003 operating system or later. A Windows Server 2008 functional level domain requires domain controllers running the Windows Server 2008 operating system or later. Forest functional levels are dependent on the domain functional level of all the domains in a forest. The Windows Server 2003 forest functional level can be set only if all of the domains in the forest are configured at the Windows Server 2003 domain functional level or higher. In addition to the Windows Server 2003 forest functional level requirement, it is necessary for the environment to meet the following conditions:

- The computer that holds the Schema Master role must be running the Windows Server 2003 operating system or later.
- The computer that functions as the Global Catalog server at each site must be running the Windows Server 2003 operating system with Service Pack 1 or later.

Although Microsoft Exchange Server 2010 became available after the release of Windows Server 2008 R2, there are many real-world networks where domains are not set at the Windows Server 2003 functional level or higher. This may be because older Windows 2000 domain controllers are still present on the network. It also may be because administrators never raised the functional level on networks that initially had Windows 2000 or Windows NT domain controllers when those domain controllers were eventually decommissioned. You can view the domain and forest functional level using the Active Directory Domains and Trusts console, as shown in Figure 1-1. You can also raise the domain and forest functional levels using this console. You will modify functional levels in the first practice exercise at the end of this chapter.

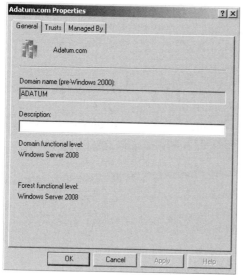

FIGURE 1-1 View functional level

Once you have ensured that the domain and forest are set to the appropriate level and that the Global Catalog servers and Schema Master meet the minimum requirements, you need to perform three steps prior to introducing the first Exchange Server 2010 server in your environment.

- Prepare the Active Directory Schema
- Prepare Active Directory
- Prepare domains that will host Exchange Server 2010

You must complete additional preliminary steps required if your organization has an existing Exchange Server 2003 deployment. You will learn about these steps later in this lesson.

 EXAM TIP

The 70-662 exam objectives do not directly address the Unified Messaging role.

Prepare Schema

If your environment does not have an existing Exchange 2003 deployment, the first step that you need to take to prepare Active Directory is to run the command *Setup /PrepareSchema*. This can be done separately, or it can be done automatically as part of the installation of the first Exchange Server 2010 server in the organization. As the 70-662 exam concentrates on the separate predeployment steps, these steps will are given separate treatment in this chapter. Prior to running the *Setup /PrepareSchema* command, you must ensure that the following conditions are met:

- You must execute this command from a user account that is a member of both the Schema Admins group and the Enterprise Admins group.
- You must execute this command on a 64-bit computer in the same Active Directory domain and same Active Directory site as the computer that holds the Schema Master role.
- The forest functional level is set to Windows Server 2003 or higher.
- The computer hosting the Schema Master role is running the Windows Server 2003 operating system or later operating system, such as Windows Server 2008.
- Computers that function as Global Catalog Servers in each site are running the Windows Server 2003 operating system with Service Pack 1 or later or a later operating system, such as Windows Server 2008.

You can determine which computer in your environment holds the Schema Master role using the Active Directory Schema snap-in. This snap-in becomes available for custom MMCs when you run the command *regsvr32 schmmgmt.dll*. You can then view the Schema Master by selecting Operations Master from the File menu, as shown in Figure 1-2. You can also determine which computer holds the Schema Master role by running the command *dsquery server –hasfsmo schema* from an elevated command prompt.

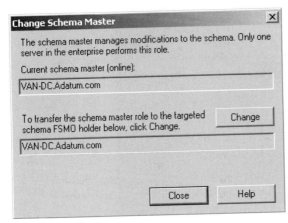

FIGURE 1-2 Locate Schema Master

You should wait for the changes that running this command makes to replicate across your organization prior to performing the step of preparing Active Directory. If your organization's domain controllers are running the Windows Server 2003 operating system, you can track replication across the domain using the Active Directory Replication Monitor tool (replmon .exe), which is part of the Windows Server 2003 Support Tools. If your organization's domain controllers are running the Windows Server 2008 operating system or later, you can use the repadmin.exe tool to monitor, diagnose, and troubleshoot replication issues.

MORE INFO **MONITOR REPLICATION WITH REPADMIN**

To learn more about monitoring Active Directory replication with the repadmin.exe tool, consult the following link on TechNet: *http://technet.microsoft.com/en-us/library/cc770963(WS.10).aspx*.

 Quick Check

- Which security group must a user be a member of to successfully run the command *setup /PrepareSchema*?

Quick Check Answer

- Enterprise Admins and Schema Admins.

Preparing Active Directory

Once the changes introduced by running *Setup /PrepareSchema* have propagated throughout the organization, you need to run the *Setup /PrepareAD* command. You will need to specify the name of the Exchange organization that you are creating if no present organization exists. Figure 1-3 shows the execution of this command in an Active Directory environment that does not have an existing Exchange organization.

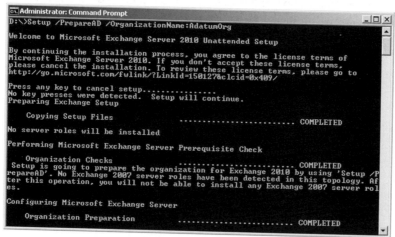

FIGURE 1-3 Configuring Active Directory with Exchange Organization information

Running the *Setup /PrepareAD /OrganizationName* command accomplishes the following:

- Creates the Microsoft Exchange container if it is not already present. A Microsoft Exchange container will be present if there is an existing Exchange organization.
- Verifies that the schema has been updated.

- Creates the containers and objects under the CN=<Organization Name>,CN=Microsoft Exchange,CN=Services,CN=Configuration,DC=<root domain>.
- Creates the default Accepted Domains entry based on the forest root namespace.
- Sets permissions in the configuration partition.
- Creates the Microsoft Exchange Security Groups OU in the root domain. Creates the following groups within this OU:
  - Exchange Organization Administrators
  - Exchange Recipient Administrators
  - Exchange Servers
  - Exchange View-Only Administrators
  - Exchange Public Folder Administrators
  - ExchangeLegacyInterop
- Prepares the local domain for the introduction of Exchange. This means that it is not necessary to run the *Setup /PrepareDomain* command in the specific domain where you ran the *Setup /PrepareAD* command.

This command must be run using a user account that is a member of the Enterprise Admins group. Like the *Setup /PrepareSchema* command, you must run this command on a computer that is in the same domain and Active Directory site as the computer that holds the Schema Master role. You learned how to determine which computer hosts the Schema Master role earlier in this lesson. You should ensure that the changes introduced by running this command are able to propagate across your organization before preparing domains for the introduction of Exchange Server 2010 using the *Setup /PrepareDomain* command. You learned how to track and verify Active Directory replication earlier in this lesson.

Preparing Individual Domains for the Introduction of Exchange

The final step in preparing Active Directory for the introduction of Exchange Server 2010 is to run the *Setup /PrepareDomain* or *Setup /PrepareAllDomains* command. The *Setup /PrepareAllDomains* command performs the same function as the *Setup /PrepareDomain* command, except that it prepares all domains in the forest rather than a specific domain. Accounts used to run this command must be configured as follows:

- The account used to run *Setup /PrepareAllDomains* command must be a member of the Enterprise Admins group.
- If the domain was created prior to the execution of the *Setup /PrepareAD* command and you are running *Setup /PrepareDomain*, the user account that is used to run this command must be a member of the Domain Admins group in the domain the command is being run against.
- If the domain was created after the execution of the *Setup /PrepareAD* command, the account used to run *Setup /PrepareDomain* must be a member of the Exchange Organization Administrators group and the Domain Admins group in the domain that the command is being run against.

Running *Setup /PrepareDomain* performs the following tasks:

- Configures permissions for Exchange Servers, Exchange Organization Administrators, Authenticated Users, Exchange Servers, Exchange Recipient Administrators, and Exchange Mailbox Administrators groups
- Creates a domain global group called *Exchange Install Domain Servers*

It is not necessary to run this command in the domain where you ran the *Setup /PrepareAD* command, as running *Setup /PrepareAD* also prepares the local domain.

> **MORE INFO** **PREPARING THE ACTIVE DIRECTORY ENVIRONMENT**
>
> For more information on preparing Active Directory and domains, consult the following document on TechNet: *http://technet.microsoft.com/en-us/library/bb125224.aspx.*

Preparing for Coexistence and Migration

As it is not possible to directly upgrade a server running Exchange Server 2003 or Exchange Server 2007 to Exchange Server 2010, it is necessary to plan for a period of coexistence between the two different versions of the messaging system. This period of coexistence will allow the migration of organizational resources from servers running the previous version of Exchange to Exchange Server 2010. Exchange Server 2010 supports coexistence with Exchange Server 2003, Exchange Server 2007, and mixed Exchange Server 2003 and Exchange Server 2007 environments. Exchange Server 2010 does not support coexistence with Exchange 2000 Server organizations. To migrate from Exchange 2000 to Exchange Server 2010, you must first migrate to either an Exchange Server 2003 or an Exchange Server 2007 organization.

> **NOTE** **UPGRADE AND MIGRATION TERMINOLOGY**
>
> In the exam objectives, "migration" in this sense means moving from one Exchange version to another. In the exam objectives, the term "upgrade" implies a direct in-place upgrade, which is not possible. In the Exchange documentation, the term "migration" is used only to discuss moving from a foreign messaging system to Exchange or from Exchange to a foreign messaging system. In the Exchange documentation, "upgrade" is used when moving data from one server, such as an Exchange Server 2007 mailbox server to an Exchange Server 2010 mailbox server. In the exam, the context is explained, and you should remember that you cannot directly upgrade a server running one version of Exchange to another.

Preparing an Exchange Server 2003 Environment for Exchange 2010

If your organization has an existing Exchange Server 2003 deployment, you must run the *Setup /PrepareLegacyExchangePermissions* command prior to running the *Setup /PrepareSchema* command. Running this command ensures that the Exchange 2003 Recipient

Update Service will function correctly after you update the Active Directory schema using the *Setup /PrepareSchema* command.

There are two ways to run *Setup /PrepareLegacyExchangePermissions*. If you run the command without any additional options, all domains in the forest are prepared for Exchange Server 2010. As an alternative, you can run the command in each domain in the forest, though you need to ensure that you run the command in the domain that holds the server that holds the schema master role first.

The user account that runs the command *Setup /PrepareLegacyExchangePermissions* with the target, as all domains in the forest must be a member of the Enterprise Admins group. If the command is being run for a specific domain, the account used to run the command must be a member of the Domain Admins group and must have been delegated the Exchange Full Administrator permissions in the existing Exchange Server 2003 infrastructure.

> **MORE INFO   PREPARE LEGACY EXCHANGE PERMISSIONS**
>
> To learn more about preparing legacy exchange permissions in an Exchange Server 2003 organization prior to the deployment of Exchange Server 2010, consult the following document on TechNet: *http://technet.microsoft.com/en-us/library/aa997914.aspx.*

When preparing for coexistence between Exchange Server 2003 and Exchange Server 2010, consider the following:

- Exchange Server 2010 can coexist with an Exchange Server 2003 organization only if that organization is configured to use Native rather than Mixed mode. An Exchange Server 2003 organization in Mixed mode will need to be converted to Native mode before Exchange Server 2010 can be introduced.

- Existing Exchange Server 2003 servers have Service Pack 2 installed prior to beginning Exchange Server 2010 deployment.

- Introduce servers in Internet-facing sites first.

- Deploy Exchange Server 2010 roles in the following order: Client Access, Hub Transport, Mailbox, and Unified Messaging. You can also choose to deploy a typical Exchange Server 2010 installation where you deploy these roles at the same time.

If the existing Exchange 2003 organization contains more than one routing group and you are intending to configure more than one routing group connector between Exchange 2003 routing groups and Exchange 2010, you will need to configure Exchange Server 2003 to suppress link state updates. You perform this procedure by using the Registry Editor to modify the registry on each Exchange Server 2003 server in the organization.

> **MORE INFO   EXCHANGE 2003 AND EXCHANGE 2010 COEXISTENCE**
>
> To learn more about deploying Exchange Server 2010 in an environment that has an existing Exchange Server 2003 deployment, consult the following TechNet document: *http://technet.microsoft.com/en-us/library/aa998186.aspx.*

Preparing Exchange 2007 Coexistence

Preparing for coexistence between Exchange Server 2007 and Exchange Server 2010 is simpler than preparing for coexistence with Exchange Server 2003. When preparing for coexistence between Exchange Server 2007 and Exchange Server 2010, consider the following:

- It is not necessary to run *Setup /PrepareLegacyExchangePermissions* when preparing to deploy Exchange Server 2010 in an existing Exchange Server 2007 organization.

- You do need to upgrade all servers running Exchange Server 2007 to Exchange Server 2007 Service Pack 2 before coexistence with Exchange Server 2010 is possible.

- You should deploy the first Exchange Server 2010 servers in Internet-facing Active Directory sites. This is because Client Access proxying works from Exchange Server 2010 Client Access servers to Exchange Server 2007 Client Access servers but does not work in the opposite direction.

- You should deploy Exchange Server 2010 roles in the following order: Client Access, Hub Transport, Mailbox, and Unified Messaging. You can also choose to deploy a typical Exchange Server 2010 installation where you deploy these roles at the same time.

EXAM TIP ACTIVE DIRECTORY PREPARATION

Know the order in which you must use the *Setup /PrepareSchema*, *Setup /PrepareAD*, and *Setup /PrepareDomain* commands. Know the circumstances under which you must use the *Setup /PrepareLegacyExchangePermissions* command.

Lesson Summary

- The forest must be at the Windows Server 2003 functional level or later before it is possible to deploy Exchange Server 2010.

- The Schema Master should be running Windows Server 2003 or later.

- At least one global catalog server in each site should be running Windows Server 2003 Service Pack 1 or later.

- You should run *Setup /PrepareLegacyExchangePermissions* if your organization has an existing Exchange Server 2003 organization. This command should be run by a user account that is a member of the Enterprise Admins group and that has been delegated the Exchange Full Administrator role.

- You should run *Setup /PrepareSchema* on a computer with an x64 operating system in the same domain and site as the computer hosting the Schema Master role. This command should be run using a user account that is a member of the Enterprise Admins and Schema Admins groups.

- After running *Setup /PrepareSchema*, run the *Setup /PrepareAD* command. This command must be run.

- The *Setup /PrepareAllDomains* command can be used to prepare all domains for Exchange Server 2010. The *Setup /PrepareAllDomains* command must be run by a member of the Enterprise Admins group. Alternatively, *Setup /PrepareDomain* can be run on a per-domain basis. User accounts that are used to run this command must be a member of the Domain Admins group and a member of the Exchange Organization Administrators group if the domain was created after Exchange Server 2010 was deployed.

- You can introduce Exchange Server 2010 into an Exchange Server 2003 environment only if the Exchange Server 2003 organization is in Native mode.

- In coexistence scenarios, deploy Exchange Server 2010 roles in the following order: Client Access, Hub Transport, Mailbox, and Unified Messaging.

Lesson Review

You can use the following questions to test your knowledge of the information in Lesson 1, "Configure the Environment for Exchange Server 2010." The questions are also available on the companion CD if you prefer to review them in electronic form.

> **NOTE ANSWERS**
>
> Answers to these questions and explanations of why each answer choice is correct or incorrect are located in the "Answers" section at the end of the book.

1. In which of the following circumstances should you run the command *Setup /PrepareLegacyExchangePermissions*?

   A. Your organization has an existing Exchange Server 2010 organization.

   B. Your organization has an existing Exchange Server 2003 organization.

   C. Your organization has an existing Exchange Server 2007 organization.

   D. Exchange has not previously been deployed in your organization.

2. You work for an Australian government department. You are preparing to deploy Exchange Server 2010 to your organization's Traralgon site. All domain controllers at the Traralgon site have Windows Server 2003 Standard edition (x86) installed. One of the domain controllers at the Traralgon site functions as a global catalog server. Which of the following steps allows you to deploy Exchange Server 2010 to this site while minimizing the amount of administrative effort involved?

   A. Upgrade all domain controllers at the Traralgon site to Windows Server 2008 Standard edition (x86)

   B. Upgrade all domain controllers at the Traralgon site to Windows Server 2008 R2 Standard edition (x64)

   C. Ensure that Service Pack 1 or later is installed on each domain controller running Windows Server 2003 Standard Edition at the Traralgon site

   D. Upgrade all domain controllers at the Traralgon site to Windows Server 2003 R2 Enterprise edition (x64)

3. Your organization has Exchange Server 2003 deployed as a messaging solution. You are planning a period of coexistence between Exchange Server 2003 and Exchange Server 2010. Which of the following steps should you take to prepare the computers that host Exchange Server 2003 for the introduction of Exchange Server 2010?

   A. Ensure that the servers are configured with Exchange Server 2003 Service Pack 1

   B. Ensure that the servers hosting Exchange Server 2003 are upgraded to Windows Server 2008

   C. Ensure that the servers hosting Exchange Server 2003 are upgraded to Windows Server 2003 R2

   D. Ensure that the servers are configured with Exchange Server 2003 Service Pack 2

4. Your existing Exchange Server 2003 organization contains three routing groups. As a part of configuring your existing organization for coexistence with Exchange Server 2010, you need to suppress minor link state updates. Which of the following tools can you use to accomplish this goal?

   A. Registry Editor

   B. Exchange Management Console

   C. Exchange Management Shell

   D. Exchange System Manager

5. Which of the following commands can you use to determine which computer in your organization holds the Schema Master role?

   A. *dsquery*

   B. *dsget*

   C. *dsadd*

   D. *dsmod*

Lesson 2: Configure the Server to Host Exchange Server 2010

You can install Exchange Server 2010 only on an appropriately prepared host server. This server must meet the minimum hardware requirements and must have an x64 version of the Windows Server 2008 Service Pack 2 or Windows Server 2008 R2 operating system installed. It is also necessary to install specific roles, role services, and features prior to attempting to deploy specific Exchange Server 2010 roles. The roles that must be deployed depend on the Exchange roles you intend the server to host. In this lesson, you will learn what steps you need to take to configure a server so that it is able to host Exchange Server 2010 roles.

> **After this lesson, you will be able to:**
>
> - Determine which software components need to be installed prior to deploying Exchange Server 2010.
> - Determine which Windows server roles and features you should configure prior to deploying Exchange Server 2010.
>
> **Estimated lesson time: 40 minutes**

Hardware and Software Requirements

Microsoft provides support for production Exchange Server 2010 servers that meet a minimum set of hardware requirements. If you deploy Exchange Server 2010 in a production environment with the expectation that Microsoft will support the configuration, you should ensure that the servers meet the minimum supported hardware requirements. When you deploy Exchange Server 2010 to a test environment, it is possible to use hardware that does not meet all of the minimum supported requirements. On top of a network card and video adapter, the minimum supported hardware requirements for Exchange Server 2010 are as follows:

- x64 architecture-based processor that supports the Intel x64 architecture or the AMD64 architecture.
- Minimum of 4 GB of RAM if one role is deployed. If the Hub Transport, Client Access, and Mailbox server roles are all deployed on the same server, a minimum of 10 GB of RAM is the minimum supported hardware configuration. An additional 3 to 30 MB of RAM should be provided for each mailbox hosted on the server.
- 1.2 GB on the volume on which you install Exchange Server 2010.
- 200 MB on the system volume of the host server.
- 500 MB on the volume that hosts the message queue database on an Edge Transport or Hub Transport server.
- Appropriate space for the number of mailboxes hosted by a mailbox server.
- All volumes that host Exchange binaries or data must be formatted with the NTFS file system.

You can also deploy all Exchange Server 2010 roles, except those with the Unified Messaging role, on Windows Server 2008 or Windows Server 2008 R2 virtual machines that meet the software requirements outlined later in this lesson. Microsoft supports production systems running Exchange Server 2010 in virtualized environments under the following conditions:

- Hardware virtualization rather than software virtualization is being used. Hardware virtualization products include:
  - Hyper-V on Windows Server 2008 and Windows Server 2008 R2.
  - Microsoft Hyper-V Server 2008 and Microsoft Hyper-V Server 2008 R2.
  - Third-party hypervisors that have been validated under the Windows Server Virtualization Validation Program.
- Exchange does not support virtual disks that dynamically expand or those that use differencing or delta mechanisms such as snapshots.

Preparing a Host for the Installation of Exchange Server 2010

In the following section, you will learn what you need to do to prepare both Windows Server 2008 and Windows Server 2008 R2 to support an Exchange Server 2010 deployment. It is important to note that the requirements for Windows Server 2008 differ from Windows Server 2008 R2, as Windows Server 2008 R2 includes several components that you must obtain separately for computers running Windows Server 2008.

You can install Exchange Server 2010 only on the x64 version of the Windows Server 2008 operating system. If you intend to use Windows Server 2008 rather than Windows Server 2008 R2 as the host platform, you must install Service Pack 2 or later before you can install Exchange Server 2010. You also need to ensure that you install several additional components on the host computer before you attempt to install Exchange Server 2010. The components that you need to install on a computer running Windows Server 2008 with Service Pack 2 are as follows:

- Microsoft .NET Framework 3.5 Service Pack 1.
- Microsoft .NET Framework 3.5 Family Update for Windows Vista x64 and Windows Server 2008 x64.
- Windows Remote Management (WinRM) 2.0.

- Windows PowerShell V2.
- 2007 Office System Converter Microsoft Filter Pack. This is necessary only if the server is going to function with the Hub Transport or Mailbox server role.

EXAM TIP

Ensure that you are clear on the difference between Windows Server 2008 and Windows Server 2008 R2, as the preparation requirements for installing Exchange Server 2010 on these operating systems are different.

Preparing a host that has the Windows Server 2008 R2 operating system installed for the installation of Exchange Server 2010 is far simpler than preparing a host that has Windows Server 2008 installed. This is because Windows Server 2008 R2 already includes many of the components that you would need to otherwise download and install from the Internet. Windows Server 2008 R2 also comes only in an x64 version, so it is not necessary for you to check that the Windows Server host supports the correct processor architecture. The only additional component that you need to obtain for the host when using Windows Server 2008 R2 as a platform for Exchange is the 2007 Office System Converter Microsoft Filter Pack. You need to obtain this software only if you are going to deploy the Hub Transport or Mailbox server role on this computer.

MORE INFO INSTALL EXCHANGE SERVER 2010 PREREQUISITES

To learn more about the command-line options you can use to install prerequisites for specific Exchange Server 2010 configurations, consult the following TechNet document: *http://technet.microsoft.com/en-us/library/bb691354.aspx.*

 Quick Check
- Which component must you download and install on a computer with the Windows Server 2008 R2 operating system if you want it to host the Exchange Server 2010 Hub Transport role?

Quick Check Answer
- You must download and install the 2007 Office System Converter Microsoft Filter Pack.

Configuring Server Roles and Features for Exchange

Each Exchange Server 2010 role is dependent on different Windows Server 2008 and Windows Server 2008 R2 roles, role services, and features. The roles, role services, and features that you install depend on the Exchange Server 2010 role that the server platform will host. To install the roles, role services, and features required to support Exchange Server 2010 require only that a user be a member of the local Administrators group on the computer that is being prepared.

The roles, role services, and features that you need to install to support each Exchange Server 2010 role are as follows:

- **Client Access** RSAT Tools, .NET Framework 3.5.1, Web Server, Web Server Basic Authentication, Web Server Windows Authentication, Web Server Digest Authentication, IIS 6 Metabase Compatibility, Web Server .NET Extensibility, IIS 6 Management Console, Windows Process Activation Service Process Model, Web Server ISAPI Extensions, Web Server Dynamic Content Compression, .NET Framework HTTP Activation, and RPC over HTTP Proxy.

- **Hub Transport** RSAT Tools, .NET Framework 3.5.1, Web Server, Web Server Basic Authentication, Web Server Windows Authentication, IIS 6 Metabase Compatibility, Web Server .NET Extensibility, IIS 6 Management Console, and Windows Process Activation Service Process Model.

- **Mailbox** RSAT Tools, .NET Framework 3.5.1, Web Server, Web Server Basic Authentication, Web Server Windows Authentication, IIS 6 Metabase Compatibility, Web Server .NET Extensibility, IIS 6 Management Console, and Windows Process Activation Service Process Model. This role has the same requirements as the Hub Transport server role.

- **Edge Transport** Active Directory Lightweight Directory Services, RSAT Tools, and .NET Framework 3.5.1.

There are several methods through which you can install the required roles, role services, and features on a server that will host Exchange Server 2010. You can use the Server Manager console to add the required components, you can use the servermanagercmd .exe command-line utility, or you can use the administrative functionality of PowerShell. The advantage of using the Server Manager console is that it is relatively straightforward to use. The disadvantage of using Server Manager console is that it requires you to know which precise roles, role services, and features must be deployed to support specific Exchange Server 2010 roles. If you accidentally overlook a required component, you may need to exit Exchange setup and start again once you install the missing component.

Rather than use the Add Roles or Add Features functionality of the Server Manager console, it is possible to use prepared XML formatted answer files located in the Scripts folder of the Exchange Server 2010 installation media with the ServerManagerCmd.exe command-line utility. The advantage of this method is that it greatly simplifies the deployment of roles, role services, and features and ensures that all required components for the deployment of specific roles are included in the answer file. The XML-formatted answer files that are relevant to the roles tested on the 70-662 exam are as follows:

- **Exchange-Typical.xml** Use this configuration file with ServerManagerCmd.exe to install the roles, role services, and features required to support a typical installation of Exchange that hosts the Client Access, Hub Transport, and Mailbox server roles.

- **Exchange-CAS.xml** Use this configuration file with ServerManagerCmd.exe to install the roles, role services, and features required to support the Client Access server role.

- **Exchange-Edge.xml**   Use this configuration file with ServerManagerCmd.exe to install the roles, role services, and features required to support the Edge Transport server role.

- **Exchange-Hub.xml**   Use this configuration file with ServerManagerCmd.exe to install the roles, role services, and features required to support the Edge Transport server role.

- **Exchange-MBX.xml**   Use this configuration file with ServerManagerCmd.exe to install the roles, role services, and features required to support the Mailbox server role.

You use the *servermanagercmd.exe* command with the following syntax, where name.xml is the name of the appropriate Exchange Server 2010 roles that you wish to deploy:

```
ServerManagerCmd.exe -ip name.xml -restart
```

It is important to note that while the ServerManagerCmd.exe utility works with Windows Server 2008 R2, the command is deprecated and may not be present in future versions of the Windows Server operating system. With this in mind, it is also possible to use PowerShell 2.0 commands to install the required roles, role services, and features if the PowerShell ServerManager module is available. You can load the server manager module into an elevated PowerShell 2.0 window by issuing the command

```
Import-Module ServerManager
```

Once this is done, you can use the *Add-WindowsFeature* cmdlet to install the appropriate roles, role services, and features. To configure a server to host a typical Exchange installation that includes the Client Access, Hub Transport, and Mailbox server roles, issue the command

```
Add-WindowsFeature NET-Framework,RSAT-ADDS,Web-Server,Web-Basic-Auth,Web-Windows-
Auth,Web-Metabase,Web-Net-Ext,Web-Lgcy-Mgmt-Console,WAS-Process-Model,RSAT-Web-
Server,Web-ISAPI-Ext,Web-Digest-Auth,Web-Dyn-Compression,NET-HTTP-Activation,RPC-Over-
HTTP-Proxy
```

To configure a host to support the Client Access server role, issue the PowerShell 2.0 command:

```
Add-WindowsFeature NET-Framework,RSAT-ADDS,Web-Server,Web-Basic-Auth,Web-Windows-
Auth,Web-Metabase,Web-Net-Ext,Web-Lgcy-Mgmt-Console,WAS-Process-Model,RSAT-Web-
Server,Web-ISAPI-Ext,Web-Digest-Auth,Web-Dyn-Compression,NET-HTTP-Activation,RPC-Over-
HTTP-Proxy
```

To configure a host to support the Hub Transport server role, issue the PowerShell 2.0 command:

```
Add-WindowsFeature NET-Framework,RSAT-ADDS,Web-Server,Web-Basic-Auth,Web-Windows-
Auth,Web-Metabase,Web-Net-Ext,Web-Lgcy-Mgmt-Console,WAS-Process-Model,RSAT-Web-Server
```

To configure a host to support the Edge Transport server role, issue the PowerShell 2.0 command:

```
Add-WindowsFeature NET-Framework,RSAT-ADDS,ADLDS
```

To configure a host to support the Mailbox server role, issue the PowerShell 2.0 command:

```
Add-WindowsFeature NET-Framework,RSAT-ADDS,Web-Server,Web-Basic-Auth,Web-Windows-
Auth,Web-Metabase,Web-Net-Ext,Web-Lgcy-Mgmt-Console,WAS-Process-Model,RSAT-Web-Server
```

As was noted earlier in the lesson, the Hub Transport role requires the same roles, role services, and features as the Mailbox server role. After these commands have installed the appropriate roles, role services, and features, it will be necessary to restart the computer prior to attempting to install Exchange Server 2010.

If the server you are configuring is going to host the Client Access server role, it is also necessary to configure the Net.TCP Port Sharing Service so that it starts automatically, as shown in Figure 1-4. You can do this through the services console or by issuing the command *sc config NetTcpPortSharing start=auto* from an elevated command prompt.

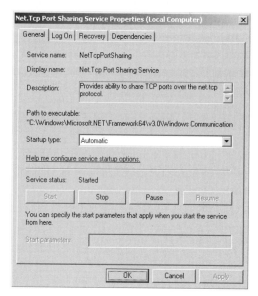

FIGURE 1-4 Net.TCP Port Sharing service configuration

Lesson Summary

- Exchange Server 2010 can be installed only on x64 versions of the Windows Server 2008 and Windows Server 2008 R2 operating system.

- You need to install Service Pack 2 on Windows Server 2008 as well as .NET Framework 3.5 Service Pack 1, Microsoft .NET Framework 3.5 Family Update, WinRM 2.0, and Windows PowerShell V2 before Windows Server 2008 can function as an Exchange Server 2010 host.

- You need to install the 2007 Office System Converter Microsoft Filter Pack if you intend to deploy the Hub Transport or Mailbox server role.

- You can use XML configuration files located in the scripts directory of the Exchange Server 2010 installation media with ServerManagerCMD.exe to install the required roles, features, and role services for specific Exchange roles.
- You must configure the Net.TCP Port Sharing Service to start automatically on computers that will host the Client Access server role.

Lesson Review

You can use the following questions to test your knowledge of the information in Lesson 2, "Configure the Server to Host Exchange Server 2010." The questions are also available on the companion CD if you prefer to review them in electronic form.

> **NOTE ANSWERS**
>
> Answers to these questions and explanations of why each answer choice is correct or incorrect are located in the "Answers" section at the end of the book.

1. Which of the following Exchange Server 2010 roles requires that you deploy Office System Converter: Microsoft Filter Pack prior to role deployment? (Choose all that apply; each answer forms a complete solution.)

   A. Mailbox

   B. Client Access

   C. Hub Transport

   D. Edge Transport

2. On computers running which of the following operating systems can you install Exchange Server 2010?

   A. Windows Server 2003 R2 (x64) Enterprise edition

   B. Windows Server 2008 Standard edition with Service Pack 2 (x64)

   C. Windows Server 2008 Enterprise edition with Service Pack 2 (x86)

   D. Windows Server 2003 Datacenter edition (x64) with Service Pack 2

3. Which of the following additional components should you install on a computer running Windows Server 2008 R2 Enterprise edition (x64) if you wanted that computer to host the Exchange Server 2010 Hub Transport server role?

   A. Silverlight 3 or later

   B. Microsoft Data Engine (MSDE)

   C. Office System Converter: Microsoft Filter Pack

   D. Microsoft Office Outlook Connector 12.1 or later

4. A Windows Server 2008 R2 (x64) server has been installed and joined to your organization's Active Directory domain. The server has undergone no additional configuration. You use the following PowerShell commands to prepare the server to host the Exchange Server 2010 Mailbox, Hub Transport, and Client Access server roles:

```
Import-Module ServerManager
Add-WindowsFeature RSAT-ADDS,Web-Server,Web-Basic-Auth,Web-Windows-Auth,Web-
Metabase,Web-Net-Ext,Web-Lgcy-Mgmt-Console,WAS-Process-Model,RSAT-Web-Server,Web-
ISAPI-Ext,Web-Digest-Auth,Web-Dyn-Compression,NET-HTTP-Activation,RPC-Over-HTTP-
Proxy
```

Which of the following additional commands would you issue to configure the server to support the designated Exchange Server 2010 roles? (Choose all that apply; each answer forms part of a complete solution.)

A. *Add-WindowsFeature NET-Framework*

B. *Add-WindowsFeature SMTP-Server*

C. *Set-Service -Name NetTcpPortSharing -StartupType Automatic*

D. *Set-Service -Name SNMPTRAP -StartupType Automatic*

Lesson 3: Deploy Exchange Server 2010 Roles

Although a typical Exchange Server 2010 installation, where the Hub Transport, Client Access, and Mailbox server roles are deployed on a single server, will be appropriate in many circumstances, there will be some circumstances where you want to customize your Exchange deployment. This may be because you want to deploy only one role on a server. Alternatively, you may wish to remove a role that has already been deployed to a server to improve the performance of other hosted server roles. In some cases, you may not wish or may not be able to perform the installation of Exchange Server 2010 yourself. In this lesson, you will learn how you can delegate this responsibility to other users without giving them unnecessary privileges in your Exchange organization.

> **After this lesson, you will be able to:**
> - Delegate server installation.
> - Perform a custom deployment of Exchange Server 2010.
> - Perform a command-line deployment of Exchange Server 2010.
> - Add roles to an existing Exchange Server 2010 deployment.
> - Troubleshoot failed installations.
>
> **Estimated lesson time: 40 minutes**

Installing Exchange Server 2010

Although in previous lessons Active Directory was prepared prior to attempting to install Exchange Server 2010, it is possible to have Active Directory prepared as a part of the setup process on the first Exchange Server 2010 server deployed in the forest. When you take this approach, the user account used to deploy Exchange Server 2010 must be a member of the Enterprise Admins, Schema Admins, and Domain Admins groups as well as a member of the local Administrators group on the server that will host Exchange. When you perform this type of deployment, you also need to install Exchange in the same site and domain as the computer that hosts the Schema Master. In general, it is better to perform environmental preparation steps separately so that you can ensure that changes replicate successfully before attempting to deploy the first Exchange server in your organization.

Consider the following factors when installing Exchange:

- You must deploy the Mailbox and Hub Transport roles in each Active Directory site for email messages to flow correctly.
- You must deploy at least one client access server in each Active Directory site that has a mailbox server.

- You can install the Mailbox, Hub Transport, Client Access, and Unified Messaging roles or a combination thereof on a single host.
- You cannot deploy the Edge Transport role on the same server as other roles.

Delegate Permission for Exchange Server Setup

In general, a user must be delegated the Organization Management role before being able to deploy Exchange Server 2010 in an existing Exchange Server 2010 organization. In some circumstances, it is necessary for an administrator at a remote branch office to install Exchange Server 2010. Rather than adding this user to the Organization Management role group, you can configure delegated setup so that the configured account is able to install a single specified Exchange server in the domain. This allows the local administrator to complete the designated task without conferring unnecessary administrative privileges.

It is not possible to use delegated setup to install the first server running Exchange Server 2010 in the domain. The first server in the domain must be installed using a user account that is a member of the Organization Management role group as well as the local Administrators group.

Administrators who are members of the Delegated Setup role group are able to deploy Exchange Server 2010 if the server that will function as the Exchange host has been provisioned by a member of the Organization Management role group. Members of the Organization Management role group can provision servers using the command

```
Setup.com /NewProvisionedServer:ServerName
```

Members of the Delegated Setup role are unable to uninstall an Exchange Server. It is possible to uninstall or remove Exchange Server 2010 only by using an account that is a member of the Organization Management role as well as the local Administrators group on the host server.

> **MORE INFO** **DELEGATED SETUP**
>
> To learn more about delegated setup, consult the following documentation on TechNet: *http://technet.microsoft.com/en-us/library/bb201741.aspx.*

Deploy Exchange Using Setup.exe

There are two general ways in which a user with appropriate permissions is able to install Exchange Server 2010. The first is to run setup.exe from within an appropriately configured Windows Server 2008 or later host by double-clicking on the executable file. Setup.exe is also run automatically when you insert the Exchange Server 2010 installation media. The second option is to run setup.com from an elevated command prompt. You will learn about this option later in the lesson.

Prior to installing Exchange Server 2010, you must choose which Exchange Language Options are going to be installed. You can choose to install all languages from the language bundle or install only languages that are included with the Exchange Server 2010 installation media. Once this is done and you have agreed to the License Agreement and determined whether you want to forward error data to Microsoft, you are given the option between performing a typical Exchange Server installation and performing a custom Exchange Server installation. When you perform a typical installation, the Hub Transport, Client Access, and Mailbox server roles are installed on the host server as well as the Exchange Management Tools. You will perform a Typical installation of Exchange Server 2010 in the final practice exercise at the end of this chapter.

If you select the custom option, you are able to install the Unified Messaging role as well as the Hub Transport, Client Access, and Mailbox server roles or a combination of those roles. You are also able to select the Edge Transport server role for deployment, though you cannot deploy this role with other roles, such as the Mailbox and Client Access server roles. The custom role selection screen is shown in Figure 1-5.

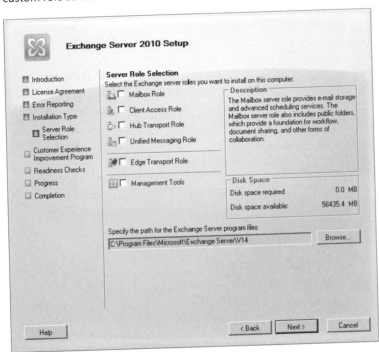

FIGURE 1-5 Custom Exchange setup

> **MORE INFO   INSTALLING THE EDGE TRANSPORT SERVER ROLE**
>
> You will learn more about installing the Edge Transport server role in Chapter 8, "Configuring Transport Servers."

If you have chosen to install the Mailbox role, you will be asked whether there are any client computers that are running Outlook 2003 or Entourage in the organization. In case the computers that use this software are present in your organization, it is necessary for setup to create a public folder database to allow these computers to connect to Exchange. If there are no client computers that use this software in your organization, it is not necessary to create a public folder database. If you select the no option and it becomes necessary to support computers running these software packages at some point in the future, you can create a public folder database as necessary. You will learn more about creating public folder databases in Chapter 2, "Exchange Databases and Address Lists," and more about public folders in Chapter 4, "Distribution Groups and Public Folders."

If you have chosen to install the Client Access server role, setup will ask you whether you want to configure the Client Access server with an Internet facing address, as shown in Figure 1-6. You will learn more about configuring the Client Access server role in Chapter 5, "Configuring Client Access." Once you have completed this step, you will be queried as to whether you wish to participate in the Customer Experience Improvement Program. This program collects information about how Exchange is used in your organization and assists Microsoft in determining which features of Exchange should be prioritized for future development.

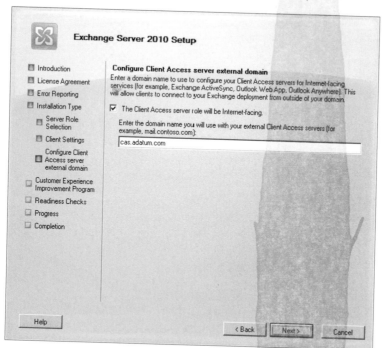

FIGURE 1-6 Client Access server external address configuration

The Exchange Server 2010 setup routine then performs a set of readiness checks based on the roles that you have chosen to install on the server. If these readiness checks complete successfully, you can proceed and install Exchange Server 2010. If the readiness checks fail, as shown in Figure 1-7, you must address the specified issues. In some cases, it will be possible to click Retry and have the readiness check occur again. In other cases, it may be necessary to log out or even reboot the host computer before Exchange Server 2010 setup can continue.

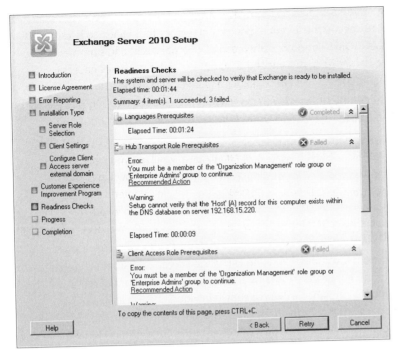

FIGURE 1-7 Failed readiness check

> **MORE INFO** **INSTALL EXCHANGE SERVER 2010**
>
> To get a more detailed overview of the process of installing Exchange Server 2010, consult the following article on TechNet: *http://technet.microsoft.com/en-us/library/bb125143.aspx*.

Command-Line Installation

You can use setup.com from an elevated command prompt to deploy and remove Exchange Server 2010 roles. The setup.com command-line utility has many options, though the options that you are most likely to be tested on in the 70-662 exam involve installing, adding, or removing roles. You can specify roles using the following terms:

- HubTransport, HT, or H
- Mailbox, MB, or M
- ClientAccess, CA, or C
- EdgeTransport, ET, or E
- UnifiedMessaging, UM, or U

For example, the command

```
Setup.com /mode:install /role:Mailbox,HubTransport
```

accomplishes the same thing as the command

```
Setup.com /mode:install /r:M,H
```

The /mode:uninstall option removes a role or the Exchange if no specific roles are selected. You can use setup.com to specify the location of a local directory that hosts updates, install language packs, and specify installation options, such as whether Exchange supports legacy Outlook clients.

> **MORE INFO** **SETUP.COM OPTIONS AND UNATTENDED INSTALLATION OF EXCHANGE SERVER 2010**
>
> Although performing an unattended installation of Exchange Server 2010 is beyond the scope of the 70-662 exam objectives, you can find out more performing unattended installations as well as a list of setup.com options at the following address: *http://technet.microsoft.com/en-us/library/aa997281.aspx.*

Adding and Removing Roles

To add or remove roles from a computer running Exchange Server 2010 after setup has completed, you need to use either the Programs and Features item in Control Panel, which puts Exchange setup into maintenance mode, as shown in Figure 1-8, or setup.com /mode:uninstall from an elevated command prompt. As you learned earlier, the user account used to uninstall or modify Exchange must be a member of the Organization Management role as well as a member of the local Administrators group on the host server.

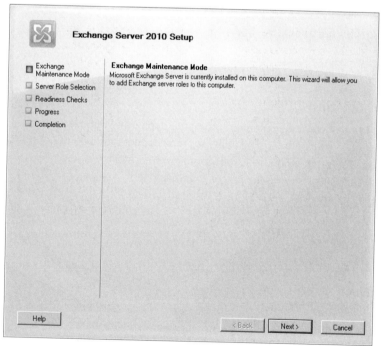

FIGURE 1-8 Exchange maintenance mode

Quick Check

- Which of the following should you use to add the Hub Transport role to an existing Exchange Server 2010 deployment from the command line, setup.exe, or setup.com?

Quick Check Answer

- Use setup.com to install or remove Exchange roles from the command line. Use setup.exe to run the Exchange Server 2010 installation routine from Windows Explorer.

Exchange Server 2010 Editions

Exchange Server 2010 comes in two editions: Standard edition and Enterprise edition. Standard edition supports five databases on each server, and Enterprise edition supports up to 100 databases on each server. Both editions support high availability through database availability groups on the Enterprise edition of Windows Server 2008 and Windows Server 2008 R2. You select an edition of Exchange Server 2010 when you enter the license key as a postinstallation task. You do not select an edition of Exchange Server 2010 during the installation process. You should choose to deploy the Enterprise edition of Exchange Server 2010 when you want to host more than five databases on a server.

Although the 70-662 exam does not cover licensing, each user or device that accesses Exchange requires a standard Client Access License (CAL). A standard CAL gives access to the majority of Exchange Server 2010 features such as Outlook Web App, Federated Calendar Sharing, and standard email functionality. If a user needs advanced Exchange Server 2010 functionality, such as custom retention policies, voicemail with Unified Messaging, and Multi-Mailbox Search and Legal Hold, it is necessary to have both a Standard user CAL and an Enterprise CAL. The Enterprise CAL is a license that is obtained in addition to the Standard CAL and is not a replacement for the Standard CAL.

> **MORE INFO EXCHANGE SERVER EDITIONS AND CALs**
>
> To find out more about the editions of Exchange and licensing, consult the following article: *http://www.microsoft.com/exchange/2010/en/us/Licensing.aspx*.

Postinstallation Tasks

When a graphical installation completes, the Exchange Management Console automatically opens. The console will display the information shown in Figure 1-9, reminding you to complete postinstallation tasks. Clicking on the Finalize Deployment Tasks item launches a browser session to a page on Microsoft that provides postdeployment advice. It is possible to view this page only if the Exchange Server is able to establish a browsing session to the Internet, either directly or through a proxy.

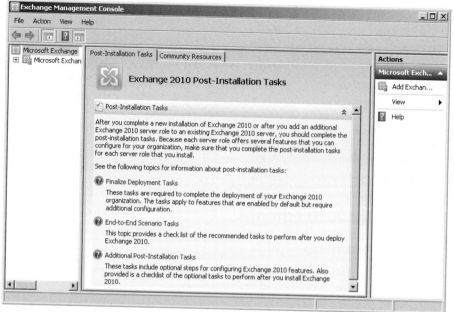

FIGURE 1-9 Postinstallation tasks

This TechNet page instructs you to perform the following tasks:

- Enter the product key for Exchange Server 2010. You can do this using the *Set-ExchangeServer* cmdlet or by navigating to Server Configuration in the Exchange Management Console and clicking on Enter Product Key Group in the Action pane. You must enter a product key within 120 days of deploying Exchange Server 2010.

- Install a product to protect Exchange Server 2010 from malware. This includes but is not limited to Forefront Security 2010 for Exchange Server. You will learn more about protecting Exchange Server 2010 from malware in Chapter 12, "Message Integrity, Antivirus and Anti-Spam."

- If you have deployed the Mailbox server role:

  - Configure an Offline Address Book and Offline Address Book distribution for Outlook clients. You will learn how to do this in Chapter 2, "Exchange Databases and Address Lists."

  - Configure High Availability and Site Resilience. You will learn more about high availability in Chapter 13, "Exchange High-Availability Solutions."

- If you have deployed the Client Access server role, configure secure access for the Client Access server role and configure Exchange ActiveSync security, authentication, and policies. You will learn more about configuring the Client Access server role in Chapter 5, "Configuring Client Access."

- If you have deployed the Hub Transport server role, configure domains for which you will accept email messages and configure Internet mail flow. You will learn to do this in Chapter 8, "Configuring Transport Servers."

- If you have deployed the Edge Transport server role, you need to configure an EdgeSync between this server and the Hub Transport servers. You will learn how to configure the Edge Transport server role in Chapter 8, "Configuring Transport Servers."

> **MORE INFO FINALIZE EXCHANGE DEPLOYMENT TASKS**
>
> You can review the document that is launched when you click on the Finalize Deployment Tasks item in Exchange Management Console by navigating to the following TechNet link: *http://technet.microsoft.com/en-us/library/bb125262.aspx.*

Firewall Configuration

The Exchange Server 2010 setup process configures Windows Firewall with Advanced Security so that all necessary ports required to support the roles that you deploy are open for server and client communication. As this process occurs automatically, it is not necessary to use the Security Configuration Wizard tool to configure these settings.

In some cases, it will be necessary to configure the ports on a separate hardware-based firewall to allow traffic to or from a server running Exchange Server 2010, such as if you have a hardware firewall separating subnets on your organization's internal network. The most commonly used ports for each role are as follows:

- **25** Hub Transport, Edge Transport server SMTP traffic

- **135** Mailbox server MAPI access

- **80** Client Access server Autodiscover, availability, Outlook Web App, Outlook Anywhere, Exchange ActiveSync

- **443** Client Access server secure (SSL) Autodiscover, availability, Outlook Web App, Outlook Anywhere, Exchange ActiveSync

> **MORE INFO EXCHANGE NETWORK PORT REFERENCE**
>
> To learn more about the network ports that are used by Exchange Server 2010, consult the following article on TechNet: *http://technet.microsoft.com/en-us/library/bb331973.aspx.*

Verifying Setup

When you install Exchange Server 2010 using the graphical setup tool, you are presented with a setup summary detailing whether each step of the setup process has completed successfully. This summary is shown in Figure 1-10 and allows you to quickly determine whether all components have installed correctly. The completion summary will detail steps that do not complete correctly should problems occur during the installation.

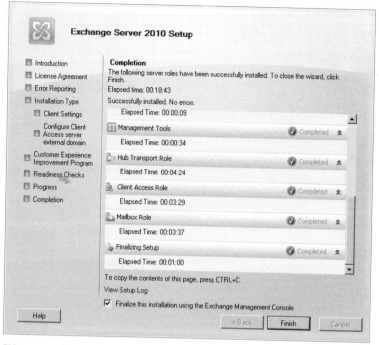

FIGURE 1-10 Successful setup

When setup completes, you can also view the setup log by clicking on View Setup Log from the completion page of the setup wizard. This file can also be opened directly using Notepad.exe and is stored at C:\ExchangeSetupLogs\ExchangeSetup.log. This log is available whether the setup fails or succeeds. This log is created and updated during the Exchange installation process, and you can examine it using notepad.exe to diagnose why a specific Exchange Server 2010 deployment has failed.

Another tool that you can use to verify that Exchange Server 2010 has been deployed successfully is the *Get-Exchange Server* cmdlet. Executing the *Get-ExchangeServer* cmdlet provides information about a specific Exchange Server. You can use the following command to view information about Exchange Server VAN-EX1:

Get-ExchangeServer -Identity VAN-EX1 | Format-List

The output of this command will inform you of which roles have been deployed, the path where Exchange files have been installed, the network name of the Exchange server, and the location of the Exchange Server's Active Directory object. You will use this command to verify the installation of Exchange Server 2010 in the final practice exercise at the end of this chapter.

MORE INFO   VERIFY AND INSTALLATION

To learn more about verifying an Exchange Server 2010 installation, consult the following TechNet link: *http://technet.microsoft.com/en-us/library/bb125254.aspx.*

Lesson Summary

- The Mailbox and Hub Transport roles must exist in each Active Directory site for email messages to flow correctly. One Client Access server must be in each Active Directory site that has a Mailbox server.
- You cannot deploy the Edge Transport role on the same server as other roles.
- User must be delegated the Organization Management role to install the first Exchange Server in an organization.
- Delegated setup allows a user who has not been delegated the Organization Management role permission to install Exchange on a provisioned server. The user must be a member of the Delegated Setup role group. The server must be provisioned using the *Setup.com /NewProvisionedServer* command.
- Exchange can be removed only by a user who has been delegated the Organization Management role.
- Setup.com is used to deploy Exchange from the command line. Setup.exe is used to start the installation of Exchange from within the Windows environment. You can use setup.com to add or remove roles from a server running Exchange once it is deployed.
- You can use the *Get-ExchangeServer* cmdlet to verify the configuration of an Exchange server after deployment.

Lesson Review

You can use the following questions to test your knowledge of the information in Lesson 3, "Deploy Exchange Server 2010 Roles." The questions are also available on the companion CD if you prefer to review them in electronic form.

> **NOTE ANSWERS**
>
> Answers to these questions and explanations of why each answer choice is correct or incorrect are located in the "Answers" section at the end of the book.

1. You want to delegate the setup of several branch office Exchange Server 2010 servers to local IT staff at the remote locations. Which of the following commands must you use before a user that is a member of the Delegated Setup role group is able to install a server named SYD-MBX02?

    A. *Setup.com /PrepareTopology*

    B. *Setup.com /RemoveProvisionedServer:SYD-MBX02*

    C. *Setup.com /NewProvisionedServer:SYD-MBX02*

    D. *Setup.com /mode:Install*

2. Your organization's network is configured with five sites. You install the Exchange Server 2010 Hub Transport, Client Access server, and Mailbox server roles in the head office site. You install the Edge Transport server role on the head office site perimeter network. You are preparing to deploy Exchange Server 2010 roles to each of the four branch office sites. Which of the following roles must you deploy to each site to ensure that email messages flow and client access at each site functions correctly? (Choose all that apply; each answer forms part of a complete solution.)

   A. Hub Transport server

   B. Edge Transport server

   C. Mailbox server

   D. Client Access server

3. Which of the following commands can you use to install the Mailbox and Hub Transport server Exchange Server 2010 roles on an appropriately configured Windows Server 2008 R2 host?

   A. *Setup.com /mode:Install /role:HT,M*

   B. *Setup.com /mode:Uninstall /role:HT,M*

   C. *Setup.com /mode:Install /role:C,M*

   D. *Setup.com /mode:Uninstall /role:C,M*

4. Each branch office site in your organization is configured so that one server hosts the Mailbox, Client Access, and Hub Transport server roles. You have installed an additional server at each site and added just the Client Access and Hub Transport Server roles to this additional server. You want to remove the Client Access and Hub Transport server roles from each of the original servers while leaving the servers functioning as Exchange Server 2010 mailbox servers. Which of the following commands allows you to accomplish this goal?

   A. *Setup.com /mode:Install /role:Mailbox*

   B. *Setup.com /mode:Uninstall /role:Mailbox*

   C. *Setup.com /mode:Install /role:ClientAccess,HubTransport*

   D. *Setup.com /mode:Uninstall /role:ClientAccess,HubTransport*

5. Which of the following Exchange Management Shell cmdlets can you use to verify that a specific set of roles has been successfully installed on a computer running Exchange Server 2010?

   A. *Test-SystemHealth*

   B. *Set-ExchangeServer*

   C. *Get-ExchangeServer*

   D. *Test-ServiceHealth*

6. Which of the following roles allows a user to install an Exchange Server 2010 mailbox server in an existing Exchange Server 2010 organization?

   A. Discovery Management

   B. Recipient Management

   C. Organization Management

   D. Public Folder Management

PRACTICE **Prepare the Environment for and Deploy Exchange Server 2010**

In this set of exercises, you will configure a computer to function as a domain controller to support the deployment of Exchange Server 2010 and then configure the domain it hosts to support the introduction of Exchange Server 2010. Once this is accomplished, you will configure a member server named VAN-EX1 so that it can host the Exchange Server 2010 Mailbox, Hub Transport, and Client Access server roles. Once this is done, you will install Exchange Server 2010 on server VAN-EX1.

EXERCISE 1   Prepare a computer to function as a Windows Server 2008 R2 domain controller in an Exchange environment

In this exercise you will configure a computer running Windows Server 2008 R2 to function as a domain controller for the Adatum.com domain, which will serve as the host network environment for the Exchange Server 2010 practice infrastructure that you will use throughout this book.

1. Log on to the first computer that you have installed Windows Server 2008 R2, using the Administrator account and the password *Pa$$w0rd*.

2. Open an elevated command prompt and issue the following commands:

   `Netsh interface ipv4 set address "Local Area Connection" static 10.10.0.10`

3. Enter the following command:

   `netdom renamecomputer %computername% /newname:VAN-DC`

4. Restart the computer and log back on using the Administrator account.

5. Click Start. In the Search Programs and Files text box, type the following:

   `Dcpromo`

6. When the Active Directory Domain Services Installation Wizard starts, click Next on the first two pages.

7. On the Choose a Deployment Configuration page, choose Create A New Domain In A New Forest and then click Next.

8. On the Name The Forest Root Domain, enter **Adatum.com** and then click Next.

9. On the Forest Functional Level page, set the Forest Functional Level to Windows Server 2008, as shown in Figure 1-11, and then click Next.

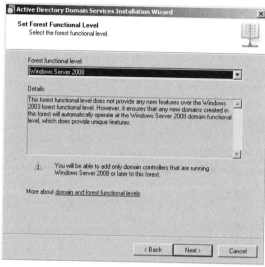

FIGURE 1-11 Set forest functional level

10. On the Set Domain Functional Level page, ensure that Windows Server 2008 is set and then click Next.

11. On the Additional Domain Controller Options page, ensure that the DNS server option is checked and then click Next. When presented with the warning describing that the delegation for the DNS server cannot be created, click Yes when asked if you want to continue.

12. Accept the default settings for the Database, Log Files, and SYSVOL locations and click Next.

13. In the Directory Services Restore Mode Administrator Password dialog box, enter the password *Pa$$w0rd* twice and then click Next.

14. On the Summary page click Next to begin the installation of Active Directory Domain Services on computer VAN-DC. When the wizard completes, click Finish. When prompted click Restart Now to reboot computer VAN-DC.

EXERCISE 2 Prepare Active Directory for the installation of Exchange

Once Active Directory has been installed, it is necessary to prepare the Active Directory environment for the installation of Exchange Server 2010. In this exercise, you will accomplish this by preparing the schema and the domain using the Exchange 2010 installation media. To complete this exercise, perform the following steps:

1. Log on to server VAN-DC using the Administrator account.

2. Using Active Directory Users and Computers, create a user account named Kim_Akers in the Users container and assign the account the password *Pa$$w0rd*. Configure the password to never expire. Add this user account to the Enterprise Admins, Domain Admins, and Schema Admins groups.

3. Open an elevated command prompt and navigate to the directory that contains the Exchange Server 2010 setup files.

4. In the elevated command prompt, run the following command:

```
Setup /PrepareSchema
```

5. Ensure that you do not press a key unless you want to cancel the process. Setup will begin to extend the Active Directory Domain Services schema to support Exchange Server 2010, as shown in Figure 1-12.

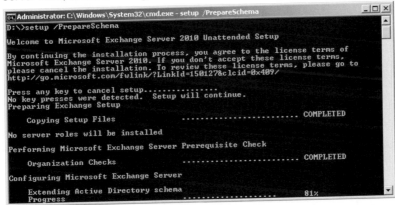

FIGURE 1-12 Prepare AD DS Schema

6. Run the following command and ensure that you do not press any keys until Active Directory preparation completes:

```
Setup /PrepareAD /OrganizationName:AdatumOrg
```

7. Verify that this command has run correctly by examining the contents of the Microsoft Exchange Security Groups OU in Active Directory and verifying that they match what is shown in Figure 1-13.

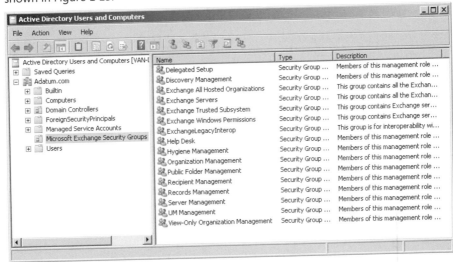

FIGURE 1-13 Groups created by setup

8. Add the Kim Akers user account that you created earlier to the Organization Management group in the Microsoft Exchange Security Groups container.

9. From the elevated command prompt, run the following command:

```
Setup /PrepareAllDomains
```

10. When this command completes, verify that the Microsoft Exchange System Objects container has been created and that the Exchange Install Domain Servers security group is located within this container.

EXERCISE 3   Preparing a computer and joining it to the domain

In this exercise, you will use the command line to configure a computer running the Windows Server 2008 R2 operating system to become a member of the adatum.com domain with the name VAN-EX1.

1. Ensure that computer VAN-DC is powered on and connected to the network or virtual network to which the second computer is connected.

2. Log on to the second computer that you have installed Windows Server 2008 R2, using the Administrator account and the password Pa$$w0rd.

3. Open an elevated command prompt and issue the following commands:

```
Netsh interface ipv4 set address "Local Area Connection" static 10.10.0.20
Netsh interface ipv4 set dnsservers "Local Area Connection" static 10.10.0.10
primary
```

4. Enter the following command:

```
netdom renamecomputer %computername% /newname:VAN-EX1
```

5. Restart the computer and then log on again using the Administrator account.

6. From an elevated command prompt issue the following command:

```
netdom join VAN-EX1 /domain:adatum
```

7. Restart the computer. When the computer restarts, log on as adatum\Administrator.

8. Transfer the Office System Converter: Microsoft Filter Pack x64 installation file to VAN-EX1. Double-click on this installation file to commence installation. Click Next on the dialog shown in Figure 1-14, accept the license terms, and then the filter pack will install.

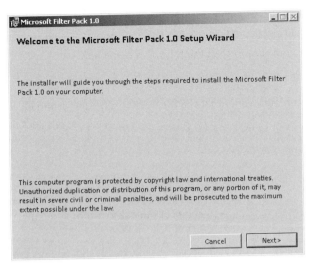

FIGURE 1-14 Install filter pack

9. Open an elevated PowerShell session and then enter the following commands:

    ```
    Import-Module ServerManager
    Add-WindowsFeature NET-Framework,RSAT-ADDS,Web-Server,Web-Basic-Auth,Web-Windows-
    Auth,Web-Metabase,Web-Net-Ext,Web-Lgcy-Mgmt-Console,WAS-Process-Model,RSAT-Web-
    Server,Web-ISAPI-Ext,Web-Digest-Auth,Web-Dyn-Compression,NET-HTTP-Activation,RPC-
    Over-HTTP-Proxy
    ```

10. Restart computer VAN-EX1 and log on using the Adatum\Administrator account. Open
    an elevated PowerShell session and then enter the following commands:

    ```
    Import-Module ServerManager
    Set-Service -Name NetTcpPortSharing -StartupType Automatic
    ```

11. Use the Server Manager console to add the Adatum\Kim_Akers user account to the
    local Administrators group on VAN-EX1.

12. Shut down the server.

EXERCISE 4   Install Exchange Server 2010 in the default configuration

In this exercise, you will perform a typical installation of Exchange Server 2010. By choosing
this option, you will install the Hub Transport, Client Access, and Mailbox server roles on
computer VAN-EX1. As you have already prepared the computer in previous exercises, you
will be able to rapidly proceed through the exercise, as all prerequisites will have been met.

1. Start computer VAN-EX1 and log on with the Adatum\Kim_Akers user account.

2. Use Windows Explorer to navigate to the location of the Exchange installation files.
    Run Setup.exe. When prompted, click Yes at the User Account Control dialog box.

3. On the splash screen shown in Figure 1-15, click on Step 3: Choose Exchange Language Option. Click on the Install Only Languages From The DVD option.

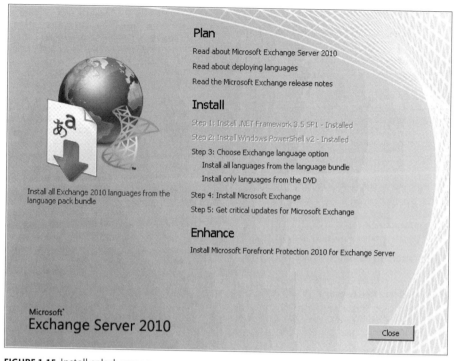

FIGURE 1-15 Install splash screen

4. Click on Step 4: Install Microsoft Exchange. On the Introduction page, click Next.

5. On the License Agreement Page, click on I Accept The Terms In The License Agreement and then click Next.

6. On the Error Reporting page, ensure that No is selected and then click Next.

7. On the Exchange Server 2010 Setup page, ensure that Typical Exchange Server Installation is selected, as shown in Figure 1-16, and then click Next.

8. On the Client Settings page, select No when asked whether you have client computers running Outlook 2003 or Entourage and then click Next.

9. On the Configure Client Access Server External Domain page, ensure that The Client Access Server Role Will Be Internet Facing option is not selected and then click Next.

10. On the Customer Experience Improvement Program page, select I Don't Wish To Join The Program At This Time and then click Next.

11. The readiness checks will now run. Verify that all readiness checks complete successfully, as shown in Figure 1-17, and then click Install.

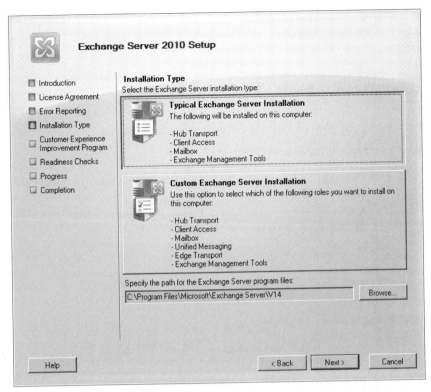

FIGURE 1-16 Setup screen

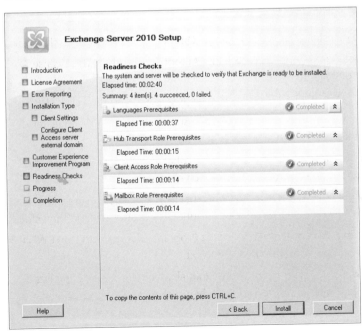

FIGURE 1-17 Exchange readiness checks

12. When setup completes, verify that all stages of the setup are marked as Completed. Click on View Setup Log to view the Exchange setup log in Notepad. Review the contents of this log by clicking on View Setup and then close the log. Click Finish.

13. On the Exchange Server Setup splash screen, click Close. At the warning that informs you about critical updates to Exchange Server, click Yes.

14. Exchange Management Console will have automatically opened at this point. Close this console and open an Exchange Management Shell. Issue the following command:

    Get-ExchangeServer VAN-EX1 | Format-List Name,Domain,Site,fqdn,ServerRole

15. Verify that the output of this command matches the output shown in Figure 1-18.

FIGURE 1-18 Verify deployment

16. Close Exchange Management Shell and Exchange Management Console. Shut down computers VAN-EX1 and VAN-DC.

Chapter Review

To further practice and reinforce the skills you learned in this chapter, you can perform the following tasks:

- Review the chapter summary.
- Complete the case scenarios. These scenarios set up real-word situations involving the topics of this chapter and ask you to create a solution.
- Complete the suggested practices.
- Take a practice test.

Chapter Summary

- An organization must have a Windows Server 2003 functional level forest or higher to deploy Exchange Server 2010.
- The computer hosting the schema master role must be running the Windows Server 2003 operating system or later.
- Run *Setup /PrepareLegacyExchangePermissions* when preparing an Exchange Server 2003 organization for the introduction of Exchange Server 2010. Run *Setup /PrepareSchema*, then *Setup /PrepareAD*, and then *Setup /PrepareDomain* to prepare the environment for Exchange.
- Exchange Server 2010 can be installed only on computers running the x64 version of Windows Server 2008 with Service Pack 2 or Windows Server 2008 R2.
- A user must be delegated the Organization Management role to install the first Exchange Server in an organization. Users must be members of this role to deploy Exchange Server 2010 unless they have been added to the Delegated Setup role group, in which case they can set up a server that has been provisioned.

Case Scenarios

In the following case scenarios, you will apply what you've learned about subjects of this chapter. You can find answers to these questions in the "Answers " section at the end of this book.

Case Scenario 1: Preparing for the Deployment of Exchange 2010 at Contoso

Contoso pharmaceuticals has an existing Exchange Server 2007 deployment spread across a number of branch offices. The contoso.com forest has a single domain running at the Windows Server 2003 functional level. Management at Contoso wants to replace its existing Exchange Server 2007 servers with servers running Exchange Server 2010. It is envisaged that there will be a period of coexistence between the servers running Exchange Server 2007 and Exchange Server 2010 as the transition occurs over the course of several months. With these facts in mind, answer the following questions:

1. What command should you run prior to running *Setup /PrepareAD* before introducing the first server running an Exchange Server 2010 role?

2. Which service pack should be installed on Exchange Server 2007 prior to the introduction of servers running Exchange Server 2010?

3. Which Exchange Server 2010 server role should you introduce to the Contoso domain first?

Case Scenario 2: Exchange Deployment at Fabrikam

Fabrikam is a new company that has decided on using Exchange Server 2010 as their messaging solution. Fabrikam has offices in the Australian east coast capital cities of Melbourne, Sydney, Brisbane, and Canberra. The Schema Master is located in the Melbourne site of the fabrikam.internal domain. Other domains in the forest include queensland.fabrikam.internal and Victoria.fabrikam.internal. One of the administrators at Fabrikam, Ken, will be responsible for preparing the existing Active Directory schema for the deployment of Exchange Server 2010. Another administrator, Laura, will be responsible for preparing the Victoria.fabrikam.internal domain. These domains all run at the Windows Server 2008 functional level and were created prior to the decision to deploy Exchange being made. With these facts in mind, answer the following questions:

1. Which groups must Dan's user account be a member of if he is going to run the *Setup /PrepareSchema* command?

2. Which site and domain must the *Setup /PrepareSchema* command be runin?

3. Which groups or roles must Laura's account be a member of if she is going to prepare the Victoria.fabrikam.internal domain using the *Setup /PrepareDomain* command?

Suggested Practices

To help you successfully master the exam objectives presented in this chapter, complete the following tasks.

Prepare the Infrastructure for Exchange

Rather than perform these exercises in a virtual lab, you will assess your organization's actual production environment. Perform these exercises only if your organization has not already deployed Exchange Server 2010.

- **Practice 1** Determine which computer in your organization holds the Schema Master role using a command-line utility.

- **Practice 2** Use appropriate tools to determine whether any global catalog servers in your organization need to be upgraded prior to the deployment of Exchange Server 2010.

Install Exchange Prerequisites

Introduce the first practice. Give guidance about which practices readers should do under which circumstances.

- **Practice 1** Use ServerManagerCmd.exe with the Exchange-Typical.xml file to prepare a computer running Windows Server 2008 for the installation of Exchange Server 2010.
- **Practice 2** Use command-line utilities to configure the Net.TCP Port Sharing service to start automatically.

Install Exchange Roles

Perform these practice exercises on a test network.

- **Practice 1** Create a new user account named Mark Lee. Delegate this user the role that will allow them to install the Exchange Server 2010 Mailbox server role.
- **Practice 2** Install the Exchange Server 2010 Mailbox and Hub Transport roles on a server running Windows Server 2008 R2 using only the command line.

Take a Practice Test

The practice tests on this book's companion CD offer many options. For example, you can test yourself on just one exam objective, or you can test yourself on all the 70-662 certification exam content. You can set up the test so that it closely simulates the experience of taking a certification exam, or you can set it up in study mode so that you can look at the correct answers and explanations after you answer each question.

> **MORE INFO** **PRACTICE TESTS**
>
> For details about all the practice test options available, see the "How to Use the Practice Tests" section in this book's Introduction.

CHAPTER 2

Exchange Databases and Address Lists

As an Exchange professional, you need to know how an Exchange Server 2010 organization stores mailboxes and public folders and how email addresses can be grouped so that a single email message is sent to multiple recipients. This chapter discusses the changes made and new features added to Exchange database technology that Exchange Server 2010 introduces to improve availability and database mobility and to increase the performance and reliability of the database engine. The chapter also discusses address list and offline address book creation and configuration.

Exam objectives in this chapter:

- Create and configure databases.
- Create and configure address lists.

Lessons in this chapter:

Before You Begin

In order to complete the exercises in the practice session in this chapter, you need to have done the following:

- Installed the Windows Server 2008 R2 domain controller VAN-DC1 and the Windows Exchange 2010 Enterprise Mailbox server VAN-EX1 as described in the Appendix "Setup Instructions for Exchange Server 2010."
- Created the Kim Akers account with the password *Pa$$w0rd* in the Adatum.com domain. This account should be placed in the Domain Admins security group and be a member of the Exchange Organization Administrator role.

- Created the Don Hall account with the password *Pa$$w0rd* in the Adatum.com domain. This account should be placed in the Backup Operators security group (so it can be used to log on to the domain controller) and should be in the Marketing organizational unit (OU).
- Created mailboxes for Kim Akers and Don Hall, accepting the default email address format for the e-mail addresses.

 REAL WORLD

Ian McLean

Email is important to almost everyone. How many people in today's world check their e-mail in the morning before they do anything else—even get their clothes on? I do.

If an organization's internal email communication is down, its operation is crippled. If its employees cannot send or receive external email, they will be very unhappy. Public folders (also an Exchange function) are important, as are Web access and access to user files on the organization's network. But first, make sure Exchange Server is up and running and properly configured.

Otherwise, your job is on the line.

Lesson 1: Deploying Exchange Databases

Exchange Server 2010 introduces a number of significant changes in Exchange database architecture. Possibly the first change you will notice is that storage groups no longer exist. When Exchange 2007 was released to run on 64-bit Windows servers, the best practice was to have a single database per storage group. In Exchange Server 2010, Microsoft has integrated the storage group functionality into the Exchange database.

Databases are no longer child objects of Exchange Mailbox servers. In Exchange Server 2010, they have the same status as servers. In the Exchange Management Console (EMC), you no longer administer databases at the server level. Databases are now configured at the organization level.

In order to support database mobility, all databases require unique names within an organization. Exchange Server 2010 also provides additional Exchange Management Shell (EMS) and EMC functionality. Some EMS cmdlets in previous versions of Exchange Server that deal with storage groups have been replaced by mailbox database and public folder database cmdlets.

> **MORE INFO** **NEW FEATURES IN EXCHANGE SERVER 2010**
>
> For more information about what is new in Exchange Server 2010, see *http://technet .microsoft.com/en-us/library/dd298136.aspx*.

> **After this lesson, you will be able to:**
> - Create and configure mailbox databases.
> - Create and configure public folder databases.
> - Mount, dismount, move, and remove Exchange databases.
>
> **Estimated lesson time: 40 minutes**

Configuring Exchange Databases

Exchange Server 2010 stores mailboxes and public folders in Exchange databases. Mailbox servers can contain both public folder and mailbox databases. Each database is stored in a single Extensible Storage Engine database (.edb) file. The database file in which a particular message is stored does not change, regardless of the type of client that sends or reads the message.

> **NOTE** **CREATING AND CONFIGURING EXCHANGE DATABASES**
>
> You must be assigned the Organization Management role to enable you to create and manage mailbox or public folder databases on any Mailbox server or the Server Management role to create databases on a specific server in an Exchange organization. Users assigned the View Only Organization Management role can view database properties but cannot modify any of those properties.

Each database has a single set of transaction logs that record changes to the database, including messages sent to or from the database. Transaction logs can be used in disaster recovery scenarios if high-availability features (described in Chapter 13, "Exchange High-Availability Solutions") are not implemented. However, their primary function is to ensure that Exchange Server 2010 follows the Atomicity, Consistency, Isolation, and Durability model for databases. Each individual database and its transaction logs are by default stored in the same folder but in a different folder from all other databases. By default, the folders that hold the databases are stored in the folder path C:\Program Files\Microsoft\Exchange\Server\v14\Mailbox, as shown in Figure 2-1.

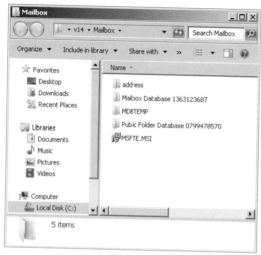

FIGURE 2-1 Exchange database folders

A single folder by default holds both the database and its transaction logs. You should, however, consider storing transaction logs in separate folders and on a different hard disk from the databases. Because transaction logs can be used in disaster recovery in situations where high-availability solutions are not implemented, you might be unable to restore to the point of failure if you lose both the database and its transaction logs in the same disk crash.

EXAM TIP

Exchange Server 2000 and Exchange Server 2003 enabled multiple databases to share a single set of transaction logs through the use of storage groups. Exchange Server 2007 also offered this functionality but only for databases that did not have high-availability features enabled. In Exchange Server 2010, each database must have its own set of transaction logs. If you see an answer in the 70-662 examination that proposes shared transaction logs or a storage group, then you can reject this answer.

The folder that contains an Exchange database (.edb) file can also contain other types of files. Figure 2-2 shows the files in a public folder database folder. The possible file types in an Exchange database folder are as follows:

- **Checkpoint file (.chk)**   Determines which transactions in the current transaction log need to be committed to the database.
- **Current transaction log file (exx.log)**   The file into which new transactions are written. When this file reaches its storage limit of 1 megabyte (MB), Exchange Server 2010 closes the log file, renames it, and creates a new current transaction log file.
- **Closed transaction log file (.log)**   Closed transaction log files have the same file type (.log) as the current transaction file but have a longer file name. For example, a current transaction file E00.log might be named E000000000001.log when its size reaches 1 MB.
- **Reserved transaction log files (.jrs)**   Exchange Server 2010 uses these files as emergency storage when the disk becomes full and it cannot create a new transaction log. The database is taken offline, and any transactions that cannot be written to the current log are written to a reserved transaction log file. Reserved transaction log files are 1 MB in size.
- **Temporary workspace file (<*log prefix*>tmp.log)**   The transaction log file for the temporary workspace (for example, E00tmp.log). The size of this file cannot exceed 1 MB.
- **Exchange database file (.edb)**   Stores content for mailbox and public folder databases. The size limit for this type of file is 64 terabytes (TB), although in practice a lower size limit will probably be imposed by disk size restrictions.

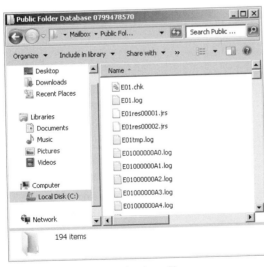

FIGURE 2-2 Public folder database files

Detailed instructions for configuring a mailbox database are given later in this lesson. However, for high-level configuration of database options in the EMC, click Mailbox under Organization Configuration and select the Database Management tab, as shown in Figure 2-3. Right-click the database you want to configure and click Properties. This accesses the General, Maintenance, Limits, and Client Settings tabs.

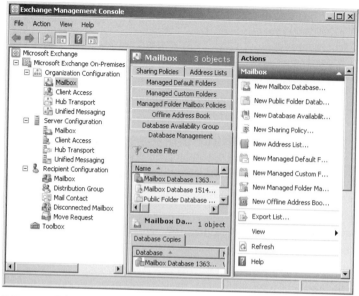

FIGURE 2-3 Selecting the Database Management tab

The General tab gives information about the database, such as its backup status, when it was last modified, the server on which it is mounted, the path to the database file, and servers that have a copy of the database.

If you are using database journaling, discussed in detail in Chapter 11, "Managing Records and Compliance," you can specify a journal recipient on the Maintenance tab. However, Microsoft recommends that you use journaling rules to configure journaling in Exchange Server 2010. On the Maintenance tab, you can configure the maintenance schedule and specify when Exchange Server 2010 performs database maintenance, such as removing deleted items and mailboxes. You can specify whether to mount the database at startup and whether the database can be overwritten by a restore. You can also enable circular logging on the database.

Circular Logging

Circular logging can be used in situations where limited storage capacity is an issue. However, Microsoft recommends that Exchange Server 2010 databases not be configured to use circular logging if you also plan to use the Volume Shadow Copy Service to enable third-party backup and recovery operations.

If circular logging is enabled, transaction logs in the same directory as a database may be deleted when that database is restored so that only point-in-time recovery operations are possible. Also, incremental and differential backup operations are not permitted if circular logging is enabled.

Finally, if circular logging is enabled while you are performing a backup or recovery operation, the restoration of individual databases will be prohibited.

On the Client Settings tab, you can specify the default public folder database and, if appropriate, the default offline address book for all mailboxes in a database.

The Limits tab, shown in Figure 2-4, lets you specify the storage limits for the database, at what database size a warning is issued, and the database file sizes at which Send and Send and Receive are prohibited. You can configure the notification schedule for sending messages to users who have exceeded these limits. The tab permits you to specify deletion settings that determine how long the database retains mailboxes and deleted items within mailboxes after a user deletes them. You can recover deleted items within their deletion period even after the user has removed them from the Deleted Items folder by using the dumpster (or Recovery Items folder). Chapter 14, "Exchange Disaster Recovery," discusses item recovery in detail. Chapter 8, "Configuring Transport Servers," discusses the dumpster.

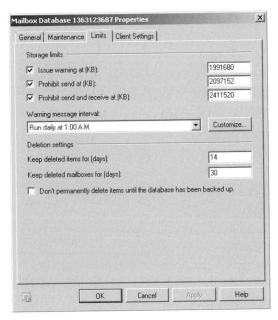

FIGURE 2-4 The Limits tab

MORE INFO   RECOVERABLE ITEMS AND THE DUMPSTER

For more information about recoverable items and single item recovery, access
http://technet.microsoft.com/en-us/library/ee364754.aspx and follow the links.

Managing Mailbox Databases

A *mailbox database* is an Exchange database for storing mailboxes. It manages the data in mailboxes, tracks deleted messages and mailbox sizes, and assists in message transfers. As an Exchange professional, you need to know how to create and remove a mailbox database, how to mount and dismount it, how to modify its size limit, and how to change the database path. You need to know how to configure database properties and how to set the maintenance schedule.

To create and configure a mailbox database, you require the Organization Management, Server Management, or Storage Management role. The following high-level procedure creates a mailbox database in the EMC:

1. In the Console tree, click Mailbox under Organization Configuration.

2. In the Action pane, click New Mailbox Database.

3. On the Introduction page of the New Mailbox Database Wizard, specify a name for the new mailbox database. Click Browse and select the server on which you want to create the database server. Click OK and then click Next.

4. If you want to change the location of the Database File Path, click Browse on the Set Paths page. To change the location of the log folder path, click Browse under Log Folder path. Select the Mount This Database check box if you want to mount the database. Mounting puts the database online so that its contents are available to users. Click Next.

5. On the New Mailbox Database page, click New. This creates the mailbox database.

6. On the Completion page, confirm that the new mailbox database was created successfully. A status of Completed indicates successful completion. If the task fails, review the summary and click Back to make any required configuration changes.

7. Click Finish to close the New Mailbox Database Wizard. The new mailbox database appears on the Database Management tab.

You can create a mailbox database in EMS using the *New-MailboxDatabase* cmdlet. For example, the following command creates the mailbox database MyMailboxDatabase and specifies the .edb database file path C:\MyDatabaseFiles\MyMailboxDatabase.edb and the log folder path D:\MyDatabaseFiles\LogFolder:

```
New-MailboxDatabase -Name "MyMailboxDatabase" -Server VAN-EX1 -EdbFilePath
C:\MyDatabaseFiles\MyMailboxDatabase.edb -LogFolderPath D:\MyDatabaseFiles\
LogFolder
```

Quick Check

■ On which tab in a mailbox database Properties dialog box can you enable or disable circular logging?

Quick Check Answer

■ The Maintenance tab.

> **MORE INFO** **NEW-MAILBOXDATABASE**
>
> For more information about the *New-MailboxDatabase* cmdlet, including its associated command syntax, see *http://technet.microsoft.com/en-us/library/aa997976.aspx*.

Mounting a Database

The procedure to mount a database is straightforward. In the EMC, click Mailbox under Organization Configuration and in the Result pane select the server on which the database is located. In the Work pane, select the mailbox database that you want to mount and then click Mount in the Action pane. If you create a new database using the EMC, you can choose to select the Mount This Database check box, in which case the newly created database is automatically mounted.

If the mailbox database is already mounted and you want to dismount it, the procedure is the same except you click Dismount in the Action pane. A warning appears asking if you want to dismount the database, and you click Yes.

In the EMS, you use the *Mount-Database* cmdlet. For example, the following command mounts the mailbox database MyMailboxDatabase. If you use the *New-MailboxDatabase* cmdlet in the EMS to create a mailbox database, you need to mount it after it is created.

```
Mount-Database –Identity MyMailboxDatabase.
```

The following command dismounts the mailbox database MyMailboxDatabase:

```
Dismount-Database –Identity MyMailboxDatabase
```

> **NOTE** **MOUNTING AND DISMOUNTING A DATABASE**
>
> The Microsoft Exchange Information Store (MSExchangeIS) service needs to be running before you can mount or dismount a database.

Removing a Database

The procedure for removing a mailbox database is also straightforward. In the EMC, you click Mailbox under Organization Configuration, click the mailbox database you want to remove in the Work pane, and then click Remove in the Action pane. A warning appears asking if you are sure you want to remove the mailbox database, and you click Yes.

To remove a mailbox database using the EMS, you use the Remove-MailboxDatabase cmdlet. For example, the following command removes the mailbox database MyMailboxDatabase:

```
Remove-MailboxDatabase -Identity MyMailboxDatabase
```

You are prompted to confirm that you want to perform the action. Type **Y**.

EXAM TIP

Bear in mind that the *New-MailboxDatabase* cmdlet syntax requires the Name parameter, while the syntax of cmdlets to configure, mount, dismount, or remove a database (for example, *Remove-MailboxDatabase*) requires the Identity parameter.

Whether you use the EMC or the EMS to remove a mailbox database, the procedure does not remove the database (.edb) file. In both cases, you are given the location of the file, and you can remove it manually. If you use the EMC, you need to click OK to close the dialog box that gives you this information.

MORE INFO   REMOVE-MAILBOXDATABASE

For more information about the *Remove-MailboxDatabase* cmdlet, see *http://technet .microsoft.com/en-us/library/aa997931.aspx*.

Configuring the Database Size Limit

The Limits tab of the Mailbox Database Properties dialog box, shown in Figure 2-4 earlier in this lesson, lets you specify the limits at which warning messages are sent, Send is prohibited, and Send and Receive are prohibited. It does not, however, let you specify the size limit for the database. To do this, you need to configure the registry of the Exchange Server 2010 server that hosts the database.

The default database size limit for Exchange 2010 Standard Edition is 50 GB. There is no default database size limit for Exchange 2010 Enterprise Edition. The Exchange store periodically checks database size limits and dismounts a database if its size limit is reached. You can modify the database size limit by adding or changing a value in the registry on the server that hosts the database. This change will be propagated to all servers that hold a copy of the database.

To specify the size limit for a mailbox database, you first need to know the global unique identifier (GUID) of the database. You can obtain this by entering a command with the following syntax in EMS:

```
Get-MailboxDatabase -Identity "<server name>\<database name>" | Format-Table Name,GUID
```

You then use the Registry Editor (regedit.exe) to locate the following registry subkey:

```
HKEY_LOCAL_MACHINE\SYSTEM\CurrentControlSet\Services\MSExchangeIS\<server name>
\Private-<database GUID>
```

If the *Database Size Limit in GB* DWORD exists for the subkey, change its value to the desired size in gigabytes. If the DWORD does not exist, create it and set its value to the desired size in gigabytes.

> **CAUTION**
>
> Ensure that size limit changes do not affect your Service Level Agreements (SLAs). If you increase the size limits of your databases, this might lead to longer backup and restore times. Take care to ensure that such changes do not contravene your SLAs.

Changing the Path to the Mailbox Database

You can use both the EMC and the EMS to change the mailbox database path. Note that if you want to move a database path, the database is automatically dismounted (if necessary) so that it is inaccessible to users. If the database was previously mounted, it is automatically remounted when the move is complete. If the database was not mounted before the path is moved, it is not automatically remounted on completion.

The high-level procedure to use the EMC is as follows:

1. Click Mailbox under Organization Configuration in the console tree.
2. On the Database Management tab in the Result pane, click the database you want to configure.
3. In the Work pane, click Move Database Path**.**
4. In the Move Database Path Wizard, on the Database Paths page, click Move to move the database path. Configure the Database File Path field. Change the location of the log folder path by configuring the Log Folder Path field. View the configuration status of the move operation. Click Back if the paths specified are not what you require.
5. On the Completion page, you confirm whether the move process completed successfully. If the task fails, review the summary and click Back to make any configuration changes required. Click Finish.

> **NOTE** **MOVING REPLICATED DATABASES**
>
> The procedure for moving database paths to replicated databases differs from the above and is described in Chapter 13.

To use the EMS to move the mailbox database path, you use the *Move-DatabasePath* cmdlet. For example, to set a new path for the mailbox database MyMailboxDatabase, enter the following command:

```
Move-DatabasePath -Identity MyMailboxDatabase -EdbFilePath C:\DifferentFolder\
MyMailboxDatabase
```

If you know the GUID of the mailbox database, you can use this instead of the database name in the Identity parameter.

Configuring Mailbox Database Properties

Earlier in this lesson, we saw that the Mailbox Database Properties dialog box offers four tabs that let you view the general properties of the mailbox database, let you set a maintenance schedule and enable circular logging, let you configure warning and prohibit limits and how long deleted items are retained, and let you view and select the default public folder database and the offline address book (OAB) for the mailbox. You can also use the *Set-MailboxDatabase* cmdlet in EMS to configure mailbox database properties.

For example, the following command configures a deleted item retention time of 14 days for the mailbox database MyMailboxDatabase:

```
Set-MailboxDatabase -Identity "MyMailboxDatabase" -DeletedItemRetention 14.00:00:00
```

Note that you can set a deleted item retention time for an individual mailbox. If you do so, this overrides the deleted item retention time set on the mailbox database that contains that particular mailbox.

Exchange database maintenance includes removing items that have passed their retention period, removing unused indexes, and other cleanup tasks. Optionally, it can also include online defragmentation, although you can configure this to occur continuously. The following command schedules maintenance to run from Sunday of each week at 10:30 PM until Monday at 1:30 AM:

```
Set-MailboxDatabase -Identity "MyMailboxDatabase" -MaintenanceSchedule "Sun.10:30 PM-
Mon.1:30 AM"
```

You can specify days by numbers, where 0 equals Sunday, 1 equals Monday, and so on. You can also specify a 24-hour clock so that you do not need to include AM and PM. For example, the following command schedules maintenance to start on Saturday at 9:00 PM and finish on the same Saturday at 11:15 PM:

```
Set-MailboxDatabase -Identity "MyMailboxDatabase" -MaintenanceSchedule 6.21:00-6.23:15
```

Quick Check

- What EMS cmdlet do you use to change a mailbox database path?

Quick Check Answer

- *Move-DatabasePath*

Managing Public Folder Databases

A *public folder database* is an Exchange database that stores public folders and system folders and assists in the replication of the folders with other Exchange servers. Exchange Server 2010 supports public folder functionality. You need to configure public folders if your clients are using Microsoft Outlook 2003 or earlier. However, Outlook 2007 and Outlook 2010 do not require public folders to implement OAB distribution or calendar information except when they need to coexist with previous versions of Exchange Server.

When you install the first Exchange Server 2010 server in an Active Directory Domain Service (AD DS) forest, you can specify whether your Exchange organization supports Outlook 2003 or Microsoft Entourage. If you say yes, Exchange Server 2010 creates a public folder database. If you say no, you can create a public folder database later on using the *New-PublicFolderDatabase* cmdlet.

> **MORE INFO** **PUBLIC FOLDER DATABASE CREATION AND CONFIGURATION**
>
> For more information about how to use the *New-PublicFolderDatabase* cmdlet to create a public folder database, see *http://technet.microsoft.com/en-us/library/bb123673.aspx*. For more information about how to use the *Set-PublicFolderDatabase* cmdlet to configure a public folder database, see *http://technet.microsoft.com/en-us/library/aa997225.aspx*. For detailed information about public folder management, access *http://technet.microsoft .com/en-us/library/bb124411.aspx* and follow the links.

Although not every Exchange organization hosts public folder databases, you, as a professional, need to know how to manage them. As with mailbox databases, you have the option of using the EMC or the EMS to carry out most tasks. In order to manage a public folder database, you need to be granted the Exchange Organization Administrator role and be a member of the Local Administrators group on the target server.

Creating a Public Folder Database

As mentioned earlier in this section, the *New-PublicFolderDatabase* cmdlet in the EMS is used to create a public folder database. For example, the following command creates a public folder database named My Public Folder database with a file path

C:\Program Files\Microsoft\Exchange Server\Mailbox\PublicDatabase.edb and a log file path D:\ExchangeDatabases\Public\Logs\ PublicDatabase:

```
New-PublicFolderDatabase -Name "My Public Folder Database" -EdbFilePath "C:\Program
Files\Microsoft\Exchange Server\Mailbox\PublicDatabase.edb" -LogFolderPath
"D:\ExchangeDatabases\Public\Logs\PublicDatabase"
```

You can also use the following procedure in the EMC:

1. In the Console pane, under Organization Configuration, click Mailbox.

2. In the Action pane, click New Public Folder Database.

3. On the Introduction page of the New Public Folder Database Wizard, specify the public folder name and select the Mailbox server on which it is to be created. Click Next.

4. On the Set Paths page, you can optionally change the default paths to the database (.edb) file and the transaction logs. Click Next. If you want to mount the database when it is created, ensure that the Mount This Database check box is selected (the default).

5. Read the summary on the New Public Folder Database page. If you agree with the settings, click New to create the public folder database. Figure 2-5 shows the New Public Folder Database page.

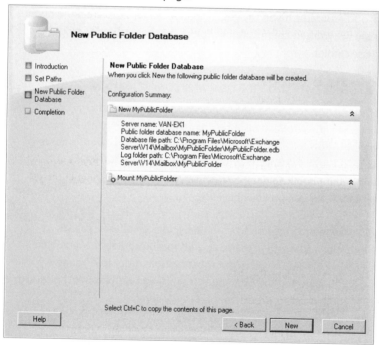

FIGURE 2-5 The New Public Folder Database page

> **NOTE   CREATING A PUBLIC FOLDER DATABASE**
>
> You cannot create a public folder database on a server on which one already exists because a Mailbox server can host a maximum of one public folder database.

Moving Public Folder Content

Two scenarios exist in which you want to move public folder content from one public folder database to another public folder database. You might want to move all public folder content in a database to the new database (for example, if you were replacing the Exchange Server 2010 server that stored the public folder database with a newer or more powerful server), or you might want to move a subtree in a tree of folders from one server to another (for example, if you wanted to share the workload involved in hosting public folders between the two servers).

You can use the MoveAllReplicas.ps1 script to move all public folders in a public folder database to a new public folder database. This script replaces a server with a new server in the replication list for all public folders, including system folders. You can use the ReplaceReplicaOnPFRecursive.ps1 script to move all the replicas of a public folder subtree from one server to another server. This script adds a new server to the replication list for a public folder and all the folders that are beneath it in the hierarchy. If the server is already listed in the replication list for a folder, nothing changes for that folder.

> **MORE INFO PUBLIC FOLDER SCRIPTS**
>
> For more information about using public folder scripts, see *http://technet.microsoft.com/ en-us/library/aa997966.aspx*.

To use the EMS to move all public folder content in a public folder database on Mailbox server MailServerA to a new public folder database on Mailbox server MailServerB, you enter the following command:

```
MoveAllReplicas.ps1 –Server MailServerA –NewServer MailServerB
```

To use the EMS to move content in a tree of folders from Mailbox server MailServerA to Mailbox server MailServerB where the top public folder in the hierarchy is called My Public Folder, you enter the following command:

```
ReplaceReplicaOnPFRecursive.ps1 –TopPublicFolder "\My Public Folder" –ServerToAdd
MailServerB –ServerToRemove MailServerA
```

Removing Public Folders from a Database

Removing user or system public folders from a public folder database is a two-stage procedure. In the EMS, you first need to identify the public folder using the *Get-PublicFolder* cmdlet and pipe the result into the *Remove-PublicFolder* cmdlet. Note that because there can be only one public folder database on a server, you identify the server rather than the database. The following command removes all user public folders from the public folder database on the Mailbox server VAN-EX1:

```
Get-PublicFolder –Server VAN-EX1 "\" –Recurse –ResultSize:Unlimited | Remove-
PublicFolder –Server VAN-EX1 –Recurse –ErrorAction:SilentlyContinue
```

The following command removes all system public folders from the public folder database on the Mailbox server VAN-EX1:

```
Get-PublicFolder -Server VAN-EX1 "\Non_Ipm_Subtree" -Recurse -ResultSize:Unlimited |
Remove-PublicFolder -Server VAN-EX1 -Recurse -ErrorAction:SilentlyContinue
```

The Recurse parameter of the *Get-PublicFolder* cmdlet specifies that the command must return the specified public folder and all its children. You do not need to specify a value with this parameter. Non_Ipm_Subtree specifies the system folder root. If this is not specified after the \ symbol, then the root public folder object Ipm_Subtree is taken as the default. In the *Remove-PublicFolder* cmdlet, the Recurse parameter indicates that the root folder and all its subfolders are removed. The ErrorAction parameter of the *Remove-PublicFolder* cmdlet determines the action to be taken if an error is detected.

> **MORE INFO** **GET-PUBLICFOLDER AND REMOVE-PUBLICFOLDER**
>
> For more information about the *Get-PublicFolder* cmdlet, see *http://technet.microsoft .com/en-us/library/aa997615.aspx*. For more information about the *Remove-PublicFolder* cmdlet, see *http://technet.microsoft.com/en-us/library/bb124894.aspx*.

Removing a Public Folder Database

If you want to remove a public folder database, you must first move any public folder replicas in the database to another server and remove all public folders in the database. Otherwise, you will receive an error stating that the public folder database cannot be removed. You can remove a public folder database that contains no public folders or public folder replicas by using either the EMC or the EMS.

To use the EMC to remove a public folder database, carry out the following procedure:

1. Click Mailbox under Organization Configuration in the Console pane.

2. On the Database Management tab in the Results pane, click the public folder database.

3. Click Remove in the Action pane.

4. A message appears asking if you are sure that you want to remove the database. Click Yes.

5. A Microsoft Exchange Warning page appears, indicating that the database was successfully removed and reminding you to manually remove the database file. The default location for a public folder database file and its associated log files is C:\Program Files\Microsoft\Exchange Server\v14\Mailbox\<public folder database name>.

You can use the *Remove-PublicFolderDatabase* cmdlet in the EMS to remove a public folder database from which all public folders have been removed and all public folder replicas moved. For example, to remove the public folder database MyPublicFolderDatabase on the server VAN-EX1, you would use the following command:

```
Remove-PublicFolderDatabase -Identity "VAN-EX1\MyPublicFolderDatabase"
```

If the public folder database you are removing is the only such database in your Exchange organization, then you need to include the RemoveLastAllowed parameter in the command.

> **MORE INFO** REMOVE-PUBLICFOLDERDATABASE
>
> For more information about the *Remove-PublicFolderDatabase* cmdlet, see *http://technet .microsoft.com/en-us/library/aa996312.aspx.*

Configuring Public Folder Database Properties

You can access the Properties dialog box for a public folder database through the EMC by using a procedure similar to the way you accessed the Properties dialog box for a mailbox database earlier in this lesson. This lets you access four tabs: General, Replication, Limits, and Public Folder Referral.

On the General tab, you can obtain details of the database, such as its file path, whether it is mounted, the server on which it is mounted, and its backup status. You can configure the database replication schedule and specify whether the database is mounted at startup, whether it can be overwritten by a restore, and whether circular logging is enabled.

On the Replication tab, shown in Figure 2-6, you can configure the replication interval and message size limit. You can specify that replication always runs, never runs, runs every hour, runs every two hours, or runs every four hours. You can click Customize to configure a custom schedule.

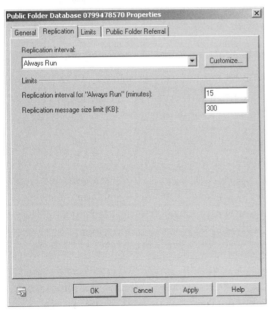

FIGURE 2-6 The Replication tab of the Public Folder Database Properties dialog box

The Limits tab is similar to the Limits tab in the Mailbox Database Properties dialog box shown earlier in Figure 2-4. You can configure Warning and Prohibit Post size limits and Maximum Item Size. You can specify the Warning Message Interval, Deletion Settings, and Age Limits. You should not set size or age limits for system folders.

On the Public Folder Referral tab, you can control how Exchange Server 2010 redirects users among the public folder servers in an organization. By default, Exchange attempts to redirect the user to a server within the AD DS site by obtaining intersite connection costs from Active Directory. You can, however, create a custom public folder server list with an individual cost for each server.

You can also use the EMS to obtain and modify public folder database settings. The *Get-PublicFolderDatabase* cmdlet can obtain the settings for all public folder databases in an Exchange 2010 organization or for a specified public folder database. For example, the following command lists the settings for all public folder databases in an Exchange organization:

```
Get-PublicFolderDatabase | fl
```

Part of the output from this command is shown in Figure 2-7.

FIGURE 2-7 Obtaining settings information for all public server databases

The following command lists the properties of the public folder database MyPublicFolderDatabase on the server ServerA:

```
Get-PublicFolderDatabase -Identity "ServerA\MyPublicFolderDatabase"
```

The *Set-PublicFolderDatabase* cmdlet in the EMS lets you configure public server database settings. For example, the following command sets the deleted items retention period to 14 days and the event history retention period to 28 days, never removes undeleted items, and retains deleted items until the next backup on the public folder database MyPublicFolderDatabase on the Mailbox server MyMailboxServer:

```
Set-PublicFolderDatabase -Identity "MyMailboxServer\MyPublicFolderDatabase"
-DeletedItemRetention 14.00:00:00 -RetainDeletedItemsUntilBackup $true
-EventHistoryRetentionPeriod 14.00:00:00 -ItemRetentionPeriod unlimited
```

The following command sets the issue warning quota to 2,000 MB and configures the quota notification schedule for all public folders in the public folder database named MyPublicFolderDatabase:

```
Set-PublicFolderDatabase -Identity MyPublicFolderDatabase -IssueWarningQuota 2000MB
-QuotaNotificationSchedule "Mon.3:00 AM-Mon.3:20 AM,Wed.3:00 AM-Wed.3:20 AM,Fri.3:00
AM-Fri.3:20 AM"
```

> **MORE INFO   GET-PUBLICFOLDERDATABASE AND SET-PUBLICFOLDERDATABASE**
>
> For more information about the *Get-PublicFolderDatabase* cmdlet, see *http://technet
> .microsoft.com/en-us/library/aa998827.aspx*. For more information about the
> *Set-PublicFolderDatabase* cmdlet, see *http://technet.microsoft.com/en-us/library/
> aa997225.aspx*.

Lesson 2, "Setting Up Public Folders," of Chapter 4, "Distribution Groups and Public Folders," provides an in-depth discussion about using and configuring public folders.

Lesson Summary

- Exchange Server 2010 stores mailboxes in mailbox databases and public folders in public folder databases.
- You can create and configure Exchange databases using the EMC or the EMS. The EMS offers more functionality than the EMC.
- You need to be assigned the Organization Management role to create and manage Exchange databases.

Lesson Review

You can use the following questions to test your knowledge of the information in Lesson 1, "Deploying Exchange Databases." The questions are also available on the companion CD if you prefer to review them in electronic form.

> **NOTE   ANSWERS**
>
> Answers to these questions and explanations of why each answer choice is correct or incorrect are located in the "Answers" section at the end of the book.

1. You have used the EMS to create a mailbox database called Marketing on the server VAN-EX1 and to set the warning quota on that database to 2.5 GB. You now want to enable it to be used to provision new mailboxes. What EMS command do you enter?

   A. *New-MailboxDatabase –Name Marketing –Server VAN-EX1*

   B. *Set-MailboxDatabase –Identity Marketing –IssueWarningQuota 2.5GB*

   C. *Mount-Database –Identity Marketing*

   D. *Dismount-Database –Identity Marketing*

2. Currently, both the database and transaction log files for the Sales mailbox database are in the same folder on the C: volume. You want to move the transaction logs to the E:\SalesTransactionLog folder. What is the first command that you enter in the EMS in order to accomplish this?

   A. *Dismount-Database –Identity Sales*

   B. *Mount-Database –Identity Sales*

   C. *Set-MailboxDatabase –Identity Sales –LogFolderPath E:\ SalesTransactionLog*

   D. *Move-DatabasePath –Identity Sales –LogFolderPath E:\ SalesTransactionLog*

3. You want to ensure that the mailbox database named Production undergoes the removal of items that have passed their retention period, the removal of unused indexes, and other cleanup tasks. You want to schedule these operations so that they occur every Sunday between 10:15 and 11:45 PM. What command do you enter in the EMS?

   A. *Get-MailboxDatabase -Identity Production -MaintenanceSchedule 0.10:15-0.11:45*

   B. *Set-MailboxDatabase -Identity Production -MaintenanceSchedule 6.22:15-6.23:45*

   C. *Set-MailboxDatabase -Identity Production -MaintenanceSchedule 0.22:15-0.23:45*

   D. *Set-MailboxDatabase -Identity Production -MaintenanceSchedule 0.10:15-0.11:45*

4. You have created a public folder database named CompanyInformation on the server VAN-EX1 running Exchange Server 2010. You want to configure this public folder database to retain items for 42 days. Which of the following EMS commands could you enter to accomplish this goal?

   A. *New-PublicFolderDatabase –Server VAN-EX1 –Name CompanyInformation*

   B. *New-PublicFolderDatabase –Server VAN-EX1 –Name CompanyInformation –ItemRetentionPeriod 42*

   C. *Set-PublicFolderDatabase –Server VAN-EX1 –Name CompanyInformation -ItemRetentionPeriod 42*

   D. *Set-PublicFolderDatabase –Identity CompanyInformation -ItemRetentionPeriod 42*

Lesson 2: Address List Configuration

An *address list* is a collection of recipient and other AD DS objects. It can contain one or more types of objects, such as users, contacts, groups, public folders, conferencing, and other resources. Address lists also provide a mechanism to partition mail-enabled objects in Active Directory for the benefit of specific groups of users. In this lesson, you will see how to create and configure an address lists and OABs.

> **After this lesson, you will be able to:**
> - Create and configure address lists.
> - Create and configure OABs.
> - Add address lists to and remove them from OABs.
>
> **Estimated lesson time: 40 minutes**

Creating and Configuring an Address List

You need to be assigned to the Organization Management role group to create an address list. You can create an address list using either the EMC or the EMS.

The procedure to create an address list in the EMC is as follows:

1. In the console tree, click Mailbox under Organization Configuration.
2. In the Action pane, click New Address List.
3. On the Introduction page of the New Address List Wizard, shown in Figure 2-8, type the name for the new address list in the Name box. The name can contain up to 64 characters, including wildcard characters, but cannot contain the backslash character (\).

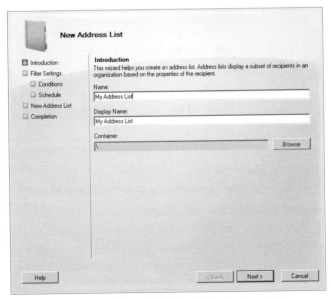

FIGURE 2-8 The New Address List Wizard Introduction page

4. In the Display Name box, type the display name for the address list. This is the name displayed to users when they view the address list from, for example, a Microsoft Outlook 2010 client. This field is automatically populated with the name you type in the Name box, but you can modify it if you want to.

5. In the Container box, you can type the path to the container for the address list, but typically you click Browse and select it. If you want to add the address list as a child to an existing address list, click the existing address list and then click OK. To create a new parent address list, click All Address Lists and then click OK. Note that if you specify All Address Lists as the container, the default (\) symbol is shown in the Container box.

6. Click Next. On the Filter Settings page, shown in Figure 2-9, select the recipient container where you want to apply the filter. The recipient container defines the OU filter for an address list. Click Browse to open the Select Organizational Unit dialog box. Use this dialog box to specify the OU from which to select the recipients.

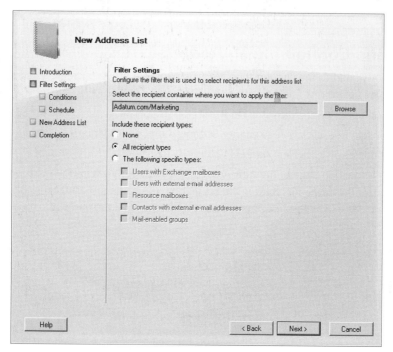

FIGURE 2-9 The Filter Settings page

7. You can select All Recipient Types or The Following Specific Types. If you select The Following Specific Types, you can select one or more of the following:

   ■ **Users With Exchange Mailboxes** You should select this check box if you want the address list to apply to users that have a user domain account and a mailbox in the Exchange organization.

- **Users With External E-Mail Addresses**   You should select this check box if you want the address list to apply to users that have user domain accounts in Active Directory but use email accounts that are external to the organization. This enables them to be included in the global address list (GAL) and added to distribution lists.

- **Resource Mailboxes**   You should select this check box if you want the address list to apply to Exchange resource mailboxes, which allow you to administer company resources, such as a conference room or video equipment, through a mailbox.

- **Contacts With External E-Mail Addresses**   You should select this check box if you want the address list to apply to contacts that have external email addresses. These contacts do not have user domain accounts in AD DS, but their external e-mail address is available in the GAL.

- **Mail-Enabled Groups**   You should select this check box if you want the address list to apply to security groups or distribution groups that have been mail-enabled. Note that you must convert any nonuniversal distribution groups to universal distribution groups to ensure that all distribution groups are displayed. Email messages that are sent to a mail-enabled group account are delivered to several recipients.

8. Click Next. The Conditions page is shown in Figure 2-10. Complete the following fields:

  - **Step 1: Select Condition(s)**   You can use this section to select one or more conditions for your address list. If you do not want to set a list condition, you do not need to select any of the following check boxes:

    - **Recipient is in a State or Province**   Select this check box if you want the address list to include only recipients from specific states or provinces.

    - **Recipient is in a Department**   Select this check box if you want the address list to include only recipients in specific departments.

    - **Recipient is in a Company**   Select this check box if you want the address list to include only recipients in specific companies.

    - **Custom Attribute equals Value**   You can specify up to 15 custom attributes for each recipient. If you want the address list to include only recipients that have a specific value set for a specific custom attribute, select the check box that corresponds to that custom attribute.

> **NOTE**   **SPECIFYING SOME CONDITIONS EXCLUDES MAIL-ENABLED DISTRIBUTION GROUPS**
>
> The State or Province, Department, and Company conditions are based on attributes that are applicable only to mailboxes, mail users, and mail contacts and do not apply to mail-enabled distribution groups. If you configure any of these conditions for an address list, you will in effect be excluding all mail-enabled distribution groups from that address list.

- **Step 2: Edit the Conditions by Selecting an Underlined Value** If you select any conditions in step 1, each condition you select will append to the definition of the address list. For example, if you select the Recipient Is In A State Or Province check box in step 1, you will see Address List Contains: All Recipient Types In The Specified State Or Province(s) condition in step 2. You click the underlined term (in this case Specified) to define the condition. You can add a new value, edit an existing value, or remove a value. You cannot specify a duplicate value. You can specify only one value for a custom attribute condition.

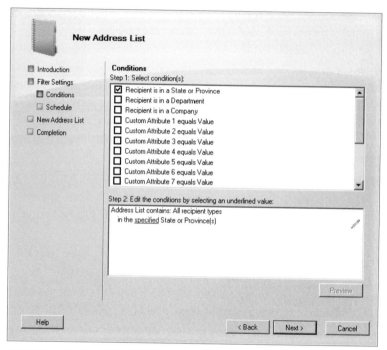

FIGURE 2-10 The Conditions page

NOTE VALUES MUST BE EXACT

The values you enter must exactly match those that appear in the recipient properties. For example, if you enter Pennsylvania in the Specify State Or Province dialog box but the Address and Phone tab in the recipient properties lists the state as PA, the condition will not be met.

9. Optionally, click Preview to view the recipients that will be contained in the address list.

10. Click Next. On the Schedule page, shown in Figure 2-11, you can specify whether you want to create the address list but do not want to apply it to recipients, whether you want to apply the address list immediately, or whether you want to apply it at a specified time. You can also specify that tasks that are still running after a configurable amount of time (by default eight hours) will be canceled.

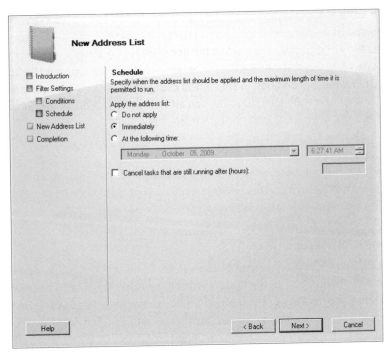

FIGURE 2-11 The Schedule page

> **MORE INFO**   **APPLYING AN ADDRESS LIST**
>
> If you choose not to apply an address list to the selected recipients, you can then use the *Update-AddressList* cmdlet in the EMS or the Apply Address List Wizard to do so retrospectively. For more information, see *http://technet.microsoft.com/en-us/library/ aa996375.aspx*.

11. Click Next and review your configuration settings on the New Address List page. Click New to create the address list or click Back to make configuration changes.

12. Click Next. A status of Completed on the Completion page indicates that the wizard completed the task successfully. In this case, click Finish. If the status is Failed, review the summary for an explanation and then click Back to make the required configuration changes.

You use the *New-AddressList* cmdlet in the EMS to create an address list. For example, the following command creates the address list PennsylvaniaAddressList by using the RecipientFilter parameter and includes recipients that are mailbox users and have StateOrProvince set to Pennsylvania:

```
New-AddressList -Name PennsylvaniaAddressList -RecipientFilter {((RecipientType -eq
'UserMailbox') -and (StateOrProvince -eq 'Pennsylvania'))}
```

The following command creates the child address list PittsburghAddressList in the PennsylvaniaAddressList parent container:

```
New-AddressList -Name "PittsburghAddressList" -Container "\PennsylvaniaAddressList"
-ConditionalCustomAttribute1 "Pittsburgh"
```

If you create an address list in the EMS, you need to apply it using the *Update-AddressList* cmdlet in the EMS or the Apply Address List Wizard in the EMC.

> **MORE INFO**   **NEW-ADDRESSLIST AND UPDATE-ADDRESSLIST**
>
> For more information about the *New-AddressList* cmdlet, see *http://technet.microsoft .com/en-us/library/aa996912.aspx*. For more information about the *Update-AddressList* cmdlet, see *http://technet.microsoft.com/en-us/library/aa997982.aspx*.

Removing an Address List

You can use the EMC or the EMS to remove an address list. To use the EMC, click Mailbox under Organization Configuration. In the Result pane, on the Address List tab, click the address list that you want to remove. If you want to remove an address list that has one or more child address lists, you need to hold down the Ctrl key and select the parent list and all its children. Next, click Remove in the Action pane. A warning appears, asking if you are sure that you want to remove the address list. Click Yes.

To remove an address list through the EMS, you use the *Remove-AddressList* cmdlet. For example, the following command removes an address list named Marketing Department that does not contain child address lists:

```
Remove-AddressList -Identity "Marketing Department"
```

The following command removes an address list named Sales Department and all of the child address lists it contains:

```
Remove-AddressList -Identity "Sales Department" -Recursive
```

In both cases, you need to enter **Y** to confirm that you want to remove the address list.

> **MORE INFO**   **REMOVE-ADDRESSLIST**
>
> For more information about the *Remove-AddressList* cmdlet, see *http://technet .microsoft.com/en-us/library/bb124342.aspx*.

Configuring Address List Properties

You can use either the EMC or the EMS to configure the properties of an address list. There are, however, limitations to using the EMC. You cannot use it to edit GALs or to move an address list from its container. Nor can you use the EMC to edit the conditions or recipient types of the default address lists All Contacts, All Groups, All Rooms, All Users, and Public Folders.

Editing an address list using the EMC uses wizard pages that are very similar to those described earlier in this lesson when you were creating the address list. You click on Mailbox under Organization Configuration in the Console tree, click the Address List tab in the Result pane, select the address list you want to configure, and then click Edit in the Action pane.

The Edit Address List Wizard has the same Introduction, Filter Settings, Conditions, and Schedule pages as does the Create Address List Wizard. The settings configured for the address list appear on these pages, and you can modify them. On the Edit Address List page, you review your configuration settings and click Edit to apply these changes or click Back if you are not satisfied with them. On the Completion page, you can click Finish to close the wizard.

You can use the *Set-AddressList* cmdlet in the EMS to configure an address list. Commands that use this cmdlet can have a lengthy syntax, principally because of the multiple custom attributes you can define. The syntax is as follows:

```
Set-AddressList -Identity <AddressListIdParameter> [-ConditionalCompany
<MultiValuedProperty>] [-ConditionalCustomAttribute1 <MultiValuedProperty>]
[-ConditionalCustomAttribute10 <MultiValuedProperty>] [-ConditionalCustomAttribute11
<MultiValuedProperty>] [-ConditionalCustomAttribute12 <MultiValuedProperty>]
[-ConditionalCustomAttribute13 <MultiValuedProperty>] [-ConditionalCustomAttribute14
<MultiValuedProperty>] [-ConditionalCustomAttribute15 <MultiValuedProperty>]
[-ConditionalCustomAttribute2 <MultiValuedProperty>] [-ConditionalCustomAttribute3
<MultiValuedProperty>] [-ConditionalCustomAttribute4 <MultiValuedProperty>]
[-ConditionalCustomAttribute5 <MultiValuedProperty>] [-ConditionalCustomAttribute6
<MultiValuedProperty>] [-ConditionalCustomAttribute7 <MultiValuedProperty>]
[-ConditionalCustomAttribute8 <MultiValuedProperty>] [-ConditionalCustomAttribute9
<MultiValuedProperty>] [-ConditionalDepartment <MultiValuedProperty>]
[-ConditionalStateOrProvince <MultiValuedProperty>] [-Confirm [<SwitchParameter>]]
[-DisplayName <String>] [-DomainController <Fqdn>] [-ForceUpgrade <SwitchParameter>]
[-IncludedRecipients <Nullable>] [-Name <String>] [-RecipientContainer
<OrganizationalUnitIdParameter>] [-RecipientFilter <String>] [-WhatIf
[<SwitchParameter>]]
```

In practice, the commands are seldom as complex as the syntax suggests. For example, the following command configures the address list Adatum Miami Branch to include recipients that work in Adatum's Miami office:

```
Set-AddressList -Identity "Adatum Miami Branch" -ConditionalCompany Adatum
-ConditionalStateorProvince Miami
```

As previously stated, if you want to reconfigure the properties of one of the default address lists, you need to use the *Set-AddressList* cmdlet and cannot use the EMC. However, you seldom need to reconfigure a default address list.

> **MORE INFO   SET-ADDRESSLIST**
>
> For more information about the *Set-AddressList* cmdlet, see *http://technet.microsoft .com/en-us/library/aa998847.aspx*.

You also cannot use the EMC to move an address list. Instead, you should use the *Move-AddressList* cmdlet in the EMS. For example, the following command moves the address list with GUID c3ffed6e-028a-22b6-88a4-8c21697bb8ad to a new location under the parent address list \All Users\Sales\:

```
Move-AddressList -Identity c3ffed6e-028a-22b6-88a4-8c21697bb8ad -Target "\All Users\
Sales\
```

> **MORE INFO MOVE-ADDRESSLIST**
>
> For more information about the *Move-AddressList* cmdlet, see *http://technet.microsoft
> .com/en-us/library/bb124520.aspx*.

> **MORE INFO OBTAINING ADDRESS LIST PROPERTIES AND VIEWING ADDRESS LIST MEMBERS**
>
> You use the *Get-AddressList* cmdlet to obtain the distinguished name (DN) of an address list and the *Get-Recipient* cmdlet to list address list members in the practice session later in this chapter. For more information about these procedures, see *http://technet
> .microsoft.com/en-us/library/bb430757.aspx*.

Creating and Configuring Global Address Lists

A *global address list* (GAL) is a directory that contains entries for every group, user, and contact within an organization's implementation of Microsoft Exchange. You cannot use the EMC to create or configure a GAL but must instead use EMS cmdlets.

To create a GAL, you use the *New-GlobalAddressList* cmdlet. For example, the following command creates a GAL named Adatum Global for recipients who are mailbox users and have their company listed as Adatum:

```
New-GlobalAddressList -Name "Adatum Global" -IncludedRecipients MailboxUsers
-ConditionalCompany Adatum
```

> **MORE INFO NEW-GLOBALADDRESSLIST**
>
> For more information about the *New-GlobalAddressList* cmdlet, see *http://technet
> .microsoft.com/en-us/library/bb123785.aspx*.

You can modify GAL properties by using the *Set-GlobalAddressList* cmdlet in the EMS. You cannot, however, change the settings of the default GAL. For example, the following command assigns the name Contoso to the GAL that has the GUID 98d0c625-eba8-6203-be4f-687a1ee4ad7b:

```
Set-GlobalAddressList -Identity 98d0c625-eba8-6203-be4f-687a1ee4ad7b -Name Contoso
```

The following command changes the recipients who will be included in the Contoso GAL to mailbox users whose company is set to Contoso:

```
Set-GlobalAddressList -Identity Contoso -RecipientFilter {Company -eq "Contoso"}
```

It may be necessary to start the update process if additional recipients that conform to the defined filter conditions are added. It can take considerable time for an update to complete, but you can start the process by using the *Update-GlobalAddressList* cmdlet, for example:

```
Update-GlobalAddressList -Identity "Contoso"
```

You remove a GAL by using the *Remove-GlobalAddressList* cmdlet, for example:

```
Remove-GlobalAddressList -Identity MyGAL
```

> **MORE INFO** **ADDRESS LIST CMDLETS**
>
> For more information about the *Set-GlobalAddressList* cmdlet, see *http://technet .microsoft.com/en-us/library/bb123877.aspx*. For more information about the *Update-GlobalAddressList* cmdlet, see *http://technet.microsoft.com/en-us/library/ aa998806.aspx*. For more information about the *Remove-GlobalAddressList* cmdlet, see *http://technet.microsoft.com/en-us/library/bb124368.aspx*.

Working with Offline Address Books

An *offline address book* (OAB) is a copy of a collection of address lists generated on an Exchange server and then downloaded to a client computer so that a Microsoft Outlook user can access the information it contains while disconnected from the Exchange organization. Exchange Server 2010 generates OAB files, compresses the files, and then places them on a local share. You can choose which address lists are available to offline users, and you can configure the distribution method. An OAB can be distributed to client computers using two methods:

- Web-based distribution
- Public folder distribution

Web-Based Distribution

Outlook 2007 and Outlook 2010 clients that are working in Cached Exchange Mode, offline, or through a dial-up connection can access the OAB using this distribution method. Web-based distribution does not require public folders. When the OAB is generated, the Client Access server replicates the files. Web-based distribution uses HTTPS and the Background Intelligent Transfer Service (BITS).

> **MORE INFO** **BITS**
>
> For more information about BITS, see *http://msdn.microsoft.com/en-us/library/ aa362708.aspx*.

Web-based distribution supports more concurrent client computers and uses less bandwidth than public folder distribution. It also provides more control over the OAB distribution points. In web-based distribution, the HTTPS web address is the distribution point from which client computers can download the OAB.

To generate or update the OAB, the OAB generation process, implemented by the OABGen service, runs on the OAB generation server (typically an Exchange Server 2010 Mailbox server). The Microsoft Exchange File Distribution service runs on Client Access servers to gather the OAB and keep its content synchronized with the content on the Mailbox server.

The OAB virtual directory provides the distribution point for the web-based distribution method. When Exchange Server 2010 is installed, a new virtual directory named OAB is by default created in the default internal web site in Internet Information Services (IIS). If you have client-side users that connect to Outlook from outside your organization's firewall, you can add an external web site. You can also use the *New-OABVirtualDirectory* cmdlet in the EMS to create a new virtual directory named OAB in the default IIS web site on the local Exchange Server 2010 Client Access server.

> **MORE INFO** **CREATING AN OAB VIRTUAL DIRECTORY**
>
> For more information about creating an OAB virtual directory, see *http://technet .microsoft.com/en-us/library/aa996917.aspx*.

The Autodiscover service in Outlook 2007, Outlook 2010, and some mobile devices automatically configures clients for Exchange access. This service runs on a Client Access server and returns the correct OAB URL for a specific client connection.

> **MORE INFO** **THE AUTODISCOVER SERVICE**
>
> For more information about the Autodiscover service, see *http://technet.microsoft.com/ en-us/library/bb124251.aspx*.

Public Folder Distribution

Outlook 2003 Service Pack 1 or earlier clients that are working offline or through a dial-up connection access the OAB through public folder distribution. The OAB generation process places files directly in a public folder, and Exchange public folder replication copies the data to other public folder distribution points.

Using this method, every request for a full OAB download is served immediately. This can lead to a large volume of traffic that could potentially overload the network for an extended period. To prevent this overload, you can set a bandwidth threshold to limit the network bandwidth that results from OAB downloads. This process is called *throttling*. By default, throttling is disabled. You can activate throttling by editing the following registry key on all public folder servers that host OAB system folders:

HKEY_LOCAL_MACHINE\System\CurrentControlSet\Services\MSExchangeIS\ParametersSystem

Hiding a Recipient from an Address List

The Microsoft Exchange System Attendant service running as Local System produces OAB data. If an administrator uses the security descriptor to prevent users from viewing certain recipients in AD DS, users who download the OAB will be able to view those hidden recipients. Therefore, you might need to hide a recipient from an address list that is included in an OAB. To do this, you configure the HiddenFromAddressListsEnabled parameter on the *Set-PublicFolder, Set-MailContact, Set-MailUser, Set-DynamicDistributionGroup, Set-Mailbox*, and *Set-DistributionGroups* cmdlets in the EMS. Alternatively, you can create a new default OAB that does not contain the hidden recipients.

> **MORE INFO** **ADDING OR REMOVING ADDRESS LISTS FROM AN OAB**
>
> For more information about how to add or remove address lists from an OAB, see *http://technet.microsoft.com/en-us/library/bb123563.aspx*.

> **MORE INFO** **UNDERSTANDING OABs**
>
> For more information about OABs, including some typical scenarios, see *http://technet .microsoft.com/en-us/library/bb232155.aspx*.

Creating an OAB

You can use the EMC to create an OAB and specify either web-based or public folder distribution. If you use the EMS, an OAB with web-based distribution is created by default. To specify public folder distribution, you set the PublicFolderDistributionEnabled parameter to a value of True.

To use the EMC to create an OAB, carry out the following procedure:

1. Open the EMC and click Mailbox under Organization Configuration in the Console tree.
2. Click New Offline Address Book in the Action pane.
3. On the Introduction page of the New Online Address Book Wizard, specify a name for the OAB, the location of the OAB generation Mailbox server, whether the GAL is included, and what other address lists (if any) are included. Figure 2-12 shows the Introduction page. Click Next.

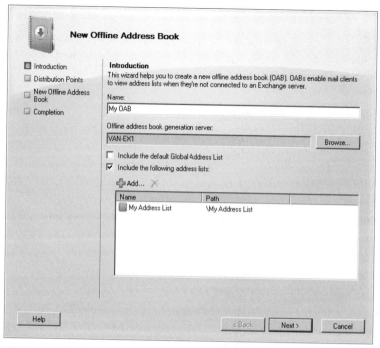

FIGURE 2-12 The Introduction page of the New Online Address Book Wizard

4. On the Distribution Points page, you can enable either web-based or public folder distribution. If you choose web-based distribution, you can specify the OAB virtual directory. If your organization uses both Outlook 2003 Service Pack 1 or earlier clients and Outlook 2007 Service Pack 1 or later clients, you can specify both distribution methods. Click Next.

5. On the Configuration Summary page, click New to create the new OAB.

6. If the wizard completes successfully, click Finish on the Completion page. Otherwise, click Back and review your settings.

You use the *New-OfflineAddressBook* cmdlet in the EMS to create an OAB. For example, the following command creates the OAB WBD-OAB on VAN-EX1 that uses the web-based distribution method and uses the default virtual directory:

```
New-OfflineAddressBook -Name "WBD-OAB" -AddressLists "\My Address List" -Server VAN-EX1
-VirtualDirectories "VAN-EX1\OAB (Default Web Site)"
```

The following command creates an OAB named PFD-OAB on VAN-EX1 that uses the public folder distribution method and uses the public folder database MyPublicDatabase:

```
New-OfflineAddressBook -Name "PFD-OAB" -AddressLists "My Address List" -Server VAN-
EX1 -PublicFolderDatabase "MyPublicDatabase" -PublicFolderDistributionEnabled $true
-Versions Version3,Version4
```

MORE INFO OAB VERSIONS

For more information on OAB versions, see "Understanding Offline Address Books" at *http://technet.microsoft.com/en-us/library/bb232155.aspx*. This link was given earlier in this section and contains a great deal of useful information.

MORE INFO NEW-OFFLINEADDRESSBOOK

For more information about the *New-OfflineAddressBook* cmdlet, see *http://technet .microsoft.com/en-us/library/bb123692.aspx*.

NOTE LEGACY OABs

OABs that use the public folder distribution method are sometimes termed *Legacy OABs*.

Creating an OAB Virtual Directory

The OAB virtual directory is the distribution point used by the OAB web-based distribution method. A virtual directory named OAB is created by default in the default internal web site in IIS when Exchange Server 2010 is installed. If you have client-side users that connect to Outlook from outside your organization's firewall, you can add an external web site. Exchange permits only one OAB virtual directory, and you need to create this directory only if there is a problem with the existing virtual directory. If you need to create a new OAB virtual directory, you use the *New-OABVirtualDirectory* cmdlet in the EMS. In order to create an OAB virtual directory, you first need to remove the existing virtual directory, as described later in this lesson.

You can create an OAB virtual directory if no such directory exists, the local Exchange Server 2010 server has the Client Access server role installed, and a default IIS web site exists. When you have created a new OAB virtual directory, you need to edit the settings on each OAB that uses web-based distribution to reconnect to the OAB virtual directory. The following command creates an OAB virtual directory on a Client Access server named DEN-CAS1 that has SSL enabled and has an external web site configured:

```
New-OABVirtualDirectory –Server DEN-CAS1 –RequireSSL $true –ExternalURL https://www
.adatum.com/OAB
```

MORE INFO REMOVING, RE-CREATING, AND RECONNECTING AN OAB VIRTUAL DIRECTORY

For more information about removing, re-creating, and reconnecting an OAB virtual directory, see *http://technet.microsoft.com/en-us/library/bb123595.aspx*.

MORE INFO NEW-OABVIRTUALDIRECTORY

For more information about the *New-OABVirtualDirectory* cmdlet, see *http://technet .microsoft.com/en-us/library/bb123735.aspx*.

Adding or Removing an Address List to or from an OAB

You can use the EMC or the EMS to add or remove an address list from an OAB. By default, there is an OAB named the Default Offline Address Book that contains the GAL. OABs are generated based on the address lists that they contain. To create custom OABs that users can download, you can add or remove address lists from OABs.

To add or remove an address list from an OAB using the EMC, click Mailbox under Organization Configuration in the Console tree, click the Offline Address Book tab in the Result pane, click the OAB that you want to edit, and then click Properties in the Action pane. This accesses the OAB Properties dialog box.

In the Address Lists tab of the Properties dialog box shown in Figure 2-13, click the Add icon (green +) to add an address list. If you want to remove an address list, click the address list. The Remove icon (red x) then becomes active, and you click it. Click Apply to save your changes without closing the dialog box or click OK to close the dialog box and save your changes.

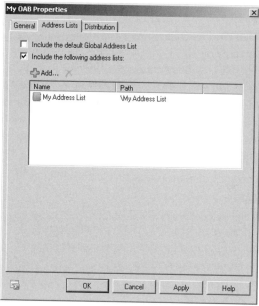

FIGURE 2-13 The Address Lists tab of an OAB Properties dialog box

You can use the *Set-OfflineAddressBook* cmdlet in the EMS to add or remove address lists from an OAB. You need to take care when using this cmdlet. Basically, it lists the address lists that should be in the OAB. So if you specify an address list that is not already in the OAB, that address list is added, and if you omit an address list that is in the OAB from the command, that address list is removed.

Suppose, for example, that you have an OAB named MyOAB that contains address lists MyAddressList01 and MyAddressList02. To add the address list MyAddressList03, you would enter the following command:

```
Set-OfflineAddressBook -Identity "MyOAB" -AddressLists
MyAddressList01,MyAddressList02,MyAddressList03
```

If you subsequently wanted to remove MyAddressList01 from the OAB, you would enter the following command:

```
Set-OfflineAddressBook -Identity "MyOAB" -AddressLists MyAddressList02,MyAddressList03
```

> **MORE INFO** **SET-OFFLINEADDRESSBOOK**
>
> For more information about the *Set-OfflineAddressBook* cmdlet, see *http://technet.microsoft.com/en-us/library/aa996330.aspx*.

Configuring OAB Properties

In addition to adding and removing address lists, you can use the OAB Properties box accessed from the EMC, as described in the previous section, to configure other OAB properties. For example, on the General tab, you can change the name of the OAB, select a predefined update schedule, or click Customize to create your own update schedule. On the Address Lists tab, you can specify whether to include the GAL on the OAB.

On the Distribution tab shown in Figure 2-14, you can specify client support, the OAB distribution method (or methods), and OAB distribution points. An OAB distribution point is the web address or public folder where client computers can download the OAB. The OAB Properties dialog box permits you to specify only web address distribution points.

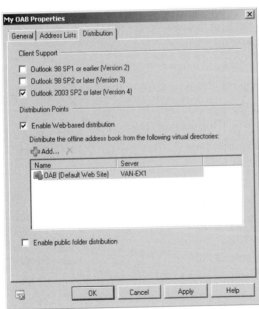

FIGURE 2-14 The Distribution tab of an OAB Properties dialog box

In the Client Support section, you can specify one or more OAB versions. As shown previously in Figure 2-14, you can specify one or more of Versions 2, 3, or 4, depending on the Outlook clients used in your organization. If you do not specify client support, the setting reverts to Version 4.

You can specify web-based distribution, public folder distribution, or both to distribute the OAB. If you specify Web-based distribution, you can specify the virtual directory.

In the previous section, you saw that you could use the *Set-OfflineAddressBook* cmdlet in the EMS to add address lists to or remove them from an OAB. You can use the same cmdlet to configure other OAB properties. For example, the following command modifies the time and date at which OAB generation occurs for MyOAB:

```
Set-OfflineAddressBook -Identity "MyOAB" -Schedule "Sat.2:00 AM-Sat.2:15 AM"
```

> **MORE INFO** **CONFIGURING OAB DISTRIBUTION POINT PROPERTIES**
>
> In addition to configuring OAB distribution properties, you may want to configure the properties of individual distribution points. For more information on this topic, see *http://technet.microsoft.com/en-us/library/bb123710.aspx.*

Moving an OAB Generation Server

OAB generation is the process by which Exchange Server 2010 creates and updates the OAB. During this process, Exchange generates new OAB files, compresses them, and then places them on a local share.

You sometimes need to move the generation task for an OAB from one server to another. You can use the EMC or the EMS to perform this task. To use the EMC to move an OAB generation server, carry out the following procedure:

1. Click Mailbox under Organization Configuration in the Console tree.
2. Click the Offline Address Book tab in the result pane and select the OAB for which you want to move the generation server.
3. Click Move in the Action pane. The Move Offline Address Book Wizard starts.
4. On the Move Offline Address Book page, click Browse, select the server to which you want to move the OAB generation process, and click OK. Click Move to move the OAB generation process to the selected server.
5. On the Completion page, determine whether the move occurred without errors. If necessary, click Back to make any required changes. Otherwise, click Finish to close the wizard.

If you choose to use the EMS to carry out this task, you should be aware that the location of the generation server is not considered to be an OAB property, and you cannot use the EMS *Set-OfflineAddressBook* cmdlet to specify a different server. Instead, you use the *Move-OfflineAddressBook* cmdlet. For example, the following command moves the generation task for a custom OAB named MarketingOAB to the server VAN-EX2:

```
Move-OfflineAddressBook -Identity "MarketingOAB" -Server VAN-EX2
```

MORE INFO   **MOVE-OFFLINEADDRESSBOOK**

For more information about the *Move-OfflineAddressBook* cmdlet, see *http://technet .microsoft.com/en-us/library/aa998191.aspx*.

Removing an OAB

You can use either the EMC or the EMS to remove an OAB. To use the EMC, click Mailbox under Organization Configuration in the Console tree, click the Offline Address Book tab in the Result pane, click the OAB that you want to remove, and then click Remove in the Action pane. You need to click Yes to confirm your action.

You can use the *Remove-OfflineAddressBook* cmdlet in the EMS to remove an OAB. For example, the following command removes the OAB MyOAB:

```
Remove-OfflineAddressBook -Identity "MyOAB"
```

You need to enter **Y** to confirm your action.

If you remove an OAB that is linked to a user or a mailbox database, the recipient downloads the default OAB unless you assign a new OAB. If you remove the default OAB, you must assign another OAB as the default.

MORE INFO   **CHANGING THE DEFAULT OAB**

For more information about how to change the default OAB, see *http://technet.microsoft .com/en-us/library/aa998569.aspx*.

MORE INFO   **REMOVE-OFFLINEADDRESSBOOK**

For more information about the *Remove-OfflineAddressBook* cmdlet, see *http://technet .microsoft.com/en-us/library/bb123594.aspx*.

Lesson Summary

- An address list is a collection of recipient and other AD DS objects. You can use both the EMC and the EMS to create and configure address lists.
- An OAB is a collection of address lists that is copied to client computers so that Outlook clients can access the information they contain offline. You can use both the EMC and the EMS to create and configure OABs.
- OABs can be distributed using web-based or public folder distribution. Public folder distribution makes OABs available to Outlook 2003 (or earlier) and other MAPI clients that cannot use web-based distribution.

Lesson Review

You can use the following questions to test your knowledge of the information in Lesson 2, "Address List Configuration." The questions are also available on the companion CD if you prefer to review them in electronic form.

> **NOTE ANSWERS**
>
> Answers to these questions and explanations of why each answer choice is correct or incorrect are located in the "Answers" section at the end of the book.

1. You have created a custom OAB named AdatumDenver. You want to move the generation task for this OAB from the server DEN-EX1 to the server DEN-EX2. What command do you enter in the EMS?

   A. *Set-OfflineAddressBook -Identity "AdatumDenver" -Server DEN-EX2*

   B. *Set-OfflineAddressBook -Identity "AdatumDenver" -Server DEN-EX1,DEN-EX2*

   C. *Move-OfflineAddressBook -Identity "AdatumDenver" -Server VAN-EX2*

   D. *Move-OfflineAddressBook -Identity "AdatumDenver" -Server Server DEN-EX1, DEN-EX2*

2. You want to create the address list ColoradoStaff that includes recipients that are mailbox users and have StateOrProvince set to Colorado. You then want to create the child address list DenverStaff in the ColoradoStaff parent container. What commands do you enter in the EMS? (Choose 2; each answer forms part of the solution.)

   A. *New-AddressList -Name ColoradoStaff -RecipientFilter {((RecipientType -eq 'UserMailbox') -and (StateOrProvince -eq 'Colorado'))}*

   B. *New-AddressList -Name "DenverStaff" -Container "\ColoradoStaff" -ConditionalCustomAttribute1 "Denver"*

   C. *New-AddressList -Name DenverStaff -RecipientFilter {((RecipientType -eq 'UserMailbox') -and (ConditionalCustomAttribute1 "Denver"))}*

   D. *New-AddressList -Name "ColoradoStaff" -Container "\DenverStaff" -RecipientFilter {((RecipientType -eq 'UserMailbox') -and (StateOrProvince -eq 'Colorado'))}*

3. You want to create an OAB named ColoradoOffline based on the ColoradoStaff address list. This OAB should be generated on the server named DEN-EX1 and should use web-based distribution. It should not be available to Outlook 2003 and other MAPI clients. Which of the following EMS commands should you enter?

   A. *New-OfflineAddressBook –Name "ColoradoOffline" –Server DEN-EX1 –AddressLists ColoradoStaff –PublicFolderDistributionEnabled $true*

   B. *New-OfflineAddressBook –Name "ColoradoOffline" –Server DEN-EX1 –AddressLists ColoradoStaff –VirtualDirectories "DEN-EX1\OAB (Default Web Site)"*

    C. *Set-OfflineAddressBook –Name "ColoradoOffline" –Server DEN-EX1 –AddressLists ColoradoStaff –PublicFolderDistributionEnabled $true*

    D. *Set-OfflineAddressBook –Name "ColoradoOffline" –Server DEN-EX1 –AddressLists ColoradoStaff –VirtualDirectories "SYDNEYMBX1\OAB (Default Web Site)"*

4. You want to create a GAL named Blue Sky Airlines – All Employees to include all mailbox users employed by Blue Sky Airlines. What command do you enter in the EMS?

    A. *Set-AddressList –Identity "Blue Sky Airlines – All Employees" -IncludedRecipients MailboxUsers –ConditionalCompany "Blue Sky Airlines"*

    B. *New-AddressList –Name "Blue Sky Airlines – All Employees" -IncludedRecipients MailboxUsers –ConditionalCompany "Blue Sky Airlines"*

    C. *Set-GlobalAddressList –Identity "Blue Sky Airlines – All Employees" -IncludedRecipients MailboxUsers –ConditionalCompany "Blue Sky Airlines"*

    D. *New-GlobalAddressList –Name "Blue Sky Airlines – All Employees" -IncludedRecipients MailboxUsers –ConditionalCompany "Blue Sky Airlines"*

PRACTICE Creating and Configuring a Mailbox Database

In this practice session, you create a mailbox database and configure it using the EMS. You then use the Edit Database Wizard in the EMC to view and modify the configuration. If you are using virtual machines, both the Exchange Server 2010 Mailbox server VAN-EX1 and the domain controller VAN-DC1 need to be running and connected.

EXERCISE 1 Using the EMS to Create and Configure a Mailbox Database

To use the EMS to create and configure a mailbox database, carry out the following procedure:

1. Log on to the Mailbox server VAN-EX1 using the Kim Akers account with the password Pa$$w0rd.

2. Open Computer and create the folders C:\MyDatabaseFiles and C:\MyLogFolder. Note that if you have a second hard drive, you can optionally create the folder D:\MyLogFolder instead of C:\MyLogFolder and amend the command in step 5 accordingly.

3. Click Start, click All Programs, and then click Microsoft Exchange Server 2010.

4. Right-click Exchange Management Shell and click Run As Administrator.

5. To create a mailbox database named Research, enter the following command:

```
New-MailboxDatabase -Name Research -Server VAN-EX1 -EdbFilePath
C:\MyDatabaseFiles\Research.edb -LogFolderPath C:\MyLogFolder
```

6. To configure the maintenance schedule, warning quota level, and deleted item retention time for the Research mailbox database, enter the following command:

```
Set-MailboxDatabase -Identity Research -MaintenanceSchedule 6.21:00-6.23:15
-IssueWarningQuota 2GB -DeletedItemRetention 21
```

7. Check that the Research mailbox database has been created and configured, as shown in Figure 2-15.

FIGURE 2-15 Creating and configuring the Research mailbox database

EXERCISE 2   Using the EMC to Edit a Mailbox Database

In this exercise, you use the Edit Mailbox Database Wizard to view and reconfigure the Research database mailbox properties.

1. If necessary, log on to the Mailbox server VAN-EX1 using the Kim Akers account with the password *Pa$$w0rd*.

2. Click Start, click All Programs, and then click Microsoft Exchange Server 2010.

3. Click Exchange Management Console. The EMC can take some time to open.

4. If necessary, expand the Console tree.

5. Click Mailbox under Organizational Configuration.

6. In the Result pane on the Database Management tab, click Research.

7. In the Action pane, click Properties.

8. On the General tab of the Research Properties dialog box, shown in Figure 2-16, check that the Database Path is C:\MyDatabasefiles\Research.edb.

9. On the Maintenance tab, check that the Maintenance Schedule setting is Use Custom Schedule. Click Customize. As shown in Figure 2-17, maintenance occurs on a Saturday between 9:00 PM and 11:15 PM. Click Cancel.

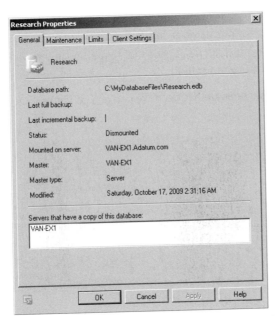

FIGURE 2-16 The General tab of the Research Properties dialog box

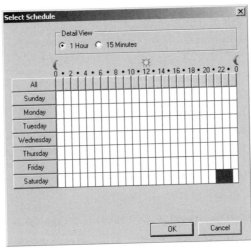

FIGURE 2-17 Viewing the maintenance schedule

10. On the Limits tab, check that the Issue Warning At (KB) setting is 2 GB (2097152) and that the Keep Deleted Items For (Days) setting is 21.

11. Click Customize beside the Warning Message Interval box. In the Select Schedule box, select 15 Minutes and select a second 15-minute interval after the interval already highlighted, as shown in Figure 2-18. Click OK. Check that the setting in the Warning Message Interval box is now Use Custom Setting.

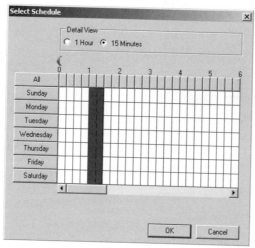

FIGURE 2-18 Configuring the warning message interval

12. On the Client Settings tab, the public folder database on the VAN-EX1 server should be specified, and no OAB should be selected. Click OK to close the Research Properties dialog box.

PRACTICE Creating an Address List

In this practice session, you configure the Company and Department properties for the user Don Hall and then use these properties to specify that Don is included in an address list you create.

EXERCISE 1 Configuring Properties for Don Hall

In this exercise, you configure organization properties for the mailbox user Don Hall.

1. Log on to the domain controller VAN-DC1 using the Kim Akers account with the password Pa$$w0rd.
2. Click Start. Click Administrative Tools. Click Active Directory Users And Computers.
3. In the Console tree, expand Adatum.com. Click the Marketing OU.
4. In the Result pane, right-click Don Hall and click Properties.
5. On the Organization tab of the Don Hall Properties dialog box, specify Job Title, Department, and Company, as shown in Figure 2-19. Click OK.

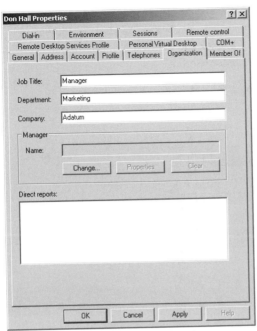

FIGURE 2-19 The Organization tab of the Don Hall Properties dialog box

EXERCISE 2   Using the EMS to Create and Populate an Address List

In this exercise, you create an address list and populate it with mailbox users who are members of the Adatum Marketing Department. Currently, only Don Hall meets this criterion. In practice, the mailing list would be populated with a number of users.

1. Log on to the Mailbox server VAN-EX1 using the Kim Akers account with the password *Pa$$w0rd.*
2. Click Start, click All Programs, and then click Microsoft Exchange Server 2010.
3. Right-click Exchange Management Shell and click Run As Administrator.
4. To create the address list AdatumMarketing, enter the following command:

    ```
    New-AddressList -Name AdatumMarketing -ConditionalCompany Adatum
    ConditionalDepartment Marketing -IncludedRecipients MailboxUsers
    ```

5. To populate the address list, enter the following command:

    ```
    Update-AddressList -Identity AdatumMarketing
    ```

6. You can view the members of an address list by specifying its distinguished name (DN). To obtain the DN of the AdatumMarketing address list, enter the following command:

    ```
    Get-AddressList -Identity AdatumMarketing | FL DistinguishedName
    ```

7. To use the DN to view the members of the AdatumMarketing address list, enter the following command:

```
Get-Recipient -Filter {AddressListMembership -eq 'CN=AdatumMarketing,CN=All
Address Lists,CN=Address Lists Container,CN=AdatumOrg,CN=Microsoft Exchange,CN=Ser
vices,CN=Configuration,DC=Adatum,DC=extest,DC=com'}
```

8. Check that Don Hall is a member of the AdatumMarketing address list, as shown in Figure 2-20.

FIGURE 2-20 Creating and populating an address list and checking its membership

Chapter Review

To further practice and reinforce the skills you learned in this chapter, you can perform the following tasks:

- Review the chapter summary.
- Review the list of key terms introduced in this chapter.
- Complete the case scenarios. These scenarios set up real-word situations involving the topics of this chapter and ask you to create a solution.
- Complete the suggested practices.
- Take a practice test.

Chapter Summary

- You can configure your Exchange Organization environment by creating and editing mailbox databases, public folder databases, address lists, and OABs.
- For most creation and configuration tasks, you can use either the EMC or the EMS. However, the EMS offers more functionality than the EMC and is the required tool for certain tasks.
- Typically, you need to be assigned the Organization Management role to create and manage Exchange objects, such as databases.

Key Terms

Do you know what these key terms mean?

- address list
- global address list (GAL)
- mailbox database
- offline address book (OAB)
- public folder database

Case Scenarios

In the following case scenarios, you will apply what you have learned about subjects of this chapter. You can find answers to these questions in the "Answers" section at the end of this book.

Case Scenario 1: Creating a Mailbox Database

James Seymour is an Exchange administrator at Blue Sky Airlines. He is tasked with creating a mailbox database named Marketing on the Mailbox server BSA-EX1. The path to the mailbox .edb file should be C:\DatabaseFiles\Marketing.edb. The transaction log files should be stored on a separate hard disk in the D:\LogFiles\Marketing folder.

After he has created the mailbox database, James wants to configure it so that deleted items are retained for 28 days and that users are sent a warning when their mailbox size reaches 2 GB.

After he has created and configured the database, James's next task is to make it available to provision new mailboxes.

With these facts in mind, answer the following questions:

1. What command does James enter in the EMS to create the mailbox database?

2. What command does James enter in the EMS to configure the mailbox database properties?

3. What command does James enter in the EMS to make the mailbox database available to provision new mailboxes?

Case Scenario 2: Creating an Address List and an OAB

North Wind Traders is a multinational holding company that controls a number of subsidiary companies, including Coho Vineyard. The holding company has a single active directory forest with a domain tree for each separate subsidiary company within the organization. Don Hall, an Exchange administrator working at North Wind Traders headquarters in Seattle, needs to create and populate an address list that includes all mailboxes used by mailbox users employed by Coho Vineyard's Sales Department. He decides to name this address list Sales-Coho-Vineyard-Addr.

When he has created and populated the Sales-Coho-Vineyard-Addr address list, Don intends to create an OAB based on that address list. This OAB, named Sales-Coho-Vineyard-Addr-OAB, should be generated on the Mailbox server named Coho-EX3. Coho Vineyard uses a range of client computers, some of which run Outlook 2010 or Outlook 2007, while others run Outlook 2003 and other MAPI clients. The OAB should be available to all clients.

With these facts in mind, answer the following questions:

1. What command does Don enter in the EMS to create the Sales-Coho-Vineyard-Addr address list?

2. What command does Don enter in the EMS to populate the Sales-Coho-Vineyard-Addr address list?

3. What distribution method or methods does Don need to use for the Sales-Coho-Vineyard-OAB OAB?

4. What command does Don enter in the EMS to create the Sales-Coho-Vineyard-OAB OAB?

Suggested Practices

To help you master the examination objectives presented in this chapter, complete the following tasks.

Use the EMC Tabs and Wizards

- **Practice 1** The EMC provides a number of tabs in the Result pane that enable you to select objects such as mailbox databases, public folder databases, address lists, OABs, and so on. The Action pane lets you specify actions that in turn start the wizard that enables you to carry out the action. Become familiar with the available tabs, especially those that appear when you click Mailbox or Hub Transport under Organization Configuration in the Console tree. Practice using the wizards that become available when you select an object and specify an action.

Become Familiar with EMS cmdlets

- **Practice 1** Some EMS cmdlets, such as *Set-MailboxDatabase* and *Get-PublicFolderDatabase*, support a large number of parameters and can appear daunting at first sight. The only way to become familiar with such commands and confident in their use is to set yourself configuration tasks, use the appropriate EMS commands to perform these tasks, and observe the results. Lots of hands-on experience is the key to examination and career success.

Create More Address Lists and OABs

- **Practice 1** Use both the EMS and the EMC to create address lists and to create OABs based on these address lists.

- **Practice 2** As this chapter is written, only two users, Don Hall and Kim Akers, have mailboxes. Create other mailbox users with different attributes (for example, that work in different departments). Create address lists based on these attributes. Create one or more OABs that contain these address lists.

Take a Practice Test

The practice tests on this book's companion CD offer many options. For example, you can test yourself on just one exam objective, or you can test yourself on all the 70-662 certification exam content. You can set up the test so that it closely simulates the experience of taking a certification exam, or you can set it up in study mode so that you can look at the correct answers and explanations after you answer each question.

> **MORE INFO** **PRACTICE TESTS**
>
> For details about all the practice test options available, see the "How to Use the Practice Tests" section in this book's Introduction.

CHAPTER 3

Exchange Mailboxes

In this chapter, you will learn how to configure new and existing users with mailboxes, modify the quotas applied to those mailboxes, move mailboxes between new servers or existing, and configure mailboxes so that other users are able to send messages on the original mailbox owner's behalf and other users are granted access to the content of those mailboxes. You will also learn about the creation of resource mailboxes, linked mailboxes, and shared mailboxes. This includes the configuration of automatic resource mailbox booking policies, which allows the resource represented by the mailbox to be automatically reserved on a first-come, first-serve basis or subject to the approval of an authorized user.

Exam objectives in this chapter:

- Create and configure mailboxes.
- Create and configure resource mailboxes and shared mailboxes.

Lessons in this chapter:

Before You Begin

In order to complete the exercises in the practice sessions in this chapter, you need to have done the following:

- Installed and configured an Exchange Server 2010 organization as outlined in the Appendix.

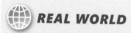

REAL WORLD

Orin Thomas

One of the most common complaints that I hear from Exchange administrators is about something that is only indirectly related to Exchange: the PST file. The first gripe is that the files are difficult to back up yet easily become corrupted. The next is an increasing awareness of the legal ramifications of allowing sensitive messages to be stored in a place that is not easily searchable. Extensive use of PST files greatly complicates the process of legal discovery. Not only must Exchange Mailboxes be checked for content that might be subject to the discovery request, but PST files must be separately scanned for similar content. In some cases, it can take longer to scan the PST files of a small number of users than it takes to scan every mailbox in the entire Exchange organization! This is why archive mailboxes are a popular feature of Exchange 2010. Archive mailboxes are additional mailboxes that allow users to store messages for historical purposes. Rather than store data that impacts on their quota in their mailbox, they can move important data that they want to keep to their archive mailbox. These messages can be stored and backed up within the Exchange organization, and when archive mailboxes are deployed correctly, there is no longer a need for PST files. They are not subject to corruption and require no special steps to back up. That they are searchable and stored on mailbox servers makes them much simpler targets for searching when complying with legal requests. Although archive mailboxes do require Enterprise Edition CALs, once decision makers in an organization understand the benefits of archive mailboxes, the days of having to deal with PST files in your organization are numbered.

Lesson 1: Mailbox Configuration

In this lesson, you will learn how to configure user mailboxes and linked mailboxes. User mailboxes are message storage containers associated with user accounts in the forest in which you have deployed Exchange Server 2010. Linked mailboxes are mailboxes that are connected to accounts hosted in forests other than the one in which you have deployed Exchange Server 2010. You will learn how to create mailboxes, apply quotas to them, move them to different mailbox servers without disrupting user access, delegate Full Control and Send As permissions, and enable or disable specific Client Access protocols.

After this lesson, you will be able to:

- Create mailboxes.
- Configure mailbox properties, including setting quotas, Client Access protocols, and permissions.
- Move mailboxes between mailbox servers.
- Delete and disable mailboxes.

Estimated lesson time: 40 minutes

Creating Mailboxes

You can create new mailboxes in two ways. You can use the New Mailbox Wizard from Exchange Management Console (EMC) or use the *New-Mailbox* cmdlet from Exchange Management Shell (EMS). To run the New-Mailbox Wizard, perform the following general steps:

1. Open the EMC and navigate to the Mailbox node, which is located under the Recipients node.

2. In the Actions pane, click on the New Mailbox item. This will bring up the first page of the New Mailbox Wizard, shown in Figure 3-1. Choose the User Mailbox option and then click Next.

3. On the next page, you choose between creating a new user account and assigning that account a mailbox or creating a mailbox and assigning that mailbox to an existing user. If you choose to create a mailbox for an existing user, a query will be performed to locate user accounts that are not currently connected to mailboxes. You can select multiple Active Directory users using this dialog box as long as those users do not have Exchange mailboxes.

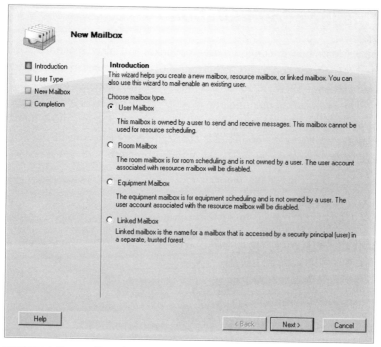

FIGURE 3-1 New mailbox dialog box

4. If you have chosen to create new Exchange mailboxes for existing Active Directory accounts, the next page allows you to have Exchange automatically select a mailbox database to host the mailbox, a managed folder mailbox policy, and an ActiveSync mailbox policy. It is also possible to specify these options should the automatically selected options not be appropriate. In general, you should place a user mailbox in a mailbox database hosted on a mailbox server in the site that the user most commonly accesses Exchange.

5. Once you have either accepted the default mailbox database and policies or specified alternates, the next page of the New Mailbox Wizard allows you to click New, which creates the mailbox. Once this step has completed, you can click Finish to close the wizard, as shown in Figure 3-2.

If you choose to create a new user account during mailbox creation, the wizard will prompt you for information similar to that required when you create a user account using the Active Directory Users and Computers console, including the ability to force users to change passwords when they initially log on with this newly created account. As Figure 3-3 shows, you can choose which OU to place the account in or have the account placed in the default Users container. Once this information has been provided, the New Mailbox Wizard functions similar to the way it functions when you are creating a mailbox for an existing user account. You will create a new user and mailbox as well as a mailbox for an existing user in the practice exercise at the end of this lesson.

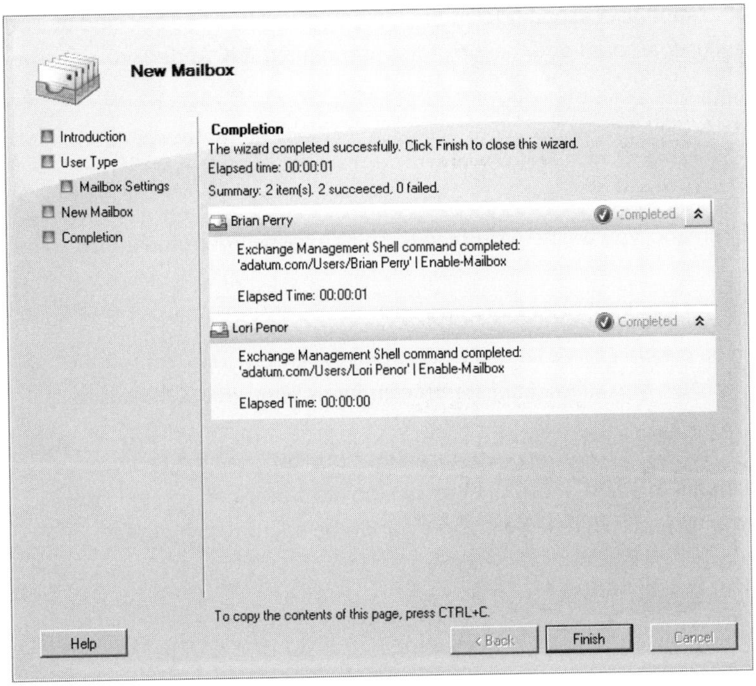

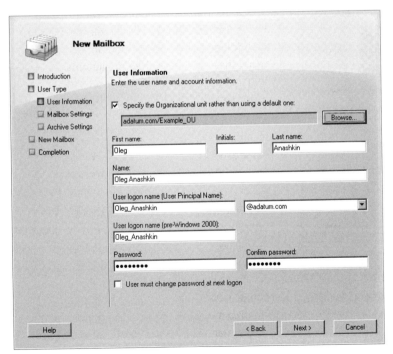

FIGURE 3-2 Complete the New Mailbox Wizard

FIGURE 3-3 Provide information for new user account

To create a new mailbox and user account from the EMS, use the *New-Mailbox* cmdlet. For example, to create a new user account and mailbox for a user named Erik Andersen, issue the following command:

```
New-Mailbox –Name 'Erik Andersen' –Alias 'Erik_Andersen' –UserPrincipalName 'Erik_
Andersen@adatum.com' –SamAccountName 'Erik_Andersen' –FirstName 'Erik' –LastName
'Andersen'
```

When you run this command, you will be prompted to enter a password for the user account.

> **MORE INFO** **CREATING NEW MAILBOXES AND USERS**
>
> For more information on creating new user mailboxes using the EMC or EMS, consult the following article on TechNet: *http://technet.microsoft.com/en-us/library/bb123809.aspx*.

To add an Exchange mailbox to an existing user account from EMS, use the *Enable-Mailbox* cmdlet. For example, to add a new Exchange mailbox to a user named Toni Poe whose existing user account resides in the Users container of the adatum.com domain, issue the following command:

```
Enable-Mailbox 'Adatum.com/Users/Toni Poe'
```

> **MORE INFO** **CREATE MAILBOXES FOR EXISTING USERS**
>
> For more information on creating Exchange mailboxes for existing users, consult the following article on TechNet: *http://technet.microsoft.com/en-us/library/aa998319.aspx*.

> **MORE INFO** **RECIPIENT PROVISIONING PERMISSIONS**
>
> To learn more about the permissions required to perform specific recipient management tasks, consult the Recipient Provisioning Permissions section of the following TechNet website: *http://technet.microsoft.com/en-us/library/dd638132.aspx*.

Linked Mailboxes

A linked mailbox is one that is associated with an external account, such as one located in a different Active Directory forest from the one in which you deployed Exchange. As mailboxes must be associated with accounts that are in the same forest as Exchange and linked mailboxes involve accounts in different forests, when you create a linked mailbox, Exchange creates a disabled user account in the local forest that is used as a stand-in for the foreign account.

To create a linked mailbox using the EMC, perform the following general steps:

1. Open the EMC and navigate to the Mailbox node, which is located under the Recipients node.

2. In the Actions pane, click on the New Mailbox item. This will bring up the first page of the New Mailbox Wizard. Choose the Linked Mailbox.

3. On the User Type page, click New User. This will allow you to create the stand-in disabled user account in the local forest.

4. On the User Information page, specify appropriate user information and a password that complies with your organization's password policies. This password, rather than the password of the user account in the account's native forest, allows user access to the mailbox.

5. On the Master Account page, click Browse to select the trusted forest or domain that hosts the account that the mailbox will be linked to. You can also specify a domain controller in the trusted forest or domain to query. Finally, click Browse to select the specific account with which the linked mailbox will be associated. Figure 3-4 shows a new linked mailbox being associated with the Dan_Hough account in the Fabrikam domain.

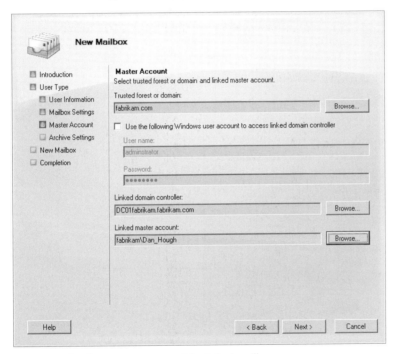

FIGURE 3-4 Configure master account for linked mailbox

6. If an Exchange Enterprise CAL is available, you will be able to associate an archive mailbox to the linked mailbox. On the final page, you create the mailbox.

You create linked mailboxes in the EMS using the *New-Mailbox* cmdlet. For example, you could use the following command to create a linked mailbox on database MBX-DB-1 for Josh Pollock in the adatum.com domain when his actual account resides in the trusted Fabrikam forest:

```
New-Mailbox -Database "MBX-DB-1" -Name "Josh Pollock" -LinkedDomain Controller
"DC01fabrikam.fabrikam.com" -LinkedMasterAccount Fabrikam\josh_pollock
-OrganizationalUnit Users -UserPrincipalName josh_pollock@adatum.com
```

Configuring Mailbox Properties

When you create a user mailbox using the EMC, it is not possible to specify settings such as mailbox quotas and proxy addresses that will be applied to or associated with the mailbox. You can configure these options after mailbox creation by editing mailbox properties using the EMC or by setting them through the *Set-Mailbox* cmdlet in the EMS.

The main difficulty that most administrators encounter when modifying mailbox properties through the EMC is determining which tab of the properties dialog box, shown in Figure 3-5, holds the setting that they wish to modify. In the following pages, you will learn how to configure specific mailbox properties, such as quota, message size, and mailbox delegation, through both the EMC and the EMS.

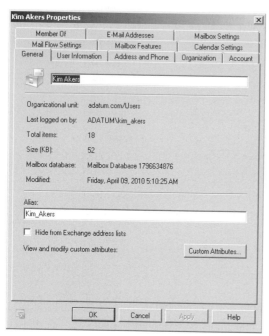

FIGURE 3-5 General tab of Mailbox properties

Configuring Mailbox Quotas and Deleted Item Retention

Although mailboxes inherit quota and deleted item retention settings from the mailbox database that hosts them, it is possible, using the EMS and EMC, to configure quota and deleted item retention settings on a per-mailbox basis. Settings applied at the mailbox level override settings applied at the mailbox database level. This allows you, as an Exchange administrator, to make exceptions for individual users should their needs reasonably diverge from everyone else in the organization without having to create a new mailbox database to cater to these specific needs.

The settings that you can configure for quota and deleted item retention are as follows:

- **Issue Warning At (KB)**   This quota value determines the threshold at which a warning will be automatically be emailed to the user.

- **Prohibit Send At (KB)**   This quota value determines the threshold at which a user will be prohibited from sending new messages. Outlook and Outlook Web App (OWA) users will be presented with a message explaining why they have been blocked when this threshold is reached.

- **Prohibit Send And Receive At (KB)**   This quota value determines when a user will be prohibited from sending and receiving messages. Any messages that are sent to a mailbox that has exceeded this threshold will be returned to the sender with an error message informing them that the destination mailbox has exceeded its storage quota.

- **Keep Deleted Items For (Days)**   This value determines the period where it is possible to recover a deleted mailbox item without performing a restore from backup. The default value is 14 days.

- **Do Not Permanently Delete Items Until You Back Up The Database**   When this option is set, deleted items are not removed until a database backup occurs, even if the deleted item retention period has expired.

You should note that while it is possible to configure mailbox item retention on a per-mailbox level, it is not possible to configure disconnected mailbox retention settings at this level. You will learn more about disconnected mailbox retention later in this lesson. To configure individual mailbox quotas using the EMC, perform the following general steps:

1. From the Recipients Configuration\Mailbox node, edit mailbox properties and navigate to the Mailbox Settings tab.

2. Click Storage Quotas and then click the Properties button.

3. Remove the check box next to Use Mailbox Database Defaults in the Storage Quotas and Deleted item retention areas shown in Figure 3-6. If you want to use the database defaults for one of these settings but not the other, do not remove the check box for the setting you want inherited from database properties. If you remove the Use Mailbox Database Defaults check box but do not configure a setting for each of the quota entries, Exchange assigns the user an unlimited quota for that entry.

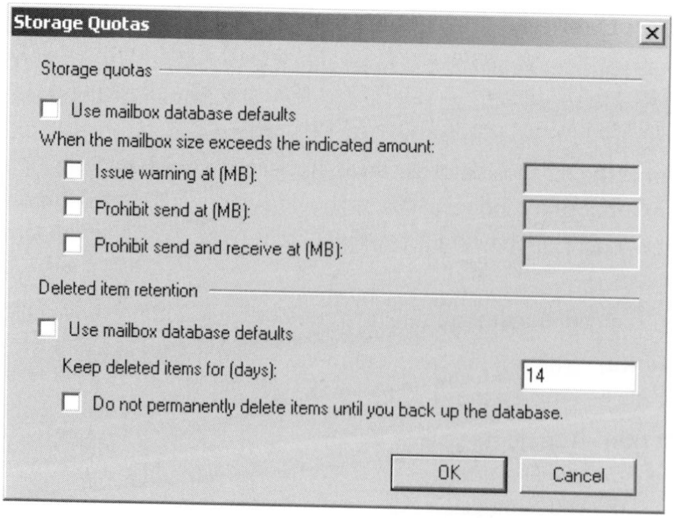

FIGURE 3-6 Configure storage quotas

To configure storage quota settings on a per-mailbox level from the EMC, use the *Set-Mailbox* command. For example, to configure Rich Haddock's mailbox so that it had a warning quota of 200 MB, a prohibit send quota of 250 MB, and a prohibit send and receive quota of 280 MB, issue the following command:

```
Set-mailbox rich_haddock –IssueWarningQuota 209715200 –ProhibitSendQuota 262144000
–ProhibitSendReceiveQuota 293601280 –RetainDeletedItemsFor 21.00:00:00
–UseDatabaseQuotaDefaults  $false –UseDatabaseRetentionDefaults $false
```

> **MORE INFO**   **CONFIGURE MAILBOX QUOTAS**
>
> For more information on configuring mailbox quotas, consult the following TechNet article: *http://technet.microsoft.com/en-us/library/aa998353.aspx*.

Message Size Restrictions

You can configure message size restrictions to limit the size of messages that a user associated with a mailbox can send and/or receive. For example, you could configure message size restrictions so that a user mailbox is able to accept only messages under 10 MB in size but the same user is able to send messages over 20 MB in size. Exchange calculates message size on the basis of the sum of the message body and attachments, though in general attachment size is significantly greater than message body size. To configure message size restrictions from the EMC, perform the following general steps:

1. From mailbox properties, select the Mail Flow Settings tab.
2. Click on Message Size Restrictions in the list and then click on the Properties button.
3. Configure the maximum sending and receiving message size in KB and then click OK.

To configure message size restrictions from the EMS, use the *Set-Mailbox* cmdlet with the MaxSendSize and MaxReceiveSize parameters. For example, to configure Kim Akers's mailbox so that she can send messages that are a maximum of 20 MB in size and receive messages that are a maximum of 15 MB in size, use the following command:

```
Set-Mailbox -Identity "Kim_Akers" -MaxSendSize 20mb -MaxReceiveSize 15mb
```

> **MORE INFO** **CONFIGURING MESSAGE SIZE**
>
> For more information about configuring message size, consult the following TechNet link: *http://technet.microsoft.com/en-us/library/bb124708.aspx.*

Additional Email Addresses

You can configure Exchange mailboxes to accept incoming messages on a variety of email addresses. For example, you might want to assign the information@adatum.com address to Kim Akers's mailbox, which is already addressable with the kim_akers@adatum.com email address. Additional email addresses assigned to Exchange mailboxes are sometimes known as proxy addresses.

To assign a proxy address to a mailbox using the EMC, perform the following general steps:

1. From mailbox properties, select the E-Mail Addresses tab.

2. Click Add. In the address dialog box, enter the new email address and click OK.
   The new email address will be shown in the list of email addresses, as Figure 3-7 shows.

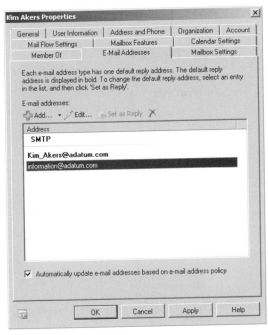

FIGURE 3-7 Add proxy address

Use the *Set-Mailbox* cmdlet to add proxy addresses to an existing mailbox using the EMC. When you use the *Set-Mailbox* command to add an address, the existing address will be removed unless an email address policy is in place. You can add additional email addresses using multivalued properties. For example, to add the sales@adatum.com proxy address to Brian Perry's mailbox, use the following command:

```
$Temp = Get-Mailbox -Identity "Brian Perry"
$Temp.EmailAddresses += ("smtp:sales@adatum.com")
Set-Mailbox -Identity "Brian Perry" -EmailAddresses $Temp.EmailAddresses
```

> **MORE INFO** **ADDING EMAIL ADDRESSES TO MAILBOXES**
>
> For more information about adding email addresses to existing user mailboxes, consult the following link: *http://technet.microsoft.com/en-us/library/bb123794.aspx*.

Configuring Mailbox Client Access Protocols

Mailbox features, such as Outlook Web App, Exchange ActiveSync, POP3, IMAP4, and MAPI Access, can be enabled or disabled on the Mailbox Features tab of a mailbox's properties, as shown in Figure 3-8. To enable or disable a feature, select the feature and then click Enable or Disable as appropriate.

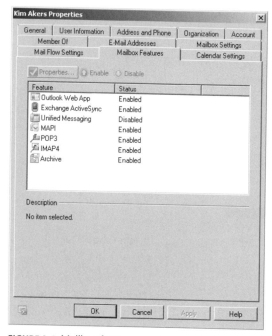

FIGURE 3-8 Mailbox features

You can configure which features are enabled or disabled using the *Set-CASMailbox* cmdlet and the ImapEnabled, MAPIEnabled, OWAEnabled, and POPEnabled parameters. For example, to disable POP3, IMAP4, and OWA access to the Don Hall mailbox, issue the following command:

```
Set-CASMailbox "Don Hall" –POPEnabled $false –ImapEnabled $false –OWAEnabled $false
```

> **MORE INFO   ENABLING AND DISABLING CLIENT ACCESS FOR MAILBOXES**
>
> To learn more about how to enable or disable certain client access features on a per-mailbox basis, consult the following link on TechNet: *http://technet.microsoft.com/en-us/library/bb125264.aspx*.

Mailbox Anti-Spam Functionality

Spam confidence level (SCL) is a figure calculated by Exchange that assigns a numeric value to the likelihood that a message contains unsolicited commercial email, also known as spam. A message assigned a value of 0 has a low probability of being spam, and a message assigned an SCL of 9 has a high probability of being spam. To configure anti-spam functionality for mailboxes using the EMS, use the *Set-Mailbox* cmdlet with the following parameters:

- **AntiSpamBypassEnabled**   This parameter specifies whether the mailbox skips anti-spam checks. Can be set to $true or $false.

- **RequireSenderAuthenticationEnabled**   Determines whether sender authentication is required. Can be set to $true or $false.

- **SCLDeleteEnabled**   Determines whether messages that meet the configured SCLDeleteThreshold are deleted. Can be set to $true, $false, or $null.

- **SCLDeleteThreshold**   A value between 0 and 9 at which a message is deleted if the SCLDeleteEnabled parameter is set to $true.

- **SCLJunkEnabled**   Determines whether messages that meet the configured SCLJunkThreshold are moved to the Junk E-Mail folder. Can be set to $true, $false, or $null.

- **SCLJunkThreshold**   Determines the SCL threshold value, between 0 and 9, at which messages will be moved into the Junk E-Mail folder if the SCLJunkEnabled parameter is set to $true.

- **SCLQuarantineEnabled**   Determines whether messages that meet the configured SCLQuarantineThreshold are placed in quarantine for later review. Can be set to $true, $false, or $null.

- **SCLQuarantineThreshold**   Determines the SCL threshold value, between 0 and 9, at which messages will be quarantined if the SCLQuarantineEnabled parameter is set to $true.

- **SCLRejectEnabled**   Determines whether messages that meet the configured SCLRejectThreshold are rejected. Can be set to $true, $false, or $null.

- **SCLRejectThreshold**   Determines the SCL threshold value, between 0 and 9, at which messages will be rejected if the SCLRejectEnabled parameter is set to $true.

You will learn how configuring anti-spam functionality at the mailbox level impacts anti-spam functionality at other levels of Exchange and learn how Reject, Quarantine, and Junk thresholds work in Chapter 12, "Message Integrity, Antivirus, and Anti-Spam."

> **MORE INFO**   **MAILBOX ANTI-SPAM FEATURES**
>
> For more information on configuring Exchange 2010 anti-spam features at the mailbox level, consult the following TechNet link: *http://technet.microsoft.com/en-us/library/bb123559.aspx.*

Mailbox Delegation

You can configure permissions so that it is possible for one user to send email messages on behalf of another user. You can also configure permissions so that one user has the ability to view the contents of another user's mailbox. This may be necessary for a variety of reasons, such as an administrative assistant needing to view the contents of a manager's mailbox or allowing that assistant to send messages on that manager's behalf. It is possible to configure the following permissions on Exchange mailboxes:

- **Send-As Permission**   When a user has been granted the Send As permission for another mailbox, the user is able to send mail as that user but is not able to receive mail as that user. The user is also unable to view that user's mailbox. For example, if Rich Haddock is granted the Send As permission on Kim Akers's mailbox, he is able to send messages to other recipients with Kim Akers's identity.
- **Full Access Permission**   When a user has been granted the Full Access permission for another mailbox, the user is able to view the contents of that mailbox but is not able to send messages as that user.

To configure Send As permission from the EMC, perform the following steps:

1. In Mailbox\Recipient Configuration node, select the mailbox that you want to delegate the Send As permission on.
2. In the Actions pane, click on the Manage Send As Permission item. This will open the Manage Send As permission dialog box, shown in Figure 3-9. Click Add and then specify the user to which you wish to assign this permission.

To configure the Send As permission from the EMS, use the *Add-ADPermission cmdlet* with the ExtendedRights parameter. For example, to configure Don Hall's mailbox so that Kim Akers has the Send As permission on the mailbox, use the following command:

```
Add-ADPermission "Don Hall" -User "adatum\kim_akers" -Extendedrights "Send As"
```

To configure the Full Access permission from the EMC, perform the following steps:

1. In the Mailbox\Recipient Configuration node, select the mailbox on which you want to delegate the Full Access permission.
2. In the Actions pane, click on the Manage Full Access Permission item.
3. In the Manage Full Access Permission dialog box, shown in Figure 3-10, click Add. Select the user that you wish to delegate the Full Access permission to, click OK, and then click Manage to close the dialog box.

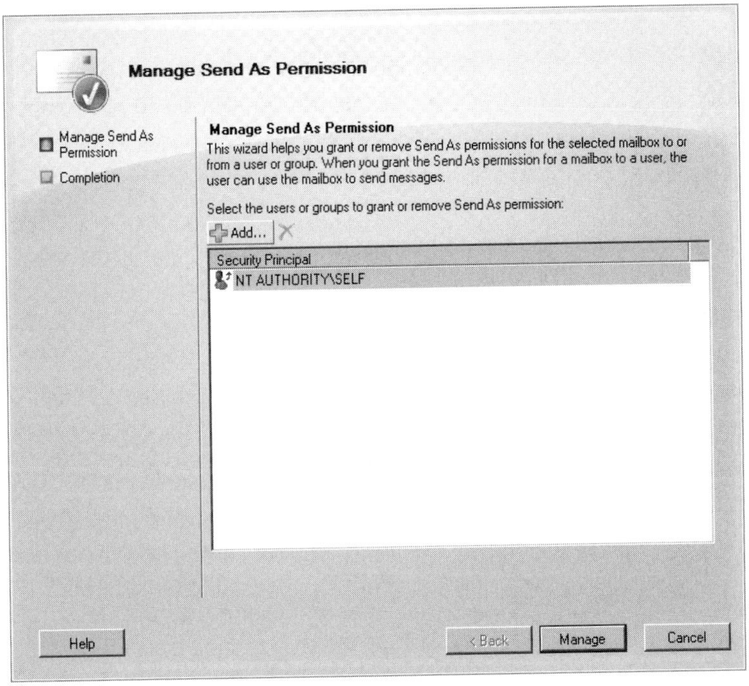

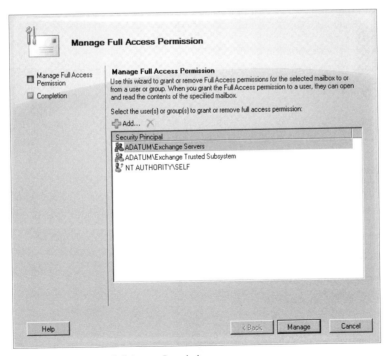

FIGURE 3-9 Manage Send As Permission

FIGURE 3-10 Manage Full Access Permission

To delegate the Full Access permission on a mailbox using the EMS, use the *Add-MailboxPermission* cmdlet with the AccessRights parameter. For example, to grant Kim Akers the Full Access permission on Oleg Anashkin's mailbox, issue the following command:

```
Add-MailboxPermission -Identity "Oleg Anashkin" -User "adatum\Kim_Akers" -AccessRights
Fullaccess -InheritenceType all
```

> **MORE INFO** **FULL ACCESS AND SEND AS PERMISSIONS**
>
> To learn more about Full Access and Send As permissions for mailboxes, consult the following TechNet article: *http://technet.microsoft.com/en-us/library/aa997244.aspx*.

Forwarding and Out-of-Office Replies

Forwarding allows all messages that are sent to one Exchange mailbox to be forwarded to another address. This address can be another mailbox or contact within the Exchange organization. When you configure forwarding, you can choose to forward messages and not have them delivered to the original mailbox or to have messages both delivered to the original destination mailbox as well as forwarded to the configured address. To configure a forwarding address using the EMC, perform the following general steps:

1. Select the mailbox in the list on the Recipient Configuration\Mailbox node and then click Properties in the Action pane.

2. On the Mail Flow Settings tab, select Delivery Options and then click Properties. This will bring up the Delivery Options dialog box.

3. In the Delivery Options dialog box, enable the Forward To: check box and then click Browse. Select the destination address and then click OK. Select the Deliver Message To Both Forwarding Address And Mailbox option if required, as shown in Figure 3-11.

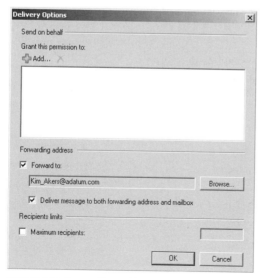

FIGURE 3-11 Forwarding address

To configure forwarding from the EMS, use the *Set-Mailbox* cmdlet with the ForwardingAddress and DeliverToMailboxAndForward parameters. For example, to configure Don Hall's mailbox so that all messages sent to it are both forwarded to Kim Akers's mailbox and delivered to Don Hall's mailbox, issue the following command:

```
Set-Mailbox -Identity "Don Hall" -ForwardingAddress "kim_akers@adatum.com"
-DeliverToMailboxAndForward $true
```

> **MORE INFO** **MAIL FORWARDING**
>
> For more information about configuring mail forwarding for a mailbox, consult the following TechNet article: *http://technet.microsoft.com/en-us/library/dd351134.aspx*.

You can use the *Set-Mailbox* cmdlet with the ExternalOofOptions parameter to specify what type of out-of-office reply can be set by a particular user mailbox. The values that you can set for the ExternalOofOptions parameter are External and InternalOnly. When you set the External option, the mailbox user is able to set an out-of-office message that will be forwarded to both Internal and External recipients. When you set the InternalOnly option, out-of-office messages will be sent only to internal recipients and will not be sent to external recipients. To configure Kim Akers's mailbox so that out-of-office messages are limited to Internal recipients only, use the following EMS command:

```
Set-Mailbox "Kim Akers" -ExternalOofOptions InternalOnly
```

 Quick Check

- You want to allow a manager's administrative assistant the ability to review the content of that manager's mailbox but not the ability to send messages as the manager. What type of permission should you grant?

Quick Check Answer

- You should grant the Full Access permission. This permission allows full access to the mailbox on which the permission has been granted but does not grant the right to send mail as the mailbox on which the permission has been granted.

Moving Mailboxes

Exchange Server 2010 makes moving mailboxes between mailbox databases easier, as it is now possible to allow users to retain access to their mailbox during a move, meaning that Exchange Administrators do not have to schedule mailbox moves during periods where users would not require access to their mailboxes. As fond as administrators are of scheduling maintenance tasks to occur at 3:00 AM, such tasks are much easier to monitor when they occur during office hours.

Using the EMS *New-MoveRequest* cmdlet and the EMC move mailbox functionality, you can perform an online mailbox move to a different mailbox database on the same server, a mailbox database on a different server, a host mailbox server in a different domain or site, and even a host mailbox server in another forest. The cmdlet used to move mailboxes was deliberately given a different name for Exchange 2010, and Exchange 2010 does not support the *Move-Mailbox* cmdlet, which was present in Exchange 2007.

Take into account the following when preparing to move mailboxes:

- You cannot use Exchange System Manager to move mailboxes from Exchange Server 2003 hosts to Exchange Server 2010 mailbox servers.

- You cannot use Active Directory Users and Computers to move mailboxes from Exchange Server 2003 to Exchange Server 2010 mailbox servers.

- When a mailbox is moved, users are unable to access message tracking information.

- You cannot use the *Move-Mailbox* cmdlet on a server running Exchange Server 2007 to move a mailbox to Exchange Server 2010. You must use *New-MoveRequest* on the server running Exchange 2010.

- Online moves are possible between Exchange 2010 databases and between Exchange 2007 Service Pack2 and Exchange 2010 databases.

- Items in the recoverable items folder are preserved during mailbox moves.

- You can perform online mailbox moves across forests. You can perform online mailbox moves between servers in the same forest or mailbox databases hosted on the same server.

- During an online move, a user is locked out for only a short period at the end of the process, when final synchronization occurs.

- It is possible to move mailboxes from Exchange Server 2010 to Exchange 2007 Service Pack 1 and RTM as well as Exchange Server 2003, but these moves will occur offline and must be managed using EMS cmdlets on a server running Exchange Server 2010.

- It is not possible to perform a mailbox move from Exchange 2007 Service Pack 1 to Exchange 2010. The Exchange 2007 server must be upgraded to Service Pack 2 before a move is possible.

- Offline moves from Exchange 2003 SP2 to Exchange Server 2010 are supported but require the use of the EMS on Exchange Server 2010. It is not possible to move mailboxes from servers running Exchange 2003 Service Pack 1 or earlier.

- If you perform a move request using the *New-MoveRequest* cmdlet, you should run the *Remove-MoveRequest* cmdlet once the move successfully completes. It is not possible to move the mailbox again until the *Remove-MoveRequest* cmdlet is executed against a moved mailbox. When you perform a move through the EMC, this process occurs automatically.

- When performing a cross-forest move, the target Exchange 2010 forest must contain a valid mail-enabled user account that has been prepared for the move.

Quick Check

- Under what conditions can you perform an online mailbox move?

Quick Check Answer

- You can perform an online mailbox move only between two mailbox servers that are running Exchange Server 2010 or a server running Exchange Server 2007 Service Pack 2 and Exchange Server 2010.

Disabling, Removing, and Reconnecting Mailboxes

The difference between removing a mailbox and disabling a mailbox is as follows:

- Disabling a mailbox disconnects the mailbox from the user account, but the user account remains in Active Directory. You can disable a mailbox by selecting the mailbox in the Recipient Configuration\Mailbox node of EMC and then clicking on Disable in the Actions pane. You can use the *Disable-Mailbox* cmdlet to disable a mailbox.

- Removing a mailbox disconnects that mailbox from the user account that it is associated with and removes this user account from Active Directory. You can remove a mailbox by selecting the mailbox in the Recipient Configuration\Mailbox node of the EMC and then clicking Remove in the Actions pane. You can use the *Remove-Mailbox* cmdlet to remove a mailbox.

When you disable or remove a mailbox, Exchange retains the mailbox in a disconnected state for the number of days specified in the mailbox retention policy. By default, Exchange retains disconnected mailboxes for 30 days. During this deleted mailbox retention duration, it is possible to connect the disconnected mailbox to an existing Active Directory user account as long as that account has no current mailbox connected.

To reconnect a mailbox, perform the following steps:

1. Open the EMC and navigate to the Disconnected Mailbox node located under the Recipient Configuration node.

2. In the Actions pane, click Connect To Server. In the Connect To Server dialog box, click Browse. In the Select Exchange Server dialog box, select the Exchange Mailbox Server that hosted the original mailbox that you wish to recover.

3. From the list of disconnected mailboxes, shown in Figure 3-12, select the mailbox you wish to recover and then click Connect in the Actions pane. This will start the Connect Mailbox Wizard.

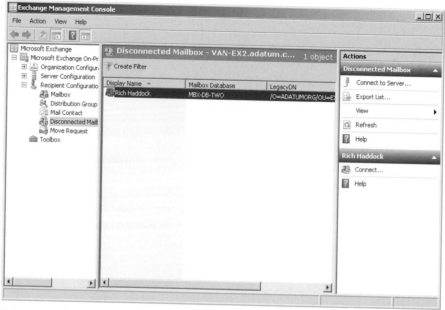

FIGURE 3-12 Disconnected mailbox

4. On the first page of the wizard, select the type of disconnected mailbox that you wish to reconnect. You can use this wizard to reconnect all mailbox types: User, Room, Equipment, and Linked.

5. You then select which user account to which you will connect the disconnected mailbox by either browsing for a matching user or selecting an existing user, as shown in Figure 3-13. The user account must exist prior to attempting to connect the disconnected mailbox. You must also provide an alias for the mailbox and specify a managed folder and Exchange ActiveSync policy if you do not want to use the default policies. Once you select the existing user account and alias, you will be able to reconnect the mailbox and close the wizard.

Occasionally, a mailbox that has been disconnected or removed does not appear in the list of disconnected mailboxes in the EMC even though the mailbox retention period has not expired. This may be because the Exchange store has not updated the status of the mailboxes yet. You can resolve this problem by running the *Clean-MailboxDatabase* cmdlet against the mailbox database that originally hosted the mailbox. When you do this, a scan is performed for disconnected mailboxes, and their status is updated in the Exchange store.

MORE INFO LOCATING MISSING DISCONNECTED MAILBOXES

To learn more about locating missing disconnected mailboxes and the *Clean-MailboxDatabase* cmdlet, consult the following link on TechNet: *http://technet .microsoft.com/en-us/library/bb124076.aspx*.

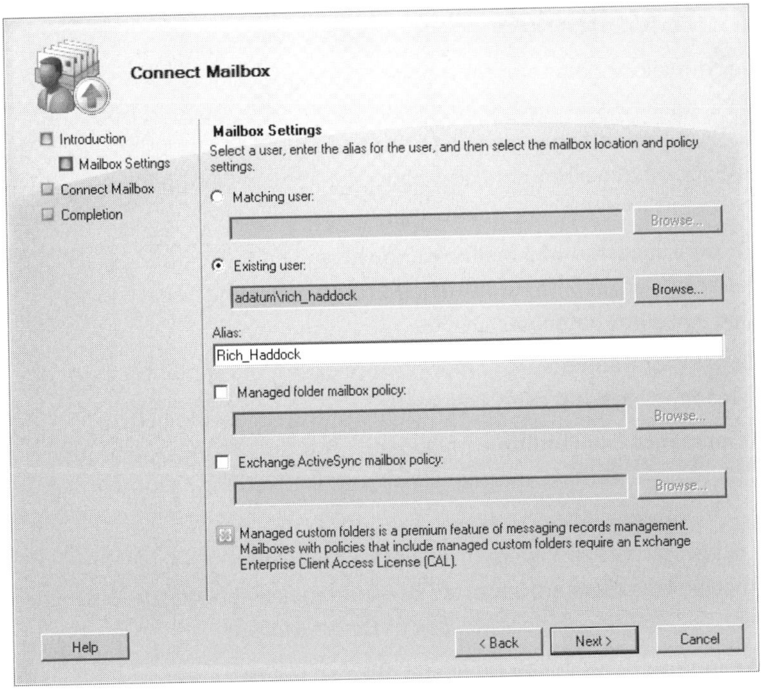

FIGURE 3-13 Reconnect mailbox

You can use the *Connect-Mailbox* EMS cmdlet to connect a disconnected mailbox to an existing Active Directory account. For example, to connect the disconnected mailbox named Jesper_Herp, which was originally located in mailbox database MBX-DB-ONE, to the Jesper_Herp user account, issue the following command:

```
Connect-Mailbox –Identity "Jesper Herp" –Database "MBX-DB-ONE" –User "Jesper Herp"
```

> **MORE INFO** **CONNECTING MAILBOXES**
>
> For more information on connecting disconnected mailboxes to Active Directory user objects, consult the following TechNet article: *http://technet.microsoft.com/en-us/library/bb123490.aspx*.

✔ **Quick Check**
  - You want to delete an Exchange mailbox but retain the Active Directory user account associated with it. Should you use the *Disable-Mailbox* or the *Remove-Mailbox* cmdlet to accomplish this goal?

Quick Check Answer
  - You should use the *Disable-Mailbox* cmdlet, as this deletes the mailbox, leaving it in a disconnected state, without removing the associated Active Directory user account.

Import and Export Mailboxes

You can import and export mailbox data to or from other Exchange mailboxes or PST files. There may be circumstances where you want to import data stored in existing PST files into Exchange mailboxes, such as if you are migrating users from using PST files to using Exchange 2010 archive mailboxes. Exporting mailbox data also allows you to perform the following tasks:

- **Create a point-in-time snapshot of a mailbox** You may need to create regular snapshots of specific mailboxes without needing to retain an extended backup set of all mailboxes on a mailbox databases.

- **Meeting compliance requirements** You may need to export the contents of specific mailboxes when meeting legal discovery requests.

- **Remove specific messages from multiple mailboxes** You can use the export mailbox process to remove sensitive messages that were inadvertently sent to multiple mailboxes.

A default import or export targets all folders, including empty folders, special folders, and subfolders. To restrict which folders are imported or exported, use the IncludeFolders or ExcludeFolders parameters when using *Import-Mailbox* or *Export-Mailbox*.

Mailbox import and export have the following limitations:

- It is possible to export only one mailbox at a time, though mailboxes can be exported sequentially.

- When you use *Export-Mailbox*, both the source mailbox and the destination mailbox are in the same Active Directory forest.

- Importing and exporting data requires a 64-bit computer that has both Exchange Server 2010 management tools installed and the 64-bit Microsoft Outlook 2010 client installed.

- *Import-Mailbox* cannot be used to import data to a mailbox hosted on previous versions of Exchange Server.

- It is not possible to import mailbox or PST data to a public folder or a public folder database.

You can perform a selective export using the RecipientKeywords, SenderKeywords, SubjectKeywords, StartDate, and EndDate parameters. When you use the *Export-Mailbox* cmdlet with the DeleteContent parameter but do not specify a target mailbox, you are able to delete specific messages in targeted mailboxes. This allows you to selectively delete messages across a number of targeted mailboxes. For example, if you wanted to remove a message that was sent to a large number of users who had mailboxes hosted on mailbox database MBX-DB-ONE called "Christmas Party Photos," which was sent by Kim Akers, you could use the following command:

```
Get-Mailbox –Database MBX-DB-ONE | Export-Mailbox –SubjectKeyWorks "Christmas Party
Photos" –SenderKeyWorks "Kim Akers" -DeleteContent
```

MORE INFO   IMPORT AND EXPORT MAILBOXES

For more information on importing and exporting mailbox data, consult the following TechNet link: *http://technet.microsoft.com/en-us/library/ee633455.aspx.*

Archive Mailboxes

Archive mailboxes are a feature new to Exchange Server 2010. Personal archives eliminate the need for PST files for Outlook 2010 by allowing users to store messages in an archive mailbox that is accessible to Outlook 2010 and OWA. This simplifies the process of legal discovery and the enforcement of message retention policies, which can be difficult to apply when messages are stored locally on users' workstations rather than on Exchange mailbox servers. Archive mailboxes are available only with Exchange Enterprise edition CALs.

You can create an archive mailbox when you create a primary user mailbox. It is also possible to create or remove an archive mailbox when a user has an existing mailbox. Archive mailboxes are stored in the same mailbox database as the user's mailbox. When you move a user's mailbox to another server, the archive mailbox is automatically moved to the destination mailbox database as well.

You can enable an archive on an existing mailbox by selecting the mailbox in the Recipient Configuration\Mailbox node of EMC and then clicking on the Enable Archive item in the Actions pane. You can use the *Enable-Mailbox* command with the Archive parameter to enable an archive mailbox for an existing mailbox. For example, to enable an archive mailbox for Rich Haddock's mailbox, issue the following EMS command:

```
Enable-Mailbox "Rich Haddock" -Archive
```

To disable an archive mailbox, select the mailbox under the Recipient Configuration\Mailbox node and then click Disable Archive in the Actions pane. You can also use the *Disable-Mailbox* cmdlet to disable an archive mailbox. For example, to disable the archive mailbox associated with Rich Haddock's mailbox, issue the following EMS command:

```
Disable-Mailbox "Rich Haddock" -Archive
```

In the event that you accidentally disable the archive mailbox for a user and you want to reconnect it and the disabled archive mailboxes is still retained in the mailbox database because of retention policies, you can reconnect it using the EMC by viewing the Disconnected Mailbox node under Recipient Configuration in EMC.

MORE INFO   ARCHIVE MAILBOXES

For more information on configuring archive mailboxes, consult the following TechNet article: *http://technet.microsoft.com/en-us/library/dd979795.aspx.*

EXAM TIP

Remember which cmdlet you use to move mailboxes in Exchange Server 2010.

Lesson Summary

- Deleted items settings are inherited from the mailbox database. It is possible to override these settings on a per-mailbox basis so that deleted items are available for a longer or shorter period.

- It is possible to configure message size limits on individual mailboxes that restrict the size of messages that a user can send and receive.

- Linked mailboxes use a disabled user account in the local forest to function as a substitute for a user account in a remote forest.

- The *New-MoveRequest* cmdlet is used to perform online mailbox moves in Exchange Server 2010.

- Delegating Full Access allows a mailbox to be read. Delegating Send As allows a user to send a message with that identity.

Lesson Review

You can use the following questions to test your knowledge of the information in Lesson 1, "Mailbox Configuration." The questions are also available on the companion CD if you prefer to review them in electronic form.

> **NOTE   ANSWERS**
>
> Answers to these questions and explanations of why each answer choice is correct or incorrect are located in the "Answers" section at the end of the book.

1. Which of the following cmdlets would you use to move a mailbox from an Exchange Server 2010 mailbox server in one site to an Exchange Server 2010 mailbox server in another Active Directory site while minimizing the disruption to the mailbox user?

   A. *Set-Mailbox*

   B. *Move-Mailbox*

   C. *New-MoveRequest*

   D. *Get-Mailbox*

2. Which of the following commands configures the Send As permission for Kim Akers on Don Hall's mailbox?

   A. *Add-MailboxPermission –Identity "Kim Akers" –User "adatum\Don_Hall" –AccessRights FullAccess –InheritanceType all*

   B. *Add-MailboxPermission –Identity "Don Hall" –User "adatum\Kim_Akers" –AccessRights FullAccess –InheritanceType all*

   C. *Add-ADPermission "Don Hall" –User "adatum\Kim_Akers" –Extendedrights "Send As"*

   D. *Add-ADPermission "Kim Akers" –User "adatum\Don_Hall" –Extendedrights "Send As"*

3. Which of the following cmdlets allows you to connect a disconnected mailbox to a newly created Active Directory user account?

   A. *New-Mailbox*

   B. *Set-Mailbox*

   C. *Enable-Mailbox*

   D. *Connect-Mailbox*

4. You want to limit the messages that Kim Akers can send and receive to 2 MB in size. Which of the following commands could you use to accomplish this goal?

   A. *Set-Mailbox "Kim Akers" –MaxReceiveSize 2097152 –MaxSendSize 2097152*

   B. *Set-Mailbox "Kim Akers" –ProhibitSendQuota 2097152 –MaxSendSize 2097152*

   C. *Set-Mailbox "Kim Akers" –MaxReceiveSize 2097152 –ProhibitSendQuota 2097152*

   D. *Set-Mailbox "Kim Akers" –IssueWarningQuota 2097152 –ProhibitSendQuota 2097152*

5. Which of the following parameters would you use with the *Set-Mailbox* cmdlet to ensure that email that had an SCL greater than 5 was sent to the junk email folder?

   A. SCLQuarantineEnabled and SCLQuarantineThreshold

   B. SCLJunkEnabled and SCLJunkThreshold

   C. SCLDeleteEnabled and SCLDeleteThreshold

   D. SCLRejectEnabled and SCLRejectThreshold

Lesson 2: Resources and Shared Mailboxes

Resource mailboxes allow people in your organization to use the calendaring function of Exchange to reserve equipment such as projectors or to book conference rooms for meetings. Acceptance policies allow these bookings to be processed automatically or moderated by an individual or individuals whose responsibilities include facilities and equipment management. Shared mailboxes are mailboxes that are accessible to multiple users but that are not associated with one specific user account.

> **After this lesson, you will be able to:**
> - Create resource mailboxes.
> - Configure shared mailboxes.
> - Modify resource mailbox properties.
>
> **Estimated lesson time: 40 minutes**

Creating and Configuring Resource Mailboxes

Resource mailboxes allow users in your organization to book resources, such as conference rooms or equipment, using Exchange's calendaring functionality. For example, if a user wants to book use of a specific conference room, a meeting request is set up, including all relevant attendees, and then the address of the room in which the meeting will be held in that request is included. Depending on how the resource mailbox has been configured, the room will automatically be booked for that meeting. The integration with Exchange calendaring means that other users will be able to check the availability of the room, with current room bookings being visible through the calendar. Exchange Server 2010 supports two types of resource mailbox:

- **Room mailboxes**   Room mailboxes represent meeting locations such as conference rooms or lecture theaters.
- **Equipment mailboxes**   Equipment mailboxes represent specific items, such as overhead projectors, scanners, or company hovercraft.

To create room or equipment mailbox, perform the following steps:

1. In the EMC, select the Mailbox node under the Recipient Configuration node.
2. In the Actions pane, click on the New Mailbox item. This will open the New Mailbox Wizard. Select Room (or Equipment) Mailbox and then click Next.
3. On the User Type page, select New User. The room mailbox needs to be associated with an Active Directory user account, even though that user account will be disabled. Click Next.
4. On the User Information page, enter the name of the room in the Name field, repeat this in the User Logon Name fields, and then enter a password. There is no need to

select the User Must Change Password At Next Logon option, and it is not necessary to specify values in the First Name, Initials, and Last Name fields. If necessary, you can specify an OU to host the disabled resource mailbox account. Click Next.

5. On the Mailbox Settings page, enter an alias for the mailbox. This can be the same name that you specified as the user logon name in step 4. You can specify a mailbox database to host the mailbox or accept the default allocation.

6. Click Next on the Archive Settings page. Click New and then click Finish.

Except for the step where you choose a Room or Equipment mailbox, the basic setup process is the same. You create Room and Equipment mailboxes using the *New-Mailbox* cmdlet. For example, to create a new room mailbox named Conference-Beta that is hosted on mailbox database MBX-DB-ONE, issue the following command:

```
New-Mailbox –UserPrincipalName conference-beta@adatum.com –Alias conference-beta –Name
Conference-Beta –Database MBX-DB-ONE –OrganizationalUnit Users -Room
```

The command for creating an equipment mailbox is the same except instead of using the Room parameter with the *New-Mailbox* cmdlet, you use the Equipment parameter. For example, to create a new equipment mailbox named Video-Camera that is hosted on mailbox database MBX-DB-ONE, issue the following command:

```
New-Mailbox –UserPrincipalName video-camera@adatum.com –Alias video-camera –Name video-
camera –Database MBX-DB-ONE –OrganizationalUnit Users -Equipment
```

Once you have created a resource mailbox, it is necessary to configure the resource mailbox. Some properties, such as Resource Capacity, which is configured on the Resource General page of the resource mailbox properties, can also be configured with the *Set-Mailbox* cmdlet. For example, to set the resource capacity of room mailbox Conference-Alpha to 40, issue the following command:

```
Set-Mailbox Conference-Alpha –ResourceCapacity 40
```

> **MORE INFO** **CUSTOM RESOURCE PROPERTIES FOR RESOURCE MAILBOXES**
>
> Exchange allows administrators to add custom resource properties to room or equipment mailboxes. For example, you could create a custom property for equipment mailboxes called Vehicle to represent company vehicles. Doing this requires modifying the resource configuration of the Exchange organization. To learn more about this process, consult the following TechNet article: *http://technet.microsoft.com/en-us/library/bb201697.aspx*.

The majority of other resource mailbox configuration tasks are performed from the EMS using the *Set-CalendarProcessing* cmdlet. You will learn about configuring additional resource mailbox properties throughout the rest of this lesson.

> **MORE INFO** **MANAGING RESOURCE MAILBOXES AND SCHEDULING**
>
> For more information on managing resource mailboxes and scheduling, consult the following TechNet article: *http://technet.microsoft.com/en-us/library/bb124374.aspx*.

Configuring Resource Policies

Resource policies determine how a resource mailbox can be booked. You can use resource policies to determine how far in advance a resource can be booked, the maximum amount of time the resource can be booked for, and which users are configured as delegates for the resource. You configure resource policies in the Resource Policy tab of the resource mailbox's properties, shown in Figure 3-14.

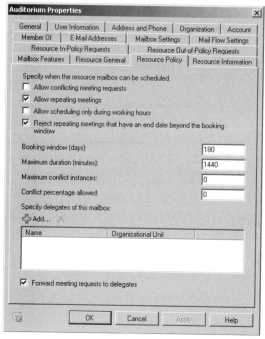

FIGURE 3-14 Configure resource policy

The settings on the Resource Policy tab have the following properties:

- **Allow Conflicting Meeting Requests** Allows meeting requests that conflict with one another to be scheduled.

- **Allow Repeating Meetings** Allows recurring meetings to be scheduled, such as if a user wants to use a particular resource every Wednesday morning at 11:00 AM.

- **Allow Scheduling Only During Working Hours** Allows the resource to be booked only during working hours. Administrators configure working hours using the *Set-MailboxCaldenarConfiguration* cmdlet.

- **Reject Meetings That Have An End Date Beyond The Booking Window** Enabling this option means that bookings that exceed the booking window are rejected.

- **Booking Window (Days)** This figure specifies how far in advance the resource can be booked.

- **Maximum Duration (Minutes)** The maximum amount of time the resource can be booked for.

- **Maximum Conflict Instances** How many conflicts with other bookings can exist prior to a meeting request being automatically denied.
- **Conflict Percentage Allowed** If a booking is configured to be recurring and a certain percentage of those recurrences conflict with existing bookings, the booking is denied.
- **Specify Delegates Of This Mailbox** Allows you to specify users who control scheduling options for the resource mailbox.
- **Forward Meeting Requests To Delegates** Specifies whether meeting requests are forwarded to specified delegates.

You can configure the Resource Properties of a resource mailbox using the Set-*CalendarProcessing* cmdlet. For example, to set a maximum booking window of 50 days and a maximum booking duration of 2 hours for the Auditorium resource mailbox, issue the following command:

```
Set-CalendarProcessing Auditorium –BookingWindowsInDays 50 –MaximumDurationInMinutes 120
```

Managing In-Policy and Out-of-Policy Requests

Exchange processes requests to use resources against the resource policy. In-policy request settings apply when a request that meets the resource policy is made. The in-policy request settings determine which users have their requests automatically approved and which in-policy requests for the resource will be subject to approval by the resource delegate. For example, if the in-policy request settings were configured as shown in Figure 3-15, where no users are set to have their in-policy requests automatically approved, all requests for the resource would be forwarded to the configured delegates for approval.

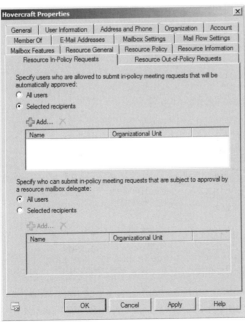

FIGURE 3-15 Configure resource in-policy requests

Out-of-policy request settings determine which users are able to submit out-of-policy requests that are subject to approval by a resource mailbox delegate. If a user is not on the list of users who can submit out-of-policy requests, the request will be automatically denied. In the case of the Resource Out-of-Policy Requests tab shown in Figure 3-16, Oleg Anaskhin is able to submit out-of-policy requests, though these requests will still require approval from a delegate. You will learn about configuring resource mailbox delegates in the next section of this lesson.

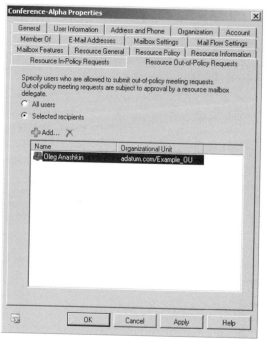

FIGURE 3-16 Out-of-policy request settings

You can configure the Resource-In-Policy Requests and Resource Out-of-Policy Request settings using the *Set-CalendarProcessing* cmdlet with the AllBookInPolicy, AllRequestInPolicy, AllRequestOutOfPolicy, BookInPolicy, RequestInPolicy, and RequestOutOfPolicy parameters.

> **MORE INFO   CONFIGURING AUTOMATIC BOOKING POLICIES**
>
> To learn more about configuring automatic booking policies, consult the following link on TechNet: *http://technet.microsoft.com/en-us/library/bb124542.aspx*.

Configure Delegates on Resource Mailboxes

Delegates are able to control the scheduling options for resource mailboxes. You can configure a resource mailbox so that all requests for the resource that the mailbox represents are forwarded to the delegate. As you learned earlier, you can configure a delegate for a resource mailbox through the EMC on the Resource Policy tab by specifying their mailboxes and enabling the Forward Meeting Requests To Delegates option.

You can configure these properties through the EMS using the *Set-CalendarProcessing* cmdlet. For example, to configure Kim Akers as a resource delegate for the Auditorium resource mailbox and to ensure that all booking requests for the resource are forwarded to her, issue the following command:

```
Set-CalendarProcessing Auditorium -ResourceDelegates "Kim_Akers@adatum.com"
-ForwardRequestsToDelegates $true
```

> **MORE INFO** **CONFIGURE DELEGATE ON A RESOURCE MAILBOX**
>
> For more information on configuring a delegate on a resource mailbox, consult the following link on TechNet: *http://technet.microsoft.com/en-us/library/bb124973.aspx*.

Configuring Automatic Booking

Once you have configured resource booking policies, you need to enable the Resource Booking Attendant. The Resource Booking Attendant enables automatic booking of resources functionality on a resource mailbox. If the Resource Booking Attendant is not enabled, the configured resource mailbox delegate must approve or decline all booking requests. The Resource Booking Attendant is enabled by selecting the Enable The Resource Booking Attendant check box on the Resource General tab of the Conference-Alpha Properties, as shown in Figure 3-17.

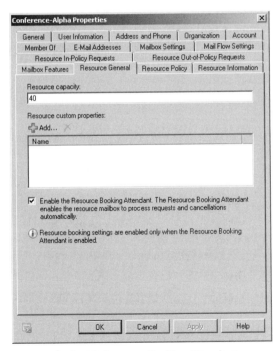

FIGURE 3-17 Enable Resource Booking Attendant

To enable the resource booking attendant from the EMS, use the *Set-CalendarProcessing* cmdlet with the AutomateProcessing parameter. For example, to enable automatic booking on the Conference-Alpha room mailbox, issue the following command:

```
Set-CalendarProcessing Conference-Alpha –AutomateProcessing AutoAccept
```

> **MORE INFO**   **ENABLE AUTOMATIC BOOKING ON A RESOURCE MAILBOX**
>
> To learn more about enabling automatic booking on a resource mailbox, consult the following TechNet article: *http://technet.microsoft.com/en-us/library/bb123495.aspx*.

 Quick Check

- Which cmdlet do you use to configure resource booking policies on a room mailbox?

Quick Check Answer

- You use the *Set-CalendarProcessing* cmdlet to configure resource booking policies on a resource mailbox.

Shared Mailboxes

A shared mailbox is a mailbox accessed by multiple users that is not associated with an enabled Active Directory user account. Although it is possible to share access to normal user mailboxes through delegation, Exchange provides shared mailboxes specifically for the shared role. This special type of mailbox appears in the recipients list with an icon different from that of other mailbox types. The Active Directory account associated with a shared mailbox is always disabled. All users that need access to the shared mailbox are delegated Full Access and Send As permissions after mailbox creation.

It is possible to create shared mailboxes only from the EMS. You create shared mailboxes using the *New-Mailbox* cmdlet with the Shared parameter. The following EMS command creates a shared mailbox named Shared-MBX on the MBX-DB-ONE mailbox database:

```
New-Mailbox –UserPrincipalName Shared-MBX@adatum.com –Alias Shared-MBX –Name Shared-MBX
–Database MBX-DB-ONE –OrganizationalUnit Users –Shared
```

Once the mailbox has been created, you can delegate Full Access and Send As permissions through either the EMS or EMC. You learned how to delegate Full Access and Send As permissions in Lesson 1, "Mailbox Configuration."

Converting Mailboxes

You can use the *Set-Mailbox* command to convert one type of mailbox to another type. One reason that you might want to convert mailboxes is when transitioning from an Exchange 2003 environment to an Exchange 2010 environment. In Exchange 2003, you can use shared mailboxes to represent resources. If you migrate these mailboxes to Exchange 2010, you will want to convert them to resource mailboxes. Although it is not possible to perform a mailbox conversion using the EMC, you can perform the following types of mailbox conversion using the *Set-Mailbox* command in the EMS:

- User mailbox to shared mailbox
- User mailbox to resource mailbox
- Shared mailbox to user mailbox
- Shared mailbox to resource mailbox
- Resource mailbox to user mailbox
- Resource mailbox to shared mailbox

For example, to convert the mailbox named Hovercraft from an Equipment mailbox to a Room mailbox, issue the following command:

```
Set-Mailbox Hovercraft -Type Room
```

MORE INFO   CONVERTING MAILBOXES

For more information about converting mailboxes, consult the following page on TechNet: *http://technet.microsoft.com/en-us/library/bb201749.aspx.*

EXAM TIP

Understand the difference between a user mailbox, a shared mailbox, a resource mailbox, and a linked mailbox.

Lesson Summary

- There are two different types of resource mailbox: equipment mailboxes and room mailboxes. Equipment mailboxes represent physical items, and room mailboxes represent locations.
- You can configure resource mailbox booking policies using the *Set-CalendarProcessing* cmdlet.
- New requests for resources are processed according to the booking policy. You can configure all or some requests to be sent to a delegate who approves or disapproves booking requests.
- A shared mailbox is a mailbox associated with a disabled user account that is accessible to multiple users.

Lesson Review

You can use the following questions to test your knowledge of the information in Lesson 2, "Resources and Shared Mailboxes." The questions are also available on the companion CD if you prefer to review them in electronic form.

NOTE ANSWERS

Answers to these questions and explanations of why each answer choice is correct or incorrect are located in the "Answers" section at the end of the book.

1. A recent renovation has increased the number of seats that are available in a conference room in your company building from 10 to 15. Which cmdlet would you use to modify the room mailbox associated with this room?

    A. *New-Mailbox*

    B. *Set-Mailbox*

    C. *Get-Mailbox*

    D. *Enable-Mailbox*

2. You have been reviewing the setup of Exchange mailboxes at one of your organization's interstate offices. You have determined that the contractor who created several mailboxes at the office incorrectly created room mailboxes when he should have created shared mailboxes. The room mailboxes currently store content that you want to retain, so you have decided to convert these mailboxes from room mailboxes to shared mailboxes. Which of the following commands would you use to reconfigure a room mailbox named SalesInfo so that it functions as a shared mailbox?

    A. *Set-Mailbox SalesInfo –Type Room*

    B. *Set-Mailbox SalesInfo –Type Shared*

    C. *Set-Mailbox SalesInfo –Type Equipment*

    D. *Set-Mailbox SalesInfo –Type Regular*

3. Which of the following cmdlets would you use to delegate control of a room mailbox to a specific user so that all requests for the room would be forwarded to that specific user for approval?

    A. *Set-Mailbox*

    B. *Set-CalendarNotification*

    C. *Set-CalendarProcessing*

    D. *Get-Mailbox*

4. Which of the following EMS cmdlets allows you to specify delegates and booking windows for resource mailboxes?

    A. *Set-Mailbox*

    B. *Set-CalendarProcessing*

    C. *Set-LinkedUser*

    D. *Set-Group*

Creating and Configuring Mailboxes

In this set of practices, you will create and configure and manage user and resource mailboxes. This practice requires that you have VAN-DC, VAN-EX1, and VAN-EX2 available and configured as described in the Appendix.

EXERCISE 1 Creating a Mailbox

In this exercise, you will create several mailboxes and then configure quota settings.

1. Ensure that the folders c:\mydatabasefiles and C:\mylogfolder have been created on computers VAN-EX1 and VAN-EX2.

2. Log on to server VAN-EX1 with the Kim_Akers user account that was created in the practice exercise at the end of Chapter 1.

3. Open the EMS and issue the following commands:

   ```
   New-MailboxDatabase –Name MBX-DB-ONE –Server VAN-EX1 –EdbFilePath
   c:\MyDatabaseFiles\mbx-db-one.edb –LogFolderPath c:\mylogfolder

   New-MailboxDatabase –Name MBX-DB-TWO –Server VAN-EX2 –EdbFilePath
   c:\MyDatabaseFiles\mbx-db-two.edb –LogFolderPath c:\MyLogFolder

   Mount-Database MBX-DB-ONE

   Mount-Database MBX-DB-TWO
   ```

4. In the Server Configuration\Mailbox node, verify that these two mailbox databases have been created and mounted.

5. Expand the Recipient Configuration node and then click on Mailbox. In the Actions pane, click on the New Mailbox item. This will launch the New Mailbox Wizard. Select the User Mailbox option, shown in Figure 3-18, and click Next.

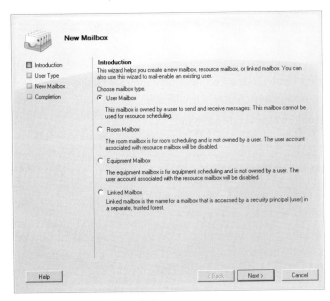

FIGURE 3-18 New mailbox choice

6. On the User Type page, select New User and then click Next.

7. Fill out the New Mailbox User Information page, as shown in Figure 3-19. Use the password *Pa$$w0rd*. Click Next.

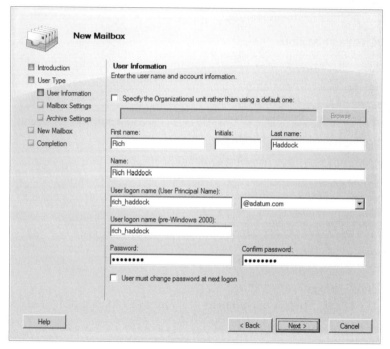

FIGURE 3-19 New user information

8. On the Mailbox Settings page, enter the alias **Rich_Haddock**. Then click the Browse button next to Specify The Mailbox Database Rather Than Using A Database Automatically Selected. In the Select Mailbox Database dialog box, select MBX-DB-ONE and click OK. Click Next.

9. On the Archive Settings page, check the Create An Archive Mailbox For This Account check box and then click Next. On the Configuration Summary page, click New. When the mailbox has been successfully created, click Finish.

10. Open the EMS and issue the following command:

```
Set-Mailbox rich_haddock -MaxReceiveSize 2097152 -MaxSendSize
2097152 -IssueWarningQuota 209715200 -ProhibitSendQuota 262144000
-ProhibitSendReceiveQuota 293601280 -UseDatabaseQuotaDefaults $false
```

11. In the EMC, select the Mailbox Node under Recipient Configuration. Right-click on the Rich Haddock mailbox and click on Properties.

12. Click on the Mail Flow Settings tab and then click on the Message Size Restrictions item. Click Properties. Verify that the maximum message that can be sent and received equals 2048 KB (2,097,152 bytes). Click Cancel to close the Message Size Restrictions dialog box.

13. On the Mailbox Settings tab, click on the Storage Quotas item and then click Properties. Verify that the figures match those in Figure 3-20 and then click Cancel.

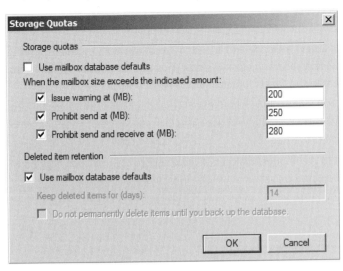

FIGURE 3-20 Storage quotas

14. Click Cancel to close the properties of Rich Haddock's mailbox.

15. Right-click on the Recipient Configuration\Mailbox node and then click New Mailbox.

16. On the Introduction page of the New Mailbox Wizard, ensure that User Mailbox is selected and then click Next.

17. On the User Type page, click Existing Users and then click Add. In the Select User dialog box, select Kim Akers and then click OK. Click Next.

18. On the Mailbox Settings page, enter **Kim_Akers** as the Alias and then click Next. Click New and then click Finish.

19. Open the EMC and issue the command:

```
New-Mailbox –Name 'Jeff Hay' –Alias 'Jeff_Hay' –UserPrincipalName 'Jeff_Hay@
adatum.com' –SamAccountName 'Jeff_Hay' –FirstName 'Jeff' –Lastname 'Hay'
```

20. When prompted, enter the password **Pa$$w0rd.**

EXERCISE 2 Move and modify a mailbox

In this exercise, you will move the mailbox that you created in the first exercise to a different mailbox database. You will then configure the Send As permission on this mailbox.

1. Ensure that you are logged on to VAN-EX1 with the Kim Akers user account. If you have not done so already, use the Server Manager console to disable Internet Explorer Enhanced Security Configuration (IE ESC) for Administrators.

2. Open Internet Explorer and navigate to *https://van-ex1/owa*. Click Continue To This Website (Not Recommended) when warned about the website security certificate.

3. Log on to Outlook Web App using the ADATUM\Rich_haddock credentials. Specify that you are using a private computer and do not use the light version of Outlook Web App.

4. When presented with the Language and Time Zone page, click OK.

5. Click New. Create a new message addressed to Kim Akers with the subject Test Message. Save the message and close the new message window. Verify that the message is present in the Drafts folder of Outlook Web App.

6. Without closing Internet Explorer, open the EMC and navigate to the Recipient Configuration\Mailbox node. Right-click on the Rich Haddock mailbox and then click on New Local Move Request.

7. In the New Local Move Request dialog box, click on Browse and then click on MBX-DB-TWO, which you created on server VAN-EX2 in Exercise 1. Click OK and then verify that the settings on the Introduction page match those shown in Figure 3-21. Click Next.

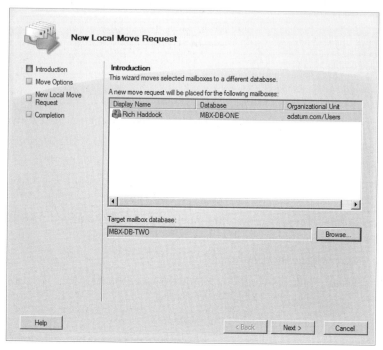

FIGURE 3-21 New local move request

8. On the Move Options page, select Skip The Mailbox and then click Next. Click New. When the move completes, click Finish.

9. Switch back to Internet Explorer and then click Reload until Outlook Web App appears again. Click on the Drafts folder and verify that the message that you were in the process of creating for Kim_Akers is still present. Close Internet Explorer.

10. In the EMC, right-click on the Rich Haddock mailbox under Recipient Configuration\ Mailbox and then click Manage Send As Permission.

11. On the Manage Send As Permission page, click Add. In the Select User Or Group dialog box, click Kim Akers and then click OK. Verify that the Manage Send As Permission dialog box is the same as that shown in Figure 3-22 and then click Manage. Click Finish to close the Manage Send As Permission dialog box.

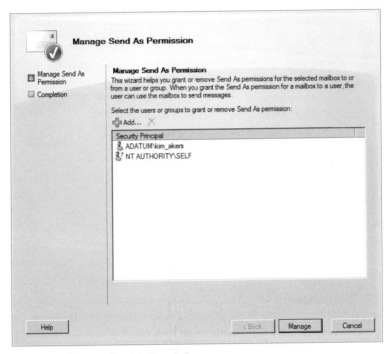

FIGURE 3-22 Manage Send As Permission

12. Open Internet Explorer and navigate to *https://van-ex1/owa*. Click Continue To This Website (Not Recommended) when warned about the website security certificate.

13. Log on to Outlook Web App using the ADATUM\Kim_Akers credentials. Specify that you are using a private computer and do not use the light version of Outlook Web App.

14. When presented with the Language and Time Zone page, click OK.

15. Click Options and then click Settings. With Mail selected, scroll down and select the Always Show From option, as shown in Figure 3-23, and then click Save.

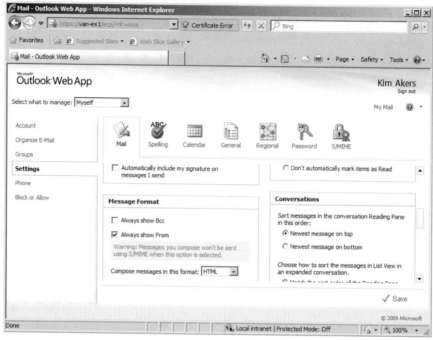

FIGURE 3-23 Configure OWA to always show From field

16. Click My Mail. Click New. If presented with a certificate warning, click Continue To This Website (Not Recommended).

17. Click on the From drop-down list and select Other E-mail Address. In the list click on Rich Haddock, click From and then click OK. In the To: Field, enter **Kim Akers,** and in the Subject and message body field, enter **Test.** Click Send.

18. Verify that a message that appears to be from Rich Haddock appears in the Kim Akers Inbox folder. Close Internet Explorer.

EXERCISE 3   Create and modify a resource mailbox

In this practice exercise, you will create and configure a room mailbox named auditorium. You will set the size of the room and configure the accept setting for this mailbox. You will also create and configure an equipment mailbox named Hovercraft and configure the accept setting for this equipment.

1. If you have not done so already, log on to server VAN-EX1 with the Kim Akers account and open the EMC.

2. Right-click on the Recipient Configuration\Mailbox node and then click New Mailbox.

3. On the Introduction page of the New Mailbox Wizard, select Room Mailbox and then click Next.

4. On the User Type page select New User and then click Next.

5. On the User Information page, set the Name and User Logon Name to Auditorium and the password to *Pa$$w0rd* and then click Next.

6. On the Mailbox Settings page, set the alias to Auditorium and then click Next.

7. On the Archive Settings page, click Next. On the New Mailbox page, click New and then, when the mailbox is created, click Finish.

8. In the list that is shown when the Recipient Configuration\Mailboxes node is selected, right-click on Auditorium and then click Properties.

9. On the Resource General tab, enter **50** in the Resource Capacity textbox. Enable the Enable The Resource Booking Attendant option and then click OK.

10. Right-click on the Recipient Configuration\Mailbox node and click New Mailbox.

11. On the Introduction page of the New Mailbox Wizard, select Equipment Mailbox and then click Next.

12. On the User Type page, select New User and then click Next.

13. On the User Information page, set the Name and User Logon Name to Hovercraft and the password to *Pa$$w0rd* and then click Next.

14. On the Mailbox Settings page, set the alias to Hovercraft and then click Next.

15. On the Archive Settings page, click Next. On the New Mailbox page, click New and then, when the mailbox is created, click Finish.

16. When the Recipient Configuration\Mailbox node is selected, locate and right-click on the Hovercraft mailbox and then click on Properties.

17. On the Resource Policy tab, click Add under Specify Delegates Of This Mailbox. In the Select Recipient dialog box, click on Kim Akers and then click OK.

18. On the Resource In-Policy Requests tab, under the Specify Users Who Are Allowed To Submit In-Policy Meeting Requests That Will Be Automatically Approved, select Selected Recipients.

19. Under Specify Who Can Submit In-Policy Meeting Requests That Are Subject To Approval By A Resource Mailbox Delegate, select All Users. Verify that the settings match those shown in Figure 3-24 and then click OK.

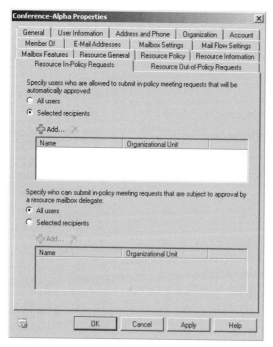

FIGURE 3-24 Resource in-policy settings

20. Open Internet Explorer and navigate to *https://van-ex1/owa*. Click Continue To This Website (Not Recommended) when warned about the website security certificate.

21. Log on to Outlook Web App using the ADATUM\Rich_haddock credentials. Specify that you are using a private computer and do not use the light version of Outlook Web App.

22. When presented with the Language and Time Zone page, click OK.

23. Click Calendar, click New, and then click Meeting Request. If presented with a certificate warning, click Continue To This Website (Not Recommended)

24. In the To field, type **Auditorium**. In the Subject field, type **Project** Update. Set the date to two days from the current date displayed, click Send, and then click OK to dismiss the warning.

25. Verify that the meeting request was accepted by viewing the acceptance e-mail in the Inbox.

26. Click Calendar. Click New and then click Meeting Request. In the To field, type **Hovercraft**. In the Resources field, type **Hovercraft**. In the Subject field, type **Research Mission**. Set the date to three days from today. Click Send and then click OK to dismiss the warning. Note that no automatic approval appears in Rich Haddock's Inbox, as Kim Akers has been configured as a delegate and must approve use of the Hovercraft resource.

Chapter Review

To further practice and reinforce the skills you learned in this chapter, you can perform the following tasks:

- Review the chapter summary.
- Review the list of key terms introduced in this chapter.
- Complete the case scenarios. These scenarios set up real-world situations involving the topics of this chapter and ask you to create a solution.
- Complete the suggested practices.
- Take a practice test.

Chapter Summary

- User mailboxes must be associated with Active Directory user accounts. It is possible to create a new Active Directory user account when creating a new mailbox.
- Exchange Server 2010 allows online mailbox moves to be performed with the *New-MoveRequest* cmdlet. You cannot use the *Move-Mailbox* cmdlet with Exchange Server 2010 mailboxes.
- Delegating the Send As permission allows a user to send a message with another user's identity. Delegating the Full Access permission grants users the ability to access the contents of the mailbox that has been delegated.
- Equipment and Room mailboxes can be configured with an automatic calendaring policy that allows automatic booking. It is also possible to configure bookings so that a delegate must manually approve.

Key Terms

Do you know what these key terms mean?

- Delegate
- Linked mailbox
- Resource mailbox

Case Scenarios

In the following case scenarios, you will apply what you've learned about subjects of this chapter. You can find answers to these questions in the "Answers" section at the end of this book.

Case Scenario 1: Provision Mailboxes at Alpine Ski House

Alpine Ski House is a small ski resort located near Jindabyne in southern New South Wales, Australia. The resort is managed by Carol Phillips. The resort is in the process of migrating to Exchange Server 2010 from an open-source mail solution, and it is necessary to create a large number of new mailboxes that are associated with existing Active Directory accounts in the alpineskihouse.local domain. One of the goals in moving to Exchange 2010 is to reduce the amount of unsolicited commercial email that appears in the mailboxes of resort staff. Only one user, Don Hall, should have an unfiltered mail feed, as he is responsible for processing resort bookings and assessing commercial opportunities, and an unsolicited commercial email filter may inadvertently block important messages. As Carol Phillips spends a lot of time out on the grounds of the resort and away from her desk, it is necessary for her administrative assistant, Dan Park, to send email messages on her behalf.

With these facts in mind, answer the following questions:

1. What steps can you take to ensure that users cannot send or receive attachments that are greater than 10 MB in size?

2. What steps can you take to stop everyone at the resort receiving messages that are rated with an SCL above 5 while allowing Don Hall, who is responsible for bookings, to receive all messages, including those rated with an SCL above 5?

3. What steps should you take to allow Dan Park to send messages on behalf of Carol Phillips?

Case Scenario 2: Fabrikam Resource Mailboxes

Fabrikam Inc. is responsible for running a chain of tropical island corporate retreats. When guests arrive, they are issued with a mailbox on the Fabrikam guest domain, a separate forest from the Fabrikam internal domain that is used by management and employees of the organization. Each guest's room has a tablet computer configured in kiosk mode that allows guests to view conference schedules and reserve conference facilities and equipment. Guests need to be able to reserve conference rooms automatically but should be able to reserve the lecture theater only after consultation with Fabrikam staff. There are 15 sailboats that are available for use by guests of the retreat. Guests should be able to the book use of a sailboat from the tablet computer in their room for a two-hour period but should not be able to book the sailboat for multiple consecutive two-hour periods.

With these facts in mind, answer the following questions:

1. What steps would you take to allow guests to book conference rooms based on the size of the meeting which they wish to hold?

2. What steps should you take to allow guests to book a sailboat for a two-hour period but not book the sailboat for multiple consecutive two-hour periods?

3. How can you ensure that guest requests to reserve the lecture theater are approved by Fabrikam management?

Suggested Practices

To help you successfully master the exam objectives presented in this chapter, complete the following tasks.

Create and Configure Mailboxes

You should complete these additional practice exercises only once you have completed practice exercise three.

- **Practice 1** Create a new mailbox and associated user named Keith Harris and have it hosted in the MBX-DB-ONE mailbox database. Configure the Keith Harris mailbox from the EMS so that it can be accessed using the POP3 protocol but cannot be accessed through Outlook Web App, Exchange ActiveSync, MAPI, or the IMAP4 protocol.
- **Practice 2** Use the EMC to perform an online mailbox move of the Keith Harris mailbox to mailbox database MBX-DB-TWO.

Create and Configure Resource Mailboxes and Shared Mailboxes

You should complete these additional practice exercises only once you have completed Exercise 3, where you configure the properties of the Hovercraft resource mailbox.

- **Practice 1** Log on to OWA as Kim Akers, open the Hovercraft shared calendar, and approve the equipment resource request made by Rich Haddock.
- **Practice 2** Create a room mailbox named Conference_Room. Configure the Conference_Room mailbox so that all bookings must be approved by Rich Haddock and that the capacity of the room is set to 15 people.

Take a Practice Test

The practice tests on this book's companion CD offer many options. For example, you can test yourself on just one exam objective, or you can test yourself on all the 70-662 certification exam content. You can set up the test so that it closely simulates the experience of taking a certification exam, or you can set it up in study mode so that you can look at the correct answers and explanations after you answer each question.

> **MORE INFO** **PRACTICE TESTS**
>
> For details about all the practice test options available, see the "How to Use the Practice Tests" section in this book's Introduction.

CHAPTER 4

Distribution Groups and Public Folders

Distribution groups simplify the task of sending messages to a group of people. Rather than having to remember the names of everyone in the target group, such as everyone in the research department, you send the message to the Research_Department group, and all the Exchange recipients in that group receive the message. A drawback of distribution groups is that they rely on someone taking responsibility for managing group membership. How accurately the distribution group mirrors the intended membership depends on the diligence of the group manager. If someone new joins the department, he or she will be a member of the group only if someone manually adds him or her. Dynamic distribution groups provide a solution for the problem of updated membership lists, as group membership is determined through a recipient filter. A recipient filter defines membership based on a property such as a recipient's association with a particular department or locality. Public folders provide a central location in Exchange for shared content. You can organize public folders in a hierarchy that allows people to file-share content in a logical manner. You can assign different permissions, through roles, to public folders, allowing some users to post and modify content while allowing other users only the ability to access that content.

Exam objectives in this chapter:
- Create and configure recipients and distribution groups.
- Create and configure public folders.

Lessons in this chapter:

Before You Begin

In order to complete the exercises in the practice sessions in this chapter, you need to have done the following:

- Installed VAN-DC, VAN-EX1, and VAN-EX2 as described in the Appendix.

REAL WORLD

Orin Thomas

Rumors of the demise of Exchange public folders have been greatly exaggerated. When Exchange 2007 was released, there was no support for public folders in the Exchange Management Console. This led to some people believing, including myself, that public folders were to be deprecated in Exchange in favor of solutions based around SharePoint technologies. I was finally corrected in my misapprehension by a member of the Exchange team at a bar during Tech.ED New Zealand in 2009. He informed me that that public folder management tools weren't included in Exchange 2007 at release not because of any policy about a future reduction of support for public folders in the product but because the tools weren't ready at that point and that the decision had been made to release them with Service Pack 1. He also mentioned that the Exchange team was always aware of how important public folders were in real-world deployments and that they weren't going to get rid of the feature at any time in the foreseeable future. He said that he often had people ask him when public folders were going to be finally removed, and he had to tell them that they weren't going anywhere anytime soon.

Although my telling you that public folders aren't going away after I heard it from a bloke at a pub in Auckland, New Zealand, might not be enough to persuade you, the inclusion of the public folder management tools in the management console in the Exchange Server 2010 should be enough to convince you that Exchange public folders aren't going anywhere soon.

Lesson 1: Managing Recipients and Distribution Groups

In Chapter 3, "Exchange Mailboxes," you learned about two recipient types: user mailboxes and resource mailboxes. In this lesson, you will learn about two additional recipient types: mail-enabled users and mail contacts. These additional recipient types allow you to integrate users with mailboxes hosted outside your organization into your organization's contact and address lists. A mail-enabled user is a person who can log on to the local Active Directory domain but who has the mailbox hosted outside the local Exchange organization. A mail contact is a special type of recipient that allows an external user's external email address to be present to Exchange clients without giving that user logon privileges in the local Active Directory environment. Distribution groups are collections of recipients. Normal distribution groups have their membership updated manually. Dynamic distribution groups have their membership updated automatically through a recipient filter that defines which recipients will and will not be members of the group.

> **After this lesson, you will be able to:**
> - Create and configure contacts.
> - Create and configure mail-enabled users.
> - Create new distribution groups.
> - Mail-enable existing groups.
> - Configure moderation for mail-enabled groups.
> - Configure Send-As permissions.
> - Configure recipient filters.
>
> **Estimated lesson time: 40 minutes**

Mail Contacts

Mail contacts allow an external user's email address to be present in Exchange address books without giving that user logon rights in the organizational forest. For example, several users at Contoso might regularly email Don Hall, a purchasing officer at a client firm but someone who never needs to log on to the Contoso network. Don Hall could be configured as an Exchange mail contact, allowing all users at Contoso to locate his address details automatically in Exchange address books or even add Don to distribution groups.

To create a mail contact using the EMC, perform the following general steps:

1. Navigate to the Recipient Configuration node. In the Actions pane, click New Mail Contact.
2. You can choose to mail-enable an existing contact or create a new contact.

3. On the Contact Information page, shown in Figure 4-1, provide information about the contact, including an alias; where the contact will be stored within Active Directory; and the associated external email address. When these details have been entered, click Next, New, and then Finish.

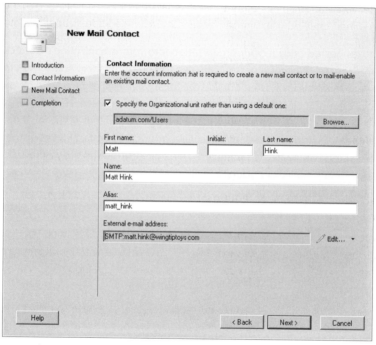

FIGURE 4-1 Creating a new mail contact

You can create a mail contact from the Exchange Management Shell (EMS) using the *New-MailContact* cmdlet. For example, to create a new mail contact for Julian Price with the address Julian.price@tailspintoys.com that will be stored in the Users container in the adatum.com domain, issue the following command:

```
New-MailContact –Name "Julian Price" –ExternalEmailAddress julian.price@tailspintoys.com
–OrganizationalUnit adatum.com/users
```

> **MORE INFO CREATING MAIL CONTACTS**
>
> To learn more about mail contacts, consult the following article on TechNet: *http://technet.microsoft.com/en-us/library/aa998858.aspx*.

Mail-Enabled Users

Mail-enabled users have user accounts in the Active Directory forest that hosts Exchange but have their mailboxes hosted by an eternal organization. Mail-enabled users are also known by the term "mail user." The external email address is associated with the user account. For example, Jim Hance is a contractor working at Contoso. To perform his job, Jim needs to be able to log on to the Contoso domain. Jim's organization does not have an Active Directory trust relationship with Contoso, so allowing local logon requires that Jim have an Active Directory user account. Rather than have a local mailbox, Jim prefers to have his email delivered to an email account that is separate from the Contoso Exchange organization. As a mail-enabled user, Jim can appear in Exchange address books, contact lists, and distribution groups even though he does not have a mailbox hosted on one of the organization's Exchange mailbox servers.

To create a mail-enabled user when no user account already exists using the Exchange Management Console (EMC), perform the following steps:

1. Click on New Mail User in the Actions Pane when the Recipient Configuration node is active in the EMC. Select New User and click Next.

2. Provide the details of the new user account, including the organizational unit (OU) that will host the user account in Active Directory and then click Next.

3. Provide an alias and the details of the external email address. Click Next, New, and then Finish.

To create a mail-enabled user using the EMS, use the *New-MailUser* cmdlet. For example, to create a mail-enabled user named Oksana with the email address oksana@contoso.com and with the account hosted in the Users container of the adatum.com domain, issue the following command:

```
New-MailUser -Name Oksana -ExternalEmailAddress Oksana@contoso.com -UserPrincipalName
oksana@adatum.com
```

When issuing this command, the EMS will prompt you to provide a password for the new user account. You can mail-enable an existing user account that is not associated with an Exchange mailbox using the EMC or the *Enable-MailUser* cmdlet in the EMS. To mail-enable an existing user account using the EMC, perform the following steps:

1. Click on New Mail User in the Actions Pane when the Recipient Configuration node is active in the EMC.

2. Select Existing User on the Introduction page. Click Browse and then select the user account that you wish to mail-enable and then click Next.

3. Provide an Exchange alias. Click Edit and then enter the external address to which Exchange will route email. Click Next, New, and then Finish.

To mail-enable an existing user account with the logon name Barry with the email address barry@contoso.com, issue the following command:

```
Enable-Mailuser -Identity Barry -ExternalEmailAddress Barry@contoso.com
```

> **MORE INFO**   **CREATE MAIL-ENABLED USER**
>
> To learn more about creating mail-enabled user, consult the following article on TechNet:
> *http://technet.microsoft.com/en-us/library/bb124381.aspx.*

Distribution Groups

Distribution groups are collections of recipients. A user sends a message to the distribution group address, and Exchange forwards that message to all members of the distribution group. Exchange supports three types of distribution groups: distribution groups, mail-enabled security groups, and dynamic distribution groups.

You manage the membership of distribution groups and mail-enabled security groups manually. Exchange adds members to dynamic distribution groups automatically. For example, you would add and remove members of a distribution group as necessary using the EMC or EMS. Exchange populates a dynamic distribution group based on its initial configuration. For example, you might define the dynamic distribution group membership as all users with an Exchange mailbox whose Active Directory properties list them as a member of the Research Department. The membership of this group is calculated automatically when a message is sent to the group, so people who are added and removed from the Research Department will automatically be added and removed from the dynamic distribution group that Exchange populates based on that attribute.

> **MORE INFO** **MANAGING DISTRIBUTION GROUPS**
>
> To learn more about managing distribution groups, consult the following article on TechNet: *http://technet.microsoft.com/en-us/library/bb125256.aspx*.

To create a distribution group using the EMC that you will use only to distribute messages and that you cannot use to assign security permissions and where the membership of the group is not generated dynamically, perform the following general steps:

1. In the EMC, select the Recipient Configuration node and then in the Actions pane click on the New Distribution Group item.

2. On the Introduction page, choose New Group. On the Group Information page, shown in Figure 4-2, specify the OU that will host the group, the group name, and the Exchange alias for the group. Click Next, New, and then Finish.

You can create a new distribution group from the EMS with the *New-DistributionGroup* cmdlet. For example, to create a new distribution group named ExemplarDG, issue the following command:

```
New-DistributionGroup –Name 'ExemplarDG' –Type 'Distribution' –SamAccountName
'ExemplarDG' –Alias 'ExemplarDG'
```

> **MORE INFO** **CREATE DISTRIBUTION GROUPS**
>
> To learn more about creating groups, consult the following article on TechNet: *http://technet.microsoft.com/en-us/library/bb124513.aspx*.

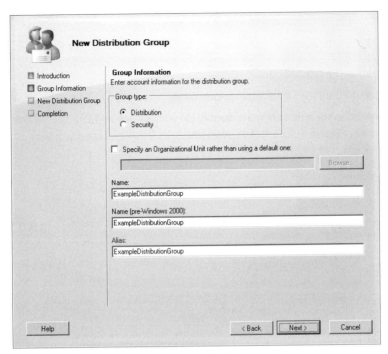

FIGURE 4-2 Example new distribution group

Mail-Enabled Security Groups

You use security groups to assign permissions to resources, such as configuring shared folder permissions. Mail-enabling a security group simply allows Exchange users to send email to the members of a security group. For example, it may be necessary to take several shared folders offline to move them to another volume or host. If the security groups assigned permissions to those folders are mail-enabled, you can send messages to the users alerting them of the downtime during this change. This is more efficient than sending a message to everyone in the organization, as mail-enabled security groups allow you to target only those people who have access to a resource.

Exchange mail-enabled security groups use universal scope. Universal groups can contain user accounts, global groups, and universal groups from any domain in the forest that hosts the Exchange organization. It is possible to mail-enable an existing security group only if the scope is already set to universal. If you want to mail-enable an existing domain local or global security group, you will need to convert the scope of that group so that it is set to universal. It is possible to convert group scopes to universal only under specific conditions. If the group is a global group, you can convert to universal only if the group you want to convert is not a member of another group that has the global scope. If the group you want to convert is domain local, it is possible to convert to the universal scope only if the group that you are converting does not have a domain local group as a member.

To create a new mail-enabled security group from the EMC, perform the following general steps:

1. Click on the Recipient Configuration node in the EMC and then click on New Distribution Group in the Actions pane.

2. Select New Group on the New Distribution Group page.

3. Select Security in the Group Type option and specify the Name, Alias, and OU that will host the group, as shown in Figure 4-3. Click Next, New, and then Finish to create the group.

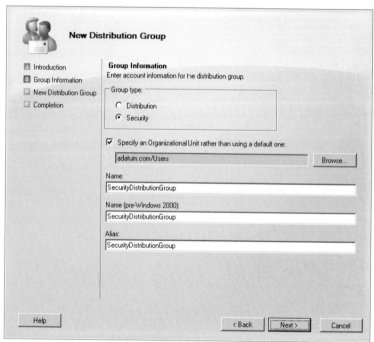

FIGURE 4-3 New mail-enabled security group

To create a new mail-enabled security group from the EMS, use the *New-DistributionGroup* cmdlet with the –Type Security parameter. For example, to create a new mail-enabled security group named SecDistGroup in the Users container of the Adatum.com domain, issue the following command:

```
New-DistributionGroup –Name SecDistGroup –OrganizationalUnit "adatum.com/Users"
–SAMAccountName SecDistGroup –Type Security
```

To mail-enable an existing security group using the EMC, run the New Distribution Group Wizard from the Actions pane when you select the Recipient Configuration node and then select the Existing Group option and browse to select the target universal security group. Enter an alias for the group and then click Next, New, and then Finish. To mail-enable an existing security group from the EMS, use the *Enable-DistributionGroup* cmdlet. For example, to mail-enable the SecGroup universal security group, issue the following command:

```
Enable-DistributionGroup –Identity SecGroup
```

Creating Dynamic Distribution Groups

Unlike a normal distribution group, where membership is managed manually, recipient filters determine the membership of a dynamic distribution group. For example, if the Development distribution group was a normal distribution group, someone would need to update the group membership as people joined and left the development team. With a dynamic distribution group, you could define group membership through a recipient filter that queries Active Directory for mailboxes, contacts, and mail users related to the development team. Group membership is updated automatically, so when a new mailbox user is associated with the development team, that mailbox user is included as a recipient for the dynamic distribution group.

There are several steps involved in configuring a recipient filter, the first of which is deciding which recipient types to include. The recipient types that can be included in a recipient filter are the following:

- Users with Exchange mailboxes
- Users with external email addresses
- Resource mailboxes
- Contacts with external email addresses
- Mail-enabled groups

As Figure 4-4 shows, you can choose one, some, or all of these types when creating a recipient filter.

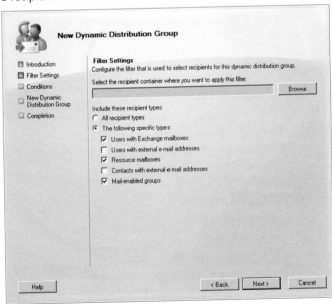

FIGURE 4-4 New recipient filter for dynamic distribution group

The next step in creating a recipient filter is to specify the conditions the filter uses to populate the group. The default conditions that you can use are that the Recipient object is associated with a state or province, a department, or a company. Figure 4-5 shows a new dynamic distribution group where the recipient filter targets mailboxes, resource mailboxes, and mail-enabled groups that are associated with the Victoria state or province and the Managers Department. You can configure the State or Province setting on the Address page of a user's account properties and the Department or Company attribute on the Organization tab. It is also possible to specify custom attributes in the event that you have populated those attributes. Custom Attributes allow you to store additional information in Active Directory without having to extend the Active Directory Schema. For example, you could use the EMS to configure Custom Attribute 1 to store employee identification numbers.

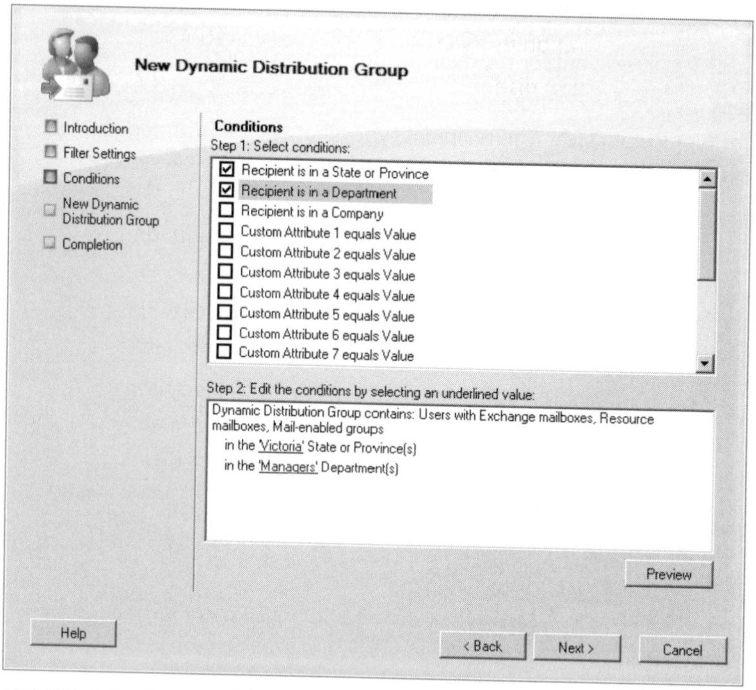

FIGURE 4-5 Configure recipients

> **MORE INFO** **CUSTOM ATTRIBUTES**
>
> To learn more about custom attributes and managing them in the EMS, consult the following article on TechNet: *http://technet.microsoft.com/en-us/library/ee423541.aspx.*

You use the *New-DynamicDistributionGroup* cmdlet to create a Dynamic Distribution Group in the EMS. For example, to create a new dynamic distribution group for all mailbox users that have accounts associated with the Sales Department called SalesDDG, issue the following command:

```
New-DynamicDistributionGroup -IncludedRecipients MailboxUsers -Name 'SalesDDG'
-ConditionalDepartment 'Sales' -Alias 'SalesDDG'
```

Configuring Moderation for Distribution Groups

The moderator for a distribution group is able to approve or block messages sent to that distribution group. For example, your organization might have a distribution group that includes all recipients in the company. Rather than allow all messages sent to the distribution group to be forwarded to all recipients, moderators would review messages before they were passed on to everyone else. Moderation settings can be configured so that specific authorized users are able to bypass the moderation process and send messages directly to the group. Moderators perform moderation using Outlook or Outlook Web App (OWA).

To configure moderation of an existing distribution group from the EMC, carry out the following general steps:

1. Navigate to the Recipient Configuration\Distribution Group node in the EMC, right-click the distribution group that you wish to configure moderation for, and then click Properties.

2. Navigate to the Mail Flow Settings tab, click on Message Moderation, and then click Properties.

3. On the Message Moderation tab, enable the Messages Sent To This Group Have To Be Approved By A Moderator option. Click Add to specify group moderators.

Figure 4-6 shows Amy Rusko configured as a moderator and Don Hall as a user who can post to the group without requiring message approval. The moderation notification settings determine which people are notified when the moderator does not approve their messages. Groups are not moderated by default. When you enable moderation for a group, the default moderator is the user who created the group.

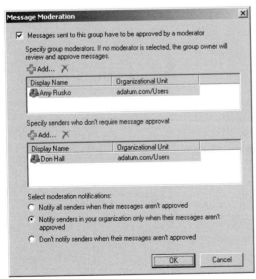

FIGURE 4-6 Message moderation

To configure message moderation from the EMS, use the *Set-DistributionGroup* cmdlet with the ModeratedBy, ModerationEnabled, and SendModerationNotifications parameters. For example, to configure moderation for the Customer_Inquiries distribution group where Amy Rusko will function as the moderator and where only senders within the organization will receive a nonapproval notification, use the following command:

```
Set-DistributionGroup -Identity "Customer_Inquiries" -ModeratedBy "Amy Rusko"
-ModerationEnabled $true -SendModerationNotifications 'Internal'
```

Configuring Distribution Group Ownership

By configuring distribution group permissions, you can grant ordinary users the ability to manage the membership of a distribution group. For example, Amy is interested in running the company charity drive. To assist her in this endeavor, you configure a new distribution group named Company_Charity and set Amy as the manager of that group. This allows Amy to add and remove people from the group as necessary.

The default manager of a distribution group is the user who created the group. Users who are managers of a distribution group are able to add and remove users from the distribution group. You can configure the manager of a distribution group on the Group Information tab of the group properties page, as shown in Figure 4-7.

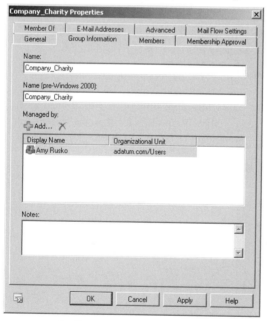

FIGURE 4-7 Configure group management

You configure ownership of a group in the EMS using the *Set-DistributionGroup* cmdlet with the ManagedBy parameter. For example, to configure the Company_Charity group so that Amy Rusko is the group owner, issue the following command:

```
Set-DistributionGroup -Identity Company_Charity -ManagedBy 'Amy Rusko'
```

A person delegating group ownership who did not originally create the group but has the appropriate privileges will need to use the BypassSecurityGroupManagerCheck parameter with the *Set-DistributionGroup* command. This is necessary only when delegating group management permissions from the EMS and occurs automatically when using the EMC.

You can configure whether approval is required for joining a group on the Membership Approval tab of a distribution group's properties, as shown in Figure 4-8. The options are open membership, which allows anyone to join without approval; closed, which requires group owners to add members manually; and owner approval, where a person can join subject to approval from a group owner. It is also possible to configure whether a recipient can leave the group without approval from the group owner.

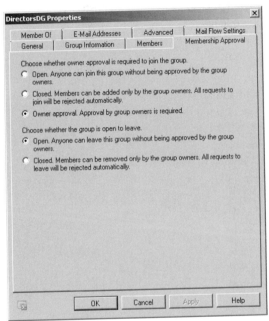

FIGURE 4-8 Membership approval settings

Membership approval settings for distribution groups can be configured using the *Set-DistributionGroup* cmdlet with the MemberJoinRestriction and MemberDepartRestriction parameters. For example, to configure the DirectorsDG distribution group so that recipients can join subject to group owner approval but can leave if they choose to without approval, the group owner should issue the following EMS command:

```
Set-DistributionGroup –MemberJoinRestriction 'ApprovalRequired' –MemberDepartRestriction
'Open' –Identity 'DirectorsDG'
```

> **MORE INFO** **CHANGE THE OWNERSHIP OF A DISTRIBUTION GROUP**
>
> To learn more about distribution group permissions, consult the following article on TechNet: *http://technet.microsoft.com/en-us/library/dd638201.aspx.*

Configuring Send As Permissions

When you grant users the Send As permission for another mailbox, they are able to send messages as that user from OWA or Outlook. When you grant a mail-enabled security group Send As permission for a mailbox, members of the mail-enabled security group are able to send messages on behalf of the mailbox from OWA or Outlook. You learned about the Send As permission in Chapter 3. You can configure the Send As permission through the EMC by clicking on the target mailbox under the Recipient Configuration node and then clicking on Manage Send As Permission item in the Actions pane. This will bring up the Manage Send As Permission dialog box, shown in Figure 4-9. You can click Add to add mail-enabled security groups to which you want to grant this permission. You cannot grant the Send As permission to a distribution group or to a dynamic distribution group, only to a mail-enabled security group.

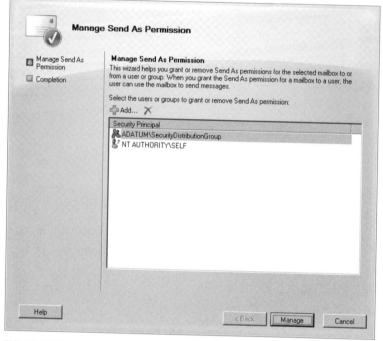

FIGURE 4-9 Manage Send As permission with group

To assign Send As permission using the EMS, use the *Add-ADPermission* cmdlet with the –Extendedrights "Send As" parameter. For example, to grant the SecurityDistributionGroup group the Send As permission on Amy Rusko's mailbox, issue the following command:

```
Add-ADPermission "Amy Rusko" –User "SecurityDistributionGroup" –Extendedrights "Send As"
```

> **MORE INFO** **MANAGING SEND AS PERMISSIONS FOR A MAILBOX**
>
> To learn more about managing Send As permissions for a mailbox, consult the following article on TechNet: *http://technet.microsoft.com/en-us/library/bb676368.aspx*.

- You want to allow Amy to manage the membership of a particular distribution group. Which EMS cmdlet would you use to accomplish this goal?

Quick Check Answer

- You use the *Set-DistributionGroup* cmdlet with the ManagedBy parameter to configure a user so that membership of a particular distribution group can be managed.

Advanced Dynamic Distribution Group Properties

Through the Advanced tab of a dynamic distribution group's properties, shown in Figure 4-10, you can configure settings such as the simple display name, expansion server, out-of-office message settings from group members, and non-delivery report options. You can configure advanced dynamic distribution group properties using the *Set-DynamicDistributionGroup* cmdlet from the EMS.

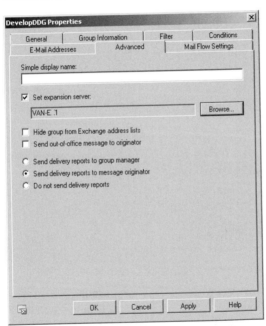

FIGURE 4-10 Dynamic distribution group advanced properties

The simple display name option allows you to provide a simplified group name for older applications that may not be able to understand dynamic distribution group names that contain some Unicode characters. The expansion server setting allows you to specify a Hub Transport server to perform distribution group expansion. Expansion is the process where Exchange routes messages to all recipients specified by the recipient filter. Expansion usually occurs on the closest available Hub Transport server. As expansion for very large groups is a resource-intensive process, you may wish to designate a specific Hub Transport server to minimize the impact on mail flow. The out-of-office setting determines whether out-of-office messages, where set, are forwarded back to the original message sender. For large groups, you may wish to stop this from occurring, as otherwise each person who sends a message to the group is likely to find one's Inbox filled with out-of-office messages, as there is always a number of people on any mailing list who are not present for one reason or another.

You can use the Message Size Restrictions item on the Mail Flow Settings tab to control the maximum size of messages that can be sent to the distribution group. You can use the Message Delivery Restrictions item on the Mail Flow Settings tab to control which users are able to send messages to the group. You can also configure Message Delivery Restrictions to block messages from specific senders. Figure 4-11 shows a group that will accept only messages from members of the DevelopDDG group and will not accept messages from Amy Rusko. As is the case with the advanced options, message size restrictions and message delivery restrictions can be configured from the EMS using the *Set-DynamicDistributionGroup* cmdlet.

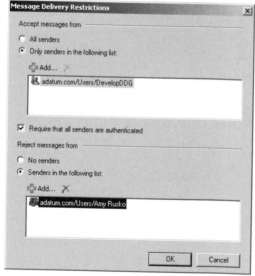

FIGURE 4-11 Message delivery restrictions

> **MORE INFO** **CONFIGURING ADVANCED DYNAMIC DISTRIBUTION GROUP PROPERTIES**
>
> To learn more about configuring advanced dynamic distribution group properties, consult the following article on TechNet: *http://technet.microsoft.com/en-us/library/bb124560.aspx.*

Distribution Group Proxy Addresses

You can configure additional addresses, also known as proxy addresses, for both distribution groups and dynamic distribution groups on the E-Mail Addresses tab. Figure 4-12 shows the address additional-group-address@adatum.com assigned to the DevelopDDG dynamic distribution group. Use the *Set-DistributionGroup* cmdlet with the EmailAddresses parameter to configure proxy addresses for distribution groups. Use the *Set-DynamicDistributionGroup* cmdlet with the EmailAddresses parameter to configure proxy addresses for a dynamic distribution group.

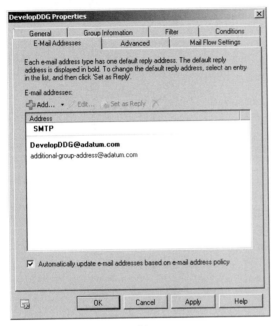

FIGURE 4-12 Group proxy addresses

EXAM TIP

Know which EMS commands allow you to modify the properties of different types of recipients.

Lesson Summary

- A mail-enabled security group is a universal Active Directory security group that has an Exchange email address that allows messages to be sent to all members of the security group that are Exchange recipients.
- A distribution group is a collection of Exchange recipients where group membership is handled on a manual rather than an automatic basis. Depending on group settings, the group manager can control the membership of the group.
- A dynamic distribution group is a collection of Exchange recipients where group membership is defined by a recipient filter. Recipient filters specify the common properties that recipients in the dynamic distribution group share.

- A moderator is able to approve messages posted to distribution groups or dynamic distribution groups. Groups can be configured so that one set of users can post to the group directly and another set of recipients can post messages to the group only if the message is approved by a moderator.

- A recipient that has been granted the Send As permission for a group is able to send messages using the email address of the group.

- A mail contact is an Exchange recipient who does not have a logon account in the Active Directory environment that hosts the Exchange organization.

- A mail-enabled user is a user who has a logon account for the Active Directory environment that hosts the Exchange organization but where messages sent to the user's address in Exchange are forwarded to an external messaging system.

- A proxy address is an additional address assigned to an Exchange recipient, distribution group, or dynamic distribution group.

Lesson Review

You can use the following questions to test your knowledge of the information in Lesson 1, "Managing Recipients and Distribution Groups." The questions are also available on the companion CD if you prefer to review them in electronic form.

> **NOTE ANSWERS**
>
> Answers to these questions and explanations of why each answer choice is correct or incorrect are located in the "Answers" section at the end of the book.

1. You are responsible for managing Exchange at Adatum. Sam Abolrous is a contractor who retrieves email from the messaging system at Contoso. Sam needs to be able to log on locally to the Adatum domain but does not yet have this right. Which of the following EMS cmdlets would you use to configure Exchange and Active Directory so that Sam could log on locally but so that all messages sent to Sam through Exchange were forwarded to the messaging system at Contoso?

   A. *Set-MailUser*

   B. *New-MailContact*

   C. *New-MailUser*

   D. *Set-MailContact*

2. Which of the following security group types can you mail-enable using the *Enable-DistributionGroup* cmdlet?

   A. Domain local

   B. Local

   C. Global

   D. Universal

3. Which of the following EMS cmdlets would you use to configure an additional proxy address for a dynamic distribution group?

   A. *Set-Contact*

   B. *Set-DistributionGroup*

   C. *Set-DynamicDistributionGroup*

   D. *Set-Group*

4. You need to set an expansion server for a large dynamic distribution group. Each server running Exchange Server 2010 in your organization hosts a separate role. Which of the following servers should you configure as the expansion server for the large dynamic distribution group?

   A. VAN-MBX-1 (Mailbox server)

   B. VAN-HT-1 (Hub Transport server)

   C. VAN-ET-1 (Edge Transport server)

   D. VAN-CAS-1 (Client Access server)

5. Which of the following cmdlets would you use to hide a sensitive distribution group from Exchange address lists?

   A. *Set-MailboxPermission*

   B. *Set-DynamicDistributionGroup*

   C. *Set-Group*

   D. *Set-DistributionGroup*

Lesson 2: Setting Up Public Folders

Public folders are an Exchange feature that provides shared access to content. Although newer technologies, such as SharePoint, may be better suited to the role that public folders play in most Exchange deployments, public folders are still an important for many organizations. In this lesson, you will learn how to create public folders, modify public folder permissions, and configure public folder limits. You will learn about making public folders highly available through replication in Chapter 13, "Exchange High-Availability Solutions."

> **After this lesson, you will be able to:**
> - Create public folders.
> - Configure public folder permissions.
> - Configure public folder limits.
>
> **Estimated lesson time: 40 minutes**

Exchange stores public folders in special databases known as public folder databases. You learned about creating public folder databases in Chapter 2, "Exchange Databases and Address Lists." You can create public folders only if there is an existing public folder database. When you install the first mailbox server in an Exchange organization, the setup wizard will prompt you as to whether computers running Outlook 2003 or Microsoft Entourage are present in your organization. If you answer yes, Exchange setup creates the public folder database and public folders necessary to support offline address book (OAB) distribution for these messaging clients. Computers running Outlook 2007 and Outlook 2010 do not require public folder infrastructure support for OAB distribution.

Exchange allows for two public folder trees: the Default Public Folders tree and the System Public Folders tree. These folder trees host the following folder types:

- **Default Public Folders (IPM_Subtree)**   The folders in this tree are commonly accessed by users through applications such as Outlook. Administrators create folders under this public folder tree.

- **System Public Folders (Non_IPM_Subtree)**   The folders in this tree are accessed indirectly by users, such as clients using older versions of Outlook accessing the OAB. System folders hosted in this tree include EFORMS REGISTRY, OFFLINE ADDRESS BOOK, and SCHEDULE+ FREE BUSY, as shown in Figure 4-13.

When designing a public folder hierarchy that will host a large number of public folders, you should aim toward a deep hierarchy rather than a wide hierarchy. A deep hierarchy is one that has many vertically nested folders. A wide hierarchy has many high-level folders but few subfolders nested under each folder. You should favor deep hierarchies over wide hierarchies, as deep hierarchies provide better performance during replication.

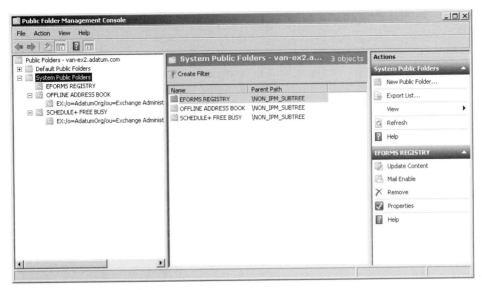

FIGURE 4-13 System public folders

Creating Public Folders

You use the Public Folder Management Console, which is located in the Toolbox node of the EMC, to create and manage public folders. To create a public folder in the EMC, perform the following general steps:

1. Open the Public Folder Management Console from the Toolbox node of the EMC.

2. In the Public Folder Management Console, navigate to Default Public Folders. If you want to create a public folder within an existing folder, navigate to that folder under the public folders node. Once you have selected the location in which you wish to create the public folder, click New Public Folder in the Actions pane. This will bring up the New Public Folder Wizard, shown in Figure 4-14. Enter the name of the public folder and then click New.

To create a new public folder using the EMS, use the *New-PublicFolder* cmdlet. For example, to create a new public folder named Child-Folder under the ExamplePublicFolder on server van-ex2.adatum.com, execute the following command:

```
New-PublicFolder -Name 'Child-Folder' -Path '\ExamplePublicFolder' -Server 'van-ex2
.adatum.com'
```

> **MORE INFO CREATING PUBLIC FOLDERS**
>
> To learn more about creating public folders, consult the following article on TechNet:
> *http://technet.microsoft.com/en-us/library/bb691104.aspx.*

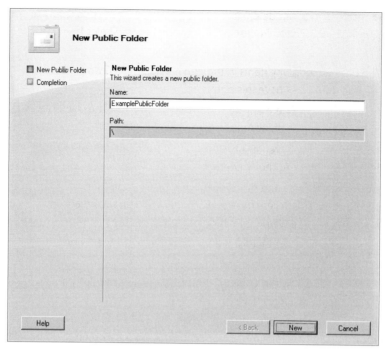

FIGURE 4-14 Create a new public folder

Configuring Public Folder Permissions

You assign permissions to public folders by assigning roles. The Exchange 2010 predefined public folder roles are Owner, PublishingEditor, Editor, PublishingAuthor, Author, Non-EditingAuthor, Reviewer, and Contributor. These predefined public folder roles are collections of client user access rights. The Owner role includes all client user access rights, whereas the Contributor role includes only two. The following is a list of client user access rights and the roles that hold them:

- **ReadItems** The user can read items in the public folder. The Owner, PublishingEditor, Editor, PublishingAuthor, Author, Non-EditingAuthor, and Reviewer roles have this right.

- **CreateItems** The user can post items to the public folder. The user can send email messages to the public folder if the public folder is mail-enabled. The Owner, PublishingEditor, Editor, Publishing Author, Author, Non-EditingAuthor, and Contributor roles have this right.

- **EditOwnedItems** The user can edit items he or she owns in the public folder. The Owner, PublishingEditor, Editor, Publishing Author, and Author roles have this right.

- **DeleteOwnedItems** The user can delete items he or she owns in the public folder. The Owner, PublishingEditor, Editor, Publishing Author, and Author roles have this right.

- **EditAllItems** The user can edit any items in the public folder. The Owner, PublishingEditor, and Editor roles have this right.

- **DeleteAllItems** The user can delete any items in the public folder. The Owner, PublishingEditor, Editor, and PublishingAuthor roles have this right.

- **CreateSubfolders** The user can create subfolders in the public folder. The Owner, PublishingEditor, and PublishingAuthor roles have this right.

- **FolderOwner** The user can view and move the folder, create subfolders, and configure permissions. This access right does not allow the user to read, edit, delete, or create items. Only the Owner role has this right.

- **FolderContact** The user is the contact for the public folder. Only the Owner role has this right.

- **FolderVisible** The user can view the public folder but does not have read or edit rights for items in the folder. All roles have this right.

You view and assign permissions to public folders using the EMS. You cannot use the EMC to view information about or assign permissions to public folders. Depending on the type of permission you are viewing, there are two different cmdlets you can use to view public folder permissions. To view administrative permissions settings, use the *Get-PublicFolderAdministrativePermission* cmdlet. To view client permissions settings, use the *Get-PublicFolderClientPermission* cmdlet. For example, to view administrative access rights for the Research public folder, issue the following command:

```
Get-PublicFolderAdministrativePermission –Identity "\Research" | Format-List
```

To view the list of client access permissions to the Research public folder, issue the following command:

```
Get-PublicFolderClientPermission –Identity "\Research" | Format-List
```

To assign client permissions to a public folder, use the *Add-PublicFolderClientPermission* cmdlet. For example, to configure Rooslan with the Publishing Editor permission to the Research folder, issue the following command:

```
Add-PublicFolderClientPermission –Identity "\Research" –AccessRights PublishingEditor
–User Rooslan
```

There are two methods through which you can grant users administrative permissions to a public folder. You can add the user to the Public Folder Management role group or you can use the *Add-PublicFolderAdministrativePermission* cmdlet. For example, to add Oksana to the Public Folder Management role group, use the following command:

```
Add-RoleGroupMember –Identity "Public Folder Management" –Member Oksana
```

You can use the *Add-PublicFolderAdministrativePermission* cmdlet to assign more detailed permissions than those provided through role group membership. For example, to add the AllExtendedRights permission to Ian for the public folder Development and all folders under it in the public folder hierarchy, issue the following command:

```
Add-PublicFolderAdministrativePermission -Identity "\Development" -User "Ian"
-AccessRights AllExtendedRights -InheritanceType SelfAndChildren
```

> **MORE INFO** **MANAGING PUBLIC FOLDER PERMISSIONS**
>
> To learn more about configuring permissions for public folders, consult the following article on TechNet: *http://technet.microsoft.com/en-us/library/bb310789.aspx*.

Mail-Enable Public Folder

Mail-enabling public folders allows people to post content to public folders by sending an email message to a configured address. This allows users that are external to the Exchange organization to post to the public folder. To mail-enable a public folder using the EMC, perform the following general steps:

1. In the EMC, open the Public Folder Management Console from the Toolbox node.

2. Select the parent of the public folder that you wish to mail-enable and then select the folder that you wish to mail-enable in the details pane. Click on Mail Enable on the Actions pane.

3. Right-click on the public folder in the Details pane and then click Properties. Verify that the E-Mail Addresses tab and the Mail Flow Settings tab are present, as shown in Figure 4-15. This indicates that the public folder is mail-enabled.

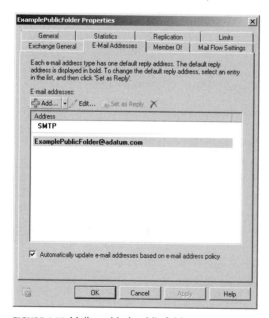

FIGURE 4-15 Mail-enabled public folder

You use the *Enable-MailPublicFolder* cmdlet to mail-enable a public folder from the EMS. For example, to mail-enable the Sales public folder, issue the following command:

```
Enable-MailPublicFolder -Identity "\Sales"
```

MORE INFO **MAIL-ENABLE PUBLIC FOLDER**

To learn more about mail-enabling a public folder, consult the following article on Tech-Net: *http://technet.microsoft.com/en-us/library/aa997560.aspx*.

 Quick Check

- Which EMS cmdlet do you use to mail-enable an existing public folder?

Quick Check Answer

- The *Enable-MailPublicFolder* cmdlet is used to mail-enable an existing public folder.

Configuring Public Folder Limits

Public folder limits allow you to configure limits on items posted to public folders, such as maximum size and age. You configure maximum item size, deleted item retention, and item age limits on the Limits tab of a public folder's properties, as shown in Figure 4-16.

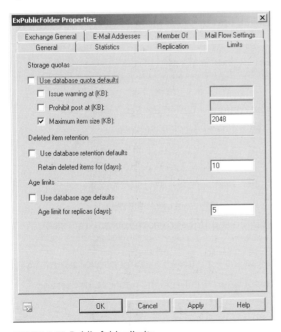

FIGURE 4-16 Public folder limits

You configure message size limits using the *Set-PublicFolder* cmdlet with the MaxItemSize parameter. For example, to set a 1 MB limit on the public folder \ExemplarFolder, issue the following command:

```
Set-PublicFolder –Identity '\ExemplarFolder' –MaxItemSize 1MB –UseDatabaseQuotaDefaults
$false
```

You can configure the maximum receive size for a mail-enabled public folder through the EMC by editing the Receiving Message Size setting in Message Size Restrictions on the Mail Flow tab. This setting controls messages that are posted to the folder through email but does not restrict posting through other methods. You can configure the maximum receive size for a mail-enabled public folder using the *Set-MailPublicFolder* cmdlet with the MaxRecieveSize parameter in the EMS. For example, to configure the ExemplarFolder public folder with a maximum receive size of 1 MB for items sent to the folder through email, issue the following command:

```
Set-MailPublicFolder –Identity '\ExemplarFolder' –MaxReceiveSize 1MB
```

To configure age limits from the EMS, use the *Set-PublicFolder* cmdlet with the AgeLimit parameter and the UseDatabaseAgeDefaults $false option. For example, to set the age limit for the ExemplarFolder public folder to 21 days, issue the following command:

```
Set-PublicFolder –Identity 'ExemplarFolder' –AgeLimit 21 –UseDatabaseAgeDefaults $false
```

> **MORE INFO   SET-PUBLICFOLDER**
>
> To learn more about configuring public folder limitations using the *Set-PublicFolder* cmdlet, consult the following article on TechNet: *http://technet.microsoft.com/en-us/library/aa998596.aspx*.

> **EXAM TIP**
>
> Remember which public folder options can be configured using the *Set-PublicFolder* cmdlet and which ones can be set using the *Set-MailPublicFolder* cmdlet.

Lesson Summary

- Most public folder administrative tasks are accomplished using the EMS.
- Use the *Set-PublicFolder* cmdlet to configure settings such as maximum item size and maximum item age.
- Use the *Enable-MailPublicFolder* cmdlet to mail-enable an existing public folder.
- Use the *Set-MailPublicFolder* cmdlet to configure mail-specific public folder settings, such as maximum item receive size.
- Public folder permissions are managed through roles. The available roles are Owner, PublishingEditor, Editor, PublishingAuthor, Author, Non-EditingAuthor, Reviewer, and

Contributor. You assign a role to a user for a specific public folder; for example, you assign Ian the Editor role for the Research folder.

- Use the *Add-PublicFolderClientPermission* cmdlet to assign PublishingEditor and PublishingAuthor roles to specific public folders.

Lesson Review

You can use the following questions to test your knowledge of the information in Lesson 2, "Setting Up Public Folders." The questions are also available on the companion CD if you prefer to review them in electronic form.

> **NOTE ANSWERS**
>
> Answers to these questions and explanations of why each answer choice is correct or incorrect are located in the "Answers" section at the end of the book.

1. Which of the following EMS cmdlets allows you to mail-enable a public folder?
    - **A.** *New-PublicFolder*
    - **B.** *Set-MailPublicFolder*
    - **C.** *Set-PublicFolder*
    - **D.** *Enable-MailPublicFolder*

2. Which of the following EMS cmdlets can you use to assign the PublishingEditor role for the Development public folder to Orin?
    - **A.** *Add-PublicFolderClientPermission*
    - **B.** *Set-PublicFolder*
    - **C.** *Set-MailPublicFolder*
    - **D.** *Add-PublicFolderAdministrativePermission*

3. Which of the following EMS cmdlets can you use to configure item age limit settings on an existing mail-enabled public folder?
    - **A.** *New-PublicFolder*
    - **B.** *Get-PublicFolder*
    - **C.** *Set-MailPublicFolder*
    - **D.** *Set-PublicFolder*

4. Which of the following EMS cmdlets can you use to configure maximum message size on a mail-enabled public folder? (Choose all that apply.)
    - **A.** *Set-MailPublicFolder*
    - **B.** *Set-PublicFolder*
    - **C.** *Set-MailboxDatabase*
    - **D.** *Set-PublicFolderDatabase*

Mail-Enabled Users, Contacts, Distribution Groups, and Public Folders

In this set of exercises, you will create and configure mail-enabled users, contacts, distribution groups, dynamic distribution groups, and public folders.

EXERCISE 1 Configure Mail-Enabled Users and Contacts

In this exercise, you will create mail-enabled users as well as mail contacts. To complete this exercise, perform the following steps:

1. Log on to computer VAN-EX2 with the Kim_Akers user account and open the EMC. Verify that the Kim_Akers account has a mailbox. If one is not present, use the New Mailbox Wizard to attach an Exchange mailbox in the default database to this account.

2. Right-click on the Recipient Configuration node and then click on New Mail Contact. This will open the New Mail Contact Wizard. Ensure that New Contact is selected and then click Next. Enter the details, as shown in Figure 4-17, and then click Edit and enter the email address roland.wacker@tailspintoys.com in the SMTP Address dialog box. Click OK to close that dialog box and then click Next.

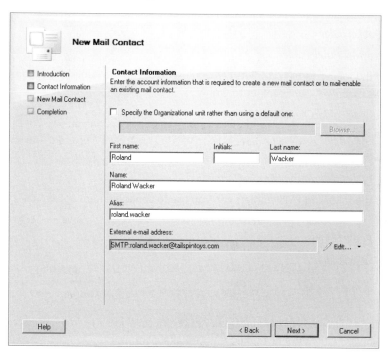

FIGURE 4-17 New Mail Contact Wizard

3. On the page that shows the configuration summary, click New and then click Finish.

4. Right-click on the Recipients node and then click on New Mail User. This will open the New Mail User Wizard. Ensure that New User is selected and then click Next.

5. In the User Information dialog box, enter the information, as shown in Figure 4-18, with *Pa$$w0rd* set as the user password and then click Next.

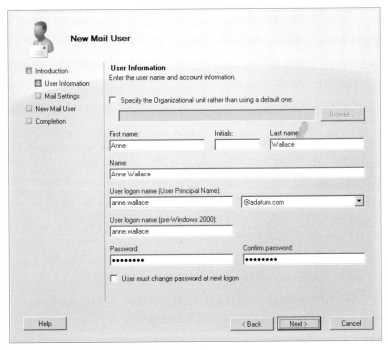

FIGURE 4-18 New Mail User Wizard

6. On the Mail Settings page, enter the alias **anne.wallace**. Click on Edit and enter the external email address **anne.wallace@tailspintoys.com**, click OK, and then click Next.

7. On the Configuration Summary page, click New and then click Finish.

8. Open the EMS and enter the following command:

```
New-MailContact -ExternalEmailAddress 'SMTP:darren.waite@tailspintoys.com' -Name
'Darren Waite' -Alias 'darren.waite' -FirstName 'Darren' -LastName 'Waite'
```

9. In the EMS, issue the following command:

```
New-MailUser -Name 'Rob Walters' -Alias 'Rob.Walters' -UserPrincipalName
'rob.walters@adatum.com' -SamAccountName 'rob.walters' -FirstName 'Rob' -LastName
'Walters' -ExternalEmailAddress 'SMTP:rob.walters@tailspintoys.com'
```

10. When prompted by the EMS, enter the password **Pa$$w0rd**.

11. Verify the creation of the Anne Wallace and Rob Walters Mail Users by entering the command **Get-MailUser**.

12. Verify the creation of the Roland Wacker and Darren Waite mail contacts by entering the command **Get-MailContact**.

EXERCISE 2   Create and Configure Distribution Groups

In this practice, you will mail-enable an existing security group, create a new distribution group, and configure membership approval settings. To complete this exercise, perform the following steps:

1. Ensure that you are logged on to computer VAN-EX2 with the Kim_Akers user account. From the Administrative Tools menu, open Active Directory Users And Computers. In the Users container, create a new universal security group named Explorers. Close Active Directory Users And Computers.

2. In the EMC, click on the Distribution Group node under the Recipient Configuration node. In the Actions pane, click on New Distribution Group.

3. On the Introduction page of the New Distribution Group Wizard, select Existing Group and then click Browse. In the Select Group dialog box, click on Explorers and then click OK. Click Next.

4. On the Group Information page, enter the alias **ExplorersDG** and then click Next. Click New and then click Finish.

5. Open the EMC and issue the following command:

    ```
    New-DistributionGroup -Name "DirectorsDG" -OrganizationalUnit "adatum.com/Users"
    -SAMAccountName "Directors" -Type "Distribution"
    ```

6. In the EMC, click on the Distribution Group node and then click on the DirectorsDG distribution group. In the Actions pane, click Properties.

7. On the Group Information tab, click on Add. Click on Ann Wallace and then click on OK.

8. On the Membership Approval tab, ensure that the owner approval settings match those in Figure 4-19 and then click OK.

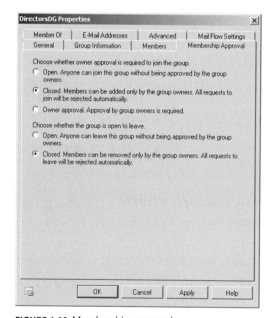

FIGURE 4-19 Membership approval

EXERCISE 3   Create and Configure a Dynamic Distribution Group

In this practice exercise, you will create and configure a dynamic distribution group called Research. To complete this exercise, perform the following steps:

1. Ensure that you are logged on to computer VAN-EX2 with the Kim_Akers user account. Navigate to the Recipient Configuration node and select the Anne Wallace Mail User. In the Actions pane, click on Properties. On the Organization tab of the Ann Wallace Properties dialog box, enter **Research** in the Department text box, as shown in Figure 4-20, and then click OK.

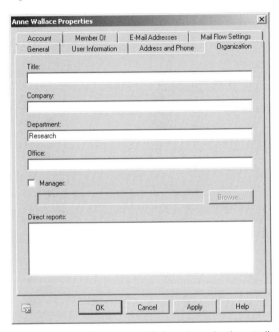

FIGURE 4-20 Configure Anne Wallace Organization attribute

2. Select the Rob Walters Mail User. In the Actions pane, click on Properties. On the Organization tab of the Rob Walters Properties dialog box, enter **Development** in the Department text box and then click OK.

3. Select the Recipient Configuration\Distribution Group node and then click on New Dynamic Distribution Group in the Actions pane. This will open the New Dynamic Distribution Group Wizard.

4. On the Introduction page, enter **ResearchDDG** in the Name and Alias text boxes and then click Next. On the Filter Settings page, click Next.

5. On the Conditions page, select the Recipient Is In A Department condition. Click on the underlined word Specified to open the Specify Department dialog box. Enter

Research and then click Add and then click OK. Verify that the Conditions page matches Figure 4-21 and then click Preview.

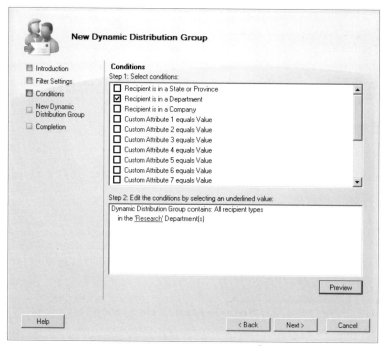

FIGURE 4-21 New Dynamic Distribution Group conditions

6. In the Dynamic Distribution Group Preview window, verify that Ann Wallace is listed and then click OK. Click Next. On the Configuration Summary page, click New. Click Finish when the group is created.

7. In the EMS, issue the following command:

```
New-DynamicDistributionGroup -Name 'DevelopDDG' -IncludedRecipients
'AllRecipients' -ConditionalDepartment 'Development' -Alias 'DevelopDDG'
```

8. In the EMC, right-click on DevelopDDG under Recipient Configuration\Distribution Group and then click Properties.

9. On the Mail Flow Settings tab, click on Message Delivery Restrictions and then click Properties.

10. On the Message Delivery Restrictions dialog box, select Only Senders In The Following List and then click Add. In the Select Recipient dialog box, click DevelopDDG and then click OK. Verify that the Message Delivery Restrictions dialog box matches Figure 4-22 and then click OK twice.

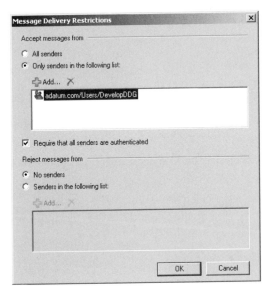

FIGURE 4-22 Message delivery restrictions

11. In the EMS, issue the following command:

```
Set-DynamicDistributionGroup –AcceptMessagesOnlyFromSendersOrMembers 'Adatum.com/
Users/ResearchDDG' –Identity 'adatum.com/Users/ResearchDDG'
```

EXERCISE 4 Create and Configure a Public Folder

In this practice exercise, you will create and configure a public folder. To complete this exercise, perform the following steps:

1. Ensure that you are logged on to computer VAN-EX2 with the Kim_Akers user account. Verify that there are no public folder databases present on VAN-EX2 by opening the EMS and issuing the command Get-PublicFolderDatabase. The output from this command should inform you that no public folder databases are present on server VAN-EX2.

> **WARNING   EXISTING PUBLIC FOLDER DATABASE**
>
> You cannot perform this practice if you have already created a public folder database on computer VAN-EX2. You may have done this to test commands when reading through the text of Chapter 2, but creating a public folder database was not directly part of any practice exercise.

2. From the EMS, issue the following command:

```
New-PublicFolderDatabase PublicFolderDB –Server VAN-EX2
```

3. When the command listed in step 2 completes, enter the following command:

```
Mount-Database PublicFolderDB
```

4. Open the EMC. From the Toolbox node, open the Public Folder Management Console. Click on the Default Public Folders node and then click on New Public Folder in the Actions pane. This will open the New Public Folder Wizard.

5. In the Name text box, enter the name **ExPublicFolder** and then click New. When the folder is created, click Finish.

6. Right-click on ExPublicFolder and then click on Mail Enable. This will enable the public folder to receive email.

7. Right-click on EXPublicFolder and then click on Properties. In the ExPublicFolderProperties dialog box, click on the E-Mail Addresses tab and verify that it matches the information, as shown in Figure 4-23.

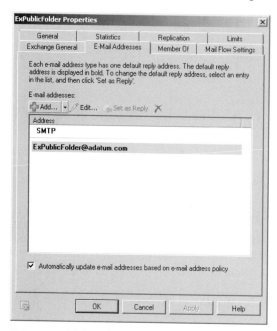

FIGURE 4-23 Mail-enable public folder properties

8. Click on the Limits tab. Configure the limits for the Public Folder, as shown in Figure 4-24, and then click Apply.

9. On the Mail Flow Settings tab, click on Message Delivery Restrictions and then click Properties. Select the Only Senders In The Following List option and then click Add. In the Select Recipient dialog box, select DevelopDDG and then click OK twice.

10. Open the EMS and issue the following commands:

```
New-PublicFolder -Name 'PublicFolderTwo' -Path '\' -Server VAN-EX2

Enable-MailPublicFolder -Identity '\PublicFolderTwo'

Set-PublicFolder -Identity "\PublicFolderTwo" -Server VAN-EX2 -AgeLimit '5.00:00:00' -
MaxItemSize 2MB -RetainDeletedItemsFor '10.00:00:00' -UseDatabaseAgeDefaults
$False -UseDatabaseQuotaDefault $false -UseDatabaseRetentionDefaults $false

Set-MailPublicFolder -Identity "\PublicFolderTwo" -Server VAN-EX2
-AcceptMessagesOnlyFromSendersOrMembers 'adatum.com/Users/ResearchDDG'
```

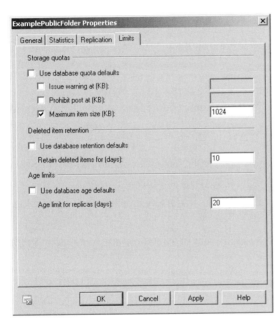

FIGURE 4-24 Public folder limits

Chapter Review

To further practice and reinforce the skills you learned in this chapter, you can perform the following tasks:

- Review the chapter summary.
- Review the list of key terms introduced in this chapter.
- Complete the case scenarios. These scenarios set up real-world situations involving the topics of this chapter and ask you to create a solution.
- Complete the suggested practices.
- Take a practice test.

Chapter Summary

- Mail contacts allow external addresses to be added to Exchange address books. Mail-enabled users are Active Directory user accounts associated with an external email address.
- Distribution group membership is managed manually. Dynamic Distribution Group membership is determined by a recipient filter. Security-enabled distribution groups can be assigned permissions to objects, such as file shares.
- Users can post items to mail-enabled public folders by emailing the public folder's email address.
- Public folder settings, such as maximum item size and age, are managed with the *Set-PublicFolder* cmdlet.
- Public folder permissions are managed through the assignment of roles to users for specific public folders.

Key Terms

Do you know what these key terms mean?

- Dynamic distribution group
- Moderation
- Proxy address
- Send as

Case Scenarios

In the following case scenarios, you will apply what you've learned about subjects of this chapter. You can find answers to these questions in the "Answers" section at the end of this book.

Case Scenario 1: Contacts and Distribution Groups at Contoso

You are the Exchange administrator at Contoso. The executive assistant to the company president has asked you to create a group named Important_Announcements that she can add users to manually. She does not want users to be able to add or remove themselves to the group, as this will allow her to strictly manage group membership. You want to create a separate group that includes all mailbox users in the Engineering Department. Group membership should be updated automatically as people join and leave the department. With these facts in mind, answer the following questions:

1. What type of group should you create for the Important_Announcements group?

2. What properties should you configure when creating the recipient filter for the EngineersDD dynamic distribution group?

3. What steps can you take to stop people from leaving the Important_Announcements group without authorization?

Case Scenario 2: Public Folders at Fabrikam

You are in the process of reviewing how public folders are used at Fabrikam. At the moment, members of the customer service team must manually post customer feedback to the Customer_Service public folder. You want to allow customers to be able to post messages to this folder by sending emails to a specific address. You want to ensure that all items posted to the Customer_Service public folder expire after 48 days. You also want to ensure that users at Fabrikam can post items of any size to the public folder but that people sending email messages to the folder are limited to sending messages that are 1,024 KB in size. With these facts in mind, answer the following questions:

1. What step can you take to ensure that customers outside Fabrikam can post items to the Customer_Service public folder?

2. What cmdlet should you use to ensure that the Customer_Service public folder will not accept email messages greater than 1,024 KB in size?

3. What cmdlet should you use to ensure that messages in the public folder older than 48 days expire?

Suggested Practices

To help you successfully master the exam objectives presented in this chapter, complete the following tasks.

Configure Recipients and Distribution Groups

You can perform these practice exercises on VAN-EX1 after you complete the main practice exercise at the end of Lesson 2.

- **Practice 1**   Use the EMC to create a dynamic distribution group named WesternAustralia that includes only the mail-enabled users in the adatum.com Exchange organization. Configure the group with the proxy address perth@adatum.com.

- **Practice 2**   Use the EMS to create a moderated distribution group where users can join or leave the group only with the permission of the group owner.

Configure Public Folders

You can perform these practice exercises on VAN-EX1 after you complete the main practice exercise at the end of Lesson 2.

- **Practice 1**   Use the EMC to create a dynamic distribution group named Tasmania that includes only the mail-enabled users in the adatum.com Exchange organization. Configure the group with the proxy address hobart@adatum.com.

- **Practice 2**   Use the EMS to create a moderated distribution group where users can join or leave the group only with the permission of the group owner.

Take a Practice Test

The practice tests on this book's companion CD offer many options. For example, you can test yourself on just one exam objective, or you can test yourself on all the 70-662 certification exam content. You can set up the test so that it closely simulates the experience of taking a certification exam, or you can set it up in study mode so that you can look at the correct answers and explanations after you answer each question.

> **MORE INFO   PRACTICE TESTS**
>
> For details about all the practice test options available, see the "How to Use the Practice Tests" section in this book's Introduction.

CHAPTER 5

Configuring Client Access

Client Access servers mediate user access to mailboxes. Users interact with the Client Access server through protocols such as Remote Procedure Call (RPC), Post Office Protocol (POP), Internet Message Access Protocol (IMAP), Outlook Anywhere, or ActiveSync or indirectly through Outlook Web App (OWA). In this chapter you will learn how to configure Exchange 2010 Client Access servers to support access to Client Access servers, including securing access through Secure Sockets Layer (SSL) certificates and appropriate authentication protocols. You will also learn how to configure Autodiscover, an Exchange functionality that allows mobile devices and Outlook clients to have settings automatically populated based on Active Directory logon information or user email address and password. This chapter will teach you how to configure the POP3 and IMAP4 services, RPC Client Access, and Exchange Control Panel settings and how to enable and disable features for OWA.

Exam objectives in this chapter:

- Configure POP, IMAP, and Microsoft ActiveSync.
- Configure Outlook Anywhere and RPC Client Access.
- Configure Outlook Web App (OWA).

Lessons in this chapter:

Before You Begin

In order to complete the exercises in the practice sessions in this chapter, you need to have done the following:

- Installed VAN-DC, VAN-EX1, and VAN-EX2 as described in the Appendix.

 **REAL WORLD**

Orin Thomas

t is no secret that most organizations do not alter the default OWA page. It is also not a secret that many people also ignore SSL certificate warnings. These nonsecrets add up to OWA being a target for password harvesting. If an attacker is able to trick a person into visiting a website that they believe is their company's OWA site, then that attacker is in a good position to collect that person's logon credentials. If you are using OWA in your organization, you should ensure that users have to change their passwords frequently. You can ensure that users are unable to change their passwords through OWA, as an attacker might once they have gained a user's password, by disabling that functionality through segmentation settings. Although OWA provides organizations with convenient email access, you need to keep in mind the security issues that it raises. In this chapter, you will learn about the options available that enable you to lock OWA down so that even if an attacker did get hold of someone's authentication credentials, their access to attachments stored on internal file servers would be minimized.

Lesson 1: IMAP, POP, and Microsoft ActiveSync

When you use SSL to secure a connection, third parties that might be intercepting your transmission are unable to access the content of that communication. This is especially important today when many clients are accessing sensitive organizational communication over insecure networks such as the wireless access point at the local coffee shop. IT departments must often support operating systems that do not support Microsoft Outlook. Alternative mail clients often use either the IMAP4 or POP3 protocols to retrieve messages from Exchange mailboxes, and you will learn how to configure that access in this lesson. Autodiscover is an automatic configuration service designed for recent versions of Outlook and mobile clients. In this lesson, you will learn how to configure SSL certificates for use with Client Access servers, the steps that you take to configure ActiveSync, what you need to do to allow clients to use the IMAP4 and POP3 protocols to access their mailboxes, and how to configure Autodiscover.

> **After this lesson, you will be able to:**
> - Configure POP and IMAP.
> - Manage certificates.
> - Configure mobile device policies.
> - Manage Autodiscover.
> - Configure ActiveSync.
>
> **Estimated lesson time: 40 minutes**

Client Access Server Certificates

Secure Sockets Layer (SSL) certificates allow clients to establish an encrypted connection to be established between a client and a Client Access server. SSL certificates, also called *server certificates*, also have the added benefit of verifying the identity of the Client Access server to the client. When you install Exchange on a computer, it installs a default self-signed certificate. As a trusted Certificate Authority (CA) did not create or sign this certificate, the certificate will be trusted only by other Exchange servers in the same organization, not by any clients in the same organization. Administrators need to take extra steps to get clients to trust these certificates, and it is often easier to look for an alternative solution, such as getting a certificate from an internal CA. The Exchange self-signed certificate will have Subject Alternative Names (SANs) that correspond to the name of the Exchange server, including the server name and the server's fully qualified domain name.

SANs are a certificate functionality that allows a certificate to be mapped to multiple fully qualified domain names. For example, Internet clients might access a server as owa.contoso .com, and internal network clients might access the same server as owa.contoso.internal. If the certificate did not support SANs, the SSL certificate would support only one name, and clients accessing the server using the other name would encounter an error. You will configure Active Directory Certificate Services to support the issuance of certificates that use SANs in the practice exercise at the end of this chapter.

SSL certificates are usually signed by an internal or a trusted third-party CA. Certificates signed by trusted third-party CAs are trusted by both internal and external clients, but obtaining these certificates can cost money. Obtaining a certificate from an internal CA has no associated charge, but clients outside your organization are unlikely to trust the certificate. You obtain a certificate by running the New Exchange Certificate Wizard and submitting the resulting certificate request file to your CA of choice.

To run the New Exchange Certificate Wizard, perform the following general steps:

1. In the Exchange Management Console (EMC), click on the Server Configuration node and then click on New Exchange Certificate in the Actions pane. This will launch the New Exchange Certificate Wizard.

2. Provide a friendly name for the certificate and click Next.

3. On the Domain Scope page, specify whether you want to apply this certificate to all subdomains using wildcards. This option allows you to add subdomains at a later stage without having to update an existing certificate.

4. On the Exchange Configuration page, use the arrows to expand access so that you can fill in details about the roles that you want the certificate to service. For example, for a Client Access server where you wanted to support Exchange Web Services, Outlook Anywhere, and Autodiscover, you would expand and configure the settings, as shown in Figure 5-1.

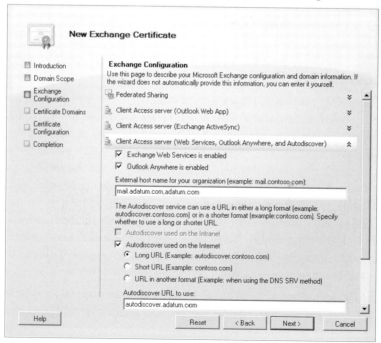

FIGURE 5-1 Certificate Request Wizard

5. You can use this page of the wizard to configure a request for all roles the server holds. To do this, expand and complete each relevant section.

6. Review the Certificate Domains that the request will contain. On this page, you can add additional SANs.

7. On the Organization and Location page, enter organization and location information. You also specify the location to which the wizard should save the certificate request file.

When an appropriate CA has processed your certificate request, you can use the Complete Pending Request option, available when the friendly name is selected within the EMC, to install the newly requested certificate.

Once you have installed the certificate, you will be able to assign services to the certificate. Assigning services configures specific services on the Exchange server to use the certificate for identification and secure communication. To assign a specific certificate to Exchange services, perform the following general steps:

1. In the EMC, select the certificate by selecting the Server Configuration node and then select the Exchange server where you installed the certificate.

2. Select the certificate and then click on Assign Services to Certificate in the Actions pane. This will bring up the Assign Services to Certificate Wizard. Select the servers where you want to assign the certificate.

3. On the Select Services page, as shown in Figure 5-2, select each service to which you want Exchange to assign the certificate.

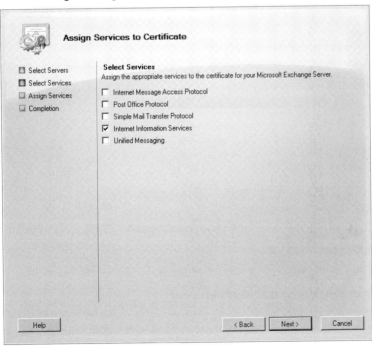

FIGURE 5-2 Assign services to certificate

When you complete the wizard, Exchange will assign the certificate to support the selected services. At the end of this chapter, you will perform a practice exercise where you will request a certificate, process that request on a CA, install the certificate, and then assign services to the certificate.

> **MORE INFO** **DIGITAL CERTIFICATES AND SSL**
>
> To learn more about using digital certificates and SSL with Client Access servers, consult the following reference on TechNet: *http://technet.microsoft.com/en-us/library/ dd351044.aspx.*

Assigning an External Name

Client Access servers are often accessed using different names, depending on whether the client is on the organization's internal or external network. You can use the Configure External Client Access Domain Wizard, shown in Figure 5-3, to configure the external name associated with OWA, ActiveSync, and the Exchange Control Panel. You can access the Configure External Client Access Domain Wizard from the EMC by clicking on the Configure External Client Access Domain item located in Actions pane when you have selected the Server Configuration\Client Access node.

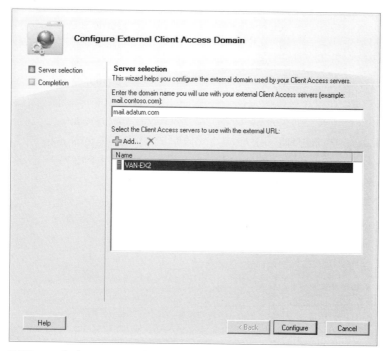

FIGURE 5-3 Assign an external name to a Client Access server

To configure the external client access domain name for OWA from the Exchange Management Shell (EMS), use the *Set-OwaVirtualDirectory* cmdlet with the ExternalUrl parameter. To configure the external client access domain name from the EMS for ActiveSync, use the *Set-ActiveSyncVirtualDirectory* cmdlet with the ExternalUrl parameter. For example, to set the external client access domain for OWA on Client Access server CAS1 to mail.contoso. com, where OWA is hosted in the default location, use the following command:

```
Set-OwaVirtualDirectory -Identity 'CAS1\owa (Default Web Site)' -ExternalUrl
'https://mail.contoso.com/owa'
```

> **MORE INFO EXTERNAL NAMESPACE**
>
> To learn more about configuring an external namespace for a Client Access server, consult the following reference on TechNet: *http://technet.microsoft.com/en-us/library/dd351198.aspx.*

Configure POP and IMAP

Most email clients support the POP3 and IMAP4 for the retrieval of messages from mail servers. Although Outlook supports the POP3 and IMAP4 protocols, Outlook defaults to RPC when interacting with Exchange Server 2010. As Exchange Server 2010 must work with clients other than Outlook, you can configure Exchange Client Access servers to support clients that use the POP3 and IMAP4 protocols.

To support POP3 and IMAP4 traffic, it is necessary to enable both of these services on the Client Access server and to ensure that you configure the mailbox user's settings to allow access to their mailbox using the appropriate protocol. To enable the POP3 or IMAP4 service on a Client Access server, perform the following general steps:

1. On the Client Access server, open the Services Console from the Administrative Tools menu.

2. Locate either the Microsoft Exchange IMAP4 service or the Microsoft Exchange POP3 service as appropriate. Right-click on the service and then click on Properties.

3. On the General tab of the service's properties, as shown in Figure 5-4, set the service startup type to Automatic. Under service status, click Start to start the service.

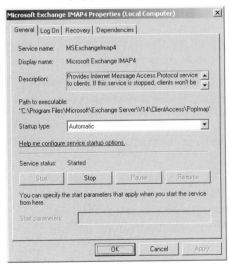

FIGURE 5-4 IMAP4 service properties

Once you have enabled the POP3 and IMAP4 services, you can configure these services by navigating to the Server Configuration\Client Access node, clicking on the POP3 and IMAP4 tab, right-clicking on either the POP3 or IMAP4 service, and then clicking on Properties. This will bring up either the POP3 or the IMAP4 properties. The tabs on these properties dialog boxes allow you to configure the following:

- **General** Allows you to configure the banner string, which is used for identification.

- **Binding** Allows you to configure which Internet Protocol version 4 (IPv4) and IPv6 addresses and ports that secure and unencrypted connections use for each service. Figure 5-5 shows the Binding tab for the POP3 service.

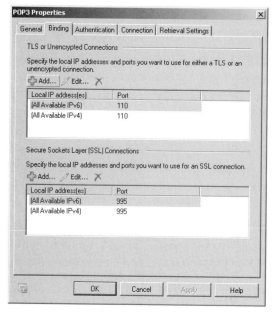

FIGURE 5-5 POP3 Binding tab

- **Authentication** On this tab, specify whether plain text (basic), plain text (Integrated Windows), or Secure logon is required. You can also specify the X.509 certificate name.

- **Connection** This tab allows you to configure connection settings, such as time-out settings, maximum connections from a single IP address, and maximum connections from a single user.

- **Retrieval Settings** This tab allows you to specify the Message MIME format, message sort order, and Calendar Retrieval Format.

You can configure all the settings on these properties dialog boxes for each service from the EMS by using the *Set-POPSettings* or *Set-IMAPSettings* cmdlets. To enable IMAP4 or POP3 for a specific user's mailbox, edit the user's mailbox properties from the recipient configuration node and enable the desired protocol on the Mailbox Features tab, as shown in Figure 5-6.

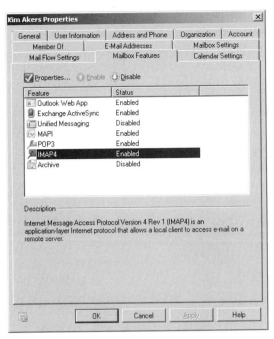

FIGURE 5-6 Enable IMAP for user

You can verify that either the POP3 or IMAP4 services are working correctly from the EMS by using one of the following commands:

- **Test-POPConnectivity** This command allows you to verify that POP3 access to Exchange mailboxes is functioning properly.

- **Test-IMAPConnectivity** This command allows you to verify that IMAP4 access to Exchange mailboxes is functioning properly.

> **MORE INFO** **UNDERSTANDING POP3 AND IMAP4 SETTINGS**
>
> To learn more about POP3 and IMAP4 settings, consult the following reference on TechNet: *http://technet.microsoft.com/en-us/library/dd297990.aspx.*

Autodiscover

The Autodiscover service provides clients running Outlook 2007, Outlook 2010, and mobile phones running Windows Mobile 6.1 or later with user profile configuration settings. To use Autodiscover, it is necessary to either provide the user's email address and password or have the user's domain credentials. For example, when Autodiscover is configured correctly, Kim Akers can log on to a new PC in the Contoso domain that has Office 2010 installed, open Outlook, and instantly interact with her Exchange mailbox as Outlook is automatically configured through Autodiscover.

You can use the *Test-OutLookWebServices* cmdlet from the EMS to verify that the Autodiscover service settings are working properly for Outlook 2007 and 2010 clients. For example, to check that Autodiscover is functioning properly on server CAS01, use the following command:

```
Test-OutlookWebServices –ClientAccessServer CAS01
```

> **MORE INFO** **UNDERSTANDING AUTODISCOVER**
>
> To learn more about Autodiscover, consult the following reference on TechNet:
> *http://technet.microsoft.com/en-us/library/bb124251.aspx.*

 Quick Check

- What type of CA should you use if you want to ensure that people using computers that do not belong to your organization can trust your organization's OWA server?

Quick Check Answer

- You should obtain a certificate from a trusted third-party CA, as this certificate will be trusted by computers used outside your organization. You should use a certificate from an internal CA only when computers accessing the service are configured to trust that CA.

ActiveSync

ActiveSync allows users to sync their Windows Mobile devices with their Exchange mailboxes. ActiveSync is optimized to work across high-latency, low-bandwidth networks, such as those likely to be encountered across a mobile phone data connection. Exchange ActiveSync is enabled automatically when you install the Client Access server role.

You can configure ActiveSync settings either by editing the ActiveSync virtual directory or by configuring ActiveSync mailbox policies. You can edit the properties of the ActiveSync virtual directory from within the EMC by navigating to the Server Configuration\Client Access node, selecting Exchange ActiveSync on the lower-middle page, right-clicking on the Client Access server that you want to modify, and then clicking on Properties. This will bring up the Microsoft-Server-ActiveSync Properties dialog box, as shown in Figure 5-7.

Through this dialog box, you can modify the following ActiveSync properties:

- **Internal URL** The URL that ActiveSync devices on the internal network use to access the Client Access server.

- **External URL** The URL that ActiveSync devices on the Internet use to access the Client Access server.

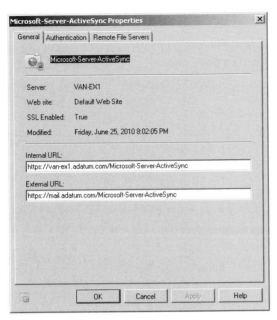

FIGURE 5-7 ActiveSync properties

- **Basic Authentication** Whether basic authentication is enabled
  - **Ignore Client Certificates** Client identification certificates are ignored during authentication.
  - **Accept Client Certificates** Client identification certificates, issued by a CA trusted by the Client Access server, are accepted for authentication.
  - **Require Client Certificates** Client identification certificates, issued by a CA trusted by the Client Access server, are required for authentication.
- **Remote File Servers Block List** A list of servers that ActiveSync devices cannot access.
- **Remote File Servers Allow List** A list of servers that ActiveSync devices can access. If a server is on both the block list and the allow list, the block list takes precedence.
- **Remote File Servers Unknown Servers** Whether the ActiveSync device should be granted access to or blocked from a server that is on neither the allow list nor the block list.
- **Internal Domain Suffix** Which domain suffixes should be treated as being internal.

You can also configure these properties using the *Set-ActiveSyncVirtualDirectory* cmdlet. The *Test-ActiveSyncConnectivity* cmdlet allows you to test that ActiveSync is functioning properly. It does this by simulating a full synchronization against a specific mailbox. For example, to test ActiveSync connectivity for the mailbox Kim_Akers on Client Access server CAS01, issue the following command:

```
Test-ActiveSyncConnectivity -ClientAccessServer CAS01 -URL http://adatum.com/mail
-MailboxCredential "Kim_Akers"
```

MORE INFO **UNDERSTANDING ACTIVESYNC**

To learn more about ActiveSync, consult the following reference on TechNet:
http://technet.microsoft.com/en-us/library/aa998357.aspx.

ActiveSync device policies

ActiveSync Mailbox Policies allow administrators to specify settings that apply to mobile devices, such as whether a device requires a password, encryption, and what the mobile phone should do if a user enters incorrect password several times in succession. To create a new ActiveSync Mailbox Policy, perform the following general steps:

1. Select the Organization Configuration\Client Access node within the EMC.

2. In the Actions pane, click on New Exchange ActiveSync Mailbox Policy.

3. On the New Exchange ActiveSync Mailbox Policy Wizard, shown in Figure 5-8, enter a policy name and configure the following settings:

   - **Allow nonprovisionable devices:** Allow devices that do not support all policies to sync with Exchange.

   - **Allow attachments to be downloaded to device:** Allow devices to retrieve attachments.

   - **Require password:** When you require a password, you can also configure password settings, such as whether an alphanumeric password is required, if password recovery is allowed; whether data stored on the device must be encrypted; whether simple passwords are allowed; minimum password length; idle time before a password is required again; whether password history is enforced; and the length of time before the password must be changed.

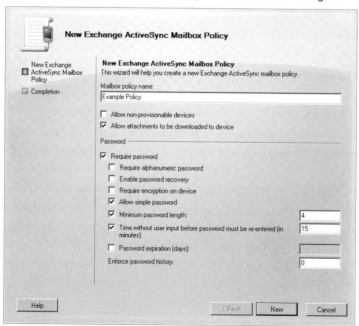

FIGURE 5-8 New ActiveSync Mailbox Policy

Once you create the policy, you can configure additional settings by editing the policy properties through the EMC or by using the *Set-ActiveSyncMailboxPolicy* cmdlet from the EMS. Editing the policy gives you access to the Sync Settings tab, shown in Figure 5-9. These settings allow you to specify which calendar and email items can be synced, whether Direct Push is enabled, whether HTML-formatted email can be sent to the device, and whether there is a limit on the size of attachments that can be sent to the device.

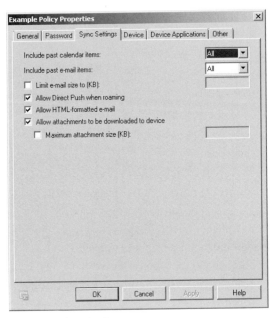

FIGURE 5-9 Sync Settings

On the Device tab, shown in Figure 5-10, you can specify what features on the device are allowed on the device. You can use this policy to allow removable storage, camera, Wi-Fi, infrared, Internet sharing (also known as tethering), remote desktop, desktop synchronization, and Bluetooth. When these features are disabled on mobile phones running compatible versions of Windows Mobile, users are unable to access them. For example, you could disable cameras on phones that have cameras through ActiveSync Mailbox policy if you worked in a sensitive environment where you did not want users taking photographs. These policies are enforced only when the associated mailbox has an Enterprise Client Access License (CAL).

The Device Applications tab allows you to specify whether the device can run a browser, consumer mail, unsigned applications, and unsigned installation packages. The Other tab, shown in Figure 5-11, gives you the option of allowing or blocking specific applications on the device. These features are also available only if the associated mailbox has an Enterprise CAL.

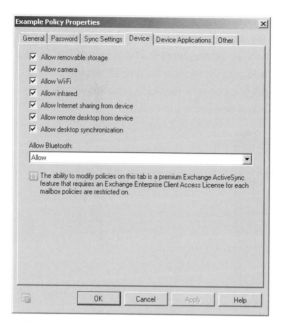

FIGURE 5-10 ActiveSync device settings

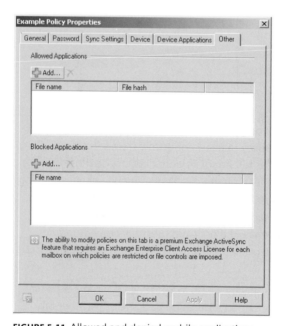

FIGURE 5-11 Allowed and denied mobile applications

You can manage mobile devices, including performing a remote wipe of the device, from the EMS. When you choose to remote-wipe a device, it resets the device to its factory default, deleting all configuration settings and personal data. There are four EMS cmdlets that you can use to manage mobile devices:

- **Get-ActiveSyncDevice**   This cmdlet can be used to list all the mobile phones that have been paired with mailboxes in the organization.

- **Get-ActiveSyncDeviceStatistics**   This cmdlet can be used to provide information about devices that are paired to specific mailbox.

- **Clear-ActiveSyncDevice**   This cmdlet can be used to wipe a mobile device.

- **Remove-ActiveSyncDevice**   This cmdlet is used to sever the relationship between a specific mailbox and a mobile device.

When OWA policies are configured appropriately, it is also possible for users to perform a remote wipe on a mobile device from OWA. You will learn more about OWA in Lesson 3, "Outlook Web App."

> **MORE INFO**   **CONFIGURING ACTIVESYNC MAILBOX POLICIES**
>
> To learn more about configuring ActiveSync mailbox policies, consult the following link on *http://technet.microsoft.com/en-us/library/bb123484.aspx*.

EXAM TIP

Remember that Client Access servers do not have the POP3 and IMAP4 services enabled by default.

Lesson Summary

- The POP3 and IMAP4 services must be manually enabled before clients can utilize them to access the content of their mailboxes.

- ActiveSync allows mobile devices to synchronize Exchange mailbox content.

- Autodiscover allows Outlook or a mobile device to be automatically configured on the basis of a user's email address or logon credentials.

- SANs allow certificates to be mapped to multiple fully qualified domain names.

- You should obtain a certificate from a trusted third-party CA when you need to support users from outside your organization.

Lesson Review

You can use the following questions to test your knowledge of the information in Lesson 1, "Configure POP, IMAP, and Microsoft ActiveSync." The questions are also available on the companion CD if you prefer to review them in electronic form.

1. Which of the following cmdlets could you use to verify that the Autodiscover service is functioning correctly for Outlook 2010 clients on an Exchange Server 2010 Client Access server?

    A. *Test-OwaConnectivity*

    B. *Test-WebServicesConnectivity*

    C. *Test-OutlookWebServices*

    D. *Test-ActiveSyncConnectivity*

2. Which of the following EMS cmdlets could you use to verify that ActiveSync is functioning correctly for a specific user?

    A. *Test-WebServicesConnectivity*

    B. *Test-OutlookWebServices*

    C. *Test-OwaConnectivity*

    D. *Test-ActiveSyncConnectivity*

3. Which of the following EMS cmdlets can you use to remotely wipe a mobile phone?

    A. *Get-ActiveSyncDeviceStatistics*

    B. *Clear-ActiveSyncDevice*

    C. *Remove-ActiveSyncDevice*

    D. *Get-ActiveSyncDevice*

4. Which of the following cmdlets can you use to enable password recovery for mobile devices that use Exchange ActiveSync?

    A. *Set-ActiveSyncMailboxPolicy*

    B. *Set-OwaMailboxPolicy*

    C. *Set-ActiveSyncVirtualDirectory*

    D. *Set-OwaVirtualDirectory*

5. Which of the following cmdlets can you use to configure Exchange ActiveSync to use basic authentication?

    A. *Set-OwaVirtualDirectory*

    B. *Set-ActiveSyncVirtualDirectory*

    C. *Set-OwaMailboxPolicy*

    D. *Set-ActiveSyncMailboxPolicy*

Lesson 2: Outlook Anywhere and RPC Clients

Outlook Anywhere, formerly known as RPC over HTTP, allows clients who use Outlook 2010, 2007, and 2003 to connect to Exchange servers on a protected network from locations over the Internet by tunneling RPC traffic over the HTTP networking protocol. Outlook Anywhere allows access to Exchange without the necessity of administrators configuring a virtual private network (VPN) or DirectAccess solution. Clients on an internal network who access Exchange mailboxes through an Exchange Server 2010 Client Access server generally do so using RPC protocol. In this lesson, you will learn how to configure both Outlook Anywhere and RPC Client Access so that clients running Outlook are able to interact with their Exchange mailboxes.

> **After this lesson, you will be able to:**
> - Prepare a server to support Outlook Anywhere.
> - Enable Outlook Anywhere.
> - Configure an external host name for Outlook Anywhere.
> - Configure RPC client access.
>
> **Estimated lesson time: 40 minutes**

Outlook Anywhere

Outlook Anywhere allows clients on the Internet to access internal Exchange resources without having to connect using a VPN or a technology such as DirectAccess. As clients on the Internet use Outlook Anywhere to access internal Exchange resources, the Client Access server hosting Outlook Anywhere needs to be accessible to clients on the Internet. The Client Access server may be on a screened subnet or may be indirectly accessible through a product such as Forefront Threat Management Gateway. To prepare a Client Access server to support Outlook Anywhere, you must first do the following:

- Obtain a valid SSL certificate from a certificate authority trusted by the potential Outlook Anywhere clients. This means obtaining an SSL certificate from a trusted third-party CA if you are supporting clients from outside your organization.
- The RPC over HTTP feature must be present on the Windows Server 2008 or Windows Server 2008 R2 host.
- The external name used with Outlook Anywhere must be able to be resolved by a client on the Internet.

Once you have met these prerequisites, you can enable Outlook Anywhere by performing the following general steps:

1. Navigate to the Server Configuration \ Client Access node in the EMC and click on Enable Outlook Anywhere in the Actions pane.

2. On the Enable Outlook Anywhere Wizard, shown in Figure 5-12, enter the external host name that clients will use for access and specify whether basic or NTLM authentication will be used. Use the SSL offloading option only if an SSL accelerator is present.

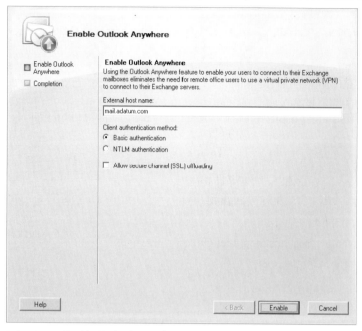

FIGURE 5-12 Enable Outlook Anywhere

You can also enable Outlook Anywhere from the EMS by using the *Enable-OutlookAnywhere* cmdlet. For example, to enable Outlook Anywhere on server CAS1 with the external host name mail.adatum.com and using NTLM for authentication, enter the following command:

```
Enable-OutlookAnywhere -Server 'CAS1' -ExternalHostname 'mail.adatum.com'
-DefaultAuthenticationMethod 'NTLM'
```

Outlook Anywhere supports NTLM and the less secure basic authentication. You can switch between authentication types using the *Set-OutlookAnywhere* cmdlet. Once you have set it up, you can verify that Outlook Anywhere is functioning by using the *Test-OutlookConnectivity* cmdlet with the protocol parameter set to http.

Once you have enabled Outlook Anywhere, you can modify its properties either using the *Set-OutlookAnywhere* cmdlet or by viewing the properties of the Client Access server when you have the Server Configuration\Client Access node selected in the EMC. On the Outlook Anywhere tab, shown in Figure 5-13, you can reconfigure the external host name and authentication method and whether the Client Access server supports SSL offloading.

> *MORE INFO* **MANAGING OUTLOOK ANYWHERE**
>
> To learn more about managing Outlook Anywhere, consult the following article on TechNet: *http://technet.microsoft.com/en-us/library/bb123513.aspx.*

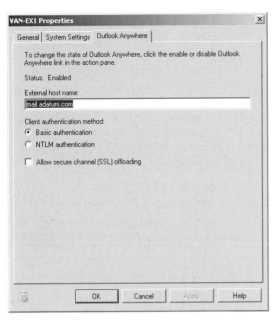

FIGURE 5-13 Configure Outlook Anywhere properties

 Quick Check

- Which EMS cmdlet can you use to verify Outlook Anywhere connectivity?

Quick Check Answer

- You can use the *Test-OutlookConnectivity* cmdlet to verify Outlook Anywhere connectivity.

Configure RPC Client Access

The method by which clients running Outlook interact with Client Access servers changed between Exchange 2007 and Exchange Server 2010. In Exchange 2007 organizations, Outlook clients could connect directly to a Mailbox server to access the contents of mailboxes. In Exchange Server 2010 organizations, Outlook access to mailboxes is mediated through a Client Access server. This ensures that high-availability functions, such as Database Availability Group failover, occur seamlessly.

Administrators should note that there may be some transition issues for clients using older versions of Outlook when an organization moves to Exchange Server 2010. Clients running Outlook 2007 and Outlook 2010 will find the transition from Exchange 2007 to Exchange 2010 to be seamless, as these clients automatically support RPC encryption. Clients running Outlook 2003 will need to be configured to use RPC encryption, which is not enabled by default and which you can accomplish through group policy. As an alternative, you can disable RPC encryption on the Client Access server, though this step is not recommended. You can accomplish this using the *Set-RpcClientAccess* cmdlet with the EncryptionRequired parameter set to $false. You can also use the *Set-RpcClientAccess* cmdlet to restrict clients by version. For example, you can use the BlockedClientVersions parameter to block all versions of Outlook, except Outlook 2010, from accessing the Client Access server.

> **MORE INFO** **RPC CLIENT ACCESS**
>
> To learn more about RPC client access, consult the following article on TechNet: *http:// technet.microsoft.com/en-us/library/ee332317.aspx.*

Configure Client Access Array

A client access array is a collection of load balanced Client Access servers. There can be one client access array per active directory site, and a single client access array cannot span multiple sites. Client access arrays are created using the *New-ClientAccessArray* cmdlet. For example, to create a new client access array named clientarray.adatum.com in the Maffra site, use the following command:

```
New-ClientAccessArray -FQDN clientarray.adatum.com -Site Maffra -Name "clientarray
.adatum.com"
```

Once the client access array is created, you assign the client access array to mailbox databases using the *Set-MailboxDatabase* cmdlet with the RpcClientAccess parameter. For example, to configure mailbox database ALPHA to use client access array clientarray.adatum. com, use the following command:

```
Set-MailboxDatabase ALPHA -RpcClientAccess clientarray.adatum.com
```

> **MORE INFO** **CLIENT ACCESS ARRAYS**
>
> To learn more about creating client access arrays, consult the following article on TechNet: *http://technet.microsoft.com/en-us/library/dd351149.aspx.* You will also learn more about Exchange 2010 high-availability strategies in Chapter 13, "Exchange High Availability Solutions."

Client Throttling Policies

Client throttling policies allow you to manage Client Access server performance by monitoring how users consume resources and enforcing bandwidth limits where necessary. Client throttling policies allow you to stop users from intentionally or unintentionally degrading Client Access server performance when they use a disproportionate amount of Client Access server resources. When you first deploy Exchange Server 2010, a default throttling policy is applied. You can view the properties of this policy by using the *Get-ThrottlingPolicy* cmdlet in the EMS. Throttling policies apply to the following Exchange components:

- Exchange ActiveSync
- Exchange Web Services

- IMAP
- OWA
- POP
- Windows PowerShell

You manage throttling policy settings using the following EMS cmdlets:

- **Get-ThrottlingPolicy**   Get the properties of existing throttling policies
- **Set-ThrottlingPolicy**   Configure the properties of an existing throttling policy
- **New-ThrottlingPolicy**   Create a new throttling policy
- **Remove-ThrottlingPolicy**   Remove an existing throttling policy

> **MORE INFO**   **CLIENT THROTTLING**
>
> To learn more about client throttling policies, consult the following article on TechNet:
> *http://technet.microsoft.com/en-us/library/dd297964.aspx.*

> **EXAM TIP**
>
> Remember what the prerequisites are for Outlook Anywhere.

Lesson Summary

- Outlook Anywhere allows clients on the Internet to access internal Exchange resources without having to use a VPN.
- A client access array is a load-balanced collection of Client Access servers that are all members of the same site.
- You can use the *Test-OutlookConnectivity* cmdlet to verify that Outlook Anywhere is functioning correctly.
- Client throttling policies ensure that no single client uses a disproportionate amount of a Client Access server's resources.
- The RPC over HTTP feature must be installed prior to the deployment of Outlook Anywhere.

Lesson Review

You can use the following questions to test your knowledge of the information in Lesson 2, "Outlook Anywhere and RPC Clients." The questions are also available on the companion CD if you prefer to review them in electronic form.

> **NOTE**   **ANSWERS**
>
> Answers to these questions and explanations of why each answer choice is correct or incorrect are located in the "Answers" section at the end of the book.

1. Which of the following cmdlets would you use to test Outlook Anywhere connectivity?

   A. *Test-WebServicesConnectivity*

   B. *Test-OutlookConnectivity*

   C. *Test-OutlookWebServices*

   D. *Test-OwaConnectivity*

2. Which if the following EMS cmdlets would you use to configure the external hostname for Outlook Anywhere for a site that has an externally facing client access array?

   A. *Set-ActiveSyncOrganizationSettings*

   B. *Set-ActiveSyncVirtualDirectory*

   C. *Set-OutlookAnywhere*

   D. *Set-OwaVirtualDirectory*

3. Which of the following EMS cmdlets would you use to create a new client access array for a specific Active Directory site?

   A. *Set-ClientAccessServer*

   B. *New-ClientAccessArray*

   C. *Set-CASMailbox*

   D. *Set-RpcClientAccess*

4. Which EMS cmdlet would you use to set the client authentication method for Outlook Anywhere to NTLM?

   A. *Set-ClientAccessArray*

   B. *Set-ActiveSyncOrganizationSettings*

   C. *Set-OutlookProvider*

   D. *Set-OutlookAnywhere*

5. Which of the following features must be installed on a computer running Windows Server 2008 R2 before that computer can support the Exchange Client Access server role with the Outlook Anywhere component?

   A. Message Queuing

   B. Peer Name Resolution Protocol

   C. RPC over HTTP Proxy

   D. Remote Differential Compression

Lesson 3: OWA

OWA, formerly known as Outlook Web Access, is a web application hosted on Client Access servers that allows users to replicate the Outlook 2010 application experience through a web browser rather than the Outlook 2010 client. OWA in Exchange Server 2010 provides several enhancements over the version provided in previous versions of Exchange, including better performance and greater compatibility with browsers other than Internet Explorer. In this lesson, you will learn how to configure OWA at both the virtual directory and the OWA mailbox policy level, including how to block password change, mediate access to specific attachments, and configure authentication.

> **After this lesson, you will be able to:**
> - Configure file and access.
> - Configure the Exchange Control Panel.
> - Configure OWA virtual directories.
> - Set up OWA authentication.
>
> **Estimated lesson time: 40 minutes**

Configure File Access and WebReady Document Viewing

One of the most common uses of email is for the sending and receiving of attachments. Although many people include attachments with their email messages, in some environments it is also common to forward a link to a file hosted on a file share or within a SharePoint library, especially when the size of the file exceeds the maximum amount allowed for attachments. You can configure OWA to either allow or deny users access to email attachments hosted within SharePoint libraries or on Windows file shares. You can also configure OWA to use WebReady document viewing, which allows users to view documents on their web browser rather than in the associated application. Exchange allows you to differentiate this access on the basis of whether users have indicated that they are accessing OWA using a public or a private computer. File access and WebReady document viewing can be configured on a per OWA mailbox policy basis using the EMC or the *Set-OWAMailboxPolicy* cmdlet or by configuring the properties of the OWA virtual directory using the EMC or the *Set-OWAVirtualDirectory* cmdlet. You enable direct file access and WebReady document viewing on both the Public and the Private Computer File Access tabs of either an OWA mailbox policy or the OWA website, as shown in Figure 5-14.

You can configure the specifics of direct file access on the Direct File Access Settings page, as shown in Figure 5-15. These settings allow you to specify whether a user can access a document without having to save the document locally. You can specify a list of files the user can always open by populating the allow list, you can specify those files the user can open after saving locally by populating the force save list, and you can populate the list of

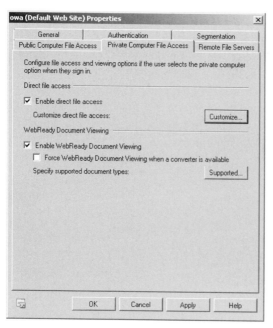

FIGURE 5-14 Configure private file access

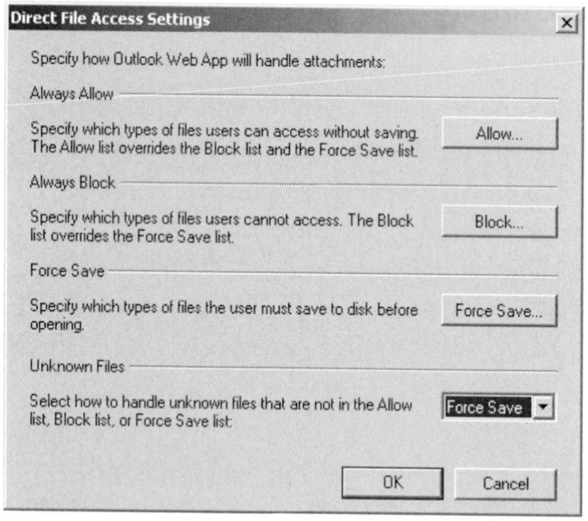

FIGURE 5-15 Direct file access settings

file types that the user is unable to open by populating the block list. The block list overrides the force save list, and the allow list overrides both the other lists. You can also set how OWA treats files of types not specified on any other the other lists, either blocking, forcing them to be saved, or allowing them to be opened.

WebReady document viewing allows OWA users to view file attachments in their browser rather than by having to open those attachments in an associated application. This can be very useful when the OWA user is using a computer that does not have the latest application software installed or is using a web terminal at an Internet café or is using an Internet access device that does not have a Microsoft operating system. You can configure WebReady Document viewing so that a user must view its documents using WebReady if a converter is available. You can configure the available converters on the WebReady Document Viewing Settings dialog box, as shown in Figure 5-16.

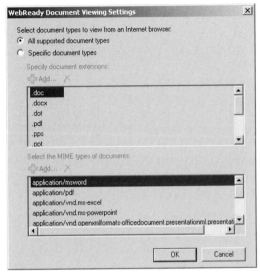

FIGURE 5-16 WebReady document viewing settings

MORE INFO   **MANAGING FILE AND DATA ACCESS IN OWA**

To learn more about managing file and data access for Outlook Web App, consult the following TechNet link: *http://technet.microsoft.com/en-us/library/bb124731.aspx*.

 Quick Check

■ Which takes precedence if the same file type is on the always allow and always block list?

Quick Check Answer

■ File extensions on the always allow list override the always block and force save lists.

Segmentation Settings

Segmentation settings in an OWA mailbox policy allow administrators to configure which features will be available to users when they connect to OWA. For example, you could use segmentation settings to block access to the Calendar or use it to restrict users from being able to change their password when connected through OWA. Segmentation settings are configured on the Segmentation tab of an OWA mailbox policy's properties, as shown in Figure 5-17, or through the use of appropriate parameters in the *Set-OWAMailboxPolicy* cmdlet. By default, all features listed on the Segmentation tab are enabled. You can also configure these settings using the *Set-OwaVirtualDirectory* cmdlet or by configuring the Segmentation tab on the OWA website properties.

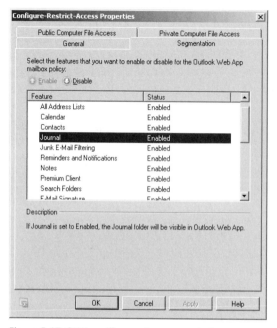

Figure 5-17 OWA mailbox policy segmentation

You can enable or disable the following features through Segmentation settings:

- **Exchange ActiveSync Integration**   This feature allows users to manage mobile phones linked to their Exchange mailbox, including remote device wipe, and view mobile device password.

- **All Address Lists**   This feature allows the user to view all address lists or, if disabled, limits them to the default global address list.

- **Calendar**   Allows calendar to be viewed from OWA.

- **Contacts**   Allows contacts to be viewed from OWA.

- **Journal**   Allows Journal to be viewed from OWA.

- **Junk E-Mail Filtering**   Allows junk email to be filtered through OWA.

- **Reminders and Notifications**   When enabled, users receive new email notifications, calendar, and task reminders.

- **Notes**   Allows notes to be viewed when connected to OWA.

- **Premium Client**   Allows the premium version of OWA to be used.

- **Search Folders**   Allows Exchange search folders, created in Outlook, to be visible in OWA.

- **E-Mail Signature**   Allows users to customize their email signature.

- **Spelling Checker**   Allows users to check their spelling on OWA.

- **Tasks**   Allows users to access Tasks from OWA.

- **Theme Selection**   Allows users to change their color scheme.

- **Unified Messaging Integration**   Allows users to access voice mail and faxes through OWA.

- **Change Password**   Allows users to change their password.

- **Rules**   Allows users to customize rules.

- **Public Folders**   Allows users to access public folders through OWA.

- **S/MIME**   Allows users to read and compose signed and encrypted messages through OWA.

- **Recover Deleted Items**   Allows users to view items that have been deleted from deleted items using OWA.

- **Instant Messaging**   Allows users to access instant messaging if users have access to this functionality.

- **Text Messaging**   Allows users to access text messages if users have access to this functionality.

OWA Virtual Directory Properties

Although you can configure public and private computer file access and segmentation both at the OWA Virtual Directory level and through individual OWA mailbox policies, you can configure the OWA authentication and Remote File Servers settings only by configuring the OWA Virtual Directory. For example, although you can block users from changing their password using OWA mailbox policies or by configuring the OWA virtual directory, you can block users from accessing file server ALPHA while allowing access to file server BETA only by configuring the OWA virtual directory.

You can access the properties of the OWA virtual directory by selecting the Server Configuration\Client Access tab from within the EMC, clicking on the Outlook Web App tab, right-clicking on the OWA website, and then clicking on Properties. In this dialog box, you can configure the following options on each of the following tabs:

- **General**   On this tab, you specify the Internal URL and the External URL used to access OWA.

- **Segmentation**   The Segmentation tab functions the same in the virtual directory properties as it does in the OWA mailbox policies that you learned about earlier. Here you configure which functionality is available or not available to OWA users.

- **Public Computer File Access**   On this tab, you specify how computers marked as public when a user logs on to OWA are able to use Direct File Access and WebReady Document Printing.

- **Private Computer File Access**   On this tab, you specify how computers marked as private when a user logs on to OWA are able to use Direct File Access and WebReady Document Printing.

- **Remote File Servers**   Use the settings on this tab to specify which servers on the internal network OWA users are able to access.

- **Authentication**   The Authentication tab, shown in Figure 5-18, allows you to configure authentication properties of OWA. You have the option of selecting standard authentication, where a dialog box will prompt users to enter their credentials, or forms-based authentication, where users will enter their credentials on a web page. You can modify the format that the credentials on the OWA web page take, so that users enter their name in the domain\username format, User Principal Name (UPN), or user name only.

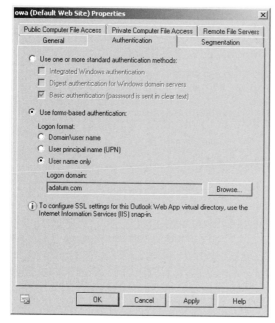

FIGURE 5-18 Configure OWA authentication

You can use the *Set-OwaVirtualDirectory* cmdlet to configure these settings from the EMC. For example, to set forms-based authentication for OWA on server CAS1, use the following command:

```
Set-OwaVirtualDirectory –Identity "CAS1\owa (default web site)" –FormsAuthentication
$true
```

> **MORE INFO   CONFIGURE OWA VIRTUAL DIRECTORY**
>
> To learn more about configuring the OWA virtual directory, consult the following TechNet link: *http://technet.microsoft.com/en-us/library/dd298140.aspx*.

Exchange Control Panel

Exchange Control Panel (ECP), shown in Figure 5-19, provides a web-based interface for administrators to manage Exchange configuration settings such as mailboxes, public groups, external contacts, administrator roles, and user roles. Administrators are also able to use the reporting functionality available through ECP to perform searches for specific messages and view delivery reports.

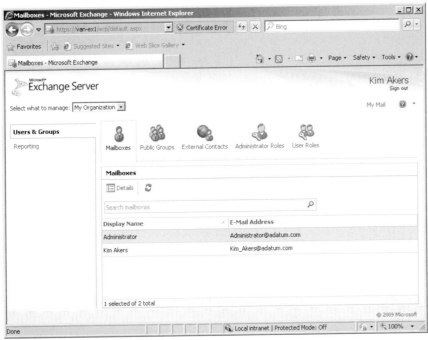

FIGURE 5-19 Exchange Control Panel

You can edit the properties of the ECP through the EMC by selecting the Server Configuration\Client Access node, selecting Exchange Control Panel, and then right-clicking on the ECP website and selecting properties. You can use this properties dialog box to edit the following:

- **Internal URL**   The URL that administrators on the internal network use to access ECP.

- **External URL**   The URL that administrators on the Internet use to access ECP.

- **Authentication**   The authentication options for ECP. This is similar to configuring the authentication options for OWA. You have the option of choosing standard authentication methods such as Integrated Windows, Digest, and Basic authentication or using Forms-Based authentication. When you choose to use Forms-Based authentication, authentication will use the same format as is used for OWA.

You can use the *Set-EcpVirtualDirectory* cmdlet to configure ECP options. For example, to disable basic authentication for the ECP on server CAS1, issue the following command:

```
Set-EcpVirtualDirectory –Identity "CAS1\ecp (default web site)" –Basicauthentication: $false
```

Lesson Summary

- Segmentation settings allow you to configure which OWA features are available to
  users. Segmentation settings can be configured through OWA mailbox policies or by
  editing the properties of the OWA virtual directory.

- You can configure public computer file access, private computer file access,
  and segmentation settings in both OWA mailbox policies and OWA virtual directory
  settings. You can configure authentication and remote server settings only in OWA
  virtual directory settings.

- The *Set-OWAMailboxPolicy* cmdlet allows you to configure OWA mailbox policies.
  These policies can be applied to individuals or groups. They allow you to configure
  segmentation settings.

Lesson Review

You can use the following questions to test your knowledge of the information in Lesson 3,
"Outlook Web App." The questions are also available on the companion CD if you prefer to
review them in electronic form.

1. Which of the following EMS cmdlets can you use to block a group of users from
    changing their password when connected to their Exchange mailbox through OWA
    without blocking this functionality from all users?

    A. *Set-OwaMailboxPolicy*

    B. *Set-OwaVirtualDirectory*

    C. *Get-OwaMailboxPolicy*

    D. *Get-OwaVirtualDirectory*

2. Which of the following EMS cmdlets can you use to verify that Outlook Web App is functional?

   A. *Test-OutlookConnectivity*

   B. *Test-ActiveSyncConnectivity*

   C. *Test-OwaConnectivity*

   D. *Test-PopConnectivity*

3. Tailspin Toys and Wingtip Toys recently merged, and you are in the process of consolidating their Exchange infrastructure. Many of the users at both companies access their email using OWA from their home computers. OWA will be hosted on a single Client Access server at the merged company. You want to ensure that these home users are able to access OWA using either the address https://owa.tailspintoys .com or the address https://owa.wingtiptoys.com and minimize the effort required to configure the computers of these users. Which of the following should you do when obtaining an SSL certificate for this Client Access server?

   A. Obtain a certificate that does not support SANs from an internal CA.

   B. Obtain a certificate that does not support SANs from a trusted third-party CA.

   C. Obtain a certificate that supports SANs from an internal CA.

   D. Obtain a certificate that supports SANs from a trusted third-party CA.

4. Which of the following cmdlets can you use to configure Exchange so that users in the Developers group are able to receive and open attachments in .EXE format from OWA while ensuring that all other users are blocked from opening this type of attachment?

   A. *Set-OwaMailboxPolicy*

   B. *Set-CASMailbox*

   C. *Set-RpcClientAccess*

   D. *Set-ActiveSyncMailboxPolicy*

5. You want to ensure that users always log on to OWA using their primary email address. Which of the following EMS cmdlets allows you to accomplish this goal?

   A. *Set-OwaMailboxPolicy*

   B. *Set-ClientAccessServer*

   C. *Set-OwaVirtualDirectory*

   D. *Set-OutlookAnywhere*

PRACTICE **Client Access Server Configuration**

In this set of practice exercises, you will configure Client Access server VAN-EX1. You will enable the POP3 and IMAP4 services on this Client Access server, configure an external client access domain, request and install a server certificate that supports the multiple names the Client Access server uses, and configure Outlook Web App.

EXERCISE 1   Enable the POP3 and IMAP4 Services on the Client Access Server

In this exercise, you will enable the POP3 and IMAP4 services on Client Access server VAN-EX1. You will also verify that Kim Akers's user mailbox can be accessed using these protocols. To complete this exercise, perform the following steps:

1. Log on to server VAN-EX1 with the Kim Akers user account.

2. Open the Services console located in the Administrative Tools menu.

3. Configure the properties of the Microsoft Exchange IMAP4 and Microsoft Exchange POP3 services so that they start automatically. Start each service manually.

4. Open the EMC and navigate to the Recipient Configuration node.

5. Right-click on the Kim Akers user mailbox and then click on Properties. Click on the Mailbox Features tab and verify that POP3 and IMAP4 are enabled, as shown in Figure 5-20.

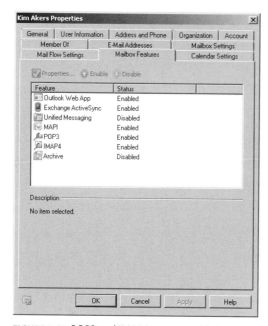

FIGURE 5-20 POP3 and IMAP4 access enabled

6. In the EMC, select the Server Configuration\Client Access node. Click on VAN-EX1. In the lower pane, select the POP3 and IMAP4 tab. Right-click on the POP3 item and then click Properties.

7. On the Authentication tab, select the Plain Text Authentication Logon (Integrated Windows Authentication) option, as shown in Figure 5-21, and then click OK.

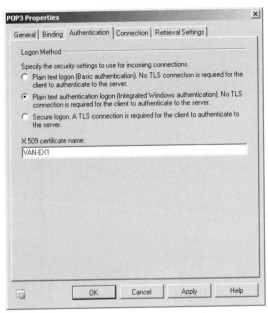

FIGURE 5-21 POP3 authentication properties

EXERCISE 2 Configure VAN-DC to issue certificates with multiple SANs and a Domain Name System (DNS) record for mail.adatum.com. To complete this exercise, perform the following steps:

1. Log on to server VAN-DC with the Kim Akers user account.

2. Use the Server Manager console to add the Active Directory Certificate Services role to server VAN-DC.

3. Ensure that you add both the Certification Authority and the Certification Authority Web Enrollment Role Services to the server. If prompted to add additional required role services, click Add Required Role Services.

4. Configure VAN-DC as an Enterprise Root CA. Select the Create A New Private Key option and select the default options for Cryptography, CA Name, Validity Period, and Certificate Database settings. Continue clicking Next until you have the option to click Install. Click Install. When Active Directory Certificate Services is installed, click Close.

5. Open an elevated command prompt and enter the command

   ```
   Certutil -setreg policy\EditFlags +EDITF_ATTRIBUTESUBJECTALTNAME2
   ```

6. Restart the Active Directory Certificate Services service using the Services console.

7. Open the DNS console. Add a host record for mail.adatum.com that maps to the IP address 10.10.0.20.

EXERCISE 3 Configure external client access domain and request and assign a certificate to the Client Access server

In this exercise, you will configure an external client access domain for Client Access server VAN-EX1. You will also request and obtain a server certificate for the Client Access server that can be used for the names mail.adatum.com and van-ex1.adatum.com. To complete this exercise, perform the following steps:

1. Log on to server VAN-ex1 with the Kim Akers user account.

2. Select the Server Configuration\Client Access node. In the Actions pane, click Configure External Client Access Domain. This will open the Configure External Client Access Domain dialog.

3. Enter the name mail.adatum.com and then click Add. On the Select Client Access server dialog click on VAN-EX1 and then click OK. Verify that the Configure External Client Access Domain dialog matches Figure 5-22 and then click Configure. When the configuration change is complete, click Finish.

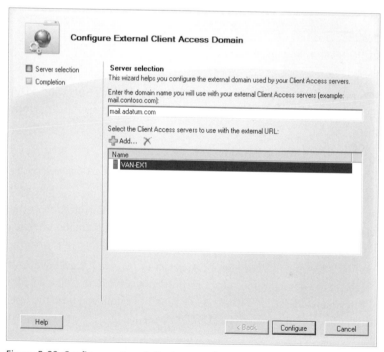

Figure 5-22 Configure external client access domain

4. Click on the Server Configuration node, right-click on VAN-EX1, and then click on New Exchange Certificate.

5. On the Introduction page, type **Adatum CAS Certificate** and then click Next twice.

6. On the Exchange Configuration page, expand Client Access server (Outlook Web App) and check the Outlook Web App Is On The Intranet option and the Outlook Web App

Is On The Internet option. Verify that the settings match those shown in Figure 5-23 and then click Next.

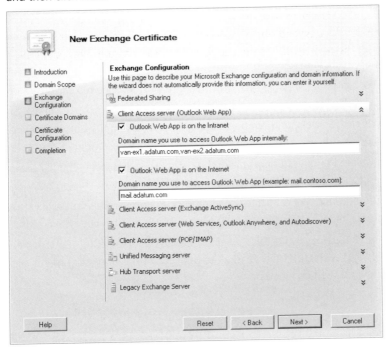

FIGURE 5-23 OWA certificate request

7. Verify that mail.adatum.com and van-ex1.adatum.com appear in the list of certificate domains and then click Next.

8. On the Organization and Location page, enter the following values:

    ■ Organization: Adatum

    ■ Organizational Unit: IT

    ■ Country/Region: Australia

    ■ City/Locality: Melbourne

    ■ State/Province: Victoria

    ■ Certificate Request Path: c:\owa-cert.req

9. Click Next, click New, and then click Finish.

10. Open the file owa-cert.req using Notepad. Press Ctrl+A to select all the text and then press Ctrl+C to place the text on the clipboard.

11. Use the Server Manager console to disable Internet Explorer Enhanced Security Configuration. Open a command prompt and issue the command: gpupdate /force.

12. Open Internet Explorer and navigate to *http://van-dc/certsrv*.

13. On the Microsoft Active Directory Certificate Services Welcome page, click Request A Certificate and then click Advanced Certificate Request.

14. On the Advanced Certificate Request page, click Submit A Certificate Request By Using A Base-64-Encoded CMC or PKCS#10 File, Or Submit A Renewal Request By Using A Base-64-Encoded CMC Or PKCS#7 File.

15. On the Submit A Certificate Request Or Renewal Request page, click on the Saved Request text box and then press Ctrl+V to paste the contents of the clipboard. Verify that the Certificate Template drop-down is set to Web Server and then click Submit.

16. On the Certificate Issued page, click Download Certificate. Save the certificate on the Desktop as certnew.cer.

17. In the EMC, click Server Configuration, click VAN-EX1, and in the bottom pane click Adatum CAS Certificate. In the Actions pane, click Complete Pending Request.

18. In the Complete Pending Request dialog box, use Browse to locate the file certnew.cer on the desktop and then click Complete. Click Finish to close the dialog box.

19. Right-click Adatum CAS Certificate and then click Assign Services To Certificate. On the Select Servers page, ensure that VAN-EX1 is selected and then click Next.

20. On the Assign Services To Certificate Select Service page, select the services shown in Figure 5-24 and then click Next. If asked to replace any existing assignments click Yes. Click Assign and then click Finish.

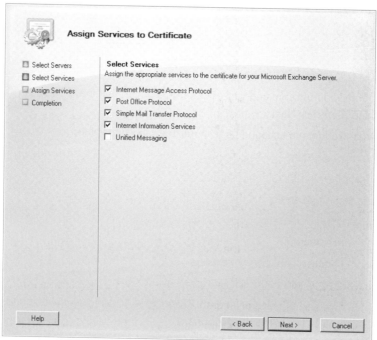

FIGURE 5-24 Assign services to certificate

21. Verify that the certificate is correctly assigned by navigating to *https://mail.adatum .com/owa* and viewing the security report by clicking the lock icon on the Internet Explorer address bar.

EXERCISE 4 Configure OWA

In this exercise, you will configure the properties of OWA for users.

1. If you have not done so already, log on to server VAN-EX1 with the Kim Akers user account.

2. Open the EMC and click on the Server Configuration\Client Access node.

3. Click on VAN-EX1. In the bottom pane, click on the Outlook Web App tab, right click on OWA (Default Web Site) and then click on Properties. This will bring up the OWA (Default Web Site) Properties dialog box.

4. On the Authentication tab, click on the User Name Only option when the Use Forms Based Authentication option is selected. Click Browse, select the adatum.com domain, and then click OK. Verify that the Authentication tab matches Figure 5-25.

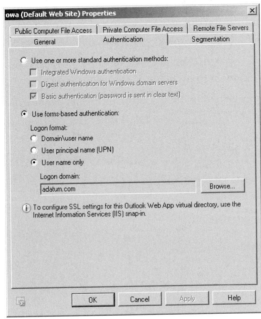

FIGURE 5-25 Configuring authentication

5. On the Segmentation tab, disable the Journal and Notes features by selecting each and clicking Disable.

6. On the Public Computer File Access tab, remove the check next to Enable Direct File Access and Enable WebReady Document Viewing.

7. On the Remote File Servers tab, click Configure. On the Internal Domain Suffix List dialog box, enter **adatum.com** and click Add. Click OK twice. Click OK at the warning informing you that you must restart Internet Information Services.

8. Open an elevated command prompt and issue the command. If the command is unsuccessful, issue it a second time:

```
iisreset /noforce
```

Chapter Review

To further practice and reinforce the skills you learned in this chapter, you can perform the following tasks:

- Review the chapter summary.
- Review the list of key terms introduced in this chapter.
- Complete the case scenarios. These scenarios set up real-world situations involving the topics of this chapter and ask you to create a solution.
- Complete the suggested practices.
- Take a practice test.

Chapter Summary

- You must configure the POP3 and IMAP4 services to start automatically before clients can access them.
- Autodiscover allows client configuration to occur automatically.
- SANs allow SSL certificates to map to multiple fully qualified domain names.
- Outlook Anywhere allows Exchange to automatically populate Outlook and mobile device configuration settings.
- Client access arrays are site-based collections of load-balanced Client Access servers.
- OWA allows users to access Exchange using a web browser.

Key Terms

Do you know what these key terms mean?

- ActiveSync
- Autodiscover
- Outlook Anywhere

Case Scenarios

In the following case scenarios, you will apply what you've learned about subjects of this chapter. You can find answers to these questions in the "Answers" section at the end of this book.

Case Scenario 1: Fabrikam Client Access

You are a consultant tasked with assisting with the configuration of Exchange Server 2010 at Fabrikam. A Fabrikam employee with little Exchange administration experience performed the original deployment. This employee has encountered some problems that inexperience has made unresolvable. The Fabrikam network has the following configuration:

- Two Mailbox servers, MBX-1 and MBX-2

- Two Hub Transport servers, HT-1 and HT-2
- One Edge Transport server, ET-1
- Two Client Access servers, CAS-1 and CAS-2

In the past, clients on the Internet accessed a web mail solution through the names mail .fabrikam.com and using an older company name, mail.adatum.com. In the past, these two separate computers hosted these web mail solutions. In the new deployment, a single web-based mail solution using OWA is preferred. CAS-2 hosts this solution. Clients are able to use OWA to connect to *https://owa.fabrikam.com* but are unable to make a secure connection to host *https://owa.adatum.com*. Management at Fabrikam wants to allow internal clients that have operating systems that do not support Outlook to access their mailboxes through CAS-1. Currently, when clients with operating systems that do not support Outlook attempt to use the IMAP4 protocol to access their mailboxes, they are unsuccessful. Clients are also unsuccessful when they attempt to use Outlook Anywhere to connect to CAS-2, although other functions on this server appear to work without a problem. With these facts in mind, answer the following questions:

1. What modification should you make to CAS-1 to support clients that have operating systems on which it is not possible to run Outlook?

2. Which operating system feature must you install on CAS-2 to support Outlook Anywhere?

3. What sort of certificate should you obtain so that clients can securely connect to OWA using either *https://owa.fabrikam.com* or *https://owa.adatum.com?*

Case Scenario 2: OWA at Tailspin Toys

You are the in the process of planning the deployment of OWA as part of a wider Exchange Server 2010 deployment at Tailspin Toys. You want to secure OWA so that every user is unable to change their password when connected to Exchange through OWA. You want to allow users that are members of the Accounting Department to be able to access XLS documents that are attached to email messages when connected to OWA but be unable to access compressed attachments in ZIP format. You also want to come up with a quick way to test that OWA is functioning properly without having to initiate a browser session. With these facts in mind, answer the following questions:

Questions

1. Which EMS cmdlet and parameters would you use to stop all users connected to OWA from changing their password regardless of the OWA mailbox policy that applies to their mailbox?

2. How do you allow users in the Accounting Department to access XLS attachments sent to them from OWA but not access compressed attachments in ZIP format while allowing users from other departments to access ZIP files as attachments?

3. Which EMS cmdlet can you use to verify OWA connectivity?

Suggested Practices

To help you successfully master the exam objectives presented in this chapter, complete the following tasks.

Configure ActiveSync

In this set of practice exercise, you will further configure ActiveSync. To complete this exercise, perform the following practices:

- **Practice 1** Use the *Set-ActiveSyncVirtualDirectory* cmdlet to disable basic authentication.
- **Practice 2** Use the *Test-ActiveSyncConnectivity* cmdlet to test synchronization against a specific mailbox.

Configure Autodiscover

In this set of practice exercises, you will further test and configure Outlook Anywhere. To complete this exercise, perform the following practices:

- **Practice 1** Use the *Set-OutlookAnywhere* cmdlet to disable SSL offloading.
- **Practice 2** Use the *Test-OutlookConnectivity* cmdlet to verify that Outlook Anywhere is functioning correctly.

Configure OWA

In this set of practice exercises, you will further configure OWA. To complete this exercise, perform the following practices:

- **Practice 1** Use the *Set-OwaVirtualDirectory* cmdlet to block users from changing passwords when connected to OWA.
- **Practice 2** Use the *New-OwaMailboxPolicy* cmdlet to create a new OWA mailbox policy that blocks access to ZIP and RTF files.

Take a Practice Test

The practice tests on this book's companion CD offer many options. For example, you can test yourself on just one exam objective, or you can test yourself on all the 70-662 certification exam content. You can set up the test so that it closely simulates the experience of taking a certification exam, or you can set it up in study mode so that you can look at the correct answers and explanations after you answer each question.

> **MORE INFO**   **PRACTICE TESTS**
>
> For details about all the practice test options available, see the "How to Use the Practice Tests" section in this book's Introduction.

CHAPTER 6

Federated Sharing and Role Based Access Control

This chapter introduces the Role Based Access Control (RBAC) permissions model. Exchange Server 2010 uses this permissions model to restrict which administrative tasks users can perform on Mailbox, Hub Transport, Unified Messaging, and Client Access servers. With RBAC, you control which resources administrators can configure and the features users can access. The chapter describes how to implement RBAC permissions in Exchange Server 2010.

Federated sharing is a concept that enables organizations running Exchange Server 2010 to share availability and contact information with other organizations and to send secure messages to these organizations. It enables a user to transparently share information, such as free or busy data or calendar details, with users in other Exchange Server organizations. Users can book meetings with users in a partner organization in exactly the same way that they book meetings with users in their own organization. This chapter discusses federated sharing and the Microsoft Federation Gateway.

Exam objectives in this chapter:

- Configure RBAC.
- Configure federated sharing.

Lessons in this chapter:

Before You Begin

In order to complete the exercises in the practice session in this chapter, you need to have done the following:

- Installed the Windows Server 2008 R2 domain controller VAN-DC1 and the Windows Exchange 2010 Enterprise Mailbox, Hub Transport, and Client Access server VAN-EX1 as described in the Appendix, "Setup Instructions for Exchange Server 2010."

- Created the Kim Akers account with the password *Pa$$w0rd* in the Adatum.com domain. This account should be placed in the Domain Admins security group and be a member of the Organization Management role group.

- Created the Don Hall account with the password *Pa$$w0rd* in the Adatum.com domain. This account should be placed in the Backup Operators security group (so it can be used to log on to the domain controller) and should be in the Marketing organizational unit (OU). This account should also be added to the local Backup Operators group on the Exchange Server 2010 server VAN-EX1.

- Created mailboxes for Kim Akers and Don Hall, accepting the default email address format for the email addresses.

 **REAL WORLD**

Ian McLean

Role Based Access Control is not a new concept. The first time I came across the term was in 1996 in an article in an Institute of Electrical and Electronics Engineers publication IEEE Computer by Messrs Sandhu, Coyne, Feinstein, and Youman (*http://csrc.nist.gov/groups/SNS/rbac/documents/sandhu96.pdf*). Of course I took it very seriously. I was studying to become a Microsoft Certified System Engineer (MCSE) at the time, and I knew IEEE publications were very important and influential.

At the same time, I wasn't sure if the framework described in the article would be totally suited to the way most organizations actually operated. The principles were sound. Roles would grant administrative privileges, each role consisting of a cohesive set of permissions, and the tasks that an administrative user could perform would be determined by the roles to which that user was added. There were far fewer rules than users in an organization so this was an efficient way of designing a permissions model. But an organization is a complex, dynamic entity, prone to changes that are not always fully understood and seldom well documented. The original model struck me as somewhat static and inflexible. This is not a criticism. Early models of almost anything tend to be static and inflexible, which doesn't stop them being invaluable.

It struck me that there needed to be an entity between the role and the user. A role or roles could be associated with that entity, and users could be added to the entity rather than directly to the role. This would provide a much more flexible system, especially when users joined or left an organization or their job descriptions changed. Remember this was 1996, and the concept of security groups was in its infancy.

Also, the tasks a user was permitted to perform in one part of an organization might not be appropriate in another. A user in Chicago might perform tasks in Chicago that would not be appropriate for the same user to perform in London, England, particularly if the Chicago and London offices had different security paradigms.

Unfortunately you can't copyright an opinion. However, looking at management role groups and management scopes in the Exchange Server 2010 implementation of RBAC, I'm comforted by the knowledge that somebody had the same sort of ideas that I had.

Lesson 1: Role Based Access Control

Role Based Access Control (RBAC) is a permissions model introduced by Exchange Server 2010 that enables you to align the roles you assign to users and administrators to the roles they hold within your organization. RBAC controls the administrative tasks that can be performed and the extent to which users can administer their own mailbox and distribution groups.

> **After this lesson, you will be able to:**
> - Describe RBAC and management role groups.
> - Create custom roles and assign roles to role groups.
> - Create and apply management scopes.
> - Identify built-in role groups.
> - Configure custom role groups.
> - Describe management role assignment policies.
>
> **Estimated lesson time: 40 minutes**

Implementing RBAC

With RBAC, you do not need modify and manage access control lists (ACLs) on Exchange Server or Active Directory Domain Services (AD DS) objects. In Exchange Server 2010, RBAC controls the administrative tasks that users can perform and the extent to which they can administer their own mailbox and distribution groups. When you configure RBAC permissions, you can define which Exchange Management Shell (EMS) cmdlets a user can run and which objects the user can modify.

RBAC assigns permissions to users in your organization depending on whether a user is an administrator or an end user. RBAC associates users with the permissions they need to perform their jobs. It does this using management role groups and management role assignment policies. The 70-662 examination focuses on management role groups, which are therefore covered in detail in this lesson. The following summarizes these methods:

- **Management role groups**   RBAC uses management role groups to assign administrator permissions. Administrators may need to manage an entire Exchange Server 2010 organization or merely part of it. Some administrators, for example, may require limited permissions to manage specific features, such as compliance or specific recipients. Such administrators, with limited permissions, are often termed "specialist users." You use management role groups by adding users to a built-in role group or to a custom role group. RBAC assigns each role group one or more management roles that define the permissions that RBAC grants to the group.

- **Management role assignment policies** You use management role assignment policies to assign end-user management roles. Role assignment policies consist of roles that control what users can do with their mailboxes or distribution groups. These roles do not allow the management of features not associated directly with an individual user or universal security group.

Using Management Role Groups

RBAC uses *management role groups*, which associate management roles with groups. Administrators manage the Exchange organization and recipient configuration. Specialist users manage specific Exchange features, such as compliance, or support the Help desk function but do not have full administrative rights. Role groups are associated with administrative management roles that enable administrators and specialist users to manage the configuration of their organization and recipients. You can assign permissions to administrators or specialist users by adding them to or removing them from role groups.

The management role group method consists of the following underlying components that define how RBAC assigns permissions:

- **Role holder** A *role holder* is a mailbox that you assign to a role group. When a mailbox becomes a role group member, RBAC grants it all of the permissions that the management roles provide. To assign a mailbox to a role group, you either add the user account to the group in AD DS or use the *Add-RoleGroupMember* cmdlet in the EMS. Note that both role group members and role group delegates are role holders. The difference between members and delegates is explained later in this lesson.

- **Management role group** A management role group is a universal security group to which one or more management roles have been assigned. It is created using Exchange Server 2010 tools but is nevertheless an AD DS object, and a domain administrator can configure its membership using the Active Directory Users and Computers console on a domain controller. It can contain mailboxes, users, other universal security groups, and other role groups. You add and remove members to management role groups, and you assign management roles to management role groups. The combination of all the roles assigned to a role group defines everything that members of that role group can manage in the Exchange organization.

- **Management role** A *management role* is a container that holds a group of management role entries, which define the specific tasks that the members of a role group can perform. RBAC assigns management roles to the role group and hence to its members using management role assignment.

- **Management role entry** A *management role entry* is an EMS cmdlet (including parameters), script, or special permission that you can add to a management role. By adding, for example, a cmdlet to a management role as a management role entry, you grant members of role groups to which that role is assigned the right to view and manage Exchange objects associated with that cmdlet.

- **Management role assignment**   A *management role assignment* assigns a role to a role group. To grant members of a role group the ability to use the cmdlets and parameters defined in the role, you assign the role to the role group. When you create a management role, you need to assign it to a role group so that role group members become role holders and can use the permissions granted by the role. (For example, they can use the cmdlets defined by the management role entries.) Role assignments can use management role scopes to control where the assignment can be used.

- **Management role scope**   When you assign a role with a *management role scope* to a role group, the scope defines the objects that the assignment is permitted to manage. The assignment and its scope are applied to the members of the role group and define what those members can manage. A scope can consist of servers, OUs, or filters on server or recipient objects. Management role scopes are sometimes known as *scopes of influence* or *scopes of impact*.

> *MORE INFO*   **MANAGEMENT ROLE GROUP COMPONENTS**
>
> For more information about management role groups, see *http://technet.microsoft.com/en-us/library/dd638105.aspx*. For more information about management roles, see *http://technet.microsoft.com/en-us/library/dd298116.aspx*. For more information about management role assignments, see *http://technet.microsoft.com/en-us/library/dd335131.aspx*. For more information about management role scopes, see *http://technet.microsoft.com/en-us/library/dd335146.aspx*.

Roles, role assignments, and role groups can be managed by administrators who have been assigned the Role Management management role. Assignees of a specific management role who have delegating role assignments can assign the role to other users. When you add a user to a role group, that user is given all the roles assigned to the role group. If scopes are applied to any of the role assignments, those scopes control what server configuration or recipients the user can manage.

If the role assignments built into Exchange Server 2010 roles do not suit your needs and you want to define which roles are assigned to a role group, you change the role assignments that link the role group to roles. Typically, the defaults are sensible, and you do not need to reconfigure them. You can, however, create a new management role based on an existing built-in role and change the role assignments for the new role. The procedure to do this is described later in this lesson.

One or more administrators or specialized users can be members of a role group. An administrator or specialized user can be a member of more than one role group. A role group can be assigned one or more role assignments. These link the role group with one or more administrative roles that define what tasks can be performed. Role assignments can contain management scopes that define where the users of the role group can perform actions.

Quick Check

- A management role consists of a number of entities that define the permissions granted to a holder of that role. What are these entities called, and of what can they consist?

Quick Check Answer

- Management entries. A management entry can be an EMS cmdlet (including parameters), script, or special permission that you can add to a management role.

Built-In Management Role Groups

Exchange Server 2010 offers several built-in role groups that provide different levels of administrative permissions to user groups. You can add users to or remove them from any built-in role group. You also can add role assignments to or remove them from most of these role groups. Table 6-1 lists and describes the built-in role groups.

TABLE 6-1 Built-In Role Groups

ROLE GROUP	DESCRIPTION
Delegated Setup	Role holders can deploy Exchange Server 2010 servers that have been previously provisioned.
Discovery Management	Role holders can search mailboxes in the Exchange organization for data that meets specific criteria.
UM Management	Role holders can manage Unified Messaging features within an Exchange organization, such as Unified Messaging server configuration, properties on mailboxes, prompts, and auto-attendant configuration.
Help Desk	Role holders can perform limited recipient management. For example, this might include managing a user's display name, address, phone number, and so on.
Organization Management	Role holders can perform (almost) any task against any Exchange Server object. This role group provides access to the entire Exchange Server 2010 organization.
Public Folder Management	Role holders can manage public folders and databases on Exchange Server 2010 servers.
Recipient Management	Role holders can create or modify recipients within the Exchange organization.
Records Management	Role holders can configure compliance features, which could include retention policy tags, message classifications, transport rules, and so on.

ROLE GROUP	DESCRIPTION
Server Management	Role holders can perform Exchange server configuration. They cannot, however, administer recipient configuration.
View-Only Organization Management	Role holders can view the properties of any object in the Exchange organization.

All the built-in management role groups are located in the Microsoft Exchange Security Groups OU in AD DS. This OU contains several other universal security groups that grant permissions to the Exchange server computer accounts. The contents of this OU are shown in Figure 6-1.

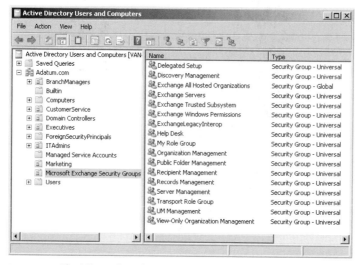

FIGURE 6-1 The Microsoft Exchange Security Groups OU

In the practice session later in this chapter, you use the Active Directory Users and Computers tool on the VAN-DC1 domain controller to add Don Hall to the Recipient Management built-in role group. You then use the Exchange Management Console (EMC) to verify that Don Hall can modify mailbox settings and create a distribution group but cannot create a mailbox database.

Setting Individual User Parameters

You can also use the *Set-user* cmdlet in the EMS to set user parameters that grant specified privileges. Note that this is not RBAC and is not the same as assigning a role to a user. It is a procedure that configures user properties on the basis of the limited set of parameters associated with the *Set-User* cmdlet. For example, the following command enables Don Hall to run remote PowerShell cmdlets:

```
Set-User -Identity "Don Hall" -RemotePowerShellEnabled $True
```

You can use the *Get-User* cmdlet to confirm your settings. The following command lists the configuration for the user Don Hall:

```
Get-User –Identity "Don Hall" | FL
```

Figure 6-2 shows the first of these commands and some of the output from the second.

FIGURE 6-2 Setting a user permission and checking that it has been applied

For more information about the *Set-User* cmdlet, see *http://technet.microsoft.com/en-us/library/aa998221.aspx*. For more information about the *Get-User* cmdlet, see *http://technet.microsoft.com/en-us/library/aa996896.aspx*.

MORE INFO **UNDERSTANDING ROLE GROUPS**

For general information about role groups and specifically built-in role groups, see *http://technet.microsoft.com/en-us/library/dd638105.aspx#Builtin*.

 Quick Check

1. What are members of a management role group called?

2. What entities can be members of a role group?

3. What is the difference between a role group member and a role group delegate?

Quick Check Answers

1. Role holders. Role holders can be role members or role delegates.

2. Users, universal security groups, or other role groups.

3. Both are role holders. However, a role delegate can also manage the role group.

The Help Desk Management Role Group

The Help Desk management role group is one of several built-in role groups that make up the RBAC permissions model in Exchange 2010. Users who are members of the Help Desk role group can perform limited recipient management of Microsoft Exchange Server 2010 recipients.

By default, membership of the Help Desk role group enables users to view and modify the Microsoft Office Outlook Web App options of any user in the organization. These options might include display name, address, phone number, and so on. They do not include options that are unavailable in Outlook Web App options, such as mailbox size or the mailbox database in which a mailbox is stored.

Members of this role group can modify only the Outlook Web App options that the user himself or herself can modify. If, for example, a user can modify his or her display name, a member of the Help Desk role group can also modify that display name. However, if a second user is not permitted to modify his or her display name, a member of the Help Desk role group cannot modify that user's display name.

If you want to, you can add management roles to the Help Desk role group to create a group that matches the needs of your organization. For example, if you want members of the Help Desk role group to manage mailboxes, mail contacts, and mail-enabled users, you can assign the Mail Recipients management role to this role group.

The limitations on the Outlook Web App options that a member of the Help Desk role group can modify are enforced by the Exchange Web interface. Note, however, that if a member of the Help Desk role group has access to the EMS, he or she can modify any Outlook Web App option for any user. You therefore need to carefully consider who you make a member of the Help Desk role group and whether that member should be given access to the EMS.

Creating a Custom Role Group

In addition to using built-in role groups, you can create custom role groups to delegate specific permissions in an Exchange organization. You would do this if none of the built-in role groups offered the management roles and associated permissions you require. When you create a custom role group, you can assign management roles to the group. You can assign built-in management roles, but you also have the option of creating new management roles and adding them retrospectively. You also need to identify the management scope for any management role you assign or add. If you want to, you can change the scope of role assignments in a role group retrospectively.

You use the *New-RoleGroup* cmdlet in the EMS to create a role group. You need to know the management roles you want to assign to the role initially, and you need to add at least one management role and at least one member. For example, the following command creates a role group called Transport Role Group that is assigned to the Transport Rules management role. The role group is assigned to Kim Akers and Don Hall and can be managed by Kim Akers. The role group (which is also a universal security group) is created in the Exchange Security Groups AD DS container:

```
New-RoleGroup -Name "Transport Role Group" -Roles "Transport Rules" -Members "Kim
Akers", "Don Hall" -ManagedBy "Kim Akers"
```

Figure 6-3 shows the output of this command.

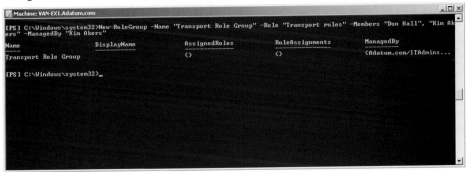

FIGURE 6-3 Creating a role group

The following command creates a role group called Melbourne Compliance Group that is assigned the Transport Rules and Journaling management roles and uses the Melbourne Recipients recipient scope:

```
New-RoleGroup -Name "Melbourne Compliance Group" -Roles "Transport Rules", "Journaling"
-CustomRecipientWriteScope "Melbourne Recipients"
```

> **MORE INFO** **NEW-ROLEGROUP**
>
> For more information about the *New-RoleGroup* cmdlet, see *http://technet.microsoft.com/ en-us/library/dd638181.aspx.*

Creating an Address Lists Management Role Group

The Address Lists management role enables administrators to create, modify, view, and remove address lists, global address lists, and offline address books in an organization. There is no built-in management role group for address list management, but it is a good idea to create a custom role group whose members can perform this function. To do this, you would enter the following in the EMS:

```
New-RoleGroup -Name "Address Lists Management " -Roles "Address Lists"
```

Adding a Role to a Role Group

To add a role to a role group, you create a role assignment. You can create a role assignment with no scope, with a predefined scope, with a recipient filter-based scope, with a configuration filter-based scope, or with an OU scope. The following command assigns the transport rules management role to the Glasgow Recipient Admins role group and scopes the assignment to the Marketing OU in the Adatum.com domain:

```
New-ManagementRoleAssignment -Name "Transport_Rules_Glasgow_Recipient_
Admins" -SecurityGroup "Glasgow Recipient Admins" -Role "Transport Rules"
-RecipientOrganizationalUnitScope Adatum.com/Marketing
```

Figure 6-4 shows the result of this command.

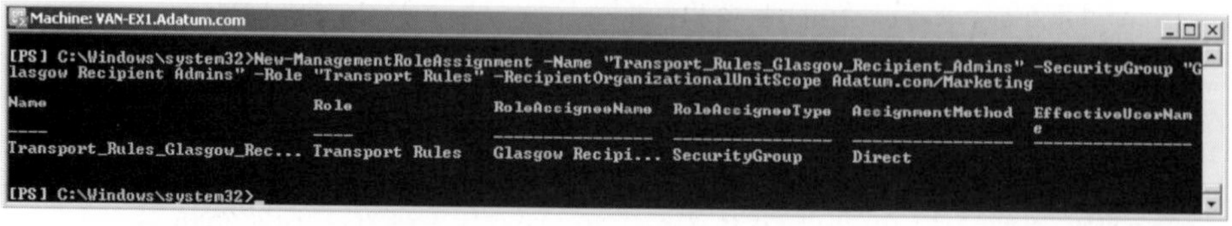

FIGURE 6-4 Adding the Transport Rules management role to the Glasgow Recipient Admins role group

As an alternative to using a scope, you can set a condition that ensures that the rights conferred by the role can be applied only to accounts located in a specific OU in a specific domain. For example, the following command assigns the Transport Rules role to the Brisbane Recipient Admins group but limits its use to accounts in the Marketing OU in the Brisbane .Adatum.com domain:

```
New-ManagementRoleAssignment -Name "Transport_Rules_Brisbane" -SecurityGroup "Brisbane
Recipient Admins" -Role "Transport Rules" -DomainOrganizationUnitRestriction Brisbane
.Adatum.com/Marketing
```

> **MORE INFO** **ADDING A ROLE TO A ROLE GROUP**
>
> For general discussion about adding a role to a role group, see *http://technet.microsoft .com/en-us/library/dd638202.aspx*.

> **MORE INFO** **NEW-MANAGEMENTROLEASSIGNMENT**
>
> For more information about the *New-ManagementRoleAssignment* cmdlet, see *http://technet.microsoft.com/en-us/library/dd335193.aspx*.

Direct User Role Assignment

You also can use direct role assignment to assign permissions. This assigns management roles directly to a user without using a role group or role assignment policy. Direct role assignments can be used when you need to provide a granular set of permissions to a specific user. You can create a role assignment directly between a user or universal security group and one or more roles. The role defines what tasks the user can perform. Role assignments can contain management scopes that define where the user can perform actions. For example, the following command assigns the Transport Rules role directly to the user Don Hall and limits its use to accounts in the Sales OU in the Adatum.com domain:

```
New-ManagementRoleAssignment –Name "Transport_Rules_Don" –Role "Transport
Rules" –User "Don Hall" –DomainOrganizationUnitRestriction Adatum.com/
Sales
```

However, Microsoft recommends that you avoid using direct role assignment because it is significantly more complicated to configure and manage. If a user leaves the organization, for example, you need to manually remove the user's assignments and add them to his or her replacement. If you have used ACLs to assign permissions, you know that it is not a good idea to assign permissions directly to users but that you should instead assign them to security groups and place users in these groups. The same is true of RBAC. You should assign roles to role groups, not to individual users.

 Quick Check

- What is the function of a management role assignment?

Quick Check Answer

- A management role assignment assigns a management role to a management group. It can also assign a management role directly to a user, but this is not recommended.

Creating a New Management Role

If none of the built-in management roles meet your needs, you can create a new management role and add it to your custom role group. You use the *New-ManagementRole* cmdlet in the EMS to create a custom management role based on one of the existing management roles. For example, the following command creates the management role MyManagementRole based on the Journaling built-in role:

```
New-ManagementRole –Name MyManagementRole –Parent Journaling
```

By default, the new management role inherits all the permissions assigned to the parent role. Note that a new management role must be based on a current management role and that the -Parent parameter is mandatory. To remove permissions from the role, you first obtain the permission you want to remove by using the *Get-ManagementRole* EMS cmdlet with a filter (Where) condition and then pipe this permission into the *Remove-ManagementRoleEntry* cmdlet to remove it. For example, the following command removes a Journaling permission from the MyManagementRole role:

```
Get-ManagementRoleEntry –Identity "MyManagementRole\*" | Where {$_.Name -NotLike "Get*"}
| Remove-ManagementRoleEntry
```

You can also use the *Get-ManagementRoleEntry* cmdlet more generally to determine which management role entries have been assigned to a specific custom management role. For example, the following command lists the management role entries assigned to the MyManagementRole role:

```
Get-ManagementRoleEntry –Identity "MyManagementRole\*"
```

You can use the *Add-ManagementRoleEntry* cmdlet to add management role entries to an existing management role. For example, the following command adds a new role entry for the *Set-Mailbox* cmdlet to the MyManagementRole management role. The role entry for the *Set-Mailbox* cmdlet is added exactly as it is configured in the Journaling parent role:

```
Add-ManagementRoleEntry "MyManagementRole\Set-Mailbox"
```

Creating a new management role, removing unnecessary management role entries, and adding role entries can be a complex procedure. Microsoft recommends that you use an existing role rather than create a new one whenever possible

> **MORE INFO**   **NEW-MANAGEMENTROLE, GET-MANAGEMENTROLE, REMOVE-MANAGEMENTROLEENTRY, AND ADD-MANAGEMENTROLEENTRY**
>
> For more information about the *New-ManagementRole* cmdlet, see *http://technet .microsoft.com/en-us/library/dd298073.aspx*. For more information about the *Get-ManagementRole* cmdlet, see *http://technet.microsoft.com/en-us/library/dd351125 .aspx*. For more information about the *Remove-ManagementRoleEntry* cmdlet, see *http://technet.microsoft.com/en-us/library/dd351170.aspx*. For more information about the *Add-ManagementRoleEntry* cmdlet, see *http://technet.microsoft.com/en-us/library/ dd351236.aspx*.

> **NOTE**   **NEW-MANAGEMENTROLEENTRY**
>
> The *New-ManagementRoleEntry* cmdlet is used to add scripts and non-Exchange cmdlets to existing top-level management roles. The scripts and cmdlets can then be used by the top-level role entries or any roles derived from the top-level roles. This, however, is beyond the scope of the 70-662 examination.

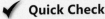 **Quick Check**

- What EMS cmdlet would you use to add a role to a role group?

Quick Check Answer

- *New-ManagementRoleAssignment*

Adding Members to a Role Group

To give a user the permissions that are granted by a role group, you need to add the user's mailbox as a member of the role group. You do this by using the *Add-RoleGroupMember* cmdlet in the EMS. You can also add members to a role group (as you can to any other security group) by using the Active Directory Users and Computers console, but you need to have domain administrator privileges (or equivalent) to use the AD DS tool.

For example, the following command adds the mailbox Don Hall to the Recipient Management role group (remember that you can also perform this operation by using the Active Directory Users and Computers console):

```
Add-RoleGroupMember -Identity "Recipient Management" -Member "Don Hall"
```

> **MORE INFO** **ADD-ROLEGROUPMEMBER**
>
> For more information about the *Add-RoleGroupMember* cmdlet, see *http://technet .microsoft.com/en-us/library/dd638207.aspx*.

Adding or Removing a Role Group Delegate

Management role group delegates are users or universal security groups that are members of the role group and can manage the role group. Adding or removing role group members or delegates to and from a role group rather than assigning roles directly to users or universal security groups is the recommended method of controlling who is granted the permissions associated with the role.

> **NOTE** **THE BYPASSSECURITYGROUPMANAGERCHECK SWITCH**
>
> A role group can be managed by the delegates on the role group or by users who are directly or indirectly assigned the role management role. If, however, a user is assigned the role management role but is not added as a delegate of the role group, that user must use the BypassSecurityGroupManagerCheck switch on the *Add-RoleGroupMember, Remove-RoleGroupMember, Update-RoleGroupMember,* and *Set-RoleGroup* cmdlets when managing a role group.

You use the ManagedBy parameter on the *Set-RoleGroup* EMS cmdlet to add a delegate to or remove a delegate from a role group. (If you view the properties of the group in Active Directory Users and Computers, the delegate list populates the Managed By area.) However, the ManagedBy parameter overwrites the entire delegate list. If you want to add delegates to the role group rather than replace the entire list of delegates, carry out the following procedure:

1. Store the role group delegate list in a variable. For example, the following command stores the delegates in the Recipient Management role group in the variable $RecipientRoleGroup:

   ```
   $RecpientRoleGroup = Get-RoleGroup "Recipient Management"
   ```

2. Add the delegate to the role group stored in the variable. For example, the following command adds the user Don Hall to the delegate list variable:

   ```
   $RecipientRoleGroup.ManagedBy += (Get-User "Don Hall").Identity
   ```

3. If you want to add more users or universal security groups, use similar commands to do so. Use the *Get-Group* cmdlet if you want to add a universal security group.

4. Apply the amended delegate list to the role group. The following command applies the list of delegates held in the $RecipientRoleGroup variable to the Recipient Management role group:

   ```
   Set-RoleGroup "Recipient Management" -ManagedBy $RecipientRoleGroup.ManagedBy
   ```

If you want to remove one or more delegates from a role group rather than replace the entire list of delegates, you follow a similar procedure. First, you store the current delegate list in a variable exactly as you did in the previous example. You then remove the delegate or delegates from the delegate list variable. For example, the following command removes the user Don Hall from the $RecipientRoleGroup variable:

```
$RecipientRoleGroup.ManagedBy -= (Get-User "Don Hall").Identity
```

When the variable stores the required list of delegates and only these delegates, use the *Set-RoleGroup* cmdlet as before to configure membership of the role group.

MORE INFO **SET-ROLEGROUP**

For more information about the *Set-RoleGroup* cmdlet, see *http://technet.microsoft.com/en-us/library/dd638182.aspx.*

EXAM TIP

Remember the difference between a role member and a role delegate. Both have access to the permissions granted by the role entries in the role group (for example, they can use the specified EMS cmdlets), but the delegate can manage the role group, while the member cannot.

 Quick Check

1. What EMS cmdlet do you use to add a member to a role group?

2. How do you add a delegate to a role group without deleting the current delegates in that role group?

Applying and Modifying Role Assignment Scopes

A management scope defines the objects that an assignment is permitted to manage. The assignment and its scope are applied to the members of the role group and define what those members can manage. If a predefined scope meets your requirements, you should apply it rather than create a new scope.

However, you can use the *New-ManagementScope* EMS cmdlet to create a new scope if you need to do so. You can use the *Set-ManagementScope* cmdlet to modify a scope, or you can apply a different scope to a role assignment by using the *Set-ManagementRoleAssignment* cmdlet. The appropriate assignment is identified using the *Get-ManagementRoleAssignment* cmdlet.

Suppose, for example, that you had assigned one or more roles to a role group called Canberra Sales Managers. Members of the Canberra Sales Managers group would then have permissions to carry out defined actions; for example, they might be able to configure properties of individual mailboxes. However, you want to ensure that members of the Canberra Sales Managers group can configure only mailboxes belonging to members of the Canberra Salespersons security group (and not, for example, mailboxes belonging to members of the Marketing Department). You would then use a command similar to the following to change the recipient scope for role assignments on the Canberra Sales Management role group to Canberra Salespersons:

```
Get-ManagementRoleAssignment -RoleAssignee "Canberra Sales Management" |
Set-ManagementRoleAssignment -CustomRecipientWriteScope "Canberra Salespersons"
```

By changing the scope of role assignments in a role group, you can change the objects that role group members can create, change, or remove. You might, for example, want to change an assignment named Recipient Admins so that roles granted through that assignment can be applied only to objects defined in the Adatum.com/RecAdmins scope. To do this, you would enter the following command, which assigns the Adatum.com/RecAdmins scope to the Recipient Admins role assignment:

```
Set-ManagementRoleAssignment -Identity "Recipient Admins" -RecipientRelativeWriteScope
adatum.com/RecAdmins
```

You can use a recipient filter to define a scope if no predefined scope meets your needs. For example, the following command creates a scope that includes all mailboxes within the Marketing OU in the Adatum.com domain:

```
New-ManagementScope -Name "Mailboxes in Marketing OU" -RecipientRestrictionFilter
{RecipientType -eq 'UserMailbox'} -RecipientRoot "Adatum.com/Marketing OU"
```

You can create a role assignment using a scope based on a recipient filter, a configuration filter, or an OU. The following command assigns the MyManagementRole role to the Marketing role group and applies the Mailboxes in Marketing OU scope:

```
New-ManagementRoleAssignment -Name "Adatum Marketing" -SecurityGroup "Marketing"
-Role "MyManagementRole" -CustomRecipientWriteScope "Mailboxes in Marketing OU"
```

You can specify a list of servers to be included in a scope. For example, the following command creates a scope called Selected Hub Transport Servers that includes the Hub Transport servers Server01, Server02, Server03, and Server04:

```
New-ManagementScope -Name "Selected Hub Transport Servers" -ServerList Server01,
Server02,Server03,Server04
```

You can use the *Set-ManagementScope* cmdlet in the EMS if you want to modify an existing scope rather than create a new one. The following command adds the Hub Transport server Server05 to the Selected Hub Transport Servers scope:

```
Set-ManagementScope -Identity "Selected Hub Transport Servers" -ServerList Server01,
Server02,Server03,Server04,Server05
```

EXAM TIP

Remember that the ServerList parameter associated with the *Set-ManagementScope* cmdlet is not additive and that you need to specify all servers, not just the server or servers you are adding. Watch out for answers in the examination that specifies only the additional servers.

To obtain details about a management scope or to obtain a list of scopes that have been configured in the Exchange organization, you use the *Get-ManagementScope* EMS cmdlet. For example, the following command returns detailed information about the management scope Selected Hub Transport Servers:

```
Get-ManagementScope -Identity "Selected Hub Transport Servers" | FL
```

> *MORE INFO* **MANAGEMENT ROLE ASSIGNMENT AND MANAGEMENT SCOPE CMDLETS**
>
> For more information about the *Get-ManagementRoleAssignment* cmdlet, see *http://technet.microsoft.com/en-us/library/dd351024.aspx*. For more information about the *Set-ManagementRoleAssignment* cmdlet, see *http://technet.microsoft.com/en-us/library/dd335173.aspx*. For more information about the *New-ManagementRoleAssignment* cmdlet, see *http://technet.microsoft.com/en-us/library/dd335193.aspx*. For more information about the *New-ManagementScope* cmdlet, see *http://technet.microsoft.com/en-us/library/dd335137.aspx*. For more information about the *Set-ManagementScope* cmdlet, see *http://technet.microsoft.com/en-us/library/dd297996.aspx*. For more information about the *Get-ManagementScope* cmdlet, see *http://technet.microsoft.com/en-us/library/dd298180.aspx*.

EXAM TIP

Remember how RBAC management role groups work:

- Role entries define individual permissions. For example, if a role entry is an EMS cmdlet and its parameters, role holders can use that cmdlet.

- Roles are made up of one or more role entries. Role holders are granted the permissions defined by the role entries contained in the role they hold.

- Exchange Server 2010 has a number of built-in roles. You can create a custom role based on a built-in role and then remove role entries from or add them to the custom role.

- Roles are assigned to role groups through role assignments.

- Role assignments can be limited by management scopes. A role assigned to a role group defines what role holders (members of a role group) can do. A scope defines what they can do it to.

- Roles can be granted directly to users rather than role groups. This, however, is bad practice and should be avoided.

- Exchange Server 2010 has a number of built-in role groups. You can also create custom role groups and assign roles to them.

- When you add members or delegates to a role group, they become role holders and are granted all the permissions defined by the role entries associated with the roles assigned to the role group. Any scope applied to the role assignment will limit the entities on which these permissions can be used.

- Role group members can apply the permissions they obtain as role holders. Role group delegates can apply the permissions and also manage the role group.

 Quick Check

- A management role is a collection of management role entries that define what a role holder can do. What defines the entities that the role holder can do it to?

Quick Check Answer

- A management scope.

Using Management Role Assignment Policies

Management role assignment policies consist of roles that control what a user can do with his or her mailbox or distribution groups. Microsoft specifies that you should use role groups to assign permissions to administrators and specialist users and role assignment policies to assign permissions to users. When you create a role assignment policy, it defines everything a user can do with his or her mailbox. For example, you could allow a user to change the display name, set up voice mail, and configure Inbox rules.

Every user with an Exchange Server 2010 mailbox (including administrators) is given a role assignment policy by default. You can define the default role assignment policy to be assigned, choose what this policy should include, and override the default for certain mailboxes. If appropriate, you can choose not to assign any role assignment policies by default. Typically, you configure permissions for users to manage their mailbox and distribution group options by assigning a user to a role assignment policy.

One or more users can be associated with a role assignment policy, which is in turn assigned one or more role assignments. These assignments link the role assignment policy with one or more end-user roles that define what the user can configure on his or her mailbox. Role assignment policies have built-in scopes that restrict the scope of assignments to the user's own mailbox or distribution groups.

> **NOTE REGULAR OR DELEGATING ROLE ASSIGNMENTS**
>
> You can assign a management role using either regular or delegating role assignments. Regular role assignments grant the permissions provided by the role to the role assignee. Delegating role assignments grant the role assignee the ability to assign the role to other role assignees.

> **NOTE ROLE MANAGEMENT**
>
> Roles, role assignments, and role groups can be managed by administrators who have been assigned the Role Management management role. Assignees of the federated sharing management role who have delegating role assignments can assign the role to other role assignees. Regular assignees are granted only the permissions provided by the role.

> **MORE INFO MANAGEMENT ROLE ASSIGNMENT POLICIES**
>
> For more information about management role assignment policies, see *http://technet .microsoft.com/en-us/library/dd638100.aspx*.

Configuring Management Role Assignment Policies

The Exchange Server 2010 default role assignment policy provides end users with the most commonly used permissions. In most Exchange organizations, the default management role assignment policy meets all requirements. However, you can, if you need to, modify the default configuration by altering the default management role assignment policy. To view the default management role assignment policy configuration, you use the *Get-ManagementRoleAssignment* cmdlet in the EMS. For example, the following command lists all the management roles assigned to the default role assignment policy:

```
Get-ManagementRoleAssignment -RoleAssignee "Default Role Assignment Policy"
```

Figure 6-5 shows the output from this command.

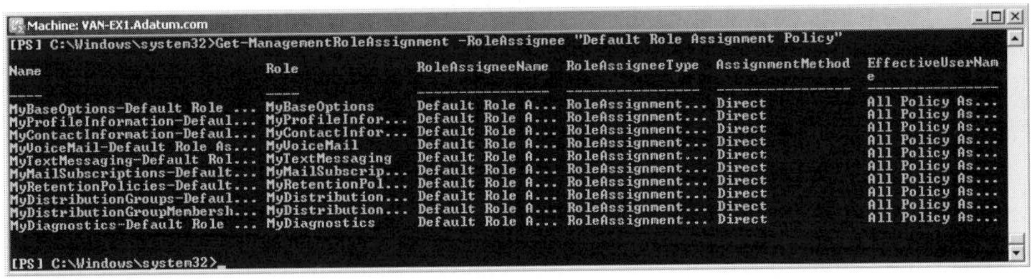

FIGURE 6-5 Management roles assigned to the default role assignment policy

To view the details of each management role, you use the *Get-ManagementRole* cmdlet in the EMS. For example, the following command displays all management role entries associated with the MyBaseOptions management role:

```
Get-ManagementRole MyBaseOptions | FL
```

This command produces a very detailed output. Figure 6-6 shows the portion of this output that is probably of most interest.

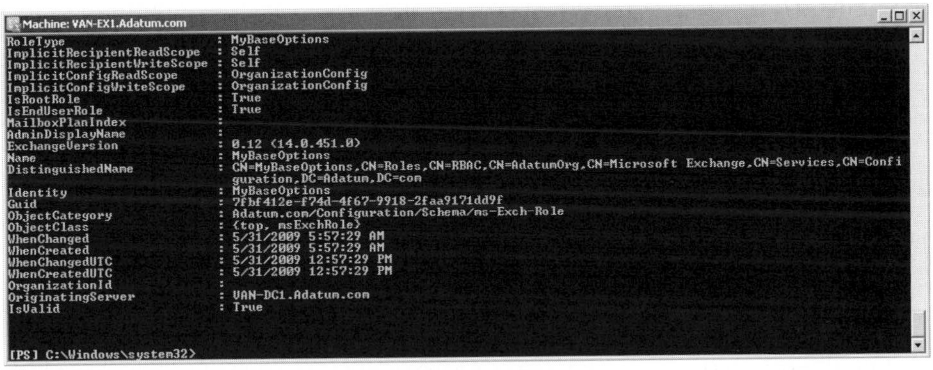

FIGURE 6-6 Details of the MyBaseOptions management role

MORE INFO *GET-MANAGEMENTROLEASSIGNMENT* **AND** *GET-MANAGEMENTROLE*

For more information about the *Get-ManagementRoleAssignment* cmdlet, see *http://technet.microsoft.com/en-us/library/dd351024.aspx*. For more information about the *Get-ManagementRole* cmdlet, see *http://technet.microsoft.com/en-us/library/dd351125.aspx*.

MORE INFO **MANAGEMENT ROLE ASSIGNMENT POLICIES**

For more information about management role assignment policies, see *http://technet.microsoft.com/en-us/library/dd638100.aspx*.

Lesson Summary

- RBAC enables you to align the roles you assign to users and administrators to the roles they hold within your organization.

- A management role holds a group of management role entries, which define the specific tasks that the members of a role group can perform.

- You can assign management roles to management role groups using management role assignments. The management role entries associated with the management roles define the permissions granted to members and delegates of the management role groups.

- You can add users or universal security groups to management role groups as members or delegates. Both members and delegates are granted all the permissions associated with the management role entries, but delegates can also manage the management group.

- A management role scope defines the objects to which the permissions granted through membership of a management role group can be applied.

Lesson Review

You can use the following questions to test your knowledge of the information in Lesson 1, "Role Based Access Control." The questions are also available on the companion CD if you prefer to review them in electronic form.

> **NOTE ANSWERS**
>
> Answers to these questions and explanations of why each answer choice is correct or incorrect are located in the "Answers" section at the end of the book.

1. You have created a scope named Hub Transport Scope that includes only the Hub Transport servers Hub01, Hub02, and Hub03. Users who are assigned management roles that have this scope can perform only tasks allowed by the role against these servers. You configure a new Hub Transport server called Hub04 and want to add it to the scope. What command do you enter in the EMS?

   A. New-ManagementScope –Name "HubTransport Scope" –ServerList Hub01,Hub02,Hub03,Hub04

   B. New-ManagementScope –Name "HubTransport Scope" –ServerList Hub04

   C. Set-ManagementScope –Identity "HubTransport Scope" –ServerList Hub01, Hub02, Hub03, Hub04

   D. Set-ManagementScope –Identity "HubTransport Scope" –ServerList Hub04

2. Jeff Hay is a delegate of the built-in Help Desk role group. Only the default roles are associated with this role group, and no management roles have been added or removed. What does delegate membership of this role group enable Jeff to do? (Choose all that apply.)

   A. Configure mailbox size.

   B. Manage mailbox databases.

   C. Modify a user's display name when that user is not permitted to modify his or her own display name.

   D. Manage membership of the role group.

   E. View and modify the Microsoft Office Outlook Web App options of any user in the organization.

3. You have created a custom management role based on the Transport Rules built-in management role, but you do not want users assigned to that role to perform certain tasks assigned to its parent role. What EMS cmdlets would you use to modify the custom management role by removing tasks that role members are permitted to carry out? (Choose all that apply; each correct answer forms part of the solution.)

   A. *Add-ManagementRoleEntry*

   B. *Remove-ManagementRoleEntry*

   C. *New-ManagementRoleAssignment*

   D. *New-ManagementRole*

   E. *Get-ManagementRole*

4. You want to create a new management role named MyManagementRole based on the built-in Journaling management role. What command should you enter in the EMS?

   A. *New-ManagementRole –Name MyManagementRole –Parent Journaling*

   B. *New-ManagementRole –Name Journaling –Parent MyManagementRole*

   C. *New-ManagementRoleAssignment –Name MyManagementRole –Parent Journaling*

   D. *New-ManagementRoleAssignment –Name Journaling –Parent MyManagementRole*

5. You want Kim Akers to be able to create or modify recipients within your Exchange organization and to configure compliance features, including retention policy tags, message classifications, and transport rules. You do not want to give her any administrative privileges other than those listed. To which built-in role groups should you add her? (Choose all that apply; each correct answer forms part of the solution.)

   A. Recipient Management

   B. Organization Management

   C. Public Folder Management

   D. Server Management

   E. Records Management

Lesson 2: Configuring Federated Sharing

This lesson defines federated sharing and describes how it works. It looks at federated sharing components, availability information access, federated message delivery, federated trusts, and organizational relationships and sharing policies. Finally, the lesson looks at how you use RBAC to assign the federated sharing role to management role groups, universal security groups, and individual users.

> **After this lesson, you will be able to:**
> - Describe federated sharing and list the components it requires.
> - Explain how federated sharing and federated message delivery work.
> - Configure a federated trust.
> - Configure organizational relationships and sharing policies.
> - Assign the federated sharing role.
>
> **Estimated lesson time: 45 minutes**

Implementing Federated Sharing

With federated sharing, you can use federation technologies to establish trusted relationships and hence enable secure Internet communications between organizations. This requires that you use Microsoft Federation Gateway as a trust broker, that each participating organization establish and manage its trust, and that federated sharing is supported for all messaging clients. To establish a federation trust, organizations exchange security certificates with public keys with each other or with a trusted third party and use those certificates to authenticate and secure all interorganizational communications.

The Microsoft Federation Gateway

The *Microsoft Federation Gateway* is an identity service that runs over the Internet and functions as a trust broker for federated sharing. It provides a broker service to establish the communication between the organizations but does not authenticate individual users or store any user account information from either organization.

To enable federated sharing, you need to register your organization with the Federation Gateway and then configure a federated sharing relationship with another organization that also registers with the Federation Gateway. The Federation Gateway then acts as a hub for all connections that the organizations make with each other, For example, Client Access servers in each organization connect through the Federation Gateway to exchange availability information and enable calendar sharing. These Client Access servers use the federated trust that you configure with the Federation Gateway to verify you partner's Client Access servers and to encrypt traffic sent between the organizations. Users can also send encrypted and authenticated email messages between the organizations.

In federated sharing, each organization needs only to manage its trust relationship with the Federation Gateway and its own user accounts. After an organization establishes a trust relationship with the Federation Gateway, you can identify other trusted organizations and the types of information you want to share with them. When you enable federation sharing, all interorganizational communication is sent through your organization's Exchange Server 2010 servers. This traffic is transparent to the messaging clients so that federated sharing works with any client that can connect to Exchange Server 2010, including Microsoft Outlook Web Access, Outlook 2003, Outlook 2007, and Outlook 2010.

> **MORE INFO FEDERATION GATEWAY**
>
> For more information about the Federation Gateway, see *http://msdn.microsoft.com/ en-us/library/cc287610.aspx*. For information about how to connect to and use the Federation Gateway, see *http://msdn.microsoft.com/en-us/library/dd164396.aspx*.

Federated Sharing Requirements

To implement federated sharing, you need to establish and configure the following components in Exchange Server 2010:

- **A federation trust**   A *federation trust* configures the Federation Gateway as a federation partner with the Exchange Server organization, which enables Exchange Server 2010 Web Services on the Client Access servers to validate all Federation Gateway authentication requests. You establish a federation trust by submitting your organization's public key and a valid X.509 certificate issued by a Certificate Authority (CA) trusted by Windows Live Domain Services to the Federation Gateway and downloading the Federation Gateway public key and certificate.

- **An organization identifier**   An *organization identifier* defines what authoritative domains in an Exchange organization are available for federation. If your organization supports multiple SMTP domains, you can include one or all of your domain names in your organization identifier. Users can participate in Federated Sharing only if they have email addresses in the domains that you configure with the organization identifier. The first domain you specify with the organization identifier is known as the account namespace. Federation Gateway creates federated user identifiers within this namespace when the Client Access server requests a delegation token for a user. This process is transparent to the Exchange Server organization.

> **NOTE OBTAINING THE ORGANIZATION IDENTIFIER OF AN EXTERNAL ORGANIZATION**
>
> The organization identifier of your own organization consists of the authoritative domains that you specify when configuring federated sharing. To obtain the organization identifier of the external organization in a federation partnership, you use the *Get-FederationInformation* EMS cmdlet. This is discussed later in this lesson.

- **Sharing relationships with the organizations with which your organization shares data** In your Exchange Server organization, you configure a sharing relationship that defines a partnership for federated sharing with an external Exchange organization. You specify the target domains configured as the organization identifier in the external Exchange organization. When you configure a sharing relationship, you can define what information your users can share with external users and which users can participate in the relationship.

> **NOTE THE FEDERATION GATEWAY AND MICROSOFT WINDOWS LIVE**
>
> Although the Federation Gateway uses Windows Live as the authentication mechanism, it does not share any user accounts with Windows Live.

 Quick Check

- What is required for your organization to set up a sharing relationship with an external Exchange organization?

Quick Check Answer

- Your organization needs to have established a trust relationship with the Federation Gateway by using a valid X.509 certificate issued by a CA trusted by Windows Live Domain Services. The external Exchange organization needs to have established a similar trust relationship with the Federation Gateway.

Accessing Availability Information

You can configure a sharing relationship that enables users from one organization to view availability information for users in another organization. Suppose, for example, that a User in Blue Sky Airlines wants to set up a meeting with a user at Consolidated Messenger and issues a meeting request. The following occurs:

1. The meeting request is sent to the Exchange Web Service on the Client Access server at Blue Sky Airlines.

2. The Blue Sky Airlines Client Access server checks with a BlueSkyAirlines.com domain controller to verify that a sharing relationship is configured with ConsolidatedMessenger.com and that the user has permission to request availability information using the sharing relationship.

3. If both verifications succeed, the Blue Sky Airlines Client Access server connects to the Federation Gateway and requests a security token for the Blue Sky Airlines user. Because you have configured BlueSkyAirlines.com in the organization identifier, the Federation Gateway issues the token.

4. The Blue Sky Airlines Client Access server sends a request for the availability information for the Consolidated Messenger user to the Consolidated Messenger Client Access server and includes the security token with the request.

5. The Consolidated Messenger Client Access server validates the security token and then checks with a domain controller in the ConsolidatedMessenger.com domain to verify that the organization has a sharing relationship with BlueSkyAirlines.com.

6. The Consolidated Messenger Client Access server retrieves the user's availability information from the Mailbox server that holds the user's mailbox.

7. The Consolidated Messenger Client Access server sends the availability information to the Blue Sky Airlines Client Access server.

8. The Blue Sky Airlines Client Access server provides the availability information to the Blue Sky Airlines user.

Federated Message Delivery

When you configure a sharing relationship, you can enable federated message delivery. This permits users from one organization to send encrypted, authenticated email messages to users in another organization. When, for example, a user in Blue Sky Airlines sends such an email message to a user in Consolidated Messenger, the following occurs (note that the first three steps are the same as those in the previous procedure):

1. The message is sent through a Blue Sky Airlines Mailbox server to a Blue Sky Airlines Hub Transport server.

2. The Blue Sky Airlines Hub Transport server accesses a BlueSkyAirlines.com domain controller to verify that a sharing relationship is configured with ConsolidatedMessenger.com and that the user has permission to send messages across the sharing relationship.

3. If both verifications succeed, the Blue Sky Airlines Hub Transport server connects to the Federation Gateway and requests a security token for the Blue Sky Airlines user. Because BlueSkyAirlines.com is configured in the organization identifier, the Federation Gateway issues the token.

4. The Blue Sky Airlines Hub Transport server encrypts the message using a key included in the security token and sends the message to the Consolidated Messenger Hub Transport server. The security token is encrypted using the Federation Gateway public key and is sent to the Consolidated Messenger Hub Transport server.

5. The Consolidated Messenger Hub Transport server validates the security token and checks with a ConsolidatedMessenger.com domain controller to verify that the organization has a sharing relationship with BlueSkyAirlines.corn.

6. The Consolidated Messenger Hub Transport server decrypts the security token and extracts the encryption key. It then decrypts the message and forwards it to the Consolidated Messenger user's Mailbox server.

Configuring a Federation Trust

Before you can configure a sharing relationship with another organization, both organizations must configure a federation trust with the Federation Gateway. You need to obtain an X.509 certificate from an external CA that is trusted by Windows Live Domain Services and hence by the Federation Gateway server. This certificate requires a private and public key pair that can act as both a client and a server certificate and that can sign and decrypt delegation tokens issued by the Federation Gateway. The certificate requires a Subject Key Identifier, and it must be deployed on all Exchange Server 2010 Client Access servers. If you want to, you can reuse an existing trusted certificate already installed on the Client Access server.

You next need to configure all SMTP domain names you want to use for federated sharing as authoritative accepted domains in your Exchange organization.

Federated sharing requires that servers from other organizations can resolve your servers' names on the Internet. You also need to configure DNS with a text (TXT) resource record that provides proof of ownership for your domain name. The Federation Gateway uses the proof-of-ownership record to ensure that your servers are authoritative for the domain name you provide.

To create this proof-of-ownership record, you need to obtain the application identifier created when you configure a federation trust. You can obtain this identifier by using the *Get-FederationTrust* cmdlet in the EMS. For example, the following command retrieves properties (including identifiers) of federation trusts configured for the organization:

```
Get-FederationTrust | FL
```

To create a new TXT record on a DNS server, you use the DNS Microsoft Management Console snap-in. Figure 6-7 shows the dialog box that enables you to create a text record. The DNS server also needs to have Internet connectivity to reach the Federation Gateway.

To use the EMC to create a federation trust, click Organization Configuration in the Console tree and then click New Federation Trust in the Action pane. This starts the New Federation Trust Wizard, shown in Figure 6-8. The EMC does not permit you to specify a name for the trust. The trust receives the name "Microsoft Federation Gateway" by default. You can browse for the *thumbprint* of a trusted third-party certificate that can validate the trust. A thumbprint is the digest of the certificate data and uniquely identifies a certificate. Click New to create the trust. Click Finish on the Completion page to close the wizard.

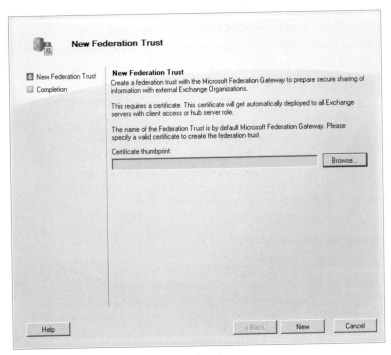

FIGURE 6-7 Creating a TXT record

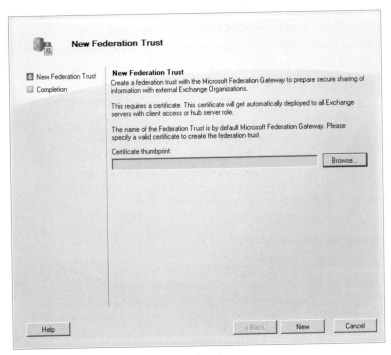

FIGURE 6-8 The New Federation Trust Wizard

You can create a federation trust in the EMS by using the *New-FederationTrust* cmdlet. However, you must first obtain the thumbprint of a valid certificate. You can use the *Get-ExchangeCertificate* EMS cmdlet to obtain the certificate thumbprint. Figure 6-9 shows two certificate thumbprints on the VAN-EX1 server. It is a good idea to redirect the output of this command to a text file so that you can paste the thumbprint into the command to create a new federation trust. Note also that the certificate whose thumbprint you choose must be exportable. You need to obtain such a certificate from a trusted third-party CA. A locally generated self-signed certificate cannot be used for this purpose.

FIGURE 6-9 Obtaining certificate thumbprints

To create a federation trust named Microsoft Federation Gateway using the thumbprint of an exportable certificate, you enter the following command:

```
New-FederationTrust -Name "Microsoft Federation Gateway" -Thumbprint <thumbprint>
```

> **NOTE INTERNET ACCESS**
>
> Your Exchange Server 2010 Client Access server requires Internet access to create a federation trust. The domain used for establishing a federation trust must be resolvable from the Internet.

Adding a Domain to a Federation Trust and Modifying the Trust Properties

If you need to configure a secondary domain with a federated organization identifier—in effect, to add it to the federated trust—the domain must exist as an accepted domain in the Exchange organization. If this condition is met, you can use the *Add-FederatedDomain* cmdlet in the EMS to add a specified domain to an existing federation trust. For example, the following command adds the domain mail.adatum.com:

```
Add-FederatedDomain -DomainName mail.adatum.com
```

As well as adding a domain to an existing federated trust, you can configure the properties of the trust using the *Set-FederationTrust* EMS cmdlet. For example, you might choose to change the certificate that you use to verify the trust, possibly because the current certificate is due to expire.

This is a multistage process. First, you use the Thumbprint parameter to specify the thumbprint of the X.509 certificate to be configured as the next certificate to be used to verify the federation trust. After the certificate is deployed on all Hub Transport and Client Access servers in the Exchange organization, you use the PublishFederationCertificate switch to configure the trust to use this certificate.

The following command configures the federation trust named Microsoft Federation Gateway to use the certificate with the thumbprint AC00F12CBA8358253F412FD0984B5CCAF2AF4F27 as the next certificate:

```
Set-FederationTrust -Identity "Microsoft Federation Gateway" -Thumbprint
AC00F12CBA8358253F412FD0984B5CCAF2AF4F27
```

You next need to verify that the certificate is available on all Hub Transport and Client Access servers. On each of these servers, you enter the *Test-FederationTrust* EMS cmdlet without parameters. The cmdlet confirms that connection to the Federation Gateway is established and that communication between the local Client Access or Hub Transport server and the Federation Gateway is working correctly. It checks that certificates, including the next certificate, are valid and can be used with the Federation Gateway, and it requests a security token from the Federation Gateway and ensures that the token can be properly retrieved and used.

Your final step is to configure the trust to use the next certificate as the current certificate. For example, to configure the federation trust Microsoft Federation Gateway to use the certificate configured as the next certificate as its current certificate, you enter the following command:

```
Set-FederationTrust -Identity "Microsoft Federation Gateway"
-PublishFederationCertificate
```

> **MORE INFO   ADD-FEDERATEDDOMAIN, SET-FEDERATIONTRUST, AND *TEST-FEDERATIONTRUST***
>
> For more information about the *Add-FederatedDomain* cmdlet, see *http://technet .microsoft.com/en-us/library/dd351208.aspx*. For more information about the *Set-FederationTrust* cmdlet, see *http://technet.microsoft.com/en-us/library/dd298034.aspx*. For more information about the *Test-FederationTrust* cmdlet, see *http://technet.microsoft .com/en-us/library/dd979787.aspx*.

Configuring Organizational Relationships

After you create the federated trust, your next step is to configure an organizational relationship. Organizational relationships determine the organizations (or domains) with which you share information and what types of information you share.

To configure organizational relationships in the EMC, carry out the following procedure:

1. Click the Organization Management node and then click New Organizational Relationship in the Action pane. The New Organizational Relationship Wizard Introduction page appears, as shown in Figure 6-10.

2. On the Introduction page, specify a descriptive name, enable or disable the organizational relationship, enable the sharing of free or busy information, specify a distribution group whose members will make their free or busy information available,

enable federated delivery, and specify the SMTP address of a remote mailbox for federated delivery. If you enable the sharing of free or busy information, you can configure the following levels of access:

- No Calendar sharing

- Calendar sharing with free or busy information only

- Calendar sharing with free or busy information, plus subject and location

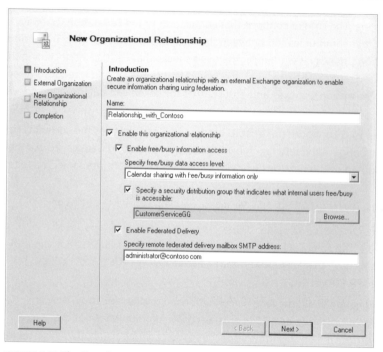

FIGURE 6-10 The New Organizational Relationship Wizard Introduction page

3. Click Next. On the External Organization page, shown in Figure 6-11, you can configure the Exchange Server 2010 Client Access server to discover the external organization's configuration information automatically. When you do this, the Exchange server contacts the Federation Gateway to locate this information. Alternatively, you can enter the external organization's information manually, including its federated domain names, application uniform resource identifier, and Autodiscover end points.

> **MORE INFO** **THE AUTODISCOVER SERVICE AND AUTODISCOVER END POINTS**
>
> For more information about the Autodiscover service and the use of Autodiscover endpoints, download the white paper at *http://technet.microsoft.com/en-us/library/ bb332063(EXCHG.80).aspx*. Although this white paper was written for Exchange Server 2007, it is highly informative and relevant to exchange Server 2010.

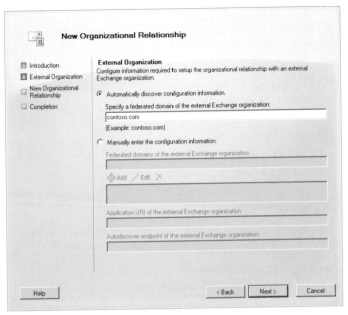

FIGURE 6-11 The New Organizational Relationship Wizard External Organization page

4. Click Next. On the New Organizational Relationship page of the wizard, shown in Figure 6-12, you can review the summary of the organizational relationship and then click New to create the organizational relationship. You can click Finish on the Completion page to close the wizard or click Back and review your settings if a problem occurred when creating the relationship.

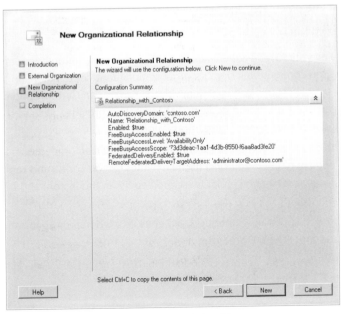

FIGURE 6-12 The New Organizational Relationship page

To use the EMS to create an organization relationship, you must use the *Get-FederationInformation* cmdlet to identify the domain names provided for the external organization. This cmdlet accesses the Federated Organization Identifier (OrgID), which defines which of the authoritative accepted domains configured in the Exchange organization are enabled for federation. You pipe the output from the *Get-FederationInformation* cmdlet into the *New-OrganizationRelationship* cmdlet, which attempts to automatically discover configuration information from the external organization and, if successful, creates the organizational relationship as specified.

The following command creates an organization relationship with the Contoso organization, enabling free or busy information and specifying that the requesting organization receives free or busy, subject, and location information from the target organization:

```
Get-FederationInformation -DomainName Contoso.com | New-OrganizationRelationship -Name
"Contoso" -FreeBusyAccessEnabled $true -FreeBusyAccessLevel -LimitedDetails
```

When you have created an organizational relationship, you can use the *Set-OrganizationRelationship* cmdlet to change its settings. For example, the following command disables the organization relationship with Contoso:

```
Set-OrganizationRelationship -Identity "Contoso" -Enabled $false
```

You can discover information about an organizational relationship by using the *Get-FederatedOrganizationIdentifier* EMS cmdlet to retrieve the Microsoft Exchange Server 2010 organization's federated organization identifier and related details, such as federated domains, organization contact, and status. You can obtain details about the status of federated domains from the Federation Gateway by including the IncludeExtendedDomainInfo parameter, such as the following:

```
Get-FederatedOrganizationIdentifier -IncludeExtendedDomainInfo
```

You can use the *Set-FederatedOrganizationIdentifier* EMS cmdlet to configure federated organization identifiers. You configure a federated organization identifier to create an account namespace for your Exchange organization with the Federation Gateway and enable federation so that you can make use of the facilities that federation provides, such as sharing calendars or contacts and accessing free or busy information.

Typically, an organization's federated organization identifier is created using the organization's primary domain name. Additional domain names can be added and removed later by using the *Add-FederatedDomain* cmdlet (described earlier in this lesson) and the *Remove-FederatedDomain* cmdlet.

For example, the following command configures and enables a federated organization identifier for the Adatum.com Exchange organization:

```
Set-FederatedOrganizationIdentifier -DelegationFederationTrust "Microsoft Federation
Gateway" -AccountNamespace "Contoso.com" -Enabled $true
```

MORE INFO **ORGANIZATIONAL RELATIONSHIP CMDLETS**

For more information about the *Get-FederationInformation* cmdlet, see *http://technet
.microsoft.com/en-us/library/dd351221.aspx*. For more information about the *New-
OrganizationRelationship* cmdlet, see *http://technet.microsoft.com/en-us/library/ee332357
.aspx*. For more information about the *Set-OrganizationRelationship* cmdlet, see *http://
technet.microsoft.com/en-us/library/ee332326.aspx*. For more information about the
Get-FederatedOrganizationIdentifier cmdlet, see *http://technet.microsoft.com/en-us/
library/dd298149.aspx*. For more information about the *Set-FederatedOrganizationIdentifier*
cmdlet, see *http://technet.microsoft.com/en-us/library/dd351037.aspx*.

Configuring Sharing Policies

Sharing policies define which users in your organization can use the organizational
relationships to share information with other organizations and what types of information
those users can share. The default sharing policy is created when you install Exchange Server
2010. This policy enables sharing with all domains but enables only calendar sharing with free
or busy information. It is assigned to no mailboxes.

If you want to enable users to participate in federated sharing, you can add their mailboxes
to the default sharing policy or create a new sharing policy. When you create a new sharing
policy, you configure the domain name for the external domain and the sharing actions that
are permitted under the policy. Sharing options include the following:

- Calendar sharing with free or busy information only
- Calendar sharing with free or busy information, subject, and location
- Calendar sharing with free or busy information, subject, location, and body
- Contacts sharing
- Calendar sharing with free or busy information only and contacts sharing
- Calendar sharing with free or busy information, subject, and location and contacts
  sharing
- Calendar sharing with free or busy information, subject, location, and body and
  contacts sharing

Configuring a sharing policy requires that a federation trust has been created between
your Exchange 2010 organization and the Federation Gateway and that the federated
organization identifier is configured. Recipients from an external domain can access your
users' information only if they have an Exchange 2010 organization and their domain is
federated. To use the EMC to configure sharing policies, carry out the following procedure:

1. Click Mailbox under Organization Configuration in the Console tree.
2. In the Result pane, click the Sharing Policies tab and then right-click the sharing policy
   you want to configure and click Properties.

3. On the General tab of the sharing policy Properties dialog box, shown in Figure 6-13, you can change the policy name, add one or more external domains, specify the sharing policy for each domain, and enable or disable the policy.

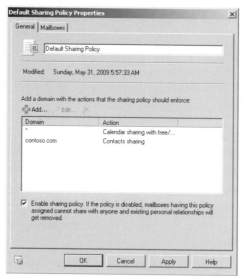

FIGURE 6-13 The General tab of the sharing policy Properties dialog box

4. On the Mailboxes tab shown in Figure 6-14, you can add or remove the mailboxes in your organization to which this sharing policy applies.

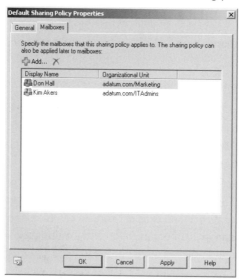

FIGURE 6-14 The Mailboxes tab of the sharing policy Properties dialog box

5. Click OK to apply your policy changes and close the dialog box.

You can use the *New-SharingPolicy* cmdlet in the EMS to create a sharing policy and the *Set-SharingPolicy* cmdlet to modify a policy. For example, the following command creates a sharing policy called Blue Sky Airlines for the mail.BlueSkyAirlines.com domain, which is external to your organization. This policy allows users in the mail.BlueSkyAirlines.com domain to see detailed free or busy information and contacts. By default, the policy is enabled:

```
New-SharingPolicy -Name "Blue Sky Airlines" -Domains 'mail.BlueSkyAirlines.com:
CalendarSharingFreeBusyDetail, ContactsSharing'
```

The following command modifies a sharing policy named Contoso for the contoso.com domain, which is external to your organization, so that users in the Contoso domain can see your users' availability (free or busy) information:

```
Set-SharingPolicy -Identity Contoso -Domains 'contoso.com:
CalendarSharingFreeBusySimple, Contacts'
```

To get details about a sharing policy, you can use the *Get-SharingPolicy* EMS cmdlet. For example, the following command displays all the available information for the sharing policy Blue Sky Airlines:

```
Get-SharingPolicy "Blue Sky Airlines" | FL
```

If you no longer require a sharing policy, you can remove it using the *Remove-SharingPolicy* EMS cmdlet. Note that you cannot remove a sharing policy that has mailboxes assigned to it and that you need to assign them to another policy first. The following command removes the sharing policy Blue Sky Airlines and suppresses the requirement that you enter Y to confirm that you want to remove the policy:

```
Remove-SharingPolicy -Identity "Blue Sky Airlines" -Confirm:$false
```

Configuring Mailboxes to Use Sharing Policies

You can configure mailboxes to use sharing policies by using the *Get-Mailbox* and *Set-Mailbox* EMS cmdlets. A command based on the *Get-Mailbox* cmdlet obtains the mailbox or mailboxes to which you want to apply the sharing policy by using the criteria you define (for example, all mailboxes that are associated with the Sales Department). You pipe the output from this command into a command based on the *Set-Mailbox* cmdlet, which applies the sharing policy.

For example, the following command configures all mailboxes associated with the Marketing Department to use the Adatum Marketing federated sharing policy:

```
Get-Mailbox -Filter {Department -eq "Marketing"}
```

You can also use a command based on the *Get-Mailbox* cmdlet to list the mailboxes that use a specific sharing policy. To give a convenient display, you can pipe the result into the format-table function. For example, the following command returns all the mailboxes in an organization that are provisioned to use the Adatum Marketing sharing policy and lists them as email addresses:

```
Get-Mailbox | Where {$._SharingPolicy -eq "Adatum Marketing" } | format-table Alias,
EmailAddress
```

> **MORE INFO** **GET-MAILBOX AND SET-MAILBOX**
>
> For more information about the *Get-Mailbox* cmdlet, see *http://technet.microsoft.com/en-us/library/bb123685.aspx*. For more information about the *Set-Mailbox* cmdlet, see *http://technet.microsoft.com/en-us/library/bb123981.aspx*.

Sharing Information with Users in an External Organization

The sharing policies you configure determine what your users can share with users from another organization. The mailboxes to which you apply the sharing policy determine which users can share this information.

Suppose, for example, that you create a sharing policy named Fabrikam01 with the external domain fabrikam.com, and this permits your users to share calendar free or busy information, subject, and location. You apply this policy to all the mailboxes belonging to users in the Marketing Department.

Suppose you create a sharing policy named Fabrikam02 with the same external domain, and this permits your users to share calendar free or busy information only and contacts. You apply this policy to all the mailboxes belonging to users in the Sales Department.

Don Hall, a user in the Marketing Department, can now send sharing invitations through his email client to users in the fabrikam.com domain. If these invitations are accepted, Don can share his calendar free and busy information, subject information, and location with these users.

Jeff Hay, a user in the Sales Department, can now send sharing invitations through his email client to users in the fabrikam.com domain. If these invitations are accepted, Jeff can share his calendar free and busy information and his contacts information with these users.

Any of your users who do not have a specific sharing policy assigned to his or her mailbox might still be able to share information with users in a federated domain. This will depend on your organization's default sharing policy.

The details that the users in the fabrikam.com domain can, in turn, share with your users depend on the sharing policies the Fabrikam administrators have configured and applied to the mailboxes in their domain.

Subject Alternative Name (SAN) Certificates

If you need to protect multiple host names with a single certificate, you can use a SAN certificate. This allows you to specify a list of host names and protect them with a single SSL certificate.

SANs enable you to secure host names on different base domains with one certificate and to host multiple virtual SSL sites using a single IP address. Typically, hosting multiple SSL-enabled sites on a single server requires a unique IP address per site, but a SAN certificate, also known as a Unified Communications SSL certificate, can solve this problem. Both Microsoft Internet Information Services version 6 or later and Apache HTTP server are able to use SAN certificates to host virtual websites.

SAN certificates can secure multiple fully qualified domain names with a single certificate. SAN certificates are used to secure Exchange Server 2010 sites where there is a need to secure multiple domains that resolve to a single IP address (such as in a shared hosting environment). Using a SAN certificate saves the time required to configure multiple IP addresses on an Exchange server and bind each IP address to a different certificate.

When browsers connect to servers using HTTPS, they check to make sure the SSL certificate matches the host name in the address bar. Browsers find a match in one of the following ways:

- The host name in the address bar exactly matches the common name in the certificate's Subject field.
- The host name matches a wildcard common name. For example, www.contoso .com matches the common name *.contoso.com.
- The host name is listed in the Subject Alternative Name field.

Normally, a browser compares the server name it connects to with the common name in the Server certificate. However, if an SSL certificate has a SAN field, then SSL clients typically ignore the common name value and seek a match in the SAN list.

Microsoft Internet Explorer, Microsoft Windows Mobile 5, Firefox, Opera, Safari, and Netscape all support SAN certificates. However, some mobile devices do not support SAN certificates, although all of them support exact common name matching.

Assigning the Federated Sharing Role

Federated sharing is a built-in management role that enables you to manage cross-forest and cross-organization sharing. It is one of several roles that make up the RBAC permissions model discussed in Lesson 1, "Role Based Access Control." This section applies the RBAC concept to the federated sharing management role.

If you want the federated sharing management role to grant permissions, it must first be assigned to a role assignee. This can be a role group, user, or universal security group. You may also need to apply either a custom or a built-in management scope to specify what recipient and server objects federated sharing role assignees can modify. If the federated sharing role is assigned to a role assignee but a management scope allows the role assignee to manage only certain objects based on a defined scope, the role assignee can use the permissions granted by the federated sharing role only on those specific objects.

The federated sharing management role is assigned to one or more role groups by default. You can use the *Get-ManagementRoleAssignment* EMS cmdlet, discussed in Lesson 1, to list these groups. To see role details, including a list of groups, users, or universal security groups assigned to this role, enter the following command in the EMS:

```
Get-ManagementRoleAssignment -Role "Federated Sharing" | FL
```

Figure 6-15 shows part of the output of this command.

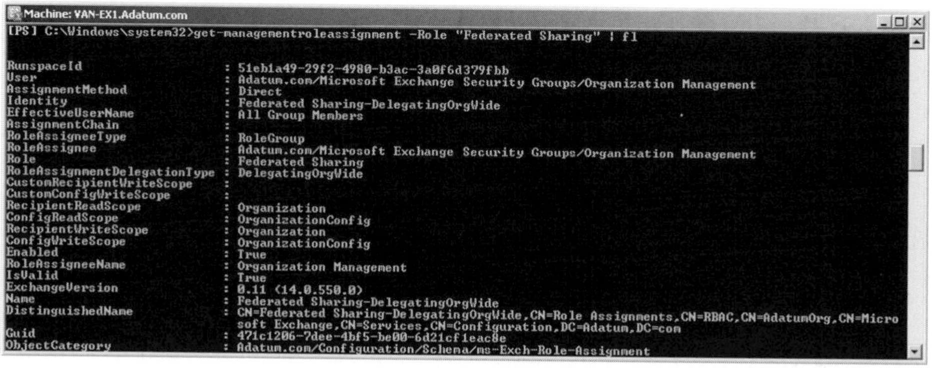

FIGURE 6-15 Management assignment details for the federated sharing role

You can also remove the federated sharing management role from built-in role groups or role groups you create and users and universal security groups. However, there must always be at least one delegating role assignment for this role granted to a role group or universal security group. You cannot delete the last delegating role assignment. This limitation helps to prevent administrators from locking themselves out of the system. Delegating role assignments was discussed in Lesson 1.

Adding the federated sharing management role to a role group gives administrators who are assigned to that management role group the ability to manage federated sharing. You can use the *New-ManagementRoleAssignment* cmdlet in the EMS, discussed in Lesson 1, to add the role to a role group. For example, the following command assigns the federated sharing management role to the Adatum Federation role group without defining a scope:

```
New-ManagementRoleAssignment -Name "Federated Sharing Adatum Federation" -SecurityGroup
"Adatum Federation" -Role "Federated Sharing"
```

The following command assigns the federated sharing role to the Adatum Federation role group and applies the Organization predefined scope:

```
New-ManagementRoleAssignment -Name "Federated Sharing Adatum Federation" -SecurityGroup
"Adatum Federation" -Role "Federated Sharing" -RecipientRelativeWriteScope Organization
```

If a predefined scope does not meet your needs, you can use a recipient filter to define a scope. For example, the following command creates a scope that includes all mailboxes within the Federation Managers OU in the Adatum.com domain:

```
New-ManagementScope -Name "Mailboxes in Federation Managers OU"
-RecipientRestrictionFilter { RecipientType -eq 'UserMailbox' } -RecipientRoot "Adatum
.com/Federation Managers OU"
```

The following command assigns the federated sharing role to the Adatum Federation role group and applies the Mailboxes in Federation Managers OU scope that you created using the previous command:

```
New-ManagementRoleAssignment -Name "Federated Sharing Adatum Federation" -SecurityGroup
"Adatum Federation" -Role "Federated Sharing" -CustomRecipientWriteScope "Mailboxes in
Federation Managers OU"
```

Removing the Federated Sharing Role from a Role Group

If you do not want members of a management role group to have permissions to manage federated sharing, you can remove the role assignment between the management role group and the federated sharing management role that grants the permissions. All members of the role group lose the ability to manage federated sharing when you remove the role assignment. If you want to remove the permissions from one member only, you need instead to remove that member from the management role group.

If you want to remove a management role assignment from a management role group, you first need to find the name of the management role assignment that assigns the role to the role group (unless you already know this). In the example given in this lesson, the role group is Adatum Federation. To find the name of the management role assignment, you enter the following command in the EMS:

```
Get-ManagementRoleAssignment -RoleAssignee "Adatum Federation"
```

This command would in this instance return the management role assignment name "Federated Sharing Adatum Federation". You could remove this role assignment by entering the following command:

```
Remove-ManagementRoleAssignment "Federated Sharing Adatum Federation"
```

This removes the management role that enables administrators assigned the Adatum Federation role group to manage federated sharing.

> **MORE INFO   REMOVE-MANAGEMENTROLEASSIGNMENT AND *GET-MANAGEMENTROLEASSIGNMENT***
>
> For more information about the *Remove-ManagementRoleAssignment* cmdlet, see *http://technet.microsoft.com/en-us/library/dd351205.aspx*. For more information about the *Get-ManagementRoleAssignment* cmdlet, see *http://technet.microsoft.com/en-us/library/dd351024.aspx* (this link was given in Lesson 1 but is repeated here for convenience).

Adding the Federated Sharing Role to a User or Universal Security Group

You can use management role assignments to assign the federated sharing management role to a user or universal security group. By assigning a role to a user or universal security group, you enable the user or group members to perform tasks dependent on cmdlets or scripts related to the federated sharing management role.

The commands to assign the federated sharing role to a universal security group are the same as those used to assign the role to a management role group except that the SecurityGroup parameter identifies a universal security group rather than a role group. To assign the role to an individual user (not recommended), you use a command similar to the following:

```
New-ManagementRoleAssignment -Name "Federated Sharing Don Hall" -User "Don Hall"
-Role "Federated Sharing"
```

To remove a role assignment from a user or universal security group, you follow the same procedure that you did for a management role group. If necessary, first use the *Get-ManagementRoleAssignment* cmdlet to determine the name of the assignment and then use the *Remove-ManagementRoleAssignment* cmdlet to remove it.

Lesson Summary

- You can establish a federated sharing relationship with an external Exchange Server 2010 organization if both your organization and the external organization have established a federation trust with the Federation Gateway.

- To establish a federation trust, you need a valid X.509 certificate issued by a third-party CA trusted by Windows Live Domain Services. The domain you use for establishing the federation trust must be resolvable from the Internet, and you need to configure DNS with a text (TXT) resource record that provides proof of ownership for your domain name.

- A federated sharing relationship permits calendar sharing with free or busy information, subject, location, and body and contacts sharing. You can send encrypted and authenticated email messages to and receive such messages from users in the external organization.

Lesson Review

You can use the following questions to test your knowledge of the information in Lesson 2, "Configuring Federated Sharing." The questions are also available on the companion CD if you prefer to review them in electronic form.

> **NOTE ANSWERS**
>
> Answers to these questions and explanations of why each answer choice is correct or incorrect are located in the "Answers" section at the end of the book.

1. You are creating a federation trust. You use the *Get-ExchangeCertificate* EMS cmdlet to obtain a list of thumbprints of the certificates available on your Client Access server, choose a certificate, and enter the *New-FederationTrust* cmdlet with the Thumbprint parameter to create a federation trust named Microsoft Federation Gateway. You get the error shown in Figure 6-16. What is the likely cause of this error?

FIGURE 6-16 Error in creating a federation trust

   A. The certificate is already being used for another purpose.

   B. You cannot use the EMS to create a federation trust named Microsoft Federation Gateway. You need to use the EMC.

   C. You cannot create a federation trust on a Client Access server. You need to do this on a domain controller.

   D. The certificate you have chosen is not trusted by Windows Live Domain Services.

2. You are testing Exchange Server 2010 configuration on a test network that is isolated from any other network. You have obtained an X.509 certificate from a trusted third-party CA and have exported it to your test network using removable media.

You attempt to create a federation trust but are unable to do so. What is the probable reason?

A. Your test network is not connected to the Internet.

B. Your certificate was exported to your test network using removable media and is therefore not valid for that network.

C. The EMS is not available on your test network.

D. The CA is not trusted by Windows Live Domain Services.

3. You want to configure all mailboxes in your Exchange organization that are associated with the Marketing Department so that they use the Adatum Marketing federated sharing policy. Which of the following commands should you use?

A. Set-Mailbox –Filter {Department –eq "Marketing"} | Get-Mailbox –SharingPolicy "Adatum Marketing"

B. Get-Mailbox –Filter {Department –eq "Marketing"} | Set-Mailbox –SharingPolicy "Adatum Marketing"

C. Set-Mailbox –Organization "Marketing" | Get-Mailbox –SharingPolicy "Adatum Marketing"

D. Get-Mailbox –Filter –Organization "Marketing" | Set-Mailbox –SharingPolicy "Adatum Marketing"

4. You want to create an account namespace for your Exchange organization with the Federation Gateway and enable federation so that you can make use of the facilities that federation provides, such as sharing calendars or contacts and accessing free or busy information. What EMS cmdlet would enable you to do this?

A. *New-OrganizationRelationship*

B. *Get-FederatedOrganizationIdentifier*

C. *Set-OrganizationRelationship*

D. *Set-FederatedOrganizationIdentifier*

5. A federated sharing relationship exists between Blue Sky Airlines and Consolidated Messenger. A user in Blue Sky Airlines sends an encrypted, authenticated email message to a user in Consolidated Messenger. Which of the following describes the first three steps of the process? (Choose all that apply; each answer forms part of the solution.)

A. The Blue Sky Airlines Hub Transport server accesses a ConsoldatedMessenger .com domain controller to verify that a sharing relationship is configured with ConsolidatedMessenger.com and that the user has permission to send messages across the sharing relationship.

B. The Blue Sky Airlines Hub Transport server accesses a BlueSkyAirlines.com domain controller to verify that a sharing relationship is configured with ConsolidatedMessenger.com and that the user has permission to send messages across the sharing relationship.

C. If both verifications succeed, the Blue Sky Airlines Hub Transport server connects to the Federation Gateway and requests a security token for the Blue Sky Airlines user. Because BlueSkyAirlines.com is configured in the organization identifier, the Federation Gateway issues the token.

D. The message is sent through a Blue Sky Airlines Mailbox server to a Blue Sky Airlines Hub Transport server.

E. If both verifications succeed, the Consolidated Messenger Hub Transport server connects to the Federation Gateway and requests a security token for the Blue Sky Airlines user. Because BlueSkyAirlines.com is configured in the organization identifier, the Federation Gateway issues the token.

F. The message is sent through a Blue Sky Airlines Mailbox server to a Consolidated Messenger Hub Transport server.

PRACTICE   Adding a User to a Built-In Role Group

In this practice session, you add Don Hall to various built-in role groups and discover the tasks that membership of these role groups enables Don to carry out. If you are using virtual machines, the domain controller VAN-DC1 and the Exchange Server 2010 server VAN-EX1 need to be running and connected.

EXERCISE 1   Add Don Hall to the Recipient Management Role Group

In this exercise, you add Don Hall to the Recipient Management built-in role group. You then use the EMC to verify that Don has only read access to the Exchange Server organization and cannot modify mailbox database settings. You check that he can modify mailbox and distribution groups. Carry out the following procedure:

1. Log on to the domain controller VAN-DC1 with the Kim Akers account and the password Pa$$w0rd.

2. Click Active Directory Users And Computers in the Administrative Tools menu.

3. In Active Directory Users And Computers, expand the Console tree and click the Microsoft Exchange Security Groups OU.

4. Right-click Recipient Management, as shown in Figure 6-17. Click Properties.

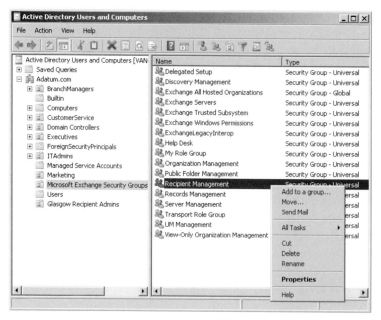

FIGURE 6-17 Accessing Recipient Management Properties

5. In the Recipient Management Properties dialog box, click the Members tab. Click Add.

6. In the Select Users, Contacts, Computers, Service Accounts, Or Groups dialog box, type Don Hall in the Enter The Object Names To Select box. Click Check Names, as shown in Figure 6-18. Click OK.

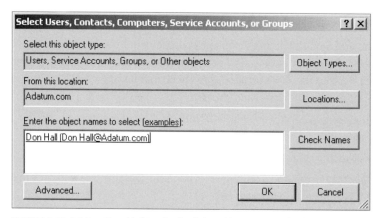

FIGURE 6-18 Adding Don Hall to the Recipient Management built-in role group

7. Click OK to close the Recipient Management Properties dialog box.

8. If you are already logged on to the Exchange Server 2010 server VAN-EX1, log off.

9. Log on to the Exchange Server 2010 server VAN-EX1 with the Don Hall account and the password Pa$$w0rd.

> **NOTE CHANGE GROUP POLICY IF YOU CANNOT LOG ON AS DON HALL**
>
> As a member of the Backup Operators security group, the Don Hall account should be able to log on locally to the VAN-EX1 server. If, however, you get the message "You cannot log on because the logon method you are using is not allowed on this computer," run gpedit.msc, expand Windows Settings\Security Settings\Local Policies, click on User Rights Assignment, and add Don Hall to the Allow Log On Locally right.

10. On the Start menu, click All Programs. Click Microsoft Exchange Server 2010. Click Exchange Management Console.

11. In the EMC, expand the Console tree. Click Mailbox under Recipient Configuration.

12. Right-click the Don Hall mailbox in the Result pane and click Properties. On the Address and Phone tab, specify an address, as shown in Figure 6-19. Click OK.

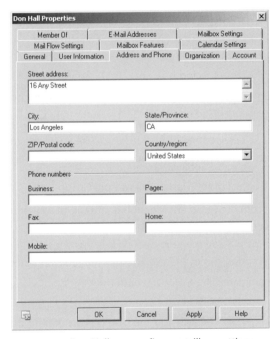

FIGURE 6-19 Don Hall can configure mailbox settings.

13. In the Console tree, click Distribution Group under Recipient Configuration. In the Actions pane, click New Distribution Group. Check that Don can run the New Distribution Group Wizard, as shown in Figure 6-20. You can create a distribution group if you want to, but all that is necessary for the exercise is to show that Don can access the wizard. Click Cancel.

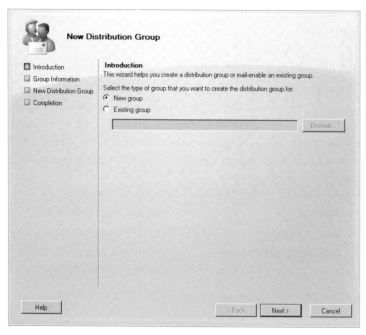

FIGURE 6-20 Don can create a distribution group.

14. In the Console tree, click Mailbox under Organization Configuration. Check that the Don Hall account cannot run the New Mailbox Database Wizard.

15. Log off from the VAN-EX1 Exchange 2010 server. (Note that you need to log off because the Don Hall account will receive the permissions associated with the role you assign in Exercise 2 only when you use it to log on.)

EXERCISE 2 Add Don Hall to the Public Folder Management Role Group

In this exercise, you remove Don Hall from the Recipient Management built-in role group and add him to the Public Folder Management built-in role group. You then use the EMS to verify that Don cannot modify mailbox settings but can manage public folder settings. You need to have completed Exercise 1 before attempting this exercise. Carry out the following procedure:

1. If necessary, log on to the domain controller VAN-DC1 with the Kim Akers account and the password Pa$$w0rd.

2. Refer to the procedure you used in Exercise 1 to add the Don Hall account to the Recipient Management role group. Use the same tools to remove the Don Hall account from the Recipient Management role group and add it to the Public Folder Management role group.

3. Log on to the Exchange Server 2010 server VAN-EX1 as Don Hall and open the EMS from the Microsoft Exchange Server 2010 menu.

4. Enter the following command:

```
New-PublicFolder –Name "Don Hall Public Folder"
```

Check that Don Hall can create a new public folder, as shown in Figure 6-21.

FIGURE 6-21 Don can create a public folder.

5. Enter the following command:

```
New-Mailbox -Name "Test Mailbox"
```

Check that Don Hall cannot create a new mailbox. The error message you should get is that "New-Mailbox" is not a recognized cmdlet. What this means is it is not a cmdlet that Don Hall has permission to use.

PRACTICE Creating a Sharing Policy and Applying It to Mailboxes

In this practice session, you create a sharing policy with a (nonexistent) external domain. You apply the policy to the Kim Akers mailbox. You then create a second policy and apply it to the Don Hall mailbox. In a production environment with federation trusts and a sharing relationship configured, Kim would be able to share calendar information with users at the external domain, while Don can share both calendar and contact information. You then display all the available information for the sharing policy applied to the Don Hall mailbox. If you are using virtual machines, the domain controller VAN-DC1 and the Exchange Server 2010 server VAN-EX1 need to be running and connected.

EXERCISE Create Sharing Policies and Apply Them to Mailboxes

In this exercise, you use the EMS to create two sharing policies and apply them to two separate mailboxes. You then view the sharing policy information for one of these policies. Carry out the following procedure:

1. Log on to the Exchange Server 2010 server VAN-EX1 using the Kim Akers account and the password Pa$$w0rd.

2. Click All Programs, click Microsoft Exchange Server 2010, and then click Exchange Management Shell.

3. Create a sharing policy named Blue Sky Airlines01 that allows users in the BlueSkyAirlines.com domain to see the detailed free or busy information and contacts

of users in your domain who have the policy applied to their mailboxes. To do this, enter the following command:

```
New-SharingPolicy -Name "Blue Sky Airlines01" -Domains 'BlueSkyAirlines.com:
CalendarSharingFreeBusyDetail, ContactsSharing'
```

4. Apply the Blue Sky Airlines01 sharing policy to the Don Hall mailbox. To do this, enter the following command:

```
Set-Mailbox -Identity "Don Hall" -SharingPolicy "Blue Sky Airlines01"
```

5. Create a sharing policy named Blue Sky Airlines02 that allows users in the BlueSkyAirlines.com domain to see the detailed free or busy information but not the contacts of users in your domain who have the policy applied to their mailboxes. To do this, enter the following command:

```
New-SharingPolicy -Name "Blue Sky Airlines02" -Domains 'BlueSkyAirlines.com:
CalendarSharingFreeBusyDetail'
```

6. Apply the Blue Sky Airlines02 sharing policy to the Kim Akers mailbox. To do this, enter the following command:

```
Set-Mailbox -Identity "Kim Akers" -SharingPolicy "Blue Sky Airlines02"
```

Figure 6-22 shows the commands that create and assign the two sharing policies.

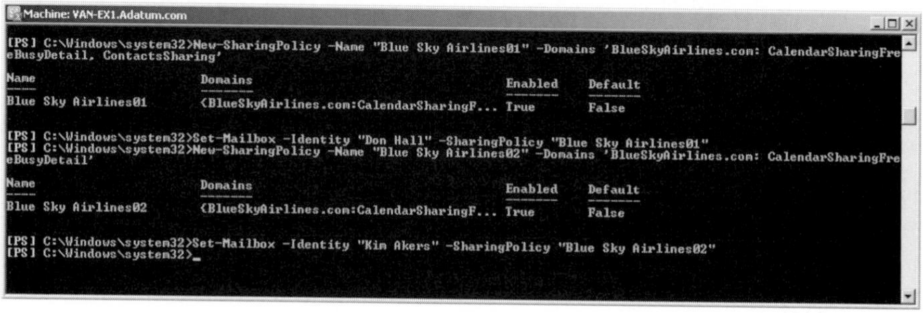

FIGURE 6-22 Creating and assigning sharing policies

7. Display all the available information for the sharing policy applied to the Don Hall mailbox. To do this, enter the following command:

```
Get-SharingPolicy "Blue Sky Airlines01" | FL
```

Figure 6-23 shows the output from this command.

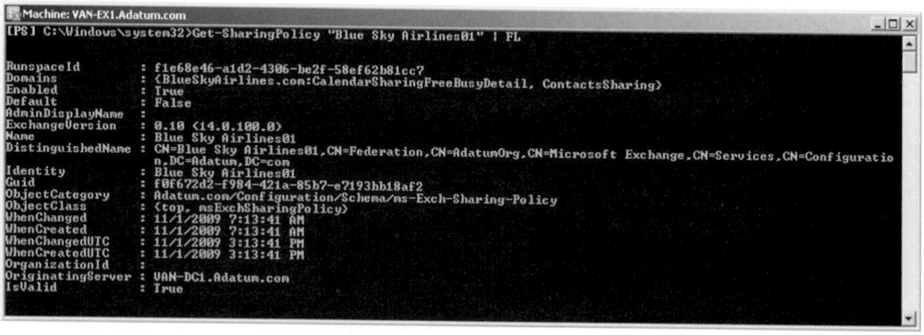

FIGURE 6-23 Information for Blue Sky Airlines01 sharing policy

Chapter Review

To further practice and reinforce the skills you learned in this chapter, you can perform the following tasks:

- Review the chapter summary.
- Review the list of key terms introduced in this chapter.
- Complete the case scenarios. These scenarios set up real-word situations involving the topics of this chapter and ask you to create a solution.
- Complete the suggested practices.
- Take a practice test.

Chapter Summary

- RBAC implements a permissions model using management role entries that grant permissions to management roles through management role assignments. Members and delegates in management role groups are added to these management roles and are granted the permissions associated with the roles. Management role scopes define the objects to which the permissions granted through membership of a management role group are applied.
- A federated sharing relationship can be established between two Exchange Server 2010 organizations provided that both organizations have configured a federated trust with the Federation Gateway authorized by a valid X.509 certificate issued by a third-party CA trusted by Windows Live Domain Services. This enables users in either organization to share calendar and contact information with users in the other organization and to send encrypted and authenticated email messages between the organizations.

Key Terms

Do you know what these key terms mean?

- Federation trust
- Management role assignment
- Management role assignment policy
- Management role entry
- Management role group
- Management role group assignment
- Management role scope
- Management role
- Microsoft Federation Gateway organization identifier
- Role Based Access Control (RBAC) role holder

Case Scenarios

In the following case scenarios, you will apply what you've learned about subjects of this chapter. You can find answers to these questions in the "Answers" section at the end of this book.

Case Scenario 1: Adding a Delegate to a Role Group

Kim Akers is an Exchange organization administrator at Northwind Traders. She wants to add Don Hall as a delegate to the role group named Recipient Managers. However, this role group already contains a number of delegates. If Kim merely adds Don to the list, she would need to enter the entire list as the argument of the ManagedBy parameter of the *Set-RoleGroup* EMS cmdlet. She knows that this would be an error-prone and time-consuming procedure. Answer the following questions:

1. What does Kim do with the current delegate list, and what does she enter in the EMS to do it?
2. How does Kim add Don to the current delegate list?
3. How does she apply the revised delegate list to the role group?
4. Kim later decides that Don should not after all be a delegate in this role group. How does she remove him from the delegate list?

Case Scenario 2: Replacing an X.509 Certificate in a Federation Trust

Jeff Hay is an Exchange organization administrator at Fabrikam, Inc. He has obtained and installed an X.509 certificate issued by a CA that is trusted by Windows Live Domain Services. He wants to use this certificate to verify the federation trust named Microsoft Federation Gateway that has been established between Fabrikam and the Federation Gateway. Answer the following questions:

1. What information does he require about the certificate, and how does he obtain it?
2. How does he specify the certificate he has obtained as the next certificate?
3. What does he then need to do in all the Client Access and Hub Transport servers in the Fabrikam Exchange Server 2010 organization?
4. How does he configure the trust to use the next certificate as the current certificate?

Suggested Practices

To help you master the examination objectives presented in this chapter, complete the following tasks.

Look More Closely at the For Info Links

■ **Practice 1** This chapter describes a considerable number of EMS cmdlets, and there is not space to discuss each of these in depth. The For Info links give you access to detailed descriptions of the cmdlets, including their syntax and parameters. You are not expected to remember every parameter, but reading through these detailed descriptions should give you a feel for the facilities available by using the cmdlets that the powerful EMS tool provides.

Find Out More about the Microsoft Federation Gateway

■ **Practice 1** This chapter describes the Federation Gateway in terms of setting up federated relationships in order to exchange calendar and contact information and secure email. There is more to the Federation Gateway than that. Use the For Info link provided in this chapter and follow subsequent links to find out just what the Federation Gateway offers you. Enter "Microsoft Federation Gateway" in a search engine and access the links.

Use Role Based Access Control

■ **Practice 1** If you are accustomed to the ACL model for configuring permissions, you will find RBAC to be considerably different. Use this permissions model to set up roles, assign role entries, and create role groups. Place users or universal security groups in the role group and test the permissions allocated to them. Experiment with role scopes. At the very least, become familiar with the built-in role groups and what members of these groups can and cannot do.

Take a Practice Test

The practice tests on this book's companion CD offer many options. For example, you can test yourself on just one exam objective, or you can test yourself on all the 70-662 certification exam content. You can set up the test so that it closely simulates the experience of taking a certification exam, or you can set it up in study mode so that you can look at the correct answers and explanations after you answer each question.

> **MORE INFO** **PRACTICE TESTS**
>
> For details about all the practice test options available, see the "How to Use the Practice Tests" section in this book's Introduction.

CHAPTER 7

Routing and Transport Rules

This chapter discusses *messaging policies*, which you can use to control and protect your email traffic, and how you can create *transport rules* and *transport protection rules* that define these policies. It considers *moderated email* traffic and how you configure moderation.

In addition to controlling and protecting message traffic, the lesson also discusses how you control the route a message takes to its final destination. It looks at how you use Receive and Send connectors to control your traffic flow, and how you obtain the necessary certificates to encrypt and authenticate confidential traffic.

In brief, this chapter is about what you send and how you send it.

Exam objectives in this chapter:

- Create and configure transport rules.
- Configure message routing.

Lessons in this chapter:

Before You Begin

In order to complete the exercises in the practice session in this chapter, you need to have done the following:

- Installed the Windows Server 2008 R2 domain controller VAN-DC1 and the Windows Exchange 2010 Enterprise Mailbox, Hub Transport, and Client Access server VAN-EX1 as described in the Appendix, "Setup Instructions for Exchange Server 2010."
- Created the Kim Akers account with the password *Pa$$w0rd* in the Adatum.com domain. This account should be placed in the Domain Admins security group and be a member of the Organization Management role group.

- Created the Don Hall account with the password *Pa$$w0rd* in the Adatum.com domain. This account should be placed in the Backup Operators security group (so it can be used to log on to the domain controller) and should be in the Marketing organizational unit.
- Created mailboxes for Kim Akers and Don Hall, accepting the default email address format for the email addresses.

🌐 REAL WORLD

Ian McLean

The thing you need to remember about test networks is that they only mimic real production networks. They cannot be exactly the same.

For example, the first time I worked with such a network, it had a single Hub Transport server and no Edge Transport servers at all. We tested any new features—including transport rules—on this network before installing them on our production system. Soon we began to realize that certain features, such as messaging policies designed to block malware and some types of external attack, should be installed on an Edge Transport server.

So we installed a messaging server with the Edge Transport role on our test network and tested a number of innovations, including some transport rules that were appropriate to the Edge Transport role. Everything seemed to work, so we implemented the changes on our production network.

Nothing actually broke down, but the results were not as expected. The production network had several Hub Transport and several Edge Transport servers. Previously, we had tested transport rules on our test Hub Transport server, and when we implemented them on our production system, Active Directory replication ensured that the rules were applied on all Hub Transport servers. This doesn't work with Edge Transport servers. If you want a transport rule to apply to all Edge Transport servers, you need to implement it on all of them (possibly by exporting and then importing such a rule).

We eventually decided to clone all our Edge Transport servers. This provided failover support and solved the transport rule problem. However, I hope we all learned a valuable lesson—I know I did. Don't believe everything you see on a test network.

Lesson 1: Managing Transport Rules

This lesson discusses transport rules and how you can use them to apply messaging policies on both Hub Transport and Edge Transport servers. You can use Windows *Rights Management Services (RMS)* to configure *Information Rights Management (IRM)* so that your users can send secure IRM-protected messages. The *RMS prelicensing agent* is installed in Exchange Server 2010 to enable you to do this. The lesson looks at how you use transport protection rules to configure rights protection.

Moderated transport is a new feature in Exchange Server 2010 that enables a moderator to intercept and check mail to a specified recipient (typically a distribution group) and allow or block delivery depending on the acceptability of the message. This lesson discusses how moderated transport works, how you configure a moderated recipient and specify a moderator, and how you configure an additional arbitration mailbox.

> **After this lesson, you will be able to:**
> - Configure transport rules on Hub Transport and Edge Transport servers.
> - Configure IRM and use a transport protection rule to apply an RMS template and IRM-protect messages.
> - Configure moderated transport.
>
> **Estimated lesson time: 50 minutes**

Using Transport Rules

Your organization may be required by law, regulatory requirements, or company policies to apply messaging policies that limit interaction between recipients and senders (both individual senders and departmental groups). Such limitations can apply both inside and outside the organization. In addition to limiting interactions inside the organization, you also need to prevent inappropriate content from entering or leaving the organization, filter confidential information, track or archive specified messages, redirect inbound and outbound messages so that they can be inspected, and apply disclaimers to messages as they pass through the organization. The mechanism that enables you to accomplish all these aims is the transport rule.

You can use transport rules to apply messaging policies to email messages that flow through the transport pipeline on Hub Transport and Edge Transport servers. These rules permit you to comply with messaging policies, secure messages, prevent information leakage, and protect messaging systems.

You create a transport rule by specifying rule conditions, exceptions, and actions. The transport rule agent (on Hub Transport servers) or the edge rules agent (on edge servers) processes the transport rule. If the condition is satisfied and none of the exceptions apply, the action is performed.

Transport Rule Conditions

You use transport rule conditions to identify messages to which a transport rule action is applied. A condition consists of one or more predicates that specify which parts of a message should be examined. Predicates can examine message fields or headers, such as To, From, or Cc. They can also examine message characteristics, such as message subject, message size, message body, attachments, and message classification. If appropriate, you can specify a comparison operator, such as equals, does not equal, or contains, and a matching value.

For example a predicate could be *MessageSize, From, FromMemberOf, FromScope, SubjectContains, FromAddressContains, SubjectMatches,* and so on. Some predicates can be used only on Hub Transport servers, whereas others can be used on both Hub and Edge Transport servers. You can obtain list of transport rule predicates by entering the following Exchange Management Shell (EMS) command:

```
Get-TransportRulePredicate | FT
```

Figure 7-1 shows some of the output from this command run on the Hub Transport server VAN-EX1. The output you obtain from the command depends on whether you run it on a Hub Transport or an Edge Transport server. If you want to save this list in a convenient format, you can redirect the output of the command to a text file.

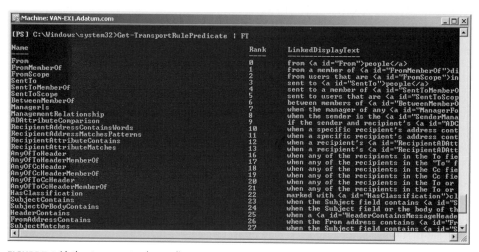

FIGURE 7-1 Listing transport rule predicates

MORE INFO **TRANSPORT RULE PREDICATES**

For more information about transport rule predicates, including lists of the predicates you can use on Hub Transport and on Edge Transport servers, see *http://technet.microsoft.com/en-us/library/dd638183.aspx.*

EXAM TIP

Do not attempt to memorize every transport rule predicate. If you come across one you do not know in the examination, the name is likely to be self-explanatory, such as *AttachmentNameMatches*. The most commonly used transport rule predicates (arguably) are included in the examples of transport rules given in this chapter and in Chapter 11, "Managing Records and Compliance."

Transport Rule Exceptions

Transport rule exceptions are based on the transport rule predicates that you use to build transport rule conditions. However, unlike conditions, exceptions identify messages to which transport rule actions should not be applied. If an exception is met, this prevents the actions specified in the transport rule from being applied to an email message, even if that message matches all configured conditions.

Exceptions include, for example, *ExceptIfFrom*, *ExceptIfFromMemberOf*, *ExceptIfFromScope*, *ExceptIfAttachmentContainsWords*, *ExceptIfAttachmentSizeOver*, *ExceptIfSCLOver*, and so on. As with predicates, the name of the exception is typically self-explanatory.

> **MORE INFO** **TRANSPORT RULE EXCEPTIONS**
>
> You can obtain a list of transport rule exceptions by examining the syntax of the *New-TransportRule* EMS cmdlet. See *http://technet.microsoft.com/en-us/library/bb125138.aspx.*

Transport Rule Actions

A transport rule action defines the action that is applied to messages that match the transport rule conditions and do not match any exceptions. You can use a transport rule to reject, delete, or redirect a message; to add recipients; to add prefixes in the message subject; to insert disclaimers and personalized signatures in the message body; and to apply a message classification (discussed in Chapter 11). You can obtain a list of transport rule actions by entering the following EMS command:

```
Get-TransportRuleAction | FL
```

Figure 7-2 shows some of the output from this command run on a Hub Transport server. As with transport rule predicates, the output you obtain from the command depends on whether you run it on a Hub Transport or an Edge Transport server. If you want to save the list in a convenient format, you can redirect the output of the command to a text file.

> **MORE INFO** **TRANSPORT RULE ACTIONS**
>
> For more information about transport rule actions, including lists of the actions that you can specify on Hub Transport and on Edge Transport servers, see *http://technet.microsoft.com/en-us/library/aa998315.aspx.*

FIGURE 7-2 Listing transport rule actions

You can use a command based on the *New-TransportRule* EMS cmdlet to create a transport rule and specify conditions, exceptions, and actions. For example, the following command creates the transport rule TransportRuleExample, which adds Kim Akers to the recipients of any email messages sent to Mark Harrington except for messages that are sent by the external user DonalMace@Contoso.com:

```
New-TransportRule –Name TransportRuleExample –SentTo "Mark Harrington" –AddToRecipients
"Kim Akers" –ExceptIfFrom DonalMace@Contoso.com
```

The output from this command is shown in Figure 7-3. If you want to try out this command, you need to first create the Mark Harrington mailbox.

FIGURE 7-3 Creating a transport rule

MORE INFO **NEW-TRANSPORTRULE**

For more information about the *New-TransportRule* EMS cmdlet, see *http://technet .microsoft.com/en-us/library/bb125138.aspx*.

 Quick Check

- An email message satisfies all the conditions of a transport rule, but it also meets one of the exceptions. Is the action specified in the transport rule implemented? Explain your answer.

Quick Check Answer

- No. All conditions need to be met before a transport rule action is implemented. However, if one or more of the exceptions are met, the rule action is blocked.

Applying Messaging Policies

Transport rules allow you to apply messaging policies to messages in the transport pipeline. Actions such as redirecting a message or adding recipients, rights-protecting a message, and rejecting or silently deleting a message can be taken on messages that match the conditions and none of the exceptions defined in the rule.

The *transport rules agent* applies transport rules on a Hub Transport server and fires on the *OnRoutedMessage* transport event. All messages in an Exchange Server 2010 organization pass though at least one Hub Transport server before they are delivered, whether they are internal messages or messages to and from external users.

Active Directory stores transport rules that are configured on Hub Transport servers so that these transport rules are accessible to all Hub Transport servers in the organization through Active Directory replication. This lets you apply a single set of rules across an entire organization. Hub Transport servers query Active Directory to retrieve an organization's current transport rule configuration and then apply the rules to messages.

The scope of transport rules applied to Hub Transport servers is the entire exchange organization, and they can be applied to all message types except system messages. These transport rules can expand distribution group membership and access Active Directory attributes, and they can inspect or modify IRM-protected message content. IRM, RMS templates, and transport protection rules are discussed later in this lesson.

EXAM TIP

Bear in mind that a transport rule can block delivery of email messages to an Exchange Server 2010 organization. However, it cannot prevent users from communicating through networked file shares, newsgroups, and forums.

MORE INFO **ACTIVE DIRECTORY REPLICATION**

For more information about Active Directory replication, see *http://go.microsoft.com/fwlink/?LinkId=129505*.

The *edge rules agent* processes transport rules on Edge Transport servers and fires on the *EndOfData* transport event. You should, as much as possible, apply messaging hygiene and policy to inbound Internet email on Edge Transport servers so that unwanted messages are not sent to your internal servers. The edge rules agent can also remove or block messages that contain harmful or objectionable content and can help block messages that contain viruses, worms, and other types of malicious code. This is particularly important during the interval between the creation of malicious code and updates to your organization's antivirus software. In addition, the edge rules agent can mitigate the impact of denial of service attacks by blocking traffic from a source that is sending an excessive number of messages.

Outbound Internet email can also be subjected to policy-based scrutiny at Edge Transport servers, and you can prevent harmful or objectionable content from leaving your organization. Message content can be checked to prevent sensitive information from being leaked to external recipients.

Transport rules that are configured on Edge Transport servers are stored in Active Directory Lightweight Directory Services (AD LDS), formerly known as Active Directory Application Mode (ADAM), on each server. Rules configured on one Edge Transport server do not automatically replicate to other Edge Transport servers in an Exchange organization. You may decide to configure each Edge Transport server with identical transport rules, and you can use the EMS commands based on the *Export-TransportRuleCollection* and *Import-TransportRuleCollection* cmdlets to do so. The section "Exporting and Importing Transport Rules" later in this lesson describes this process in more detail.

You also have the option of configuring different transport rules on each of your Edge Transport servers to address the email message traffic patterns of each server. The scope of a transport rule configured on an Edge Transport server is the local server. Edge server transport rules apply to all types of message, cannot expand distribution group membership, cannot access Active Directory attributes, and cannot inspect or modify IRM-protected message content.

> **MORE INFO** **APPLYING TRANSPORT RULES**
>
> For more information about how transport rules are applied, see *http://technet.microsoft .com/en-us/library/bb124703.aspx*.

Expressions in Transport Rules

When you are matching text patterns in different parts of a message (such as message headers, sender, recipients, message subject, and body) as specified in a transport rule, you can use expressions in transport rule predicates to determine whether a configured action should be applied to an email message.

You can use *simple expressions* or *regular expressions*. A simple expression is a specific value that you want to match exactly in a message. For example, a simple expression could be the title of a document such as Sales_Forecast.doc. Data in an email message identified by a simple expression must exactly match that simple expression to satisfy either a condition or an exception in a transport rule.

A regular expression contains flexible notation that you can use to find a text pattern in a message. The notation consists of literal characters and *metacharacters*. Literal characters must exist in the target string. They are normal characters, as typed. Metacharacters are special characters that indicate how the text can vary in the target string. For example the \d character matches any single numeric digit (note that metacharacters are case sensitive), the \D pattern string matches any nonnumeric digit, the \s pattern string matches any single white-space character, the \S pattern string matches any single character that is not a space, and so on.

For example, the following EMS command creates a transport rule named "Check For Number Pattern" that redirects any email message containing a number in the format *xx-xxx-xx-xxxx* in its subject or body to the Kim Akers mailbox:

```
New-TransportRule –Name "Check For Number Pattern" –SubjectOrBodyMatchesPatterns
'\d\d-\d\d\d-\d\d-\d\d\d\d' –RedirectMessageTo "Kim Akers"
```

MORE INFO   REGULAR EXPRESSIONS IN TRANSPORT RULES

For more information about regular expressions in transport rules, including a full list of metacharacters, see *http://technet.microsoft.com/en-us/library/aa997187.aspx*.

Coding a Transport Rule That Uses an Expression

Because regular expressions can appear to be complex and lead to lengthy EMS commands being written to interpret such expressions, administrators often write code in the EMS to implement such rules. This code is not complex programming but consists mainly of defining variables that simplify the final statement of the rule.

A typical example detects that a number pattern is in the format of a U.S. Social Security number. For the benefit of those not based in the United States, Social Security numbers take the form *xxx-xx-xxxx* (for example, 123-45-6789). The transmission of such numbers in email messages is typically prohibited. The following code, entered into the EMS, creates a transport rule that prohibits the transmission of a U.S. Social Security number:

```
$Condition = Get-TransportRulePredicate SubjectMatches
$Condition.Patterns = @("\d\d\d-\d\d-\d\d\d\d")
$Action = Get-TransportRuleAction RejectMessage
$Action.RejectReason = "You are not permitted to transmit Social Security Numbers."
New-TransportRule –Name "Block Social Security Numbers" –Condition $Condition –Action
$Action
```

Note that this code, given as an example, blocks email messages that contain any number that takes the form *xxx-xx-xxxx*. Code that can specifically identify Social Security numbers by detecting their valid prefixes would be much more complex.

EXAM TIP

The 70–662 examination is unlikely to ask you to generate a program script under examination conditions. You could, however, be presented with such a script and asked to identify the line that is incorrect.

Managing Transport Rules

You can use either the Exchange Management Console (EMC) or the EMS to create, modify, view, enable, disable, remove, export, or import a transport rule on both Hub Transport and Edge Transport servers.

Creating a Transport Rule

You can create transport rules on Hub Transport or Edge Transport servers. Both server roles have many common predicates and actions, but some predicates and actions are exclusive to each Transport server role. Earlier in this lesson, you saw examples of the use of EMS commands based on the *New-TransportRule* cmdlet to create transport rules. You can also use the EMC to create a transport rule. The high-level procedure to do this on a Hub Transport server is as follows:

1. In the EMC Console pane, expand Organization Configuration and click Hub Transport.

2. Click the Transport Rules tab on the Result pane.

3. Click New Transport Rule on the Actions pane. This starts the New Transport Rule Wizard.

4. Complete the following fields on the Introduction page of the wizard:

   - **Name** Provide a name for the transport rule.

   - **Comment** Optionally, use this field to describe what the rule does.

   - **Enable Rule** New rules are enabled by default. If you want to create the rule in a disabled state, clear this check box.

5. If you want the rule to be applied to all email messages, do not select any conditions on the Conditions page. Otherwise, complete the following fields:

   - In the Step 1. Select Condition(s) box, select all the conditions that you want to apply to the rule.

   - If you have selected conditions in the Select Conditions box, click each blue underlined word in turn in the Step 2. Edit The Rule Description By Clicking An Underlined Value box. When you click a blue underlined word, a new window opens to prompt you for the values to apply to the condition. Select the values that you want to apply or type the values manually and click Add. Repeat this process until you have entered all the values and then click OK.

6. On the Actions page, shown in Figure 7-4, select all the actions that you want to apply to this rule in the Step 1. Select The Actions box.

7. Click each blue underlined word in turn in the Step 2. Edit The Rule Description By Clicking An Underlined Value box. Specify actions in the same way that you specified conditions in the previous step.

8. If you do not want to define any exceptions, do not make any selections on the Exceptions page. Otherwise, complete the following fields:

   - Select all the exceptions that you want to apply to the rule in the Step 1. Select The Exceptions If Necessary box.

   - If you select exceptions, click each blue underlined word in turn in the Step 2. Edit The Rule Description By Clicking An Underlined Value box. Specify exceptions in the same way that you specified conditions and actions in previous steps.

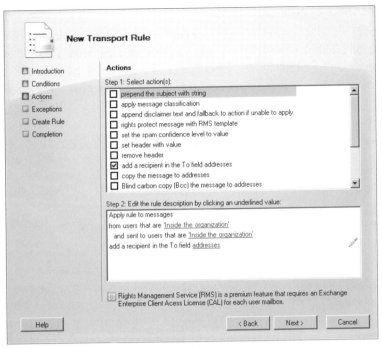

FIGURE 7-4 The Actions page of the New Transport Rule Wizard

9. Review the Configuration Summary on the Create Rule page. If you are satisfied with the configuration of the rule, click New.

10. A status of Completed on the Completion page indicates that the wizard completed the task successfully. In this case, click Finish to close the wizard. Otherwise, review the summary for an explanation of the failure and click Back to make any required configuration changes.

> **MORE INFO**   **CREATING A TRANSPORT RULE**
>
> For more information about creating a transport rule, see *http://technet.microsoft.com/en-us/library/bb124737.aspx*.

Modifying a Transport Rule

You can use the EMS or the EMC to modify an existing transport rule. To use the EMC, you access the Transport Rules tab, as previously described in the procedure, to create a transport rule. You then select the transport rule you want to modify and click Edit Rule in the Actions pane. The Introduction, Conditions, Actions, and Exceptions pages of the Edit Transport Rule Wizard are the same as those in the New Transport Rule Wizard, and you can edit the settings on these pages. You can review the changes displayed in the Configuration Summary on the Update Rule page and click Update if you are satisfied with them. Otherwise, click Back to make a revision. Finally, click Finish on the Completion page.

You can use an EMS command based on the *Set-TransportRule* cmdlet to modify a transport rule. The following command modifies the transport rule TransportRuleExample so that messages sent to Mark Harrington are sent to both Kim Akers and Don Hall, unless they come from DonalMace@Contoso.com:

```
Set-TransportRule -Identity TransportRuleExample -AddToRecipients "Kim Akers","Don Hall"
-ExceptIfFrom DonalMace@Contoso.com
```

> **MORE INFO** **MODIFYING A TRANSPORT RULE AND THE *SET-TRANSPORTRULE* CMDLET**
>
> For more information about modifying a transport rule, see *http://technet.microsoft.com/en-us/library/aa998262.aspx*. For more information about the *Set-TransportRule* EMS cmdlet, see *http://technet.microsoft.com/en-us/library/bb123534.aspx*.

Viewing Transport Rules

You may want to list all the transport rules stored in Active Directory in an Exchange Server 2010 organization or in AD LDS on an Edge Transport server. You may also want to view the properties of a specific transport rule. You can see a list of transport rules that apply to a Hub Transport server (and to all other Hub Transport servers in the Exchange organization) by expanding Organization Configuration and clicking Hub Transport on the EMC pane. You then click the Transport Rules tab in the Result pane, and a list of the transport rules appears on that tab. On an Edge Transport server, the procedure is similar except that you click Edge Transport on the Console pane, and the list on the Transport Rules tab applies only to the current server.

If you want to view the properties of a transport rule, you can click on the rule on the Transport Rules tab and then click Edit Rule on the Actions pane. You can step through the pages of the Edit Transport Rule Wizard without making any changes and hence view the transport rule configuration.

You can use the EMS to view a summary list of all transport rules configured on all Hub Transport servers or an Edge Transport server by entering the following command:

```
Get-TransportRule
```

Figure 7-5 shows the output of this command on Hub Transport server VAN-EX1. You might have a different list on the same server on your test network. The list of transport rules on a Hub Transport server in a production network is likely to be considerably longer.

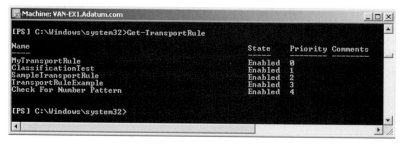

FIGURE 7-5 Listing transport rules

You can obtain a list of the properties of a specific transport rule by entering an EMS command similar to the following:

```
Get-TransportRule TransportRuleExample | FL
```

Figure 7-6 shows some of the output of this command.

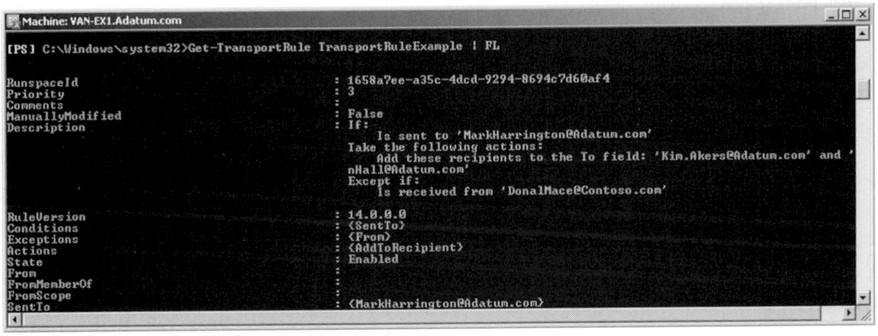

FIGURE 7-6 Listing the properties of a transport rule

> **MORE INFO** **VIEWING TRANSPORT RULES AND THE *GET-TRANSPORTRULE* CMDLET**
>
> For more information about viewing transport rules, see *http://technet.microsoft.com/ en-us/library/aa998187.aspx*. For more information about the *Get-TransportRule* EMS cmdlet, see *http://technet.microsoft.com/en-us/library/aa998585.aspx*.

EXAM TIP

You use the *New-TransportRule* EMS cmdlet to create a new transport rule. You use the *Set-TransportRule* EMS cmdlet to modify a transport rule. This includes adding conditions, exceptions, or actions to the rule. You use the *Get-TransportRule* EMS cmdlet to display the properties of an existing rule. The *Get-TransportRuleAction* EMS cmdlet allows you to view the actions that the transport rule performs.

Enabling or Disabling and Removing a Transport Rule

The transport rule agent must be enabled before you can apply transport rules to email messages that pass through a Hub Transport server, and the edge rule agent must be enabled before you can apply transport rules to messages that pass through an Edge Transport server. These agents are enabled by default, but if an agent becomes disabled, all transport rules are disabled. This is an unusual event possibly caused by a software fault, but if you need to, you can use the following EMS command on either a Hub Transport or an Edge Transport server to check the status of the appropriate transport agent:

```
Get-TransportAgent
```

Figure 7-7 shows the output of this command.

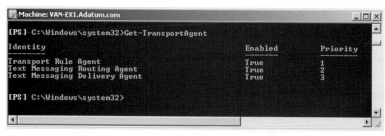

FIGURE 7-7 Checking the status of the transport agent

More typically, you may want to temporarily stop the execution of a single transport rule. To use the EMC to disable a transport rule, you list the transport rules on the Transport Rules tab, as described in the previous section, "Viewing Transport Rules"; right-click the transport rule you want to disable; and then click Disable Rule. You need to click Yes to confirm this action. If a rule is already disabled and you want to enable it, you right-click it and click Enable Rule. Note that disabling a rule on a Hub Transport server disables that rule for all Hub Transport servers in the Exchange organization. Disabling a rule on an Edge Transport server disables that rule only on that particular server.

If a transport rule is no longer required, the procedure to remove it is the same as the procedure to disable it, except that you click Remove instead of Disable Rule. As with disabling a rule, you need to click Yes to confirm the action. Take care that although you can enable a disabled rule, you cannot retrieve a rule that you remove, and you need to re-create it (or restore from backup) if you removed it in error.

You can use the EMS to disable and enable and to remove a transport rule. For example, the following EMS command disables the transport rule TransportRuleExample:

```
Disable-TransportRule TransportRuleExample
```

Note that this command requires confirmation unless you set the Confirm switch to suppress this requirement. The following command enables the transport rule that was previously disabled:

```
Enable-TransportRule TransportRuleExample
```

You can use a command based on the *Remove-TransportRule* EMS cmdlet to remove a transport rule. However, because this action is irreversible, it is a good idea to use the WhatIf switch to determine the results of removing a rule before you do so. You would enter a command similar to the following:

```
Remove-TransportRule TransportRuleExample -WhatIf
```

If you are sure it is what you want to do, you could then use a command similar to the following to remove the transport rule:

```
Remove-TransportRule TransportRuleExample
```

You need to confirm this command unless you have configured the Confirm switch so that confirmation is not required.

> **MORE INFO** **ENABLING, DISABLING, AND REMOVING TRANSPORT RULES**
>
> For more information about enabling and disabling transport rules, see *http://technet*
> *.microsoft.com/en-us/library/bb267004.aspx*. For more information about removing
> transport rules, see *http://technet.microsoft.com/en-us/library/aa996918.aspx*.

Exporting and Importing Transport Rules

If you want to duplicate the same transport rule on more than one Edge Transport server, you
can export it from the server on which you created it and import it to other Edge Transport
servers. Note that if you want to replicate the entire Exchange configuration on all Edge
Transport servers, you should instead clone the Edge Transport servers. This is discussed in
Chapter 14, "Exchange Disaster Recovery."

Another situation in which you might want to export and import transport rules is if
you are configuring coexistence while updating an Exchange Server 2007 organization to
Exchange Server 2010. Exchange Server 2007 stores transport rules in a container that is
different than that used by Exchange Server 2010. Any existing transport rules that exist in the
Exchange 2007 container need to be converted and stored in the Exchange 2010 container so
that the Exchange organization has the same set of transport rules for both Exchange Server
versions and the same messaging policies apply. You export Exchange Server 2007 rules so
that you can import them into Exchange Server 2010 by entering an EMS command based
on the *Export-TransportRuleCollection* cmdlet and the ExportLegacyRules parameter. This
command runs on an Exchange Server 2010 Hub Transport server.

EXAM TIP

You can export Exchange Server 2007 transport rules and then import them into Exchange
Server 2010. However, you cannot export Exchange Server 2010 transport rules and import
them into Exchange Server 2007.

You can use the EMS but not the EMC to export and import transport rules. The following
two EMS commands export transport rules on an Exchange Server 2010 server running the
Hub Transport or Edge Transport server role by exporting transport rule data to the variable
$transportfile and then writing it to the Exchange2010TransportRules.xml file in the
C:\MyDocs folder:

```
$transportfile = Export-TransportRuleCollection
Set-Content -Path "C:\MyDocs\Exchange2010TransportRules.xml" -Value $transportfile
.FileData -Encoding Byte
```

The following two EMS commands, entered on an Exchange Server 2010 Hub Transport
server, export legacy transport rules created in Exchange 2007:

```
$transportfile = Export-TransportRuleCollection -ExportLegacyRules
Set-Content -Path "C:\MyDocs\LegacyRules.xml" -Value $transportfile.FileData -Encoding
Byte
```

You export transport rules to an XML file and define the path of that file in the EMS command. You can then import transport rules from that file. The following EMS commands import transport rules from the ExportedRules.xml file:

```
[Byte[]]$transportdata = Get-Content -Path "C:\MyDocs\ExportedRules.xml" -Encoding Byte
-ReadCount 0
Import-TransportRuleCollection -FileData $transportdata
```

Configuring Disclaimers

A disclaimer is a statement that is added to email messages when they enter or leave an Exchange Server 2010 organization. You can apply multiple disclaimers to a single email message when that message matches more than one transport rule on which a disclaimer action is configured. The messages in disclaimers are typically of a legal nature, although you can use the same technique to add signatures or other organizational information.

You create a new disclaimer by creating a new transport rule (or modifying an existing one), and you have the option of specifying conditions or exceptions. If, however, you want the disclaimer to be added to all messages, you should not configure any conditions or exceptions.

You can use either the EMC or the EMS to configure a disclaimer. Step-by-step procedures to do this are listed in practice exercises later in this chapter. The high-level procedure to configure a disclaimer using the EMC is as follows:

1. Start the New Transport Rule Wizard, as described in the section "Creating a Transport Rule" earlier in this lesson.

2. On the Introduction page, provide a name and (optionally) a comment. Ensure that the Enable Rule check box is selected.

3. On the Conditions page, add any conditions that you want the transport rule to meet if the disclaimer is to be added. Typically, when configuring a disclaimer, you would not make any changes on this page.

4. On the Actions page, complete the following fields:

   ■ In the Step 1. Select Actions field, select Append Disclaimer Text And Fallback To Action If Unable To Apply.

   ■ In the Step 2. Edit The Rule Description By Clicking An Underlined Value field, complete the following tasks:

      ● Click Disclaimer Text. In the Specify Disclaimer Text dialog box, type the plain-text or HTML disclaimer text message that you want to add to messages.

      ● If you want to change the position of the disclaimer in messages, click Append and select Prepend in the Select Position dialog box.

      ● If you want to change the fallback action, click Wrap. Select the desired fallback action in the Select Fallback Action dialog box.

5. On the Exceptions page, add any exceptions that would prevent the transport rule from adding the disclaimer. Typically, when configuring a disclaimer, you would not make any changes on this page.

6. Review the Configuration Summary on the Create Rule page. If you are satisfied with the configuration of the new rule, click New.

7. If the status on the Completion page is Failed, click Back to make any additional changes. A status of Completed indicates that the wizard completed the task successfully. In this case, click Finish.

You can use the EMS to create a transport rule that applies a disclaimer. The following command applies the disclaimer "The Adatum Corporation supports all Government initiatives to control global warming." to all messages sent outside the Adatum organization and sets the fallback action to wrap:

```
New-TransportRule -Name ExternalDisclaimer -Enabled $true -SentToScope
'NotInOrganization' -ApplyHtmlDisclaimerLocation 'Append' -ApplyHtmlDisclaimerText
"<h3>Adatum Corporation Policy</h3><p> The Adatum Corporation supports all Government
initiatives to control global warming.</p>" -ApplyHtmlDisclaimerFallbackAction Wrap
```

> **MORE INFO** **CONFIGURING DISCLAIMERS**
>
> For more information about configuring disclaimers, see *http://technet.microsoft.com/ en-us/library/bb124352.aspx.*

Ethical Walls

An ethical wall prohibits communication between departments of a business or organization. This prevents conflicts of interest that result in the inappropriate release of sensitive information and helps implement your organization's compliance with applicable regulations and laws.

To create an ethical wall, you use the same procedure that you use to create a transport rule. When you implement an ethical wall by creating a transport rule, you can configure conditions and exceptions to control which email messages the ethical wall blocks. Typically, you create an ethical wall between two distribution groups using either the EMC New Transport Rule Wizard or the EMS *New-TransportRule* cmdlet with the *BetweenMemberOf* transport rule predicate and the *RejectMessage* transport rule action. This transport rule action uses the enhanced status code 5.7.1. You can modify the delivery status notification (DSN) code returned by specifying a custom DSN code. A custom DSN code must be associated with a custom DSN message. Chapter 11 discusses ethical walls and custom DSN messages.

For more information about ethical walls, see *http://technet.microsoft.com/en-us/library/bb123878.aspx*. For more information about custom DSN codes and messages, see *http://technet.microsoft.com/en-us/library/bb123506.aspx*.

Configuring Rights Protection

Organizations typically transmit sensitive and confidential information through email on a daily basis. Such organizations need to protect the privacy of individuals and the confidentiality of communications. You can implement privacy and confidentiality requirements by configuring IRM. This permits your organization and your users to apply persistent protection to messages so that access is restricted to authorized users and permitted actions (such as forwarding, copying, and printing messages).

RMS includes all the server and client technologies that are required to support IRM in an organization. Exchange Server 2010 ships with the Do Not Forward RMS template. When this template is applied to a message, only the recipients addressed in the message can decrypt the message. Recipients cannot forward the message to anyone else, copy content from the message, or print the message.

Installing an AD RMS Server

If the Do Not Forward RMS template is not adequate for your needs, you can apply for other templates from an AD RMS server installed on your organization. This server role is typically installed on a member server and preferably not on a domain controller, although it can be installed on the domain controller in a small network. An AD RMS server is a good candidate for virtualization. The AD RMS role should not be installed on an Exchange Server 2010 server because Microsoft does not support this configuration in a production environment.

A full AD RMS installation is beyond the scope of this book and the 70-662 examination. However, if you want to study AD RMS and the facilities it provides out of professional interest, the steps to install an AD RMS server are as follows:

- Create a CNAME Domain Name System (DNS) record to use in the AD RMS cluster URL.
- Create a service account and four global security groups that are required for AD RMS administration delegation.
- Create and install a Web server certificate. This is required because AD RMS requires Secure Sockets Layer (SSL)–encrypted web connections.
- Install the AD RMS server role.

> **NOTE AD RMS CLUSTERS**
>
> An *AD RMS cluster* is the term used for an AD RMS deployment in an organization. It can include a single server deployment. AD RMS is a Web service and does not require you to set up a Windows Server 2008 (or Windows Server 2008 R2) failover cluster.

> **MORE INFO INSTALLING AND USING AD RMS**
>
> For more information about installing and using AD RMS, see *http://technet.microsoft.com/en-us/library/cc753531(WS.10).aspx.*

Prelicensing

Configuring and using IRM features requires that the RMS prelicensing agent is enabled on a Hub Transport server. This agent is installed by default and enabled when you enable the IRM feature.

To access IRM-protected content, RMS-enabled applications must procure a use license for the authorized user, and this can be obtained from the prelicensing agent without the need to apply to an AD RMS server. This permits you to apply RMS templates to messages sent to a specified Simple Mail Transport Protocol (SMTP) address and configure rights protection by using transport rules.

The following EMS command enables licensing and hence enables IRM features for messages sent to internal recipients. Internal licensing is disabled by default for internal recipients:

```
Set-IRMConfiguration -InternalLicensingEnabled $true
```

In on-premises deployments, licensing is disabled for external messages by default. Note that IRM-protected messages sent to external recipients require that a federated trust exist between your Active Directory forest and that of the recipient organization. The following command enables licensing and hence enables IRM features for messages sent to external recipients:

```
Set-IRMConfiguration -ExternalLicensingEnabled $true
```

Enabling IRM enables the RMS prelicensing agent by default. If, however, the prelicensing agent is disabled, you can enable it by entering the following EMS command:

```
Enable-TransportAgent "Prelicensing Agent"
```

You then need to restart the MSExchangeTransport service for the agent to become active.

If you want to disable the RMS prelicensing agent, you enter the following command:

```
Disable-TransportAgent "Prelicensing Agent"
```

To obtain details about the RMS prelicensing agent, you enter the following command:

```
Get-TransportAgent "Prelicensing Agent"
```

Configuring IRM

Typically, company mailboxes contain large amounts of potentially sensitive information, and information leakage poses a serious threat. In addition, company policy and industry regulations govern how certain types of information are stored, transmitted, and secured. To help address these issues, Exchange Server 2010 offers IRM features that provide persistent online and offline protection of email messages and attachments.

Exchange Server 2010 IRM uses the Windows Server 2008 and Windows Server 2008 R2 information protection technology AD RMS. AD RMS uses Extensible Rights Markup Language (XrML)–based certificates and licenses to certify computers and users and to protect content. When content is protected by using AD RMS, an XrML license containing the rights that authorized users have to the content is attached. To access IRM-protected content, AD RMS–enabled applications must procure a use license for the authorized user from the AD RMS cluster. In Exchange 2010, the prelicensing agent attaches a use license to protected messages without needing to access an AD RMS server.

IRM enables an organization and its users to control the rights that recipients are granted for email messages. It also helps control recipient actions, such as forwarding a message to other recipients, printing a message or attachment, or extracting message or attachment content by copying and pasting. Users can apply IRM protection in Microsoft Outlook or Outlook Web App (OWA). As an administrator, you can configure your organization's messaging policies and apply them by using transport protection rules or Outlook protection rules. IRM also enables your organization to decrypt protected content and enforce policy compliance.

IRM protection is configured by applying an AD RMS rights policy template. You can use policy templates to control permissions that recipients have on a message.

> **NOTE   RMS-ENABLED APPLICATIONS**
> Microsoft Office applications, such as Microsoft Word, Microsoft Excel, and Microsoft PowerPoint, are RMS enabled and can be used to create protected content.

Quick Check

- What EMS command enables licensing and hence enables IRM features for
  messages sent to internal recipients?

Quick Check Answer

- *Set-IRMConfiguration –InternalLicensingEnabled $true*

AD RMS Rights Policy Templates

AD RMS uses XrML-based rights policy templates to allow compatible IRM-enabled
applications to apply consistent protection policies. Exchange 2010 ships with the Do Not
Forward template. When this template is applied to a message, only the recipients addressed
in the message can decrypt the message, and these recipients cannot forward the message
to anyone else, copy content from the message, or print the message. If an AD RMS server
is present in your organization, you can create additional RMS templates to meet your IRM
protection requirements.

The following EMS command retrieves the list of active rights management services policy
templates that are currently available to the Exchange Server 2010 Hub Transport server on
which the command is run:

```
Get-RMSTemplate
```

Note, however, that because the Do Not Forward template ships with Exchange
Server 2010, it is not listed by this command. The *Get-RMSTemplate* command lists any
additional templates that you obtain from an AD RMS server and returns a blank list by
default.

Applying IRM Protection

IRM protection can be applied to messages manually by Outlook users. This process uses the IRM functionality in Outlook, but you can use Exchange to take actions (such as applying transport rules) that enforce your organization's messaging policy. OWA users can protect messages they send and view IRM-protected messages they receive.

In Outlook 2010, you can create Outlook protection rules that automatically IRM-protect messages. Outlook 2010 applies IRM protection when a user is composing a message. You can also create transport rules on Hub Transport servers that automatically IRM-protected messages. Note that you cannot IRM-protect a message that is already IRM protected. If a user IRM-protects a message in Outlook, you cannot then apply IRM protection using a transport rule.

You can IRM-protect messages sent to mailbox users or distribution groups within your Exchange organization, but you cannot directly IRM-protect messages sent to recipients outside your organization unless you create a federated trust between your Active Directory forest and the forest that contains the external users by using Active Directory Federation Services. Because external distribution list or distribution group expansion does not occur within the sending Exchange organization, IRM-protected messages sent to external distribution groups contain a license for the group but not for group members, who are therefore unable to access the message.

 Quick Check

- What EMS command retrieves the list of active rights management services policy templates that are currently available to the Exchange Server 2010 server on which the command is run (other than templates that ship with Exchange Server 2010)?

Quick Check Answer

- *Get-RMSTemplate*

Decrypting IRM-Protected Messages

Administrators need to be able to access encrypted message content so that they can enforce messaging policies and ensure regulatory compliance. They must also be able to search encrypted messages to meet the requirements of litigation, regulatory audits, or internal investigations. To help with these tasks, Exchange 2010 includes the following IRM features:

- **Transport decryption**   This allows transport agents (such as the transport rules agent) installed on Exchange 2010 servers to access message content.

> **MORE INFO**   **TRANSPORT DECRYPTION**
>
> For more information about transport decryption, see *http://technet.microsoft.com/ en-us/library/dd638122.aspx*.

- **Journal report decryption**   You can use journaling to preserve messaging content and meet compliance or business requirements. The Exchange Server 2010 journaling agent creates a journal report for messages subject to journaling and includes metadata about the message in the report. If the message in a journal report is IRM protected, journal report decryption attaches a clear text copy. Journaling is discussed in Chapter 11.

> **MORE INFO**   **JOURNAL REPORT DECRYPTION**
>
> For more information about journal report decryption, see *http://technet.microsoft .com/en-us/library/dd876936.aspx*.

- **IRM decryption for Exchange Search**   This enables Exchange Search to index content in protected messages. When a discovery manager uses a Multi-Mailbox Search to perform a discovery operation, indexed protected messages are returned in the search results.

> **MORE INFO**   **EXCHANGE SEARCH AND MULTI-MAILBOX SEARCH**
>
> For more information about Exchange Search, see *http://technet.microsoft.com/ en-us/library/bb232132.aspx*. For more information about Multi-Mailbox Search, see *http://technet.microsoft.com/en-us/library/dd335072.aspx*.

To enable these decryption features, Exchange servers must be able to access the message. This is accomplished by adding the Federated Delivery mailbox, a system mailbox created by Exchange Setup, to the super users group on the AD RMS server. If a distribution group has been created and configured as a superusers group in the AD RMS cluster, you can add the Exchange 2010 Federated Delivery mailbox as a member of that group. If a superusers group is not configured, you need to create a distribution group and add the Federated Delivery mailbox as a member.

The following command adds the Federated Delivery mailbox FederatedEmail .4c1f4d8b-8179-4148-93bf-00a95fa1e042 to the ADRMSSuperUsers distribution group:

```
Add-DistributionGroupMember ADRMSSuperUsers -Member FederatedEmail.4c1f4d8b-8179-4148
-93bf-00a95fa1e042
```

IRM Agents

Transport agents, known as IRM agents, enable IRM functionality on Hub Transport servers. IRM agents are installed by Exchange Setup. Table 7-1 lists the IRM agents implemented on Hub Transport servers.

TABLE 7-1 IRM Agents

AGENT	FUNCTION
RMS decryption agent	Decrypts messages to allow access to transport agents.
Transport rules agent	Flags messages that match rule conditions in a transport protection rule so they can be protected by the RMS encryption agent.
RMS encryption agent	Applies IRM protection to messages flagged by the transport rules agent and reencrypts decrypted messages.
Prelicensing agent	Attaches a use license to protected messages.
Journal report decryption agent	Decrypts protected messages attached to journal reports and embeds clear-text versions along with the original encrypted messages.

Configuring IRM Features and Testing IRM Configuration

You can use the EMS but not the EMC to configure IRM features. The *Set-IRMConfiguration* EMS cmdlet is used to enable or disable IRM for internal messages and to enable or disable transport decryption, journal report decryption, IRM for Exchange Search, and IRM in OWA.

As discussed previously in the prelicensing section of this lesson, the following command enables licensing and hence enables IRM features for messages sent to internal recipients:

```
Set-IRMConfiguration -InternalLicensingEnabled $true
```

IRM features can be applied to messages to external recipients only if an appropriate federated trust has been configured. Federated trusts are discussed in Chapter 6, "Federated Sharing and Role-Based Access Control." As discussed previously, the following command enables licensing and hence enables IRM features for messages sent to external recipients if external licensing is currently disabled and a federated trust is configured:

```
Set-IRMConfiguration -ExternalLicensingEnabled $true
```

IRM features are enabled in OWA by default. The following command disables IRM features in OWA:

```
Set-IRMConfiguration -OWAEnabled $false
```

The following command enables IRM features in OWA if they have previously been disabled:

```
Set-IRMConfiguration -OWAEnabled $true
```

If transport decryption is mandatory, any message that cannot be decrypted is rejected and a non-delivery report (NDR) is returned to the sender. The following command sets transport decryption to mandatory:

```
Set-IRMConfiguration -TransportDecryptionSetting mandatory
```

If transport decryption is disabled, no attempt is made to decrypt internal or external messages before delivery. The following command sets transport decryption to disabled:

```
Set-IRMConfiguration -TransportDecryptionSetting disabled
```

Setting transport decryption to optional provides a best-effort approach to decryption. Messages are decrypted if possible but are delivered even if decryption fails. The following command sets transport decryption to optional:

```
Set-IRMConfiguration -TransportDecryptionSetting optional
```

> **MORE INFO** **SET-IRMCONFIGURATION**
>
> For more information about the *Set-IRMConfiguration* EMS cmdlet, including the parameters that apply only to the Outlook Live service, see *http://technet.microsoft.com/en-us/library/dd979792.aspx*.

> **MORE INFO** **CONFIGURING IRM FEATURES**
>
> For more information about configuring IRM features, see *http://technet.microsoft.com/en-us/library/dd351212.aspx*.

EXAM TIP

Notice that parameters such as OWAEnabled that take Boolean values are set to $true or $false. However, non-Boolean parameters, such as TransportDecryptionSetting, are not set to values that have an initial $ symbol.

If you want to view the current IRM configuration—either the default values before you configure it or the values after configuration—you enter the following command:

```
Get-IRMConfiguration | FL
```

Figure 7-8 shows a typical output of this command.

FIGURE 7-8 IRM configuration

After you configure IRM, you can use a command based on the *Test-IRMConfiguration* EMS cmdlet to perform end-to-end tests of your IRM deployment. These tests verify IRM functionality immediately after initial IRM configuration and on an ongoing basis. Commands based on this cmdlet perform the following tests:

- Inspect IRM configuration in your Exchange Server 2010 organization.
- Check the AD RMS server for version and hotfix information.
- Verify whether an Exchange server can be activated for RMS by retrieving a Rights Account Certificate and Client Licensor Certificate.
- Acquire AD RMS rights policy templates from the AD RMS server.
- Verify that the specified sender can send IRM-protected messages.
- Retrieve a superuser use license for the specified recipient.
- Acquire a prelicense for the specified recipient.

For example, the following command tests the IRM configuration for messages that Kim Akers sends to Don Hall:

```
Test-IRMConfiguration -Sender KimAkers@adatum.com -Recipient DonHall@adatum.com
```

MORE INFO **TEST-IRMCONFIGURATION**

For more information about the *Test-IRMConfiguration* EMS cmdlet, see *http://technet .microsoft.com/en-us/library/dd979798.aspx.*

Quick Check

- Which IRM agent flags messages that match rule conditions in a transport protection rule so that they can be protected by the RMS encryption agent?

Quick Check Answer

- The transport rules agent

Using Transport Protection Rules

Email messages and attachments typically contain business critical information, including personally identifiable information (PII), such as contact details, credit card numbers, and employee records. Industry-specific and local regulations govern the collection, storage, and disclosure of PII. Organizations create messaging policies that provide guidelines about how to handle sensitive information. In Exchange Server 2010, transport protection rules implement messaging policies by inspecting message content, encrypting sensitive email content, and using rights management to control access. Transport protection rules are transport rules that apply an AD RMS rights policy template to protect messages through the IRM.

Exchange Server 2010 ships with the Do Not Forward template. When this template is applied to a message, only the recipients addressed in the message can decrypt it. These recipients cannot forward the message to anyone else, copy content from the message, or print the message. Additional RMS templates can be created using your organization's AD RMS server to meet your rights protection requirements.

> **MORE INFO** **CREATING AD RMS TEMPLATES**
>
> For more information about creating AD RMS templates, see *http://go.microsoft.com/ fwlink/?LinkId=136593*.

Creating a Transport Protection Rule

You can use transport protection rules to apply persistent rights protection to messages based on message properties such as sender, recipient, message subject, and content. You can use either the EMC or the EMS to create a transport protection rule. To use the EMC, carry out the following procedure:

1. Open the EMC and expand the tree on the Console pane.
2. Under Organization Configuration, click Hub Transport.
3. Click New Transport Rule on the Actions pane. This opens the New Transport Rule Wizard.
4. On the Introduction page, provide a name and, optionally, a comment. If you do not want the new rule to be enabled automatically when it is created, clear the Enabled check box.

5. Click Next. On the Conditions page, shown in Figure 7-9, complete the following fields:

- In the Step 1. Select Condition(s) box, select all the conditions that you want to apply to this rule. Note that if you do not select any conditions, all messages handled by Hub Transport servers are IRM protected. In a production environment, this can lead to a considerable resource requirement.

- If you selected conditions in the Step 1. Select Condition(s) box, click each blue underlined word in the Step 2. Edit The Rule Description By Clicking An Underlined Value box.

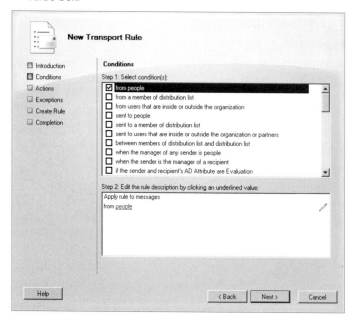

FIGURE 7-9 The Conditions page

6. When you click a blue underlined word, a window opens, as shown in Figure 7-10, to prompt you for the values to apply to the condition. Select the values that you want to apply or type the values manually. If the window requires that you manually add values to a list, type a value and then click Add. Repeat this process until you have entered all the values and then click OK to close the window.

7. Repeat the previous step for each condition that you selected. After you configure all the conditions, click Next on the Conditions page.

8. On the Actions page, shown in Figure 7-11, complete the following fields:

- In the Step 1. Select Actions box, select the Rights Protect Message With RMS Template check box.

- In the Step 2: Edit The Rule Description By Clicking An Underlined Value box, click the underlined words RMS Template.

9. In the Select RMS Template dialog box, select an available RMS template and then click OK.

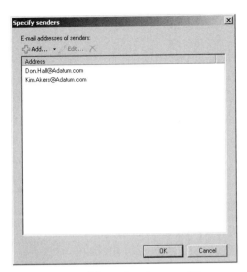

FIGURE 7-10 Applying values to a condition

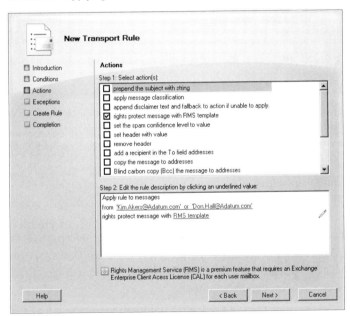

FIGURE 7-11 The Actions page

10. Click Next. Optionally, on the Exceptions page, select an exception you want to use and specify the appropriate value as required.

11. Click Next. On the Create Rule page, review the Configuration Summary. Make sure that the RMS template selected is the one you intend to use.

12. Click New to create the transport rule.

13. On the Completion page, if the status is Failed, click Back and review your settings. Otherwise, the status is Completed, in which case click Finish to close the wizard.

You can also use the EMS to create a transport protection rule. The following command creates the transport protection rule Protect-Confidential. The rule IRM-protects messages that contain the word "Confidential" in the Subject field using the Do Not Forward template:

```
New-TransportRule -Name "Protect-Confidential" -SubjectContainsWords "Confidential"
-ApplyRightsProtectionTemplate "Do Not Forward"
```

> **MORE INFO   GET-RMSTEMPLATE AND NEW-TRANSPORTRULE**
>
> For more information about the *Get-RMSTemplate* EMS cmdlet, see *http://technet .microsoft.com/en-us/library/dd297960.aspx*. For more information about the *New-TransportRule* EMS cmdlet, see *http://technet.microsoft.com/en-us/library/bb125138.aspx*.

> **MORE INFO   TRANSPORT RULES AND TRANSPORT PROTECTION RULES**
>
> For more information about transport rules, access *http://technet.microsoft.com/en-us/ library/dd351127.aspx* and follow the links. For more information about transport protection rules, see *http://technet.microsoft.com/en-us/library/dd298166.aspx*.

Protecting Outlook and OWA Messages

Outlook and OWA users can apply IRM protection to messages by applying an AD RMS rights policy template. However, this gives users the option of sending messages in clear text without IRM protection. In organizations that use email as a hosted service, information leakage can occur as a message leaves the client and is routed and stored outside the boundaries of the organization. Email hosting companies might have well-defined procedures and checks to help mitigate the risk of information leakage, but an organization loses control of the information after a message leaves its boundary. *Outlook protection rules* can help protect against this type of information leakage.

Outlook protection rules help an organization protect against the risk of information leakage by automatically applying IRM protection to messages. In Outlook 2010, messages are IRM-protected before they leave the Outlook client. This protection is also applied to any attachments using supported file formats. When you create Outlook protection rules on an Exchange Server 2010 server, these rules are automatically distributed to Outlook 2010 by Exchange Web services. Outlook 2010 can then apply the rule, provided that the AD RMS rights policy template is available on client computers.

Outlook protection rules are applied in Outlook 2010 before the message leaves the user's computer. Messages protected by an Outlook protection rule enter the transport pipeline with IRM protection already applied and are saved in an encrypted format in the Sent Items folder of the sender's mailbox.

If you use transport protection rules, users have no indication of whether a message will be automatically protected on the Hub Transport server. When, on the other hand, an Outlook protection rule is applied to a message in Outlook 2010, users know whether a message will be IRM protected. If required, users can also select a different rights policy template.

You can use the EMS but not the EMC to create an Outlook protection rule. For example, the following command creates the Outlook protection rule MyProject. This rule protects messages sent to the TechnicalAuthors distribution group with the AD RMS template Do Not Forward:

```
New-OutlookProtectionRule -Name "MyProject" -SentTo "TechnicalAuthors"
-ApplyRightsProtectionTemplate "Do Not Forward"
```

You can specify whether the user can override the rule, either by removing IRM protection or by applying a different AD RMS rights policy template. If a user overrides the IRM protection applied by an Outlook protection rule, Outlook 2010 inserts the X-MS-Outlook-Client-Rule-Overridden header in the message. This allows an administrator to discover that the user overrode a rule.

You can use the *Get-OutlookProtectionRule* EMS cmdlet to obtain the configuration of an existing Outlook protection rule and the *Set-OutlookProtectionRule* EMS cmdlet to change that configuration. You can also use the EMS *Remove-OutlookProtectionRule* cmdlet to remove an Outlook protection rule. For example, the following command removes the MyProject Outlook protection rule:

```
Remove-OutlookProtectionRule -Identity "MyProject"
```

> **MORE INFO** **NEW-OUTLOOKPROTECTIONRULE, GET-OUTLOOKPROTECTIONRULE, SET-OUTLOOKPROTECTIONRULE, AND REMOVE-OUTLOOKPROTECTIONRULE**
>
> For more information about the *New-OutlookProtectionRule* EMS cmdlet, see *http://technet.microsoft.com/en-us/library/dd298182.aspx*. For more information about the *Get-OutlookProtectionRule* EMS cmdlet, see *http://technet.microsoft.com/en-us/library/dd298004.aspx*. For more information about the *Set-OutlookProtectionRule* EMS cmdlet, see *http://technet.microsoft.com/en-us/library/dd297994.aspx*. For more information about the *Remove-OutlookProtectionRule* EMS cmdlet, see *http://technet.microsoft.com/en-us/library/dd297961.aspx*.

 Quick Check

1. What EMS cmdlet do you use to create a transport protection rule?
2. What parameter associated with this cmdlet configures the rule as a transport protection rule?

Quick Check Answers

1. *New-TransportRule*
2. ApplyRightsProtectionTemplate

Enabling or Disabling IRM in OWA

If you enable IRM in OWA in your organization, OWA users can IRM-protect messages by applying an AD RMS template created on your AD RMS cluster. This also enables OWA users to view IRM-protected messages. Note that before you enable IRM in OWA, you must add the Federated Delivery mailbox to the super users group on the AD RMS cluster, as described earlier in this lesson.

You can use commands based on the *Set-IRMConfiguration* EMS cmdlet to enable or disable IRM in OWA for your entire Exchange Server 2010 organization. You can also control IRM in OWA at the following levels:

- **Per-OWA virtual directory**   To enable or disable IRM for an OWA virtual directory, use the *Set-OWAVirtualDirectory* cmdlet and set the IRMEnabled parameter to $true (the default) or $false. This allows you to disable IRM for one OWA virtual directory on a Client Access server while keeping it enabled on another virtual directory on a different Client Access server.

- **Per-OWA mailbox policy**   To enable or disable IRM for an OWA mailbox policy, use the *Set-OWAMailboxPolicy* cmdlet and set the IRMEnabled parameter to $true (the default) or $false. This allows you to enable IRM in OWA for one set of users and disable it for other users by assigning them a different OWA mailbox policy.

You can use the EMS but not the EMC to enable or disable IRM in OWA. The following command enables IRM in OWA for an entire Exchange Server 2010 organization:

```
Set-IRMConfiguration -OWAEnabled $true
```

The following command disables IRM in OWA for the virtual directory MyVirtualDirectory on Client Access server VAN-EX1:

```
Set-OWAVirtualDirectory -Identity VAN-EX1\MyVirtualDirectory -IRMEnabled $false
```

EXAM TIP

Note that the *Set-IRMConfiguration* cmdlet supports the OWAEnabled parameter, whereas the *Set-OWAVirtualDirectory* and *Set-OWAMailboxPolicy* cmdlets support the IRMEnabled parameter.

MORE INFO   SET-IRMCONFIGURATION, SET-OWAVIRTUALDIRECTORY, AND *SET-OWAMAILBOXPOLICY*

For more information about the *Set-IRMConfiguration* EMS cmdlet, see *http://technet .microsoft.com/en-us/library/dd979792.aspx*. For more information about the *Set-OWAVirtualDirectory* EMS cmdlet, see *http://technet.microsoft.com/en-us/library/ bb123515.aspx*. For more information about the *Set-OWAMailboxPolicy* cmdlet EMS cmdlet, see *http://technet.microsoft.com/en-us/library/dd297989.aspx*.

Implementing Moderated Transport

The moderated transport feature introduced by Exchange Server 2010 enables you to specify that all email messages sent to specific recipients are approved by moderators. You can configure any type of recipient as a moderated recipient, and an Exchange Server 2010 Hub Transport server ensures that all messages sent to those recipients go through an approval process.

Note that Exchange Server 2007 and earlier Hub Transport servers do not understand moderated transport and that if a moderated distribution group is expanded on an Exchange Server 2007, the message is sent to all recipients and bypasses the moderation process.

Typically, moderated transport is used to control messages sent to large distribution groups. Depending on organizational requirements, messages sent to specific mailboxes or partner contacts may also require moderation. You use moderated recipients to accomplish these tasks.

Moderated transport makes use of the Exchange Server 2010 approval framework. Exchange uses the approval framework for making decisions about email messages. The approval framework uses a special mailbox called the *arbitration mailbox* for each workflow. This mailbox stores the original message and the decision state during the approval process.

> **MORE INFO** **THE APPROVAL FRAMEWORK**
>
> For more information about the approval framework, see *http://technet.microsoft.com/ en-us/library/dd351166.aspx*.

The following components are included in the moderated transport application:

- **Categorizer**   The transport categorizer initiates the approval process. When it detects a moderated recipient while processing a message, the categorizer reroutes the message to the arbitration mailbox.

- **Information Assistant**   The Information Assistant process monitors the arbitration mailbox and resubmits approved messages to the submission queue for delivery to intended recipients. Otherwise, it deletes rejected messages. This component is also responsible for sending rejection notifications to the sender and cleaning the arbitration mailbox by deleting any stale or orphaned messages. For example, if a moderator deletes an approval request rather than making a decision, the Information Assistant removes the message that is waiting for approval in the arbitration mailbox.

- **Store driver**   The store driver processes messages that the categorizer marks for moderation by storing the original message in the arbitration mailbox, sending approval requests to the moderators, and marking the moderator decision on the message stored in the arbitration mailbox. If the Information Assistant submits a previously approved message, the store driver reconfigures the message so that it is identical to the original message submitted by the sender.

- **Arbitration mailbox**   The arbitration mailbox stores the original message that is awaiting approval. During setup, one arbitration mailbox is created for moderated transport by default and is used for all moderated recipients. If appropriate, you can add additional arbitration mailboxes for load-balancing purposes. If you use multiple arbitration mailboxes, you need to specify which mailbox is used for each moderated recipient.

When a user sends a message to a recipient and moderation is enabled, the message follows the path to its destination, as described by the following procedure (illustrated in Figure 7-12):

1. The sender creates a message that is sent to the moderated recipient.

2. The categorizer intercepts the message and marks it for moderation. It then reroutes it to the arbitration mailbox.

3. The store driver stores the message in the arbitration mailbox and sends an approval request to the moderator.

4. The moderator accepts or rejects the message.

5. The store driver marks the moderator's decision on the original message in the arbitration mailbox.

6. The Information Assistant reads the approval status on the message stored in the arbitration mailbox. It then processes the message depending on the moderator's decision:

   ■ If the moderator approves the message, the Information Assistant resubmits it to the submission queue. The message is delivered to the recipient (process 6a in Figure 7-12).

   ■ If the moderator rejects the message, the Information Assistant deletes it from the arbitration mailbox and notifies the sender that the message was rejected (process 6b in Figure 7-12).

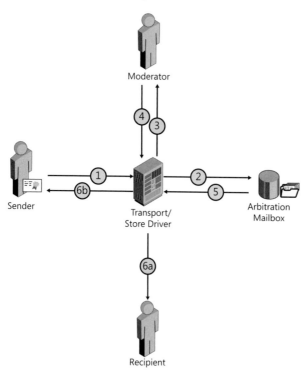

FIGURE 7-12 Moderated transport message flow

Configuring a Moderated Recipient

When you configure a recipient for moderation, all messages sent to that recipient are subject to approval by the designated moderator or moderators. You typically moderate email messages sent to a distribution group, although you can moderate email sent to an individual user. You can use either the EMC or the EMS to configure a moderated distribution group (or a moderated user). To use the EMC to configure the global distribution group FirstDistributionGroup as a moderated distribution group and identify Don Hall as the moderator, carry out the following procedure (note that the mail-enabled distribution group FirstDistributionGroup must exist for this procedure to work):

1. On the EMC Console pane, click Recipient Configuration.

2. Click the distribution group FirstDistributionGroup on the Result pane and then click Properties on the Actions pane.

3. Click the Mail Flow Settings tab in the FirstDistributionGroup Properties dialog box. This tab is shown in Figure 7-13.

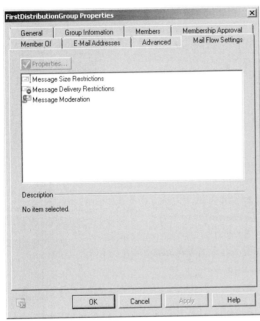

FIGURE 7-13 The Mail Flow Settings tab in the FirstDistributionGroup Properties dialog box

4. Click Message Moderation and then click Properties.

5. In the Message Moderation dialog box, select the Messages Sent To This Group Have To Be Approved By A Moderator check box.

6. In the Specify Group Moderators section, click Add.

7. In the Select Recipient dialog box, select Don Hall and then click OK.

8. Select the Notify Senders In Your Organization Only When Their Message Is Not Approved option. The Message Moderation dialog box should look similar to Figure 7-14.

9. Click OK to close the Message Moderation dialog box.

10. Click OK to close the FirstDistributionGroup Properties dialog box.

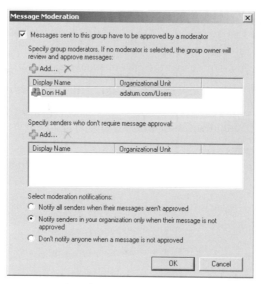

FIGURE 7-14 Specifying Message Moderation settings

This example shows how to configure a distribution group for moderation, but the same steps can be followed to configure any recipient for moderation.

You can also use the EMS to configure a moderated distribution group or user. The following EMS command enables moderation for the distribution group SecondDistributionGroup (which must exist or else the command returns an error), designates Kim Akers as the moderator, permits the members of the distribution group ThirdDistributionGroup (which must also exist) to bypass moderation, and notifies internal senders if their message to the distribution group is rejected but does not send any notifications to senders external to the organization:

```
Set-DistributionGroup SecondDistributionGroup -ModerationEnabled $true -ModeratedBy
"Kim Akers" -ByPassModerationFromSendersOrMembers ThirdDistributionGroup
-SendModerationNotifications Internal
```

This command completes without output. Note that because no arbitration mailbox is specified, the default arbitration mailbox is used.

> **MORE INFO** **SET-DISTRIBUTIONGROUP**
>
> For more information about the *Set-DistributionGroup* EMS cmdlet, see *http://technet .microsoft.com/en-us/library/bb124955.aspx*.

You can configure any recipient for moderation. For example, to configure a moderated mailbox user, you would enter a command with a similar syntax except that you would use the *Set-Mailbox* cmdlet instead of the *Set-DistributionGroup* cmdlet.

Creating and Deploying an Additional Arbitration Mailbox

You can, if required for load balancing, create an additional arbitration mailbox by entering an EMS command based on the *New-Mailbox* cmdlet and using the Arbitration parameter. It is possible to configure an existing mailbox as an additional arbitration mailbox by using the *Set-Mailbox* EMS cmdlet with the same parameter, but this could lead to confusion, and it is typically preferable to create an additional arbitration mailbox from scratch.

The following EMS command creates an arbitration mailbox named Arbitration. You need to provide other information, such as the user principal name, when prompted:

```
New-Mailbox –Name Arbitration –Arbitration
```

When you have created an additional arbitration mailbox, you can assign it to a moderated recipient by using the ArbitrationMailbox parameter. For example, the following command assigns the arbitration mailbox Arbitration to the FirstDistributionGroup moderated recipient:

```
Set-DistributionGroup FirstDistributionGroup –ArbitrationMailbox Arbitration
```

Figure 7-15 shows the EMS commands to create and deploy the additional arbitration mailbox named Arbitration.

FIGURE 7-15 Creating and deploying an arbitration mailbox

EXAM TIP

Distinguish between the Arbitration and ArbitrationMailbox parameters. The Arbitration parameter defines a new or reconfigured mailbox as an additional arbitration mailbox. The ArbitrationMailbox parameter specifies which arbitration mailbox is used when moderating email messages to a specific recipient. If the ArbitrationMailbox parameter is not included in the command, the default arbitration mailbox is used.

Moderated and Nonmoderated Recipients

If a message is sent to a group of recipients that includes both moderated and nonmoderated recipients, a separate approval process occurs for each moderated recipient.

Suppose, for example, the user Don Hall sends a message to five recipients, one of which is a moderated distribution group. The categorizer splits this message into two. The first message is delivered immediately to the four nonmoderated recipients, and the second message is submitted to the approval process for the moderated distribution group. If a message is intended for more than one moderated recipient, a separate copy is created for each moderated recipient and submitted to the approval process.

A moderated distribution group can contain other moderated recipients. In this case, a separate approval process occurs for each moderated recipient in the distribution group after the message to the distribution group is approved. You can enable the automatic approval of the distribution group members after the message to the moderated distribution group is approved by setting the BypassNestedModerationEnabled parameter of the moderated distribution group to $true. In this case, you enter an EMS command similar to the following:

```
Set-DistributionGroup -Identity Research -BypassNestedModerationEnabled $true
```

> **MORE INFO** **SET-DISTRIBUTIONGROUP**
>
> For more information about the *Set-DistributionGroup* EMS cmdlet, see *http://technet .microsoft.com/en-us/library/bb124955.aspx.*

Bypassing Moderation

Messages from moderators are delivered to the moderated recipient immediately and bypass the approval process. A moderator has the authority to determine what messages are appropriate for a moderated recipient.

Owners of distribution groups and dynamic distribution groups are not, by default, trusted senders, and messages from these senders are subject to the approval process. A distribution group owner can be responsible for managing the distribution group membership but may not be able to moderate messages sent to it.

For example, the Technical Support Department may be the owners of a distribution group called Marketing, but only specific people in the Marketing Department may have moderator rights for this distribution group. To bypass moderation for owners, you must either designate them as moderators or add them to the list of senders explicitly allowed to send messages to the moderated recipients.

> **MORE INFO** **MODERATED TRANSPORT**
>
> For more information about moderated transport, see *http://technet.microsoft.com/ en-us/library/dd297936.aspx.*

Lesson Summary

- You use transport rules to apply messaging policies on both Hub Transport and Edge Transport servers.

- You can configure IRM to use an RMS template that enables users to send secure IRM-protected messages.

- Transport protection rules and Outlook protection rules are used to IRM-protect messages.

- Moderated transport enables a moderator to intercept and check mail to a specified recipient.

Lesson Review

You can use the following questions to test your knowledge of the information in Lesson 1, "Managing Transport Rules." The questions are also available on the companion CD if you prefer to review them in electronic form.

> **NOTE ANSWERS**
>
> Answers to these questions and explanations of why each answer choice is correct or incorrect are located in the "Answers" section at the end of the book.

1. You want to create a transport rule named AddPaulWest that adds Paul West to the recipients whenever an email message is sent to Don Hall, except when the message subject includes the word "holiday." What command do you enter on a Hub Transport server?

   A. *New-TransportRule –Name AddPaulWest –SentTo "Don Hall" –AddToRecipients "Paul West" –ExceptIfSubjectOrBodyContainsWords "holiday"*

   B. *New-TransportRule –Name AddPaulWest –SentTo "Don Hall" –AddToRecipients "Paul West" –ExceptIfSubjectContainsWords "holiday"*

   C. *New-TransportRule –Name AddPaulWest –SentTo "Paul West" –AddToRecipients "Don Hall" –ExceptIfSubjectContainsWords "holiday"*

   D. *New-TransportRule –Name AddPaulWest –SentTo "Paul West" –AddToRecipients "Don Hall" –ExceptIfSubjectOrBodyContainsWords "holiday"*

2. You want to amend the transport rule AddPaulWest so that both Paul West and Kim Akers are added to the recipients when email is sent to Don Hall. What EMS cmdlet would you use?

   A. *Get-TransportRule*

   B. *New-TransportRule*

   C. *Set-TransportRule*

   D. *Set-TransportRulePredicate*

3. You are using a regular expression in a transport rule and specify that an action is to be implemented when a pattern in the subject or body matches the expression \D\D\S\S\ d\d\d\d\S\S\S\d\d\d\d. Which of the following patterns trigger the action? (Choose all that apply.)

   A. ABCA1221YZz3333

   B. A12A3421YZU6234

   C. AB986556+++9688

   D. 1Aaa9865fg99999

   E. Good4444bad2222

   F. 4leggood2legbad

4. You are using the EMC New Transport Rule Wizard to create a transport protection rule that IRM-protects email traffic. What check box do you need to select on the Action page of the wizard, shown in Figure 7-16?

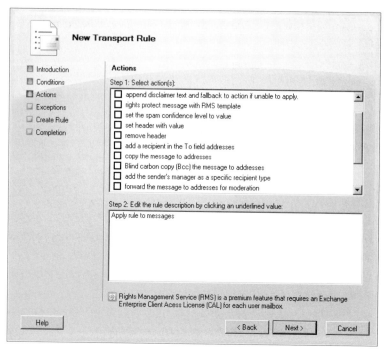

FIGURE 7-16 The Action page of the New Transport Rule Wizard

   A. Append Disclaimer Text And Fallback Action If Unable To Apply

   B. Rights Protect Message With RMS Template

   C. Add A Recipient In The To Field Address

   D. Forward The Message To Addresses For Moderation

5. You want to configure a transport rule that appends an HTML disclaimer to all messages sent outside your organization (Adatum.com). The disclaimer should read, "All messages sent by the Adatum Corporation have been checked for viruses and other malware using the best and most up-to-date software available." If, for any reason, this disclaimer cannot be appended to an email message, the message should be rejected. What EMS command creates the transport rule AppendDisclaimer that implements this requirement?

   A. *New-TransportRule -Name AppendDisclaimer -Enabled $true -SentToScope 'NotInOrganization' -ApplyHtmlDisclaimerLocation 'Append' -ApplyHtmlDisclaimerText "<h3>Adatum Corporation Policy</h3><p>All messages sent by the Adatum Corporation have been checked for viruses and other malware using the best and most up-to-date software available.</p>" -ApplyHtmlDisclaimerFallbackAction Reject*

B. *New-TransportRule -Name AppendDisclaimer -Enabled $true -SentToScope 'InOrganization' -ApplyHtmlDisclaimerLocation 'Append' -ApplyHtmlDisclaimerText "<h3>Adatum Corporation Policy</h3><p>All messages sent by the Adatum Corporation have been checked for viruses and other malware using the best and most up-to-date software available.</p>" -ApplyHtmlDisclaimerFallbackAction Reject*

C. *New-TransportRule -Name AppendDisclaimer -Enabled $true -SentToScope 'NotInOrganization' -ApplyHtmlDisclaimerLocation 'Append' -ApplyHtmlDisclaimerText "<h3>Adatum Corporation Policy</h3><p>All messages sent by the Adatum Corporation have been checked for viruses and other malware using the best and most up-to-date software available.</p>" -ApplyHtmlDisclaimerFallbackAction Ignore*

D. *New-TransportRule -Name AppendDisclaimer -Enabled $true -SentToScope 'InOrganization' -ApplyHtmlDisclaimerLocation 'Append' -ApplyHtmlDisclaimerText "<h3>Adatum Corporation Policy</h3><p>All messages sent by the Adatum Corporation have been checked for viruses and other malware using the best and most up-to-date software available.</p>" -ApplyHtmlDisclaimerFallbackAction Ignore*

Lesson 2: Setting Up Message Routing

This lesson considers how email traffic is routed from one Active Directory site to another and how the path it takes is controlled by the cost of site links, based in turn on the speed and bandwidth these links provide. It looks at how you configure *Send connectors* to send email messages to specified destinations both inside and outside your organization and how you configure parameters, such as maximum message size, on these connectors.

The lesson discusses *Receive connectors* and how you configure such a connector to listen on a specific port at a specific Internet Protocol (IP) address for email traffic from specified external sources. Some traffic needs to be encrypted and its source and destination authenticated, and the lesson looks at how this is accomplished.

After this lesson, you will be able to:

- Explain how site-link costs determine message routing and distinguish between Active Directory and Exchange site-link costs.
- Assign an Exchange cost to a site link.
- Create and configure Send connectors.
- Create and configure Receive connectors.
- Use Foreign connectors to connect to non-SMTP messaging systems.
- Use *Transport Layer Security (TLS)* and *Mutual TLS (MTLS)* to encrypt and authenticate email traffic.

Estimated lesson time: 50 minutes

Routing Messages

Hub Transport and Edge Transport servers route messages received from internal and external senders to their ultimate destinations. The message is first categorized and is next processed by the store driver, delivery agents, or the foreign gateway connection handler. The component that is used depends on the ultimate destination. This section describes the stages of message categorization and the various messaging components that implement message routing.

Categorizing Messages

As discussed in Lesson 1, "Managing Transport Rules," the categorizer is a message routing component of the Exchange Server 2010 transport service that processes incoming messages and determines what to do with these messages based on information about the intended recipients. After a message is received by an Exchange Server 2010 Hub Transport or Edge Transport server, it undergoes preliminary processing and is delivered to the submission queue. Messages then move from the submission queue through the categorizer. This process can be divided into several phases as follows:

- **Initial agent processing** Agents such as the Microsoft Forefront Protection for Exchange Server antivirus agent and the journaling agent process messages on Hub Transport servers.

> **MORE INFO** **MICROSOFT FOREFRONT PROTECTION**
>
> For more information about Microsoft Forefront Protection, access *http://www.microsoft.com/forefront/en/us/default.aspx* and follow the links.

- **Recipient resolution** The recipient email address is resolved. This determines whether the recipient has an internal mailbox or an external email address.
- **Routing** The categorizer's routing component determines the message's ultimate destination and the route to that destination. It then selects the next segment (or hop) for message relay and resolves the next hop information to a list of physical servers and IP addresses.
- **Content conversion** This transforms email messages into a format that is readable by the recipient and that is specific to the recipient's email client. Conversion occurs before a message is relayed to its next hop.
- **Routed message agent processing** After the routing decisions for a message are made, the transport rules agent and the journaling agent are applied on a Hub Transport server. Note that the journaling agent is applied both at the initial agent processing stage and when the message has been routed. This enables any changes that are made to the message by the transport rules agent to be processed by the journaling agent.
- **Message assembly and DSN generation** The categorized message is assembled and moved to a delivery queue. A DSN message may also be generated during this phase.

Messaging Components

When they have been categorized, messages are processed by the store driver, delivery agents, or the foreign gateway connection handler. The processing component that is used depends on the ultimate message destination. A delivery queue is dynamically generated for each hop, and messages are queued in delivery queues after a routing decision is made. If a route to a recipient cannot be found, the messages are queued to the unreachable queue.

Exchange Server 2010 accesses configuration information stored in Active Directory to make routing decisions on a Hub Transport server. On an Edge Transport server, configuration information is stored in and accessed from AD LDS on the local server. Windows Server 2008 (or 2008 R2) and Exchange Server 2010 services create mappings of the configuration data and cache these mappings in routing tables that Exchange Server 2010 references when making routing decisions. The mappings cache is updated whenever the routing topology changes. Note that Edge Transport servers cannot cache information about Active Directory topology.

The following configuration and service components are used in message routing:

- **Active Directory sites**   These represent routing boundaries for Hub Transport servers. A Hub Transport server delivers email messages directly to Mailbox servers, distribution group expansion servers, and source servers for connectors in its local Active Directory site. It can also route messages to Edge Transport servers that are subscribed to that site. However, when routing email messages to remote Active Directory sites, a Hub Transport server must relay these messages to a Hub Transport server in the remote site.

- **Active Directory IP site links**   IP site links define logical paths between Active Directory sites. Exchange Server 2010 uses IP site links to determine the least-cost routing path to remote Active Directory sites.

- **Send connectors**   These are used to send messages to other SMTP hosts. If your Exchange organization routes messages to more than one email domain, you may decide to create Send connectors that are dedicated to each address space.

> **MORE INFO**   **ROUTING MESSAGES TO EXTERNAL DOMAINS**
>
> For more information about using Send connectors to route messages to external domains, see *http://technet.microsoft.com/en-us/library/bb232045.aspx*.

- **Delivery agents**   These are used to route messages to foreign systems that do not use the SMTP protocol.

- **Foreign connectors**   These use drop directories to send messages to foreign systems that do not use SMTP protocol for message transfer. Exchange uses the configuration of Foreign connectors when making routing decisions.

> **MORE INFO**   **DROP DIRECTORIES**
>
> For more information about drop directories used with foreign connectors, see *http://technet.microsoft.com/en-us/library/aa998275.aspx*.

- **Routing groups**   All computers running Exchange Server 2010 deployed in an organization belong to a single, global routing group. This is to implement compatibility with Exchange Server 2003.

- **Routing group connectors**   These define logical paths between Exchange routing groups. They are used when Exchange Server 2010 is deployed in an existing Exchange 2003 organization.

> **MORE INFO**   **ROUTING MESSAGES BETWEEN DIFFERENT EXCHANGE SERVER VERSIONS**
>
> For more information about message routing in an environment where more than one version of Exchange Server is deployed, see *http://technet.microsoft.com/en-us/library/bb232193.aspx*.

- **Microsoft Exchange Transport service**   This service is the SMTP provider for Exchange Server 2010. A series of SMTP Receive agents are triggered by various SMTP events, and the Microsoft Exchange Transport service enables these agents to process messages as they pass through SMTP transport and to perform anti-spam, antivirus, and other tasks before messages are submitted to the categorizer.

- **Microsoft Exchange Active Directory Topology service**   This service locates the domain controllers and global catalog servers that Exchange Server 2010 uses to retrieve configuration and recipient data from Active Directory.

- **Routing tables**   These hold the information that the routing component uses to make routing decisions. The routing table is composed of a map of topology components and their relationship to one another.

- **SMTP**   The SMTP protocol is used for communication when messages are relayed between SMTP servers. An SMTP server can be a Hub Transport server, Edge Transport server, or smart host. A Hub Transport server uses remote procedure call to deliver messages directly to Mailbox servers that have the same Active Directory site membership as the Hub Transport server.

- **DNS**   Exchange Server 2010 uses the enhanced DNS client component of the Microsoft Exchange Transport service to resolve the next hop selection to a list of target server names. The standard DNS client is used to resolve that list of server names to IP addresses. Enhanced DNS also provides round-robin load-balancing functionality for Exchange 2010 Transport servers.

Using Active Directory Sites and Site Costs for Routing

An Active Directory site is based on the physical aspects of the network and defines which subnets in the network are connected. The aim of site design is to optimize Active Directory replication traffic. The Active Directory site represents a routing boundary for Exchange Server 2010, and Hub Transport servers make routing decisions based on Active Directory site topology.

Site Membership

By default, an Active Directory forest contains a single Active Directory site named Default-First-Site-Name. If no other Active Directory sites are created, all domain member computers in the forest are members of Default-First-Site-Name, and you do not need to configure a subnet-to-site association. If you create additional Active Directory sites, you must specify the subnets that are assigned to each site. Table 7-2 shows a typical site-to-subnet association.

TABLE 7-2 Active Directory Site-to-Subnet Association

SITE NAME	ASSOCIATED IP SUBNETS
Site 01	10.10.10.0/24
	10.10.11.0/24
Site02	10.10.20.0/24
	10.10.21.0/24
Site03	10.10.30.0/24
	10.10.31.0/24

A Domain or Enterprise administrator assigns Active Directory site membership to domain controllers and global catalog servers. Other member computers in the domain, such as Exchange servers, are assigned Active Directory site membership automatically when they are configured to use an IP address in an IP subnet that is associated with an Active Directory site. Computers within the same Active Directory site are presumed to have good network connectivity. A member server is always in only one Active Directory site.

A site-aware application, such as Exchange Server 2010, can determine the Active Directory site membership of the computer on which it is installed and of other computers in the forest and then use that information to control communication flow. When a site-aware application needs to access another server, such as a domain controller or global catalog server, it first attempts to access servers that have the same Active Directory site membership as the computer on which it runs. An Exchange Server 2010 server uses Active Directory topology for message routing and to communicate with the services that are running on computers with other Exchange Server 2010 server roles installed. The Active Directory site acts as both a routing boundary and a service discovery boundary.

The process of determining the site membership of a computer in a domain uses a series of DNS queries to compare the local IP address to defined subnets and thus determine the appropriate site membership association. To reduce the overhead associated with DNS queries, Exchange Server 2010 adds the *msExchServerSite* attribute to the Active Directory schema. This attribute is a property of each Exchange server object, and the value of this attribute is the distinguished name of the Active Directory site of the Exchange server. Because site membership affinity is stored as an attribute of the server object, the current topology can be read directly from the Active Directory. This also enables a site membership association for a non-domain computer, such as a subscribed Edge Transport server.

 Quick Check

1. What entities represent routing boundaries for Hub Transport servers?

2. Which service locates the domain controllers and global catalog servers that Exchange Server 2010 uses to retrieve configuration and recipient data from Active Directory?

IP Site Links and Site-Link Costs

Site links are logical paths between Active Directory sites. A site-link object represents a set of sites that can communicate at a uniform cost through a specified intersite transport. Site links do not correspond to the actual paths that network packets follow on the physical network, but the cost that an administrator assigns to a site link typically relates to the reliability, speed, and available bandwidth of the underlying network. For example, an administrator would assign a lower cost to a network connection with a speed of 100 megabits per second (Mbps) than to a network connection with a speed of 10 Mbps.

By default, all site links are transitive. This means that if Site 01 links to Site 02 and Site 02 links to Site 03, then Site 01 links to Site 03. The transitive link between Site 01 and Site 03 is known as a *site-link bridge*.

You can configure a site link to use either IP or SMTP as the communication transport protocol. An SMTP site link is designed to provide a store and forward mechanism for replication of a limited number of data types between Active Directory sites that do not have a reliable network link. All types of data can be replicated across an IP site link, and Exchange Server 2010 uses IP site links to determine its routing topology. The routing component of Exchange Server 2010 takes into account the cost assigned to an IP site link when calculating a routing table. IP site-link costs are used to calculate the least-cost routing path to the ultimate destination for a message.

Every Active Directory site must be associated with at least one IP site link and a single IP site link named DEFAULTIPSITELINK is implemented by default. When you create an Active Directory site, you associate that site to an IP site link and you can either create additional IP site links to implement the desired topology or associate every Active Directory site with the DEFAULTIPSITELINK site link. Each Active Directory site that is part of an IP site link can communicate directly with every other site in that link at a uniform cost.

Figure 7-17 shows a full mesh topology that uses only the single default IP site link DEFAULTIPSITELINK. Each site communicates directly with every other site by using the same cost metric. Although more than one communication path is configured, only a single IP site link is defined.

A hub-and-spoke topolgy requires additional site links. For example, in Figure 7-18, four sites are connected in this topology. The central site, Site A, can communicate directly with each of the spoke sites, and the spoke sites can communicate with each other through the central site.

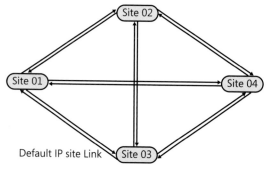

FIGURE 7-17 Full mesh topology using the single default IP site link

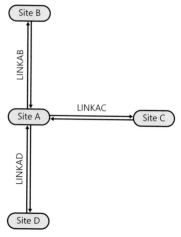

FIGURE 7-18 Hub-and-spoke site topology

Exchange uses site links when determining the least-cost path but will always attempt to deliver messages directly to the destination Hub Transport server. For example, if a user in Site B in the topology shown in Figure 7-18 sends a message to a user in Site C, the Hub Transport server in Site B will connect directly to the Hub Transport server in Site C. If you want to force messages to go through Site A, you need to enable that site as a hub site. Hub sites are discussed later in this lesson.

> **MORE INFO** **SITE CONFIGURATION**
>
> For more information about Active Directory site configuration, see *http://go.microsoft .com/fwlink/?linkid=33551*.

Assigning Exchange Costs to Site Links

The default cost for a site link is 100. A valid site-link cost can be any number from 1 through 99,999. If you specify more than one path, the link with the lowest cost assignment is always preferred. You can assign an Exchange-specific cost to an IP site link. If an Exchange cost is assigned to an IP site link, it is used by Exchange Server 2010. Otherwise, the Active Directory cost is used.

In most cases, existing IP site-link costs, based on network speeds, work well for Exchange Server 2010 message routing. However, if costs and traffic flow patterns are not optimal for Exchange traffic, you can assign Exchange costs by using an EMS command based on the *Set-AdSiteLink* cmdlet. For example, the following command sets an Exchange cost of 1,000 on the IP site link LINK0304:

```
Set-AdSiteLink -Identity LINK0304 -ExchangeCost 1000
```

In Figure 7-19, messages from Site 01 to Site 04 would normally be routed through Site 03 based on Active Directory IP site-link costs. However, because the Exchange cost of the IP site link between Site 03 and Site 04 has been set at 1,000, Exchange will route messaging traffic from Site 01 to Site 04 through Site 02.

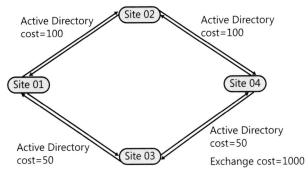

FIGURE 7-19 Using Exchange site-link cost to route messaging traffic

Adjusting IP site-link costs can be useful when the message routing topology needs to diverge from the Active Directory replication topology. You can use Exchange costs to force all messages to pass through a hub site. You can also use Exchange costs to control situations where messages are queued because communication to an Active Directory site fails or if a network connection between sites is a low-bandwidth connection used only for Active Directory replication.

Configuring Maximum Message Size on Site Links

By default, Exchange Server 2010 does not limit the size of messages that are relayed between Hub Transport servers in different Active Directory sites. If it becomes necessary to specify size limits because of traffic considerations, you can use an EMS command based on the *Set-AdSiteLink* EMS cmdlet to configure a maximum message size on an Active Directory IP site link. For example, the following command sets the maximum message size on the Active Directory IP site link LINKAB to 1 gigabyte (GB):

```
Set-AdSiteLink -Identity LINKAB -MaxMessageSize 1GB
```

Exchange routing generates an NDR for any message that has a size larger than the maximum message size limit configured on any Active Directory site link in the least-cost routing path. You can use this facility to restrict the size of messages sent to remote Active Directory sites with low-bandwidth connections.

> **MORE INFO   SET-ADSITELINK**
>
> For more information about the *Set-ADSiteLink* EMS cmdlet, see *http://technet.microsoft .com/en-us/library/bb123696.aspx*.

Implementing Hub Sites

Sometimes you want to ensure that all message delivery is relayed through a particular Active Directory site, such as to comply with your Exchange organization's internal policies. You can use an EMS command based on the *Set-AdSite* cmdlet to designate an Active Directory site as a hub site. If a hub site exists along the least-cost routing path for message delivery, the messages queue is processed by the Hub Transport servers in the hub site before messages are relayed to their ultimate destination. If several hub sites exist along the least-cost routing path, messages stop at each hub site along that path.

The following command designates the Active Directory site MyADSite as a hub site:

```
Set-AdSite -Identity MyADSite -HubSiteEnabled $true
```

> **MORE INFO   SET-ADSITE**
>
> For more information about the *Set-ADSite* EMS cmdlet, see *http://technet.microsoft.com/ en-us/library/bb124548.aspx*.

Exchange 2010 Routing Tables

When the Microsoft Exchange Transport service starts, it calculates a set of routing tables based on a snapshot of information retrieved from Active Directory (or on an Edge Transport server from AD LDS). Routing tables determine how messages are routed to recipients. When configuration changes are made, the routing tables are rebuilt, and the new routing tables are used to route incoming messages.

Exchange Server 2010 retrieves the following configuration data from Active Directory and makes it available to the routing component on Hub Transport servers:

- Active Directory sites
- Active Directory IP site links
- Exchange servers and their relationship to Active Directory sites
- SMTP connectors
- Non-SMTP connectors (these include delivery agent connectors, Foreign connectors, and non-SMTP connectors hosted by Exchange Server 2003)
- Routing groups
- Routing group connectors

- Mailbox stores
- Public folder stores
- Public folder hierarchies

Based on this data, the routing component of the Microsoft Exchange Transport service populates routing tables. The routing table correlates the data and maps the topology. This topology map contains the following elements:

- **Linked connectors map**   This map identifies the Receive connectors on the local server that are linked to the Send connector.

- **Server map**   This contains all Exchange Server 2010 and Exchange Server 2007 Hub transport, Edge Transport, and Mailbox servers, in addition to any Exchange Server 2003 servers in the organization. The map includes the total cost to reach any specific server.

- **Legacy server map**   This contains all Exchange Server 2007 Hub Transport, Edge Transport, and Mailbox servers, in addition to any Exchange Server 2003 servers in the organization. The map includes the total cost to reach any specific server.

- **Message Database (MDB) map**   This contains all MDBs in the organization and correlates the distinguished name of each MDB to routing data that includes the total cost to reach the server that hosts a specific MDB.

- **Active Directory site map**   This contains all Active Directory sites and a structure that holds the least-cost routing path from the local site to every other site. The map includes any hub sites along the least-cost routing path. Each routing path hop also identifies all Hub Transport servers on that site that will be used by the Enhanced DNS component. DNS is discussed later in this lesson.

- **Routing groups map**   This contains the total cost and first hop routing group connector for the least-cost routing path from the Exchange 2010 routing group to each legacy routing group.

- **Send connectors map**   This identifies the Send connectors configured in the organization and the source servers for each connector.

The information in the routing tables is logged to routing logs. These logs are located by default in the C:\Program Files\Microsoft\Exchange Server\V14\TransportRoles\Logs\Routing folder. A new log is generated every time the routing tables are recalculated. If a Hub Transport server is unable to contact Active Directory, routing decisions are based on the currently cached data, even though that data may not be up to date.

 Quick Check

- What EMS command would you use to configure the Active Directory site ContosoSite as a hub site?

Quick Check Answer

- *Set-AdSite -Identity ContosoSite -HubSiteEnabled $true*

Using and Configuring Send Connectors

Send connectors are configured on Hub Transport or Edge Transport servers. The Send connector on a Transport server represents a logical gateway through which outbound messages are sent to the next hop on the way to their destination. No explicit Send connectors are created by default when the Hub Transport or Edge Transport server role is installed. However, implicit and invisible Send connectors are automatically computed based on the site topology and are used to route messages internally between Hub Transport servers.

End-to-end mail flow requires that Edge Transport servers be subscribed to the Active Directory site by using the Edge subscription process. If your organization has an Internet-facing Hub Transport server or an unsubscribed Edge Transport server, you need to manually configure Send connectors to establish end-to-end mail flow.

A Send connector created on a Hub Transport server is stored in Active Directory and is available to all Hub Transport servers in the organization. If a Send connector is configured to send messages to an external domain, any Hub Transport server in the organization routes a message for that domain to a source server for that connector. The message is then relayed to the destination domain.

Send Connector Usage Type

You can use the New Send Connector Wizard in the EMC or an EMS command based on the *New-SendConnector* cmdlet to create a Send connector. You use the EMC to do this in the practice session later in this chapter. When you use the EMC, you need to specify a usage type for the connector. When you use the EMS, the default usage type is set to Custom.

The usage type determines the default permissions that are assigned on the connector and grants those permissions to trusted security principals, such as users, computers, and security groups. A security principal is identified by a security identifier. The usage type also defines the default smart host authentication mechanism. Note that if DNS resolution delivery is selected for a Send connector instead of a smart host, no smart host authentication mechanism is configured. Send connector permissions and smart host authentication mechanisms are discussed in detail later in this lesson. The available usage types are as follows:

- **Custom** This usage type has no default permissions and no smart host authentication mechanism. You would select the Custom usage type for a Send connector on an unsubscribed Edge Transport server that sends email to a Hub Transport server. You would also select the Custom usage type for a cross-forest Send connector on a Hub Transport server that sends email to an Exchange Server 2010 or an Exchange Server 2007 Hub Transport server, or to an Exchange Server 2003 bridgehead server in a second forest. You would also select this usage type for a Send connector on a Hub Transport server that sends email to a third-party smart host and for an Edge Transport server that sends email to a third-party smart host or to an external relay domain.

- **Internal**   The default permission sets for this usage type are ms-Exch-Send-Headers-Organization, ms-Exch-SMTP-Send-Exch50, ms-Exch-Send-Headers-Routing, and ms-Exch-Send-Headers-Forest. Default permissions are granted to Hub and Edge Transport servers, externally secured servers, the Exchange Legacy Interop universal security group, and Exchange Server 2003 and Exchange 2000 Server bridgehead servers. The Default smart host authentication mechanism is Exchange Server Authentication. You would select this usage type for a Send connector on a subscribed Edge Transport server that sends email to a Hub Transport server or to an Exchange 2003 bridgehead server. This connector is automatically created by the edge subscription process, and if email is being sent to an Exchange 2003 bridgehead server, that server needs to be configured as a smart host.

- **Internet**   The default permissions set for this usage type is Ms-Exch-Send-Headers-Routing. Default permissions are granted to anonymous user accounts and there is no smart host authentication mechanism. You would select this usage type for a Send connector on an Edge Transport server that sends email to the Internet. Note that a Send connector that is configured to send email to all domains is created automatically when the Edge Transport server is subscribed to the Exchange organization. If you wanted to send email directly on to the Internet from a Hub Transport server, you would need to configure a Send connector with the Internet usage type. However, this is not considered best practice.

- **Partner**   The default permissions set for this usage type is Ms-Exch-Send-Headers-Routing, and default permissions are granted to partner servers. The smart host authentication mechanism is not applicable because this usage type is selected when you establish MTLS authentication with a remote domain. You would apply the Partner usage type to a Send connector on an Edge Transport server that sends email to a domain with which you have established MTLS authentication.

Send Connector Address Space

The Send connector address space, specified, for example, in the AddressSpace parameter of the *New-SendConnector* EMS cmdlet, specifies the names of domains to which the Send connector routes mail. You need to specify the AddressSpace parameter unless the Send connector you are creating is linked to a Receive connector. If a linked Receive connector is specified by using the LinkedReceiveConnector parameter, the value of the AddressSpace parameter must be $null. Receive connectors are discussed later in this lesson.

> *NOTE*   **THE ADDRESSSPACE PARAMETER**
>
> You can use AddressSpace or AddressSpaces interchangeably with the *New-SendConnector* cmdlet. Both parameters specify one or more address spaces.

The syntax for entering an address space is as follows:
<AddressSpaceType>:<AddressSpace>;<AddressSpaceCost>

On an Edge Transport server, the address space type must be SMTP. On a Hub Transport server, it may be SMTP, X400, or another text string. If you omit the address space type, SMTP is assumed.

For SMTP address space types, the address space that you enter must be RFC 1035 compliant, for example, *.*.com, and *.adatum.com. For X.400 address space types, the address space that you enter must be RFC 1685 compliant, such as o=ThisSite;p=ThisOrg; a=adatum;c=us. For all other values of address space type, there are no format restrictions on the text for the address space.

The valid input range for the address space cost is from 1 through 100. A lower cost indicates a better route. This parameter is optional; if you omit the address space cost, a cost of 1 is assumed. If you enter a non-SMTP address space that contains the semicolon character (;), you must specify the address space cost.

If you specify the address space type or the address space cost, you must enclose the address space in quotation marks ("), for example, "SMTP:adatum.com;1."

You can specify multiple address spaces by separating the address spaces with commas, for example, contoso.com,fabrikam.com or "SMTP:adatum.com;1","SMTP:Fabrikam.com;2".

> **NOTE** **NON-SMTP ADDRESS SPACE**
>
> If you specify a non-SMTP address space type on a Send connector configured on a Hub Transport server, you must use a smart host to route email by specifying a value for the SmartHosts parameter, and you must set the DNSRoutingEnabled parameter to $false.

The following EMS command creates a Send connector named SendConnector01 with a usage type of Internet that sends email to all .com Internet sites:

```
New-SendConnector -Internet -Name SendConnector01 -AddressSpace "SMTP:*.com;1"
```

Figure 7-20 shows the output of this command.

FIGURE 7-20 Creating a Send connector

The following EMS command reconfigures the Send connector SendConnector01 to send email to an address space of the adatum.com domain and all its subdomains:

```
Set-SendConnector -Identity SendConnector01 -AddressSpace *.adatum.com
```

> ***NOTE*** **CHANGING THE USAGE TYPE**
>
> **You cannot reconfigure the usage type using the *Set-SendConnector* cmdlet. To do this, you need to delete the connector using the *Remove-SendConnector* cmdlet and then re-create it with a different usage type. You can (optionally) use the Usage parameter in the *New-Send-Connector* cmdlet to specify the usage type for a new Send connector, but this parameter does not exist for the *Set-SendConnector* cmdlet.**

The following EMS command lists the properties of the Send connector SendConnector01:

```
Get-SendConnector -Identity SendConnector01
```

Figure 7-21 shows the output of this command.

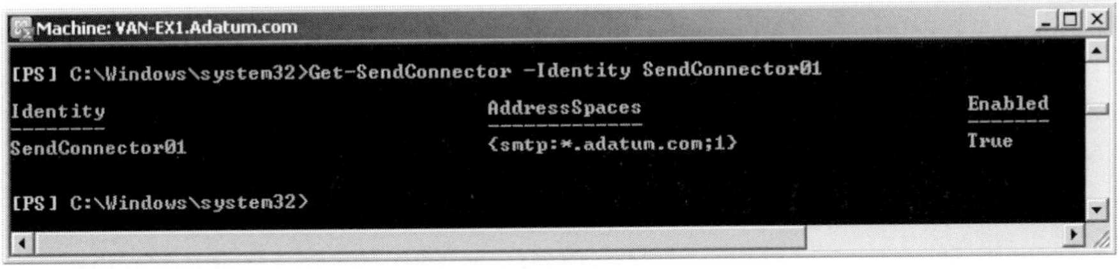

FIGURE 7-21 Listing properties for a Send connector

> ***NOTE*** **DISABLING OR REMOVING A SEND CONNECTOR**
>
> **If you want to temporarily disable a Send connector, you would use the *Set-SendConnector* EMS cmdlet and set the Enabled parameter to $false. If you use the Remove-SendConnector parameter, this deletes the Send connector, and you would subsequently need to create it again.**

Send Connector Permissions

When a security principal establishes a session with a Send connector, the Send connector permissions assigned to that security principal determine the types of header information that can be sent with the email message. If an email message includes header information that is not allowed by the Send connector permissions, those headers are stripped from the message. Table 7-3 describes the permissions that can be assigned on a Send connector to security principals. You can use the *Add-ADPermission* EMS cmdlet to modify the default permissions for a Send connector.

TABLE 7-3 Send Connector Permissions

SEND CONNECTOR PERMISSION	DESCRIPTION
ms-Exch-Send-Exch50	Allows the session to send a message that contains the *EXCH50* command.
Ms-Exch-Send-Headers-Routing	Allows the session to send a message that has all received headers intact.

SEND CONNECTOR PERMISSION	DESCRIPTION
Ms-Exch-Send-Headers-Organization	Allows the session to send a message that has all organization headers intact.
Ms-Exch-Send-Headers-Forest	Allows the session to send a message that has all forest headers intact.

Send Connector Scope

You can use the scope of a Send connector to control the visibility of the connector within the Exchange organization. By default, all Send connectors that you create are usable by all the Hub Transport servers in the Exchange organization. However, you can limit the scope of any Send connector so that it is usable only by other Hub Transport servers in the same Active Directory site.

You can use the EMS IsScopedConnector parameter in the *New-SendConnector* cmdlet or the *Set-SendConnector* cmdlet. When the value of this parameter is $true, the connector can be used only by Hub Transport servers in the same Active Directory site. When the value of this parameter is $false, the connector can be used by all Hub Transport servers in the Exchange organization.

For example, the following EMS command configures the Send connector SendConnector01 so that it can be used only by Hub Transport servers in the same Active Directory site:

```
Set-SendConnector -Identity SendConnector01 -IsScopedConnector $true
```

Using DNS Resolution to Deliver Email

You can configure Send connectors so that they deliver email by using DNS address resolution or by routing the email to a smart host. When the Send connector is set to use DNS Mail Exchange (MX) resource records to route mail automatically, the DNS client on the source server must be able to resolve public DNS records. By default, the DNS server that is configured on the source server's internal network adapter is used for name resolution.

You can configure a specific DNS server to use internal and external DNS lookups by using the EMC to modify the DNS settings on the Exchange server properties. If you configure a DNS on the Transport server to use external DNS lookups and use the New SMTP Send Connector wizard in the EMC to create a Send connector, you can select Use DomainName System (DNS) "MX" Records To Route Mail Automatically on the Network Settings page of the wizard. Whether you select this option or the alternative Route Mail Through The Following Smart Hosts, you can choose to select the Use The External DNS Lookup Settings On The Transport Server check box.

You can configure a Send connector to use DNS resolution by setting the UseExternalDNSServersEnabled parameter with the *Set-SendConnector* or *New-SendConnector* EMS cmdlets. When this parameter is set to $true (the default is $false), the

Send connector uses the external DNS list that you can specify by using the *Set-TransportServer* EMS cmdlet with the ExternalDNSServers parameter, such as follows:

```
Set-TransportServer -Identity VAN-EX1 -ExternalDNSServers 192.168.30.2,10.10.50.10
Set-SendConnector -Identity SendConnector01 -UseExternalDNSServersEnabled $true
```

> **MORE INFO   SET-TRANSPORTSERVER**
>
> For more information about the *Set-TransportServer* EMS cmdlet, see *http://technet .microsoft.com/en-us/library/bb124238.aspx.*

Using a Smart Host to Route Email

You must specify a smart host if you select the Internal usage type for a Send connector. When you route mail through a smart host, this host handles delivery to the next hop in the delivery destination. You can use an IP address or the fully qualified domain name (FQDN) of the smart host to specify the smart host identity. The smart host identity can be the FQDN of a smart host server, an MX record, or an Address (A) resource record. If you configure an FQDN as the smart host identity, the source server for the Send connector uses DNS name resolution to locate the smart host server.

If you specify the Internet usage type for a Send connector, the smart host for that connector may be a server that is hosted by your Internet service provider. The smart host for a Send connector with the Custom or Internal usage types may be another email server in your organization or an email server in a remote domain.

The following EMS command creates a Send connector named Contoso that transmits messages through a smart host named smarthost.contoso.com to Contoso's mail domain mail.contoso.com (note that the usage type is Internet and that you would create such a connector on an Edge Transport server):

```
New-SendConnector -Internet -Name Contoso -Addresspaces smtp:mail.contoso.com
-Smarthosts smarthost.contoso.com
```

When you route mail through a smart host, you must specify how the source server will authenticate to the smart host computer. You cannot require security settings for a Send connector unless a smart host destination is specified.

Table 7-4 lists the smart host authentication mechanisms that you can configure for a Send connector.

TABLE 7-4 Smart Host Authentication Mechanisms

SECURITY SETTING	DESCRIPTION
None	Anonymous access is allowed.
Basic authentication	This requires a user name and password. Basic authentication sends credentials in clear text. All smart hosts with which this Send connector is authenticating must accept the same user name and password.

SECURITY SETTING	DESCRIPTION
Basic authentication over TLS	TLS encrypts the transmission of the credentials. The receiving server must have a server certificate. The exact FQDN of the smart host, MX record, or A record that is defined on the Send connector as the smart host identity must also exist in the server certificate. The Send connector performs Basic authentication only after the TLS session has been established. A client certificate is also required to support MTLS authentication.
Exchange Server authentication	This uses Generic Security Services application programming interface (GSSAPI) and Mutual GSSAPI.
Externally Secured (for example, with IPsec)	The network connection is secured using a method that is external to the Exchange server.

You must select at least one source server for a Send connector. The source server is the Transport server to which messages are routed for delivery through the selected Send connector. You can set more than one source server on a Send connector. When you specify more than one source server, this provides load balancing and redundancy if a server fails. The source servers associated with Send connectors that are configured for the Exchange organization can be Hub Transport servers or subscribed Edge Transport servers.

Configuring Maximum Message Size and Connection Inactivity Time-Out

You can configure the maximum size of messages sent through a Send connector. Take care to distinguish this from the maximum message size sent over an IP site link. By no means do all the messages that are sent through a Send connector pass over an IP site link. If a message is subject to both Send connector and site-link restrictions, the smaller of the two maximum message sizes is enforced.

You can use the MaxMessageSize parameter with both the *New-SendConnector* and the *Set-SendConnector* EMS cmdlets to specify maximum message size. The default value is 10 MB. To remove the message size limit on a Send connector, you can enter a value of unlimited.

You can also use the ConnectionInactivityTimeOut parameter with both the *New-SendConnector* and the *Set-SendConnector* EMS cmdlets to specify the maximum time that an idle connection can remain open. The default value is 10 minutes. To specify a value, you enter it as a time span in the format *dd.hh:mm:ss*, where d = days, h = hours, m = minutes, and s = seconds. The valid input range for this parameter is from 00:00:01 through 1.00:00:00.

The following command configures the send connector SendConnector01 with a maximum message size of 5 MB and a maximum time for which an idle connection can remain open for 20 minutes:

```
Set-SendConnector -Identity SendConnector01 -MaxMessageSize 5MB
-ConnectionInactivityTimeOut 00:20:00
```

Using and Configuring Receive Connectors

Exchange Server 2010 Hub Transport and Edge Transport servers use Receive connectors
to receive messages from the Internet, from email clients, and from other email servers.
A Receive connector controls inbound connections to your Exchange organization. The
Receive connectors you require on a Hub Transport server for internal mail flow are, by
default, automatically created when the Hub Transport server role is installed. A Receive
connector that can receive email from the Internet (and from Hub Transport servers) is
automatically created when the Edge Transport server role is installed. End-to-end mail flow
can be implemented by subscribing an Edge Transport server to your Active Directory site by
using the Edge subscription process. Other scenarios, such as an unsubscribed Edge Transport
server, require manual connector configuration to establish end-to-end mail flow.

In Exchange Server 2010, the Receive connector listens for inbound connections that
match its settings, such as connections that are received through a particular local IP address
and port or from a specified IP address range. You create Receive connectors when you want
to control which servers receive messages from a particular IP address or IP address range
and when you want to configure special connector properties for messages that are received
from a particular IP address, such as specifying a larger message size, more recipients per
message, or more inbound connections.

Receive connectors are scoped to a single server and determine how that specific server
listens for connections. When you create a Receive connector on a Hub Transport server, it
is stored in Active Directory as a child object of the server on which it is created. When you
create a Receive connector on an Edge Transport server, it is stored in AD LDS on that server.

If you need additional Receive connectors for specific scenarios, you can create them by
using the EMS. You will create a Receive connector in the practice session later in this chapter.
Each Receive connector uses a unique combination of IP address bindings, port number
assignment, and remote IP address ranges from which mail will be accepted by this connector.

Default Receive Connectors Created During Setup

When you install the Hub Transport server role, two Receive connectors are created. Typically,
additional Receive connectors are not required, and in most cases the default Receive
connectors do not require reconfiguration change. You can, however, amend default Receive

connector settings or create additional Receive connectors if you consider it appropriate to do so.

The default Receive connectors created when the Hub Transport server role is installed are named Client <servername> and Default <servername>, for example, Client VAN-EX1 and Default VAN-EX1. The Client <servername> Receive connector accepts SMTP connections from all non–Messaging Application Programming Interface (MAPI) clients, such as POP and IMAP. The configuration of the Client <servername> Receive connector is as follows:

- Status: Enabled.
- Protocol logging level: None.
- Connector FQDN: *Servername.forestroot.extension* (for example, VAN-EX1 .adatum.com).
- Bindings: All available IP addresses. The server accepts mail received through any network adapter on the Hub Transport server.
- Port: 587. This is the default port for receiving messages from all non-MAPI clients for SMTP relay.
- Remote server IP address range: 0.0.0.0 through 255.255.255.255 for IPv4 and 0000:0000:0000:0000:0000:0000:0.0.0.0 through ffff:ffff:ffff:ffff:ffff:ffff:255.255.255.255 for IPv6. The Hub Transport server accepts mail from any IP address.
- Available authentication methods: TLS, Basic authentication, Exchange Server authentication, Integrated Windows authentication.
- Permission groups: Exchange users.

The Default <servername> Receive connector accepts connections from other Hub Transport servers and any Edge Transport servers in your organization. The configuration of the Default <servername> Receive connector is as follows:

- Status: Enabled.
- Protocol logging level: None.
- Connector FQDN: *Servername.forestroot.extension*
- Local server Receive connector bindings: All available IP addresses. The server accepts mail received through any network adapter on the Hub Transport server.
- Port: 25.
- Remote server IP address range: 0.0.0.0 through 255.255.255.255 for IPv4 and 0000:0000:0000:0000:0000:0000:0.0.0.0 through ffff:ffff:ffff:ffff:ffff:ffff:255.255.255.255 for IPv6. The Hub Transport server accepts mail from any IP address.
- Available authentication methods: TLS, Basic authentication, Integrated Windows authentication.
- Permission groups: Exchange users, Exchange servers, Legacy Exchange servers.

During installation of the Edge Transport server role, one Receive connector is created. This is configured to accept SMTP communications from all IP address ranges and is bound to all IP addresses on the local server. It is configured to have the Internet usage type and accepts anonymous connections. Typically, no additional Receive connectors are required on an Edge Transport server. If you use EdgeSync, you do not need to make any configuration changes because the Edge subscription process automatically configures permissions and authentication mechanisms. Anonymous sessions and authenticated sessions are granted different permission sets.

> **MORE INFO** **THE EDGE SUBSCRIPTION PROCESS AND EDGESYNC**
>
> For more information about the Edge subscription process and EdgeSync, see *http:// technet.microsoft.com/en-us/library/aa997438.aspx.*

You can list all the Receive connectors configured on Hub Transport servers in your Exchange organization by entering the following EMS command on a Hub Transport server (the same command entered on an Edge Transport server lists all the Receive connectors configured on that server):

```
Get-ReceiveConnector
```

Figure 7-22 shows the output from this command entered on the VAN-EX1 Hub Transport server. This lists the two connectors created by default when this server was added to the Hub Transport role. The other Receive connectors listed were created during experimentation and are unlikely to be configured on your test network.

FIGURE 7-22 Listing Receive connectors

Receive Connector Usage Types

As with Send connectors, the usage type of a Receive connector determines the default security settings for that connector and hence specifies the permissions that are granted to sessions that connect to that connector and the supported authentication mechanisms.

When you use the *New-ReceiveConnector* EMS cmdlet to create a Receive connector, you can specify the usage type by using the Usage parameter or by specifying the usage type directly with the appropriate parameter switch, such as Custom.

The valid Receive connector usage types are Client, Custom, Internal, Internet, and Partner. You need to supply a value for the Bindings parameter if you specify the Internet, Partner, or Custom usage type. You need to supply a value for the RemoteIPRanges parameter if you specify the Client, Internal, Partner, or Custom usage type. If you do not specify a value for a required parameter, the command ends unsuccessfully and does not prompt you for the missing required parameters.

You would configure the Internet usage type for a Receive connector on an Edge Transport server that is receiving email from the Internet. If a Hub Transport server was Internet facing, you would also specify this usage type; however, Internet-facing Hub Transport servers are not recommended.

You would configure the Internal usage type for a Receive connector on a Hub Transport server that is receiving email from a Hub Transport server in another forest (you can also use the Custom usage type for cross-forest connections), from a message transfer agent (MTA), or from an Exchange Server 2003 bridgehead server in the same forest (in which case a routing group must also exist). You would also configure this usage type on an Edge Transport server that is receiving email from a Hub Transport server or from an Exchange Server 2003 bridgehead server that is configured to use the Edge Transport server as a smart host.

A Receive connector with the Client usage type is automatically created on every Hub Transport server when the role is installed. By default, this Receive connector is configured to receive email through TCP port 587.

You would configure the Custom usage type for a Receive connector on a Hub Transport server receiving email from a Hub Transport server or an Exchange Server 2003 bridgehead server in another forest. You would also configure this usage type for a Receive connector on an Edge Transport server receiving email from a third-party MTA, an external relay domain, or an Exchange Hosted Services server.

You would configure the Partner usage type for a Receive connector on a Hub Transport server receiving email from a domain with which you have established MTLS authentication.

Creating and Configuring a Receive Connector

If you need to create and configure Receive connectors for specific purposes, you can use commands based on the *New-ReceiveConnector* and *Set-ReceiveConnector* EMS cmdlets.

For example, the following command creates the Receive connector ReceiveConnector01 with the Custom usage type; this connector listens for incoming SMTP connections on the IP address 10.10.10.1 and port 25 and accepts incoming SMTP connections only from the IP range 192.168.8.1 through 192.168.8.127:

```
New-ReceiveConnector -Name ReceiveConnector01 -Usage Custom -Bindings 10.10.10.1:25
-RemoteIPRanges 192.168.8.1-192.168.8.127
```

Note that the Bindings parameter specifies the local Hub or Edge Transport server IP address and the port through which the Receive connector accepts connections. These settings bind the Receive connector to a particular network adapter and TCP port on the Hub or Edge Transport server. By default, a Receive connector is configured to use all available network adapters and TCP port 25. If the server on which it is created has multiple network adapters, you may want the Receive connector to be bound to a particular network adapter or to accept connections through an alternative port. For example, you may want to configure one

Receive connector on an Edge Transport server to accept anonymous connections through an external network adapter and to configure a second Receive connector on the server to accept connections only from local Hub Transport servers through the internal network adapter.

The IP address or IP address range for the remote servers from which a Receive connector will accept inbound connections, as specified by the RemoteIPRanges parameter, can use one of the following formats:

- **IP address**   For example, 192.168.20.1
- **IP address range**   For example, 192.168.20.10-192.16820.20
- **IP address with subnet mask**   For example, 192.168.20.0(255.255.255.0)
- **IP address with Classless Interdomain Routing notation subnet mask**   For example, 192.168.1.0/24

The following EMS command sets the authentication mechanism of the Receive connector ReceiveConnector01 to Integrated Windows authentication:

```
Set-ReceiveConnector -Identity ReceiveConnector01 -AuthMechanism Integrated
```

The usage type you specify for a Receive connector defines its default authentication method, but you can use the *Set-ReceiveConnector* EMS cmdlet with the AuthMechanism parameter as in the previous command to configure one of the following mechanisms:

- None
- TLS
- Integrated
- BasicAuth
- BasicAuthRequireTLS
- ExchangeServer
- ExternalAuthoritative

Typically, you create and configure additional Receive connectors in order to specify a maximum message size, a connection time-out, or a connection activity time-out for traffic from specified IP addresses where these settings are different from those specified by default Receive connectors. The following EMS command specifies a maximum message size of 100 MB, a connection time-out of 20 minutes, and a connection inactivity time-out of 15 minutes for the ReceiveConnector01 Receive connector (note that the connection time-out must be greater than the connection inactivity time-out):

```
Set-ReceiveConnector -Identity ReceiveConnector01 -MaxMessageSize 100MB
-ConnectionTimeout 00:20:00 -ConnectionInactivityTimeout 00:15:00
```

When you have made significant configuration changes to a Receive connector, it is a good idea to list these configuration changes and check for errors. The following command displays the configuration changes made on the Receive connector ReceiveConnector01:

```
Get-ReceiveConnector -Identity ReceiveConnector01 | FL Identity,AuthMechanism,Bindings,
ConnectionTimeout,ConnectionInactivityTimeout,MaxMessageSize
```

Figure 7-23 shows the output from this command.

FIGURE 7-23 Listing configuration changes on a Receive connector

Finally, if you no longer need a Receive connector, you can delete it—note that this is not the same as temporarily disabling it. The following command deletes the Receive connector ReceiveConnector01:

```
Remove-ReceiveConnector –Identity ReceiveConnector01
```

> **MORE INFO**   *NEW-RECEIVECONNECTOR, SET-RECEIVECONNECTOR, GET-RECEIVECONNECTOR,* **AND** *REMOVE-RECEIVECONNECTOR*
>
> For more information about the *New-ReceiveConnector* EMS cmdlet, see *http://technet .microsoft.com/en-us/library/bb125139.aspx.* For more information about the *Set-ReceiveConnector* EMS cmdlet, see *http://technet.microsoft.com/en-us/library/bb125140 .aspx.* For more information about the *Get-ReceiveConnector* EMS cmdlet, see *http:// technet.microsoft.com/en-us/library/aa998618.aspx.* For more information about the *Remove-ReceiveConnector* EMS cmdlet, see *http://technet.microsoft.com/en-us/library/ aa996005.aspx.*

Using a Receive Connector to Restrict Anonymous Relay

Anonymous relay on Internet SMTP messaging servers is a serious security risk that could be (and probably will be) exploited by unsolicited commercial email senders to hide the source of their messages. Therefore, you need to place restrictions on Internet-facing messaging servers to prevent relaying to unauthorized destinations.

In Exchange Server 2010, you typically tackle this problem by configuring accepted domains on Edge Transport server or Hub Transport servers. Accepted domains can be authoritative, internal relay, and external relay.

In Exchange Server 2010, an accepted SMTP domain is considered authoritative when the Exchange organization hosts mailboxes for recipients in this domain. The Edge Transport servers should always accept email that is addressed to any of the organization's authoritative domains. By default, when the first Hub Transport server role is installed, one accepted domain is configured as authoritative for the Exchange organization. The default accepted domain is the FQDN for your forest root domain. If your internal domain name differs from the external domain name, you must create an accepted domain to match your external domain name. No accepted domains are configured by default on Edge Transport servers.

When an Edge Transport server receives email from the Internet and the recipient of the message is not part of an authoritative domain, the sending server attempts to relay the message through the Exchange server. When a server acts as a relay server that has no restrictions, this can put a large burden on Internet-connected servers. You can prevent this open relay scenario by rejecting all email that is not addressed to a recipient in your organization's authoritative domains. However, there are scenarios in which an organization wants to let partners or subsidiaries relay email through their Exchange servers. In Exchange Server 2010, you can configure accepted domains as relay domains. Your organization receives the email messages and then relays the messages to another email server.

You can configure a relay domain as an internal relay domain or as an external relay domain. When you configure an internal relay domain, some or all of the recipients in this domain do not have mailboxes in your Exchange organization. Email from the Internet is relayed for this domain through your Hub Transport servers. To support this scenario, you need to create an accepted domain that is configured as an internal relay domain. The accepted domain that is configured as an internal relay domain first tries to deliver to a recipient in the Exchange organization. If the recipient is not found, the message is routed to the Send connector that has the closest address space match.

When you configure an external relay domain, messages are relayed by an Edge Transport server to an email server that is outside the Exchange organization and outside the organization's network perimeter. In this scenario, the MX resource record for the external relay domain references a public IP address for the Exchange Server 2010 organization that is relaying messages. The Edge Transport server receives the messages for recipients in the external relay domain and then routes the messages to the email system for the external relay domain. You need to configure a Send connector from the Edge Transport server to the external relay domain. The external relay domain may also use your organization's Edge Transport server as a smart host for outgoing mail.

> **MORE INFO** **ACCEPTED DOMAINS**
>
> For more information about configuring accepted domains, see *http://technet.microsoft .com/en-us/library/bb124423.aspx.*

You can also restrict anonymous relay by examining the source of incoming messages. This method can be useful when an unauthenticated application or messaging server uses a Hub Transport server or an Edge Transport server as a relay server. When you create a Receive connector that is configured to relay email traffic, you should implement the following restrictions:

- For local network settings, restrict the Receive connector to listen only on the appropriate network adapter on the Hub Transport or Edge Transport server.
- For remote network settings, restrict the Receive connector so that it accepts connections only from a specified server or servers. This restriction is necessary because this Receive connector is configured to accept relay from anonymous users. Restricting the source servers by IP address is the only measure of protection possible on this Receive connector.

Configuring Foreign Connectors for Compliance

Exchange Server 2010 Hub Transport servers use Foreign connectors to deliver messages to gateway servers that do not use SMTP to transmit messages. For example, third-party fax gateway servers are foreign gateway servers. A Foreign connector controls outbound connections from the Hub Transport server to the foreign gateway server. The outbound messages are put in a Drop directory on the Hub Transport server or in a network file share on a remote server. Each Foreign connector uses its own Drop directory. The foreign gateway server is configured to obtain messages from the Drop directory that is specified for the Foreign connector.

Foreign connectors that you create on Hub Transport servers are stored in Active Directory and are available to all Hub Transport servers in your Exchange organization. When a Hub Transport server in your organization routes messages to an address space configured on a Foreign connector, the message is delivered to a source Hub Transport server for that Foreign connector and is relayed to the destination domain.

You can specify several different Hub Transport servers as source servers for a Foreign connector to provide fault tolerance. In this case, you need to ensure that the Drop directory that is specified by the Foreign connector can be accessed by all Hub Transport servers designated as source servers for that Foreign connector.

Foreign gateway servers send messages into an Exchange Server 2010 organization by using the Replay directory on the Hub Transport server. Email message files in the Replay directory are submitted for delivery.

Address Spaces and Connector Scope

The address space for a Foreign connector specifies the recipient domains to which this connector routes email. You can specify either SMTP address spaces or non-SMTP address spaces. You can use the scope of a Foreign connector to control the visibility that connector within your Exchange organization. By default, all Foreign connectors you create can be used by all Hub Transport servers in your Exchange organization. You can, however, limit the scope of a Foreign connector so that it is usable only by other Hub Transport servers in the same Active Directory site.

Creating and Configuring a Foreign Connector

You can create a Foreign connector by entering an EMS command based on the *New-ForeignConnector* cmdlet on a Hub Transport server. You can configure an existing Foreign connector by using commands based on the *Set-ForeignConnector* cmdlet. In either case, the connector scope is specified by using the IsScopedConnector parameter. When the value of this parameter is set to $false, the connector can be used by all Hub Transport servers in the Exchange organization. When the value of the parameter is $true, the connector can be used only by Hub Transport servers in the same Active Directory site.

When you create or configure a Foreign connector, the AddressSpaces parameter specifies the domain names to which the Delivery Agent connector Foreign connector sends messages. In Exchange Server 2010, the syntax for specifying an address space is as follows:

```
<AddressSpaceType>:<AddressSpace>;<AddressSpaceCost>
```

The address space type can be SMTP, X400, or any other text string. If you omit the address space type, an SMTP address space type is assumed. For SMTP address space types, the address space that you enter must be RFC 1035 compliant, such as *.*.com, and *.adatum .com. For X.400 address space types, the address space that you enter must be RFC 1685 compliant, such as follows:

```
o=MySite;p=MyOrg;a=adatum;c=us
```

The valid input range for the address space cost is from 1 through 100. A lower cost indicates a better route. If you omit the address space cost, a cost of 1 is assumed. If you enter a non-SMTP address space that contains the semicolon character (;), you are required to specify the address space cost. If you specify the address space type or the address space cost, you must enclose the address space in quotation marks ("), for example, "SMTP:adatum .com;1". You can specify multiple address spaces by separating the address spaces with commas, for example, adatum.com, fabrikam.com.

The following EMS command creates a Foreign connector named ForeignConnector01. The address space type is X.400, and the X.400 address space is c=US;a=Adatum;P=Contoso. The address space cost is 5, and the source Hub Transport server is VAN-EX1:

```
New-ForeignConnector -Name ForeignConnector01 -AddressSpaces "X400:c=US;a=Adatum;P=Conto
so;5" -SourceTransportServers VAN-EX1
```

Figure 7-24 shows the output of this command.

FIGURE 7-24 Creating a Foreign connector

You use EMS commands based on the *Set-ForeignConnector* cmdlet to configure an existing Foreign directory. For example, the maximum message size for a Foreign connector is unlimited. The following EMS command configures the maximum message size on this connector to be 50 MB:

```
Set-ForeignConnector -Identity ForeignConnector01 –MaxMessageSize 50MB
```

> **MORE INFO** **NEW-FOREIGNCONNECTOR** AND **SET-FOREIGNCONNECTOR**
>
> For more information about the *New-ForeignConnector* EMS cmdlet, see *http://technet .microsoft.com/en-us/library/aa996310.aspx*. For more information about the *Set-ForeignConnector* EMS cmdlet, see *http://technet.microsoft.com/en-us/library/ bb123789.aspx*.

Delivery Agent Connectors

Exchange Server 2010 introduces the Delivery Agent connector. Like the Foreign connector, this can be used to route messages to foreign systems that do not use the SMTP protocol. When a message is routed to a Delivery Agent connector, the associated delivery agent performs the content conversion and message delivery. Delivery Agent connectors allow queue management of Foreign connectors and eliminate the need to store messages on the file system in a Drop directory. They provide greater control over the message delivery to the foreign systems.

> **MORE INFO** **DELIVERY AGENT CONNECTORS**
>
> For more information about Delivery Agent connectors, see *http://technet.microsoft.com/ en-us/library/dd638118.aspx*.

Using TLS and MTLS

Chapter 12, "Message Integrity, Antivirus, and Anti-Spam," discusses the TLS and MTLS protocols in detail, and they are therefore covered only briefly here. These protocols and their associated certificates provide encrypted communications and end-point authentication over network connections. Server-to-server connections use MTLS for mutual authentication. On an MTLS connection, the server originating a message and the server receiving it exchange certificates from a mutually trusted certification authority (CA). The certificates prove the identity of each server to the other.

The TLS protocol enables clients to authenticate servers and (optionally) servers to authenticate clients. It provides a secure channel by encrypting communications. However, when TLS is deployed, it typically provides only encryption. Sometimes no authentication occurs between the sender and the receiver, and only the receiving server is authenticated. For example, SSL, which is an implementation of TLS, authenticates only the receiving server.

Exchange Server 2010 Setup creates a self-signed certificate, and TLS is enabled by default. You can clone this certificate to use it on additional servers or, if appropriate, replace it with certificates that are issued by a trusted third-party CA. Exchange Server 2010 attempts to use TLS for all remote connections, and all traffic between Edge Transport servers and Hub Transport servers is authenticated and encrypted using MTLS.

You can require TLS authentication on Send and Receive connectors. For example, the following EMS command creates a Receive connector for incoming messages on port 25 from the IP address range 10.10.0.1 through 10.10.0.24 and specifies that all messages coming from this range must use TLS:

```
New-ReceiveConnector –Name Secure –Bindings 0.0.0.0:25 –RemoteIPRanges 10.10.0.1-
10.10.0.24 –RequireTLS $true
```

Generating and TLS Certificates

Chapter 5, "Configuring Client Access," introduced certificates and the Active Directory Certificate Services role. TLS and MTLS require a certificate for authentication of inbound connections to and outbound connections from a front-end server. Each Edge Transport server must have a certificate for MTLS communication with other servers on the network, in particular, Hub Transport servers.

You can use commands based on the *New-ExchangeCertificate* cmdlet to generate TLS keys, which consist of the TLS certificate and related private keys. You can specify certificate metadata that enables different services to use the same certificate and private key. This metadata is stored in fields in the resulting certificate. You can also generate a certificate request from a third-party or other public key infrastructure CA.

The subject name field is specified by using the SubjectName parameter. This information is used by DNS-aware services and binds a certificate to a particular server or domain name. A subject name is an X.500 distinguished name that consists of one or more relative distinguished names (RDNs). Table 7-5 lists frequently used RDNs for identifying organizations or server entities.

TABLE 7-5 RDNs Used to Create a Subject Name

NAME	ABBREVIATION
Country/Region	c
Domain Component	dc
State or Province	s
Locality	l
Organization	o
Organizational Unit	ou
Common Name	cn

Subject names are represented as a single parameter that consists of a series of comma-separated RDNs. Each name is identified by the RDN abbreviation. For example, the following subject name represents Country/Region = US, Organization = Adatum, and Common Name = mail.adatum.com:

```
"c=US,o=adatum,cn=mail.adatum.com"
```

If the SubjectName parameter is not specified, the host name of the server where the cmdlet is run is used as the common name in the resulting certificate. For example, for the server VAN-EX1, the SubjectName parameter value cn=VAN-EX1 is used.

For example, if you run the *New-ExchangeCertificate* EMS cmdlet without parameters on the Hub Transport server VAN-EX1, this generates a self-signed certificate with the FQDN of the VAN-EX1 server as the subject name. You can use this certificate for direct trust authentication and encryption between Edge Transport servers and Hub Transport servers. The certificate is published to Active Directory so that Exchange direct trust can validate the authenticity of the server for MTLS. The following EMS command generates this certificate:

```
New-ExchangeCertificate
```

Note that this command generates a new default certificate that overwrites the current default certificate and that you need to confirm this action.

The following command run on a Hub Transport server lists all the Exchange certificates published in Active Directory (on an Edge Transport server, the same command would list the certificates stored on the server):

```
Get-ExchangeCertificate
```

Figure 7-25 shows a typical output for this command. You need to know a certificate's thumbprint in order to renew it, and it is a good idea to redirect the output of this command into a text file so that you can paste thumbprints into commands as necessary.

FIGURE 7-25 Listing certificates

The following EMS command renews a self-signed certificate that has the thumbprint listed in the code:

```
Get-ExchangeCertificate -Thumbprint C4248AB7065B62BC972A60F7293BDA7F533A4FCA | New-
ExchangeCertificate
```

The following EMS command creates a certificate with an exportable private key and a subject name defined by Country/Region = US, Organization = Adatum, and Common Name = mail.adatum.com:

```
New-ExchangeCertificate -SubjectName "c=US,o=adatum,cn=mail.adatum.com"
-PrivateKeyExportable $true
```

Depending on the certificates that already exist in Active Directory, you may need to confirm this command. Figure 7-26 shows the command output.

FIGURE 7-26 Creating a certificate with a specified subject name

Generating a Certificate Request

You can use the *New-ExchangeCertificate* EMS cmdlet to generate a certificate request and output it to the command-line console. You can send the certificate request to a CA within your organization, a trusted CA outside your organization, or a commercial CA by pasting the certificate request output into an email message or into the appropriate field on the CA's certificate request web page. You can also save the certificate request to a text file.

The following EMS command generates a certificate request with a subject name c=UK, o=Blue Sky Airlines, cn=mail.blueskyairlines.co.uk, a subject alternate name blueskyairlines. co.uk, and an exportable private key:

```
New-ExchangeCertificate -GenerateRequest -SubjectName "c=UK,o=Blue Sky Airlines,cn=mail
.blueskyairlines.co.uk" -DomainName blueskyairlines.co.uk -PrivateKeyExportable $true
```

Figure 7-27 shows this certificate request.

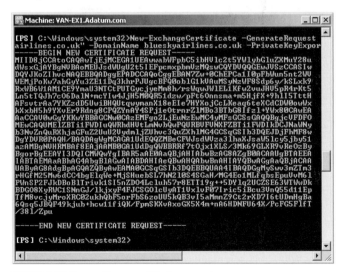

FIGURE 7-27 Generating a certificate request

As Figure 7-27 demonstrates, the certificate request is lengthy and complex, and it is advisable to automate storing this request in a request file. You can store the output of the command to generate a certificate request in a variable and use the *Set-Content* PowerShell cmdlet to generate a request file. The following two commands create the same certificate request as before and then save it in the file CertRequest01.req in the C:\Requests folder:

```
$Request = New-ExchangeCertificate -GenerateRequest -SubjectName "c=UK,o=Blue
Sky Airlines,cn=mail.blueskyairlines.co.uk" -DomainName blueskyairlines.co.uk
-PrivateKeyExportable $true
Set-Content -Path "C:\Requests\CertRequest01.req" -Value $Request
```

> **MORE INFO** **NEW-EXCHANGECERTIFICATE AND GET-EXCHANGECERTIFICATE**
>
> For more information about the *New-ExchangeCertificate* EMS cmdlet, see *http://technet .microsoft.com/en-us/library/aa998327.aspx*. For more information about the *Get-ExchangeCertificate* EMS cmdlet, see *http://technet.microsoft.com/en-us/library/ bb124950.aspx*.

Lesson Summary

- You can use Exchange costs on IP site links to control the route that email traffic takes to a remote Active Directory site without affecting other intersite traffic.
- Send connectors send email traffic to specified destinations. You can control the characteristics of this traffic by configuring Send Connector parameters.
- Receive connectors listen for incoming traffic from specified sources on a specific IP address and TCP port. You can accept or reject email messages depending on how you configure your Receive connectors.
- You can use TLS and MTLS to encrypt and authenticate email traffic.

Lesson Review

You can use the following questions to test your knowledge of the information in Lesson 2, "Setting Up Message Routing." The questions are also available on the companion CD if you prefer to review them in electronic form.

> **NOTE** **ANSWERS**
>
> Answers to these questions and explanations of why each answer choice is correct or incorrect are located in the "Answers" section at the end of the book.

1. You want to designate the Active Directory site MySite as a hub site for the purposes of Exchange message routing. What EMS command do you enter?

    A. *Get-AdSite -Identity MyADSite -HubSiteEnabled $true*

    B. *Get-AdSiteLink -Identity MyADSite -HubSiteEnabled $true*

C. *Set-AdSite -Identity MySite -HubSiteEnabled $true*

D. *Set-AdSiteLink -Identity MyADSite -HubSiteEnabled $true*

2. Email traffic from Active Directory site Site01 destined for Site03 currently passes through Site02. The Active Directory cost of the route from Site01 to Site03 through Site02 is 200. An alternative path exists through Site04, but the Active Directory cost of this route is 300. You want to ensure that email traffic from Site01 to Site03 is routed through Site04 rather than Site02. You do not want to affect other, non-Exchange network traffic. You want to implement this change by configuring the IP site link Site02-Site03. What EMS command do you use?

   A. *Set-AdSiteLink -Identity Site02-Site03 -ExchangeCost 100*

   B. *Set-AdSiteLink -Identity Site02-Site03 -ExchangeCost 400*

   C. *Set-AdSite -Identity Site03 -ExchangeCost 400*

   D. *Set-AdSite -Identity Site02 -ExchangeCost 400*

3. You are creating a Send connector to send email to a domain with which you have established MTLS authentication. Which usage type would you specify?

   A. Custom

   B. Internal

   C. Internet

   D. Partner

4. You want to ensure that the maximum size of any email message sent to the contoso.com domain and all its subdomains is 5 MB. You have already configured a Send connector named ContosoSend that sends email to the *.contoso.com address space. What command reconfigures this Send connector to enforce this limitation?

   A. *Set-SendConnector –Identity ContosoSend –MaxMessageSize 5MB*

   B. *Set-SendConnector –Identity ContosoSend –Usage Custom –MaxMessageSize 5MB*

   C. *Set-SendConnector –Identity ContosoSend –AddressSpace contoso.com,mail .contoso.com –MaxMessageSize 5MB*

   D. *Set-SendConnector –Identity ContosoSend –IsScopedConnector $true –MaxMessageSize 5MB*

5. You want to create a Receive connector named MyRC with the Custom usage type. The connector listens for incoming SMTP connections on the IP address 10.10.123.123 and port 25. It accepts incoming SMTP connections only from the IP range 10.10.8.1 through 10.10.8.127. You want to set the authentication mechanism of the Receive connector to be Integrated Windows authentication. What command do you use to create this connector?

   A. *Set-ReceiveConnector -Name MyRC -Usage Custom -Bindings 10.10.123.123:25 -RemoteIPRanges 10.10.8.1-10.10.8.127 –AuthMechanism Integrated*

   B. *Set-ReceiveConnector -Name MyRC -Usage Custom -Bindings 10.10.8.1-10.10.8.127 –RemoteIPRanges 10.10.123.123:25 AuthMechanism Integrated*

C. *New-ReceiveConnector -Name MyRC -Usage Custom -Bindings 10.10.123.123:25 -RemoteIPRanges 10.10.8.1-10.10.8.127 –AuthMechanism Integrated*

D. *New-ReceiveConnector -Name MyRC -Usage Custom -Bindings 10.10.8.1- 10.10.8.127 –RemoteIPRanges 10.10.123.123:25 AuthMechanism Integrated*

PRACTICE **Configuring a Disclaimer**

In this practice session, you will use both the EMC and the EMS to add a disclaimer message to email messages sent by all users in your organization.

EXERCISE 1 Using the EMC to Configure a Disclaimer

In this exercise, you will use the EMC to add a disclaimer to all messages sent by all users in your Exchange organization. The disclaimer is appended to both internal and external messages. If, for any reason, the disclaimer cannot be added to a message, this is ignored, and the message is sent without the disclaimer. Carry out the following procedure:

1. Log on to the Hub Transport server VAN-EX1 with the Kim Akers account and start the EMC.

2. Expand Organization Configuration in the Console pane and click Hub Transport.

3. Click New Transport Rule on the Actions pane. This starts the New Transport Rule Wizard.

4. On the Introduction page shown in Figure 7-28, type the name **Disclaimer01** and the comment **"This adds a disclaimer."** Ensure that the Enable Rule check box is selected. Click Next.

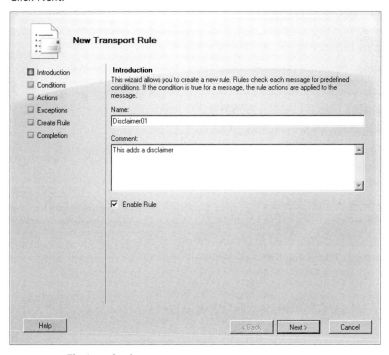

FIGURE 7-28 The Introduction page

5. Because you want the disclaimer to be appended to all email messages from all your users, you should not make any changes on the Conditions page. Click Next. Click Yes to clear the Warning dialog box.

6. On the Actions page in the Step 1. Select Actions field, select the Append Disclaimer Text And Fallback To Action If Unable To Apply check box.

7. In the Step 2. Edit The Rule Description By Clicking An Underlined Value field, click Disclaimer Text.

8. In the Specify Disclaimer Text dialog box, type the disclaimer text message **"All email sent by the Adatum Corporation has been checked by the latest antivirus software."** Figure 7-29 shows this dialog box. Click OK.

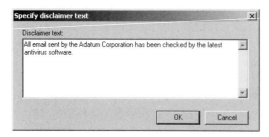

FIGURE 7-29 Specifying the text for the disclaimer

9. In the Step 2. Edit The Rule Description By Clicking An Underlined Value field, click Wrap.

10. In the Select Fallback Action dialog box, shown in Figure 7-30, click Ignore. Click OK.

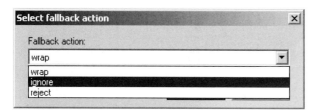

FIGURE 7-30 Specifying the fallback action

11. The Actions page should now look similar to Figure 7-31. Click Next.

12. You want to append the disclaimer to all email messages from all your users. Therefore, you should not make any changes on the Exceptions page. Click Next.

13. Review the Configuration Summary on the Create Rule page shown in Figure 7-32. If you are satisfied with the configuration of the new rule, click New.

14. On the Completion page, click Finish.

15. Optionally, use OWA to send email internally (for example, from Kim Akers to Don Hall). Check that the disclaimer message is added to all emails.

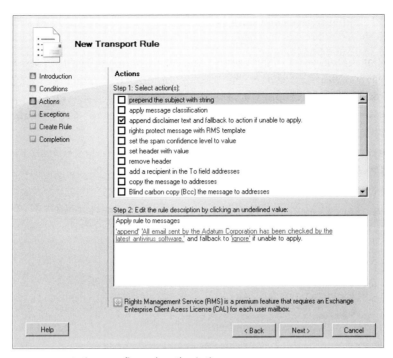

FIGURE 7-31 Actions configured on the Actions page

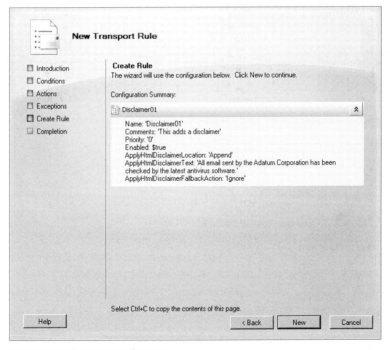

FIGURE 7-32 The Create Rule page

EXERCISE 2 Using the EMS to Configure a Disclaimer

In this exercise, you will first delete the transport rule that you created in the previous exercise because it might affect the results of this exercise. You will then use the EMS to create a transport rule that applies the disclaimer "The Adatum Corporation is committed to quality and all of our products bear the appropriate kite mark." to all messages sent outside the Adatum organization. The transport rule sets the fallback action to Reject. Carry out the following procedure:

1. If necessary, log on to the Hub Transport server VAN-EX1 with the Kim Akers account and start the EMS.

2. Enter the following command:

   ```
   Remove-TransportRule Disclaimer01
   ```

3. When prompted, enter **Y** to confirm this action.

4. Enter the following command:

   ```
   New-TransportRule -Name Disclaimer02 -Enabled $true -SentToScope
   'NotInOrganization' -ApplyHtmlDisclaimerText "The Adatum Corporation is
   committed to quality and all of our products bear the appropriate kite mark."
   -ApplyHtmlDisclaimerFallbackAction Reject
   ```

   Figure 7-33 shows these commands.

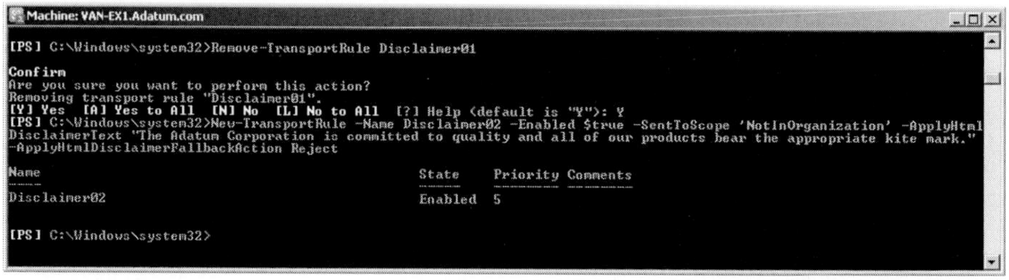

FIGURE 7-33 Using the EMS to configure a disclaimer

PRACTICE **Creating Send and Receive Connectors**

In this practice session, you will use the EMC to create a Send connector and the EMS to create a Receive connector on the Hub Transport server VAN-EX1.

EXERCISE 1 Using the EMC to Create a Send Connector

In this exercise, you will create a Send connector with the Custom usage type that sends email internally within the Adatum Exchange organization. Carry out the following procedure:

1. Log on to the Hub Transport server VAN-EX1 with the Kim Akers account and start the EMC.

2. Expand Organization Configuration in the Console pane and click Hub Transport.

3. On the Actions pane, click New Send Connector. This starts the New SMTP Send Connector Wizard.

4. In the Name box, enter **AdatumSendConnector**. Ensure that the Intended Use For This Send Connector drop-down box is set to Custom and click Next.

5. On the Address Space page, click Add. In the SMTP Address Space dialog box, enter **Adatum.com** in the Address box and select the Include All Subdomains check box. Ensure the Type is SMTP and Cost is 1. Figure 7-34 shows this dialog box. Click OK.

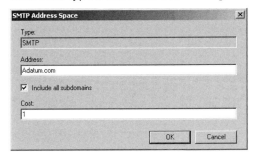

FIGURE 7-34 The SMTP Address Space dialog box

6. The Address Space page should look similar to Figure 7-35. Click Next.

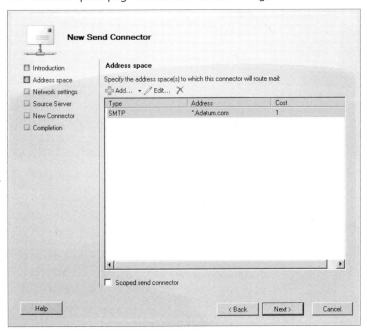

FIGURE 7-35 The configured Address Space page

7. On the Network Settings page, select the Use DomainName System (DNS) "MX" Records To Route Mail Automatically option. Click Next.

8. On the Source Server page, ensure that the server VAN-EX1 is selected and click Next.

9. Check the settings on the New Connector page. They should be similar to Figure 7-36. Click New.

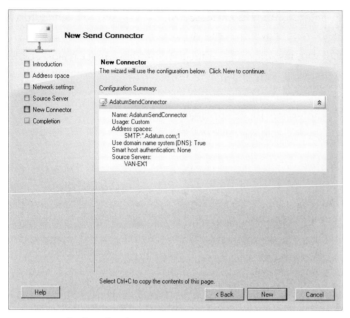

FIGURE 7-36 Settings for the new connector

10. On the Completion page, click Finish.

EXERCISE 2 Using the EMS to Create a Receive Connector

In this exercise, you will use the EMS to create a Receive connector named AdatumReceiveConnector with the Custom usage type. This connector receives internal email from within the Adatum Exchange organization. The Receive connector listens on IP Address 10.10.0.10 and on TCP port 24, which is the TCP port used for private mail. It accepts email messages from any source within the address range 10.10.10.1 through 10.10.10.255. It uses Integrated Windows Authentication as its authentication mechanism. Carry out the following procedure:

1. If necessary, log on to the Hub Transport server VAN-EX1 with the Kim Akers account and start the EMS.

2. Enter the following command:

```
New-ReceiveConnector -Name AdatumReceiveConnector -Usage Custom -Bindings
10.10.10.10:24 -RemoteIPRanges 10.10.10.0/24 -AuthMechanism Integrated
```

Figure 7-37 shows the output of this command.

FIGURE 7-37 Creating the AdatumReceiveConnector Receive connector

Chapter Review

To further practice and reinforce the skills you learned in this chapter, you can perform the following tasks:

- Review the chapter summary.
- Review the list of key terms introduced in this chapter.
- Complete the case scenarios. These scenarios set up real-world situations involving the topics of this chapter and ask you to create a solution.
- Complete the suggested practices.
- Take a practice test.

Chapter Summary

- Transport rules and transport protection rules enable you to apply messaging policies that both control and protect email messages. Moderated transport permits a nominated person or group to check and approve messages sent to users and distribution groups.
- Exchange costs on IP site links can be used to route intersite email traffic. Send connectors send email traffic both within your organization and to other organizations. Receive connectors enable your Transport servers to receive traffic from specified sources over specified TCP ports.
- You can configure parameters on Send and Receive connectors to control the traffic your users send and receive. TLS and MTLS can encrypt and authenticate sensitive traffic.

Key Terms

Do you know what these key terms mean?

- Edge rules agent
- Information Rights Management (IRM)
- Messaging policy
- Moderated email
- Mutual Transport Layer Security (MTLS)
- Outlook protection rule
- Receive connectors
- Regular expression
- Rights Management Services (RMS)
- RMS prelicensing agent
- Send connectors

- Simple expressions
- Transport Layer Security (TLS)
- Transport protection rule
- Transport rule
- Transport rule agent

Case Scenarios

In the following case scenarios, you will apply what you've learned about subjects of this chapter. You can find answers to these questions in the "Answers" section at the end of this book.

Case Scenario 1: Configuring Moderation

Kim Akers is the Exchange administrator at Margie's Travel. Kim wants to moderate all email sent to members of the Sales distribution group and to specify herself as the moderator. She wants to notify internal senders if their message to the distribution group is rejected but does not want to send any notifications to senders external to the organization. Answer the following questions:

1. What EMS command does Kim use to moderate the Sales distribution group and specify herself as the moderator?

2. Don Hall is a member of the Sales distribution group, but Kim does not need to moderate email sent to Don. What EMS command specifically exempts Don's email from being moderated because of his Sales group membership?

3. Several distribution groups within the Sales distribution group, for example, OnlineSales and InsuranceSales, are already moderated. Kim does not want members of these groups to be moderated twice. What EMS command does she use to prevent this?

Case Scenario 2: Setting Up MTLS-Protected Email Communication with a Partner Organization

You are the senior Exchange administrator at the Adatum Corporation. You are implementing secure, encrypted email communications with Adatum's partner organization Trey Research, and you want to use MTLS for this purpose. Answer the following questions:

1. You need to obtain a TLS certificate with exportable private key and a subject name defined by Country/Region = US, Organization = Adatum Corporation, and Common Name = mail.adatum.com. To do this, you need to generate a certificate request. You want to save this request in the file TreyProjectRequest.req in the C:\Requests folder on the server on which you generate the request. You intend to post information from this file into the website of the commercial CA from which you intend to obtain the certificate. What EMS commands do you use to generate and store this certificate request?

2. You intend to create a Receive and a Send connector on an Edge Transport server specifically for this encrypted traffic. What usage type of Send and Receive connector should you specify?

3. You want to create a Send connector named TreySendConnector that sends email to the domain treyresearch.com and all its subdomains. You do not need to specify cost, maximum message size, or any other optional parameters. What EMS command do you use?

4. You want to create a Receive connector named TreyReceiveConnector on an Edge Transport server with the IP address 192.168.20.6. The connector listens on TCP port 25. The IP addresses of the Trey Research Edge Transport servers that will send traffic to Adatum are 10.100.10.15 and 10.100.10.16. You want to specify that the maximum size of messages received on this connector is 15 MB. What EMS command do you use?

Suggested Practices

To help you master the examination objectives presented in this chapter, complete the following tasks.

Investigate the Transport Rule Cmdlets

- **Practice 1**   The *New-TransportRule* and *Set-TransportRule* EMS cmdlets are very powerful and support a large number of parameters. Practice using these cmdlets and their parameters. Investigate the messaging policies you can configure and how these affect internal email traffic.

- **Practice 2**   Investigate the use of the *Get-TransportRule* EMS cmdlet. In particular, look at how the output of commands that use this cmdlet can be piped into other commands.

- **Practice 3**   Optionally, if you are using virtual machines, configure a second Exchange organization in a separate forest and investigate the messaging policies you can configure for external email traffic. This practice requires a great deal of configuration and is therefore optional.

Investigate IRM and AD RMS

- **Practice 1**   Install the AD RMS role on your domain controller (VAN-DC1) and investigate the additional RMS templates that this lets you use when configuring IRM protection.

- **Practice 2**   Optionally, if you have created a second Exchange organization, as suggested in Practice 1, investigate the use of transport protection rules to IRM-protect external traffic.

Investigate the Send and Receive Connector Cmdlets

- **Practice 1** The *New-SendConnector, Set-SendConnector, New-ReceiveConnector,* and *Set-ReceiveConnector* EMS cmdlets are very powerful. Practice using them and their parameters.

- **Practice 2** If you have a second Exchange server configured on your test network (VAN-EX2), install the Edge Transport role on that server (if not already installed) and investigate configuring Send and Receive connectors on Edge and Hub Transport servers and how these affect internal email traffic between these servers.

- **Practice 3** Optionally, if you are using virtual machines, configure a second Exchange organization in a separate forest and configure Send and Receive connectors to send email traffic between the two organizations. This practice requires a great deal of configuration and is therefore optional.

Investigate TLS and MTLS

- **Practice 1** Obtain a TLS certificate from your internal CA (if this server role is not already installed in VAN-DC1, install it). Use this certificate to encrypt internal traffic.

- **Practice 2** Optionally, if you have configured a second Exchange organization, set up MTLS to authenticate and encrypt email traffic between the two organizations.

Take a Practice Test

The practice tests on this book's companion CD offer many options. For example, you can test yourself on just one exam objective, or you can test yourself on all the 70-662 certification exam content. You can set up the test so that it closely simulates the experience of taking a certification exam, or you can set it up in study mode so that you can look at the correct answers and explanations after you answer each question.

> **MORE INFO** **PRACTICE TESTS**
>
> For details about all the practice test options available, see the "How to Use the Practice Tests" section in this book's Introduction.

CHAPTER 8

Configuring Transport Servers

Transport servers are responsible for routing messages in an Exchange 2010 organization. There are two different types of transport server. Hub Transport servers route messages within the organization, moving messages from site to site and delivering messages to mailboxes. Edge Transport servers route messages sent to and received from outside the organization, such as those sent to and from hosts on the Internet. By reading this chapter, you will learn about the following transport server concepts: accepted domains, remote domains, email address policies, the transport dumpster, the EdgeSync process, and address rewrite policies.

Exam objectives in this chapter:

- Configure hub transport.
- Configure Edge transport.

Lessons in this chapter:

Before You Begin

In order to complete the exercises in the practice sessions in this chapter, you need to have done the following:

- Installed servers VAN-DC, VAN-EX1, and VAN-EX2 as described in the Appendix.
- Prepare an additional server running Windows Server 2008 R2 Enterprise edition using the default configuration. Ensure that you configure this server with two separate network adapters. Do not join this computer to a domain. Set the Administrator account password to *Pa$$w0rd*.

Orin Thomas

One thing that is important to remember is that when you are configuring an Edge Transport server, ensure that you work out how you are going to remotely manage that Edge Transport server before you deploy it. A friend of mine was doing some work for a company based out of Alice Springs in Australia's Northern Territory. One team was responsible for managing the firewall, and his team was in the process of upgrading to Exchange. When the firewall team asked what network ports he needed open between the protected network and the perimeter network, he replied with the standard answer involving the ports used for Simple Mail Transfer Protocol (SMTP) and the EdgeSync process. What he forgot was also ensuring that a port was open allowing him to RDP to the server from the protected network so that he could actually set the EdgeSync process up. By the time he had figured out his error, it was approaching 2:00 PM, and he couldn't get in contact with anyone on the firewall team. To resolve the problem, he had to drive across to the hosting facility, which was located on the other side of Alice Springs, and log onto the server manually to start the EdgeSync process. Now 2:00 PM is about the hottest part of the day. and it just happened to be late January, which is the middle of the Aussie summer. (Did I mention that Alice Springs has some of the highest daytime temperatures in the Australian Outback?) What should have been a quick 20-minute drive turned into a four-hour adventure after his car broke down in the extreme heat. My friend ended up being rehydrated in an Alice Springs hospital—all because he didn't remember that he had to have a port open to perform remote management tasks on a computer on the perimeter network. So when you see an exam question asking you what ports to open between the perimeter network, be sure to pick the answer that doesn't leave you driving across an Australian Outback town in the middle of a scorching summer day to undo your mistake.

Lesson 1: Hub Transport Servers

The core function of a Hub Transport server is to route an Exchange organization's internal messages. In addition to this primary task, Hub Transport servers apply transport rules, enforce journaling policies, and deliver messages to user's mailboxes. In this lesson, you will learn how to configure and organize accepted and remote domains, configure appropriate email address policies, and modify transport dumpster settings.

After this lesson, you will be able to:

- Organize accepted domains.
- Manage remote domains.
- Configure email address policies.
- Modify transport dumpster settings.

Estimated lesson time: 30 minutes

Hub Transport Servers

Hub Transport servers process all messages that transit an Exchange Server 2010 organization. Hub Transport servers deliver internal or externally sourced messages to user mailboxes and forward messages bound for hosts on the Internet to Edge Transport servers. A component on the Hub Transport server, called the *categorizer,* determines what to do with each message based on recipient information in the message header. The categorizer expands distribution lists, identifies alternative recipients, and processes recipient forwarding addresses. The categorizer also applies policies, routes messages, and converts content. Hub Transport servers receive messages through the SMTP protocol from other transport servers or by picking them up from a sender's Outbox using the store driver. Hub Transport servers use send and receive connectors to transmit messages to other locations. You learned about how send and receive connectors work in Chapter 7, "Routing and Transport Rules."

If your organization does not use an Edge Transport server, you can configure the Hub Transport server to relay messages directly to hosts on the Internet, such as a third-party smart host. It is also possible to enable the Edge Transport server anti-spam agents on the Hub Transport server role as well as configure a Hub Transport server to scan messages for malicious content by deploying antivirus protection. You will learn about antivirus and anti-spam functionality in Chapter 12, "Message Integrity, Antivirus, and Anti-Spam."

You must deploy a Hub Transport server in each Active Directory site that hosts an Exchange server with the Mailbox server role. You can install the Hub Transport role on servers that already host the Client Access and Mailbox server roles. You can deploy more than one Hub Transport server in each site to provide redundancy without having to configure Domain Name System (DNS) round-robin or network load balancing. You will learn more about high availability in Chapter 13, "Exchange High-Availability Solutions."

Accepted Domains

An Exchange organization can accept messages for a particular email domain only if that mail domain is set up as an accepted domain. Accepted domains are also domains for which Exchange is able to send email. For example, if your organization needs to send and accept email for the Contoso.com and Fabrikam.com domains, you need to configure both of these domains as accepted domains. By default, the domain name associated with the forest in which you install Exchange is the default accepted domain for your Exchange organization. You can configure an email address policy, which you will learn about later in this chapter, only for domains that are on the list of accepted domains.

When you configure an accepted domain, you need to specify whether the accepted domain will be authoritative, an internal relay domain, or an external relay domain. Figure 8-1, the first page of the New Accepted Domain Wizard, displays this choice. The differences between each of these types of accepted domain is as follows:

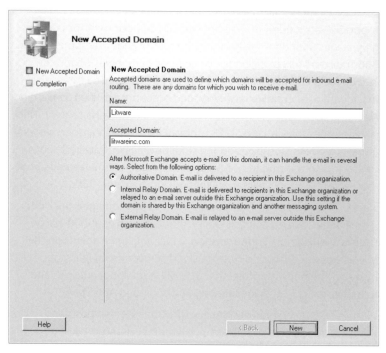

FIGURE 8-1 Choose between authoritative, internal, and external relay

- **Authoritative Domains**   Accepted domains for which the Exchange organization accepts and stores email messages from external locations. For example, at Contoso, Contoso.com is an authoritative domain, as Contoso.com transport servers deliver messages addressed to Contoso.com recipients to mailboxes hosted on Contoso .com mailbox servers. The default authoritative domain for an organization is the fully qualified domain name of the forest root domain.

- **Internal Relay Domains**   Accepted domains for which the Exchange organization will accept email messages from an external location but forwards them to another mail system located on the internal network. For example, a subsidiary company of Contoso is running a third-party mail system on the internal network. The domain related to this mail system is configured as an accepted domain, but Hub Transport servers route messages directed to recipients at this domain to those internal mail servers rather than delivering the messages to Exchange mailbox servers. You can also use internal relay domains when an organization has more than one Active Directory forest or when recipients in a single email domain are spread between Exchange and a third-party email system. To function properly, internal relay domains require that you configure a send connector to that domain on your organization's Hub Transport servers.

- **External Relay Domains**   An accepted domain for which the Exchange organization will accept email messages from external locations but does not process them locally and forwards these incoming messages to an external mail server. For example, Contoso.com transport servers might accept messages to recipients with email addresses associated with the domain proseware.com domain, but these transport servers automatically route these messages to a mail server that exists outside the organization's internal or perimeter network. To function properly, external relay domains require that you configure a send connector to the external domain on your organization's Edge Transport servers.

You can create a new accepted domain by clicking on New Accepted Domain in the Actions pane when the Organization Configuration\Hub Transport node is selected in Exchange Management Console (EMC). Creating an accepted domain involves specifying the domain name and a label for the name, choosing between the domain being an authoritative, internal, or external relay domain.

You can use one of the following Exchange Management Shell (EMS) cmdlets to manipulate accepted domains:

- **New-AcceptedDomain**   This cmdlet is used to create new accepted domains. Use the DomainType parameter to specify whether the domain will function as an authoritative, external relay, or internal relay domain.

- **Get-AcceptedDomain**   This cmdlet can be used to list the properties of existing accepted domains.

- **Set-AcceptedDomain**   This cmdlet allows you to modify the properties of an existing accepted domain.

- **Remove-AcceptedDomain**   This cmdlet allows you to remove an existing accepted domain.

MORE INFO **ACCEPTED DOMAINS**

For more information on understanding accepted domains, consult the following link on TechNet: *http://technet.microsoft.com/en-us/library/bb124423.aspx*.

Remote Domains

Remote domains allow you to control the types of messages and message formats sent from users in your organization to a specific external domain. When you install Exchange, a default remote domain is created that has the label represented by an asterisk (*). This default remote domain is responsible for the settings applied to all outgoing messages except those configured for specific remote domains. You can edit the properties of a remote domain or create new remote domains through the Organization Configuration\Hub Transport node in the EMC.

You create a new remote domain by clicking on New Remote Domain when the Organization Management\Hub Transport server node is selected from within the EMC and then clicking on New Remote Domain in the Actions pane. When you create a new remote domain, you need to provide a label and the domain name and specify whether all subdomains of that domain will be included. You configure items such as MIME character sets and out-of-office message settings after you create the remote domain by editing the properties of the remote domain.

By configuring a remote domain, you can configure whether specific external domains receive out-of-office messages from recipients in your organization, as shown in Figure 8-2. For example, you may have configured the default remote domain so that no out-of-office messages are sent to external recipients but decide to configure a special remote domain for a partner so that he or she receives out-of-office notifications.

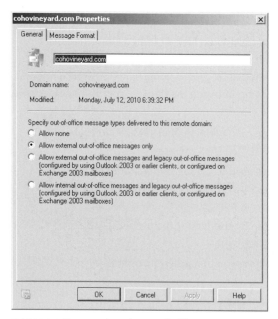

FIGURE 8-2 Remote domain out-of-office settings

Remote domain message format options allow you to configure whether automatic replies, automatic forward, delivery reports, and the sender's name are forwarded to a remote domain. It also allows you to specify whether Exchange rich text format is used and which MIME and non-MIME character set is used. Figure 8-3 shows the cohovineyard.com remote domain configured to use the Cyrillic (ISO) character set. You would configure a specific remote domain message format when the default is appropriate. For example, there are four separate Cyrillic MIME character sets, and when messages are sent using the wrong character set, messages are not formatted correctly for their intended recipient. In general, you will need to discuss which character set is appropriate for a specific remote domain with a representative of the recipients in that domain.

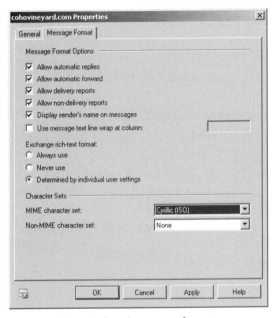

FIGURE 8-3 Remote domain message format

Four EMS cmdlets allow you to configure and manage remote domains:

- **New-RemoteDomain**   Create a new remote domain entry
- **Set-RemoteDomain**   Modify an existing remote domain entry
- **Get-RemoteDomain**   View the properties of an existing remote domain
- **Remove-RemoteDomain**   Remove an existing remote domain entry

MORE INFO   **REMOTE DOMAINS**

For more information on understanding remote domains, consult the following link on TechNet: *http://technet.microsoft.com/en-us/library/aa996309.aspx.*

Quick Check

- What kind of accepted domain would you configure if some of your organization's recipients have Exchange mailboxes and others are hosted on a third-party messaging system?

Quick Check Answer

- You would configure an internal relay domain.

Email Address Policies

Email address policies generate the primary and secondary email addresses for recipients in an Exchange organization based on a combination of first name, last name, middle initial, and accepted domain. The default email address policy for an organization involves the user's alias, the "at" sign (@), and the default accepted domain, which is the forest root domain's fully qualified domain name.

To create an email address policy, perform the following general steps:

1. Navigate to the Organization\Hub Transport node in the EMC and click on New E-Mail Address Policy in the Actions pane.

2. Enter a name for the policy and specify which recipient types to which the policy applies. As Figure 8-4 shows, policies can apply to all recipient types or a selection of mailboxes, external email addresses, resource mailboxes, contacts, and mail-enabled groups. On this screen, you can also select the recipient container, such as a specific organizational unit, to which the policy will apply.

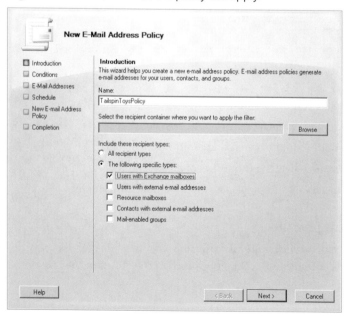

FIGURE 8-4 New address policy

3. Specify the conditions under which the policy applies. This could mean that the user's state or province, department, or company attribute matches a certain value.

4. Specify the format of the email address and the accepted domain to which the email address applies. You can add multiple email address formats at this point and set the default reply to address of addresses, as shown in Figure 8-5.

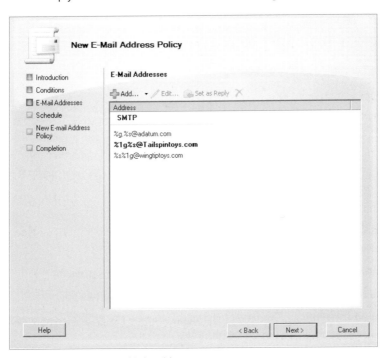

FIGURE 8-5 Policy with multiple addresses

5. Specify whether the policy will apply immediately or at a specific time in the future or whether the policy does not apply.

Each recipient can have multiple email addresses applied either through a single policy or through the application of multiple policies. The reply-to address set in the policy with the highest priority becomes the user's default reply-to address. You can manually configure the default reply address for a single user by selecting an address on the E-Mail Addresses tab of a recipient's properties, disabling the Automatically Update E-Mail Addressed Based On E-Mail Address Policy, and then clicking Set-As-Reply, as shown in Figure 8-6.

To configure email address policy priority, use the *Set-EmailAddressPolicy* cmdlet with the Priority parameter. The policy that has priority 1 overrides other policies. When you set a policy to priority 1, all other policies increment their priority so that no conflicts occur. For example, the existing policy that was priority 1 becomes priority 2 and so on. You can also select a policy in the Organization\Hub Transport node of the EMC and then click on Change Priority.

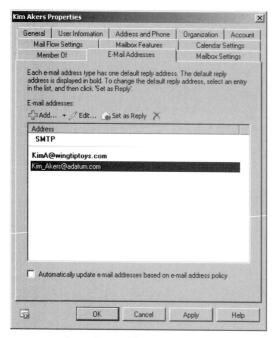

FIGURE 8-6 Set reply-to address

You can use the following EMS cmdlets to manage email address policies:

- **New-EmailAddressPolicy**   This cmdlet allows you to create a new policy.
- **Get-EmailAddressPolicy**   This cmdlet allows you to view the properties of an existing policy or list existing policies and their priorities.
- **Set-EmailAddressPolicy**   This cmdlet allows you to modify the properties of an existing policy, including setting the policy priority.
- **Update-EmailAddressPolicy**   This cmdlet updates the email address policy to apply any changes made by the *Set-EmailAdressPolicy* cmdlet to all recipients within the scope of the policy.
- **Remove-EmailAddressPolicy**   This cmdlet removes an existing policy but does not remove email addresses that have been applied to users through that policy.

MORE INFO   **EMAIL ADDRESS POLICIES**

For more information on understanding email address policies, consult the following link on TechNet: *http://technet.microsoft.com/en-us/library/bb232171.aspx*.

Transport Settings and Transport Dumpster

Transport settings properties allow you to configure the maximum receive size, send size, and maximum number of recipients that transport servers will allow for messages that they route in your Exchange organization.

By editing the properties of transport settings, you can also configure the properties of the transport dumpster. The transport dumpster holds copies of messages that are replicating to other mailbox databases in a database availability group. In the event that a mailbox database fails before replication has occurred, messages will be kept safely in the transport dumpster up until the specified limits. You will learn more about database availability groups in Chapter 13, "Exchange High-Availability Solutions."

You can access transport settings properties by selecting the Organization Configuration\ Hub Transport node and clicking on the Global Settings tab, selecting Transport Settings, and clicking on Properties in the actions pane. Figure 8-7 shows this properties dialog box.

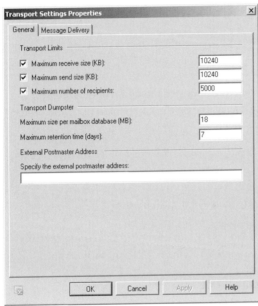

FIGURE 8-7 Dumpster settings

You can configure transport settings at the organizational level by using the *Set-TransportConfig* cmdlet. Use the *Set-TransportConfig* cmdlet with the MaxReceiveSize, MaxRecipientEnvelopeLimit, and MaxSendSize parameters to configure maximum receive size, send size, and number of recipients for the organization. Use the *Set-TransportConfig* cmdlet with the MaxDumpsterSizePerDatabase and MaxDumpsterTime parameters to configure transport dumpster properties.

MORE INFO **TRANSPORT SETTINGS**

For more information on understanding the transport settings dumpster, consult the following link on TechNet: *http://technet.microsoft.com/en-us/library/bb676532.aspx*.

EXAM TIP

Understand the difference between an accepted domain and a remote domain.

Lesson Summary

- An accepted domain is an email domain for which an Exchange organization will accept and send messages.

- There are three types of accepted domain: authoritative domain, internal relay domain, and external relay domain.

- Remote domains allow you to configure message format settings and out-of-office settings on a per-external-recipient-domain basis.

- Email address policies allow you to configure the format of email addresses.

- The transport dumpster provides redundancy for database availability group replication.

Lesson Review

You can use the following questions to test your knowledge of the information in Lesson 1, "Hub Transport Servers." The questions are also available on the companion CD if you prefer to review them in electronic form.

> **NOTE ANSWERS**
>
> Answers to these questions and explanations of why each answer choice is correct or incorrect are located in the "Answers" section at the end of the book.

1. Which of the following EMS cmdlets would you use to configure an existing accepted domain to change it from being an internal relay domain to being Authoritative?

   A. *Set-ForeignConnector*

   B. *Set-SendConnector*

   C. *Set-AddressRewriteEntry*

   D. *Set-AcceptedDomain*

2. Your organization is partnered with Contoso. You want to allow recipients at Contoso to receive internal out-of-office messages from users in your organization. You want to ensure that other partners do not receive these messages. Which of the following EMS cmdlets would you use to accomplish this goal?

   A. *New-RemoteDomain*

   B. *New-ForeignConnector*

   C. *New-SendConnector*

   D. *New-AcceptedDomain*

3. You are configuring Exchange to accept incoming email for the domain Fabrikam. com. Messages to addresses in Fabrikam.com are delivered to mailboxes hosted on your organization's Exchange Server 2010 mailbox servers. Which of the following should you configure with respect to the Fabrikam.com domain on your organization's transport servers to support this configuration?

   A. Internal relay domain

   B. Authoritative domain

   C. External relay domain

   D. Foreign connector

4. Your organization is in the process of changing its name. It is currently known as Wingtip Toys but will be changing its name to Tailspin Toys. You want to ensure that users are able to receive email at addresses either for the domains wingtiptoys. com and tailspintoys.com. You have configured Tailspin Toys and Wingtip Toys as authoritative domains. Which of the following commands should you use to configure email addresses for users that reflect the new company name?

   A. *New-AddressRewriteEntry*

   B. *New-AcceptedDomain*

   C. *New-EmailAddressPolicy*

   D. *New-AddressList*

5. Which of the following EMS cmdlets would you use to configure transport dumpster settings on your organization's Hub Transport servers?

   A. *Set-TransportServer*

   B. *Set-TransportAgent*

   C. *Set-TransportConfig*

   D. *Set-SendConnector*

Lesson 2: Edge Transport Servers

Edge Transport servers are responsible for transmitting messages to and receiving messages from email servers on the Internet. As the entry point for external messages, Edge Transport servers are responsible for message hygiene, that is, cleaning messages that contain malware and discarding messages that contain unsolicited commercial or phishing-related content. Edge Transport servers store configuration information in an Active Directory Lightweight Directory Services database. A special unidirectional replication process called EdgeSync populates this database. The unidirectional nature of this replication process ensures that Active Directory is not compromised in the event that attackers compromise the Edge Transport server.

After this lesson, you will be able to:

- Install the Edge Transport server role.
- Configure EdgeSync.
- Clone Edge Transport server configurations.
- Configure Edge Transport server settings.

Estimated lesson time: 40 minutes

Edge Transport Role

The Edge Transport role is different from other Exchange server roles in that you can install the role on a computer that is not a member of a domain. Edge Transport servers are designed to be deployed in perimeter networks. Edge Transport servers form a bridge between mail servers on the Internet and Hub Transport servers on the internal network. You can use the Edge Transport server to scan and discard incoming messages if these messages are found to contain malware or have unsolicited commercial or phishing-related content. You will learn more about anti-malware technologies in Chapter 12.

Like other Exchange Server 2010 roles, you can deploy the Edge Transport server role on computers running Windows Server 2008 or Windows Server 2008 R2. Prior to deploying the Edge Transport role, you need to install the following operating system features:

- .NET FrameWork 3.51
- Remote System Administration Tools for Active Directory Directory Services
- Active Directory Lightweight Directory Services

Prior to running Exchange setup, you also need to ensure that the server's fully qualified domain name is set. You can set the fully qualified domain name of the host server by performing the following general steps:

1. In the Computer Name tab of the System Properties dialog box, click on the Change button.

2. In the Computer Name/Domain Changes dialog box, click on the More button.

3. On the DNS Suffix and NetBIOS Computer Name page, enter the DNS suffix of the computer.

You will install the Edge Transport server role on a computer in the practice exercise at the end of the chapter.

MORE INFO   EDGE TRANSPORT SERVER ROLE

To learn more about the Edge Transport server role, consult the following article on TechNet: *http://technet.microsoft.com/en-us/library/bb124701.aspx.*

EdgeSync

EdgeSync is a unidirectional process that replicates transport server configuration information, such as transport rules, from Hub Transport servers on protected networks to Edge Transport servers on perimeter networks. EdgeSync subscriptions mean that Edge Transport servers can be configured centrally rather than having to make a remote desktop connection to the server on the protected network. EdgeSync subscriptions replicate information from the Hub Transport server to the Edge Transport server. This way, should the Edge Transport server become compromised by an attacker, it is not possible for the attacker to replicate information back to the internal network.

Once you configure EdgeSync, you will be unable to perform certain configuration tasks on the Edge Transport server. The following cmdlets are disabled on an Edge Transport server when you configure EdgeSync:

- *Set-SendConnector*
- *New-SendConnector*
- *Remove-SendConnector*
- *New-AcceptedDomain*
- *Set-AcceptedDomain*
- *Remove-AcceptedDomain*
- *New-MessageClassification*
- *Set-MessageClassification*
- *Remove-MessageClassification*
- *New-RemoteDomain*
- *Set-RemoteDomain*
- *Remove-RemoteDomain*

If you want to create an additional send connector after you have configured an edge transport solution, you need to create it within the Exchange organization. The new send connector configuration will then replicate through the EdgeSync process to the Edge Transport server.

When configuring the firewall between the screened subnet and the internal network, you will need to open port 25 between the Hub Transport and Edge Transport servers to allow for the transmission of messages. To allow the EdgeSync process to function, you need to open TCP port 50636 between the Edge Transport server and the Hub Transport servers on the site connected to the perimeter network. This port must be open before you attempt to configure the Edge subscription.

To create an Edge subscription, perform the following general steps:

1. Ensure that the Hub Transport and Edge Transport servers are able to resolve each other's DNS names.

2. On the Edge Transport server, use the EMS to run the *New-EdgeSubscription* cmdlet.

3. Transfer the file generated by running the *New-EdgeSubscription* cmdlet to a Hub Transport server.

4. On the Hub Transport server, open the EMC and navigate to the Organization Configuration\Hub Transport node. Click on the Edge Subscriptions tab and then click New Edge Subscription in the Actions pane. This will open the New Edge Subscription Wizard.

5. On the New Edge Subscription Wizard, specify the location of the Edge Subscription file that you copied to the Hub Transport server. Select the Active Directory site to which the Edge Transport server will subscribe. Select the Automatically Create A Send Connect For This Edge Subscription if you want to route messages through the Edge Transport server to the Internet.

6. Click New to create the subscription and then click Finish to dismiss the wizard.

You can use the following EMS cmdlets to manage Edge subscriptions:

- **New-EdgeSubscription** This cmdlet, when run on an Edge Transport server, allows you to create a subscription file. You can also use this cmdlet on a Hub Transport server to import a subscription file.

- **Get-EdgeSubscription** This cmdlet allows you to retrieve information about existing Edge subscriptions.

- **Remove-EdgeSubscription** You can use this cmdlet to delete an existing Edge subscription.

- **Start-EdgeSynchronization** You can use this cmdlet to force the edge synchronization process.

- **Test-EdgeSynchronization** This cmdlet allows you to diagnose the synchronization status of currently subscribed Edge Transport servers.

- **New-EdgeSyncServiceConfig** Create a new edge synchronization schedule.

- **Get-EdgeSyncServiceConfig** Get the properties of an existing edge synchronization schedule.

- **Set-EdgeSyncServiceConfig** Modify the properties of an existing edge synchronization schedule.

If you add additional Hub Transport servers to a site where there is an existing subscription, the new hub transport will not participate in the synchronization process. To allow the new Hub Transport server to participate in the Edge subscription, you must resubscribe each Edge Transport server to the Active Directory site. Removing a Hub Transport server from a subscribed site does not cause problems unless the removed Hub Transport server is the last server in that site. When you deploy a new Edge Transport server on the perimeter network, you must subscribe that Edge Transport server to the Active Directory site, but it is not necessary to resubscribe the existing Edge Transport servers.

> **MORE INFO   EDGESYNC**
>
> To learn more about EdgeSync, consult the following link on TechNet: *http://technet .microsoft.com/en-us/library/aa997438.aspx.*

 Quick Check

- Under what conditions is it necessary to resubscribe existing Edge Transport servers to an Active Directory site?

Quick Check Answer

- You must resubscribe existing Edge Transport servers to an Active Directory site if you add new Hub Transport servers to the site.

Clone Edge Transport Server

If you want to configure a second or third Edge Transport server on your organization's perimeter network, you are likely to want to ensure that each Edge Transport server has the same configuration. Rather than manually attempt to replicate the server's configuration, you can use special scripts to import and export the server's configuration.

Cloning the configuration of an Edge Transport server does not replicate EdgeSync subscription settings or server certificates. You will need to create a new EdgeSync subscription for the new Edge Transport server.

The following settings are replicated to the new server when you clone the configuration:

- Send and receive connectors
- Accepted domains
- Remote domains
- IP allow list
- IP block list
- The following anti-spam configuration settings are cloned: content filter configuration, recipient filter configuration, address rewrite entries, and attachment filter entries.

To clone an Edge Transport server, perform the following general steps:

1. Ensure that you have already installed the Edge Transport server role on the target server.

2. From the EMS, run ExportEdgeConfig.ps1 on the prepared Edge Transport server. Running this command will create an XML file. Transfer this file across to the target server.

3. You will need to edit the XML file to include the following information:
   - Data and log file paths
   - Source IP addresses for send connectors
   - Network bindings for each receive connector

4. After you have edited the XML file, from the EMS run ImportEdgeConfig.ps1 on the target server to verify and apply the configuration.

> **MORE INFO**   **EDGE TRANSPORT SERVER CLONED CONFIGURATION**
>
> To learn more about Edge Transport server cloned configuration, consult the following link on TechNet: *http://technet.microsoft.com/en-us/library/aa998622.aspx*.

Address Rewriting

In some cases, it is necessary to rewrite email addresses into a more consistent format when they are sent to hosts on the Internet. For example, two organizations may merge into a third organization that has a new name. Users in each original organization may continue to receive email using their original addresses, but address rewriting would allow mail flow to be configured so that all outbound messages would have the sender address associated with them rewritten so that it matched the domain name of the new third organization. For example, Fabrikam and Contoso are merging into a new organization named Adatum. Kim Akers's email address is kim.akers@contoso.com, and Sam Abolrous's email address is abolrous.s@fabrikam.com. An address rewriting policy can ensure that both Kim's and Sam's email addresses are rewritten so that they appear in the format first initial.surname@adatum .com even though neither address is originally in that format. This would make Kim's and Sam's addresses, when rewritten, k.akers@adatum.com and s.abolrous@adatum.com.

Address rewriting on an Edge Transport server requires that address rewriting agents be enabled. To enable the inbound and outbound transport agents, run the following EMS commands:

```
Enable-TransportAgent –Identity "Address Rewriting Inbound agent"
Enable-TransportAgent –Identity "Address Rewriting Outbound agent"
```

You can verify that the address rewriting agent is enabled by using the *Get-TransportAgent* cmdlet and verifying that both the Address Rewriting Inbound Agent and the Address Rewriting Outbound Agent are enabled.

You use the *New-AddressRewriteEntry* cmdlet to configure address rewrite entries. You can configure address rewrite entries for single addresses, single domains, or multiple domains.

For example, to change the address sam.abolrous@contoso.com to helpdesk@adatum
.com, issue the following command:

```
New-AddressRewriteEntry -name "Sam to Helpdesk" -Internal sam.abolrous@contoso.com
-ExternalAddress helpdesk@adatum.com
```

To change all email addresses from the tailspintoys.com domain to the wingtiptoys.com
domain, issue the following command:

```
New-AddressRewriteEntry -name "Tailspintoys to Wingtiptoys" -InternalAddress
tailspintoys.com -ExternalAddress wingtiptoys.com
```

To change all email addresses from Contoso.com subdomains, such as Australia
.contoso.com and Fiji.contoso.com, issue the following command:

```
New-AddressRewriteEntry -Name "All Contoso Subdomains" -InternalAddress *.contoso.com
-ExternalAddress Contoso.com -OutboundOnly $True
```

> **MORE INFO** **ADDRESS REWRITING**
>
> To learn more about address rewriting, consult the following link on TechNet:
> *http://technet.microsoft.com/en-us/library/aa996806.aspx.*

EXAM TIP

Know under which circumstances it is necessary to resubscribe Edge Transport servers.

Lesson Summary

- EdgeSync is a process that binds the configuration of Edge Transport servers to those of the organization's Hub Transport servers.
- You create the EdgeSync subscription on the Edge Transport server and then import the XML file on the Hub Transport server.
- When you add a Hub Transport server to the site where the EdgeSync subscription exists, you need to re-create the Edge subscription for each subscribed Edge Transport server for the Edge Transport servers to be aware of the new Hub Transport server.
- You do not need to resubscribe an existing Edge Transport server when you add a new Edge Transport server, though the new Edge Transport server will require its own separate EdgeSync subscription.
- You can use a script to export the configuration of an Edge Transport server and then import that configuration on a separate Edge Transport server. It is necessary to create a new Edge Transport subscription for the newly cloned server.
- Address rewriting policies allow you to rewrite inbound and outbound email addresses so that they appear in a consistent format.
- You need to enable address rewriting transport agents before you can use address rewriting policies.

Lesson Review

You can use the following questions to test your knowledge of the information in Lesson 2, "Edge Transport Servers." The questions are also available on the companion CD if you prefer to review them in electronic form.

> **NOTE ANSWERS**
>
> Answers to these questions and explanations of why each answer choice is correct or incorrect are located in the "Answers" section at the end of the book.

1. Which of the following features or roles must be installed on a computer running Windows Server 2008 R2 before you can install the Hub Transport role? (Choose all that apply.)

   A. .NET Framework 3.5.1

   B. Active Directory Lightweight Directory Services

   C. RPC over HTTP

   D. Active Directory Domain Services

2. You are configuring a third-party firewall device that is used to demarcate your internal network from the screened network on which your organization's Edge Transport server resides. You have opened port 25 between the Edge Transport server and the Hub Transport servers on your internal network. Which other ports should you open to support the EdgeSync synchronization process?

   A. TCP port 443

   B. TCP port 110

   C. TCP port 50636

   D. TCP port 80

3. Your organization's Edge Transport server, VAN-EX-A, recently failed. While the server was unavailable, users were unable to send or receive messages from external locations. As this had a negative impact on the business, management authorized the purchase of a second server to hold the Edge Transport role. The name of this server is VAN-EX-B. There are custom transport rules present on the existing server. You want to ensure that the new server has an identical configuration. Which of the following steps should you take to accomplish this goal? (Choose 2; each answer forms part of the solution.)

   A. Run the ExportEdgeConfig.ps1 script on VAN-EX-A

   B. Run the ImportEdgeConfig.ps1 script on VAN-EX-B

   C. Run the ImportEdgeConfig.ps1 script on VAN-EX-A

   D. Run the ExportEdgeConfig.ps1 script on VAN-EX-B

4. You are about to perform the EdgeSync process between an Edge Transport server named VAN-ET and a Hub Transport server named VAN-HT. Which of the following commands would you run as a part of that process? (Choose 2; each answer forms part of the solution.)

   A. *Start-EdgeSynchronization on VAN-HT*

   B. *Start-EdgeSynchronization on VAN-ET*

   C. *New-EdgeSubscription on VAN-HT*

   D. *New-EdgeSubscription on VAN-ET*

5. Your organization uses a multitude of different internal email addresses based on which business unit a user is located in. You want to keep these internal addresses but also want to ensure that all email addressed to recipients on the Internet uses a consistent email address format for your organization's parent email domain, Contoso.com. Which of the following cmdlets would you use to accomplish this goal?

   A. *New-SendConnector*

   B. *New-EmailAddressPolicy*

   C. *New-AddressRewriteEntry*

   D. *New-RemoteDomain*

PRACTICE Configuring Transport Servers

In this set of practice exercises, you will configure a Hub Transport server and an Edge Transport server.

EXERCISE 1 Configure accepted domains

In this practice exercise, you will configure the domains wingtiptoys.com and tailspintoys.com as accepted domains. To complete this exercise, perform the following steps:

1. Log on to server VAN-EX1 using the Kim Akers user account.

2. In the EMC, select the Organization Configuration\Hub Transport node. In the Actions pane, click on New Accepted Domain.

3. In the New Accepted Domain dialog box, enter **wingtiptoys.com** in the Name and Accepted Domain fields. Select the Authoritative Domain option, as shown in Figure 8-8, and then click New. Click Finish.

4. Open the EMS and issue the following command:

   ```
   New-AcceptedDomain -Name 'Tailspintoys.com' -DomainName 'Tailspintoys.com'
   -DomainType 'Authoritative'
   ```

5. Use the EMC to verify that both the tailspintoys.com and the wingtiptoys.com domains have been configured as accepted domains in the Exchange organization.

FIGURE 8-8 New Accepted Domain

EXERCISE 2 Configure remote domains

In this exercise, you will configure cohovineyard.com and fabrikam.com as remote domains. To complete this exercise, perform the following steps:

1. In the EMC, ensure that the Organization Configuration\Hub Transport node is selected.
2. In the Actions pane, click on New Remote Domain. In the New Remote Domain dialog box, enter **fabrikam.com** in the Name and Domain Name fields, as shown in Figure 8-9, and then click New. Click Finish.

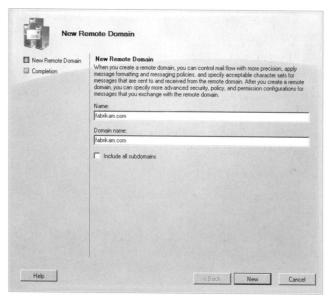

FIGURE 8-9 New Remote Domain

3. In the EMS, issue the following command:

```
New-RemoteDomain -Name 'cohovineyard.com' -DomainName 'cohovineyard.com'
```

4. Use the *Get-RemoteDomain* cmdlet to verify the creation of the fabrikam.com and cohovineyard.com remote domains.

EXERCISE 3 Configure email address policies

In this exercise, you will configure an email address policy that so that users who are members of the Wingtip Toys Department are able to receive mail with a wingtiptoys.com email address as well as their adatum.com e-mail address. To complete this exercise, perform the following steps:

1. From the EMC, select the Organization Configuration\Hub Transport node. In the Actions pane, click on New E-Mail Address Policy.

2. On the Introduction page of the New E-Mail Address Policy Wizard, enter the name **WingTip Toys Policy** and then click Next.

3. On the Conditions page, select Recipient is in a Department. Click on the underlined word specified. In the Specify Department dialog box, type **Wingtip Toys**, click Add, and then click OK. Click Next.

4. On the E-Mail Addresses tab, click Add. In the SMTP E-Mail Address dialog box, select Last Name.First Name and then select the Select The Accepted Domain For The E-Mail Address and click Browse. Click on Wingtiptoys.com and then click OK. Verify that the SMTP E-Mail Address dialog box matches what is shown in Figure 8-10 and then click OK.

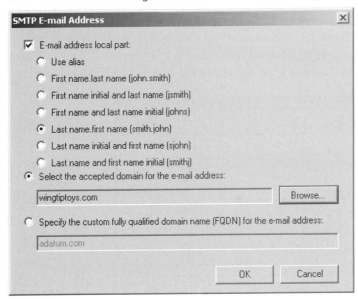

FIGURE 8-10 New Email Address Policy

5. Click Next twice and then click New. Click Finish to close the New E-Mail Address Policy Wizard.

EXERCISE 4 Prepare server for and install the Edge Transport server role

In this exercise, you will prepare a new server to function as an Edge Transport server for your existing Exchange Server 2010 deployment. To complete this exercise, perform the following steps:

1. Log on to server VAN-DC and create a new DNS record et.adatum.com that maps to the IP address 10.10.0.50. Ensure that when you create the host record, you also create the PTR record in the reverse lookup zone.

2. Log on to the computer that you have installed Windows Server 2008 R2 on using the Administrator account and the password *Pa$$w0rd*.

3. Open an elevated command prompt and issue the following commands:

   ```
   Netsh interface ipv4 set address "Local Area Connection" static 10.10.0.50

   Netsh interface ipv4 set dnsservers "Local Area Connection" static 10.10.0.10 primary

   Netdom renamecomputer %computername% /newname:VAN-ET
   ```

4. Restart the computer and log back on using the Administrator account. Open an elevated PowerShell session and then enter the following commands:

   ```
   Import-Module ServerManager

   Add-WindowsFeature NET-FrameWork,RSAT-ADDS,ADLDS –Restart
   ```

5. After the server restarts, log in as Administrator. From the Start menu, right-click on Computer and then click on Properties. Click on Advanced System Settings, click on the Computer Name tab, and then click on Change. Click on the More button. In the DNS Suffix And NetBIOS Computer Name dialog box, shown in Figure 8-11, enter **adatum.com** and then click OK. Restart the computer when prompted.

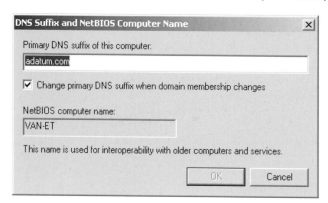

FIGURE 8-11 DNS suffix settings

6. After the server restarts, log in as Administrator and use Windows Explorer to navigate to the location of the Exchange installation files. Run Setup.exe. If prompted, click Yes in the User Account Control dialog box.

7. On the splash screen, click on Step 3: Choose Exchange Language Option. Click on the Install Only Languages From The DVD option. Click on Step 4: Install Microsoft Exchange. On the Introduction screen, click Next.

8. On the License Agreement screen, select I Accept The Terms In The License Agreement and then click Next.

9. On the Error Reporting screen, verify that No is selected and then click Next.

10. On the Installation Type screen, click Custom Exchange Server Installation and then click Next.

11. On the Server Role Selection screen, shown in Figure 8-12, click on the Edge Transport Role and then click Next.

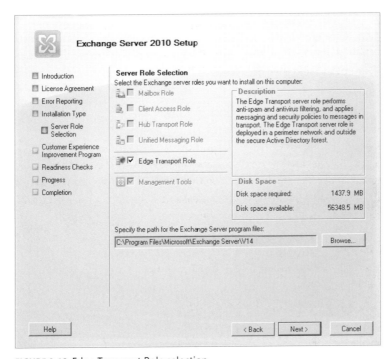

FIGURE 8-12 Edge Transport Role selection

12. Ensure that I Don't Wish To Join The Program At This Time is selected on the Customer Experience Improvement Program page and then click Next.

13. After the readiness checks complete, click Install.

14. After the install completes, de-select the Finalize Installation Using Exchange Management Console option and then restart the server.

EXERCISE 5 Configure and perform Edge Transport server synchronization

In this exercise, you will configure the Edge Transport server that you installed in Exercise 4 to perform an edge synchronization. To complete this exercise, perform the following steps:

1. If you have not already done so, log on to server VAN-ET with the Administrator account.

2. From the EMS, issue the following command:

   ```
   New-EdgeSubscription –FileName "C:\VAN-ET.xml"
   ```

3. When prompted, press Y.

4. Click Start. In the search box, type **\\van-ex1\c$** and then press Enter.

5. Copy c:\VAN-ET.xml to the \\VAN-EX1\c$ directory.

6. Log on to server VAN-EX1 using the Kim Akers user account.

7. Click on the Organization Configuration\Hub Transport node and then click on New Edge Subscription. This will bring up the New Edge Subscription dialog box.

8. Click Browse next to Active Directory Site, select Default First Site Name, and then click OK. Click Browse next to Subscription File, navigate to C:\VAN-ET.xml, and click Open. Verify that the New Edge Subscription dialog box matches what is shown in Figure 8-13 and then click New.

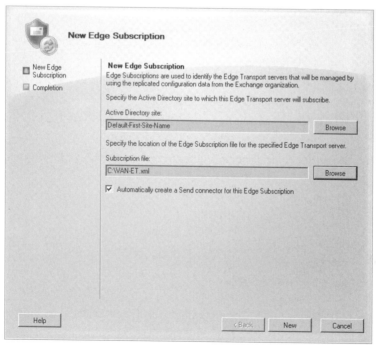

FIGURE 8-13 New Edge Subscription

9. Click Finish to close the New Edge Subscription Wizard.

10. From the EMS, issue the *Get-EdgeSubscription* command. Verify that VAN-ET is returned as a subscription.

Chapter Review

To further practice and reinforce the skills you learned in this chapter, you can perform the following tasks:

- Review the chapter summary.
- Review the list of key terms introduced in this chapter.
- Complete the case scenarios. These scenarios set up real-world situations involving the topics of this chapter and ask you to create a solution.
- Complete the suggested practices.
- Take a practice test.

Chapter Summary

- Accepted domains are email address domains that the Exchange organization accepts messages for. Authoritative domains are processed by Exchange, internal relay domains are forwarded to a location within the internal network, and external relay domains forward email to trusted partner organizations on external networks.
- Remote domains allow you to configure the message format and out-of-office settings for specific external mail domains.
- Email address policies allow you to configure the format of email addresses used by recipients in an organization.
- The transport dumpster holds copies of messages while they replicate to other members of the database availability group.
- EdgeSync subscriptions allow Edge Transport servers to be connected to Hub Transport servers for the purposes of using a centralized configuration.
- You can clone the configuration of an Edge Transport server by exporting its configuration and then importing it on a new Edge Transport server.
- Address rewrite policies allow you to rewrite addresses as messages pass to and from the organization's Edge Transport servers.

Key Terms

Do you know what these key terms mean?

- Accepted domains
- Authoritative domains
- EdgeSync
- Email address policy
- Remote domains
- Transport dumpster

Case Scenarios

In the following case scenarios, you will apply what you've learned about subjects of this chapter. You can find answers to these questions in the "Answers" section at the end of this book.

Case Scenario 1: Hub Transport Configuration at Coho Winery

You are in the process of optimizing the deployment of Exchange Server 2010 at Coho Winery. This optimization will involve integrating a subsidiary business, Coho Vineyard, into the existing Coho Winery Exchange organization. To this end, you want recipients to be able to receive email in the Coho Winery exchange organization if they have @cohovineyard.com email addresses. An additional problem that you must address is the use of inconsistent email addresses. Some users have email addresses with just their first name, and others have last name. You want to have a consistent format for email addresses that includes first name, middle initial, and last name. Another problem that you have been asked to resolve involves messages to a Russian supplier that occasionally use an incorrect Cyrillic character set. You need to ensure that all messages to this supplier use a consistent character set so that they are intelligible to the intended Russian recipients. With these facts in mind, answer the following questions:

1. How can you ensure that mail addressed to users in the cohovineyard.com domain can be received by users in the Coho Winery Exchange organization?

2. How can you ensure that each user's email addresses is in a consistent format, including first name, middle initial, and last name?

3. How can you ensure that email to the Russian supplier arrives with the correct character set?

Case Scenario 2: Edge Transport Configuration at Tailspin Toys

You have been asked to consult on the configuration of three Edge Transport servers at Tailspin Toys. These servers all reside on the organization's perimeter network and have the names mail1.tailspintoys.com, mail2.tailspintoys.com, and mail3.tailspintoys.com. One of the issues that management wants you to address is to ensure that inbound and outbound message traffic is distributed as evenly as possible among the three Edge Transport servers. At this time, management does not want to deploy a network load-balancing solution, though this is a possible option in the future. Management also wants you to ensure that all transport servers have the same transport rules. They have noticed that sometimes the legal disclaimer that should accompany all outbound messages is not added, depending on which transport server the outbound email passes through. Management would also like you to ensure that users who have email addresses in the australia.tailspintoys.com and newzealand.tailspintoys.com mail domains have their reply to email address formatted simply as @tailspintoys.com when they are sending messages to external recipients. With this information in mind, answer the following questions:

1. How can you ensure that all Edge Transport servers have the same set of transport rules?

2. What sort of solution can you use so that each transport server gets an approximately equal amount of traffic?

3. What steps can you take to ensure that external recipients receive messages from addresses that appear to have the same email domain?

Suggested Practices

To help you successfully master the exam objectives presented in this chapter, complete the following tasks.

Further Configuration of Hub Transport Servers

Perform the following practice exercises after you have completed the main practice exercise at the end of the chapter.

- **Practice 1** Configure an email address policy that uses the format first name and first initial of last name for the wingtip toys domain.

- **Practice 2** Configure the tailspintoys.com and cohovineyard.com domains as accepted domains.

Further Configuration of Edge Transport Servers

Perform the following practice exercises after you have completed the main practice exercise at the end of the chapter.

- **Practice 1** Configure an address rewriting policy on server VAN-ET.
- **Practice 2** Clone the ET configuration of server VAN-ET.

Take a Practice Test

The practice tests on this book's companion CD offer many options. For example, you can test yourself on just one exam objective, or you can test yourself on all the 70-662 certification exam content. You can set up the test so that it closely simulates the experience of taking a certification exam, or you can set it up in study mode so that you can look at the correct answers and explanations after you answer each question.

> **MORE INFO** **PRACTICE TESTS**
>
> For details about all the practice test options available, see the "How to Use the Practice Tests" section in this book's Introduction.

CHAPTER 9

Monitoring Exchange Server 2010

To ensure that your Microsoft Exchange Server 2010 organization is operating reliably and efficiently, you need to monitor your Exchange Servers and make sure they are healthy. Proactive monitoring and preventive maintenance can help you identify potential errors before a serious problem interferes with Exchange operation.

In this chapter, you will look at monitoring Exchange databases and database statistics, how you configure message tracking and monitor transport queues and mail flow, and how you test and monitor connectivity for the various protocols that implement connectivity between both clients and servers and between the various Exchange Server roles.

Exam objectives in this chapter:

- Monitor databases.
- Monitor mail flow.
- Monitor connectivity.

Lessons in this chapter:

Before You Begin

In order to complete the exercises in the practice session in this chapter, you need to have done the following:

- Installed the Windows Server 2008 R2 domain controller VAN-DC1 and the Windows Exchange 2010 Enterprise Mailbox, Hub Transport, and Client Access server VAN-EX1 as described in the Appendix "Setup Instructions for Exchange Server 2010."

- Created the Kim Akers account with the password *Pa$$w0rd* in the Adatum.com domain. This account should be placed in the Domain Admins security group and be a member of the Organization Management role group.

- Created the Don Hall account with the password *Pa$$w0rd* in the Adatum.com domain. This account should be placed in the Backup Operators security group (so it can be used to log on to the domain controller) and should be in the Marketing organizational unit.

- Created mailboxes for Kim Akers and Don Hall, accepting the default email address format for the email addresses.

REAL WORLD

Ian McLean

As an Exchange professional, you understand the connection between sound operational practices and procedures and a healthy infrastructure. You regularly check the health of your servers, your mailbox and public databases, and all other aspects of your Exchange organization. You know that monitoring is a task that is—and definitely should be—invisible to the user. The problem with invisibility is that if monitoring is skipped one day, who is to know?

Administrators are very busy people, and we are all human. It is tempting to reduce the frequency of checks or even stop monitoring completely during particularly busy and stressful periods. But if monitoring is skipped for long enough, minor problems become major problems that affect your organization's messaging infrastructure.

So it's not sufficient to know how to monitor the various components of your exchange organization. You also need to formalize the procedures, roles, and responsibilities that are involved in monitoring operations. There needs to be an audit trail. A responsible person (probably you) needs to sign a piece of paper or an electronic document saying exactly what monitoring has been carried out, what the results were, and, if necessary, what actions were taken. The documentation should track trends so that it helps you detect the operations that are currently still proceeding in a satisfactory manner but aren't running as well as they did a month ago. A senior person in your organization needs to check that the documentation has been completed as specified and to ask hard questions if it is not.

The procedures themselves need to be clearly described. If you and your entire team fell ill, would the consultants your organization brings in (hopefully as a temporary measure) have clear instructions about what to measure and what results to expect? I've seen some very capable and skillful administrators fall down when it comes to fully documenting their work. Please do not fall into the same trap.

Lesson 1: Monitoring Exchange Databases

Database monitoring involves regularly checking the health of your databases. Typically, your monitoring procedures are complemented by a notification system that sends alerts to administrators when problems occur. You can use the Exchange Management Console (EMC) and the Exchange Management Shell (EMS) to obtain database information and statistics. Additional tools, such as Microsoft Operations Manager, can also assist in monitoring your Exchange organization, but this chapter concentrates on the facilities provided directly by Microsoft Exchange Server 2010.

Microsoft recommends monitoring your databases on a daily basis. The main advantages to daily monitoring are as follows:

- You can quickly detect and address issues that may affect the messaging service or data availability.
- You can ensure the successful completion of specific administrative tasks, such as daily backup operations.
- It helps you meet the requirements of your Service Level Agreements.

In this lesson, you consider how you monitor public folder and mailbox database statistics to detect anomalies and indications of current and future problems and how you check the status of an Exchange Server 2010 database. You also consider how you monitor status information about mailbox database copies included in a database availability group (DAG).

After this lesson, you will be able to:

- Monitor public folder database information and statistics.
- Monitor mailbox database information and statistics.
- Monitor the status of Exchange databases.
- Monitor status of mailbox database copies included in a DAG.

Estimated lesson time: 45 minutes

Monitoring Exchange Database Information and Statistics

In order to check the health of your Exchange databases and of the replication process (if configured), you need to monitor your databases. You can obtain general information about both public folder and mailbox databases and statistics related to the public folders and mailboxes they contain. You can obtain more specific information about mailboxes and mailbox databases, such as usage information, information about queues, information about lagged mailbox database copies, and information about disconnected mailboxes.

Obtaining Information about Mailbox Databases

When you are monitoring a mailbox database you first need to obtain general information about the database, such as the server where it is located, its mailbox retention period, deleted item retention period, quota limits, associated public folder database, and so on. You can use the *Get-MailboxDatabase* cmdlet to obtain general information for mailbox databases. For example, the following command returns detailed information about all the mailbox databases in an Exchange 2010 organization:

```
Get-MailboxDatabase | FL
```

The previous command typically returns a lot of information that you would likely redirect into a text file for analysis. In a large organization that has a lot of databases, this command returns an excessive volume of information. You have the option of refining this information by specifying the Mailbox server, the mailbox database identity, or both. For example, the following command returns detailed information about the mailbox database named Mailbox Database 1363123687:

```
Get-MailboxDatabase -Identity "Mailbox Database 1363123687" | FL
```

Figure 9-1 shows some of the output from this command.

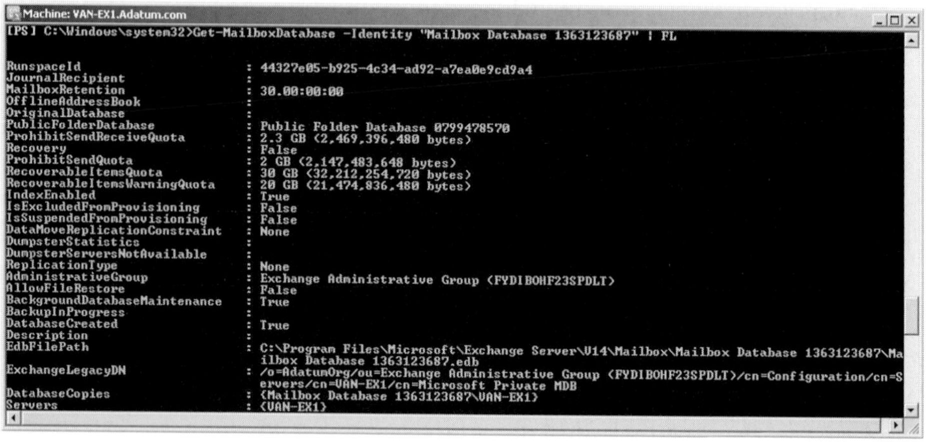

FIGURE 9-1 Detailed information about a mailbox database

The transport dumpster is described in Chapter 8, "Configuring Transport Servers." You can obtain statistics (if available) about the transport dumpster, such as dumpster deletes per second, dumpster inserts per second, and dumpster item count by including the DumpsterStatistics parameter, as demonstrated by the following command:

```
Get-MailboxDatabase -Identity "Mailbox Database 1363123687" -DumpsterStatistics | FL
```

You can also determine the status of the mailbox database, if this is available, by including the Status parameter. This tells you whether the status of the mailbox database is one of the following: BackupInProgress, Mounted, or OnlineMaintenanceInProgress. It also tells you the available free space in the database root. Checking the status of mailbox databases is an important step in monitoring replication health. The following command uses the Status parameter:

```
Get-MailboxDatabase -Identity "Mailbox Database 1363123687" -Status | FL
```

> **NOTE** **THE DATABASE ROOT**
>
> The Extensible Storage Engine (ESE) organizes database storage in a three-level hierarchy: database root, tables, and indexes and long values. The database root owns all the space in the database. Tables request chunks of space, which they then own in conjunction with the database root. Index and long-value trees request space from a table that in turn owns space allocated from the database root.

You can also use the EMC to determine the properties of a mailbox database. The procedure is as follows:

1. On your Mailbox server, open the EMC.

2. Click Mailbox under Organization Configuration in the Console tree.

3. In the Result pane, click the Database Management tab and then click the mailbox database whose status you want to determine.

4. Click Properties in the Actions pane.

The tabs on a mailbox database Properties dialog box are General, Maintenance, Limits, and Client Settings, as shown in Figure 9-2. The information available on these tabs was discussed in detail in Chapter 2, "Exchange Databases and Address Lists."

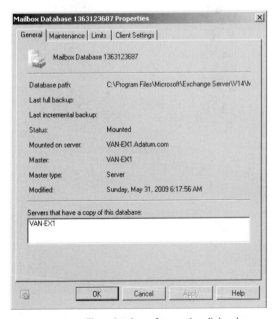

FIGURE 9-2 A mailbox database Properties dialog box

Viewing Mailbox Statistics

You can use the *Get-MailboxStatistics* EMS cmdlet to view the statistics for all the mailboxes on a server, for all the mailboxes in a mailbox database, or for a single mailbox. Note that you cannot use the cmdlet without arguments to view the statistics for all mailboxes in an Exchange organization. The cmdlet requires the Server, the Database, or the Identity parameter.

For example, the following command lists the statistics for all the mailboxes on the VAN-EX1 Mailbox server:

```
Get-MailboxStatistics -Server VAN-EX1 | FL
```

The following command lists the statistics for all the mailboxes in the mailbox database Mailbox Database 1363123687:

```
Get-MailboxStatistics -Database "Mailbox Database 1363123687" | FL
```

Figure 9-3 shows the output from this command.

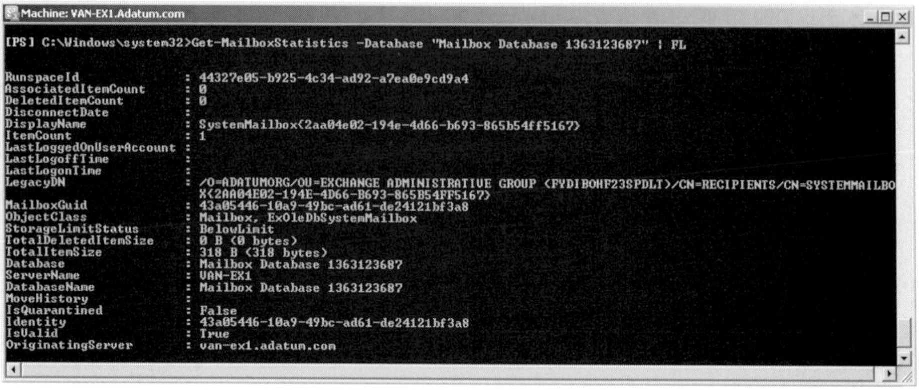

FIGURE 9-3 Viewing the statistics for mailboxes in a mailbox database

If a user mailbox has been created but has never been accessed, that mailbox is not included when you list the statistics of mailboxes on a server or in a mailbox database. If you attempt to obtain statistics for a mailbox that has not been accessed, you will get no statistical information but will instead receive a warning message. Suppose, for example, that the Don Hall mailbox has never been accessed and you enter the following command:

```
Get-MailboxStatistics -Identity "Don Hall" | FL
```

This results in the message shown in Figure 9-4.

FIGURE 9-4 A mailbox needs to have been accessed before it will return statistics

If a mailbox returns statistics, you can use the PowerShell *format-list* (FL) cmdlet to display the value of one or more specified statistics. This is more convenient than searching through the list of all the statistical values. For example, the following command displays the last logon time for the Kim Akers mailbox:

```
Get-MailboxStatistics -Identity "Kim Akers" | FL LastLogonTime
```

You can use the *Sort-Object* PowerShell cmdlet to sort the mailboxes in a mailbox database or on a Mailbox server by the value of one or more mailbox statistics. You can do this in either descending or ascending order and use the *format-table* (FT) PowerShell cmdlet to display the results as a table. For example, the following command lists the mailboxes in the Research mailbox database in descending order of item count:

```
Get-MailboxStatistics -Database Research | Sort-Object ItemCount -Descending | FT
DisplayName,ItemCount
```

The following command lists the mailboxes in the Research mailbox database in descending order of total item size:

```
Get-MailboxStatistics -Database Research | Sort-Object TotalItemSize -Descending | FT
DisplayName,TotalItemSize
```

> **NOTE MAILBOX SIZE**
>
> The size of a mailbox is the sum of its total item size and total deleted item size. This is not returned directly as a statistical value. If you want to display total mailbox sizes, you need to use a PowerShell routine that combines the TotalItemSize and TotalDeletedItemSize statistics for this mailbox.

If you do not want to list all the mailboxes in a mailbox database or on a Mailbox server but instead want to list, for example, the top five mailboxes in terms of total item size, you can pipe the results of your search into the *Select-Object* PowerShell cmdlet. For example, the following command lists the top five mailboxes in Mailbox Database 1363123687 in descending order of total item size:

```
Get-MailboxStatistics -Database "Mailbox Database 1363123687" | Sort-Object
TotalItemSize -Descending | Select-Object -First 5 | FT DisplayName,TotalItemSize
```

The following command lists the top 10 mailboxes on the Mailbox server VAN-EX1 in descending order of item count:

```
Get-MailboxStatistics -Server VAN-EX1 | Sort-Object ItemCount -Descending | Select-
Object -First 10 | FT DisplayName,ItemCount
```

> **NOTE USING THE *SORT-OBJECT* AND *SELECT-OBJECT* POWERSHELL CMDLETS**
>
> You can use the *Sort-Object* and *Select-Object* PowerShell cmdlets with other EMS cmdlets such as *Get-MailboxDatabase* if, for example, you want to list the top five mailbox databases on a Mailbox server in terms of database size.

Monitoring Resource Usage

Sometimes pressure on a mailbox database can be the result of certain users consuming a disproportionate amount of resources, such as by sending an excessive number of large attachments to a large number of recipients. To detect this situation, you can use the *Get-StoreUsageStatistics* EMS cmdlet to generate a report on the 25 accounts that are using the greatest amount of resources within a mailbox database. For example, the following command returns the 25 users with the largest mailboxes in Mailbox Database 1363123687:

```
Get-StoreUsageStatistics -Database "Mailbox Database 1363123687"
```

You can also use the *Get-StoreUsageStatistics* cmdlet to obtain statistics about a specific mailbox, but only if this mailbox account is one of the 25 top resource users. Under these circumstances, the following command would generate a report about the Kim Akers account:

```
Get-StoreUsageStatistics -Identity "Kim Akers"
```

Using Performance Monitor Counters

You can use the Exchange Server Performance Monitor tool to monitor counters that can indicate whether resources in your Exchange organization are coming under stress. This is the same tool as Performance Monitor (PerfMon) except that the Performance and Logs Alerts snap-in has been prepopulated with a large number of Exchange-related performance counters. You can access Exchange Server Performance Monitor from the EMC by clicking the Toolbox node, clicking Performance Monitor, and clicking Open Tool.

As an experienced administrator, you should have used PerfMon on both server and client operating systems to monitor current performance, create data records, and generate reports. The tool provided by Exchange Server 2010 works in the same way, but you have the option of monitoring performance counters specific to Exchange. More than 100 MSExchange countergroups exist, each one of which offers a significant number of counters.

You are not expected to be familiar with every counter that populates the Exchange Server PerfMon. It is probable that no single person could list and describe all of them. Nor can you be expected to know the acceptable values that every counter returns. Although some countervalues exist that definitely indicate a fault while other values indicate that a process is operating in a satisfactory manner, absolute good or bad values are not typical. If you want to use PerfMon counters to monitor performance, you would normally record baseline counter values when your Exchange organization is working in a satisfactory manner—possibly during a quiet period, under normal conditions, and during busy times. Recording values on a regular basis under the same conditions and comparing these to baseline values would indicate whether performance is deteriorating over time and help you track trends.

For example, to ensure that your mailbox databases continue to operate efficiently, you need to check that they are being defragmented online on an ongoing basis. Online defragmentation is a background task that operates continuously by default. Exchange Server 2010 provides the following performance counters for monitoring the behavior of online database defragmentation:

- **MSExchange Database → Online Defrag Average Log Bytes**   Shows average size of the log records being generated by online defragmentation

- **MSExchange Database → Online Defrag Data Moves/Sec**   Shows the number of times that data is moved from one page to another by the online defragmentation process

- **MSExchange Database → Online Defrag Log Records/Sec**   Shows the number of times per second that data is moved from one page to another by the online defragmentation process

- **MSExchange Database → Online Defrag Page Moves/Sec**   Shows the number of times that data is moved from one page to a new page by the online defragmentation process

- **MSExchange Database → Online Defrag Pages Dirtied/Sec**   Shows the rate at which online defragmentation is modifying clean database pages

- **MSExchange Database → Online Defrag Pages Freed/Sec**   Shows the number of pages per second that are freed from the database by the online defragmentation process

- **MSExchange Database → Online Defrag Pages Preread/Sec**   Shows the rate at which database pages are read in anticipation of future use by online defragmentation

- **MSExchange Database → Online Defrag Pages Read/Sec**   Shows the rate of database read operations being performed by online defragmentation

- **MSExchange Database → Online Defrag Pages Re-Dirtied/Sec** Shows the rate at which online defragmentation is modifying database pages that already contained modifications

- **MSExchange Database → Online Defrag Pages Referenced/Sec** Shows the rate at which online defragmentation is touching database pages

> **NOTE USING EXCHANGE SERVER PERFORMANCE MONITOR TO MONITOR QUEUES**
>
> Exchange Server PerfMon can monitor a large number of Exchange-related counters. In particular, you can use it to obtain information about transport queues by monitoring counters in the MSExchange Transport Queues group, such as MSExchange Transport Queues→ Active Mailbox Delivery Queue Length, MSExchange Transport Queues→ Aggregate Delivery Queue Length (All Queues), MSExchange Transport Queues→ Items Queued For Delivery/Sec, MSExchange Transport Queues→ Items Completed Delivery/ Sec, and MSExchange Transport Queues→ Poison Queue Length. Transport queues are described in Lesson 2 of this chapter, "Monitoring Mail Flow."

Obtaining Information about Public Folder Databases

When you are monitoring a public folder database, you first need to obtain general information about the database, such as the server where it is located, what public folders it contains, its maximum item size, quota limits, replication schedule, and so on. You can use EMS commands based on the *Get-PublicFolderDatabase* cmdlet for this purpose. For example, the following command gets detailed information about every public folder database in an organization:

```
Get-PublicFolderDatabase | FL
```

Figure 9-5 shows some of the output from this command.

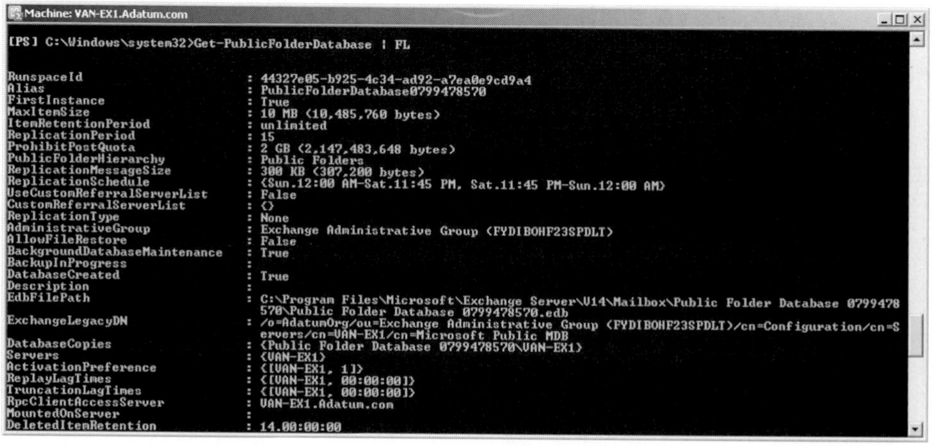

FIGURE 9-5 Detailed information about public folder databases

If you want to obtain detailed information about a specific public folder database, you can specify the Exchange Server 2010 Mailbox server on which it is located. For example, the following command gets detailed information about the public folder database on the VAN-EX1 server.

```
Get-PublicFolderDatabase -Server VAN-EX1 | FL
```

It is typically easier to analyze and store this information if the output of the command is redirected to a text file. For example, the following command redirects detailed information about the public folder database on the VAN-EX1 server to the text file PublicFolderDetails .txt in the DatabaseInformation folder on the VAN-EX1 server:

```
Get-PublicFolderDatabase -Server VAN-EX1 | FL >
C:\DatabaseInformation\PublicFolderDetails.txt
```

You can use the Status parameter of the *Get-PublicFolderDatabase* cmdlet to obtain backup and mount status information (if available). Checking the status of public folder databases is an important step in monitoring replication health. The following command gets detailed information about the public folder database on the VAN-EX1 server, including status information:

```
Get-PublicFolderDatabase -Server VAN-EX1 -Status | FL
```

> **MORE INFO GET-PUBLICFOLDERDATABASE**
>
> For more information about the *Get-PublicFolderDatabase* cmdlet, see *http://technet .microsoft.com/en-us/library/aa998827.aspx*.

You can use the EMC to obtain information about a public folder database. This information, such as database path, status, maintenance schedule, replication interval, storage limits, public folder referral information, and so on, is the same as that returned by EMS commands based on the *Get-PublicFolderDatabase* cmdlet. It does not tell you about database usage or the size and number of the public folders within the database.

The procedure to view public folder database properties is very similar to that for viewing mailbox database properties described earlier in this lesson. The procedure is as follows:

1. On your Mailbox server, open the EMC.

2. Click Mailbox under Organization Configuration in the Console tree.

3. In the Result pane, click the Database Management tab and then click the public folder database whose status you want to determine.

4. Click Properties in the Actions pane.

5. The General, Replication, Limits, and Public Folder Referral tabs of the public folder database Properties dialog box, shown in Figure 9-6, show the properties of the public folder database.

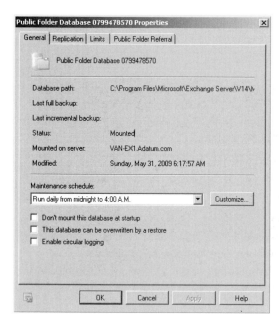

FIGURE 9-6 The public folder database Properties dialog box

Viewing Public Folder Statistics

No EMS cmdlet exists that returns the statistics for an entire public folder database. However, you can use the *Get-PublicFolderStatistics* EMS cmdlet to obtain statistics for each individual public folder within a public folder database. You would, for example, obtain public folder statistics if you had created a new public folder database on another Mailbox server and you wanted to replicate a public folder on your current server to the new public folder database.

You can check replication by ensuring that, for example, the number and size of items in the public folder replica are the same as in the original public folder. You could use the same procedure if you replicate an entire public folder database and want to check that replication is working correctly.

The following command obtains statistics for every public folder in an Exchange 2010 organization:

```
Get-PublicFolderStatistics | FL
```

The previous command can return an excessive volume of information, particularly if you have a large number of public folders. As with mailbox databases, you can refine the information. If, for example, you want to obtain statistics for every public folder in the public folder database on the Mailbox server VAN-EX1, you would enter the following command:

```
Get-PublicFolderStatistics –Server VAN-EX1 | FL
```

If you want to obtain statistics for the public folder MyPublicFolder on the Mailbox server VAN-EX1, you would enter the following command:

```
Get-PublicFolderStatistics –Identity \MyPublicFolder –Server VAN-EX1 | FL
```

Figure 9-7 shows the output from this command. Note that this command runs only if you have previously created a public folder named MyPublicFolder as a child of the public folder root.

```
Machine: VAN-EX1.Adatum.com

[PS] C:\Windows\system32>Get-PublicFolderStatistics -Identity \MyPublicFolder -Server VAN-EX1 | FL

RunspaceId                  : 44327e05-b925-4c34-ad92-a7ea0e9cd9a4
AdminDisplayName            : MyPublicFolder
AssociatedItemCount         : 0
ContactCount                : 1
CreationTime                : 11/1/2009 4:43:47 AM
DeletedItemCount            : 0
EntryId                     : 000000001A447390AA6611CD9BC800AA002FC45A03004759F11A31B7E74C8B3F1C2DE213956300005632D9340000
ExpiryTime                  :
FolderPath                  : MyPublicFolder
IsDeletePending             : False
ItemCount                   : 0
LastAccessTime              : 11/11/2009 2:52:14 AM
LastModificationTime        : 11/1/2009 4:43:48 AM
LastUserModificationTime    :
LastUserAccessTime          :
Name                        : MyPublicFolder
OwnerCount                  : 1
TotalAssociatedItemSize     : 0 B (0 bytes)
TotalDeletedItemSize        : 0 B (0 bytes)
TotalItemSize               : 0 B (0 bytes)
ServerName                  :
StorageGroupName            :
DatabaseName                : Public Folder Database 0799478570
Identity                    : 000000001A447390AA6611CD9BC800AA002FC45A03004759F11A31B7E74C8B3F1C2DE213956300005632D9340000
IsValid                     : True
OriginatingServer           : van-ex1.adatum.com
```

FIGURE 9-7 Statistics for the public folder MyPublicFolder

Detecting Database Errors

Database corruption occurs, for example, when the Exchange Server Database (EDB) file is damaged during improper server shut down, through virus infection, or because of physical damage to the storage media. If an entire Exchange database becomes corrupt, the ESE writes error messages to Event Viewer, such as "Unable to read database header—database may have moved, or data was moved or was missing during recovery" or "Database page read failed verification because of a 1018 error (page checksum mismatch)." You can use tools such as Eseutil and Isinteg to repair a corrupt database or to fix database integrity problems. However, Microsoft recommends restoring a corrupt database from backup because the use of a tool such as Eseutil can lead to data loss. Chapter 14, "Exchange Disaster Recovery," discusses repairing a corrupt database.

Sometimes a database is not itself corrupt but holds items such as email messages, which are. Corrupt email messages can cause problems with mail flow and lead to excessive queuing. If you move an Exchange database to another server or copy its contents to a new database, corrupt messages do not move or copy. You can then delete such messages, typically with a non-delivery report (NDR).

Monitoring DAGs

A DAG is a set of up to 16 Exchange Server 2010 Mailbox servers that provide automatic database-level recovery from the failure of a database, server, or network. DAGs use continuous replication and Windows failover clustering technologies to provide continuous mailbox availability. Mailbox servers in a DAG monitor each other for failures. When a Mailbox server is added to a DAG, it works with the other servers in the DAG to provide automatic, database-level recovery from database failures. Chapter 13, "Exchange High-Availability Solutions," discusses DAGs in detail. This lesson briefly discusses how you monitor the status information about mailbox database copies included in a DAG.

Exchange 2010 provides several built-in tools and features that are used for regular proactive monitoring when the Exchange organization is configured for high availability or site resilience through the creation of DAGs. The primary tools for monitoring mailbox database copies included in DAGs are the EMS cmdlets *Get-MailboxDatabaseCopyStatus* and *Test-ReplicationHealth*.

Exchange Server 2010 also introduces a new event log stream that uses the crimson channel capabilities in Windows Server 2008 and Windows Server 2008 R2 and built-in scripts that can collect data from these event channels.

Crimson Channel Event Logging

Applications and Services logs is a new category of event logs in Windows Server 2008 and Windows Server 2008 R2. Logs in this category store events from a single application or component rather than events that have systemwide impact. The Applications and Services logs category includes four subtypes: Admin, Operational, Analytic, and Debug logs.

Typically, you would use event log records in the Admin logs subtype to troubleshoot problems. These events typically provide guidance about what action you should take when the event is logged. Events in the Operational log require more interpretation. Analytic logs (hidden and disabled by default) store events that trace an issue and, if enabled, typically log a high volume of events. Developers use Debug logs when debugging applications.

An application's *crimson channel* contains event logs in the Applications and Services category that are specific to that particular application. Exchange Server 2010 has two crimson channels: HighAvailability and MailboxDatabaseFailureItems. To view Exchange Server 2010 crimson channel event logs, carry out the following steps on the Exchange server:

1. Open Event Viewer in the Administrative Tools menu.

2. Expand Applications and Services Logs in the Console tree. Expand Microsoft. Expand Exchange.

3. You should see two crimson channels under Exchange: High Availability and MailboxDatabaseFailureItems. Expand High Availability. This gives you access to the Debug and Operational logs. Figure 9-8 shows the Operational log.

4. Expand MailboxDatabaseFailureItems. This gives you access to the Operational log, shown in Figure 9-9.

The MailboxDatabaseFailureItems channel logs events (including failure events) that affect a replicated mailbox database.

The High Availability channel contains events related to startup and shutdown of the Microsoft Exchange Replication service and the components that run within that service, such as Active Manager, the Third Party Synchronous Replication Application Program Interface (API), the Tasks Remote Procedure Call (RPC) Server, Tcp Listener, and Volume Shadow Copy

Service writer. Active Manager uses this channel to log events related to Active Manager role monitoring and database action events, such as a database mount operation and log truncation, and to record events related to the DAG's underlying cluster.

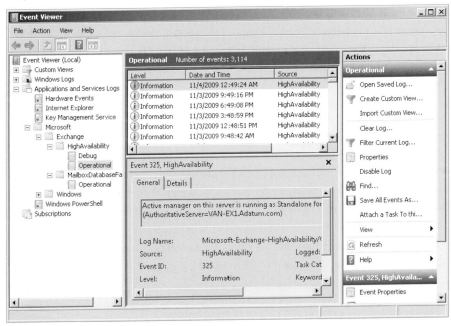

FIGURE 9-8 The HighAvailability Operational log

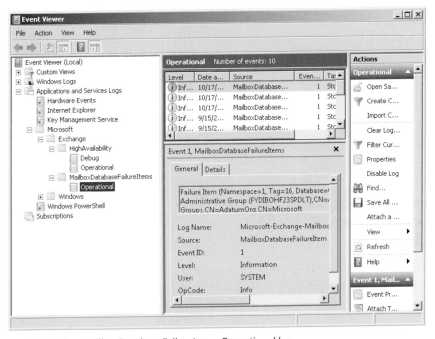

FIGURE 9-9 The MailboxDatabaseFailureItems Operational log

Obtaining the Status of Mailbox Database Copies

When you are investigating the condition of your mailbox database copies, you typically need to determine whether the status of a particular database copy is, for example, failed or healthy. You can use the *Get-MailboxDatabaseCopyStatus* EMS cmdlet to view status information about mailbox database copies. This lets you obtain information about all copies of a database, information about a specific copy of a database on a specific server, or information about all database copies on a specific server.

For example, the following command returns status information for all copies of a mailbox database copy named MyMailboxDatabase in an Exchange Server 2010 organization:

```
Get-MailboxDatabaseCopyStatus -Identity MyMailboxDatabase | FL
```

Note that commands based on the *Get-MailboxDatabaseCopyStatus* cmdlet also return information about mailbox databases on a server if mailbox database copies are not implemented. However, the status information for a mailbox database returns fewer possible values than that for a mailbox database copy. For example, a mailbox database that is not a copy cannot have the status "seeding."

The following command returns the status for all mailbox database copies (and mailbox databases) on a Mailbox server named VAN-EX1:

```
Get-MailboxDatabaseCopyStatus -Server VAN-EX1 | FL
```

Figure 9-10 shows some of the output of this command.

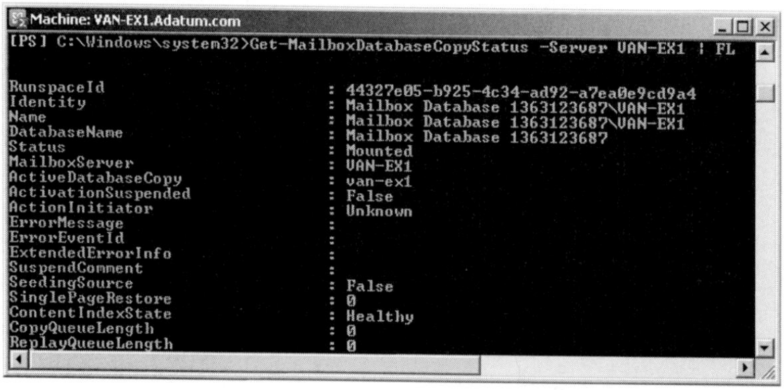

FIGURE 9-10 Status information for a mailbox database on server VAN-EX1

The following command returns the status for all mailbox database copies on the Mailbox server on which the command is entered:

```
Get-MailboxDatabaseCopyStatus -Local | FL
```

The following command returns the status and log shipping and seeding network information for a mailbox database copy named MyMailboxDatabase on a Mailbox server named VAN-EX1 (log shipping and seeding information for a mailbox database copy are discussed in detail in Chapter 13):

```
Get-MailboxDatabaseCopyStatus -Identity MyMailboxDatabase\VAN-EX1 -ConnectionStatus | FL
```

Table 9-1 lists and describes possible values for the copy status of a mailbox database copy.

TABLE 9-1 Mailbox database copy status

COPY STATUS	DESCRIPTION
ActivationSuspended	An administrator has manually blocked the mailbox database copy from activation.
DisconnectedAndHealthy	The mailbox database copy is no longer connected to the active database copy and was in the Healthy state when the loss of connection occurred. This status represents the database copy's view of connectivity to its source database copy. It may be reported during DAG network failures between the source copy and the target database copy.
DisconnectedAndResynchronizing	The mailbox database copy is no longer connected to the active database copy and was in the Resynchronizing state when the loss of connection occurred. This status represents the database copy's view of connectivity to its source database copy. It may be reported during DAG network failures between the source copy and the target database copy.
Dismounted	Only the active copy of a mailbox database copy can have a copy status of Dismounted. In this state, the active copy is offline and not accepting client connections.
Dismounting	Only the active copy of a mailbox database copy can have a copy status of Dismounting. In this state, the active copy is going offline and terminating client connections.
Failed	The mailbox database copy is in a Failed state and cannot copy or replay log files. While the database copy is in a failed state and not suspended, the system will periodically check to see if the problem that caused the failed copy status has been resolved. If the system detects that the problem has been resolved and no other issues are causing the database copy to fail, the copy status automatically changes to Healthy.

COPY STATUS	DESCRIPTION
FailedAndSuspended	The Failed and Suspended states have been set simultaneously by the system because a failure was detected, the resolution of which explicitly requires administrator intervention, such as if the system detects unrecoverable divergence between the active mailbox database and a database copy. Unlike when the mailbox database copy status is Failed, the system does not periodically check to see if the problem has been resolved. Instead, an administrator must intervene to resolve the underlying cause of the failure before the mailbox database copy can be transitioned to a Healthy state.
Healthy	The mailbox database copy is successfully copying and replaying log files, or it has successfully copied and replayed all available log files.
Initializing	The mailbox database copy status is set as Initializing when a new database copy has been created, when the Microsoft Exchange Replication service is starting up or has just been started, and during transitions from Suspended, ServiceDown, Failed, Seeding, SinglePageRestore, LostWrite, or Disconnected to another status. While a mailbox database copy is set to the Initializing status, the system is verifying that the database and log stream are in a consistent state. In most cases, the Initializing mailbox database copy status will last for about 15 seconds, but in all cases, this status should not last for more than 30 seconds.
Mounted	Only the active copy of a mailbox database copy can have a copy status of Mounted. In this state, the active copy is online and accepting client connections.
Mounting	Only the active copy of a mailbox database copy can have a copy status of Mounting. In this state, the active copy is coming online and not yet accepting client connections.
Resynchronizing	The mailbox database copy and its log files are being compared with the active copy of the database to check for any divergence between the two copies. The mailbox database copy status will remain as Resynchronizing until any divergence is detected and resolved.

COPY STATUS	DESCRIPTION
Seeding	The mailbox database copy is being seeded, the content index for the mailbox database copy is being seeded, or both. After seeding has successfully completed, the copy status changes to Initializing.
SeedingSource	In Exchange Server 2010, any healthy database or database copy can be used as the seeding source for an additional copy of that database. When a database is being used as a seeding source, its copy status is SeedingSource.
ServiceDown	The Microsoft Exchange Replication service is not running on the server that hosts the mailbox database copy.
SinglePageRestore	A single page restore operation is occurring on the mailbox database copy.
Suspended	The mailbox database copy is in a Suspended state. You can manually suspend a database copy by entering a command based on the *Suspend-MailboxDatabaseCopy* EMS cmdlet.

> **NOTE   THE CONNECTIONSTAUS PARAMETER**
>
> The *Get-MailboxDatabaseCopyStatus* EMS cmdlet also supports the **ConnectionStatus** parameter, which returns details about the in-use replication networks. If you use this parameter, two additional output fields—IncomingLogCopyingNetwork and SeedingNetwork—are populated in the output of the command.

> **MORE INFO   GET-MAILBOXDATABASECOPYSTATUS**
>
> For more information about the *Get-MailboxDatabaseCopyStatus* cmdlet, see
> *http://technet.microsoft.com/en-us/library/dd298044.aspx*.

Viewing the Continuous Replication Status of Mailbox Database Copies

If you need to check all aspects of the replication and replay status of mailbox database copies and obtain a complete overview of replication on a specific Mailbox server in a DAG, you can use commands based on the Test-ReplicationHealth EMS cmdlet. This functionality implements proactive monitoring of continuous replication and the continuous replication pipeline. It indicates the availability of Active Manager and the health and status of the underlying cluster service, quorum, and network components. You can run the commands locally on or remotely against any Mailbox server in a DAG.

For example, the following tests replication health for the Mailbox server VAN-EX1:

```
Test-ReplicationHealth -Identity VAN-EX1 | FL
```

Figure 9-11 shows the output from this command.

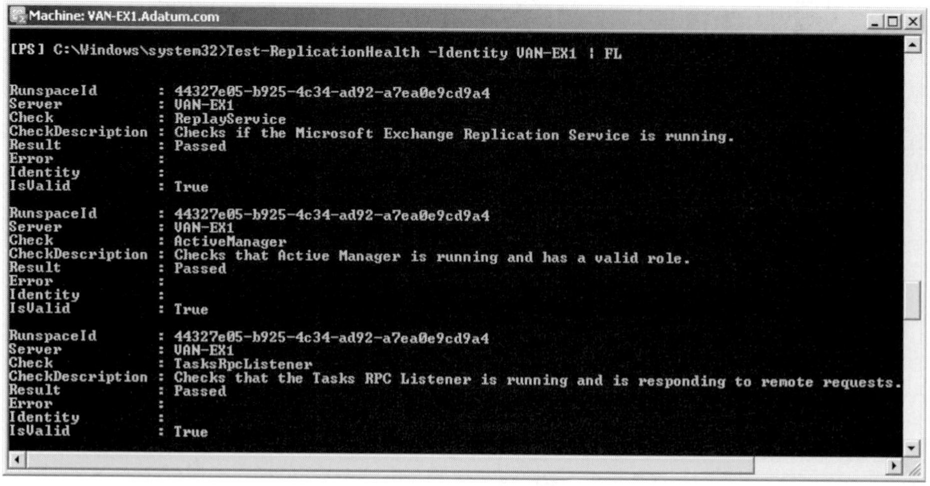

FIGURE 9-11 Testing replication health on Mailbox server VAN-EX1

The *Test-ReplicationHealth* cmdlet supports the OutputObjects parameter, which enables a command that uses this cmdlet to output an array of information regarding failures. The information returned can include the following:

- **ServerName**   The server on which a failure occurs
- **CheckID**   A unique identifier for every check performed
- **CheckTitle**   The title of the check that was run
- **InstanceIdentity**   A unique string identifying the instance that failed (for example, a database Global Unique Identifier [GUID])
- **DbFailureEventID**   The Event identity (ID) of the failure event logged by the Microsoft Exchange Replication Service for a database copy that is in a Failed state
- **CheckResult**   A check result (for example, pass, fail, or warning)
- **ErrorMessage**   A failure message logged by the check for the specific failure instance

For example, the following command tests replication health on server VAN-EX1 and returns failure information:

```
Test-ReplicationHealth -Identity VAN-EX1 -OutputObjects | FL
```

Figure 9-12 shows the output from this command. Note that if no failure has occurred, then no failure information is recorded.

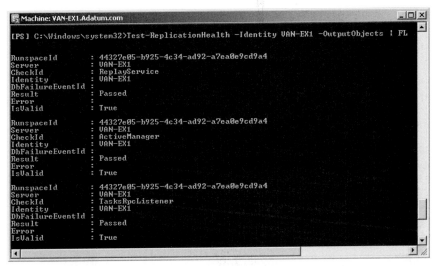

FIGURE 9-12 Using the OutputObjects parameter with the *Test-ReplicationHealth* cmdlet

Table 9-2 lists and describes the tests you can perform by using the *Test-ReplicationHealth* cmdlet.

TABLE 9-2 Continuous replication status tests

TEST	DESCRIPTION
ActiveManager	Verifies that the instance of Active Manager running on the specified DAG member (or, if no DAG member is specified, on the local server) is in a valid role (Primary, Secondary, or Standalone).
ClusterNetwork	Verifies that all cluster-managed networks on the specified DAG member (or, if no DAG member is specified, on the local server) are available.
ClusterService	Verifies that the Cluster service is running and can be reached on the specified DAG member. If no DAG member is specified, this tests if the service is reachable on the local server.
DagMembersUp	Verifies that all DAG members are up and running and reachable.
DBCopyFailed	Checks whether any mailbox database copies are in a Failed state on the specified DAG member or, if no DAG member is specified, on the local server.
DBCopySuspended	Checks whether any mailbox database copies are in a Suspended state on the specified DAG member or, if no DAG member is specified, on the local server.
DBDisconnected	Checks whether any mailbox database copies are in a Disconnected state on the specified DAG member or, if no DAG member is specified, on the local server.

TEST	DESCRIPTION
DBInitializing	Checks whether any mailbox database copies are in an Initializing state on the specified DAG member or, if no DAG member is specified, on the local server.
DBLogCopyKeepingUp	Verifies that log copying and inspection by the passive copies of databases on the specified DAG member (or, if no DAG member is specified, on the local server) is able to keep up with log generation activity on the active copy.
DBLogReplayKeepingUp	Verifies that replay activity for the passive copies of databases on the specified DAG member (or, if no DAG member is specified, on the local server) is able to keep up with log copying and inspection activity.
FileShareQuorum	Verifies that the witness server, witness directory, and share configured for the DAG are reachable.
QuorumGroup	Verifies that the default cluster group (quorum group) is in a healthy and online state.
ReplayService	Verifies that the Microsoft Exchange Replication service is running and can be reached on the specified DAG member, or if no DAG member is specified, this tests if the service is reachable on the local server.
TasksRpcListener	Verifies that the tasks RPC server is running and reachable on the specified DAG member or, if no DAG member is specified, on the local server.
TcpListener	Verifies that the TCP log copy listener is running and reachable on the specified DAG member or, if no DAG member is specified, on the local server.

Obtaining Switchover and Failover Statistics

If you are monitoring mailbox database copies, you sometimes need to monitor when switchovers or failovers occur and how frequently this is happening. Exchange Server 2010 provides the *CollectOverMetrics.ps1* script. This collects information about switchover- and failover-related statistics that have already been recorded. It is a passive monitoring script and does not generate any new statistics. The script supports parameters that enable you to customize the script's behavior and output. For a full list of these parameters, refer to the More Info link at the end of this section. Examples of the (arguably) more significant parameters are as follows:

- **DatabaseAvailabilityGroup**   The DAG from which you want to collect metrics. If this parameter is omitted, the local server's DAG is used.
- **Database**   One or more databases for which the report is generated. This parameter supports wildcards.

- **StartTime** The time from which event data is collected. If this parameter is omitted, the start time is 12:00 AM on the preceding day.

- **EndTime** The time at which event data collection stops. If this parameter is omitted, events are collected up to 11:59 PM on the preceding day.

- **IncludeAppLogs** Specifies if events in the Application event log should also be collected, merged, and processed. The following providers are included by default: MSExchangeIS, MSExchangeIS Mailbox Store, and MSExchangeRepl.

- **ShowHtmlReport** Specifies that an HTML report should be displayed in a web browser after it is generated.

- **GenerateHtmlReport** Specifies that the report should be output in simple HTML table format.

For example, the following command collects metrics for all databases whose names start with MyData in the DAG named MyDAG and generates and displays an HTML report after the metrics are collected:

```
CollectOverMetrics.ps1 -DatabaseAvailabilityGroup MyDAG -Database:"MyData*"
-GenerateHTMLReport -ShowHTMLReport
```

This command collects metrics for all databases in a DAG named SecondDAG and generates and displays an HTML report after the metrics are collected:

```
CollectOverMetrics.ps1 -DatabaseAvailabilityGroup SecondDAG -GenerateHTMLReport
-ShowHTMLReport
```

> **NOTE   RUNNING THE *COLLECTOVERMETRICS.PS1* SCRIPT**
>
> This script will not run, and an error is returned if the server on which it is entered is not part of a DAG.

> **MORE INFO   *COLLECTOVERMETRICS.PS1***
>
> For more information about the *CollectOverMetrics.ps1* script, see *http://technet .microsoft.com/en-us/library/dd351258.aspx*. This link gives general information about monitoring high availability and site resilience but includes a description of the *CollectOverMetrics.ps1* parameters.

Monitoring Replication Metrics

If you need to collect and monitor metrics actively in real time, you can use the Exchange Server 2010 CollectReplicationMetrics.ps1 script. The script supports parameters that enable you to customize its behavior and output. It does not have a StartTime or an EndTime parameter because it starts immediately. Instead, you can specify a duration parameter. The script does not support the ShowHTMLReport or GenerateHTMLReport parameters, but you can specify Verbose to display the script output on the screen.

For example, the following command collects metrics for all databases in the DAG named MyDAG and displays the collected data in an on-screen report:

```
CollectReplicationMetrics.ps1 -DagName MyDAG -Verbose
```

As with the *CollectOverMetrics.ps1* script, the CollectReplicationMetrics.ps1 script will not run if the server is not part of a DAG.

> **MORE INFO** **COLLECTREPLICATIONMETRICS.PS1**
>
> You can obtain detailed information about the CollectReplicationMetrics.ps1 script parameters in the same monitoring high-availability report that gave information about the *CollectOverMetrics.ps1* script. As before, see *http://technet.microsoft.com/en-us/ library/dd351258.aspx*.

Lagged Mailbox Database Copies

A *lagged mailbox database copy* is a passive mailbox database copy that has a log replay lag time greater than zero. You can create lagged mailbox database copies as insurance against corruption caused by, for example, damage to the EDB file during improper server shutdown. If you activate and recover a lagged mailbox database copy, the database replays all log files and makes the database copy current. The database copy thus created replaces the corrupted database. If you want to replay log files up to a specific point in time, you need to manually manipulate log files and run the Eseutil utility.

If you want to configure a lagged mailbox database copy of a mailbox database, you can use the *Add-MailboxDatabaseCopy* EMS cmdlet. If you specify the SeedingPostponed parameter, the new copy remains in a Suspended state because the database needs to be seeded.

The ReplayLagTime parameter specifies the amount of time that the Microsoft Exchange Replication service waits before replaying log files that have been copied to the passive database copy. If you set this parameter to a value greater than zero, this creates a lagged database copy. The TruncationLagTime parameter specifies the amount of time that the Exchange Replication service waits before truncating log files that have replayed into the passive copy of the database. This time period begins after the log has been successfully replayed into the copy of the database.

If you want to configure a lagged mailbox database copy of the database Mailbox Database 1363123687 that is hosted on Mailbox server VAN-EX1 and you want to configure a replay lag time of 10 minutes and truncation lag time of two days, you would enter the following command:

```
Add-MailboxDatabaseCopy -Identity "Mailbox Database 1363123687" -MailboxServer VAN-EX1
-ReplayLagTime 00:10:00 -TruncationLagTime 02:00:00
```

If you want to change the replay lag time for the lagged mailbox database copy Mailbox Database 1363123687 to a value of one hour, you would enter the following command:

```
Set-MailboxDatabaseCopy -Identity "Mailbox Database 1363123687" -ReplayLagTime 00:01:00
```

Lesson Summary

- You can use EMS commands based on the *Get-PublicFolderDatabase* and
  Get-PublicFolderStatistics cmdlets to monitor public folder databases.

- You can use EMS commands based on the *Get-MailboxDatabase* and
  Get-MailboxStatistics cmdlets to monitor mailbox databases.

- You can view the Crimson Channel logs in Event Viewer or use commands based on
  the *Get-MailboxDatabaseCopyStatus* EMS cmdlet to obtain the status of mailbox
  database copies.

Lesson Review

You can use the following questions to test your knowledge of the information in Lesson 1,
"Monitoring Exchange Databases." The questions are also available on the companion CD if
you prefer to review them in electronic form.

1. You want to view detailed information, including backup and mount status
   information, about the public folder database on the ContosoMail01 mailbox
   server. What EMS command do you enter?

   A. *Get-PublicFolderDatabase –Identity ContosoMail01 | FL*

   B. *Get-PublicFolderDatabase –Server ContosoMail01 | FL*

   C. *Get-PublicFolderDatabase –Identity ContosoMail01 -Status | FL*

   D. *Get-PublicFolderDatabase –Server ContosoMail01 -Status | FL*

2. You want to discover whether the status of the mailbox database MyMailboxDatabase is BackupInProgress, Mounted, or OnlineMaintenanceInProgress. You also want to find how much free space is available in the database root. What EMS command do you enter?

   A. *Get-MailboxDatabase -Identity MyMailboxDatabase –Status | FL*

   B. *Get-MailboxDatabase -Server MyMailboxDatabase –Status | FL*

   C. *Get-MailboxDatabase -Identity MyMailboxDatabase – DumpsterStatistics | FL*

   D. *Get-MailboxDatabase -Server MyMailboxDatabase – DumpsterStatistics | FL*

3. You want to obtain statistics for the Jeff Hay mailbox in the mailbox database MyMailboxDatabase on the Mailbox server Mai01. You enter the following command:

   ```
   Get-MailboxStatistics -Identity "Jeff Hay" | FL
   ```

   Mailbox statistics are not returned, but instead you get a warning message. What is the likely reason for this?

   A. You need to use the Server parameter and specify the value Mai01.

   B. You need to use the Database parameter and specify the value MyMailboxDatabase.

   C. Jeff Hay has never logged on to his mailbox, and the mailbox has not been accessed in any other way (for example, an email message has not been sent to it).

   D. You need to use the *Get-StoreUsageStatistics* cmdlet, not the *Get-MailboxStatistics* cmdlet.

4. Which mailbox database copy status indicates that the mailbox database copy is no longer connected to the active database copy and that it was in the Resynchronizing state when the loss of connection occurred?

   A. DisconnectedAndResynchronizing

   B. ActivationSuspended

   C. Seeding

   D. DisconnectedAndHealthy

5. Which EMS cmdlet can you use to generate a report on the 25 accounts that are using the greatest amount of resources within a mailbox database?

   A. *Get-MailboxStatistics*

   B. *Get-StoreUsageStatistics*

   C. *Get-MailboxDatabase*

   D. *Get-MailboxDatabaseCopyStatus*

Lesson 2: Monitoring Mail Flow

One of the most important things you need to monitor in your Exchange organization is how well messages are flowing through your email system. Message queues are probably inevitable in a busy Exchange environment, but are the correct messages in the appropriate queues, are they staying in queues for too long, are queues being retried when appropriate, and how do you track messages that appear to have been lost or stuck in the system?

In this lesson, you will look at how you configure message tracking and message tracking log files. You will look at how you view, retry, and delete message queues. The lesson covers back-pressure thresholds and whether NDRs are sent when specific types of messages (for example, suspected spam messages) are deleted.

After this lesson, you will be able to:

- Configure message tracking and message tracking logs.
- Enable or disable message subject logging.
- Monitor and manage transport queues.
- Manage messages.
- Test mail flow.

Estimated lesson time: 40 minutes

Configuring Message Tracking

Message tracking tracks all messages transferred to and from an Exchange Server 2010 Hub Transport, Edge Transport, or Mailbox server. Message tracking logs assist in mail flow analysis, reporting, and troubleshooting. By default, message tracking is enabled on all Exchange Server 2010 Hub Transport, Edge Transport, or Mailbox servers. You can use the EMS and (for a limited number of settings) the EMC to configure message tracking. Note that this section discusses message tracking configuration. How you track messages and view message tracking reports is covered later in this lesson.

> **NOTE LIMITATION TO USING THE EMC**
> You can use the EMC to configure some message tracking settings on a Hub Transport or Edge Transport server. You cannot use the EMC to configure message tracking on a Mailbox server that does not also have the Hub Transport role installed. Also, you cannot use the EMC to configure the maximum size or age of message tracking log files or the maximum size of the message tracking log file directory. You cannot use the EMC to configure message subject logging in message tracking logs.

Enabling or Disabling Message Tracking and Changing the Log Path

To use the EMC to enable or disable message tracking on a Hub Transport server, carry out the following procedure:

1. Open the EMC and expand the Console tree.

2. In the Console tree, select Hub Transport under Server Configuration.

3. In the Action pane, click Properties directly under the server name.

4. In the Properties dialog box, click the Log Settings tab, as shown in Figure 9-13.

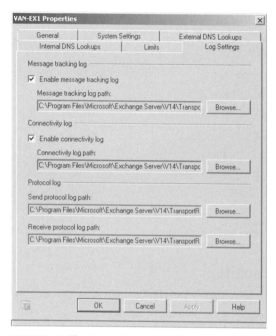

FIGURE 9-13 The Log Settings tab of the server Properties dialog box

5. In the Message Tracking Log section, you can select or clear the Enable Message Tracking Log check box to enable or disable message tracking. If message tracking is enabled, you can, if required, change the default path to the message tracking log. Note that you cannot use the EMC to change the path to the message tracking log on Mailbox servers that do not also have the Hub Transport role installed.

6. Click OK to save your changes and close the Properties dialog box.

To use the EMS to enable or disable message tracking and to change the path to the message tracking log, you enter a command based on the *Set-TransportServer* or *Set-MailboxServer* cmdlet. For example, the following command disables message tracking on the Exchange Server 2010 Hub Transport server VAN-EX1:

```
Set-TransportServer –Identity VAN-EX1 –MessageTrackingLogEnabled:$false
```

The following command enables message tracking on the Exchange Server 2010 Mailbox server VAN-EX2:

```
Set-MailboxServer -Identity VAN-EX2 -MessageTrackingLogEnabled:$true
```

The following command changes the path to the message tracking log on Hub Transport server VAN-EX1 to C:\Logfiles\MessageTracking:

```
Set-TransportServer -Identity VAN-EX1 -MessageTrackingLogPath C:\Logfiles\
MessageTracking
```

The following command changes the path to the message tracking log on Mailbox server VAN-EX2 to C:\Logfiles\Tracking\MessageLogs:

```
Set-TransportServer -Identity VAN-EX2 -MessageTrackingLogPath C:\Logfiles\Tracking\
MessageLogs
```

Configuring the Size and Age of Message Tracking Log Files

By default, the maximum size for each message tracking log file is 10 megabytes (MB). When a message tracking log file reaches its maximum size, Exchange Server 2010 opens a new message tracking log file. This continues until the message tracking log directory reaches its specified maximum size (by default 250 MB) or until a message tracking log file reaches its specified maximum age (by default 30 days). In either of these cases, Exchange Server 2010 deletes the oldest message tracking log file.

You can use the EMS (but not the EMC) to change the maximum size of each message tracking log file, the maximum age of each message tracking log file, and the maximum size for the entire message tracking log directory on Hub Transport, Edge Transport, and Mailbox servers.

The following command changes the maximum size of each message tracking log file on the Hub Transport server VAN-EX1 to 15MB (the same command would work on an Edge Transport server):

```
Set-TransportServer -Identity VAN-EX1 -MessageTrackingLogMaxFileSize 15MB
```

The following command changes the maximum age of each message tracking log file on the Hub Transport server VAN-EX1 to 35 days (as before, the same command would work on an Edge Transport server):

```
Set-TransportServer -Identity VAN-EX1 -MessageTrackingLogMaxAge 35.00:00:00
```

The following command changes the maximum size of the message tracking log file directory on the Hub Transport server VAN-EX1 to 300 MB (again the same command would work on an Edge Transport server):

```
Set-TransportServer -Identity VAN-EX1 -MessageTrackingLogMaxDirectorySize 300MB
```

The commands to configure maximum log size and age and the maximum size of the message tracking log file directory on a Mailbox server are similar, except that the *Set-MailboxServer* cmdlet is used. Note that if an Exchange Server 2010 server holds both the Mailbox and the Hub Transport roles, the effective maximum size of its message tracking log file directory is twice the size that is specified because message tracking log files for the mailbox and the transport functions have different prefixes. File prefixes are discussed later in this lesson.

The following command changes the maximum size of each message tracking log file on the Mailbox server VAN-EX2 to 20 MB:

```
Set-MailboxServer –Identity VAN-EX2 -MessageTrackingLogMaxFileSize 20MB
```

The following command changes the maximum age of each message tracking log on the Mailbox server VAN-EX2 to 40 days:

```
Set-MailboxServer –Identity VAN-EX2 -MessageTrackingLogMaxAge 40.00:00:00
```

The following command changes the maximum size of the message tracking log file directory on the Mailbox server VAN-EX2 to 350 MB:

```
Set-MailboxServer –Identity VAN-EX2 -MessageTrackingLogMaxDirectorySize 350MB
```

 Quick Check

- What command would disable message tracking on the Edge Transport server CAN-Edge1?

Quick Check Answer

- *Set-TransportServer –Identity CAN-Edge1 -MessageTrackingLogEnabled:$false*

File Name Prefixes and the Maximum Size of the Message Tracking Log Directory

Message tracking log files for Hub Transport or Edge Transport servers have the name prefix MSGTRK (for example, MSGTRK20100215-1.log). Message tracking log files for Mailbox servers have the name prefix MSGTRKM (for example, MSGTRKM20100214-2.log). The maximum size of the message tracking log directory is calculated as the total size of all log files that have the same name prefix. Files that do not follow the name prefix convention are not counted when calculating the total directory size. Renaming old log files or copying other files into the message tracking log directory could cause the physical size of the directory to exceed its specified maximum size.

When the Hub Transport and Mailbox server roles are installed on the same server, the maximum physical size of the message tracking log directory is not the specified maximum size because the message tracking log files generated by the different server roles have different name prefixes. In this case, the maximum physical size of the message tracking log directory is two times the specified value.

Configuring Message Subject Logging in Message Tracking Logs

By default, the subject line of a Simple Mail Transfer Protocol (SMTP) email message is stored in the message tracking log. However, you may want to disable message subject logging to comply with security or privacy requirements. Before you enable or disable message subject logging, you need to verify your organization's policy about revealing subject-line information. As with previous message tracking configurations, you use the *Set-TransportServer* and *Set-MailboxServer* EMS cmdlets to enable or disable message subject logging on Hub Transport and Edge Transport servers and on Mailbox servers, respectively.

For example, the following command disables message subject logging in message tracking logs on the Hub Transport server VAN-EX1:

```
Set-TransportServer –Identity VAN-EX1 -MessageTrackingLogSubjectLoggingEnabled $false
```

The following command enables message subject logging in message tracking logs on the Mailbox server VAN-EX2:

```
Set-MailboxServer –Identity VAN-EX2 -MessageTrackingLogSubjectLoggingEnabled $true
```

> **MORE INFO** **SET-MAILBOXSERVER AND SET-TRANSPORTSERVER**
>
> For more information about the *Set-MailboxServer* cmdlet, see *http://technet.microsoft .com/en-us/library/aa998651.aspx*. For more information about the *Set-TransportServer* cmdlet, see *http://technet.microsoft.com/en-us/library/bb124238.aspx*.

Monitoring Transport Queues

If a mailbox database is experiencing performance problems, this typically manifests itself in excessively long transport queues associated with the database. If a Hub Transport or Edge Transport server becomes overloaded, this can result in an excessive number of messages in the transport queues on that server. It is a good idea to monitor transport queues on a regular basis, and you would typically look at queue statistics as a matter of course when you encounter performance problems.

You can use both the EMC and the EMS to monitor transport queues. To use the EMC on a Hub Transport server, carry out the following procedure:

1. Open the EMC on the Hub Transport server and expand the Console tree.
2. Click Toolbox in the Console tree.
3. Click Queue Viewer in the Result pane.
4. Click Open Tool in the Actions pane.
5. Click the Queues tab in Queue Viewer, shown in Figure 9-14. This displays a list of the queues on the server to which you are connected. Note that you are unlikely to see any queues on your isolated test network.

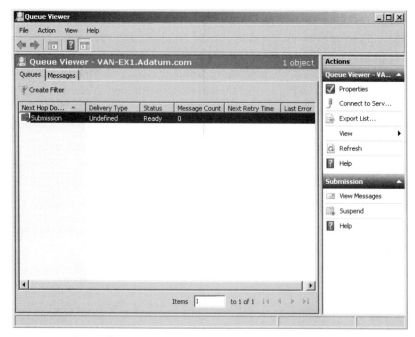

FIGURE 9-14 Queue viewer

6. If you want to export the list of queues, click Export List in the Actions pane. If you want a list of messages in a queue, click the queue in the Queues tab in the Result pane and click View Messages in the Actions pane.

You can use the *Get-Queue* EMS cmdlet to view transport queues. For example, the following command lets you view all the queues on the Hub Transport or Edge Transport server on which it is entered:

```
Get-Queue | FL
```

The following command displays detailed information for a queue that exists on the server VAN-EX1:

```
Get-Queue -Server VAN-EX1 | FL
```

Figure 9-15 shows the output from this command.

FIGURE 9-15 Viewing information about queues on a server

Filtering Queues

In a busy Exchange Server 2010 organization, the number of queues can become very large, depending on the current mail flow. The queue list can change frequently as messages enter and leave a server. You can filter queues to search for specific criteria and locate queues that are experiencing mail flow problems. You can use the Exchange Queue Viewer in the EMC and EMS commands to filter queues. You can then perform operations that modify the status of those queues.

To use the Queue Viewer to filter queues on a Hub Transport server, carry out the following procedure:

1. Open the EMC on the Hub Transport server and expand the Console tree.

2. Click Toolbox in the Console tree.

3. Click Queue Viewer in the Result pane.

4. Click Open Tool in the Actions pane.

5. Click the Queues tab in Queue Viewer.

6. Click Create Filter.

7. In the queue property drop-down list, select a queue property. The options available are shown in Figure 9-16.

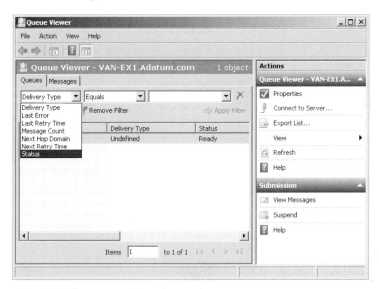

FIGURE 9-16 Queue property options

8. Select a comparison operator from the comparison operator drop-down list (for example, Equals).

9. Depending on the queue property you have chosen, either type a value in the value drop-down list or select a value from the drop-down list. If the property requires a date/time expression, change the current date/time values or click the drop-down list

to select a date from the calendar interface. Figure 9-17 shows the options available for the Status queue property.

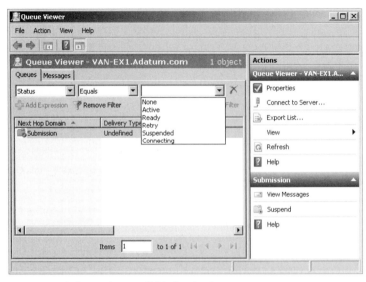

FIGURE 9-17 Value options available for the Status queue property

10. Optionally, click Add Expression and specify additional filter criteria. Only queues that meet all filter criteria are displayed.

11. Click Apply Filter to display only queues that meet the filter criteria.

You can also use the *Get-Queue* EMS cmdlet with the Filter parameter to filter queues. For example, the following command lists all the queues on the Hub Transport or Edge Transport server on which it is entered that contain more than 50 messages:

```
Get-Queue -Filter {MessageCount -gt 50}
```

You can also use the Filter parameter of the *Get-Queue* cmdlet to display the number of messages in queues bound for a particular destination. For example, the following command displays the number of messages in queues on the Hub Transport or Edge Transport server on which it is entered where the next-hop destination is the Contoso.com domain:

```
Get-Queue -Filter{NextHopDomain -eq "contoso.com"}
```

You can also use a remote server name or site name in place of the SMTP domain name.

In general, the Filter parameter requires an expression that identifies the queues that you want to display. The expression includes a property name followed by a comparison operator and value. The following queue properties are valid for the Filter parameter:

- **DeliveryType**   The delivery type for a queue must be one of the following values:
  - DNSConnectorDelivery
  - NonSMTPGatewayDelivery

- SmartHostConnectorDelivery
- SmtpRelayWithinAdSitetoEdge
- MapiDelivery
- SmtpRelayWithinAdSite
- SmtpRelaytoRemoteAdSite
- SmtpRelaytoTiRg
- Undefined
- Unreachable

- **Identity**   The queue identity takes the form Server\destination, where destination is a remote domain, Mailbox server, or persistent queue name.

- **LastError**   A text string that contains the last error recorded for a queue.

- **LastRetryTime**   The time when a connection was last tried for this queue.

- **MessageCount**   The number of items in the queue.

- **NextHopConnector**   The GUID of the connector that was used to create the queue.

- **NextHopDomain**   The next hop domain of the queue, specified as a remote SMTP domain, a server name, the name of an Active Directory site, or a message database identifier.

- **NextRetryTime**   The time when a connection will next be tried for this queue.

- **Status**   The status of the queue. The queue status can be Active, Ready, Retry, or Suspended.

NOTE   **QUEUE STATUS**

You can manually suspend and resume queues. The delivery queue on a Hub Transport or Edge Transport server is automatically put in a Retry status when the server cannot connect to the next hop. You can use either the EMC or the EMS to retry a queue.

EXAM TIP

The list of queue properties that are valid for the Filter parameter can look daunting. However, you are unlikely to be asked to generate a complex filter condition in the examination, although you might need to do so as part of your job. You might be asked to identify a valid filter condition that, for example, displays queues marked as unreachable or queues that are suspended. The best way to become familiar with filter conditions is to generate and enter commands that use them. This is one of the suggested practices at the end of this chapter.

MORE INFO **VIEWING AND MANAGING QUEUES**

For more information about the *Get-Queue* cmdlet, see *http://technet.microsoft.com/ en-us/library/bb124904.aspx*. For more information about using the EMS to manage queues, see *http://technet.microsoft.com/en-us/library/aa998047.aspx*.

Queue Types

How a message is routed determines the type of queue in which it is stored. The following types of queues are used in Exchange Server 2010:

- **Submission queue** A submission queue is a persistent queue that the categorizer uses to store messages that need to be resolved, routed, and processed by transport agents. All messages that are received by a Transport server are held in the submission queue before processing. Messages are submitted through SMTP-receive, the Pickup directory, or the store driver. The categorizer retrieves messages from this queue and determines the location of the recipient and the route to that location. After categorization, the message is moved to a delivery queue or to the unreachable queue. Only one submission queue exists on each Exchange Server 2007 Transport server. Messages that are in the submission queue cannot be in other queues at the same time.

NOTE **THE CATEGORIZER**

The categorizer is an Exchange transport component that processes all inbound messages and determines what to do with them on the basis of information about their intended recipients. In Exchange 2010, a server with the Edge Transport role uses the categorizer to route messages to their appropriate destinations. A server with the Hub Transport role uses the categorizer to expand distribution lists and to identify alternative recipients and forwarding addresses. After the categorizer retrieves full information about recipients, it uses that information to apply policies, route the message, and perform content conversion.

- **Mailbox delivery queue** A mailbox delivery queue holds messages that are delivered to a Mailbox server by using an encrypted Exchange RPC. Mailbox delivery queues exist only on servers with the Hub Transport role. A mailbox delivery queue holds messages that are being delivered to mailbox recipients whose mailbox data is stored on a Mailbox server located in the same site as the Hub Transport server. Several mailbox delivery queues can exist on a server with the Hub Transport role. The next hop for a mailbox delivery queue is defined by the distinguished name of the mailbox store.

- **Remote delivery queue** A remote delivery queue holds messages that are being delivered to a remote server by using SMTP. Remote delivery queues can exist on servers with both the Hub Transport and the Edge Transport role, and more than one remote delivery queue can exist on each server. A remote delivery queue contains messages that are being routed to recipients that have the same delivery destination. On a server with the Edge Transport role, these destinations are external SMTP domains or SMTP connectors. On a server with the Hub Transport role, the destinations are outside the Active Directory site in which the server with the Hub Transport role is located. A server with the Hub Transport role can also route Internet email. Remote delivery queues are created dynamically as required and are automatically deleted from the server when they no longer hold messages and when their (configurable) expiration time has passed. By default, a remote delivery queue is deleted three minutes after the last message has left the queue. The next hop for a remote delivery queue is an SMTP domain name, a smart host name or Internet Protocol (IP) address, or an Active Directory site name.

■ **Poison message queue** The poison message queue is a special queue that is used to isolate messages that are potentially harmful to Exchange Server 2010. This queue is typically empty. If no poison messages exist, the queue does not appear in queue-viewing interfaces such as Queue Viewer. The poison message queue is always in a Ready state. By default, all messages in this queue are suspended. You can delete the messages if you judge that they are harmful to the system. If an event that causes a message to enter the poison message queue is unrelated to the message, message delivery can be resumed. If delivery is resumed, the message enters the submission queue.

> **MORE INFO**   **DETERMINING WHETHER A MESSAGE IS A POISON MESSAGE**
>
> A poison message is a message that has exceeded the maximum number of delivery attempts to an application. For more information about poison message identification and how these messages are handled, see *http://msdn.microsoft.com/en-us/library/ms789028.aspx.*

■ **Unreachable queue** The unreachable queue contains messages that cannot be routed to their destinations. An Edge Transport or Hub Transport server can have only one unreachable queue. Typically, an unreachable destination can be created when configuration changes modify the delivery routing path. All messages that have unreachable recipients reside in the unreachable queue.

When a message is received, a transport mail item is created and saved to the database, and a unique identifier is assigned to the item. If a message or transport mail item is being sent to more than one recipient, the item can have more than one destination. Each destination represents a separate routing solution for the transport mail item, and each routing solution causes a routed mail item to be created.

The routed mail item refers to the transport mail item. If a transport mail item has more than one routing solution, more than one routed mail item references the same transport mail item. A single message addressed to recipients in two different domains appears as two distinct messages in the delivery queues, even if there is only one transport mail item in the database.

MORE INFO **QUEUES AND QUEUE TYPES**

For more information about transport queue types and managing queues, see *http:// technet.microsoft.com/en-us/library/bb125022.aspx*.

Suspending, Resuming, and Retrying Queues

Sometimes if you are experiencing message flow problems on a Hub Transport or Edge Transport server, you need to stop queued messages from being sent so that you can investigate problems within the queue. You then need to enable the queue to resume normal operations. If a queue is experiencing problems sending messages, it will try again to do so at configured intervals. Sometimes you need to force an immediate retry. This section investigates all these situations.

Suspending Queues

You can suspend a transport queue on a Hub Transport or Edge Transport server if you want to prevent messages from leaving the queue. Suspending a queue does not change the status of messages in that queue. Messages that are in the process of delivery will finish operations. You can suspend a queue to stop mail flow and then suspend one or more messages in the queue. When you resume the queue, the messages that were suspended will not leave the queue.

You can suspend a queue that has a status of Active or Retry. You can also suspend the Unreachable queue and the Submission queue. If you suspend the Unreachable queue, items are not resubmitted to the categorizer when the Transport server receives configuration updates until the queue is resumed. If you suspend the Submission queue, messages are not picked up by the categorizer until the queue is resumed.

The Queue Viewer can be used to suspend a queue. You access the Queues tab as described earlier in this lesson, right-click the queue, and click Suspend. You can also select several queues and then click Suspend in the Actions pane.

You can use commands based on the *Suspend-Queue* EMS cmdlet. Like the *Get-Queue* cmdlet, this supports the Filter parameter. For example, the following command suspends all queues that have a message count equal to or greater than 500 and have a status of Active:

```
Suspend-Queue -Filter {MessageCount -ge 500 -and Status -eq "Active"}
```

The cmdlet supports the Confirm switch, which you can use to suppress the confirmation prompt that appears by default when the cmdlet is run. For example, the following command suspends the same queues as the previous command, but you do not need to confirm the action:

```
Suspend-Queue -Filter {MessageCount -ge 500 -and Status -eq "Active"} -Confirm:$False
```

> **NOTE SUSPENDING A MESSAGE IN A QUEUE**
>
> You can use the *Suspend-Message* cmdlet, discussed later in this lesson, to prevent delivery of a particular message in a queue on a computer that has the Hub Transport server role or the Edge Transport server role installed. Suspending a message in a queue does not suspend the entire queue.

Resuming Queues

When you resume a suspended queue on a Hub Transport or Edge Transport server, this restarts the queue's outgoing activities. The queue must have a status of Suspended for this action to have any effect. When you resume a queue, the status of messages in the queue does not change. Messages that have a status of Suspended remain suspended and do not leave the queue.

To use the Queue Viewer to resume queues, you must first list all the queues that have a status of Suspended. Open the tool, access the Queues tab, and click Create Filter, as described in the procedure to filter queues earlier in this lesson. Then set the queue property, comparison operator, and value drop-down lists to Status, Equals, and Suspended, respectively. Click Apply Filter, and all the queues with a status of Suspended on the server are displayed. You can then right-click an individual queue and click Resume or select a number of queues and click Resume in the Actions pane.

You can use the *Resume-Queue* EMS cmdlet to resume queues. This cmdlet also supports the Filter parameter. For example, the following command resumes all the suspended queues on the Hub Transport or Edge Transport server on which it is entered:

```
Resume-Queue -Filter {Status -eq "Suspended"}
```

Retrying Queues

When a Hub Transport or Edge Transport server cannot connect to the next hop, the delivery queue is put in a status of Retry. You can retry a delivery queue by using the EMC Queue Viewer or the EMS. This forces an immediate connection attempt and overrides the next scheduled retry time. If the connection is unsuccessful, the retry interval timer is reset. The delivery queue must be in a status of Retry for this action to have any effect.

To use Queue Viewer to retry a queue, you first need to display all the queues that have a status of Retry. To do this, you open the tool, access the Queues tab, and click Create Filter, as described in the procedure to filter queues earlier in this lesson. You then set the queue property, comparison operator, and value drop-down lists to Status, Equals, and Retry, respectively. Click Apply Filter, and all the queues with a status of Retry on the server are displayed. You can then right-click an individual queue and click Retry or select a number of queues and click Retry in the Actions pane.

You can also use commands based on the *Retry-Queue* cmdlet to retry transport queues. For example, the following command retries all queues with the status of Retry on the Hub Transport or Edge Transport server on which it is entered:

```
Retry-Queue -Filter {status -eq "Retry"}
```

The following command forces a connection attempt for all queues on a Hub Transport or Edge Transport server that are holding messages for the domain fabrikam.com and have a status of Retry:

```
Retry-Queue -Filter {NextHopDomain -eq "fabrikam.com" -and Status -eq "Retry"}
```

 Quick Check

- You want to resume all suspended queues on a Hub Transport server. You open the EMS on that server. What command do you enter?

Quick Check Answer

- *Resume-Queue -Filter {Status -eq "Suspended"}*

Managing Messages

In addition to managing message queues, you also need to manage messages within queues. Problems with a single message can prevent an entire queue of messages from being delivered. Sometimes you want to identify and view messages that are greater than a specified size, that are from a particular address, or that you suspect are spam.

Filtering Messages

You can filter messages on a Hub Transport or Edge Transport server by message properties, search using specific criteria, and locate messages that may be causing a mail flow problem. You can then modify the status of those messages. You can use Queue Viewer or the EMS to search for messages by using filter criteria.

To use Queue Viewer to set up a filter that identifies messages by specified criteria, carry out the following procedure:

1. Open the tool, as previously described in this lesson.

2. Click the Messages tab, as shown in Figure 9-18. A list of all messages in all queues on the server is displayed.

3. Alternatively, because there can be a large number of messages on a busy Exchange Server 2010 server, you might find it easier to first click the Queues tab and search

for the queue in which the messages you want to access are contained. You can then right-click the queue name and click Messages. A tab for the queue you selected then appears.

FIGURE 9-18 The Message tab in Queue Viewer

4. If you elected to access the Messages tab directly, click Create Filter. Note that this control is not available on tabs that identify specific queues, which permit you to specify message filter settings immediately.

5. Select a message property from the message property drop-down list. For example, if you want to identify messages that are possible spam, click SCL. The available options are shown in Figure 9-19.

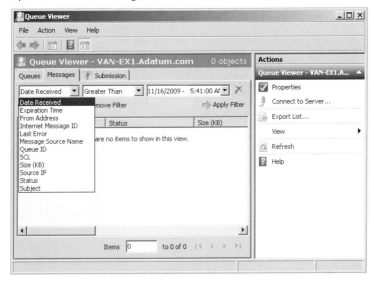

FIGURE 9-19 Available message property options

6. Select a comparison operator from the comparison operator drop-down list. For example, if you had selected SCL in the message property drop-down list, you might select Greater Than Or Equals in the comparison operator drop-down list.

7. Type a value in the value drop-down list or select a value if the property has fixed values. If the property requires a date/time expression, change the current date/time values or click the drop-down list to select a date from the calendar interface. For example, to list all messages with a spam confidence level (SCL) greater than or equal to 6, you set the filter conditions, as shown in Figure 9-20.

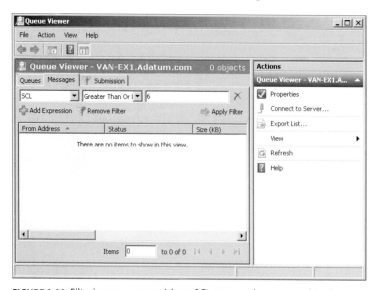

FIGURE 9-20 Filtering messages with an SCL greater than or equal to 6

8. Optionally, click Add Expression to specify additional filter criteria. Only messages that meet all filter criteria are displayed.

9. Click Apply Filter. Messages that meet the filter criteria are displayed.

MORE INFO SPAM CONFIDENCE LEVEL

For more information about the SCL and SCL thresholds, see *http://technet.microsoft.com/en-us/library/aa995744.aspx*.

You can use the *Get-Message* EMS cmdlet with the Filter parameter to filter messages. For example, the following command lists all messages that have an SCL equal to or greater than 6 and were sent from any sender in the Adatum.com domain:

```
Get-Message -Filter {SCL -ge 6 -and FromAddress -eq "*adatum.com"}
```

Viewing Message Properties

When you have used Queue Viewer to identify and list a specific message, you can right-click that message and click Properties. The Properties dialog box for a message has two tabs: General and Recipient Information.

The General tab displays the following fields:

- Identity
- Subject
- Internet Message ID
- From Address
- Status (Active, Pending Remove, Pending Suspend, Ready, Retry, or Suspended)
- Size (KB)
- Message Source Name
- Source IP
- SCL
- Date Received
- Expiration Time
- Last Error
- Queue ID
- Recipients
- Retry Count

The Recipient Information tab displays the following fields:

- Address
- Status
- Last Error

You can also use the *Get-Message* cmdlet to view the properties of a message that is queued for delivery. The following command tabulates the sender address, recipients, subject, and received date information for all messages that are currently in the Retry state:

```
Get-Message -IncludeRecipientInfo -Filter {Status -eq "Retry"} | FT FromAddress,
Recipients,Subject,DateReceived
```

MORE INFO **GET-MESSAGE**

For more information about the *Get-Message* cmdlet, see *http://technet.microsoft.com/ en-us/library/bb124738.aspx*.

Suspending and Resuming Messages

You can suspend one or more messages in a queue on a Hub Transport or Edge Transport server. When you suspend a message, you prevent its delivery. However, a message that appears in the queue but is already in the process of delivery will not be suspended. Instead, delivery will continue, and the message status will be set to Pending Suspend. If the delivery fails, the message will reenter the queue, and it will then be suspended. You cannot suspend a message in the Submission queue or in the Poison Message queue. A message that is addressed to multiple recipients might be located in multiple queues. To suspend a message in more than one queue in a single operation, you use a filter.

> **MORE INFO** **POISON MESSAGE QUEUE**
>
> For more information about poison message handling and the Poison Message queue, see *http://msdn.microsoft.com/en-us/library/ms789028.aspx.*

You can suspend a message that is listed in Queue Viewer by right-clicking the message and clicking Suspend. You can also use the *Suspend-Message* EMS cmdlet. If you want to suspend a message identified by filter criteria or a message that appears in more than one queue (for example, a message sent to multiple recipients), you can use the Filter parameter. For example, the following command suspends all messages in queues that are from any sender in the domain BlueSkyAirlines.com:

```
Suspend-Message -Filter {FromAddress -eq "*blueskyairlines.com"}
```

The following suspends a message with the message ID 2 in the unreachable queue on Hub Transport server VAN-EX1:

```
Suspend-Message -Identity VAN-EX1\Unreachable\2
```

> **MORE INFO** **SUSPEND-MESSAGE**
>
> For more information about the *Suspend-Message* cmdlet, see *http://technet.microsoft .com/en-us/library/aa997457.aspx.*

You can resume a message that currently has a status of Suspended on a Hub Transport or Edge Transport server. When you resume a message, you enable its delivery. If you resume a message located in the Poison Message queue, the message will be sent to the categorizer for processing.

You can use the Queue Viewer to list all suspended messages on a server or in a selected queue by applying a filter with the message property drop-down list set to Status, the comparison operator drop-down list set to Equals, and the value drop-down list set to Suspended. Click Apply Filter, and all messages that have a status of Suspended are displayed. You can now right-click a message on the list and click Resume.

You can use the *Resume-Message* EMS cmdlet with the Filter parameter to resume one or more suspended messages. For example, the following command resumes all messages being sent from any sender in the Fabrikam.com domain:

```
Resume-Message -Filter {FromAddress -eq "*fabrikam.com"}
```

MORE INFO   RESUME-MESSAGE

For more information about the *Resume-Message* cmdlet, see *http://technet.microsoft
.com/en-us/library/bb124421.aspx.*

✓ **Quick Check**

- What command tabulates the sender address, recipients, subject, and received
  date information for all messages that are currently in the Retry state on the Hub
  Transport server on which the command is entered?

Quick Check Answer

- *Get-Message -IncludeRecipientInfo -Filter {Status -eq "Retry"} | FT FromAddress,
  Recipients,Subject,DateReceived*

Removing and Exporting Messages

You can remove messages that are in a queue on a Hub Transport or Edge Transport server.
When you remove a message, you can select whether to send an NDR. You cannot remove
a message from the Submission queue.

To remove a message listed in Queue Viewer, right-click it and select either Remove
Messages (with NDR) or Remove Messages (without NDR). When a confirmation dialog box
appears, click Yes.

You can use the *Remove-Message* EMS cmdlet with the Filter parameter to remove messages. For example, the following command removes messages that have the subject "Weight
Loss" without sending an NDR:

```
Remove-Message -Filter {Subject -eq "Weight Loss"} -WithNDR $false
```

Figure 9-21 shows the output from this command.

FIGURE 9-21 Removing all messages with the subject "Weight Loss"

If you want the command to run without requiring confirmation, you can use the
Confirm switch, for example:

```
Remove-Message -Filter {Subject -eq "Weight Loss"} -WithNDR $false -Confirm:$False
```

When you want to investigate message content, you can export a message from a queue
to a file. When you do this, the message is not removed from the queue; instead, a copy
of the message is created in the specified location as a text file that you can open using an
application such as a text editor or an email client. Optionally, you can resubmit the message
by using the Replay directory on any Hub Transport server or Edge Transport server inside or
outside your Exchange organization.

You need to use an EMS command to export a message. Queue Viewer cannot perform
this function, although you can use this tool to locate, identify, and suspend messages before
you export them. Before you export messages, the following prerequisites must be in place:

- The target directory must exist. It can be local to the Exchange Server 2010 server on
  which the messages exist or a share on a remote server. The command does not create
  the target directory for you. If you do not specify a path, the current EMS working
  directory is used.

- The account you use must have Write permission to the destination directory.

- You need to locate and suspend messages to be exported to prevent their delivery
  during the export process. A message will not be exported unless it is suspended.
  Messages in the poison message queue are already suspended. You cannot suspend
  messages in the Submission queue and therefore cannot export messages from that
  queue.

- The destination file must have a .eml extension.

You can use the *Export-Message* EMS cmdlet to export a message that you have located,
identified, and suspended. You need to identify the message, for example, by specifying
its InternalMessageID. The following command exports the message that has an InternalMessageID
of 6391 and that is located in the remote delivery queue for the domain Fabrikam.com on the
server VAN-EX1 to the path C:\ExportedMessages\Fabrikam\export001.eml:

```
Export-Message -Identity VAN-EX1\Fabrikam.com\6391 -Path
"C:\ExportedMessages\Fabrikam\export001.eml"
```

If you want to export all messages from a specific queue, you first retrieve the messages
using the *Get-Message* cmdlet. You need to export each message individually, so you pipe the
results of the Get-Message operation into the *ForEach-Object* PowerShell cmdlet. You need
to provide an individual path and file name for each message. In the example given below
you do this by specifying a variable, $Destination, that consists of the Internet Message ID
and a .eml extension. The Internet Message ID field contains angled brackets (> and <), which
need to be removed because they are invalid characters in a file name. This is done using the
Replace method in the temporary variable. When the appropriate path is created for each
message, that message is exported to it.

The following command exports a copy of all the messages from the Fabrikam.com remote delivery queue on the server VAN-EX1 to the directory C:\ExportedMessages\Fabrikam on the local computer using the Internet Message IDs of each message as the file name (note that this command hangs but does not return an error if the queue Contoso.com does not exist on server VAN-EX1):

```
Get-Message -Queue "VAN-EX1\Contoso.com" | ForEach-Object {$Destination="C:\
ExportedMessages\Fabrikam\"+$_InternetMessageID+".eml";$Destination=$Destination.
Replace("<","_");$Destination=$Destination.Replace(">","_");Export-Message $_.Identity |
AssembleMessage -Path $Destination
```

The following command exports a copy of all the messages from senders in the BlueSkyAirlines.com domain from all queues on the server VAN-EX1 to the directory C:\ExportedMessages\BlueSkyAirlines on the local computer using the Internet Message IDs of each message as the file name:

```
Get-Message -Filter {FromAddress -like "@BlueSkyAirlines.com"} -Server "VAN-
EX1" | ForEach-Object {$Destination="C:\ExportedMessages\BlueSkyAirlines"+$_
InternetMessageID+".eml";$Destination=$Destination.Replace("<","_");$Destination=$Destin
ation.Replace(">","_");Export-Message $_.Identity | AssembleMessage -Path $Destination}
```

EXAM TIP

The commands to export multiple messages look more complex than they are, mainly because of the requirement to replace the < and > characters in the file name. Experiment with similar commands until you are comfortable with this syntax. You will probably not be asked to generate such commands under examination conditions, but you could be asked to identify the correct syntax.

MORE INFO   *EXPORT-MESSAGE* **AND** *FOREACH-OBJECT*

For more information about the *Export-Message* cmdlet, see *http://technet.microsoft.com/ en-us/library/aa997214.aspx*. For more information about the *ForEach-Object* PowerShell cmdlet, see *http://technet.microsoft.com/en-us/library/dd347608.aspx*.

Tracking Messages

The configuration of message tracking logs on transport and Mailbox servers was discussed earlier in this lesson. This section describes their use and how an administrator would obtain a message tracking report for troubleshooting purposes.

A unique message tracking log exists on every Windows Server 2010 Hub Transport, Mailbox, or Edge Transport server. This is a comma-separated value (CSV) file that contains detailed information about the history of each email message as it travels through an individual server. You can use the *Get-MessageTrackingLog* EMS cmdlet to search message information stored in the message tracking log.

You can specify parameters such as Sender to view entries sent from a specific email address or Recipients to view entries sent to one or more email addresses. You can specify start and end dates and times. Typically, you want to look at the message tracking log on the server on which you are working, but you also have the option of using the Server parameter to specify another Hub Transport, Mailbox, or Edge Transport server in your organization.

You can view entries for messages with a specific EventID (for example, BadMail, Defer Deliver, PoisonMessage, Fail, and so on). You can specify an InternalEventID to get tracking information about a specific message. The ResultSize parameter specifies how many messages are returned. If you want to see all the messages that meet the other specified conditions but you do not know how many there are, set ResultSize to Unlimited.

For example, the following command retrieves message tracking log entries that were created between November 13, 2010, at 09:00 hours and March 21, 2011, at 17:00 hours with a Sender parameter value of DonHall@adatum.com:

```
Get-MessageTrackingLog –ResultSize Unlimited –Start "11/13/2010 9:00AM" –End "03/21/2011
5:00PM" –Sender "DonHall@adatum.com"
```

> **MORE INFO** **GET-MESSAGETRACKINGLOG**
>
> For more information about the *Get-MessageTrackingLog* cmdlet, see *http://technet .microsoft.com/en-us/library/aa997573.aspx.*

A *message tracking report* gives detailed information about a specific email message, and you typically use message tracking reports during troubleshooting. Suppose, for example, that Don Hall at the Adatum Corporation is expecting an email message from Jeff Hay at Fabrikam, but the message does not arrive. Don contacts the Adatum Help desk, and Kim Akers views the message tracking report for that message.

Kim uses a command based on the *Get-MessageTrackingReport* EMS cmdlet. As an administrative user, Kim can enter a command that uses the BypassDelegateChecking parameter to enable her to view a message sent from another user to a different user. She can specify whether the report is a summary or a verbose report. She can use the DoNotResolve parameter to prevent the resolution of email addresses to display names and hence improve performance.

However, the *Get-MessageTrackingReport* cmdlet requires the ID for the message tracking report. Therefore, Kim needs first to use the *Search-MessageTrackingReport* EMS cmdlet to find the message tracking report ID for the message and pass this information to the *Get-MessageTrackingReport* cmdlet. Typically, Kim might find all message tracking reports for messages from Jeff Hay to Don Hall and use the *ForEach-Object* PowerShell cmdlet to generate a report for each message.

The message tracking report typically identifies where the message is held in the transport queues. The message could be in the unreachable queue or the poison message queue, in which case it will not be delivered. It could be in a queue that is currently suspended, or the message itself could be suspended. The message could be in a queue with the status of

Retry, which would indicate that connectivity problems may be preventing next-hop delivery. You can resume a message or a message queue or manually retry a queue as appropriate. If this does not result in message delivery, further investigation of the message properties (described earlier in this lesson) may be required.

The following command, entered by Kim Akers on a server in the Adatum Exchange organization, gets the message tracking reports for all email messages Jeff Hay has sent to Don Hall and displays a detailed message tracking report for each email message, without resolving display names:

```
Search-MessageTrackingReport -Identity "Don Hall" -Sender "JeffHay@fabrikam
.com" -ByPassDelegateChecking -DoNotResolve | ForEach-Object { Get-MessageTrackingReport
-Identity $_.MessageTrackingReportID -DetailLevel Verbose -BypassDelegateChecking
-DoNotResolve -RecipientPathFilter "DonHall@adatum.com" -ReportTemplate RecipientPath }
```

> **MORE INFO** **GET-MESSAGETRACKINGREPORT** AND **SEARCH-MESSAGETRACKINGREPORT**
>
> For more information about the *Get-MessageTrackingReport* cmdlet, see *http://technet .microsoft.com/en-us/library/dd351082.aspx*. For more information about the *Search-MessageTrackingReport* cmdlet, see *http://technet.microsoft.com/en-us/library/dd351138.aspx*.

Testing Mail Flow

Exchange Server 2010 provides you with tools to test mail flow and resolve situations where email messages are not delivered. The EMC provides the Microsoft Exchange Mail Flow Troubleshooter as part of the Microsoft Exchange Troubleshooting Assistant, but the primary tool for resolving mail flow and resolving nondelivery situations is the EMS *Test-Mailflow* cmdlet.

You can use this cmdlet to diagnose whether mail can be successfully sent from and delivered to the system mailbox on a Mailbox server. You can also use it to verify that email is sent between Mailbox servers within a specified time (sometimes termed the *latency threshold*). The *Test-Mailflow* cmdlet tests mail submission, transport, and delivery. It verifies that each Mailbox server can successfully send itself a message. You can also use this cmdlet to verify that the system mailbox on one Mailbox server can successfully send a message to the system mailbox on another Mailbox server.

The *Test-Mailflow* cmdlet supports the AutoDiscoverTargetMailboxServer parameter. This specifies whether a command will automatically populate a list of target Mailbox servers to which a test message is sent. The task queries Active Directory Directory Services (AD DS) to discover all Mailbox servers and then sends each server a test message.

You can use the TargetDatabase parameter to specify a target mailbox database to which messages are sent. You can also use the TargetEmailAddress parameter to specify a target email address when you want to send test messages to a Mailbox server in a remote forest. The TargetMailboxServer parameter specifies one or more Mailbox servers in the local Exchange organization to which test messages are sent. If more than one of these parameters is specified, the AutoDiscoverTargetMailboxServer parameter takes precedence over the TargetEmailAddress and TargetMailboxServer parameters. The TargetMailboxServer parameter takes precedence over the TargetEmailAddress parameter. A system mailbox must be present on all servers involved in the test.

> ✔ **Quick Check**
>
> 1. You want to copy an email message into a text file so that you can view it, but you do not want to remove the message from its queue. You have suspended the message. What EMS cmdlet do you use to copy the message to a file?
>
> 2. What file extension should you use for a file into which you are copying an email message?
>
> **Quick Check Answers**
>
> 1. *Export-Message*
>
> 2. The .eml file extension.

Several parameters specify time-outs. The ActiveDirectoryTimeout parameter specifies the number of seconds that elapse before the task provides an informational message about the delay. The default value is 15 seconds. The ErrorLatency parameter specifies the number of seconds that elapse before an error event is logged in Microsoft System Center Operations Manager 2007. The default value when a test message is sent to the local Mailbox server is 15 seconds. When a test message is sent to a remote Mailbox server, the default value is 180 seconds.

The ExecutionTimeout parameter specifies the maximum time that the task can run before the test is determined to be a failure. If no test message or delivery report arrives before the execution time expires, the task ends, and an error is reported. When the task is run in the EMS, the default setting is 240 seconds. When you include the MonitoringContext parameter, which specifies that System Center Operations Manager 2007 is being used for server monitoring, the default setting is 15 seconds.

> **MORE INFO** **SYSTEM CENTER OPERATIONS MANAGER 2007**
>
> For more information about System Center Operations Manager 2007, see *http://technet .microsoft.com/en-us/library/bb687791.aspx#scop07*.

The Identity parameter specifies the source Mailbox server name or source mailbox SMTP address from which a test message is sent. The default value is the local Mailbox server. If you include the Confirm switch, this causes the command to pause and requires you to acknowledge that you want the task to proceed before processing continues. You do not specify a value with the Confirm switch.

The following command tests message flow from the Mailbox server VAN-EX1 to the Mailbox server VAN-EX2:

```
Test-Mailflow VAN-EX1 -TargetMailboxServer VAN-EX2
```

The following command tests message flow from the server VAN-EX1 to the email address DonHall@adatum.com:

```
Test-Mailflow VAN-EX1 -TargetEmailAddress DonHall@adatum.com
```

Figure 9-22 shows that this test was successful.

FIGURE 9-22 A successful mail flow test

> **MORE INFO   TEST-MAILFLOW**
>
> For more information about the *Test-Mailflow* cmdlet, see *http://technet.microsoft.com/en-us/library/aa995894.aspx*.

Back Pressure

Back pressure is a system resource monitoring feature of the Microsoft Exchange Transport service that exists on Hub Transport and Edge Transport servers. System resources such as available hard disk drive space and available memory are monitored. If utilization of a system resource exceeds its specified limit, the Exchange server stops accepting new connections and messages. This prevents the system resources from being completely overwhelmed and enables the server to deliver the existing messages. When utilization of the system resource returns to a normal level, the Exchange server accepts new connections and messages.

The following system resources are monitored as part of the back-pressure feature:

- Free space on the hard disk drive that stores the message queue database
- Free space on the hard disk drive that stores the message queue database transaction logs
- The number of uncommitted message queue database transactions that exist in memory
- The memory that is used by the EdgeTransport.exe process
- The memory that is used by all processes

For each monitored system resource on a Hub Transport server or Edge Transport server, the following three levels of resource utilization are applied:

- **Normal**   The resource is not overused. The server accepts new connections and messages.
- **Medium**   The resource is slightly overused. Back pressure is applied to the server in a limited manner. Mail from senders in the authoritative domain can flow. However, the server rejects new connections and messages from other sources.
- **High**   The resource is severely overused. Full back pressure is applied. All message flow stops, and the server rejects all new connections and messages.

Configuration options for back pressure are available in the EdgeTransport.exe .config application configuration file that is located in the C:\Program Files\ Microsoft\Exchange Server\V14\Bin directory. The EdgeTransport.exe.config file is an XML application configuration file that is associated with the EdgeTransport.exe file. EdgeTransport.exe and MSExchangeTransport.exe are executable files located in the same directory that are used by the Microsoft Exchange Transport service. This service runs on every Hub Transport or Edge Transport server. Changes that are saved to the EdgeTransport.exe.config file are applied after the Microsoft Exchange Transport service is restarted.

However, Microsoft strongly discourages modifying the back-pressure settings in the EdgeTransport.exe.config file because such modification may result in poor performance or data loss. You should instead investigate and correct the root causes of any back-pressure events. In other words, find out what resource is under pressure and why and take the appropriate action such as upgrading server hardware or moving tasks to another server. In general, events with event source MSExchangeTransport and event category Resource Manager that indicate problems due to excessive resource usage are regarded as back-pressure events.

Scanning for Disconnected Mailboxes

A connected mailbox requires that a mailbox object exists in the Exchange store and the corresponding user object exists and has Exchange properties in AD DS. A disconnected mailbox is a mailbox object in the Exchange store that is not connected to a user object in Active Directory. You can use the *Disable-Mailbox* EMS cmdlet to disconnect a mailbox and the *Connect-Mailbox* cmdlet to reconnect a disconnected mailbox to an AD DS user account. You can use the *Remove-Mailbox* cmdlet to disconnect a mailbox and remove the user object from AD DS. Using the *Remove-Mailbox* cmdlet permanently removes the mailbox object from the Exchange store.

Under normal circumstances, a mailbox is marked as disconnected immediately after the *Disable-Mailbox* or *Remove-Mailbox* command completes. However, if you use the *Disable-Mailbox* cmdlet or the *Remove-Mailbox* cmdlet while the Microsoft Exchange

Information Store service is stopped or if a mailbox is disabled by external means other than the *Disable-Mailbox* cmdlet or the *Remove-Mailbox* cmdlet, it is possible that the disconnected mailbox is not marked as disconnected in AD DS, and this can lead to problems if email messages are sent to the user.

In this situation, you can use the *Clean-MailboxDatabase* EMS cmdlet to scan a mailbox database for disconnected mailboxes that have not been marked as disconnected within AD DS. Commands based on this cmdlet also update the status of those mailboxes so that they are correctly marked as disconnected.

For example, the following command scans the database Mailbox Database 1363123687 for disconnected mailboxes that are not marked as disconnected within AD DS and updates their status so that they are correctly marked as disconnected:

```
Clean-MailboxDatabase –Identity "Mailbox Database 1363123687"
```

> **MORE INFO** **CONNECTING, DISCONNECTING, AND REMOVING A MAILBOX**
>
> For more information about the *Connect-Mailbox* cmdlet, see *http://technet.microsoft .com/en-us/library/aa997878.aspx*. For more information about the *Disable-Mailbox* cmdlet, see *http://technet.microsoft.com/en-us/library/aa997210.aspx*. For more information about the *Remove-Mailbox* cmdlet, see *http://technet.microsoft.com/en-us/ library/aa995948.aspx*.

> **MORE INFO** **CLEAN-MAILBOXDATABASE**
>
> For more information about the *Clean-MailboxDatabase* cmdlet, see *http://technet .microsoft.com/en-us/library/bb124076.aspx*.

Lesson Summary

- The EMS is the primary tool for configuring message tracking and tracking logs. You can use the EMC to perform some tasks, but its functionality is limited.
- You can use Queue Viewer in the EMC to monitor or EMS commands to monitor, filter, and manage transport queues on a Hub Transport or Edge Transport server.
- You can use Queue Viewer in the EMC to filter messages but the primary tool for managing messages and testing mail flow is the EMS.

Lesson Review

You can use the following questions to test your knowledge of the information in Lesson 2, "Monitoring Mail Flow." The questions are also available on the companion CD if you prefer to review them in electronic form.

> **NOTE** **ANSWERS**
>
> Answers to these questions and explanations of why each answer choice is correct or incorrect are located in the "Answers" section at the end of the book.

1. You want to enable message tracking on the Mailbox server AdatumMail02. What EMS command do you use?

   A. *Set-TransportServer –Identity AdatumMail02 -MessageTrackingLogEnabled:$false*

   B. *Set-MailboxServer –Identity AdatumMail02 -MessageTrackingLogEnabled:$false*

   C. *Set-TransportServer –Identity AdatumMail02 -MessageTrackingLogEnabled:$true*

   D. *Set-MailboxServer –Identity AdatumMail02 -MessageTrackingLogEnabled:$true*

2. You want to change the maximum size of each message tracking log file on the Edge Transport server NY-Edge01 to 15 MB. What command do you enter in the EMS?

   A. *Set-TransportServer –Identity NY-Edge01 -MessageTrackingLogMaxDirectorySize 15MB*

   B. *Set-TransportServer –Identity NY-Edge01 -MessageTrackingLogMaxFileSize 15MB*

   C. *Set-MailboxServer –Identity NY-Edge01 -MessageTrackingLogMaxDirectorySize 15MB*

   D. *Set-MailboxServer –Identity NY-Edge01 -MessageTrackingLogMaxFileSize 15MB*

3. You want to display the number of messages in queues on an Edge Transport server in the Contoso.com domain that are bound for the BlueSkyAirlines.com domain. What command do you enter in the EMS?

   A. *Get-Queue –Filter {NextHopDomain –eq "blueskyairlines.com"}*

   B. *Get-Queue -Filter {MessageCount -gt 50}*

   C. *Get-Queue –Filter {NextHopDomain –eq "adatum.com"}*

   D. *Get-Queue -Filter {MessageCount -ge 50}*

4. You want to suspend all queues on a Hub Transport server that have a message count equal to or greater than 450 and have a status of Retry. The command should work immediately without requiring confirmation. What EMS command do you enter on the server?

   A. *Suspend-Queue -Filter {MessageCount -ge 450 -and Status -eq "Retry"}*

   B. *Suspend-Queue -Filter {MessageCount -gt 450 -and Status -eq "Retry"} -Confirm:$False*

   C. *Suspend-Queue -Filter {MessageCount -ge 450 -and Status -eq "Active"} -Confirm:$False*

   D. *Suspend-Queue -Filter {MessageCount -ge 450 -and Status -eq "Retry"} -Confirm:$False*

5. You want to test the message flow from the Mailbox server NY-EX1 to the Mailbox server NY-EX2. What command do you enter in the EMS?

   A. *Test-Mailflow NY-EX1 -TargetMailboxServer NY-EX2*

   B. *Test-Mailflow NY-EX2 -TargetMailboxServer NY-EX1*

   C. *Test-Mailflow NY-EX1 -TargetDatabase NY-EX2*

   D. *Test-Mailflow NY-EX1 -TargetEmailAddress NY-EX2*

Lesson 3: Monitoring Exchange Connectivity

This lesson looks at communication between the various server and client computers that make up an Exchange Server organization. Computers need to be correctly configured so that they can communicate with each other over IP networks and (unless your email requirements are fully internal) with external networks such as extranets or the Internet. Clients need to be able to connect to servers using the appropriate client protocols, and servers need to be able to communicate with each other.

> **After this lesson, you will be able to:**
> - Test and debug network connectivity.
> - Use the Telnet tool to test protocol connectivity over various ports and particularly SMTP and Extended Simple Mail Transfer Protocol (ESMTP) connectivity over port 25.
> - Test connectivity using the various client-to-server and server-to-server protocols that enable users to access and read email messages.
> - Test Microsoft Exchange Web Services (EWS), Microsoft Outlook Anywhere, and Microsoft Exchange ActiveSync operation.
>
> **Estimated lesson time: 40 minutes**

Debugging Network Connectivity

The standard tools for troubleshooting network connectivity, such as Ping, Tracert, Nslookup, and Ipconfig, are well known but sometimes do not provide the answers you are looking for, particularly on servers such as Windows Server 2008 and Windows Server 2008 R2, whose internal firewalls by default block the Internet Control Message Protocol Echo command.

However, the main thrust of this lesson is the use of the Telnet tool and EMS cmdlets to obtain network connection information and to test connectivity over the various client-to-server and server-to-server protocols used to implement an Exchange Server 2010 organization.

Using Telnet to Test SMTP Communication

On client computers that have a Telnet client installed, you can use the Telnet tool to test connectivity for protocols defined by their port numbers. For example, opening a Telnet session and entering open `VAN-EX1.contoso.com` 25 tests connectivity to server VAN-EX1 .contoso.com on port 25, and if this connection can be made, the Telnet command ELHO tests that ESMTP connections can be made to that server.

You can use the Telnet utility to connect to and verify the functionality of the SMTP service on an Edge Transport server and to test whether this server is able to receive email sent from other SMTP servers on the Internet. By default, SMTP listens on port 25. If you use Telnet on port 25, you can enter the SMTP commands that are used to connect to an SMTP server and send a message exactly as if your Telnet session were an SMTP messaging server.

However, before you use Telnet to test SMTP communication, you need to consider a number of factors. For example, message transfers that occur between Hub Transport servers are encrypted and authenticated by default. You can use Telnet on port 25 to submit messages only to an internal Hub Transport server that has a Receive connector configured to allow anonymous access or basic authentication. Anonymous access is required for Internet-facing servers. When you send a message to a Receive connector that accepts basic authentication, you must have a utility to convert the text strings that are used for the user name and password into the Base64 format. Chapter 7, "Routing and Transport Rules," discusses Receive connectors.

> **CAUTION BASIC AUTHENTICATION CAN BE A SECURITY RISK**
>
> Because the user name and password are easily discernible when basic authentication is used, Microsoft recommends that you do not use basic authentication without encryption.

Typically, Internet-facing SMTP messaging servers are configured to validate the source IP address, the corresponding Domain Name System (DNS) domain name, and the reverse-lookup IP address of any Internet host that tries to send a message to the server. If you connect a client computer to the Internet and try to send a test message to a remote messaging server by using Telnet on port 25, your message is likely to be rejected. In this case, you should connect to the remote messaging server from your Edge Transport server. The accepted domains that are configured on the Edge Transport server have the appropriate DNS mail exchanger (MX) records, address (A) records, and reverse-lookup records that identify the Edge Transport server as a legitimate and traceable email message source.

You can use Telnet to connect to your organization's Edge Transport server from a host that is located outside your perimeter network and send a test message. You can also use Telnet to connect to a remote messaging server from your organization's Edge Transport server and send a test message. Note that the syntax of Telnet commands may differ depending on the third-party Telnet client you use. Remember that you cannot use the backspace key after you have connected to a destination SMTP server within the Telnet session. If you make a mistake as you type an SMTP command, you must press Enter and then type the command again.

To use Telnet on port 25 to connect to a destination SMTP server, you must first discover the fully qualified domain name (FQDN) or the IP address of the SMTP server. You can use the Nslookup command-line tool to find the MX record for the destination domain and hence the address of the SMTP server by carrying out the following procedure:

1. On the computer you are using to run the Telnet session and to connect to a remote SMTP server on the Internet, right-click Command Prompt on the Accessories menu and click Run As Administrator. If you are not logged on with an Administrator-level account, you need to supply credentials.

2. Enter the following command:

```
nslookup
```

3. Enter the following command:

```
set type=mx
```

4. Enter the following command:

```
set timeout=20
```

> **NOTE DNS QUERY TIME-OUT**
>
> By default, Windows DNS servers have a 15-second recursive DNS query time-out limit.

5. Enter the name of the domain for which you want to find the MX record, followed by a trailing period. For example, to find the MX record for the contoso.com domain, enter the following command:

```
contoso.com.
```

> **NOTE USING A TRAILING PERIOD**
>
> The trailing period indicates a FQDN. The use of the trailing period prevents any default DNS suffixes configured for your network from being unintentionally added to the domain name. Note also that the domain must be reachable on the Internet and must contain at least one messaging server.

6. Obtain the FQDN and IP address for the server to which you want to connect. The portion of the command's output that is of significance to you should look similar to the following (note that the IP addresses will be public Internet addresses and not the private addresses shown here as an illustration):

```
contoso.com mx preference=10, mail exchanger = mail1.contoso.com
contoso.com mx preference=20, mail exchanger = mail2.contoso.com
mail1.contoso.com internet address = 10.0.10.20
mail2 contoso.com internet address = 10.0.10.30
```

7. To end the Nslookup session, enter the following command:

```
exit
```

The above procedure discovers the FQDNs and IP addresses of messaging servers in an external Exchange organization reachable over the Internet. To find the FQDNs of Hub Transport and Edge Transport servers within your internal Exchange Server 2010 organization, enter the following command in the EMS:

```
Get-ExchangeServer | where {$_.isHubTransportServer -eq $true -or $_.isEdgeServer -eq
$true} | FL Fqdn,ServerRole
```

Figure 9-23 shows the output from this command.

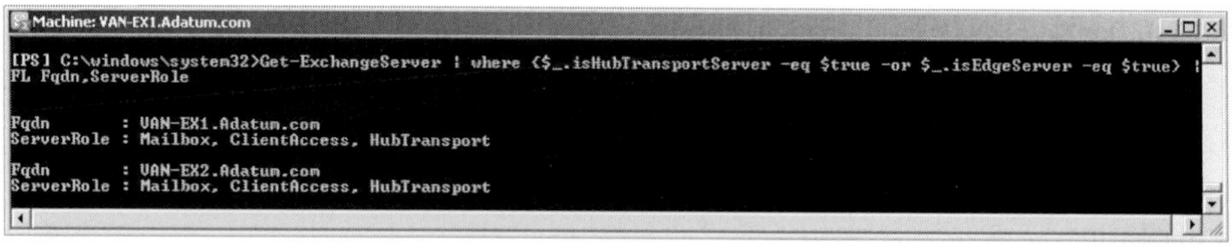

FIGURE 9-23 Messaging servers in the adatum.com internal organization

> **MORE INFO   GET-EXCHANGESERVER**
>
> For more information about the *Get-ExchangeServer* cmdlet, see *http://technet.microsoft .com/en-us/library/bb123873.aspx.*

When you have obtained the FQDN of the target messaging server, you can use Telnet on port 25 to test SMTP communication (assuming that a Telnet client is installed in your source computer—remember that Microsoft Windows Vista and Microsoft Windows 7 client computers do not have a Telnet client installed by default). The procedure described below uses the following values:

- **Destination SMTP server**   mail01.contoso.com
- **Source domain**   adatum.com
- **Sender's email address**   KimAkers@adatum.com
- **Recipient's email address**   TerryAdams@contoso.com
- **Message subject**   Test from Adatum
- **Message body**   Test message

To use Telnet on port 25 to test SMTP communication, carry out the following procedure:

1. On an Edge Transport server in the Adatum.com domain, open a command prompt by specifying Run As Administrator and enter the following command to open the Telnet session:

    ```
    telnet
    ```

2. Optionally, to view the characters as you type them, enter the following command:

    ```
    set localecho
    ```

3. Optionally, to enable logging of the Telnet session to the log file telnet.log, enter the following command:

    ```
    set logfile C:\Logfiles\telnet.log
    ```

4. To access the server mail01.contoso.com on port 25, enter the following command:

    ```
    open mail01.contoso.com 25
    ```

    If access is successful, you receive a response similar to the following:

    ```
    220 mail01.contoso.com Microsoft ESMTP MAIL Service ready at <day-date-time>
    ```

5. To test that ESMTP is operating in the Contoso.com domain, enter the following command:

```
EHLO contoso.com
```

If ESMTP is working correctly, you receive a response similar to the following:

```
250 mail01.contoso.com Hello [<sourceIPaddress>]
```

6. To specify the sender's email address, enter the following command:

```
MAIL FROM:KimAkers@adatum.com
```

If the sender's email address is recognized as valid, you receive a response similar to the following:

```
250 2.1.0 Sender OK
```

7. To specify the recipient's email address and to define the particular delivery status notification (DSN) messages that the destination SMTP server must provide to the sender, enter the following command:

```
RCPT TO:TerryAdams@fabrikam.com NOTIFY=success,failure
```

If the recipient's email address is recognized as valid, you receive a response similar to the following:

```
250 2.1.5 Recipient OK
```

MORE INFO   DSN MESSAGES

DSN messages are defined in RFC 1891. For more information, see *http://www.faqs.org/rfcs/rfc1891.html.*

8. To start mail input, enter the following command:

```
DATA
```

You receive a response similar to the following:

```
354 start mail input; end with <CLRF>.<CLRF>
```

9. Enter Subject: Test from Adatum.
10. Press Enter. You need a blank line between the Subject: header field and the message body.
11. Enter Test message.
12. Press Enter, type a period, and then press Enter again. You receive a response similar to the following:

```
250 2.6.0 <GUID> Queued mail for delivery
```

13. To disconnect from the destination SMTP server, enter the following command:

```
QUIT
```

You receive a response similar to the following:

```
221 2.0.0 Service closing transmission channel
```

14. To close the Telnet session, enter the following command:

```
QUIT
```

Using Nslookup to Test MX Record Configuration

You can use the Nslookup tool to verify MX record configuration on an external or Internet DNS server. In order to receive incoming email, an MX record for each of your mail servers that you use as bridgehead servers or Internet mail servers must exist on your external DNS server or servers. For external DNS servers to resolve a mail server's MX record and contact that mail server, the mail server must be accessible from the Internet and must be configured to contact a correctly configured DNS server to resolve DNS names.

In order to send outgoing mail, you can configure Exchange Server 2010 to use internal DNS servers that resolve external names locally or use a forwarder to an external DNS server. Typically, you configure computers running Exchange Server 2010 as DNS clients of your internal DNS server. On your internal DNS server, you can configure an external forwarder to point to trusted external DNS servers. Alternatively, to send outgoing mail, you can configure computers running Exchange Server 2010 to use a dedicated external DNS server.

To use Nslookup to verify that your MX records are configured correctly for ingoing and outgoing email, you can perform the following procedure on your Mailbox server:

1. Open the Command Prompt console and enter the following command:

```
nslookup
```

2. Where <IP address> is the IP address of the external DNS server, enter the following command:

```
server <IP address>
```

3. Enter the following command:

```
set q=MX
```

4. Type the name of your domain (for example, contoso.com) and then press Enter. If DNS is configured correctly, the MX record for the domain you entered is displayed.

Viewing Network Adapter Configuration

If you are experiencing network connectivity problems on a particular Exchange Server 2010 server, you can use a command based on the *Get-NetworkConnectionInfo* EMS cmdlet to view the network configuration information for all network adapters configured on that server. Typically, you run this cmdlet locally, and it returns information about the network adapters on the server on which it runs. You can optionally specify another server on the network and the FQDN of the domain controller that retrieves data from AD DS. Note that you cannot use the DomainController parameter when obtaining configuration information on an Edge Transport server.

Commands based on the *Get-NetworkConnectionInfo* cmdlet can display the following fields:

- **RunspaceID**   This displays a GUID that uniquely identifies the session in which an event occurs.

- **Name**   This displays the name of the network adapter. This can indicate the manufacturer and model of the network adapter or an administrator-specified network adapter name.

- **DnsServers**   This displays the DNS servers the network adapter uses. If more than one DNS server exists, the server names are separated by commas.

- **IPAddresses**   This displays the IP addresses used by the network adapter.

- **AdapterGuid**   This displays the GUID that Microsoft Windows assigns to the network adapter.

- **MacAddress**   This displays the media access control address of the network adapter.

The following command returns network connection information for the local server:

```
Get-NetworkConnectionInfo
```

Figure 9-24 shows the output from this command. Some of the fields on the Exchange Server 2010 server on your test network will return different information.

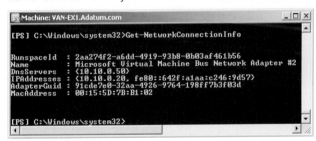

FIGURE 9-24 Connection information

> **MORE INFO   GET-NETWORKCONNECTIONINFO**
>
> For more information about the *Get-NetworkConnectionInfo* cmdlet, see *http://technet .microsoft.com/en-us/library/aa998845.aspx*.

Testing Post Office Protocol Version 3 (POP3) Connectivity

The POP3 service provides email access to clients on port 110. Secure Socket Layer (SSL)-protected POP3 uses port 995. POP3 is a client-to-server protocol in which email is received and held for the user on the Client Access server. Periodically, users check their mailboxes and download mail using the POP3 service. POP3 is built into, for example, Microsoft Outlook Express. It is also built into the Microsoft Internet Explorer browser.

You can use commands based on the *Test-PopConnectivity* EMS cmdlet to verify that the POP3 service is running correctly. The *Test-PopConnectivity* cmdlet can be used to test the POP3 functionality on a specified Client Access server for all mailboxes on servers running Exchange Server 2010 in the same AD DS site. You can also specify a single Mailbox server in the site by using the MailboxServer parameter. You can identify a single mailbox by using the MailboxCredential parameter, but to do this, you need to first get the credential information for a specific mailbox by using the *Get-Credential* PowerShell cmdlet.

For example, the following command prompts for the credentials for the Kim Akers mailbox user and tests POP3 connectivity to the Kim Akers mailbox on the VAN-EX1 Mailbox server:

```
Test-PopConnectivity -MailboxServer:VAN-EX1 -MailboxCredential:(Get-Credential "adatum\
Kim Akers") | FL
```

Note that this command prompts for credentials even when you are logged on with the Kim Akers user. Figure 9-25 shows that connectivity failed in this instance because the MSExchangePOP3 service is not running.

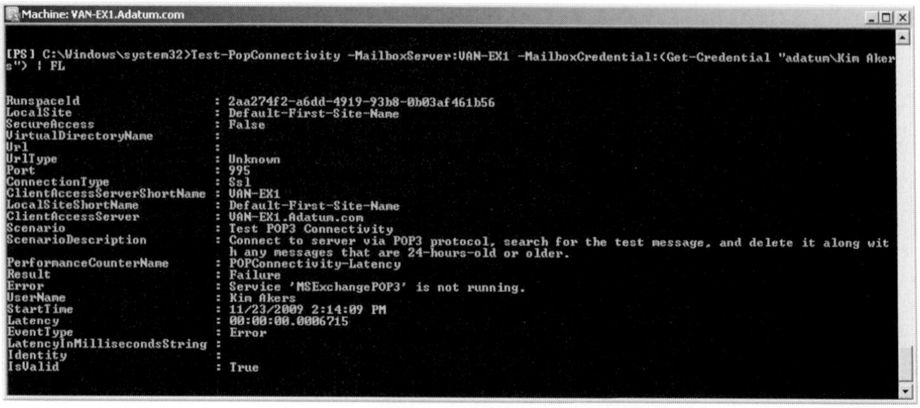

FIGURE 9-25 POP3 connectivity failure message

Commands based on the *Test-PopConnectivity* cmdlet are typically run against the Client Access server on which they are entered. However, you can specify a remote Client Access server in the same Exchange Server 2010 organization by using the ClientAccessServer parameter. You can also use the ConnectionType parameter to specify whether the connection type is Plaintext, SSL, or Transport Layer Security (TLS). For example, the following command tests POP3 connectivity between the Client Access server CAS01 and all mailboxes on all Mailbox servers in the same organization and specifies the connection type as SSL:

```
Test-PopConnectivity -ClientAccessServer:CAS01 -ConnectionType:SSL
```

> **NOTE CREATING A USER TO TEST CLIENT ACCESS SERVER CONNECTIVITY**
>
> You need to create a test user account to test connectivity to Client Access servers. To do this, enter the following command in the EMS and follow the prompts:
>
> ```
> New-TestCasConnectivityUser.ps1
> ```

You can use the TrustAnySSLCertificate parameter to instruct the command to check the POP3 service without generating an error when the SSL certificate does not match the URL of the Client Access server. You can use the MonitoringContext parameter to specify whether the command is run by System Center Operations Manager 2007. Take care, however, that if System Center Operations Manager 2007 is not running, including this parameter causes the command to fail.

If you want to perform only a test logon to a Mailbox server using the POP3 protocol and do not require the command to test the sending and receiving of a message, you can specify the LightMode parameter. If you are using a port other than port 110 to connect to the Client Access server, you need to use the PortClientAccessServer parameter to specify the port used.

> **MORE INFO**   **TEST-POPCONNECTIVITY** AND **GET-CREDENTIAL**
>
> For more information about the *Test-PopConnectivity* cmdlet, see *http://technet.microsoft* *.com/en-us/library/bb738143.aspx*. For more information about the *Get-Credential* cmdlet, see *http://technet.microsoft.com/en-us/library/dd315327.aspx*.

 Quick Check

- What fields can EMS commands based on the *Get-NetworkConnectionInfo* cmdlet display?

Quick Check Answer

- RunspaceID, Name, DnsServers, IPAddresses, AdapterGuid, and MacAddress.

Testing Internet Message Access Protocol Version 4 (IMAP4) Connectivity

IMAP4 is a standard client-to-server protocol for accessing email from an Exchange Server 2010 server local to the email client. Email messages are received and held by the server. A mailbox user can view the heading and the sender of the message and then decide whether to download it. A user can create and manipulate multiple folders or mailboxes on the server, delete messages, or search for messages. IMAP4 requires continual access to the server during the time that a user is working with his or her email messages.

The default port for IMAP4 is 143. SSL-protected IMAP4 uses TCP port 993 to retrieve email through a Client Access server. Note that both POP3 and IMAP4 enable users to receive email messages. SMTP or ESMTP enables users to send email messages.

You can use commands based on the *Test-ImapConnectivity* EMS cmdlet to verify that the IMAP4 service is working as expected. You can test IMAP4 functionality on a specified Client Access server for all mailboxes on Exchange Server 2010 Mailbox servers in the same Active Directory site, for a specific Mailbox server, or for a specific mailbox identified by its credentials.

The *Test-ImapConnectivity* cmdlet supports the MailboxServer, -MailboxCredential, ClientAccessServer, ConnectionType, TrustAnySSLCertificate, MonitoringContext, LightMode, and PortClientAccessServer parameters in the same way as previously described for the *Test-PopConnectivity* cmdlet. For example, the following command tests IMAP4 connectivity from the Client Access server on which it is entered to all mailboxes on the Mailbox server VAN-EX1:

```
Test-ImapConnectivity -MailboxServer:VAN-EX1 | FL
```

The following example tests IMAP4 connectivity from the Client Access server CAS01 to all mailboxes on all Mailbox servers on the local site:

```
Test-ImapConnectivity -ClientAccessServer:CAS01 | FL
```

The following example tests IMAP4 SSL-protected connectivity from the Client Access server CAS01 to all mailboxes on all Mailbox servers on the local site:

```
Test-ImapConnectivity -ClientAccessServer:CAS01 -ConnectionType:SSL
-PortClientAccessServer:993 | FL
```

> **MORE INFO   TEST-IMAPCONNECTIVITY**
>
> For more information about the *Test-ImapConnectivity* cmdlet, see *http://technet .microsoft.com/en-us/library/bb738126.aspx*.

Testing Messaging Application Programming Interface (MAPI) Connectivity

MAPI is a messaging architecture and Component Object Model designed by Microsoft and based on the Application Programming Interface for Microsoft Windows. It allows client programs to become email messaging enabled or aware by calling MAPI subsystem routines that interface with messaging servers. While MAPI is designed to be protocol independent, it is usually used with the RPC protocol. MAPI/RPC is the proprietary protocol that Microsoft Outlook uses to communicate with Microsoft Exchange and is usually termed the *MAPI protocol*. MAPI uses a negotiated dynamic port (above 1024). RPC uses port 135.

The MAPI version that ships with Exchange Server 2010 and Microsoft Office Outlook is sometimes known as Extended MAPI. It allows complete control over the messaging system on the client computer, creation and management of messages, management of the client mailbox, and so on. Extended MAPI includes facilities to access message transports, message stores, and directories.

You can use commands based on the *Test-MapiConnectivity* EMS cmdlet to test MAPI connectivity and verify server functionality. You use the Identity parameter to specify a logon mailbox. The SystemMailbox is used if you do not include the Identity parameter. The cmdlet retrieves a list of items in the Inbox. Logging on to the mailbox tests two protocols used when a client connects to a Mailbox server: MAPI and Lightweight Directory Application Protocol. During authentication, the *Test-MapiConnectivity* cmdlet verifies that the MAPI server, Exchange store, and Directory Service Access (DSAccess) service are working.

Commands based on the *Test-MapiConnectivity* cmdlet log on to the specified mailbox using the credentials of the account with which you are logged on to the local computer. After successful authentication, the command accesses the mailbox to verify that the database is working. Note that you do not run the *Test-MapiConnectivity* cmdlet against the Client Access server. This cmdlet must be run against the Mailbox server.

The *Test-MapiConnectivity* cmdlet supports the Database parameter. This parameter specifies a mailbox database identity so that the command can test whether it is possible to log on to the system mailbox on the specified database. The cmdlet also supports the Identity parameter, which specifies a mailbox identity so that the command can test whether it is possible to log on to a specific mailbox. The Server parameter specifies a server identity and tests whether it is possible to log on to each system mailbox on the specified server.

For example, the following command tests MAPI connectivity to the system mailboxes in each mailbox database on the Mailbox server VAN-EX1 and returns detailed results:

```
Test-MapiConnectivity -Server VAN-EX1 | FL
```

Figure 9-26 shows the output of this command.

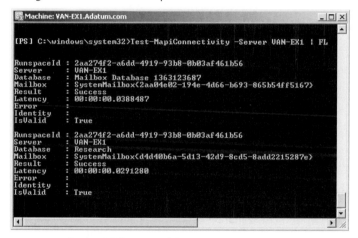

FIGURE 9-26 Testing MAPI connectivity

The following command tests MAPI connectivity to the system mailbox in the mailbox database Research and returns detailed results:

```
Test-MapiConnectivity -Database Research | FL
```

The following command tests MAPI connectivity to the Don Hall mailbox in the Adatum.com domain and returns detailed results:

```
Test-MapiConnectivity -Identity "adatum\Don Hall" | FL
```

MORE INFO   **TEST-MAPICONNECTIVITY**

For more information about the *Test-MapiConnectivity* cmdlet, see *http://technet .microsoft.com/en-us/library/bb123681.aspx*.

Quick Check

- What parameter enables you to specify that EMS commands based on the *Test-PopConnectivity* cmdlet are run by System Center Operations Manager 2007?

Quick Check Answer

- MonitoringContext.

Testing EWS and Outlook Anywhere

The EWS-managed API provides a managed interface for developing client applications that use EWS. This API communicates with the Exchange Client Access server by means of EWS Simple Object Access Protocol (SOAP) messages.

EWS uses standard industry protocols that provide interoperability between servers and client applications. SOAP XML messages provide the communication between the computer that is running Exchange Server 2010 and web services client applications. The following changes and enhancements are included in Exchange Server 2010 EWS:

- Distribution Lists are renamed Contact Groups.
- The FindItems interface is redesigned.
- The Autodiscover implementation supports DNS SRV record lookup.
- The notifications interface is redesigned.
- New methods have been added for getting and setting free or busy information.

EXAM TIP

EWS is a developer tool. As such, it is unlikely to be tested in the 70-662 examination. You should, however, know how to verify EWS functionality as described in this section.

Outlook Anywhere enables Microsoft Office Outlook clients to connect to their Exchange servers over the Internet by using the RPC-over-HTTP networking component. It integrates RPCs with an HTTP layer and allows email traffic to traverse network firewalls without requiring RPC ports to be opened. To deploy Outlook Anywhere in your Exchange messaging environment, you need to enable at least one Client Access server by using the Enable Outlook Anywhere Wizard.

You can use the Enable Outlook Anywhere Wizard on an Exchange Server 2010 Client Access server to allow a user to connect to his or her Exchange mailbox from the Internet. Outlook Anywhere eliminates the need for mobile users or users in remote offices or to use a virtual private network to connect to Exchange servers.

Outlook Anywhere is enabled on your Client Access server after a configuration period of approximately 15 minutes. To verify that Outlook Anywhere has been enabled, you can check the application event log on the Client Access server. Before you can use Outlook Anywhere, you need to do the following:

- Install a valid SSL certificate from a certification authority trusted by the client.
- Install the Microsoft Windows RPC-over-HTTP Proxy component (if this not installed by default). Note that if you use the XML files included with Exchange Server 2010 and the install and setup instructions in the Appendix, you should not need to install RPC-over-HTTP Proxy.
- Enable Outlook Anywhere on the Client Access server.

> **MORE INFO** **INSTALLING THE WINDOWS RPC OVER HTTP PROXY COMPONENT**
>
> If you require more information about how to install the Windows RPC-over-HTTP proxy component, see *http://technet.microsoft.com/en-us/library/dd776122.aspx*.

> **NOTE** **THE DEFAULT SSL CERTIFICATE IS NOT SUFFICIENT FOR OUTLOOK ANYWHERE**
>
> When you install Exchange Server 2010, you can install a default SSL certificate created by Exchange Setup. However, this certificate is not trusted by the client. To use Outlook Anywhere, you must install an SSL certificate that is trusted by the client.

If you use Outlook Anywhere, you must allow port 443 through your firewall because Outlook Anywhere requests use HTTP-over-SSL. If you already use Outlook Web App (OWA) with SSL or Exchange ActiveSync with SSL, you do not need to open any additional ports from the Internet. By default, when you enable Outlook Anywhere on a Client Access server, all users who have mailboxes on Mailbox servers are enabled for Outlook Anywhere.

> **MORE INFO** **OUTLOOK ANYWHERE**
>
> For more information about Outlook Anywhere, access *http://technet.microsoft.com/en-us/library/bb123513.aspx* and follow the links.

You can test the connectivity needed for EWS and Outlook Anywhere to work by entering commands based on the *Test-WebServicesConnectivity* EMS cmdlet. You can use such commands to verify the functionality of EWS on an Exchange Server 2010 Client Access server. The *Test-WebServicesConnectivity* cmdlet tests the functionality of EWS and performs basic operations to verify the functionality of Outlook Anywhere. By default, the following operations are tested:

- GetFolder
- CreateItem
- DeleteItem
- SyncFolderItems

However, if you specify the LightMode parameter in the command, only the GetFolder operation is tested.

By default, the test runs on the Client Access server on which the command is entered. However, you can use the ClientAccessServer parameter to specify a remote Client Access server in the same Exchange organization. As with other test cmdlets described earlier in this lesson, you can use the MailboxServer and MailboxCredential parameters to test connectivity to a specific Mailbox server or to a specific user mailbox. The MonitoringContext parameter specifies whether the test result is passed to System Center Operations Manager 2007. If this parameter is set to a value of $false, the test result appears only on the command line.

The Timeout parameter specifies the amount of time, in seconds, allowed for the test operation to finish. The default value for the Timeout parameter is 300 seconds. The time-out value you specify must be greater than 0 seconds. Microsoft recommends configuring this parameter with a value of 5 seconds or greater.

The ResetTestAccountCredentials parameter resets the password for the test account used to run *Test-WebServicesConnectivity* commands. This is typically reset every seven days. When the ResetTestAccountCredential parameter is used, a password reset is forced any time it is required for security reasons. You can specify whether a secure SSL channel is required or whether the test can run over an unsecured channel by using the AllowUnsecureAccess switch parameter. If the test runs over a secure channel, the TrustAnySSLCertificate parameter allows it to use any SSL certificate available.

The UseAutodiscoverForClientAccessServer parameter specifies whether the test uses the *Autodiscover service* to locate the Client Access server. The Autodiscover service configures client computers that are running Outlook 2007 or Outlook 2010. The service can also configure supported mobile devices. It provides access to Exchange Server 2010 features for Outlook clients that are connected to the Exchange Server 2010 messaging environment. The service enables clients to automatically connect to features, such as the Outlook Address Book (OAB), the Availability service, and Unified Messaging (UM). The service uses the user's email address and password to provide profile settings to Outlook clients and supported mobile devices. If the Outlook client is joined to the domain, the user's domain account credentials are used.

The following command tests Web services continuity for the Getfolder operation between the Client Access server on which it is entered and all mailboxes in the same Exchange organization. The test operates over a secure channel authenticated by any available SSL certificate; if a secure channel cannot be established, the command attempts to test connectivity over an insecure channel:

```
Test-WebServicesConnectivity -LightMode:$true -TrustAnySSLCertificate:$true
-AllowUnsecureAccess:$true | FL
```

Figure 9-27 shows the output from this command.

> **MORE INFO** **TEST-WEBSERVICESCONNECTIVITY**
>
> For more information about the *Test-WebServicesConnectivity* cmdlet, see *http://technet .microsoft.com/en-us/library/aa998328.aspx*.

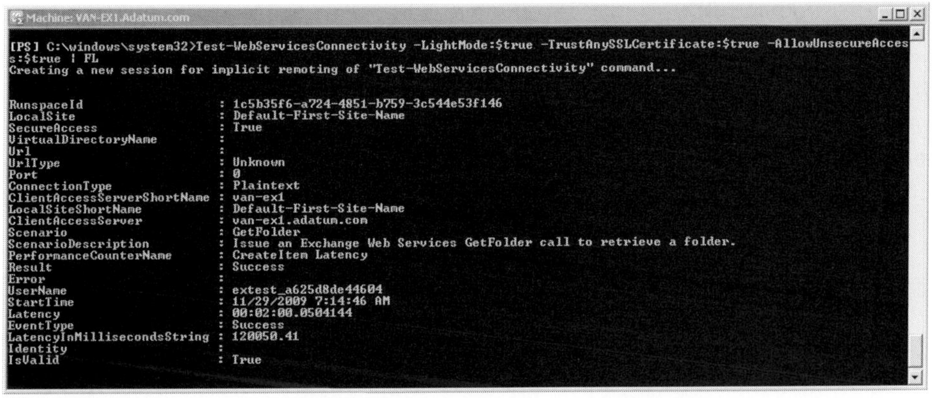

FIGURE 9-27 Testing web services connectivity

You can use commands based on the *Test-OutlookWebServices* EMS cmdlet to verify that the Autodiscover settings for Microsoft Outlook are configured correctly. This cmdlet supports an Identity parameter that can specify any valid email address in the forest, and this address is used to test the Outlook provider. It is typically an SMTP address, but you can specify the domain and user name or an Active Directory GUID, and the command resolves this information to an SMTP address. The TargetAddress parameter specifies the recipient used to test whether Availability service data can be retrieved.

Typically, commands based on this cmdlet run against the Client Access server on which they are entered, but, as with previously described cmdlets, you can use the ClientAccessServer parameter to specify the Client Access server that the client accesses. The MonitoringContext parameter specifies whether the results of the command include monitoring events and performance counters. If you specify this parameter with the value $true, the test results include monitoring events and performance counters in addition to information about the MAPI transaction.

The following command verifies the service information returned to the Outlook client from the Autodiscover service for the user DonHall@adatum.com:

```
Test-OutlookWebServices -Identity:DonHall@adatum.com -MonitoringContext:$true | FL
```

The above command tests the following:

- The Availability service
- Outlook Anywhere
- The OAB
- UM

Figure 9-28 shows the output from this command.

> **MORE INFO** **THE AUTODISCOVER SERVICE**
>
> For more information about the Autodiscover service, access *http://technet.microsoft.com/en-us/library/aa995956.aspx* and follow the links.

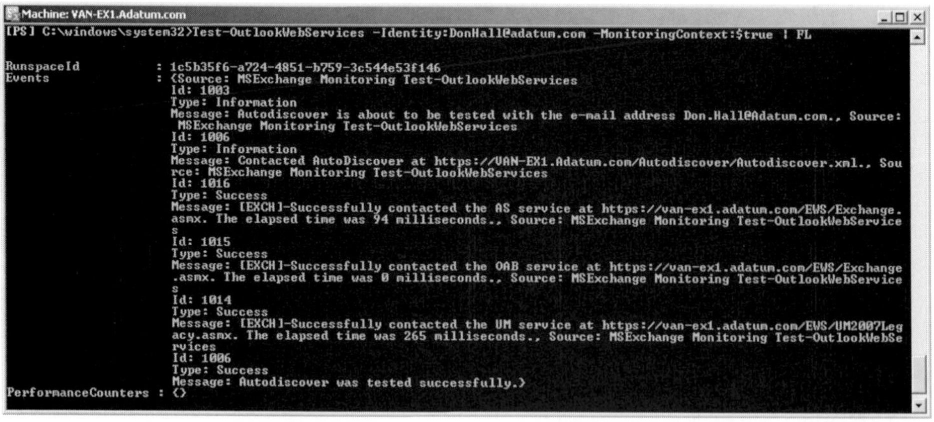

FIGURE 9-28 Verifying Autodiscover settings

MORE INFO   **TEST-OUTLOOKWEBSERVICES**

For more information about the *Test-OutlookWebServices* cmdlet, see *http://technet*
.microsoft.com/en-us/library/bb124509.aspx.

Using Exchange Server ActiveSync

Exchange Server ActiveSync is the messaging component of Exchange Server 2010 that
relays messages to mobile devices. Windows Server 2008 and Windows Server 2008 R2 use
Windows Mobile Device Center version 6.1, which is a version of ActiveSync.

You can use the EMS to create a Microsoft Exchange ActiveSync virtual directory in
Microsoft Exchange Server 2010. When Exchange server 2010 is installed, a new ActiveSync
virtual directory named Microsoft-Server-ActiveSync is created in the default Internet
Information Services (IIS) website. You can optionally create additional Exchange Server 2010
ActiveSync virtual directories in websites other than the default website. All the ActiveSync
virtual directories you create have the name Microsoft-Server-ActiveSync.

For example, the following EMS command creates a new ActiveSync virtual directory in the
adatum.com website:

```
New-ActiveSyncVirtualDirectory -WebSiteName "Adatum.com"
```

MORE INFO   **NEW-ACTIVESYNCVIRTUALDIRECTORY**

For more information about the *New-ActiveSyncVirtualDirectory* cmdlet, see *http://*
technet.microsoft.com/en-us/library/aa997160.aspx.

When you install the Client Access server role on Exchange Server 2010, ActiveSync is
enabled by default, and an ActiveSync virtual directory is created on the Client Access server.
You can then configure the virtual directory using either the EMC or the EMS.

To use the EMC to configure ActiveSync virtual directory properties, open the EMC, expand the Console tree, and carry out the following procedure:

1. In the console tree under Server Configuration, click Client Access.

2. In the Work pane, click the Exchange ActiveSync tab. Right-click Microsoft-Server-ActiveSync and click Properties.

3. In the General tab, you can view display-only information about the ActiveSync virtual directory and set internal and external URLs.

4. On the Authentication tab, shown in Figure 9-29, you can control the authentication methods for the Exchange ActiveSync virtual directory.

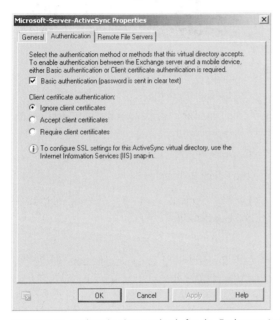

FIGURE 9-29 Authentication methods for the Exchange ActiveSync virtual directory

5. On the Remote File Servers tab, you specify allowed and blocked host names for ActiveSync clients. This tab also allows you to configure which domains are treated as internal. You can use the Block List to configure a list of host names of servers to which clients are denied access and the Allow List to configure a list of host names of servers on which clients are allowed to access files. The Block list takes precedence over the Allow list. You can use the Unknown Servers list to specify how to access files from host names not listed in either the Block list or the Allow list. The default value is Allow. Use the Enter The Domain Suffixes That Should Be Treated As Internal control to configure specific host names as internal host names.

You can also use the EMS to configure the Exchange ActiveSync virtual directory properties. For example, the following command configures the Exchange ActiveSync virtual

directory with Basic authentication and an External URL of http://adatum.com/
Microsoft-Server-ActiveSync:

```
Set-ActiveSyncVirtualDirectory -Identity "http://adatum/microsoft-server-activesync"
-BasicAuthEnabled:$true -ExternalURL http://adatum.com/Microsoft-Server-ActiveSync
```

The following example configures the Exchange ActiveSync virtual directory with Basic
authentication:

```
Set-ActiveSyncVirtualDirectory -Identity "adatum\microsoft-server-activesync"
-BasicAuthEnabled:$true
```

> **MORE INFO** **SET-ACTIVESYNCVIRTUALDIRECTORY**
>
> For more information about the *Set-ActiveSyncVirtualDirectory* cmdlet, see *http://technet*
> *.microsoft.com/en-us/library/bb123679.aspx.*

By default, users are enabled for ActiveSync in Exchange Server 2010. You can disable
Exchange ActiveSync for a user by using the EMC or the EMS.

To use the EMC to disable Exchange ActiveSync for a user, open the EMC and expand
the Console tree, then carry out the following procedure:

1. Click Mailbox under Recipient Configuration in the Console tree.

2. Right-click the user's mailbox and then click Properties.

3. Click the Mailbox Features tab.

4. Click Exchange ActiveSync and then click Disable.

5. Click OK.

To enable Exchange ActiveSync for a user for whom it has previously been disabled, you
carry out the same procedure except that you click Enable after you have clicked Exchange
ActiveSync.

You can also use the EMS to disable Exchange ActiveSync for a user. The following
command disables Exchange ActiveSync for the mailbox user Don Hall in the Adatum.com
domain:

```
Set-CASMailbox -Identity DonHall@adatum.com -ActiveSyncEnabled $false
```

To use the EMS to enable Exchange ActiveSync for a user for whom it has previously been
disabled, you would enter a command similar to the following:

```
Set-CASMailbox -Identity DonHall@adatum.com -ActiveSyncEnabled $true
```

You can restrict access to ActiveSync by using the device ID. This feature prevents users
from synchronizing, for example, unauthorized mobile phones with Exchange Server 2010.
By default, if ActiveSync is enabled for a user, that user can synchronize the Exchange
mailbox with any mobile phone. To restrict a user to a specific mobile phone, you use the
ActiveSyncAllowedDeviceIDs parameter of the *Set-CASMailbox* cmdlet. For example, the

following command permits Don Hall to synchronize two mobile phones identified by their device IDs, where these IDs are specified by the variables <DeviceID_01> and <DeviceID_02>":

```
Set-CASMailbox -Identity: -Identity DonHall@adatum.com -ActiveSyncAllowedDeviceIDs:
"<DeviceID_01>","<DeviceID_02>"
```

> **MORE INFO** **MANAGING EXCHANGE SERVER ACTIVESYNC**
>
> For more information about managing Exchange Server ActiveSync, access *http://technet .microsoft.com/en-us/library/bb124396.aspx* and follow the links.

> **MORE INFO** **SET-CASMAILBOX**
>
> For more information about the *Set-CASMailbox* cmdlet, see *http://technet.microsoft.com/ en-us/library/bb125264.aspx*.

 Quick Check

- What port do you need to allow through your firewall if you use Outlook Anywhere?

Quick Check Answer

- You must allow port 443 because Outlook Anywhere requests use HTTP-over-SSL. This port may already be opened if you also use, for example, OWA.

Lesson Summary

- You can use the Telnet tool from a computer that has a Telnet client installed to test SMTP and ESMTP connectivity on Port 25.
- EMS commands are available to enable you to display network adapter settings and test POP3, IMAP4, and MAPI connectivity.
- You can also use EMS commands to test EWS connectivity and Outlook Anywhere operability. You can use either the EMC or the EMS to configure Exchange Server ActiveSync.

Lesson Review

You can use the following questions to test your knowledge of the information in Lesson 2, "Monitoring Exchange Connectivity." The questions are also available on the companion CD if you prefer to review them in electronic form.

> **NOTE** **ANSWERS**
>
> Answers to these questions and explanations of why each answer choice is correct or incorrect are located in the "Answers" section at the end of the book.

1. You have opened a Telnet session on an Edge Transport server and want to access the Mailbox server Mailbox02.fabricam.com in the remote Fabrikam.com domain using SMTP and ESMTP. What Telnet session command do you enter to access the server Mailbox02.fabricam.com?

   A. *open Mailbox02.fabrikam.com*

   B. *EHLO fabrikam.com*

   C. *open Mailbox02.fabrikam.com 25*

   D. *set localecho*

2. You want to view the network configuration information for all network adapters configured on a Mailbox server. What EMS cmdlet enables you to do so?

   A. *Get-NetworkConnectionInfo*

   B. *Test-WebServicesConnectivity*

   C. *Test-OutlookWebServices*

   D. *Set-ActiveSyncVirtualDirectory*

3. You want to test POP3 connectivity over an SSL connection between the Client Access server VAN-CAS01 and all mailboxes in your Exchange organization. What EMS command do you use?

   A. *Test-PopConnectivity -MailboxServer:VAN-CAS01 –ConnectionType:TLS*

   B. *Test-PopConnectivity -ClientAccessServer:VAN-CAS01 –ConnectionType:TLS*

   C. *Test-PopConnectivity -MailboxServer:VAN-CAS01 –ConnectionType:SSL*

   D. *Test-PopConnectivity -ClientAccessServer:VAN-CAS01 –ConnectionType:SSL*

4. Your organization provides email access to third-party email clients on TCP port 143 on the Client Access server NY-CAS01. Some clients are unable to retrieve email. What EMS cmdlet would you use to verify that the relevant service on MY-CAS01 is functioning correctly?

   A. *Test-ImapConnectivity*

   B. *Test-PopConnectivity*

   C. *Test-MapiConnectivity*

   D. *Test-WebServicesConnectivity*

5. You want to test Web services continuity for only the Getfolder operation between a Client Access server and all mailboxes in the same Exchange organization. You want the test to operate over a secure channel authenticated by any available SSL certificate. What EMS command do you enter on the Client Access server?

   A. *Test-WebServicesConnectivity –TrustAnySSLCertificate:$true | FL*

   B. *Test-WebServicesConnectivity –LightMode:$true –TrustAnySSLCertificate:$true | FL*

   C. *Test-WebServicesConnectivity –AllowUnsecureAccess:$true | FL*

   D. *Test-WebServicesConnectivity –LightMode:$true–AllowUnsecureAccess:$true | FL*

PRACTICE **Creating a Mailbox Database and Obtaining Mailbox Database Information and Statistics**

In this practice session, you will create a mailbox database (if necessary), obtain general information about this database, and view mailbox database statistics, The information and statistics you obtain for a mailbox database in an isolated test network are not especially interesting, but the same procedure can be used to obtain significant data in a production environment.

EXERCISE 1   Creating and Configuring a Mailbox Database (Optional)

If you already created and configured the Research mailbox database in Chapter 2, "Exchange Databases and Address Lists," you do not need to carry out this exercise. If not, create and configure this mailbox database using the following procedure:

1. Log on to the Mailbox server VAN-EX1 using the Kim Akers account with the password *Pa$$w0rd*.

2. Open Computer and create the folders C:\MyDatabaseFiles and C:\MyLogFolder. Note that if you have a second hard drive, you can optionally create the folder D:\MyLogFolder instead of C:\MyLogFolder and amend the command in step 5 accordingly.

3. Click Start, click All Programs, and then click Microsoft Exchange Server 2010.

4. Right-click Exchange Management Shell and click Run As Administrator.

5. To create a mailbox database named Research, enter the following command:

```
New-MailboxDatabase -Name Research -Server VAN-EX1 -EdbFilePath
C:\MyDatabaseFiles\Research.edb -LogFolderPath C:\MyLogFolder
```

6. To configure the maintenance schedule, warning quota level, and deleted item retention time for the Research mailbox database, enter the following command:

```
Set-MailboxDatabase -Identity Research -MaintenanceSchedule 6.21:00-6.23:15
-IssueWarningQuota 2GB -DeletedItemRetention 21
```

7. Check that the Research mailbox database has been created and configured, as shown in Figure 9-30.

FIGURE 9-30 Creating and configuring the Research mailbox database

EXERCISE 2   Obtaining Mailbox Database Information and Statistics

In order to carry out this exercise, you need to have created the Research mailbox database either by carrying out Exercise 1 or previously in Chapter 2. Obtain general information for this mailbox database using the following procedure:

1. If necessary, log on to the Mailbox server VAN-EX1 using the Kim Akers account with the password *Pa$$w0rd*. Open the EMS using Run As Administrator, as described in the previous exercise.

2. To obtain detailed information about the Research mailbox database, enter the following command:

    ```
    Get-MailboxDatabase -Identity Research | FL
    ```

    Figure 9-31 shows some of the output from this command.

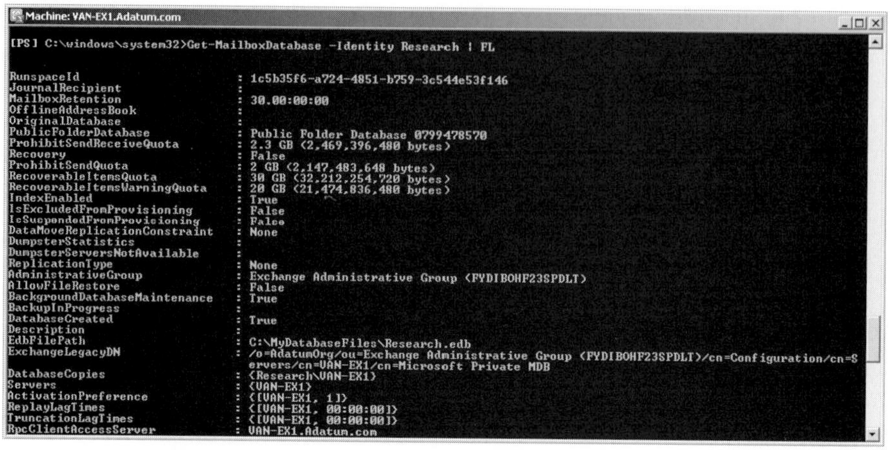

FIGURE 9-31 Detailed information about the Research mailbox database

3. To obtain mailbox statistics, enter the following command:

    ```
    Get-MailboxStatistics -Database Research | FL
    ```

    Figure 9-32 shows some of the output from this command.

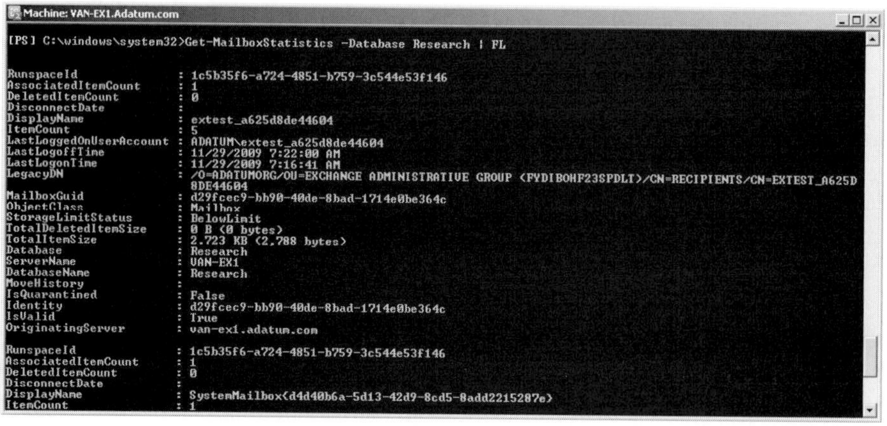

FIGURE 9-32 Statistics for the Research mailbox database

Configuring the Size and Age of Message Tracking Log Files on a Hub Transport and a Mailbox Server

The Exchange Server 2010 server VAN-EX1 is configured with both the Hub Transport and the Mailbox server roles. You need to configure the size and age of message tracking log files and the size of the message tracking log file directory separately for each role. You perform these tasks in this practice session.

EXERCISE 1 Configuring Message Tracking Log File Settings on a Hub Transport Server

In this exercise, you change the maximum size of each message tracking log file on the Hub Transport server VAN-EX1 to 25 MB and the maximum age of each message tracking log file to 45 days. You change the maximum size of the message tracking log file directory on the same server to 350 MB. To complete these tasks, carry out the following procedure:

1. If necessary, log on to the Mailbox server VAN-EX1 using the Kim Akers account with the password *Pa$$w0rd*. Open the EMS using Run As Administrator, as described in the previous practice session.

2. To change the maximum size of each message tracking log file to 25 MB, enter the following command:

   ```
   Set-TransportServer –Identity VAN-EX1 –MessageTrackingLogMaxFileSize 25MB
   ```

3. To change the maximum age of each message tracking log file to 45 days, enter the following command:

   ```
   Set-TransportServer –Identity VAN-EX1 –MessageTrackingLogMaxAge 45.00:00:00
   ```

4. To change the maximum size of the message tracking log file directory to 350 MB, enter the following command:

   ```
   Set-TransportServer –Identity VAN-EX1 –MessageTrackingLogMaxDirectorySize 350MB
   ```

   If all three commands complete without error, as shown in Figure 9-33, you have successfully made the changes.

FIGURE 9-33 The Hub Transport server configuration changes have been successfully made.

EXERCISE 2 Configuring Message Tracking Log File Settings on a Mailbox Server

In this exercise, you change the maximum size of each message tracking log file on the Mailbox server VAN-EX1 to 35 MB and the maximum age of each message tracking log file to

40 days. You change the maximum size of the message tracking log file directory on the same server to 400 MB. To complete these tasks, carry out the following procedure:

1. If necessary, log on to the Mailbox server VAN-EX1 using the Kim Akers account with the password *Pa$$w0rd*. Open the EMS using Run As Administrator, as described in the previous practice session.

2. To change the maximum size of each message tracking log file to 35 MB, enter the following command:

   ```
   Set-MailboxServer –Identity VAN-EX1 –MessageTrackingLogMaxFileSize 35MB
   ```

3. To change the maximum age of each message tracking log file to 40 days, enter the following command:

   ```
   Set-MailboxServer –Identity VAN-EX1 –MessageTrackingLogMaxAge 40.00:00:00
   ```

4. To change the maximum size of the message tracking log file directory to 400 MB, enter the following command:

   ```
   Set-MailboxServer –Identity VAN-EX1 –MessageTrackingLogMaxDirectorySize 400MB
   ```

   If all three commands complete without error, as shown in Figure 9-34, you have successfully made the changes.

FIGURE 9-34 The Mailbox server configuration changes have been successfully made.

PRACTICE **Testing MAPI Connectivity to a Mailbox Database and to a Specific Mailbox**

In this practice session, you test MAPI connectivity from the Client Access server VAN-EX1 to the Research mailbox database and to the Kim Akers mailbox in the adatum.com domain. The Research mailbox database and the Kim Akers mailbox must exist on the server VAN-EX1 before you can carry out this practice.

EXERCISE   Testing MAPI Connectivity

To test MAPI connectivity to a specified mailbox database, you connect to the system mailbox in the mailbox database. To test MAPI connectivity to a specified mailbox in a domain, you specify the mailbox name and the domain. To perform both these tasks, carry out the following procedure:

1. If necessary, log on to the Client Access server VAN-EX1 using the Kim Akers account with the password *Pa$$w0rd*. Open the EMS using Run As Administrator, as described in the previous practice session.

2. Enter the following command to test MAPI connectivity to the Research mailbox database and return detailed results:

```
Test-MapiConnectivity –Database Research | FL
```

Figure 9-35 shows the output of this command.

FIGURE 9-35 Testing MAPI connectivity to the Research mailbox database

Enter the following command to test MAPI connectivity to the Kim Akers mailbox in the Adatum.com domain and return detailed results:

```
Test-MapiConnectivity –Identity "adatum\Kim_Akers" | FL
```

Figure 9-36 shows the output of this command.

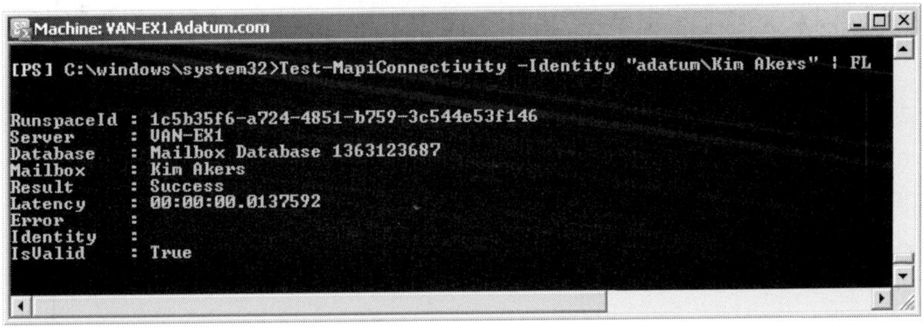

FIGURE 9-36 Testing MAPI connectivity to the Kim Akers mailbox

Chapter Review

To further practice and reinforce the skills you learned in this chapter, you can perform the following tasks:

- Review the chapter summary.
- Review the list of key terms introduced in this chapter.
- Complete the case scenarios. These scenarios set up real-world situations involving the topics of this chapter and ask you to create a solution.
- Complete the suggested practices.
- Take a practice test.

Chapter Summary

- Exchange Server 2010 provides graphical and command-line tools that enable you to monitor public folder and mailbox database properties and view database statistics. You can view the status of database copies and monitor DAGs.
- You can monitor and manage mail flow on Edge Transport and Hub Transport servers by configuring message tracking, managing transport queues, and filtering and managing messages. You can discover why a specific message or group of messages has not been delivered to the recipient or recipients.
- Exchange Server 2010 provides tools that let you test connectivity over the various protocols that permit users to send and receive email messages. You can test connectivity between a client and a Client Access server and between Client Access servers and servers assigned other Exchange Server 2010 server roles.

Key Terms

Do you know what these key terms mean?

- Applications and Services log category
- Autodiscover service
- Back-pressure
- Crimson channel
- Database availability group (DAG)
- Database monitoring
- Exchange Server ActiveSync
- Lagged mailbox database copy Message tracking

- Message tracking log
- Message tracking report
- Outlook Anywhere

Case Scenarios

In the following case scenarios, you will apply what you have learned about monitoring Exchange Server 2010. You can find answers to these questions in the "Answers" section at the end of this book.

Case Scenario 1: Monitoring Mailboxes and Viewing the Continuous Replication Status of Mailbox Database Copies

Jeff Hay holds the Exchange Organization Administrator role for the Exchange 2010 organization at Northwind Traders. One of Jeff's responsibilities is to monitor mailbox databases and mailbox statistics. Another responsibility is to check all aspects of the replication and replay status of mailbox database copies in a DAG. Answer the following questions:

1. What EMS command does Jeff enter to obtain general information, including status information, about all the mailbox databases on the Mailbox server WWT-Mail01?

2. What EMS command does Jeff enter to obtain statistical information about all the mailboxes on all the databases, including recovery databases, on the Mailbox server WWT-Mail01?

3. Jeff needs to obtain a list of the 25 mailbox users that are consuming the most resource for the top 25 mailboxes on all the active databases on the Mailbox server WWT-Mail01. What EMS command returns this information?

4. What EMS command does Jeff enter to test replication health on server WWT-Mail01and view failure information?

Case Scenario 2: Managing Queues

Terry Adams is managing queues on the Hub Transport server BSA-Hub02, which is part of the Exchange 2010 organization at Blue Sky Airlines. A large number of messages can be contained in various queues at any one time, and Terry needs to use filter conditions to identify the messages that are of interest. Answer the following questions:

1. What EMS command does Terry enter to list all the queues on the Hub Transport server BSA-Hub02 that contain more than 50 messages?

2. What EMS command does Terry enter to display the number of messages in queues on the Hub Transport server BSA-Hub02 where the next-hop destination is the Adatum. com domain?

3. What EMS command does Terry enter to resume all suspended queues on the Hub Transport server BSA-Hub02?

Case Scenario 3: Testing Protocol Connectivity

You are an Exchange Organization administrator at Contoso Inc. Your company offers an email service, and users access your Exchange 2010 organization using a wide range of client software. You need to ensure that users can access their Inboxes whatever client they are using. Answer the following questions:

1. You need to test connectivity between a Client Access server and user mailboxes on ports 110 and 995. What EMS cmdlet do you use?

2. You need to test IMAP4 connectivity between a Client Access server and all mailboxes on the Mailbox server NY-EX1. What EMS command do you enter on the Client Access server?

3. You are encountering problems with the Kim Akers mailbox on the Mailbox server CON-EX1. What EMS command, entered on a Client Access server, tests MAPI connectivity between that server and the Kim Akers mailbox in the Contoso.com domain?

Suggested Practices

To help you master the examination objectives presented in this chapter, complete the following tasks.

Investigate Public Folder Database and Mailbox Database Cmdlets

- **Practice 1**   You need to know how to view general information and statistics related to public folder and mailbox databases, Review the following EMS cmdlets and become familiar with their parameters: *Get-PublicFolderDatabase*, *Get-PublicFolderStatistics*, *Get-MailboxDatabase*, and *Get-MailboxStatistics*.

Investigate Get-Queue Filtering

- **Practice 1**   Investigate the Filter parameter of the *Get-Queue* cmdlet. Specify filter conditions, enter commands that use these conditions, and look carefully at any conditions where the command does not operate as you suspect.

Investigate Multiple Message Export

- **Practice 1**   Experiment with commands that export multiple messages by using the *Get-Message* and *Export-Message* EMS commands and the *ForEach-Object* PowerShell commands. Such commands can look complex because of the requirement to replace the < and > characters in file names. The only way to become comfortable with them is to use them.

Investigate Protocol Connectivity Cmdlets

- **Practice 1**   The *Test-PopConnectivity*, *Test-ImapConnectivity*, and *Test-MapiConnectivity* cmdlets support similar sets of parameters. Study the syntax of these parameters and practice using the associated commands.

Take a Practice Test

The practice tests on this book's companion CD offer many options. For example, you can test yourself on just one exam objective, or you can test yourself on all the 70-662 certification exam content. You can set up the test so that it closely simulates the experience of taking a certification exam, or you can set it up in study mode so that you can look at the correct answers and explanations after you answer each question.

> **MORE INFO**   **PRACTICE TESTS**
>
> For details about all the practice test options available, see the "How to Use the Practice Tests" section in this book's Introduction.

CHAPTER 10

Logging and Reports

Chapter 9, "Monitoring Exchange Server 2010," discussed mailbox statistics and the *Get-MailboxStatistics* Exchange Management Shell (EMS) cmdlet. The chapter gave examples of using the *Format-List (FL)* and *Format-Table (FT)* PowerShell cmdlets to select the statistics you want and to display statistics in a convenient format. You also saw examples of the use of the *PowerShell Sort-Object* and *Select-Object* cmdlets that enabled you, for example, to list the five largest mailboxes on a Mailbox server in order of size. However, Chapter 9 discussed these topics only briefly and presented commands to display mailbox statistics as examples. This chapter discusses the tools for reporting mailbox statistics in more depth.

A considerable number of logs are available that enable you to log activity on a computer running Windows Exchange 2010 Server or in an Exchange 2010 organization. This chapter discusses the various Exchange Server 2010 logs, such as the Protocol, Message Tracking, Agent, Administrator Audit, and Routing Table logs. It looks at Exchange Store logging and how you configure logging levels and analyze logging results.

Exam objectives in this chapter:

- Generate reports.
- Configure logging.

Lessons in this chapter:

Before You Begin

In order to complete the exercises in the practice session in this chapter, you need to have done the following:

- Installed the Windows Server 2008 R2 domain controller VAN-DC1 and the Windows Exchange 2010 Enterprise Mailbox, Hub Transport, and Client Access server VAN-EX1 as described in the Appendix, "Setup Instructions for Exchange Server 2010."

- Created the Kim Akers account with the password *Pa$$w0rd* in the Adatum.com domain. This account should be placed in the Domain Admins security group and be a member of the Organization Management role group.
- Created the Don Hall account with the password *Pa$$w0rd* in the Adatum.com domain. This account should be placed in the Backup Operators security group (so it can be used to log on to the domain controller) and should be in the Marketing organizational unit (OU).
- Created mailboxes for Kim Akers and Don Hall, accepting the default email address format for the email addresses.

REAL WORLD

Ian McLean

I once had a slow delivery complaint that I solved very easily indeed. However the follow-up was, to say the least, instructive. A senior manager had sent an email to his daughter, arranging to telephone her at 7:00 PM that evening. He sent the email from his office desk in the United Kingdom at 3:00 PM.

"She told me it didn't arrive until she was in bed asleep," he said, "and she didn't read it until the next morning." He wanted me to check the office email system for excessive delays. I had only recently checked message queues and mailbox health and was confident the delay wasn't at my end, but I told him I'd track the message. I asked him for the recipient email address or, failing that, the message subject.

"I happen to have the email address written down," he said. "She moved recently, and she sent it to me." I looked at the address and noticed it ended .au. Problem solved. I reminded him about time differences. He looked a bit embarrassed and admitted that the earth's rotation wasn't really the responsibility of technical support. To be fair I think he knew about the time difference between the United Kingdom and Australia, but his daughter's family had only recently emigrated, and it had slipped his mind.

Then he paused. "You said subject," he remarked. "You can see the subjects of my emails?" I told him that I could track email messages by a number of criteria including the subject line. "I don't want anyone seeing the subjects of my emails," he snapped. "Disable this immediately."

Pausing only to wonder exactly what he was putting into what was supposed to be company email, I explained that written company policy stated that message subject logging should be enabled and that I couldn't disable it just for him. Fortunately, I was able to identify and quote from the relevant document. The ramifications rumbled on for months, but message subject logging wasn't disabled.

The moral of this story is that, for your own protection, know exactly what your organization's policy is for matters as sensitive as message subject logging. And know where to find the document that states that policy.

Lesson 1: Generating Reports

In this lesson, you will look at the various mailbox and mailbox folder statistics that you can use to generate reports that keep you informed about the current condition and status of the mailboxes in your Exchange organization. The lesson describes EMS cmdlets that you can use to obtain these statistics and PowerShell cmdlets you can use to display the results in list or table format, to sort mailboxes and folders into the order determined by a specific statistic, and to display a limited number of results (for example, the five largest mailboxes on a server in terms of total item size). This lesson also discusses how you can save your results in a comma-separated values (CSV) file for analysis by report-generating software packages.

This lesson discusses testing mail flow between servers and to a specific mailbox. It looks at the tools available through the Exchange Management Console (EMC) that enable you to generate reports about the health of your entire Exchange organization or of a single server within that organization and to report on the flow of mail within your organization.

After this lesson, you will be able to:

- Create mailbox statistics, mailbox folder statistics, and mailbox logon statistics reports in various formats.
- Save report statistics in CSV format files.
- Test mail flow and generate mail flow reports.
- Order the information in your reports depending upon the value of a particular statistic.
- Carry out a health scan and generate a health scan report.

Estimated lesson time: 45 minutes

Generating Mailbox Statistics Reports

Although it is possible to write scripts that use Windows Management Instrumentation or Messaging Application Programming Interface (MAPI) to generate mailbox statistics reports, and such scripts can still be found on the Internet, Exchange Server 2010 (and Exchange Server 2007) provides a less complex method of achieving the same results. EMS cmdlets provide direct access to the statistics you require, and PowerShell cmdlets offer you the facility to generate formatted reports from the command line or to export information in text or CSV files that can be read and manipulated by other software packages, such as Microsoft Office Excel.

If you run the *Get-MailboxStatistics* EMS cmdlet against a Mailbox server or against a mailbox database or an individual mailbox on the Mailbox server on which the command is entered, it lists the display name of the mailbox, the number of items in the mailbox, the mailbox storage limit status, and the last logon time. If you want to find out what other statistics are available for a mailbox, you can pipe the output into the PowerShell *FL* cmdlet.

Doing this for every mailbox on a server would typically provide too much information, so you would typically specify a mailbox. For example, the following command lists all the statistics for the Don Hall mailbox:

```
Get-MailboxStatistics -Identity "Don Hall" | FL
```

Figure 10-1 shows the output from this command.

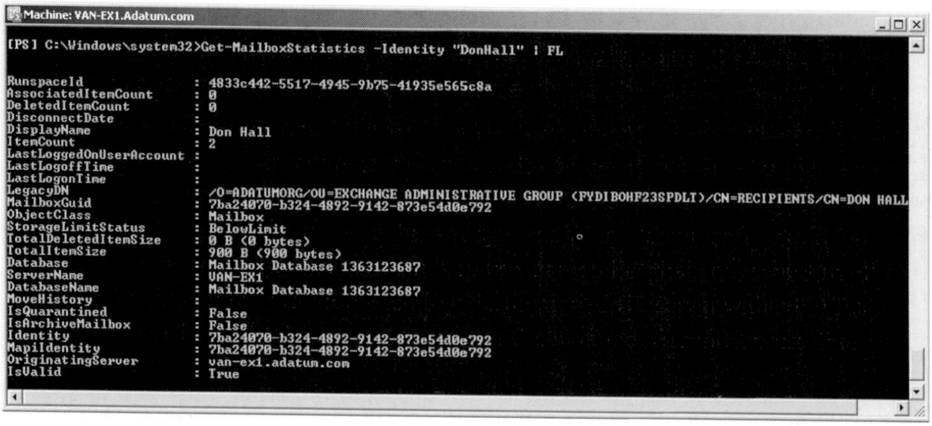

FIGURE 10-1 Statistics available for a mailbox

Even for a single mailbox you obtain a significant amount of information, and you might find it convenient to redirect the output of *Get-MailboxStatistics* commands to a text file. The following example places the statistics for the Don Hall Mailbox in the file donstats.txt in the folder C:\MailboxStats on the server on which the command is run:

```
Get-MailboxStatistics -Identity "Don Hall" | FL > C:\MailboxStats\donstats.txt
```

Note that if the file donstats.txt did not already exist, this command would create it. However, the folder C:\MailboxStats must already exist; otherwise, the command returns an error.

Running the *Get-MailboxStatistics* cmdlet against a mailbox and piping the result into the *FL* cmdlet helps identify the names of the mailbox statistics that the cmdlet returns, for example, ItemCount, LastLogonTime, LastLogoffTime, TotalItemSize, ServerName, DatabaseName, and so on. If you want to return the values of only the statistics you are interested in, you can use these names (known as attribute identifiers) with the *FL* cmdlet. For example, the following command returns the display name, total item size, and item count for the Don Hall mailbox:

```
Get-MailboxStatistics -Identity "Don Hall" | FL DisplayName,TotalItemSize,ItemCount
```

Displaying Data in Tables

Displaying the statistics for a single mailbox in list format is usually satisfactory, but if you are displaying several statistics for several mailboxes, the result is typically clearer in tabular format. In this case, you pipe the output of the *Get-MailboxStatistics* cmdlet into the *FT* PowerShell cmdlet. The following example lists the display name, total item size, and item count for all the mailboxes in the mailbox database named Mailbox Database 1363123687:

```
Get-MailboxStatistics -Database "Mailbox Database 1363123687" | FT DisplayName,
TotalItemSize,ItemCount
```

Figure 10-2 shows the output from this command.

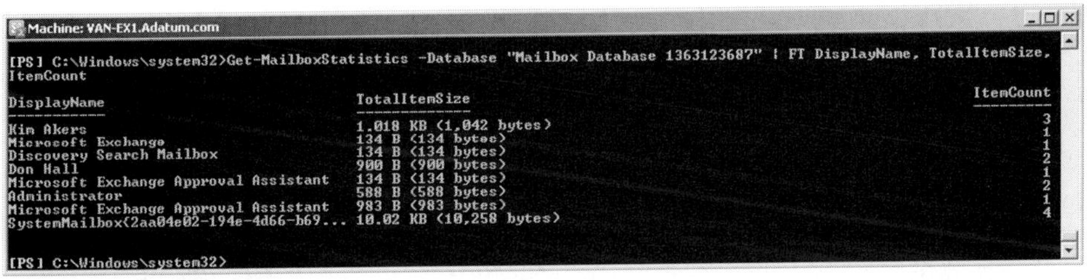

FIGURE 10-2 Mailbox statistics in tabular form

A table on an EMS screen is, however, not the best way to display a report. You can convert the output of the *Get-MailboxStatistics* cmdlet to CSV format by using the *Export-CSV* PowerShell cmdlet and storing the output in a CSV file. You can then display or manipulate the file by using software that reads CSV files, such as Microsoft Excel. The following command creates the file MailboxStats.csv in the C:\MailboxStats folder:

```
Get-MailboxStatistics -Database "Mailbox Database 1363123687" | Export-CSV
C:\MailboxStats\MailboxStats.csv
```

This command captures all the statistics for all the mailboxes in the Mailbox Database 1363123687 database. Typically, you would use reporting software to manipulate the CSV file and display the information you want to see. Data is saved in ASCII format by default. If you want to save the data in, for example, Unicode format, you can use the Encoding parameter followed by the desired format, such as follows:

```
Get-MailboxStatistics -Database "Mailbox Database 1363123687" | Export-CSV
C:\MailboxStats\MailboxStats.csv -Encoding unicode
```

By default, the first line of any CSV file you create with *Export-CSV* lists the .NET object type in its first line, for example, #TYPE Microsoft.Exchange.Data.Mapi.MailboxStatistics. If you do not want to list this information, you can specify the Notype parameter, such as follows:

```
Get-MailboxStatistics -Database "Mailbox Database 1363123687" | Export-CSV
C:\MailboxStats\MailboxStats.csv -Notype
```

MORE INFO **EXPORT-CSV**

For more information about the *Export-CSV* PowerShell cmdlet, see *http://technet .microsoft.com/en-us/library/ee176825.aspx*.

Listing Results by Statistic Values

You can use the values of mailbox statistics to generate reports that list mailboxes that meet specific conditions. For example, if you wanted a report that gave details of all disconnected mailboxes on the Mailbox server VAN-EX1, you could use the PowerShell Where clause, such as follows:

```
Get-MailboxStatistics -Server VAN-EX1 | Where {$_.DisconnectDate -ne $null}| FT
```

Figure 10-3 shows the output of this command. (Note that the Don Hall mailbox was disconnected using the *Disable-Mailbox* cmdlet before the command was entered.)

FIGURE 10-3 Listing disconnected mailboxes

As before, you can place the output of the previous command into a CSV file, such as follows

```
Get-MailboxStatistics -Server VAN-EX1 | Where {$_.DisconnectDate -ne $null} | Export-Csv
C:\ \MailboxStats\DisconnectedMailboxes.csv -Notype
```

The Where clause can also be used to list all mailboxes that are greater than or equal to a defined size or hold a defined number of messages or more. You could, for example, list all mailboxes on a Mailbox server that have a size of 1 GB or greater. However, on your isolated test network, it would be most unlikely that the size of any mailbox would exceed 1 GB or even 1 MB. Therefore, the following command lists all the mailboxes on the Mailbox server VAN-EX1 with a total item size greater than or equal to 1 KB:

```
Get-MailboxStatistics -Server VAN-EX1 | Where ($_.TotalItemSize -ge 1KB) | FT
DisplayName,TotalItemSize
```

Figure 10-4 shows the output from this command.

Similarly, the item counts in the mailboxes on your test network will be much lower than they would be on a production Exchange organization. The following command lists all the mailboxes on the Mailbox server VAN-EX1 with an item count greater than or equal to 2:

```
Get-MailboxStatistics -Server VAN-EX1 | Where ($_.ItemCount -ge 2) | FT
DisplayName,ItemCount
```

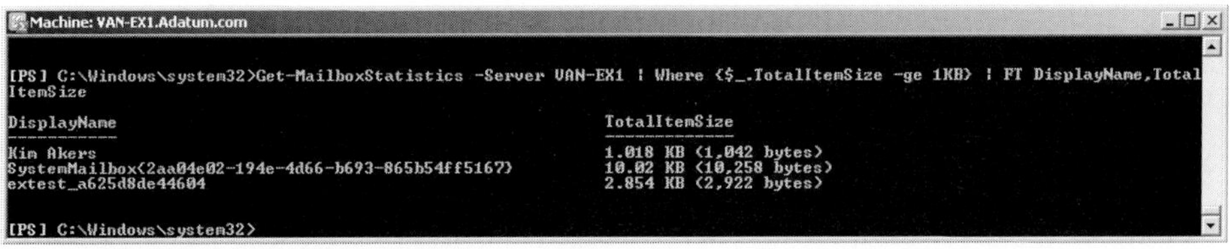

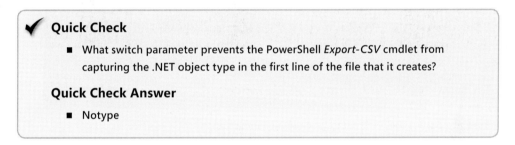

FIGURE 10-4 Mailboxes with a total item size greater than or equal to a specified value

Figure 10-5 shows the output of this command.

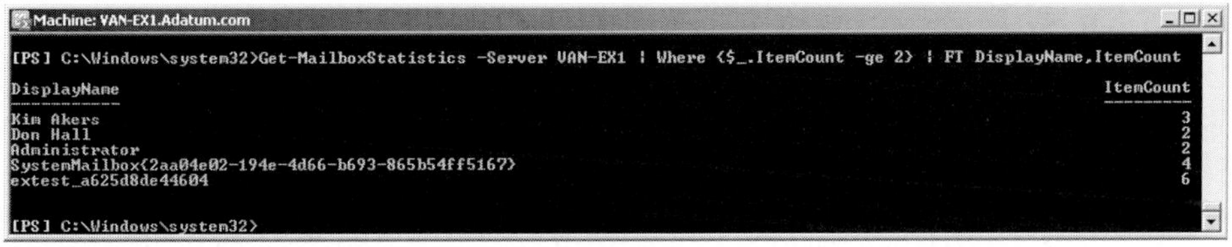

FIGURE 10-5 Mailboxes with an item count greater than or equal to a specified value

As before, you can redirect this information to a CSV file that you can use to generate a report.

> ✔ **Quick Check**
>   - What switch parameter prevents the PowerShell *Export-CSV* cmdlet from capturing the .NET object type in the first line of the file that it creates?
>
> **Quick Check Answer**
>   - Notype

Listing Mailboxes in a Defined Order

Sometimes you do not want to know the absolute item size of mailboxes but instead want to list them in a specified order. You can use the PowerShell *Sort-Object* cmdlet, introduced in Chapter 9, to sort mailboxes in the order defined by a mailbox statistic, such as TotalItemSize or ItemCount. By default, the list will be in ascending order, but you can use the Descending parameter to order the list so that the largest values are first. For example, to list the display name, total item size, and total item count of the mailboxes on the Mailbox server VAN-EX1 in descending order of total item size, you would enter the following command:

```
Get-MailboxStatistics -Server VAN-EX1 | Sort-Object TotalItemSize -Descending |
FT DisplayName,TotalItemSize,ItemCount
```

Figure 10-6 shows the output from this command. As before, you have the option of capturing this output in a CSV file.

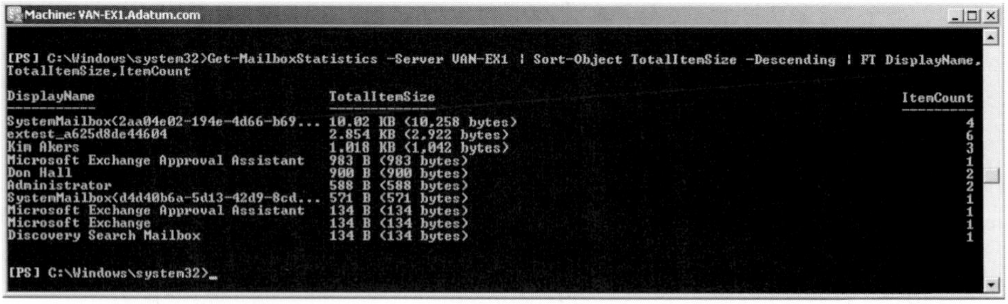

FIGURE 10-6 Mailboxes on the Mailbox server VAN-EX1 in descending order of total item size

If you do not want to list all the mailboxes in a mailbox database or Mailbox server (typically this would be too much information) but instead want to list, for example, the five largest mailboxes in terms of item count, you can use the PowerShell *Select-Object* cmdlet (introduced in Chapter 9). For example, the following command lists the top five mailboxes on the Mailbox server VAN-EX1 in descending order of item count:

```
Get-MailboxStatistics –Server VAN-EX1 | Sort-Object ItemCount –Descending | Select-
Object –First 5 | FT DisplayName,ItemCount
```

Figure 10-7 shows the output from this command.

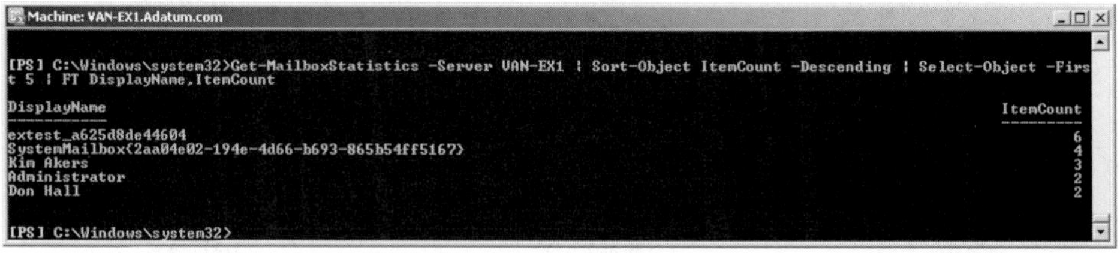

FIGURE 10-7 Sorting the first five results in order of item count

---

MORE INFO   GET-MAILBOXSTATISTICS

For more information about the *Get-MailboxStatistics* cmdlet, see *http://technet.microsoft .com/en-us/library/bb124612.aspx*. This link was given in Chapter 9 but is repeated here for convenience.

MORE INFO   SORT-OBJECT AND SELECT-OBJECT

For more information about the *Sort-Object* cmdlet, see *http://technet.microsoft.com/ en-us/library/dd347688.aspx*. For more information about the *Select-Object* cmdlet, see *http://technet.microsoft.com/en-us/library/dd315291.aspx*. As before, these links were given in Chapter 9 but are repeated here for convenience.

Reporting Mailbox Folder Statistics

If you need to generate a report that presents information about the folders in a specific mailbox, including the number and size of items in the folder, the folder name and identity, and other information, you can use the *Get-MailboxFolderStatistics* EMS cmdlet.

You can identify the mailbox by specifying its Global Unique Identifier (GUID), Active Directory object identity (ADObjectID), distinguished name (DN), domain\account information, user principal name, LegacyExchangeDN, Simple Mail Transport Protocol (SMTP) address, or alias. Optionally, you can use the DomainController parameter to specify the fully qualified domain name of the domain controller that retrieves data from Active Directory. For example, the following command returns mailbox folder statistics for the Kim Akers mailbox:

```
Get-MailboxFolderStatistics -Identity "Kim Akers"
```

Figure 10-8 shows some of the output from this command.

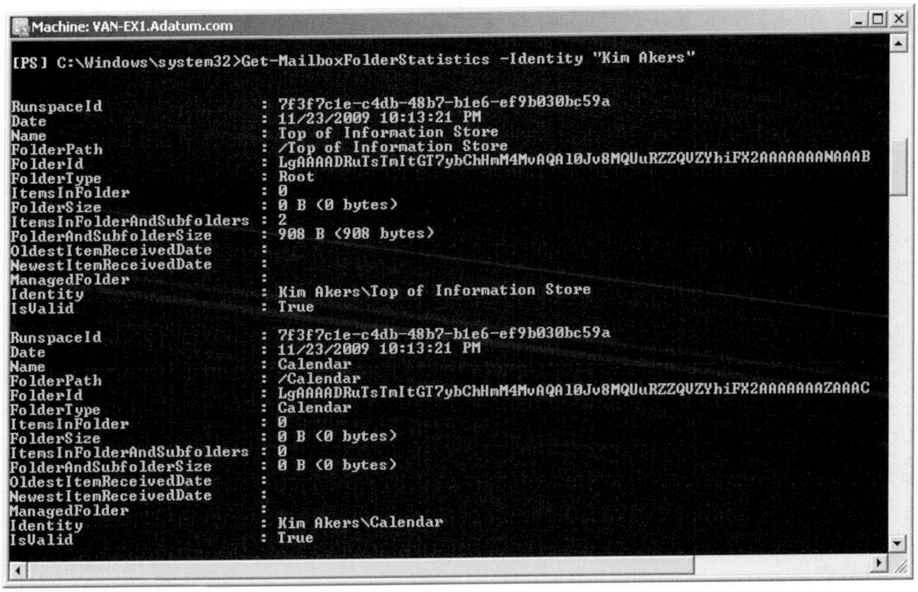

FIGURE 10-8 Listing folder statistics for a mailbox

Using the *Get-MailboxFolderStatistics* cmdlet without filtering the information returns a large number of statistical values in a format that is not well suited to a report. As with the *Get-MailboxStatistics* cmdlet, you can use the *FL* or *FT* PowerShell cmdlets to refine the information. For example if you want to list the name of each folder in the Kim Akers mailbox and the number of items in each folder, you would enter the following command:

```
Get-MailboxFolderStatistics -Identity "Kim Akers" | FT Name,NumberOfItems
```

Figure 10-9 shows the output from this command. Note that there were no items in any of the folders in this mailbox when this command was entered. This can happen on a small test network, but you are unlikely to obtain the same result on a production Exchange organization.

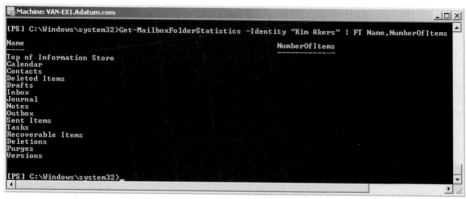

FIGURE 10-9 Tabulating folder statistics for all folders in a mailbox

Sometimes you are interested in one or more specific folders in a mailbox. You can use the FolderScope parameter to define the folders in which you are interested. The FolderScope parameter specifies the scope of the search by folder type. Valid parameter values include the following:

- All
- Calendar
- Contacts
- ConversationHistory
- DeletedItems
- Drafts
- Inbox
- JunkEmail
- Journal
- ManagedCustomFolder
- Notes
- Outbox
- RecoverableItems
- RssSubscriptions
- SentItems
- SyncIssues
- Tasks

If the ManagedCustomFolder value is used, the command returns the output for all managed custom folders. If the RecoverableItems value is entered, the command returns the output for the Recoverable Items folder and the Deletions, Purges, and Versions subfolders.

The following command returns the folder statistics for the Calendar folder in the Don Hall mailbox:

```
Get-MailboxFolderStatistics –Identity "Don Hall" –FolderScope Calendar
```

Figure 10-10 shows the output from this command.

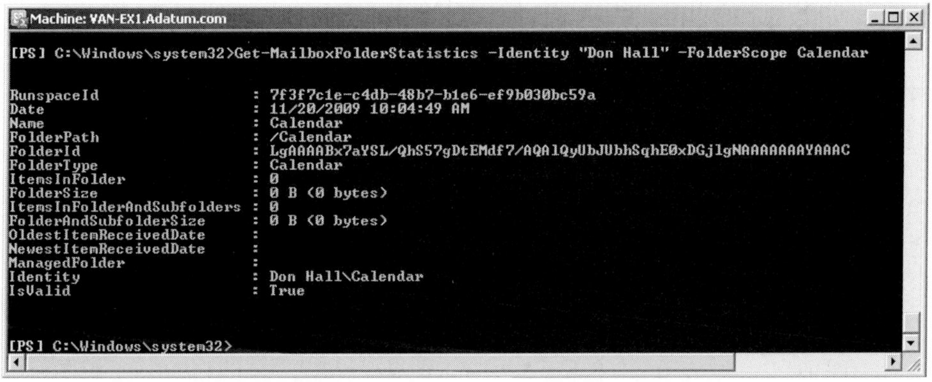

FIGURE 10-10 Folder statistics for the Calendar folder in the Don Hall mailbox

You can decide whether you want a command to return the dates of the oldest and newest items in each folder by specifying the IncludeOldestAndNewestItems parameter. This can take the value $true or $false.

As with commands based on the *Get-MailboxStatistics* cmdlet, you can redirect the output from *Get-MailboxFolderStatistics* commands into .txt or .csv files for analysis by other software packages. You can use the *Sort-Object* and *Select-Object* PowerShell cmdlets to list folders in order of size or item count and to list, say, the five largest or smallest folders.

If you need to analyze the folders on several mailboxes (for example, to list the mailboxes with the largest DeletedItems folders), you can retrieve mailboxes using the *Get-Mailbox* EMS cmdlet and then use the *ForEach-Object* PowerShell cmdlet (introduced in Chapter 9) to obtain folder statistics for each mailbox. You could, for example, use the *Where-Object* PowerShell cmdlet to list all mailboxes that have items in their Outboxes. However, this involves PowerShell programming and is beyond the scope of the 70-662 examination.

Testing Mail Flow

Testing mail flow has two main purposes. The first is to ensure that messages pass through the system without excessive delay (latency). The second is to determine the volume of messages passing through the system in a given time. If the message volume is increasing, maybe you need to plan for future investment so that your organization can seamlessly cope with the anticipated expansion. Monitoring mail flow was discussed in detail in Chapter 9, and this chapter therefore concentrates on mail flow testing.

Using the *Test-Mailflow* Cmdlet

You can use commands based on the *Test-Mailflow* EMS cmdlet to verify that each of your Mailbox servers can successfully send itself a message and to verify that the system mailbox on one Mailbox server can successfully send a message to the system mailbox on another Mailbox server.

A system mailbox must be present on all servers involved in the test. For example, the following command tests that the Mailbox server VAN-EX1 can send email to the mailbox with the SMTP address Administrator@adatum.com.

```
Test-Mailflow -Identity VAN-EX1 -TargetEmailAddress Administrator@adatum.com
```

Figure 10-11 shows the output from this command.

FIGURE 10-11 Testing mail flow to a mailbox

The following command tests that the Mailbox server VAN-EX1 can send email to the Mailbox server VAN-EX2:

```
Test-Mailflow -Identity VAN-EX1 -TargetMailboxServer VAN-EX2
```

Figure 10-12 shows the output from this command. Note that unless you have installed a second Mailbox server VAN-EX2 on your test network, this command returns a test mail flow result failure.

FIGURE 10-12 Testing mail flow to another Mailbox server

You can also use the *Test-Mailflow* cmdlet to verify that email is sent between Mailbox servers within a defined latency threshold. The ErrorLatency parameter specifies how long Exchange Server 2010 waits for a test message to be delivered before an error event is logged in Microsoft System Center Operations Manager 2007. The default value when a test message is sent to the local Mailbox server is 15 seconds. When a test message is sent to a remote Mailbox server, the default value is 180 seconds. You can specify in the command whether error events are logged using System Center Operations Manager 2007 by setting the MonitoringContext parameter to $true (the default value is $false). If you set the value to of this parameter to $true the command populates the MonitoringContext object with events and performance counters used by System Center Operations Manager 2007.

You can specify the maximum time that the test runs before the result is determined to be a failure using the ExecutionTimeout parameter. If no test message or delivery report arrives before this time expires, the task ends, and Exchange Server 2010 reports an error. When the task is run in the EMS, the default setting is 240 seconds. When you use the MonitoringContext parameter set to $true to specify that System Center Operations Manager 2007 is being used for server monitoring, the default execution time-out setting is 15 seconds.

The ActiveDirectoryTimeout parameter specifies the number of seconds that elapse before the task provides an informational message about the delay. The default value is 15 seconds. You can specify the display name of the mailbox to which test messages are sent by using the TargetEmailAddressDisplayName parameter. For example, the following command sends a message to the Kim Akers mailbox if a test message from Mailbox server VAN-EX1 to Mailbox server VAN-EX2 experiences a delay greater than 100 seconds:

```
Test-Mailflow –Identity VAN-EX1 -TargetMailboxServer VAN-EX2 –ActiveDirectoryTimeout 100
-TargetEmailAddressDisplayName "Kim Akers"
```

MORE INFO   TEST-MAILFLOW

For more information about the *Test-Mailflow* cmdlet, see *http://technet.microsoft.com/ en-us/library/aa995894.aspx*.

NOTE   USING PROTOCOL LOGS TO GENERATE REPORTS ON EXTERNAL MAIL FLOW

If protocol logging (described in Lesson 2 of this chapter, "Managing Logging") is enabled, you can use protocol logs to generate reports on external message traffic. Protocol log files are in CSV format and can be read by software such as Microsoft Office Excel or report generation packages.

NOTE   SYSTEM CENTER OPERATIONS MANAGER 2007

System Center Operations Manager 2007 does not have built-in cmdlets. If you are using this facility you can set the MonitoringContext parameter to $true.

 Quick Check

■ What EMS command tests that the Mailbox server DEN-EX1 can send email to the Mailbox server DEN-EX2?

Quick Check Answer

■ *Test-Mailflow –Identity DEN-EX1 -TargetMailboxServer DEN-EX2*

Using the Microsoft Exchange Server Mail Flow Troubleshooter

The Microsoft Exchange Server Mail Flow Troubleshooter is a diagnostic tool that helps you troubleshoot mail flow problems. The tool diagnoses retrieved data, presents an analysis of possible root causes of problems, and suggests corrective actions. You can use the Mail Flow Troubleshooter to troubleshoot common mail flow problems and identify the root causes of symptoms such as the following so that you can corrective actions:

- Users receive unexpected non-delivery reports (NDRs) when sending messages.
- Expected messages from senders are delayed or are not received.
- Messages sent to recipients are delayed or are not received.
- Messages are backing up in one or more queues on a server.
- Specifically, messages are remaining in the pending submission queue on a Mailbox server.
- Edge Transport servers are not synchronizing with Active Directory.

The Exchange Mail Flow Troubleshooter is part of the Exchange Server 2010 Exchange Troubleshooting Assistant. You can access the tool from the EMC by clicking Tools and double-clicking Microsoft Mail Flow Troubleshooter. As with all Troubleshooting Assistant tools, the first time you access the Mail Flow Troubleshooter, you are given the choice as to whether to check for updates at start-up and whether you want to join the Microsoft Customer Experience Improvement Program. If you choose not to check for updates (a choice you would make on your isolated test network but not on a production network), then accessing the tool subsequently takes you straight to the Welcome screen.

On the Welcome screen, shown in Figure 10-13, you specify a name for your analysis and select a symptom from the list in a drop-down box. You can also specify whether to hide the detailed analysis results until the end of the analysis. The symptoms you can choose in the drop-down box are as follows:

- Users are receiving unexpected NDRs when sending messages.
- Expected messages from senders are delayed or are not received by some recipients.
- Messages are not received by some of the intended recipients.
- Messages are backing up in one or more queues on a server.
- Messages sent by users are pending submission on their Mailbox servers.
- Problems with edge server synchronization with Active Directory.

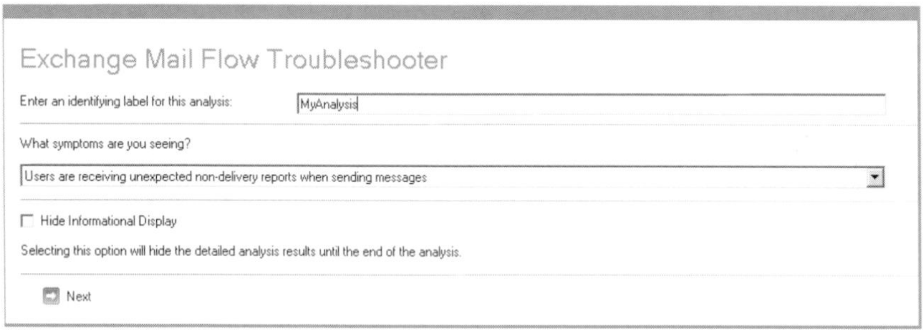

FIGURE 10-13 Mail Flow Troubleshooter Welcome screen

USERS RECEIVING UNEXPECTED NDRS

When you or your users receive an unexpected NDR, you can select Users Are Receiving Unexpected Non-Delivery Reports When Sending Messages. When you click Next, the troubleshooter asks you what delivery status notification (DSN) code the NDR contains and provides you with guidance on what the DSN code typically means and what actions are suggested. For some DSN codes, the tool checks whether the records in DNS are consistent.

MESSAGES FROM SENDERS DELAYED OR NOT RECEIVED

If your Exchange organization is not receiving any messages from the Internet or if some users can receive mails from the Internet but some cannot, you would choose Expected Messages From Senders Are Delayed Or Are Not Received By Some Recipients. When you click Next, the troubleshooter carries out several tests because the root causes of mail flow issues can vary from a transient network condition to a suboptimal SMTP configuration. Depending on the results it receives, the troubleshooter will perform one or more of the following troubleshooting steps:

- Ping the designated gateway or bridgehead server
- Test connectivity over port 25 and other designated SMTP ports to the designated gateway or bridgehead server
- Check the status of the SMTP service and SMTP virtual server
- Check filtering configurations
- Send a test mail from a designated gateway or bridgehead to a designated address
- Check for known SMTP proxies that may be blocking SMTP conversations
- Scan message tracking logs from the sending server to the destination server to determine how far the test message has traveled and start the queue troubleshooter if a backup is detected
- Verify that local domains are correctly registered in the metabase

If one or more of these tests fail, you are presented with a hyperlink with the message Tell Me More About The Issue And How To Resolve It.

MESSAGES TO RECIPIENTS DELAYED OR NOT RECEIVED

If no messages are going out to the Internet, you cannot send messages to a specific domain, or you cannot send messages to a specific external address, you should select Messages Destined To Recipients Are Delayed Or Are Not Received By Some Recipients. The troubleshooter will perform some or all of the following actions:

- Locate the most recent message submitted by a specified sender to a specified recipient
- Scan message tracking logs beginning from the sending server to see how far the message has traveled and start queue troubleshooting if a backup is detected
- Check the status of the SMTP service or SMTP virtual server
- Check SMTP connector configuration
- Check address space (remote domain) settings in the SMTP connector and the metabase

MESSAGES BACKING UP IN QUEUES

If you suspect problems related to queues, you can select Messages Are Backing Up In One Or More Queues On A Server. Queue testing can also be triggered automatically from the mail flow tests described earlier in this section. The actions the troubleshooter carries out could include the following:

- Detect retry or frozen queues and also queues that contain large numbers of messages
- Test whether DNS servers can be accessed from a specified server
- Check whether DNS returns valid records for the remote hosts
- Test connectivity to remote hosts
- Check remote SMTP virtual server configuration and status
- Check the metabase for event sink registrations
- Check whether SMTP Proxies exist
- Check whether antivirus software is blocking SMTP ports
- Check link states
- Check Categorizer performance
- Check journaling configurations
- Check for dismounted databases
- Check for missing SMTP system mailboxes

MESSAGES PENDING SUBMISSION ON MAILBOX SERVERS

If you suspect that email messages are being held for too long in pending submission queues on Mailbox servers, you should select Messages Sent By Users Are Pending Submission On Their Mailbox servers. Symptoms of this problem include Outlook Web App (OWA) user messages being stored in the Drafts folder and Microsoft Outlook 2007 and 2010 user messages being placed in the Sent Items folder but not being sent. The Mail Flow Troubleshooter will check registry settings and MAPI connectivity.

EDGE SERVER SYNCHRONIZATION

The configuration and recipient data on Edge Transport servers is kept up to date by periodically synchronizing changes from Active Directory to Active Directory Lightweight Directory Services (AD LDS). By default, configuration data is synchronized to AD LDS once every hour, and recipient data is synchronized to AD LDS once every four hours. If you observe that your Edge Transport servers are not maintaining synchronization and suspect problems in this area, you should select Problems With Edge Server Synchronization With Active Directory.

The troubleshooter will check the synchronization intervals (it is possible that another administrator has altered these using the *Set-EdgeSyncService* EMS cmdlet) and will suggest other steps you can take. It is possible to force synchronization using the *Start-EdgeSynchronization* cmdlet, but this is not a long-term solution to this problem.

Reporting Logon Statistics

You can use the *Get-LogonStatistics* EMS cmdlet to retrieve logon statistics, such as user name, logon time, last access time, client version, and adapter speed for a single mailbox, for all the mailboxes in a mailbox database, or for all the mailboxes on a Mailbox server. You can use the *FL* and *FT* PowerShell cmdlets to display the results in list or table format, and you can redirect the results into a TXT or CSV file for use by reporting software. For example, the following command obtains all available logon statistics for the Kim Akers mailbox:

```
Get-LogonStatistics -Identity "Kim Akers" | FL
```

Note that this command returns no information if the user has not logged on to his or her mailbox.

The following command displays logon statistics for the mailbox database Mailbox Database 1514648952:

```
Get-LogonStatistics -Database "Mailbox Database 1514648952" | FT
```

Figure 10-14 shows the output of this command.

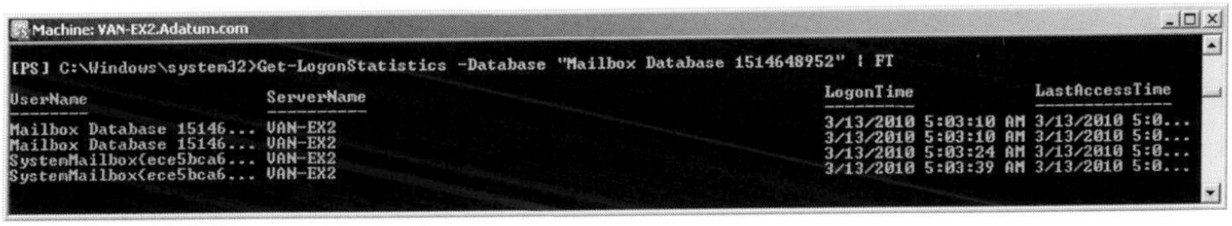

FIGURE 10-14 Available logon statistics for a mailbox database

You can specify the particular logon statistics you want to display. For example, the following command displays the mailbox name and last logon time (if available) for all the mailboxes on Mailbox server VAN-EX1:

```
Get-LogonStatistics -Server VAN-EX1 | FT Name,LastLogonTime
```

> **MORE INFO   GET-LOGONSTATISTICS**
>
> For more information about the *Get-LogonStatistics* cmdlet, see *http://technet.microsoft .com/en-us/library/bb124415.aspx*.

Creating Reports on Number of Users of a Particular Protocol

You can use the EMS to determine how many mailbox-enabled users are configured to use specific client protocols, such as Post Office Protocol version 3 (POP3), Internet Message Access Protocol version 4 (IMAP4), and OWA. It is more difficult to discover how much network traffic is being generated by these protocols. This requires a network monitoring tool, such as Microsoft Network Monitor.

> ***MORE INFO*** **MICROSOFT NETWORK MONITOR 3.4**
>
> For more information about Microsoft Network Monitor 3.4 and to download the tool, see *http://www.microsoft.com/downloads/details.aspx?familyid=983b941d-06cb-4658-b7f6-3088333d062f&displaylang=en.*

To list the client settings on a Client Access server, you can use EMS commands based on the *Get-CASMailbox* cmdlet. For example, to get client settings for all mailboxes in an Exchange organization, you would enter the following command:

```
Get-CasMailbox
```

Figure 10-15 shows the output from this command.

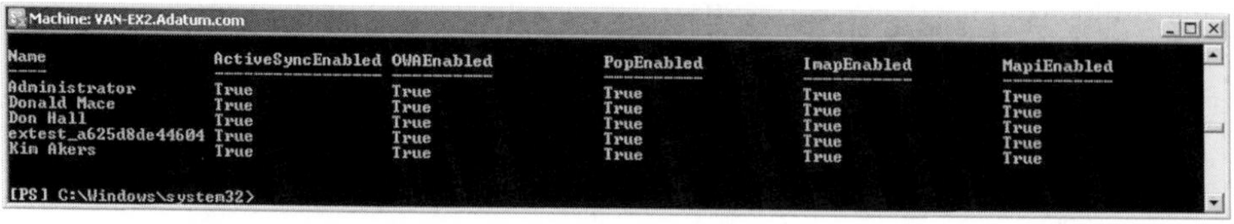

FIGURE 10-15 Client protocols enabled on mailboxes

You specify parameters with the *Get-CasMailbox* cmdlet to get client settings for a single mailbox or for all mailbox-enabled users in an OU. Also, the *Get-CasMailbox* cmdlet supports the Filter parameter, but properties such as OWAenabled and PopEnabled are not filterable. Therefore, you need to use the *PowerShell Where-Object* (?) cmdlet. For example the following command returns the client settings for all the mailboxes on the server on which it runs that have OWA enabled:

```
Get-CasMailbox | ? { $_.OWAEnabled -eq $True }
```

The following command saves information about client access settings in an Exchange organization to a CSV file for further processing:

```
Get-CasMailbox | Export-CSV C:\ClientSettings.csv -NoType
```

This command returns a great deal of information, particularly about OWA settings. In a production environment, this would be a very large file and would be processed by powerful data manipulation software, such as SQL Server.

Using Exchange Server Performance Monitor

You can use counters provided by the MSExchange OWA object in Exchange Server Performance Monitor to monitor, for example, the number of OWA users, the number of unique users, the number of proxy users, and logons per second. You can view the current values in these counters with System Monitor, or you can capture a log over an extended period with the Performance Logs and Alerts tool and compare the results with baseline logs. Exchange Server Performance Monitor can be accessed from the EMC and is described in Chapter 9.

Figure 10-16 shows the MSExchange OWA performance object and some of its associated counters.

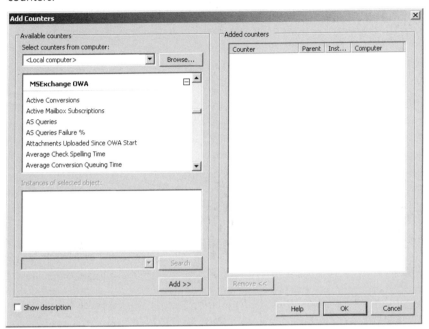

FIGURE 10-16 The MSExchange OWA performance object

✔ **Quick Check**

■ What command returns the client settings for all the mailboxes on the server on which it runs that have OWA enabled?

Quick Check Answer

■ *Get-CasMailbox | ? { $_.OWAEnabled –eq $True }*

Using the Microsoft Exchange Best Practices Analyzer (ExBPA) to Create Reports

The *ExBPA* is an EMC tool that helps you determine the overall health of your Exchange Server 2010 servers and check their topology. You can access this tool from the EMC by clicking the Toolbox node, clicking Best Practices Analyzer, and then clicking Open Tool. It scans Exchange Server 2010 servers and identifies items that do not conform to Microsoft best practices. ExBPA automatically examines the Exchange Server 2010 deployment and determines whether the configuration is set according to Microsoft best practices.

ExBPA can examine your Active Directory and Exchange Server 2010 servers and generate a list of issues, such as suboptimal configuration settings or unsupported or not-recommended options. You can also use it to report on the general health of a system.

You can run ExBPA against an entire deployment, against a specific server, or against a set of servers. When you open ExBPA for the first time, you have the option of selecting to automatically check whether updates to the tool are available (the default) and whether to join the Microsoft Customer Experience Improvement Program. On your isolated test network, you should select not to check for updates and not to join the Customer Experience Improvement Program. On a production network, your settings should be the opposite. When you have configured these settings, you can click Check For Updates Now or Go To The Welcome Screen.

On the Welcome screen, shown in Figure 10-17, you have the choice of carrying out a new scan or accessing an existing scan. You carry out a Best Practices scan in the practice session later in this chapter.

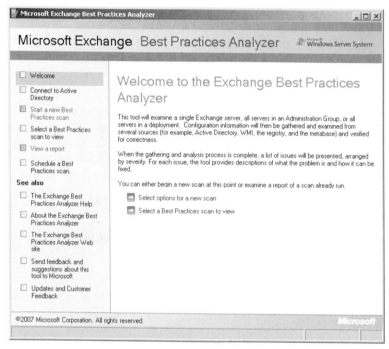

FIGURE 10-17 The ExBPA Welcome screen

Reporting on an Existing Scan

If one or more scans already exist, you can enable the reporting features of ExBPA. Choose to access an existing scan and then select the scan you want to view. You can then click View A Report Of This Scan, as shown in Figure 10-18.

On the View Best Practices Report page, you can select List Reports, Tree Reports, and Other Reports. If you select List Reports, you can view Critical Issues, All Issues, Non-Default Settings, Recent Changes, or Informational Items. List Reports can be arranged by Class, Severity, or Issue. If you select Tree Reports, you can access Detailed View or Summary View tabs. Figure 10-19 shows a List Report with All Issues selected.

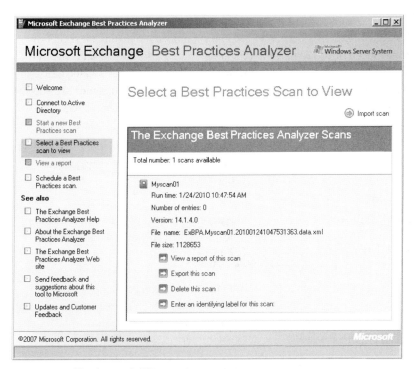

FIGURE 10-18 Viewing an ExBPA report

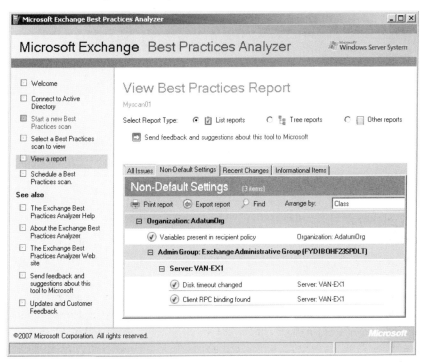

FIGURE 10-19 An ExBPA List Report with All Issues selected

If you select Other Reports, you can access the Run Time Log or Hidden Items. For example, some critical issues, such as Unrecognized Exchange Signature, can appear in List Reports, and you can choose not to display them, an unrecognized Exchange signature can be caused by the version of DomainPrep that was last run, and you can reasonably choose to ignore this message in Critical Issues of List Reports, but if you do so, this is recorded under Hidden Items in Other Reports.

If you click Export Report, you can export reports as Hypertext Markup Language (HTML), CSV, or Extended Markup Language (XML) files. HTML and CSV files contain only the information on the displayed tab of the report. XML files contain all the information in the report.

Carrying Out a Scan

If you are carrying out a scan rather than generating a report from a previous scan, you can specify the type of scan ExBPA carries out. If you select Health Scan, you have the option of specifying Performance Baseline. Typically, this adds two hours to the time taken by the scan. Figure 10-20 shows this option. You can also specify the speed of your local or wide area network. At the foot of the screen (not shown in the figure), you can specify whether to start scanning immediately or to schedule a Best Practices scan. When scanning is complete, you can click View A Report Of This Best Practices Scan if you want to view the report immediately.

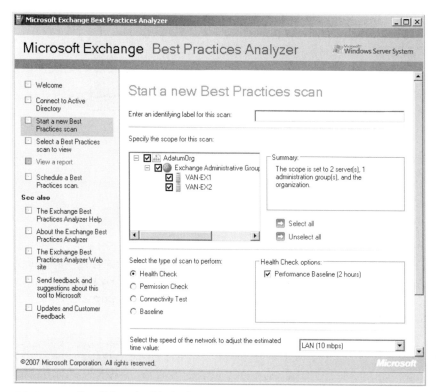

FIGURE 10-20 Specifying a health check with performance baseline scan

Figure 10-21 shows part of the extensive list of items on the Informational Items tab of a performance baseline List Report. You would typically capture a performance baseline after you first install Exchange Server 2010 or if you make any major changes to the software, Exchange organization, or network infrastructure.

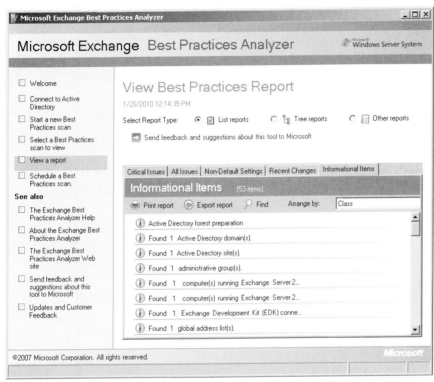

FIGURE 10-21 Informational items for a performance baseline report in ExBPA

You can use ExBPA to carry out one of the following types of scans:

- Health check (with or without performance baseline)
- Permission check
- Connectivity test
- Baseline

If you carry out a health check without specifying the Performance Baseline option, then the scan takes less time and returns fewer items. You should carry out such scans on a regular basis. Figure 10-22 shows the Detailed View tab of the report type Tree Reports for a health scan without the Performance Baseline option.

> **MORE INFO** ExBPA
>
> For more information about ExBPA, see *http://technet.microsoft.com/en-us/exchange/ bb288481.aspx.*

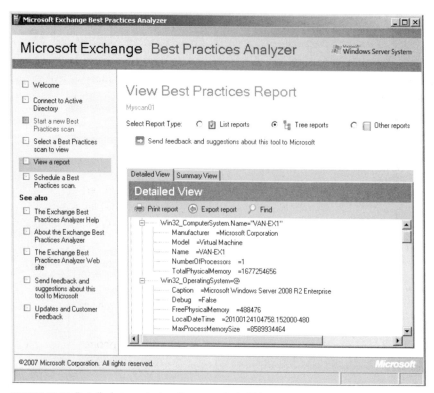

FIGURE 10-22 Detailed view of a health report in ExBPA

> ✔ **Quick Check**
>
> 1. What can you use the ExBPA tool for?
>
> 2. What scans can ExBPA carry out?
>
> **Quick Check Answer**
>
> 1. ExBPA examines your Active Directory and Exchange Server 2010 servers and generates a list of issues, such as suboptimal configuration settings or unsupported or not-recommended options. You can also use it to report on the general health of a system.
>
> 2. ExBPA carries out the following scans:
>
>   ■ Health check (with or without performance baseline)
>
>   ■ Permission check
>
>   ■ Connectivity test
>
>   ■ Baseline

EXAM TIP

It is not unusual for an examination question to ask what tools perform a particular function and list both EMS commands and the EMC graphic tools in the answers. You should know, for example, that you can test mail flow using both the *Test-Mailflow* cmdlet and the Mail Flow Troubleshooter.

Obtaining Exchange ActiveSync Reports

When you install the Client Access server (CAS) role on a computer running Microsoft Exchange Server 2010, you enable Microsoft Exchange ActiveSync. This feature lets users synchronize their mobile phones with their Exchange 2010 mailboxes. This enables a user to access email, calendar, contacts, and tasks and to continue to be able to access this information while working offline.

You can perform the following Exchange ActiveSync administrative tasks:

- Enable and disable Exchange ActiveSync for individual users
- Set policies such as minimum password length, device locking, and maximum failed password attempts
- Initiate a remote wipe to clear all data from a lost or stolen mobile phone
- Generate a variety of reports for viewing or exporting into reporting software

Exchange ActiveSync reporting is a Windows PowerShell task that compiles a set of Internet Information Services (IIS) logs and processes to create a series of reports. You can generate Exchange ActiveSync reports using the *Export-ActiveSyncLog* EMS cmdlet that exports the information in the ActiveSync log, which in turn generates a series of reports. Available ActiveSync reports include the following:

- **Exchange ActiveSync usage report**   This report includes the total bytes that were sent and received and a count of each type of item sent and received. Item types include email messages, calendar items, contact items, and task items.

- **Hits report**   This report tells you the total number of synchronization requests processed per hour and the total number of unique devices that are initiating synchronization requests.

- **HTTP status report**   This report provides an overview of the CAS server performance. It includes a summary of the different error response codes and how often each code was generated.

- **Policy compliance report**   This report provides information about the number of fully compliant, partially compliant, and noncompliant devices. A fully compliant device is one that has accepted the Exchange ActiveSync policy and can implement all aspects of the policy. A partially compliant device is one that has accepted the policy but has a mobile device operating system that is unable to enforce all aspects of the policy. A noncompliant device is either unable to accept the policy or has rejected the policy.

- **User agent list** This report returns the total number of unique users, organized by a mobile phone operating system.

The *Export-ActiveSyncLog* cmdlet lets you specify input parameters such as the location of the IIS log files, the start dates and the end dates for the reports, and the location of the reports folder. For example, the following command exports the ActiveSync log for the date range 03/09/10 to 03/11/10. The times are in Coordinated Universal Time (UTC), and the reports are saved in C:\Reports\ActiveSyncReports:

```
Export-ActiveSyncLog -Filename: "C:\Windows\System32\LogFiles\W3SVC1\ex030910.log"
-StartDate:"03/09/10" -EndDate:"03/11/10" -UseGMT:$true -OutputPath:"C:\Reports\
ActiveSyncReports"
```

Note that the file C:\Windows\System32\LogFiles\W3SVC1\ex030910.log and the folder C:\Reports\ActiveSyncReports must exist; otherwise, the command returns an error. For example, you cannot generate reports if no ActiveSync devices are synchronized with your server.

> **MORE INFO   EXPORT-ACTIVESYNCLOG**
>
> For more information about the *Export-ActiveSyncLog* cmdlet, see *http://technet .microsoft.com/en-us/library/bb123821.aspx*.

Lesson Summary

- You can use EMS commands to obtain mailbox statistics, mailbox folder statistics, and mailbox logon statistics. You can use PowerShell functions to display these statistics in list or table format.

- PowerShell commands enable you to rank mailboxes in order of a specified statistic and to limit your results to, for example, the five largest mailboxes or the 10 mailboxes that contain the largest numbers of messages.

- You can use PowerShell functions to capture statistics in CSV files for use by reporting software.

- The *Test-Mailflow* EMS cmdlet and the Mail Flow Troubleshooter provided by the EMC enable you to test mail flow and generate mail flow reports.

- The ExBPA tool helps you determine the overall health of your Exchange Server 2010 servers and check their topology.

Lesson Review

You can use the following questions to test your knowledge of the information in Lesson 1, "Generating Reports." The questions are also available on the companion CD if you prefer to review them in electronic form.

1. You want to list the top 10 mailboxes in the mailbox database Research in descending order of item count. What command do you enter in the EMS?

    A. *Get-MailboxStatistics –Database Research | Sort-Object ItemCount | Select-Object –First 10 | FT DisplayName,ItemCount*

    B. *Get-MailboxStatistics –Database Research | Select-Object ItemCount –Descending | Sort-Object –First 10 | FT DisplayName,ItemCount*

    C. *Get-Mailbox –Database Research | Sort-Object ItemCount –Descending | Select-Object –First 10 | FT DisplayName,ItemCount*

    D. *Get-MailboxStatistics –Database Research | Sort-Object ItemCount –Descending | Select-Object –First 10 | FT DisplayName,ItemCount*

2. Which Exchange tool would you use to generate a health scan report on a computer running Exchange Server 2010?

    A. System Center Operations Manager 2007

    B. Exchange Server Mail Flow Analyzer

    C. ExBPA

    D. EMS

3. The Mailbox server DEN-EX1 has three mailbox databases: Research, Manufacturing, and Production. You want to generate a report about the logon statistics of only those mailboxes hosted in the Research database. You want this data outputted in table format. Which of the following EMS commands would you enter?

    A. *Get-LogonStatistics –Database Research | FT*

    B. *Get-LogonStatistics –Server DEN-EX1 | FT*

    C. *Get-LogonStatistics –Database Research | FL*

    D. *Get-LogonStatistics –Server DEN-EX1 | FL*

4. You want to list all folders in the Kim Akers mailbox in descending order of item count. You want to report the result in list format and display only the folder name and the number of items. What command do you enter in the EMS?

    A. *Get-MailboxStatistics –Identity "Kim Akers" | Sort-Object NumberOfItems –Descending | FL Name,NumberOfItems*

    B. *Get-MailboxFolderStatistics –Identity "Kim Akers" | Sort-Object NumberOfItems –Descending | FL Name,NumberOfItems*

    C. *Get-MailboxStatistics –Identity "Kim Akers" | Sort-Object NumberOfItems –Descending | FT Name,NumberOfItems*

    D. *Get-MailboxFolderStatistics –Identity "Kim Akers" | Sort-Object NumberOfItems –Descending | FT Name,NumberOfItems*

5. You want to test that the system mailbox on the Mailbox server DEN-EX1 can send email to the mailbox with the SMTP address KimAkers@adatum.com. What command do you enter in the EMS?

    A. *Test-Mailflow –Identity system –TargetEmailAddress KimAkers@adatum.com*

    B. *Test-Mailflow –Identity DEN-EX1 –TargetEmailAddress KimAkers@adatum.com*

    C. *Get-Message –Server DEN-EX1 –TargetEmailAddress KimAkers@adatum.com*

    D. *Test-Mailflow –Identity KimAkers@adatum.com -TargetEmailAddress system*

Lesson 2: Managing Logging

Connectivity logs record the connection activity of outgoing message delivery queues. *Protocol logs* record SMTP activity between messaging servers as part of messaging delivery. *Message Tracking logs* record all message activity on Hub Transport, Edge Transport, and Mailbox servers. *Agent logs* record all activity by anti-spam and antivirus agents. *Routing table logs* record routing table data. *Administrator Audit logs* record the use of EMS cmdlets and parameters. Exchange store logs implement transaction logging, which is central to the operation of Exchange databases. This lesson looks at how you configure logging, set logging levels, and analyze logging results.

> **After this lesson, you will be able to:**
> - Configure connectivity log settings.
> - Configure protocol log settings.
> - Configure message tracking and use the Tracking Log Explorer to view message activity and track messages.
> - Configure administrator audit logging and view administrator audit log settings.
> - Configure routing table logging and use the Routing Log Viewer to view and search routing table logs.
> - Configure Agent logging.
> - Describe Exchange store logging and explain how this is used to maintain Exchange databases.
>
> **Estimated lesson time: 50 minutes**

Managing Connectivity Logging

Connectivity logs record the connection activity of the outgoing message delivery queues. A connectivity log tracks connection activity from the sending queue to the destination Mailbox server, smart host, or domain. You can use both the EMC and the EMS to configure connectivity logging in Microsoft Exchange Server 2010. However, you must use the EMS to configure size and age restrictions on the connectivity log files.

Enabling or Disabling Connectivity Logging

Connectivity logging is disabled by default on Hub Transport or Edge Transport servers. To use the EMC to enable connectivity logging or disable it if it has already been enabled, carry out the following procedure:

1. Open the EMS.
2. On an Edge Transport server, click Edge Transport. On a Hub Transport server, expand Server Configuration and select Hub Transport.

3. On the Actions pane, under the Transport server you want to configure, click Properties.

4. On the Properties page, click the Log Settings tab.

5. In the Connectivity Log section, shown in Figure 10-23, either select Enable Connectivity Log to enable connectivity logging or clear Enable Connectivity Log to disable connectivity logging.

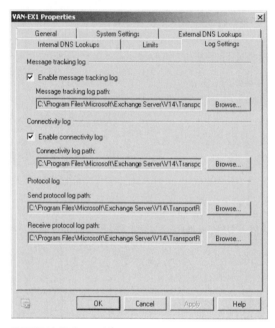

FIGURE 10-23 Log settings

6. Click OK.

You can use the *Set-TransportServer* cmdlet to enable or disable connectivity logging. For example, the following command enables connectivity logging on the Hub Transport server VAN-EX1:

```
Set-TransportServer VAN-EX1 -ConnectivityLogEnabled $true
```

The following command disables connectivity logging on the Edge Transport server DEN-EX2:

```
Set-TransportServer DEN-EX2 -ConnectivityLogEnabled $false
```

Configuring the Location of the Connectivity Log Files

By default, the connectivity log files are stored in the C:\Program Files\Microsoft\Exchange Server\V14\TransportRoles\Logs\Connectivity directory. You can change this location, but the directory must be local to the Exchange Server 2010 computer.

To use the EMC to change the location of the connectivity log files, carry out the following procedure:

1. Access the Log Settings tab of the hub or edge server Properties page, as described in the previous procedure, where you enabled or disabled connectivity logging.

2. In the Connectivity Log section, click Browse next to Connectivity Log Path.

3. In the Browse For Folder window, browse to the new location where you want to store the connectivity log files. If you want to create a folder, select a parent folder, click Make New Folder, and then type the name of the new folder. After you select or create a folder, click OK to close the Browse For Folder window.

4. Click OK.

You can also use an EMS command to change the connectivity log file location. For example, the following command changes the location of the connectivity log file to C:\ConnectivityLogFile on the Hub Transport server VAN-EX1:

```
Set-TransportServer VAN-EX1 -ConnectivityLogPath "C:\ConnectivityLogFile"
```

> **NOTE DISABLING CONNECTIVITY LOGGING**
>
> If you set the value of the ConnectivityLogPath parameter to $null, this effectively disables connectivity logging. However, this can generate errors, and Microsoft does not recommend the procedure. If you want to disable connectivity logging, you should instead set the value of the ConnectivityLogEnabled parameter to $false, as described previously in this lesson.

Changing the Maximum Size of Individual Connectivity Log Files and the Connectivity Log Directory

The maximum size for each connectivity log file is by default 10 MB. When a connectivity log file reaches its maximum size, Exchange Server 2010 opens a new log file. This process continues until the connectivity log directory reaches its specified maximum size or a connectivity log file reaches its specified maximum age. After the maximum size or age limit is reached, circular logging deletes the oldest connectivity log files.

If you want to change the maximum size of individual connectivity log files, you need to use the EMS. You cannot use the EMC to perform this function. For example, the following command sets the maximum size of any connectivity log file on the hub server VAN-EX1 to 15 MB:

```
Set-TransportServer VAN-EX1 -ConnectivityLogMaxFileSize 15MB
```

Similarly, you can use the EMS but not the EMC to change the maximum size of the connectivity log directory. The default maximum size for the connectivity log directory is 250 MB. Circular logging deletes the oldest connectivity log files when either the connectivity log directory reaches its specified maximum size or a connectivity log file reaches its specified maximum age. The size of individual connectivity log files cannot be larger than the size of the entire directory (in practice, the individual file size will be much less than the directory size). The permitted range for both the individual log file size and the directory size is 1 through 9,223,372,036,854,775,807 bytes.

To change the maximum size of the connectivity log directory on the Hub Transport server VAN-EX1 to 300 MB, you would enter the following command:

```
Set-TransportServer VAN-EX1 -ConnectivityLogMaxDirectorySize 300MB
```

Changing the Maximum Age of the Connectivity Log Files

You can use the EMS but not the EMC to change the maximum age of the connectivity log files. The maximum age for any connectivity log file is 30 days by default. Circular logging deletes the oldest connectivity log files when the connectivity log directory reaches its specified maximum size and deletes a connectivity log file when that file reaches its specified maximum age.

You can specify an age value by entering it as a time span using the format *dd.hh:mm:ss*. The valid range for the ConnectivityLogMaxAge parameter is 00:00:00 through 24855.03:14:07. Setting the parameter value to 00:00:00 prevents the automatic removal of connectivity log files because they have reached a maximum age, although the oldest files will still be removed if the connectivity log directory reaches its specified maximum size.

The following command changes the maximum age of the connectivity log files on the Hub Transport server VAN-EX1 to 40 days:

```
Set-TransportServer VAN-EX1 -ConnectivityLogMaxAge 40.00:00:00
```

> **MORE INFO** **SET-TRANSPORTSERVER**
>
> For more information about the *Set-TransportServer* cmdlet, see *http://technet.microsoft .com/en-us/library/bb124238.aspx*.

 Quick Check

- For which of the following operations can you use either the EMC or the EMS?
  - Enabling or disabling connectivity logging
  - Configuring the location of the connectivity log files
  - Changing the maximum size of individual connectivity log files
  - Changing the maximum size of the connectivity log directory
  - Changing the maximum age of the connectivity log files

Quick Check Answer

- Enabling or disabling connectivity logging.

Managing Protocol Logging

Protocol logging logs the SMTP communication between email servers that occurs as part of message delivery. This traffic, known as SMTP conversations, occurs on Send connectors and Receive connectors configured on computers running Exchange Server 2010 that have the Hub Transport or Edge Transport server role installed. In addition to the techniques described earlier in this chapter, you can use the information in protocol logs to help you diagnose mail flow problems.

Protocol logging is disabled on all Send and Receive connectors by default and is enabled or disabled on a per-connector basis. All the Receive connectors on a Hub Transport or Edge Transport server share the same protocol log files and protocol log options. Similarly, all the Send connectors on a Hub Transport or Edge Transport server share the same protocol log files and protocol log options. The Receive connector protocol log files and protocol log options are independent of the Send connector protocol log files and protocol log options on the same server.

By default, the Exchange 2010 server uses circular logging to limit the protocol logs based on file size and file age to help control the hard disk space used by the log files. You can perform the following configuration tasks for the protocol logs of all Send connectors or all Receive connectors on a Transport server:

- Specify the location of the Send or Receive connector protocol log files.
- Specify a maximum size for the Send or Receive connector protocol log files. The default size is 10 MB.
- Specify a maximum size for the directory that contains the Send or Receive connector protocol log files. The default size is 250 MB.
- Specify a maximum age for the Send or Receive connector protocol log files. The default maximum age is 30 days.

Configuring the Intraorganization Send Connector

The intraorganization Send connector is a special Send connector that exists on every Hub Transport server. It is implicitly created and invisible and requires no management. The intraorganization Send connector is used to relay messages to Exchange Server 2010 and Exchange Server 2007 Hub Transport servers, to Exchange Server 2003 servers, and to Edge Transport servers in the Exchange organization.

Protocol logging for the intraorganization Send connector is disabled by default. The following EMS command enables protocol logging for the intraorganization Send connector:

```
Set-TransportServer -IntraOrgConnectorProtocolLoggingLevel Verbose
```

The following command disables protocol logging for the intraorganization Send connector if this has previously been enabled:

```
Set-TransportServer -IntraOrgConnectorProtocolLoggingLevel None
```

If the IntraOrgConnectorProtocolLoggingLevel parameter of the *Set-TransportServer* cmdlet is set to Verbose, logging occurs in the Send connector protocol logs configured on the Hub Transport server. The information is written to the Send connector protocol log specified by the SendProtocolLog parameter.

Protocol Log File Structure

The default locations for the protocol log files are as follows:

- Receive connector protocol log files are located at C:\Program Files\Microsoft\ Exchange Server\V14\TransportRoles\Logs\ProtocolLog\SmtpReceive
- Send connector protocol log files are located at C:\Program Files\Microsoft\Exchange Server\V14TransportRoles\Logs\ProtocolLog\SmtpSend

The naming convention for log files in each protocol log directory is *prefixyyyymmdd-nnnn*.log. The variables represent the following information:

- The variable *prefix* is SEND for Send connectors or RECV for Receive connectors.
- The variable *yyyymmdd* is the UTC date on which the log file was created.
- The variable *nnnn* is an instance number that starts at the value of 1 for each day.

Information is written to the log file until the file size reaches its maximum specified value. At this point, a new log file with an incremented instance number opens. Circular logging deletes the oldest log files when the protocol log directory reaches its maximum specified size or when a log file reaches its maximum specified age.

The protocol log files are text files that contain data in CSV format. Each protocol log file has a header that contains the following information:

- **#Software** The software that created the protocol log file. Typically, this value is Microsoft Exchange Server.
- **#Version** The version number of the software that created the protocol log file. Currently, this value is 14.0.0.0.
- **#Log-Type** The log type value, which is either SMTP Receive Protocol Log or SMTP Send Protocol Log.
- **#Date** The UTC date-time when the log file was created. This is in the date-time format: *yyyy-mm-ddThh:mm:ss.fffZ*, where *yyyy* = year, *mm* = month, *dd* = day, *hh* = hour, *mm* = minute, *ss* = second, *fff* = fractions of a second, and *Z* signifies Zulu, which is another designation for UTC.
- **#Fields** A comma-delimited list of names of the fields used in the protocol log files.

The protocol log stores each SMTP protocol event on a single line. The information stored on each line is organized into fields, separated by commas.

A single SMTP conversation represents the sending or receiving of a single email message. However, this generates multiple SMTP events that cause multiple lines to be written to the protocol log. Multiple SMTP conversations that represent the sending or receiving of multiple email messages can occur simultaneously, which creates interspersed protocol log entries. You need to use the session-id and sequence-number fields to identify protocol log entries by SMTP conversation.

Analyzing External Message Traffic

Send and Receive connectors handle external messages. Protocol logging records the SMTP conversations that occur between email servers as part of message delivery. If protocol logging is enabled, you can use protocol logs to generate reports on external message traffic. Protocol log files are in CSV format and can be read by report generation software.

You can determine fairly easily how many mailbox-enabled users are configured to use specific client protocols, for example, POP3, IMAP4, and OWA. It is more difficult to discover how much network traffic is being generated by these protocols. This requires a network monitoring tool such as Network Monitor (Netmon.exe).

You can use EMS commands based on the *Get-CASMailbox* cmdlet to list the client settings on a Client Access server. For example, as mentioned previously in this chapter, you can obtain client settings for all mailboxes in an Exchange organization.

You can specify parameters for the *Get-CASMailbox* cmdlet to get client settings for a single mailbox or for all mailbox-enabled users in an Active Directory OU. Also, the *Get-CASMailbox* cmdlet supports the Filter parameter, but properties such as OWAenabled and PopEnabled are not filterable. Therefore, you need to capture the client settings details and process the information in the report generation software or use the *where-object (?)* cmdlet. For example, as mentioned earlier in this lesson, the following command returns the client settings for all the mailboxes that have OWA enabled on the server on which the command runs:

```
Get-CasMailbox | ? { $_.OWAEnabled -eq $True }
```

Using the HTTP Monitoring Service

You can also generate reports specific to the OWA servers in your Exchange organization by using the HTTP Monitoring (HTTPMon) service. Although this utility has been around for some time, it remains a powerful tool for monitoring websites and applications and, in particular, OWA servers. You should be aware that HTTPMon exists, although it is not mentioned in the examination objectives.

HTTPMon can check several websites, OWA servers, or applications simultaneously and export the results to a log file in CSV format or to the Windows Server event log. After you install HTTPMon, you need to run HTTPMon Configuration Manager to configure global settings for your organization and add the OWA servers you want to monitor and for which you need to generate reports. HTTPMon runs a series of tests that generate CSV files that you review and analyze to detect problems with your OWA servers. You can also review the events logged by HTTPMon in Event Viewer.

Enabling and Disabling Protocol Logging

You can use the EMC or the EMS to enable or disable protocol logging on connectors. The following procedure describes how you enable use the EMC to enable protocol logging on a Hub Transport server:

1. Open the EMC.

2. Expand Server Configuration in the Console tree and click Hub Transport.

3. In the Result pane, select the server that has the Receive connector that you want to modify and then click the Receive Connectors tab.

4. Click the Receive connector you want to modify.

5. Under the name of the Receive connector in the Actions pane, click Properties.

6. On the General tab, use the drop-down box next to Protocol Logging Level to enable or disable protocol logging. Figure 10-24 shows protocol logging being enabled for the Default VAN-EX2 Receive connector on the VAN-EX2 Transport server.

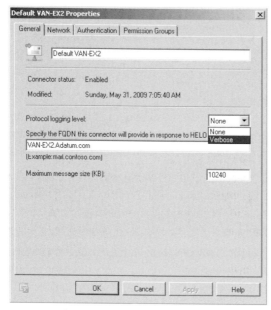

FIGURE 10-24 Using the EMC to enable protocol logging on a Receive connector

7. Click OK.

The procedure to enable or disable protocol logging on Send connectors is similar, except that to access Send connectors, you expand Organization Configuration and click Hub Transport. You then click the Send Connectors tab.

You can also use the EMS to enable or disable protocol logging on connectors. For example, to enable protocol logging for the Default VAN-EX2 Receive connector, you would enter the following command:

```
Set-ReceiveConnector "Default VAN-EX2" -ProtocolLoggingLevel Verbose
```

To disable protocol logging for the Send connector MySendConnector, you would enter the following command:

```
Set-SendConnector MySendConnector -ProtocolLoggingLevel None
```

You can use the EMS but not the EMC to enable or disable protocol logging for the intraorganization Send connector. The following command enables protocol logging for the intraorganization Send connector on the Hub Transport server VAN-EX1:

```
Set-TransportServer –Identity VAN-EX1 –IntraOrgConnectorProtocolLoggingLevel Verbose
```

> **MORE INFO** *SET-RECEIVECONNECTOR* **AND** *SET-SENDCONNECTOR*
>
> For more information about the *Set-ReceiveConnector* cmdlet, see *http://technet .microsoft.com/en-us/library/bb125140.aspx*. For more information about the *Set-SendConnector* cmdlet, see *http://technet.microsoft.com/en-us/library/aa998294.aspx*.

> **NOTE** **LOGGING LEVELS**
>
> The logging levels for protocol logging are Verbose and None. However, for diagnostic logs used for troubleshooting, you can specify a number of logging levels that control the events that are written to event logs. Diagnostic logging levels are discussed later in this lesson.

Changing the Location of Protocol Log Files

By default, the Receive connector protocol log files are located at C:\Program Files\ Microsoft\Exchange Server\V14\TransportRoles\Logs\ProtocolLog\SmtpReceive, and the Send connector protocol log files are located at C:\Program Files\Microsoft\Exchange Server\V14\ TransportRoles\Logs\ProtocolLog\SmtpSend. The directory must be local to the Exchange Server 2010 computer. You can use either the EMC or the EMS to change these locations.

To use the EMC to change the location of the Receive connector protocol log files on a Hub Transport server, carry out the following procedure:

1. Open the EMC.
2. In the Console tree, expand Server Configuration and select Hub Transport.
3. In the Actions pane, click Properties directly under the server name.
4. Click the Log Settings tab in the Properties dialog box.
5. In the Protocol Log section, click Browse next to Receive Connector Protocol Log File Path.
6. In the Browse For Folder window, shown in Figure 10-25, browse to the new location where you want to store the Receive connector protocol log files. If you want to create a folder, select a parent folder, click Make New Folder, and then type the name of the new folder. After you make your folder selection, click OK to close the Browse For Folder window.

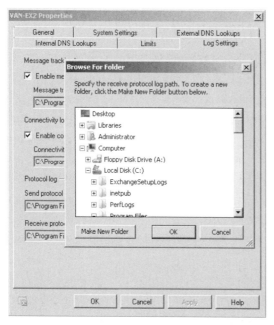

FIGURE 10-25 Browsing to a location for Receive connector protocol log files

7. Click OK.

To change the location of the Send connector protocol log files on a Hub Transport server, the procedure is similar, except that you click Browse next to Send Connector Protocol Log File Path in the Protocol Log section of the Log Settings tab.

You can also use the EMS to change the location of the Receive connector and Send connector protocol log files and log directories. For example, to set the Receive connector protocol log directory to C:\ProtolcolLogs\Receive on the Hub Transport server VAN-EX1, you would enter the following command:

```
Set-TransportServer –Identity VAN-EX1 -ReceiveProtocolLogPath C:\ProtocolLogs\Receive
```

To change the location of the Send connector protocol log files directory to C:\ProtolcolLogs\Send on the Hub Transport server VAN-EX1, you would enter the following command:

```
Set-TransportServer –Identity VAN-EX1 -SendProtocolLogPath C:\ProtocolLogs\Send
```

> **NOTE** **DISABLING PROTOCOL LOGGING**
>
> Setting the value of the SendProtocolLogPath parameter or ReceiveProtocolLogPath parameter to $null disables protocol logging for all Send connectors and all Receive connectors, respectively, on the server. However, if you set either of these parameters to $null when protocol logging is enabled on any Receive connector or any Send connector, including the intraorganization Send connector, this can generate event log errors.

Microsoft therefore recommends that you disable protocol logging using the *Set-SendConnector* or *Set-ReceiveConnector* cmdlet to set the ProtocolLogging-Level parameter to None. You can also use the *Set-TransportServer* cmdlet to set the IntraOrgProtocolConnectorLoggingLevel parameter to None.

Configuring the Maximum Size of Protocol Log Files

The maximum size for each protocol log file is 10 MB by default. All Receive connectors on a Transport server share the same protocol log files. All Send connectors on the server share the same protocol log files. However, the log files that the Receive connectors use are not the same as the log files that the Send connectors use.

When a protocol log file reaches its maximum size, a new protocol log file opens. This process continues until either the protocol log directory reaches its specified maximum size or a protocol log file reaches its specified maximum age. After the maximum size or age limit is reached, circular logging deletes the oldest protocol log files.

You can use the EMS but not the EMC to set the maximum size of Receive connector and Send connector protocol log files. For example, to set the maximum size of Receive connector protocol log files to 15 MB on the Hub Transport server VAN-EX1, you would enter the following command:

```
Set-TransportServer –Identity VAN-EX1 -ReceiveProtocolLogMaxFileSize 15MB
```

To set the maximum size of Send connector protocol log files to 20 MB on the Edge Transport server DEN-EDGE1, you would enter the following command:

```
Set-TransportServer –Identity DEN-EDGE1 -SendProtocolLogMaxFileSize 20MB
```

Configuring the Maximum Size of the Protocol Log Directory

The maximum size for the whole protocol log directory is 250 MB by default. All Receive connectors on a Transport server share the same protocol log directory, and all Send connectors on a Transport server share the same protocol log directory. However, the Receive protocol directory is not the same directory as the Send protocol log directory. Circular logging deletes the oldest protocol log files when either the protocol log directory reaches its specified maximum size or a protocol log file reaches its specified maximum age.

You can use the EMS but not the EMC to configure the maximum size of the Receive connector protocol log directory and the Send connector protocol log directory. For example, to change the maximum size of the Receive connector protocol log directory to 300 MB on the Hub Transport server VAN-EX2, you would enter the following command:

```
Set-TransportServer –Identity VAN-EX2 -ReceiveProtocolLogMaxDirectorySize 300MB
```

To set the maximum size of the Send connector protocol log directory to 400 MB on the Hub Transport server VAN-EX1, you would enter the following command:

```
Set-TransportServer –Identity VAN-EX1 -SendProtocolLogMaxDirectorySize 400MB
```

Configuring the Maximum Age of Protocol Log Files

The maximum age for a protocol log file is 30 days by default. Circular logging deletes the oldest protocol log files if either the protocol log directory reaches its specified maximum size or a protocol log file reaches its specified maximum age.

You can use the EMS but not the EMC to configure the age limit of the Receive connector protocol log files and the Send connector protocol log files. You specify an age value by entering it as a time span in the format *dd.hh:mm:ss,* where *dd* = days, *hh* = hours, *mm* = minutes, and *ss* = seconds. The valid input range for this parameter is 00:00:00 through 24855.03:14:07. Setting the value of the ReceiveProtocolLogMaxAge parameter or the SendProtocolLogMaxAge parameter to 00:00:00 prevents the automatic removal of protocol log files because of their age.

For example, to change the age limit of the Receive connector protocol log files to 45 days on Edge Transport server DEN-EDGE2, you would enter the following command:

```
Set-TransportServer -Identity DEN-EDGE2 -ReceiveProtocolLogMaxAge 45.00:00:00
```

To set the age limit of the Send connector protocol log files to 40 days on the Hub Transport server VAN-EX2, you would enter the following command:

```
Set-TransportServer -Identity VAN-EX2 -SendProtocolLogMaxAge 40.00:00:00
```

 Quick Check

- For which of the following operations can you use either the EMC or the EMS?
  - Enabling or disabling protocol logging
  - Configuring the location of the protocol log files
  - Changing the maximum size of individual protocol log files
  - Changing the maximum size of the protocol log directory
  - Changing the maximum age of the protocol log files

Quick Check Answers

- Enabling or disabling protocol logging.
- Configuring the location of the protocol log files.

Managing Agent Logging

You can use agent logs to record actions performed on a message by specified anti-spam agents that you have installed and configured on an Edge Transport or Hub Transport sever. The following agents can write information to the agent log:

- Connection and content filter agents
- Edge rules agent

- Recipient and sender filter agents
- Sender identity (ID) agent

Information written to the agent log depends on the agent, the SMTP event, and the action performed on the message. By default, agent logging is enabled on Hub Transport servers or Edge Transport servers. The following are default values:

- The path where the agent logs are stored; this is C:\Program Files\Microsoft\ Exchange Server\V14\TransportRoles\Logs\AgentLog.
- The maximum size for the individual agent log files. This is 10 MB.
- The maximum size for the directory that contains the agent log files. This is 250 MB.
- The maximum age for the agent log files. This is 30 days.

Exchange Server 2010 uses circular logging to limit the agent logs based on file size and file age and to help limit the hard disk space used by the log files. If you need to keep agent log files longer than allowed by file age or directory size values, you should create a scheduled task that periodically moves agent log files to a different location for archiving.

Transport Agents

Transport agents act on messages at specific access points in the SMTP command sequence that transports messages through a Hub Transport server or Edge Transport server. These access points are called *SMTP events*. Each agent has a priority value, but SMTP events must always occur in a specific order, and agent priority depends on the SMTP event. If two agents act on a message during the same SMTP event, the agent that has the highest priority acts on the message first.

Table 10-1 lists SMTP events and the agents that write information to the agent log for each SMTP event.

TABLE 10-1 SMTP Events and Their Associated Transport Agents

SMTP EVENT	AGENT
OnConnect	Connection Filter agent
OnMailCommand	Connection Filter agent
	Sender Filter agent
OnRcptCommand	Connection Filter agent
	Recipient Filter agent
OnEndOfHeaders	Connection Filter agent
	Sender ID agent
	Sender Filter agent
OnEndOfData Edge Rules agent	Content Filter agent

Agent Log Location and File Structure

The anti-spam agent logs on a Transport server are located in the folder C:\Program Files\
Microsoft\Exchange Server\V14\TransportRoles\Logs\AgentLog. If no agent logging has
occurred on the server, this folder will not exist. The naming convention for these files is
AGENTLOG*yyyymmdd-nnnn*.log. The placeholder *yyyymmdd* is the UTC date when the log
file was created. The variables *yyyy* = year, *mm* = month, and *dd* = day. The variable *nnnn* is
an instance number that starts at the value of 1 for each day.

Information is written to the log file until the file size reaches 10 MB, at which point a new
log file is opened with an incremented instance number. This process is repeated throughout
the day. Circular logging deletes the oldest log files when the agent log directory reaches
250 MB or when a log file is 30 days old.

Agent log files are text files that contain data in CSV format. Each agent log file has
a header that contains the same information that was previously described for protocol log
files earlier in this lesson. Specifically, the headers are #Software, #Version, #Log-Type, #Date,
and #Fields.

The agent log stores each agent transaction on a single line in the log. The information
stored on each line is organized by fields. These fields are separated by commas. Typically,
the field name is sufficiently descriptive to determine the type of information it contains, such
as Timestamp, SessionId, MessageId, Recipient, and so on. Some of the fields may be blank,
and the type of information stored in the field may change based on the agent or the action
performed on the message by the agent.

 Quick Check

- What transport agents write information to agent logs for the OnMailCommand
  SMTP event?

Quick Check Answer

- The Connection Filter agent and the Sender Filter agent.

Searching Agent Logs

You can use commands based on the *Get-AgentLog* EMS cmdlet on an Edge or Hub Transport
server to access the information in an agent log. For example, the following command returns
a report containing statistics collected between 09:00 (9:00 AM),
October 4, 2010, and 18:00 (6:00 PM), November 5, 2010:

```
Get-AgentLog -StartDate "10/04/2010 9:00:00 AM" -EndDate "11/05/2010 6:00:00 PM"
```

If the C:\Program Files\Microsoft\Exchange Server\V14\TransportRoles\Logs\AgentLog folder does not exist on the server, this command returns an error. You can also use the Get-AntiSpamFilteringReport.ps1 script to search the agent logs and obtain anti-spam filtering statistics. The script displays statistics for each agent, taking one of the following values as a mandatory parameter:

- Connections
- Commands
- MessageRejected
- Messagesdeleted
- Messagesquarantined

MORE INFO **GET-AGENTLOG**

For more information about the *Get-AgentLog* cmdlet, see *http://technet.microsoft.com/en-us/library/aa996044.aspx.*

Configuring Agent Logging

By default, agent logging is enabled on a Hub Transport or an Edge Transport server. You can enable or disable agent logging by modifying the EdgeTransport.exe.config file located in the folder C:\Program Files\Microsoft\Exchange Server\V14\Bin. By default, only the AgentLogEnabled key is present in the EdgeTransport.exe.config file.

To configure the maximum file size for individual logs, the maximum age of the agent log files, and the maximum size for the agent log directory, you need to add the AgentLogMaxFileSize, AgentLogMaxAge, and AgentLogMaxDirectorySize keys. You do this in the practice session later in this lesson. The files EdgeTransport.exe.config and MSExchangeTransport.exe are used by the Microsoft Exchange Transport service. You need to restart this service before any configuration changes you make take effect.

NOTE **CONFIGURABLE AGENT LOGGING SETTINGS**

Because the AgentLogMaxFileSize, AgentLogMaxAge, and AgentLogMaxDirectorySize keys do not exist by default in the EdgeTransport.exe.config file, some documentation states that the only configurable option for agent logging is to disable or enable it. However, if you add the keys to the file, as described in the practice session later in this lesson, you can then configure the maximum file size for individual logs, the maximum age of the agent log files, and the maximum size for the agent log directory.

MORE INFO **AGENT LOGGING**

For more information about agent logging, see *http://technet.microsoft.com/en-us/library/bb124795.aspx.*

EXAM TIP

Remember that agent logging assists in spam filtering and is configured by amending a configuration file rather than by using EMS commands.

Managing Exchange Store Logging

The Exchange store provides a single repository for managing several types of information and is the core data storage repository for Exchange Server 2010. It contains mailbox databases and public folder databases that can reside on a single server or can be distributed across multiple servers.

Exchange Server 2010 stores data in a specialized set of data files, such as Exchange database (EDB) files, transaction logging (LOG) files, and checkpoint (CHK) files. Exchange Server 2010 writes operations such as creating or modifying a message to a LOG file for a specific database. Committed transactions are later written to an EDB file in the database itself. All completed and in-progress transactions are logged, so data integrity is maintained in case of a service interruption. The databases share a single set of transaction logs that are named using consecutive numbers (for example, E0000000001.log and E0000000002.log).

Checkpoint files store information that indicates when a transaction is successfully saved to the database files on the hard disk. Exchange Server 2010 uses checkpoint files to allow an instance of the Extensible Storage Engine (ESE) to automatically replay log files into an inconsistent database when recovering from a service interruption, starting with the next unwritten transaction. The checkpoint files are placed in the same log location as the log files.

Transaction Logging

Exchange store logging, or transaction logging, is an ESE recovery mechanism designed to restore an Exchange database to a consistent state after any sudden stoppage. The logging mechanism is also used when restoring online backups. You will learn more about this in Chapter 14, "Exchange Disaster Recovery." Before changes are made to an Exchange database file, Exchange writes the changes to a transaction log file. After a change has been logged, it can be written to the database file. Changes are securely written to a transaction log file and can be made available if required.

Changes are not lost when a database suddenly stops. When the database restarts, Exchange scans the log files and reconstructs and applies any changes not yet written to the database file. This process is called *replaying log files*. Exchange can determine whether any operation in a log file has already been applied to the database, whether it needs to be applied to the database, or whether it does not belong to the database.

Exchange uses a series of log files, each exactly 1 MB in size. When a log file is full, Exchange closes it and renames it with a sequential number. The first log that is filled ends with the name E*nn*00000001.log, where the variable *nn* refers to a two-digit number known as the base name or log prefix.

Log files for each database are distinguished by file names with sequentially numbered prefixes (for example, E00, E01, E02, or E03). The log file currently open for a database is named E*nn*.log—it does not have a sequence number until it has been filled and closed. The checkpoint file (E*nn*.chk) tracks how far Exchange has progressed in writing logged information to the database files. Each log stream has a checkpoint file, and all the databases share a single log stream. Thus, a single log file often contains operations for multiple databases.

NOTE   LOG FILE NUMBERING

Log files are numbered in a hexadecimal manner, so the log file after E0000000009.log is E000000000A.log, not E0000000010.log.

You can examine the header of a log file by using the Eseutil utility. For example, the following command redirects header information for the log file E000000000B.log into the text file C:\logheader.txt:

```
Eseutil /ml E000000000B.log > C:\Logheader.txt
```

The information in a log file header tells you the base name of the file and whether it is the current log file. If the file is current, the header information tells you what its sequence number will be when it is filled and closed. The Checkpoint value in the header tells you how far into the log file the checkpoint is. If the checkpoint file has been destroyed, the Checkpoint value reads NOT AVAILABLE. In this event, Exchange can still recover and replay log files appropriately. To do so, it scans all the log files, beginning with the oldest file available. Exchange ignores data that has already been applied to the database and works sequentially through the logs until it encounters data that needs to be applied.

Figure 10-26 shows some lines of log file header information that has been redirected into a text file. You know that this is the current log file because the log file name does not have a sequence number. The 1Generation value shows that when the log is filled and closed, its sequence number will be A, corresponding to the decimal value 10. The base name is e01, and therefore the final log file name will be *E010000000A.log*.

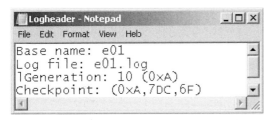

FIGURE 10-26 Log file header information

When an Exchange database shuts down normally, all outstanding data is written to the database files. After normal (clean) shutdown, the database file set is considered to be consistent, and Exchange detaches it from its log stream. This means that the database files are now completely up to date. The transaction logs are not required to start consistent database files.

Circular Logging

You can configure Exchange Server 2010 to save disk space by enabling circular logging, although Microsoft does not recommend this as a best practice. Circular logging allows Exchange to overwrite transaction log files after the data that the log files contain has been committed to the database. However, if circular logging is enabled, you can recover data only up to the last full backup. You will learn more about this in Chapter 14.

In standard transaction logging, each database transaction is written to a log file and then to the database. When a log file reaches 1 MB in size, it is renamed, and a new log file is created. Over time, this results in a set of log files. If Exchange stops unexpectedly, you can recover the transactions by replaying the data from these log files into the database. Circular logging overwrites and reuses the first log file after the data it contains has been written to the database.

Circular logging is disabled by default on Exchange databases. By enabling it, you reduce drive storage space requirements. However, without a complete set of transaction log files, you cannot recover any data more recent than the last full backup.

Managing Administrator Audit Logging

Administrator audit logging enables you to create a log entry each time an EMS cmdlet that you specify is run. The log entries tell you which cmdlet was run, which parameters were used, who ran the cmdlet, and what objects were affected. When you keep a log of the cmdlets that are run, you can attribute a change to the person who made it, augment your change logs with detailed records of changes, and comply with regulatory requirements and requests for discovery.

Changes in audit log configuration are refreshed every 60 minutes on computers that have the EMS open at the time a configuration change is made. If you want to apply changes immediately, close and then open the EMS on each computer.

Specifying the Cmdlets to Audit

By default, audit logging creates a log entry for every cmdlet that runs. If you are enabling audit logging for the first time and want to audit all cmdlets, you do not have to change the cmdlet audit list. If you previously specified cmdlets to audit and now want to audit all cmdlets, you would enter the following command:

```
Set-AdminAuditLogConfig -AdminAuditLogCmdlets *
```

If you want to specify a list of cmdlets to audit, you can use the AdminAuditLogCmdlets parameter of the *Set-AdminAuditLogConfig* cmdlet. You can provide single cmdlets, cmdlets with wildcard characters (*), or a mix of both. For example the following command specifies all cmdlets that start with "Set-Transport," all cmdlets that contain "Management," all cmdlets that end with "TransportRule," and the *New-MailboxDatabase* cmdlet:

```
Set-AdminAuditLogConfig -AdminAuditLogCmdlets Set-Transport*,*Management*,*TransportRule,
New-MailboxDatabase
```

Specifying the Parameters to Audit

By default, audit logging creates a log entry for every parameter of every cmdlet that it audits. If you have previously specified parameters to audit and now want to audit all parameters, you would enter the following command:

```
Set-AdminAuditLogConfig -AdminAuditLogParameters *
```

You can specify which parameters you want to audit by using the AdminAuditLogParameters parameter of the *Set-AdminAuditLogConfig* cmdlet. You can provide single parameters, parameters with wildcard characters (*), or a mix of both. Each entry in the list is separated by commas. For example, the following command specifies that you want to audit all parameters that start with "Custom," contain "Address," or end with "Region," in addition to all instances of the Database parameter:

```
Set-AdminAuditLogConfig -AdminAuditLogParameters Custom*,*Address*,*Region,Database
```

The command must include at least one parameter that exists on at least one cmdlet you have specified for auditing. Otherwise, the audit log entry will not be created.

Specifying the Auditing Mailbox

You can use the AdminAuditLogMailbox parameter of the *Set-AdminAuditLogConfig* cmdlet to specify the SMTP address of the mailbox where you want to store administrator audit logs. The SMTP address should be a mailbox in your Exchange 2010 organization. For example, the following command stores the audit logs in the mailbox with the SMTP address KimAkers@adatum.com:

```
Set-AdminAuditLogConfig -AdminAuditLogMailbox KimAkers@adatum.com
```

Enabling and Disabling Administrator Audit Logging

If you have not previously configured administrator audit logging, you need to specify the cmdlets and parameters you want to be audited (or accept the defaults) and to specify an auditing mailbox before you enable administrator audit logging.

You can enable administrator audit logging by setting the AdminAuditLogEnabled parameter of the *Set-AdminAuditLogConfig* cmdlet to $True. To disable administrator audit logging after it has been enabled, you can set the same parameter to $False. The following command enables administrator audit logging:

```
Set-AdminAuditLogConfig -AdminAuditLogEnabled $True
```

The following command disables administrator audit logging:

```
Set-AdminAuditLogConfig -AdminAuditLogEnabled $False
```

Viewing Administrator Audit Logging Settings

You can view the administrator audit logging settings that you have configured for your organization by entering the following command:

```
Get-AdminAuditLogConfig
```

Figure 10-27 shows the output of this command for the configuration settings discussed earlier in this section.

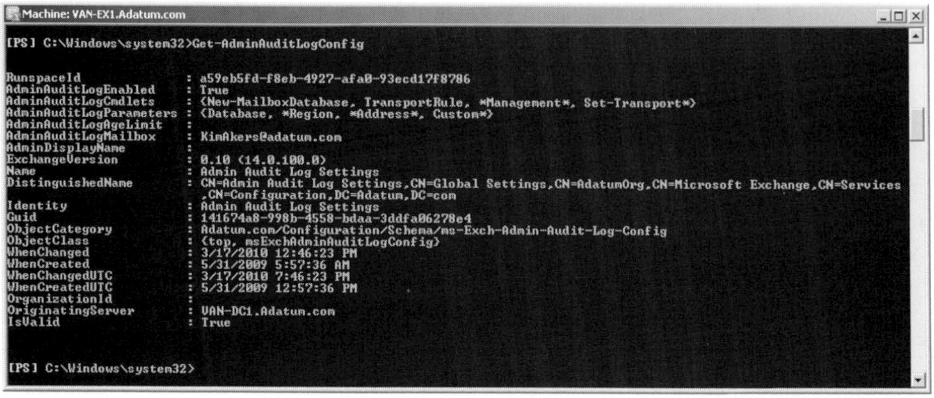

FIGURE 10-27 Viewing administrator audit logging settings

> **MORE INFO** **SET-ADMINAUDITLOGCONFIG AND GET-ADMINAUDITLOGCONFIG**
>
> For more information about the *Set-AdminAuditLogConfig* EMS cmdlet, see *http://technet.microsoft.com/en-us/library/dd298169.aspx*. For more information about the *Get-AdminAuditLogConfig* EMS cmdlet, see *http://technet.microsoft.com/en-us/library/dd298077.aspx*.

Managing Routing Table Logging

Routing table logging records a snapshot of the routing table used by a computer running Microsoft Exchange Server 2010 that has the Hub Transport or Edge Transport server role installed. The routing table is used to route messages to their destinations. The routing table log is recorded periodically after a fixed time interval, whenever the Microsoft Exchange Transport service is started, and after a routing configuration change is detected. You can use the routing table log to help troubleshoot mail flow and routing issues.

You can control the automatic routing table recalculation interval in the EdgeTransport. exe.config application configuration file. The routing table recalculation interval controls how frequently the routing table is automatically recalculated and how frequently the routing table is logged. As shown in Figure 10-28, the default interval is 12 hours. However, recalculation may occur sooner than scheduled if one of the other trigger conditions (for example, the Microsoft Exchange Transport service starts) occurs.

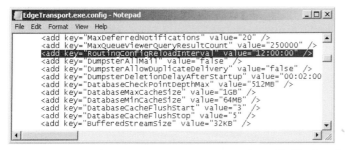

FIGURE 10-28 The routing table recalculation interval specified in the EdgeTransport.exe.config file

You can perform all other routing table log configuration tasks using the *Set-TransportServer* EMS cmdlet. For example, the following command sets the maximum size of the routing table log directory to 70 MB (the default is 50 MB) on the Hub Transport server VAN-EX2:

```
Set-TransportServer -Identity VAN-EX2 -RoutingTableLogMaxDirectorySize 70MB
```

The default maximum age for the routing table log files is seven days. You can change this value using the RoutingTableLogMaxAge parameter of the *Set-TransportServer* EMS cmdlet. The valid input range for this parameter is 00:00:00 through 24855.03:14:07. Setting the value of the RoutingTableLogMaxAge parameter to 00:00:00 prevents the automatic removal of routing table log files because of their age. The following command changes the maximum age of a routing table log file to 14 days on the Hub Transport server VAN-EX2:

```
Set-TransportServer -Identity VAN-EX2 -RoutingTableLogMaxAge 14.00:00:00
```

By default, the routing table log files exist in the directory C:\Program Files\Microsoft\ Exchange Server\V14\TransportRoles\Logs\Routing. You can change this path using the parameter RoutingTableLogPath. However, the directory must be local to the Exchange Server 2010 computer.

The following command changes the location of the routing table log to C:\Logfiles\ RoutingTable on the Hub Transport server VAN-EX2:

```
Set-TransportServer -Identity VAN-EX2 -RoutingTableLogPath C:\Logfiles\RoutingTable
```

By default, Exchange Server 2010 uses circular logging to limit the routing table logs based on file size and file age to help control the hard disk space used by the log files.

Viewing Routing Table Logs

You can use the Routing Log Viewer in the EMC to view and search routing table logs. You access this tool by clicking Toolbox on the EMC Console, clicking Routing Log Viewer, and clicking Open Tool on the Actions pane. On the File menu, you click Open Log File, then either specify a Transport server or click Browse Local Files and navigate to the routing table log directory (by default, C:\Program Files\Microsoft\Exchange Server\V14\TransportRoles\Logs\Routing). You can then select a file and click Open.

The Routing Log Viewer has four tabs:

- Active Directory Sites & Routing Groups
- Servers
- Send Connectors
- Address Spaces

On the Active Directory Sites & Routing Groups tab, shown in Figure 10-29, you can obtain a listing of Active Directory sites and routing groups in the Exchange organization. Only those Active Directory sites that have Exchange servers are listed. If a site is enabled as a hub site, this is indicated on this tab. The server names have hyperlinks to other tabs.

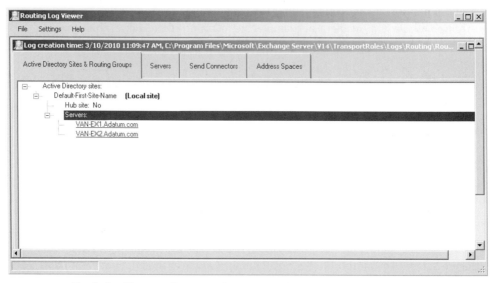

FIGURE 10-29 The Active Directory Sites & Routing Groups tab

The Servers tab, shown in Figure 10-30, displays a list of all Exchange servers in the Exchange organization. The local server where the routing logs were generated is identified. The following information is generated for each server when you access the Servers tab:

- The distinguished name (DN) of the server
- The server's proximity to the local server
- The Active Directory site or routing group that the server belongs to
- The server roles installed, such as Mailbox or Hub Transport
- The total AD cost
- The message databases available

- The Legacy DN
- Whether you are using Exchange Server 2007 or a subsequent version (in this case Exchange Server 2010)

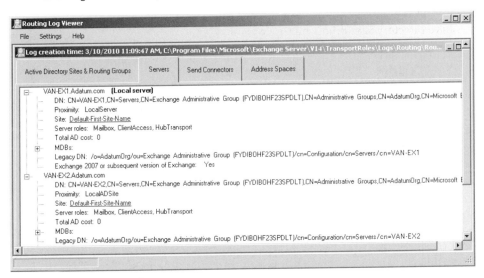

FIGURE 10-30 The Servers tab

Some properties, such as Site, have hyperlinks that link to their counterpart in related tabs.

The Send Connectors tab, shown in Figure 10-31, displays a list of all SMTP connectors, foreign connectors, and routing group connectors available in the Exchange organization. Legacy gateway connectors on legacy servers are also listed.

Information for each connector type includes some or all of the following:

- Name
- GUID
- DN
- Proximity to the local server
- Maximum message size of a message that passes through a connector (the default is unlimited)
- Total site cost to reach the connector
- Whether this is scoped connector
- Address spaces
- Whether DNS routing is enabled
- What smart hosts are defined

If the connector uses connected routing groups, this information is available on the Connected Domains property. For foreign connectors, the value specified by the drop directory (not shown in the figure) is also provided.

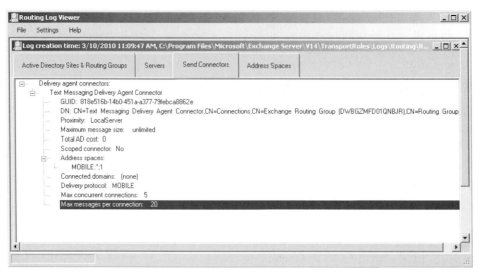

FIGURE 10-31 The Send Connectors tab

The Address Spaces tab provides a list of all address spaces in the Exchange organization, separated by the address type, such as SMTP. Each address space lists all the associated connectors with their cost. As Figure 10-32 demonstrates, a small, isolated test network does not provide many address spaces. The Test Messaging Delivery Agent Connector, shown on the tab in Figure 10-32, provides a hyperlink that links to its properties on the Send Connectors tab.

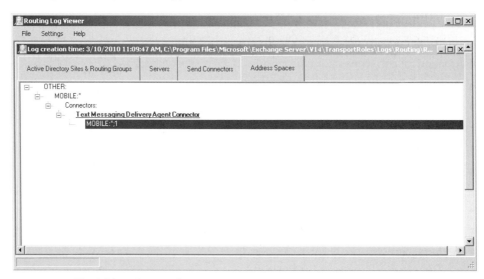

FIGURE 10-32 The Address Spaces tab

You can use the information in the Routing Log Viewer to, for example, find the lowest cost path to a site or to find the preferred connector for a specific address.

The Structure of the Routing Table Log Files

The naming convention for the routing table log files is RoutingConfig#1@UTCcreationdate-time.xml. For example, a routing table log file may be named RoutingConfig#1@03_20_2010 10_52_06.xml. This file was created on March 20, 2010, at six seconds after 10:52 AM.

The routing table log is a snapshot of the routing table stored in memory. Routing table log files are text files that contain data in XML format. They contain a large amount of information. However, their actual file size depends on the size and complexity of the Exchange organization.

The routing table log is composed of several sections. Each section identifies a particular element of the Exchange organization, such as the routing table identity, Exchange topology, connectors, address spaces, Active Directory site, and so on. The information defined in one section is connected to the information defined in another section to build a complete routing table for the whole Exchange organization.

Specifying Diagnostic Logging Levels

Protocol logging, described earlier in this lesson, has only two logging levels, Verbose and None. However, diagnostic logs such as Agent logs can be configured with one of five logging levels. The logging level for each Exchange process determines which events are written to the Application event log in Event Viewer. Event sources can include the MSExchangeAL service, the MSEXchangeTransport service, and so on.

Changing the diagnostic logging level for a given process may cause additional events to be written to the event log, depending on the actions being performed by the current process and the Event Viewer logging levels associated with a specific diagnostic logging level. Table 10-2 shows the relationship between Exchange diagnostic logging levels and Event Viewer logging levels. The default logging level is Lowest.

TABLE 10-2 Exchange Diagnostic Logging Levels and Events Logged

LOGGING LEVEL	EVENTS LOGGED
Lowest	Critical events, error events, and events with a logging level of zero (0)
Low	Events with a logging level of 1 or lower
Medium	Events with a logging level of 3 or lower
High	Events with a logging level of 5 or lower
Expert	Events with a logging level of 7 or lower

To use the EMC to set logging levels, carry out the following procedure:

1. Open the EMC and expand the tree on the Console pane.

2. Under Server Configuration, click Mailbox. On the Result pane, click the server you want to configure.

3. On the Actions pane, click Manage Diagnostic Logging Properties.

4. On the Manage Diagnostic Logging Properties Wizard page, expand the Exchange service for which you want to change the logging level (for example, MSExchangeAL). Click the process that you want to configure (for example, Account Management).

5. Select the logging level (for example, High).

6. Click Configure. (Note that you can return to the default logging levels by selecting Reset All Services To Default Logging Levels and then clicking Configure.)

7. If the status on the Completion page indicates that the wizard completed successfully, click Finish to close the wizard. Otherwise, click Back and review your settings.

You can also use the EMS to examine and set logging levels. The following command identifies all processes and their current logging levels:

```
Get-EventLogLevel
```

This command generates a large amount of information, and you may find it convenient to redirect its output into a text file.

The following command changes the MSExchangeTransport\Agents logging level to High:

```
Set-EventLogLevel -Identity "MSExchangeTransport\Agents" -Level High
```

> **MORE INFO** *SET-EVENTLOGLEVEL* **AND** *GET-EVENTLOGLEVEL*
>
> For more information about the *Set-EventLogLevel* cmdlet, see *http://technet.microsoft .com/en-us/library/aa998905.aspx*. For more information about the *Get-EventLogLevel* cmdlet, see *http://technet.microsoft.com/en-us/library/bb125129.aspx*.

> **NOTE** **RETURN LOGGING LEVELS TO THEIR DEFAULT SETTINGS**
>
> Microsoft recommends that you return logging levels to their default settings after completing your troubleshooting activities.

Managing Message Tracking

Message tracking records the SMTP transport activity of all messages transferred to and from a Hub Transport, Edge Transport, or Mailbox server. You can use message tracking logs to analyze mail flow, generate reports, and locate problems.

By default, message tracking is enabled on Hub Transport, Edge Transport, and Mailbox servers. You can use the EMC to disable or enable message tracking on Hub Transport and Edge Transport servers but not on Mailbox servers. You can use the EMS to disable or enable message tracking for all three server roles. For example, to use the EMC to enable or disable message tracking on a Hub Transport server, carry out the following procedure:

1. Open the EMC.

2. In the Console tree, expand Server Configuration and click Hub Transport. In the Actions pane, click the Properties link directly under the server name.

3. Click the Log Settings tab on the Properties dialog box. This tab is shown in Figure 10-33.

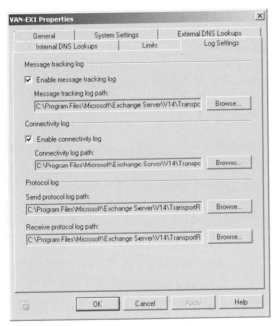

FIGURE 10-33 The Log Settings tab

4. In the Message Tracking Log section, select or clear the Enable Message Tracking check box as appropriate.

5. Click OK.

You can use the EMS to enable or disable message tracking on Edge Transport, Hub Transport, and Mailbox servers. For example, the following command disables message tracking on the Hub Transport server VAN-EX2:

```
Set-TransportServer –Identity VAN-EX2 –MessageTrackingLogEnabled:$false
```

The following command enables message tracking on the Mailbox server VAN-EX1 (assuming this has previously been disabled):

```
Set-MailboxServer –Identity VAN-EX1 –MessageTrackingLogEnabled:$true
```

Configuring Message Tracking Log Location

By default, message tracking logs are located in the folder C:\Program Files\Microsoft\
Exchange Server\V14\TransportRoles\Logs\MessageTracking. You can use the EMC to
reconfigure the message tracking log location on Hub Transport and Edge Transport servers
but not on Mailbox servers. You can use the EMS to reconfigure the message tracking log
location for all three server roles. For example, to use the EMC to reconfigure the message
tracking log location on a Hub Transport server, carry out the following procedure:

1. Open the EMC and access the server Properties dialog box, as described in the
    previous procedure. This tab was shown in Figure 10-33.

2. In the Message Tracking Log section, click Browse next to Message Tracking Log Path.

3. In the Browse For Folder window, browse to the new location where you want to store
    the message tracking log files. If you want to create a folder, select a parent folder,
    click Make New Folder, and then type the name of the new folder.

4. Click OK to close the Browse For Folder window.

5. Click OK.

You can use the EMS to reconfigure the message tracking log location on Edge Transport,
Hub Transport, and Mailbox servers. For example, the following command changes the
message tracking log location on the Hub Transport server VAN-EX2 to C:\Logfiles\
MessageTracking:

```
Set-TransportServer -Identity VAN-EX2 -MessageTrackingLogPath C:\Logfiles\
MessageTracking
```

The following command changes the message tracking log location on the Mailbox server
VAN-EX1 to C:\Logfiles\MessageTracking:

```
Set-MailboxServer -Identity VAN-EX1 -MessageTrackingLogPath C:\Logfiles\MessageTracking
```

> **NOTE** **DISABLING MESSAGE TRACKING**
>
> If you set the value of the MessageTrackingLogPath parameter to $null, this effectively
> disables message tracking. However, if you set the value of the MessageTrackingLogPath
> parameter to $null when the value of the MessageTrackingLogEnabled attribute is $true, this
> generates event log errors. As a result, Microsoft does not recommend this procedure. The
> preferred method of disabling message tracking is to use the MessageTrackingLogEnabled
> parameter with the *Set-TransportServer* cmdlet or the *Set-MailboxServer* cmdlet.

Configuring the Size of Individual Message Tracking Log Files

By default, the maximum size for each message tracking log file is 10 MB. When a message
tracking log file reaches its maximum size, Exchange Server 2010 opens a new message
tracking log file. This process continues until either the message tracking log directory reaches
its specified maximum size or a message tracking log file reaches its specified maximum age.
After the maximum size or age limit is reached, circular logging deletes the oldest message

tracking log files. You can use the EMS but not the EMC to change the maximum size of each message tracking log file on Edge Transport, Hub Transport, and Mailbox servers.

To change the maximum size of each message tracking log file on Hub Transport and Edge Transport servers, you can use the MessageTrackingLogMaxFileSize parameter of the *Set-TransportServer* EMS cmdlet. For example, the following command changes maximum size of each message tracking log file on the Hub Transport server VAN-EX2 to 15 MB:

```
Set-TransportServer -Identity VAN-EX2 -MessageTrackingLogMaxFileSize 15MB
```

To change the maximum size of each message tracking log file on Mailbox servers, you can use the MessageTrackingLogMaxFileSize parameter of the *Set-MailboxServer* EMS cmdlet. For example, the following command changes the maximum size of each message tracking log file on the Mailbox server VAN-EX1 to 20 MB:

```
Set-MailboxServer -Identity VAN-EX1 -MessageTrackingLogMaxFileSize 20MB
```

Configuring the Maximum Size of the Message Tracking Log Directory

By default, the maximum size of the message tracking log directory is 250 MB. Circular logging deletes the oldest message tracking log files when either a message tracking log file reaches its specified maximum age or the message tracking log directory reaches its specified maximum size. You can use the EMS but not the EMC to reconfigure the maximum size of the message tracking log directory on Edge Transport, Hub Transport, and Mailbox servers.

For example, the following command changes the maximum size of the message tracking log directory to 300 MB on Hub Transport server VAN-EX2:

```
Set-TransportServer -Identity VAN-EX2 -MessageTrackingLogMaxDirectorySize 300MB
```

The following command changes the maximum size of the message tracking log directory to 400 MB on Mailbox server VAN-EX1:

```
Set-MailboxServer -Identity VAN-EX1 -MessageTrackingLogMaxDirectorySize 400MB
```

 Quick Check

- What command changes maximum size of each message tracking log file on the Hub Transport server VAN-HUB1 to 25 MB?

Quick Check Answer

- *Set-TransportServer -Identity HUB-EX2 -MessageTrackingLogMaxFileSize 25MB*

Configuring the Maximum Age of Message Tracking Logs

The maximum age for an individual message tracking log file is 30 days by default. Circular logging deletes the oldest message tracking log files if the message tracking log directory reaches its specified maximum size or a message tracking log file reaches its specified maximum age. You can use the EMS but not the EMC to reconfigure the maximum age for message tracking log files on a Hub Transport, Edge Transport, or Mailbox server.

For example, to change the maximum age of message tracking logs on the Hub Transport server VAN-EX2 to 25 days, you would enter the following command:

```
Set-TransportServer –Identity VAN-EX2 -MessageTrackingLogMaxAge 25.00:00:00
```

To change the maximum age of message tracking logs on the Mailbox server VAN-EX1 to 40 days, you would enter the following command:

```
Set-MailboxServer –Identity VAN-EX1 -MessageTrackingLogMaxAge 40.00:00:00
```

Configuring Message Subject Logging

By default, the subject line of an SMTP email message is stored in the message tracking log. However, this setting can prove contentious. Some users might not want you to be able to see the subjects of their email messages, while others might ask you to find a message that they can identify only by its subject. You may be required to disable message subject logging to comply with increased security or privacy requirements. This is a managerial decision, and you need to verify your organization's policy about revealing subject-line information. You can enable or disable message subject logging on individual servers (but not on an individual user basis). However, organizational policy typically dictates that you use the same setting throughout an Exchange organization.

You can use the EMS but not the EMC to enable or disable message subject logging in message tracking logs on Edge Transport, Hub Transport, and Mailbox servers. For example, to disable message subject logging in message tracking logs on the Hub Transport server VAN-EX2, you would enter the following command:

```
Set-TransportServer –Identity VAN-EX2 -MessageTrackingLogSubjectLoggingEnabled $false
```

To enable message subject logging in message tracking logs on the Mailbox server VAN-EX1 (assuming it had previously been enabled), you would enter the following command:

```
Set-MailboxServer –Identity VAN-EX1 -MessageTrackingLogSubjectLoggingEnabled $true
```

EXAM TIP

It is important to know about message subject logging because it can be a contentious issue in a production organization.

Viewing Message Activity and Tracking Messages

The *Tracking Log Explorer*, part of the Troubleshooting Assistant, provides details of all message activity as messages are transferred to and from an Exchange server that has the Hub Transport server role, the Mailbox server role, or the Edge Transport server role installed. Exchange servers that have the Client Access server role or Unified Messaging server role installed (and none of the other three roles) do not have message tracking logs.

You access the Tracking Log Explorer by opening the EMC, clicking Toolbox, and double-clicking Tracking Log Explorer. The Welcome screen is shown in Figure 10-34. By default, the RECEIVE EventID is enabled with a 10-minute interval specified, depending on when you opened the tool. You can specify parameters shown in the figure, such as Recipients, Sender, Server, and so on. If message subject logging is enabled, you can also specify Subject.

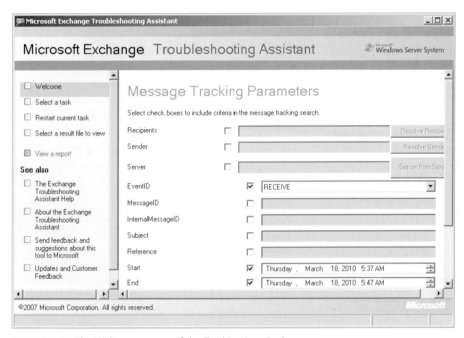

FIGURE 10-34 The Welcome screen of the Tracking Log Explorer

You can use the EMS to locate all messages with a RECEIVE EventID (there are likely to be a lot of them, so you would probably specify other parameters, such as Start, End, and Sender). The command to access the same messages as would be listed by the settings displayed in Figure 10-34 is as follows:

```
Get-MessageTrackingLog -EventID RECEIVE -Start 3/18/2010 5:37:00 AM -End 3/18/2010
5:47:00 AM
```

When you have specified all your search parameters on the Welcome screen, you click Next. An Executing Message Tracking Request screen appears, followed by a Message Tracking Results screen. If you want to repeat the request but change the search parameters, you can click Restart Current Task on the left pane, respecify your settings, and repeat the task. If the request highlights message tracking problems, you can select a symptom and obtain further information.

When the Tracking Log Explorer successfully completes a tracking request, a result file is generated. You can view the results of previous tracking requests by clicking Select A Result File To View on the left pane. This aborts any tasks currently running (you receive a warning and click OK) and accesses the Select A Result File To View screen, shown in Figure 10-35.

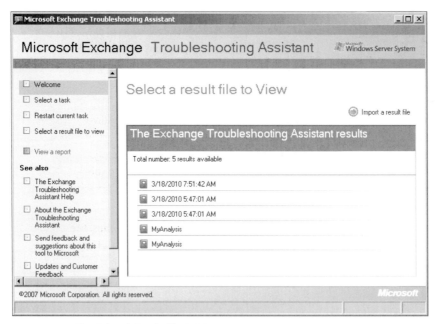

FIGURE 10-35 The Select A Result File To View screen

You can then double-click a report and either export it to a file for further analysis by reporting software or click View Results. The View Results screen lets you view List Reports, Tree Reports, or Other Reports. A Tree Report is illustrated in Figure 10-36. You can export the report, print it, or find a text string in the report.

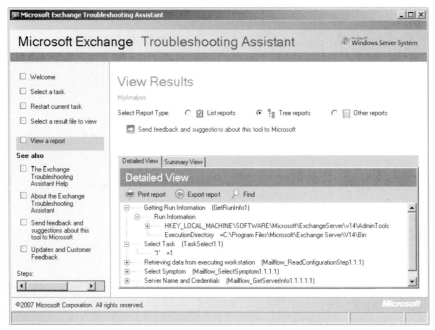

FIGURE 10-36 A Tree Report

EXERCISE Generating a Health Scan Report

This exercise assumes that you have already opened ExBPA and have selected not to check for updates and not to join the Customer Experience Improvement Program. The tool will then open at the Welcome screen. If you have never opened the tool, configure these settings first and then click Go To The Welcome Screen. If you have configured the tool differently and it starts to check for updates, cancel this action and go to the Welcome screen.

1. Log on to the Exchange Server 2010 server VAN-EX1 as Kim Akers.

2. Open the EMC and select Toolbox.

3. Click Best Practices Analyzer and then click Open Tool.

4. On the Welcome screen (shown previously in Figure 10-17), click Select Options For A New Scan.

5. In the Connect To Active Directory screen, shown in Figure 10-37, ensure that the Active Directory Server is VAN-DC1 and then click Connect To The Active Directory Server.

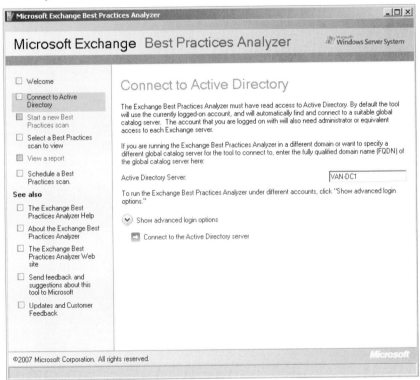

FIGURE 10-37 Specifying an Active Directory server

6. On the Start A New Best Practices scan screen, specify VAN-EX1HealthScan as the identifying label, ensure that the VAN-EX1 server is the only server selected, select Health Scan, and ensure that the Performance Baseline [2 Hours] check box is not selected. Do not change the Select The Speed Of The Network To Judge The Estimated Time Value setting. Your screen should look similar to Figure 10-38.

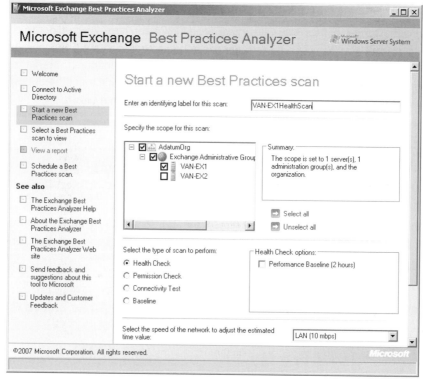

FIGURE 10-38 Specifying an ExBPA health scan

7. Click Start Scanning.

8. When the scan completes, click View A Report Of This Best Practices Scan.

9. On the View Best Practices Report page, select List Reports and look in turn at the Critical Issues, All Issues, Non-Default Settings, Recent Changes, and Informational Items tabs. Note that depending on previous configuration (such as a decision to hide certain items), the Critical Issues tab might not be displayed. Figure 10-39 shows the Recent Changes tab. Your report might contain other items.

10. Click the All Issues tab. Select any issue and then click Tell Me More About This Setting.

11. Read the resulting Help screen and then close it.

12. Select Tree Reports and look in turn at the Detailed Review and Summary Review tabs. Figure 10-40 shows the Detailed Review tab.

13. Select Other Reports and view the Run-Time Log.

14. Return to the All Issues tab in List Reports.

15. Click Export Report.

16. Identify the path to saved files, for example, C:\Users\Kim Akers.ADATUM\AppData\ Roaming\Microsoft\ExBPA.

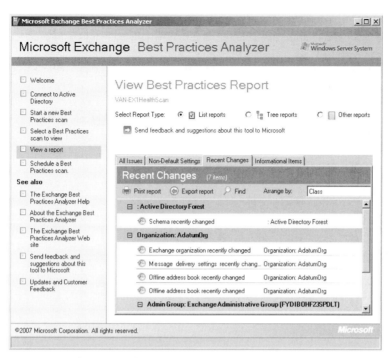

FIGURE 10-39 The Recent Changes tab in the List Report in an ExBPA health scan

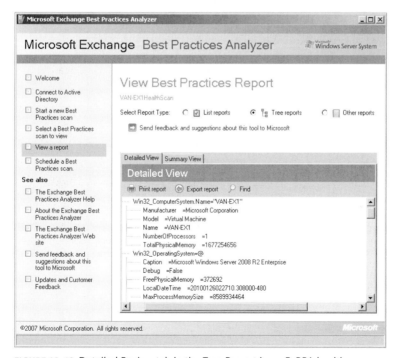

FIGURE 10-40 Detailed Review tab in the Tree Report in an ExBPA health scan

17. In the Export Report dialog box, click the report identified by ExBPA.VAN-EX1HealthScan and change the Save As Type to HTML, as shown in Figure 10-41.

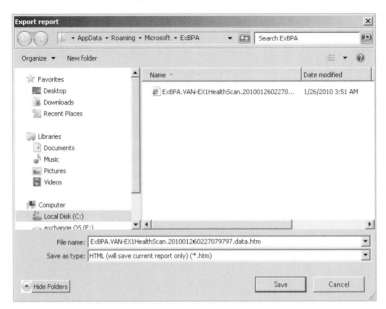

FIGURE 10-41 Specifying the report to export and the file type

18. Click Save.

19. Browse to the ExBPA folder you identified earlier. This contains files such as those shown in Figure 10-42. Identify the HTML file that starts with ExBPA.VAN-EX1HealthReport. Double-click this file to open it.

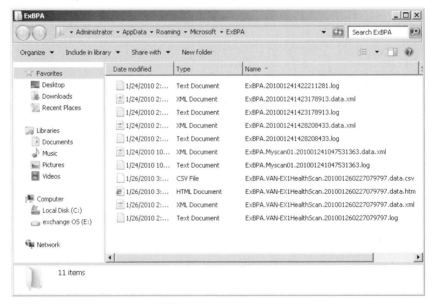

FIGURE 10-42 Files in the ExBPA folder

20. Figure 10-43 shows the file you created opened with Microsoft Internet Explorer. Optionally, if you have a spreadsheet package installed that can read CSV files (for example, Microsoft Excel), you can save the file in CSV format and use that application to open it. If you have a third-party XML Reader installed, you can save the file in XML format and use that application to open it. Although you can open both CSV and XML files in Microsoft Notepad, the result is less informative.

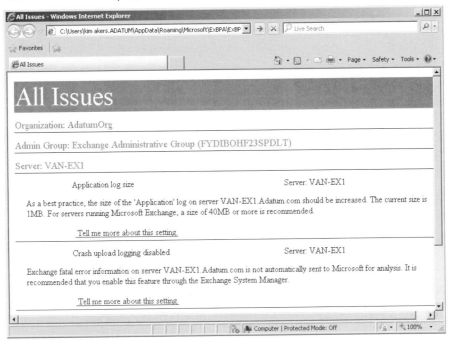

FIGURE 10-43 ExBPA health scan report opened in Internet Explorer

PRACTICE   Configuring Protocol and Agent Logging

In this practice, you will configure protocol logging for both Send and Receive connectors. You will amend the EdgeTransport.exe.config file to configure agent logging.

EXERCISE 1   Configuring Send Connector Protocol Logging

In this exercise, you will set the maximum size of each Send connector protocol log file on a Hub Transport server to 20 MB, the maximum age of the Send connector protocol log files to 35 days, and the maximum size of the Send connector protocol log directory to 350 MB.

1. If necessary, log on to the VAN-EX1 Hub Transport server with the Kim Akers account.
2. Open the EMS.
3. Enter the following command:

   ```
   Set-TransportServer –Identity VAN-EX1 –SendProtocolLogMaxFileSize 20MB
   ```

4. Enter the following command:

   ```
   Set-TransportServer –Identity VAN-EX1 –SendProtocolLogMaxAge 35.00:00:00
   ```

5. Enter the following command:

```
Set-TransportServer -Identity VAN-EX1 -SendProtocolLogMaxDirectorySize 350MB
```

Figure 10-44 shows these commands.

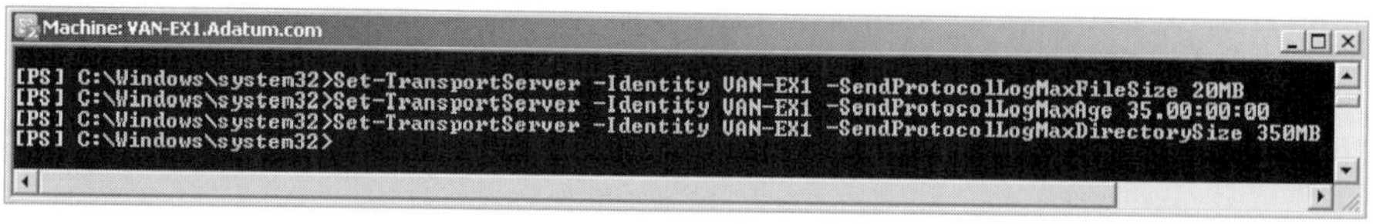

FIGURE 10-44 Configuring protocol logs for a Send connector

EXERCISE 2 Configuring Receive Connector Protocol Logging

In this exercise, you will set the maximum size of each Receive connector protocol log file on a Hub Transport server to 10 MB, the maximum age of the Receive connector protocol log files to 25 days, and the maximum size of the Receive connector protocol log directory to 200 MB.

1. If necessary, log on to the VAN-EX1 Hub Transport server with the Kim Akers account.
2. Open the EMS.
3. Enter the following command:

```
Set-TransportServer -Identity VAN-EX1 -ReceiveProtocolLogMaxFileSize 10MB
```

4. Enter the following command:

```
Set-TransportServer -Identity VAN-EX1 -ReceiveProtocolLogMaxAge 25.00:00:00
```

5. Enter the following command:

```
Set-TransportServer -Identity VAN-EX1 -ReceiveProtocolLogMaxDirectorySize 200MB
```

Figure 10-45 shows these commands.

FIGURE 10-45 Configuring protocol logs for a Receive connector

EXERCISE 3 Configuring Agent Logging

In this exercise, you will ensure that agent logging is enabled and then add keys to the EdgeTransport.exe.config file that enable you to set the maximum size of each agent log file on a Hub Transport server to 20 MB, the maximum age of the agent log files to 35 days, and the maximum size of the agent log directory to 350 MB.

1. If necessary, log on to the VAN-EX1 Hub Transport server with the Kim Akers account.
2. Navigate to the C:\Program Files\Microsoft\Exchange Server\V14\Bin directory.
3. Use Microsoft Notepad to open the EdgeTransport.exe.config file.

4. Locate the AgentLogEnabled key directly under <appsettings> and ensure that this is set to "true."

5. Add the following lines to the EdgeTransport.exe.config file directly under the AgentLogEnabled key:

   <add key="AgentLogMaxDirectorySize" value="350MB" />

   <add key="AgentLogMaxFileSize" value="20MB" />

   <add key="AgentLogMaxAge" value="35.00:00:00" />

   Figure 10-46 shows the amended file.

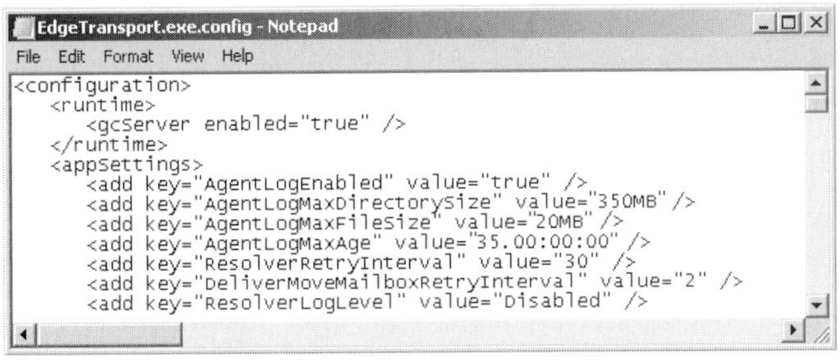

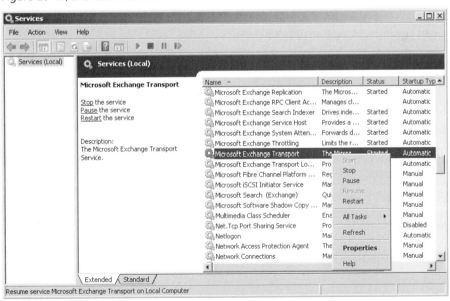

FIGURE 10-46 Adding keys to the EdgeTransport.exe.config file

6. Open the Services Console on VAN-EX1.

7. Locate the Microsoft Exchange Transport service. Right-click this service, as shown in Figure 10-47, and click Restart.

FIGURE 10-47 Restarting the Microsoft Exchange Transport service

8. When the service restarts, close the Services Console.

Chapter Review

To further practice and reinforce the skills you learned in this chapter, you can perform the following tasks:

- Review the chapter summary.
- Review the list of key terms introduced in this chapter.
- Complete the case scenarios. These scenarios set up real-world situations involving the topics of this chapter and ask you to create a solution.
- Complete the suggested practices.
- Take a practice test.

Chapter Summary

- You can use EMS commands and PowerShell functions to generate Exchange statistics reports and save your data in CSV files for use by report generation software.
- The EMC provides a number of troubleshooting and report generation tools, such as the Mail Flow Troubleshooter and the ExBPA.
- Exchange Server 2010 provides a range of log file types, such as Connectivity logs, Protocol logs, the Message Tracking log, Agent logs, Routing table log, and Administrator Audit logs, that enable you to track activity on your servers and generate reports. Transaction logs are central to the operation of Exchange databases. You can manage logging by configuring various log parameters.
- The EMC provides a number of tools for viewing log files, such as the Tracking Log Explorer and the Routing Log Viewer. You can also use EMS cmdlets to view the information in log files.

Key Terms

Do you know what these key terms mean?

- Administrator Audit logs
- Agent logs
- Connectivity logs
- Exchange Best Practices Analyzer (ExBPA)
- Exchange Server Mail Flow Troubleshooter
- Message Tracking logs
- Protocol logs
- Tracking Log Explorer

Case Scenarios

In the following case scenarios, you will apply what you have learned about planning server installs and upgrades. You can find answers to these questions in the "Answers" section at the end of this book.

Case Scenario 1: Obtaining a Server Health Report and Detecting Suboptimal Settings

You are a senior Exchange administrator at Trey Research. You suspect that other administrators in your team have configure suboptimal settings on Trey's Exchange Server 2010 servers and Windows Server 2008 R2 domain controllers. You need to investigate and obtain health checks for all Exchange servers in the organization. Answer the following questions:

1. What tool can you use to examine your domain controllers and Exchange Server 2010 servers?
2. What type of information does this tool give you?
3. Do you need to examine each server separately?
4. What types of scan are available?
5. What report formats are available?

Case Scenario 2: Auditing Protocol Log Configuration

You are a senior Exchange administrator at NorthWind Traders. You know that members of your team are reconfiguring protocol logging on NorthWind Traders' Edge Transport and Hub Transport servers. You want to audit this activity. Answer the following questions:

1. What procedure do you use to do this?
2. What EMS cmdlets do you need to audit?
3. What parameters do you need to audit?
4. What EMS commands do you enter to set this up?

Suggested Practices

To help you master the examination objectives presented in this chapter, complete the following tasks.

Investigate the EMS Commands That Access Statistics

- **Practice 1** Investigate the *Get-MailboxStatistics* and *Get-MailboxFolderStatistics* cmdlets and the parameters they support. Note that investigating the first of these cmdlets is also a suggested practice in Chapter 9. Revisit the cmdlet. It is important.

Investigate the PowerShell Commands and Clauses That Enable You to Format Statistical Reports

- **Practice 1**   Investigate *FL*, *FT*, *Export-CSV*, *Sort-Object*, *Select-Object*, and the Where clause. Learn the parameters and switches they support. Determine the effect of combining more than one of these commands.

Further Investigate the ExBPA

- **Practice 1**   This is a powerful and significant tool. You will use it in your job, and the examination will probably test your knowledge of the facilities it offers.

Look at Log Files

- **Practice 1**   This chapter gives you the location of various log files. Look at the content of these files. You may find it useful to install software, such as Microsoft Office Excel, that reads CSV files. You may also get more information by examining the log files on a production system. The log files on your isolated test network are likely to contain very little information.

Install or Access an Edge Transport Server (Optional)

- **Practice 1**   The examples in this chapter use a Hub Transport server (or a Mailbox server). Running the same EMS commands or graphics tools on an Edge Transport server can generate results that look different (although they are basically the same). Optionally, create a virtual machine that runs the Edge Transport server role, or if you have access to a production network that supports an Edge Transport server, look at the output of the various tools and commands on it.

Take a Practice Test

The practice tests on this book's companion CD offer many options. For example, you can test yourself on just one exam objective, or you can test yourself on all the 70-662 certification exam content. You can set up the test so that it closely simulates the experience of taking a certification exam, or you can set it up in study mode so that you can look at the correct answers and explanations after you answer each question.

> **MORE INFO**   **PRACTICE TESTS**
>
> For details about all the practice test options available, see the "How to Use the Practice Tests" section in this book's Introduction.

CHAPTER 11

Managing Records and Compliance

Organizational email contains messages that are important from a business, legal, or regulatory perspective. Such messages may need to be retained for a certain period, depending on organizational policy or for legal reasons. Other email messages may not have a retention value beyond a limited period, if at all. In this chapter, you will learn how to manage messages and control their retention behavior.

Organizations frequently need to produce evidence during litigation or to provide documentation to prove that they are complying with regulations. Checks must also be in place to ensure that an organization is complying with its own internal regulations and written company policy. An organization is implementing compliance when it plans its information technology infrastructure and, in particular, its email infrastructure to supply the required documentation on demand. This chapter considers the various features in Exchange Server 2010 that can be configured for compliance and help you respond to current or future discovery requirements.

Exam objectives in this chapter:

- Configure records management.
- Configure compliance.

Lessons in this chapter:

Before You Begin

In order to complete the exercises in the practice session in this chapter, you need to have done the following:

- Installed the Windows Server 2008 R2 domain controller VAN-DC1 and the Windows Exchange 2010 Enterprise Mailbox, Hub Transport, and Client Access server VAN-EX1 as described in the Appendix, "Setup Instructions for Exchange Server 2010."

- Created the Kim Akers account with the password *Pa$$w0rd* in the Adatum.com domain. This account should be placed in the Domain Admins security group and be a member of the Organization Management role group.

- Created the Don Hall account with the password *Pa$$w0rd* in the Adatum.com domain. This account should be placed in the Backup Operators security group (so that it can be used to log on to the domain controller) and should be in the Marketing organizational unit (OU).

- Created mailboxes for Kim Akers and Don Hall, accepting the default email address format for the email addresses.

REAL WORLD

Ian McLean

Compliance is one of these issues that everyone thinks is important to administrators and nobody else. It's a bit like parking an automobile. Everyone thinks the rules are merely unnecessary fuss—until they find a vehicle blocking emergency access when they fall ill in a shopping mall.

Nobody wants restrictions on their email. They want to send what they want to whomever they want. Of course, they will act responsibly. They would never dream of sending confidential company information to an external recipient. Well, clicking Reply All was an accident, wasn't it? How were they to know that the innocent-looking distribution list they sent to contained members of an organization that most definitely should not have the information?

Compliance to company policy, industry rules, and national and international laws and regulations is indeed a fussy business. I am not a lawyer, much less an international lawyer, and I want an email system that automatically prevents me from accidentally sending confidential information to where it should not go. Not only that—I want what I send and receive recorded so that I can prove absolutely that whoever leaked that important piece of information, it wasn't me.

Administration (forgive me if I've said this before) involves people skills as much as technical skills. You can configure the various aspects of compliance described in this chapter. You can and should take legal advice on what you can and cannot do. You still need to explain to the irate senior executive why his or her email bounced. To have a good explanation, you need to know not only how to configure compliance and what your company's policies are but also why a particular configuration was essential—even when applied to your chief executive officer.

Lesson 1: Managing Records

Typically, email messages related to business strategy, transactions, product development, or customer interactions need to be retained, whereas messages such as newsletter subscriptions or personal email likely do not. In this lesson, you will look at two methods of managing messaging records and implementing message retention—retention tags and policies and managed folders—that together make up Message Records Management (MRM).

> **After this lesson, you will be able to:**
> - Create and configure retention tags of the three available types.
> - Create and configure retention policies that group retention tags.
> - Assign retention policies to user mailboxes.
> - Apply retention hold to a user mailbox.
> - Create and configure managed folders.
> - Create and configure managed folder policies.
> - Apply managed folder policies to user mailboxes.
>
> **Estimated lesson time: 45 minutes**

Using MRM

MRM helps you ensure that your Exchange Server 2010 organization retains the messages needed to comply with company policy, government regulations, or legal needs and that content that has no legal or business value is discarded. MRM accomplishes this by using retention policies or managed folders. Chapter 2, "Exchange Databases and Address Lists," briefly introduced retention policies and retention tags.

Retention policies use retention tags to apply retention settings. Later in this lesson, you will see how to create retention tags and link them to a retention policy. Mailboxes that have a retention policy applied to them are processed by the Managed Folder Assistant, which runs when scheduled and provisions retention tags in mailboxes. This utility is also described in detail later in this lesson.

Managed folders were introduced in Exchange Server 2007 and are also available in Exchange 2010. You can apply managed content settings to managed folders. This lesson describes how you create managed folders and link them to a managed folder mailbox policy. Mailboxes that have managed folder mailbox policies applied are also processed by the Managed Folder Assistant.

When a message reaches its retention age, the retention action is taken as specified by the retention tag or the managed content settings in a managed folder. For example, a message could be moved to the Deleted Items folder, moved to the Recoverable Items folder, or permanently deleted. If you use retention tags, you can specify the additional option of moving the message to the user's archive mailbox (if it exists). Managed content settings for managed folders provide the additional option of moving a message to a managed custom folder.

Comparing Retention Tags and Managed Folders

You can use managed folders to enforce basic MRM policies on default folders and on the entire mailbox. If you take this approach, users need to participate in the process of classifying messages based on their nature and retention value.

Alternatively, you can use retention tags to apply default retention settings to default folders, such as the Inbox folder, and apply a default policy tag (DPT) to the entire mailbox. DPT retention settings are then applied to untagged items that may reside in folders without a retention tag, such as custom folders created by the user. Users are not required to store messages in folders based on the folder's retention settings. They can apply any personal tag to custom folders and also explicitly apply a different tag to individual messages.

Configuring Retention Tags and Retention Policies

You can formulate your organization's MRM policies to specify the retention period for different classes of email messages by creating and configuring retention tags and retention policies. Typically you would assign a retention policy tag (RPT). An RPT is a retention tag applied to default folders, such as Inbox and Deleted Items. You would apply a DPT to specific mailboxes to manage the retention of all untagged items. A DPT is a retention tag that applies to all items in a mailbox that do not already have a retention tag applied. You can apply only one DPT in a retention policy. Optionally, you would assign personal tags (or allow users to assign them in Outlook or Outlook Web App [OWA]). A personal tag is a retention tag available to OWA and Outlook 2010 users for applying retention settings to custom folders and to individual items such as email messages.

You use retention tags to apply retention settings to folders and individual items, such as messages, notes, and contacts. These settings specify how long a message remains in a mailbox and the action to be taken when the message reaches the specified retention age. Retention tags allow users to tag mailbox folders and individual items for retention. You can create three types of retention tags:

- DPTs
- RPTs
- Personal tags

DPTs apply retention settings to untagged mailbox items that do not already have a retention tag applied, either by inheritance from the folder in which they are located or specified by the user. A retention policy cannot contain more than one DPT.

RPTs apply retention settings to default folders, such as Inbox, Deleted Items, and Sent Items. Mailbox items in a default folder that have an RPT applied inherit the folder's tag. Users cannot apply a different tag to a default folder, but they can apply a different tag to the individual items within a default folder. You cannot include more than one RPT for the same default folder type in a single retention policy. For example, if a retention policy has an Inbox tag, you cannot add another RPT of type Inbox to that retention policy.

The folders to which you can apply retention tabs were listed in Chapter 2, but this information is repeated here for convenience. You can create RPTs for the following default folders:

- Deleted Items
- Drafts
- Inbox
- Junk E-mail
- Outbox
- Sent Items
- RSS Feeds
- Sync Issues
- Conversation History

EXAM TIP

Exchange Server 2010 does not support RPTs for the Calendar, Contacts, Journal, Notes, and Tasks default folders.

Personal tags are available to Outlook 2010 and OWA users as part of their retention policies. Users can apply personal tags to folders they create or to individual items, even if those items already have a different tag applied. You see how to create a personal tag later in this lesson.

Configuring Retention Age Limit Actions

You can select from one of the following actions to specify what retention action should apply to a mailbox item when it reaches its retention age:

- **MoveToArchive** Messages are moved to a folder in the archive mailbox that has the same name as the source folder in the user's primary mailbox. This allows users to more easily find messages in their archive mailbox.

- **MoveToDeletedItems** This emulates the behavior experienced by users when they delete a message. Items in the Deleted Items folder can be moved back to the Inbox or any other mailbox folder.

- **DeleteAndAllowRecovery** This emulates the behavior when the Deleted Items folder is emptied or the user hard-deletes a message. If deleted item retention is configured for the mailbox database or the user, messages move to the Recoverable Items folder (or dumpster).

- **PermanentlyDelete** This action permanently purges a message from the mailbox.
- **MarkAsPastRetentionLimit** This action marks a message as past its retention limit. Outlook 2010 and Office Outlook 2007 clients use strikethrough text when displaying messages that are past their retention limit.

Creating and Configuring Retention Tags

You can use the Exchange Management Shell (EMS) but not the Exchange Management Console (EMC) to create and modify RPTs, DPTs, and personal tags. For example, the following command creates an RPT for the default folder Deleted Items. When the tag is applied to a mailbox, items in the Deleted Items folder are permanently deleted in 45 days:

```
New-RetentionPolicyTag "Tag-EXAMPLE-DeletedItems" -Type "DeletedItems" -Comment
"Deleted Items purged in 45 days" -RetentionEnabled $true -AgeLimitForRetention
45 -RetentionAction PermanentlyDelete
```

Figure 11-1 shows some of the output from this command.

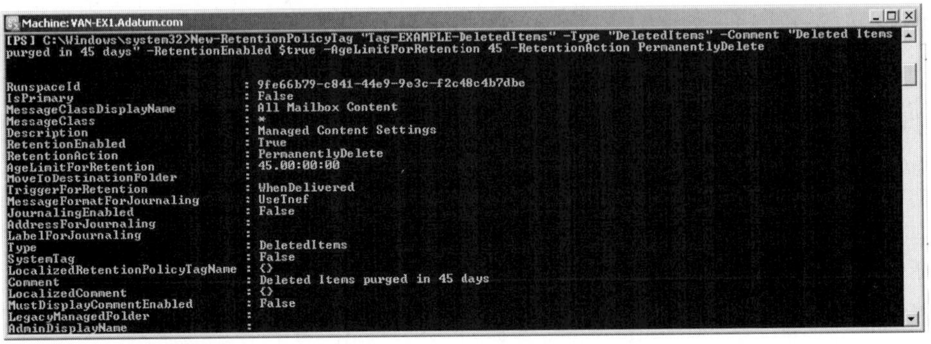

FIGURE 11-1 Creating an RPT

> **NOTE** **THE MESSAGECLASS PARAMETER AND THE ISPRIMARY PARAMETER**
>
> The *New-RetentionPolicyTag* cmdlet supports the MessageClass parameter. However, in Windows Exchange Server 2010, only the default value of this parameter (*) is supported. The IsPrimary parameter specifies that the tag should be displayed as the primary Default Tag in Microsoft Outlook 2010. A tag designated as primary should be of type All. A retention policy cannot have more than one tag set as primary.

✔ **Quick Check**
- What types of retention tags can you create?

Quick Check Answer
- DPTs, RPTs, and personal tags.

The following command creates a DPT. When the tag is applied to a mailbox, items without an inherited or explicitly applied retention tag are moved to the Deleted Items folder after 180 days:

```
New-RetentionPolicyTag "Tag-EXAMPLE-Default" -Type All -Comment "Items
without a retention tag are deleted after 180 days." -RetentionEnabled $true
-AgeLimitForRetention 180 -RetentionAction MoveToDeletedItems
```

Figure 11-2 shows some of the output from this command.

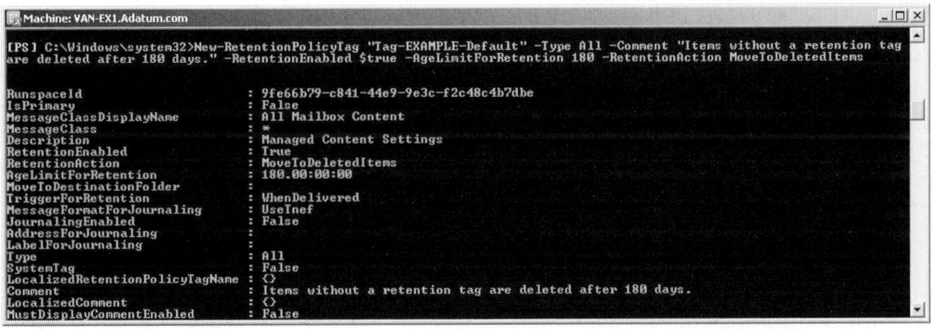

FIGURE 11-2 Creating a DPT

The following command creates a personal tag named *Tag-PersonalArchive*. Items to which the tag is applied are moved to the personal archive after 365 days:

```
New-RetentionPolicyTag "Tag-PersonalArchive" -Type Personal -Comment "Tagged messages
are moved to the archive after 365 days." -RetentionEnabled $true -AgeLimitForRetention
365 -RetentionAction MoveToArchive
```

The following command amends the RPT *Tag-EXAMPLE-DeletedItems* so that items in the Deleted Items folder are permanently deleted after 30 days:

```
Set-RetentionPolicyTag "Tag-EXAMPLE-DeletedItems" -AgeLimitForRetention 30
```

> **MORE INFO** *NEW-RETENTIONPOLICYTAG* AND *SET-RETENTIONPOLICYTAG*
>
> For more information about the *New-RetentionPolicyTag* cmdlet, see *http://technet .microsoft.com/en-us/library/dd335226.aspx*. For more information about the *Set-RetentionPolicyTag* cmdlet, see *http://technet.microsoft.com/en-us/library/ dd298042.aspx*.

> **MORE INFO** **RETENTION TAGS**
>
> For more information about retention tags, including an informative diagrammatic illustration of how they work, see *http://technet.microsoft.com/en-us/library/ dd297955.aspx*.

Creating a Retention Policy and Applying It to Mailboxes

You can use retention policies to group one or more retention tags and apply them to mailboxes. Retention tags can be linked to or unlinked from a retention policy at any time, and a mailbox cannot have more than one retention policy.

A retention policy can support one or more RPTs, one DPT of type All, and any number of personal tags. Note that if you configure a retention policy with no retention tags linked to it, this may result in mailbox items that never expire.

You create a retention policy in the EMS by entering a command with the following syntax:

```
New-RetentionPolicy -Name <String> [-Confirm [<SwitchParameter>]] [-DomainController
<Fqdn>] [-Organization <OrganizationIdParameter>] [-RetentionPolicyTagLinks
<RetentionPolicyTagIdParameter[]>] [-WhatIf [<SwitchParameter>]]
```

For example, the following command creates a retention policy called *Accounting* that uses the RPT *Tag-EXAMPLE-DeletedItems*:

```
New-RetentionPolicy -Name "Accounting" -RetentionPolicyTagLinks "Tag-EXAMPLE-
DeletedItems"
```

Figure 11-3 shows the output from this command.

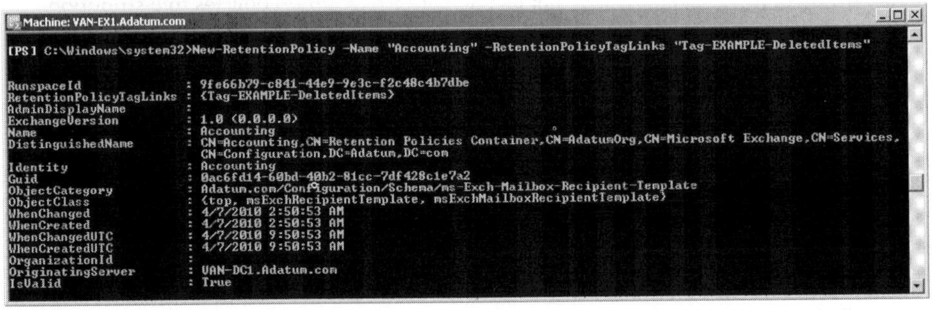

FIGURE 11-3 Creating a retention policy

You can use a retention policy to group one or more retention tags and assign them to mailboxes and thus enforce message retention settings. A mailbox cannot have more than one retention policy assigned to it at any one time. If you assign a retention policy to an individual mailbox (or to a mailbox that is in a distribution group) that already has a policy assigned, the new policy assignment will overwrite the existing policy assignment. You can use the EMS but not the EMC to assign a retention policy to a mailbox or a distribution group. For example, the following command assigns the retention policy Accounting to the Don Hall mailbox:

```
Set-Mailbox "Don Hall" -RetentionPolicy "Accounting"
```

Figure 11-4 shows the output from this command. Note that you receive a warning that this operation is not supported on client computers running Microsoft Office Outlook 2007 or earlier and that you need to confirm that you want the command to complete.

FIGURE 11-4 Applying a retention policy to a mailbox

If you assign a retention policy to a distribution group, the policy is assigned to all mailboxes in the group. Any mailbox that previously had a different policy assigned to it would have its policy assignment overwritten. The following command assigns the Retention policy Accounting to members of the distribution group Accountants:

```
Get-DistributionGroupMember -Identity "Accountants" | Set-Mailbox -RetentionPolicy
"Accounting"
```

> **NOTE ADDING USERS TO OR REMOVING THEM FROM A DISTRIBUTION GROUP**
>
> When users are added to or removed from a distribution group, their mailbox retention policy is not automatically updated. To ensure that a policy is applied to new distribution group members, you need to rerun the command that applies the policy. Microsoft recommends that you schedule commands that allocate retention policies to distribution groups so that they run automatically at regular intervals.

> **MORE INFO GET-DISTRIBUTIONGROUPMEMBER AND SET-MAILBOX**
>
> For more information about the *Get-DistributionGroupMember* cmdlet, see *http://technet .microsoft.com/en-us/library/aa996367.aspx*. For more information about the *Set-Mailbox* cmdlet, see *http://technet.microsoft.com/en-us/library/bb123981.aspx*.

The command to replace a current retention policy with a new retention policy is relatively complex when compared to the commands that apply a retention policy to a mailbox or distribution group. You need to use the *Get-RetentionPolicy* cmdlet to obtain details of the current policy and store these in a variable. You then filter using this variable to obtain the mailboxes that have the current retention policy applied to them and apply the new policy to each of these mailboxes. The following command applies the new retention policy New-Retention-Policy to all mailboxes that currently have the policy Old-Retention-Policy applied to them:

```
$OldPolicy={Get-RetentionPolicy "Old-Retention-Policy"}.distinguishedName | Get-
Mailbox -Filter {RetentionPolicy -eq $OldPolicy} -Resultsize Unlimited | Set-Mailbox
-RetentionPolicy "New-Retention-Policy"
```

> **MORE INFO GET-RETENTIONPOLICY AND GET-MAILBOX**
>
> For more information about the *Get-RetentionPolicy* cmdlet, see *http://technet.microsoft .com/en-us/library/dd298086.aspx*. For more information about the *Get-Mailbox* cmdlet, see *http://technet.microsoft.com/en-us/library/bb123685.aspx*.

Quick Check

- Which EMS cmdlet would you use to assign a retention policy to an individual user mailbox?

Quick Check Answer

- *Set-Mailbox*

Starting, Stopping, and Scheduling the Managed Folder Assistant

The Managed Folder Assistant is a Mailbox Assistant utility that applies the message retention settings you configure using retention policies or managed folder mailbox policies. If a mailbox uses a managed folder mailbox policy, the Managed Folder Assistant also creates any managed folders required and applies managed content settings to them. When the Managed Folder Assistant applies retention policies and managed folder mailbox policies to user mailboxes it processes mailboxes that have an applied retention policy or a managed folder mailbox policy. It applies the retention tags included in the policy to default folders and the entire mailbox. Any personal tags included in the policy are provisioned and become available to users in Microsoft Outlook 2010 and Microsoft Office OWA.

Messages that have some retention value are retained, although users can still delete or remove messages from their mailboxes. If your organization requires that messages be retained outside a user's mailbox for long-term storage, you should consider implementing journaling as described in Lesson 2 of this chapter, "Implementing Compliance."

The Managed Folder Assistant applies a retention policy by inspecting items in the mailbox and determining whether they are subject to retention. It then stamps items with the appropriate retention tags and takes the specified retention action on items that are past their retention age. It does not take any action on messages that are not subject to retention. When an item is not subject to retention, its retention tag's RetentionEnabled property is set to $false. You can manually set this property to $false to temporarily suspend items with a particular tag from being processed.

By default, the Managed Folder Assistant runs daily from 1:00 AM until 5:00 AM. However, it stops as soon as all mailboxes are processed rather than running continuously until the end of the scheduled period. You can schedule the assistant to run at a time when the Mailbox server is relatively idle or not under a heavy load. If you decide to reschedule the Managed Folder Assistant, you need to take into account other processes that compete for Mailbox server resources, such as offline defragmentation of the mailbox database and antivirus scans.

You can use either the EMC or the EMS to schedule the Managed Folder Assistant. If you use the EMC, the procedure is as follows:

1. Open the EMC and expand the tree in the Console pane.

2. Under Server Configuration, click Mailbox.

3. In the Result pane, right-click the Mailbox server for which you want to schedule the Managed Folder Assistant and click Properties.

4. Click the Messaging Records Management tab in the Properties dialog box.

5. In the Schedule The Managed Folder Assistant box, select Use Custom Schedule. Click Customize.

6. In the Select Schedule dialog box, shown in Figure 11-5, select the times and days during which you want the Managed Folder Assistant to run.

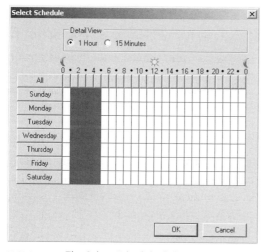

FIGURE 11-5 The Select Schedule dialog box

7. Click OK to close the Select Schedule dialog box. Click OK again to close the Properties dialog box.

You can use the EMS to schedule the Managed Folder Assistant or to start it immediately. For example, the following command sets the Managed Folder Assistant schedule on Mailbox server VAN-EX1 to start running at 15:00 (3:00 PM) on a Sunday and continue running until all mailboxes are processed or until 13:00 (1:00 PM) on the following Sunday, whichever comes first:

```
Set-MailboxServer -Identity VAN-EX1 -ManagedFolderAssistantSchedule "Sun.15:00
-Sun.13:00"
```

When you manually start the Managed Folder Assistant, it continues running until all mailboxes on the Mailbox server are processed or until the Managed Folder assistant is stopped manually. The following commands start and stop the Managed Folder Assistant, respectively:

```
Start-ManagedFolderAssistant
Stop-ManagedFolderAssistant
```

When you stop the Managed Folder Assistant manually, you are prompted for confirmation.

> **MORE INFO**   *SET-MAILBOXSERVER, START-MANAGEDFOLDERASSISTANT, AND STOP-MANAGEDFOLDERASSISTANT*
>
> For more information about the *Set-MailboxServer* cmdlet, see *http://technet.microsoft .com/en-us/library/aa998651.aspx*. For more information about the *Start-ManagedFolderAssistant* cmdlet, see *http://technet.microsoft.com/en-us/library/ aa998864.aspx*. For more information about the *Stop-ManagedFolderAssistant* cmdlet, see *http://technet.microsoft.com/en-us/library/bb123532.aspx*.

> **NOTE**   **MOVING ITEMS BETWEEN FOLDERS**
>
> A mailbox item moved from one folder to another inherits any tags applied to the folder to which it is moved. If you move an item to a folder that has no tag assigned, the DPT is applied to it. If the item has a tag explicitly assigned to it, the assigned tag always takes precedence over any folder-level tags or the default tag.

Removing or Deleting a Retention Tag from a Retention Policy

When you remove a retention tag from the retention policy applied to a mailbox, the tag is no longer available to the user and cannot be applied to items in the mailbox. Existing items that have been stamped with the tag continue to be processed by the Managed Folder Assistant, and any retention action specified in the tag is applied to those messages. Any existing mailbox items with the tag applied will continue to expire based on the tag's settings.

However, if you use the *Remove-RetentionPolicyTag* cmdlet to delete the tag, the tag definition stored in Active Directory is removed. The next time the Managed Folder Assistant runs, it processes all items that have the removed tag applied and restamps them.

If you disable retention for a retention tag, the Managed Folder Assistant ignores items that have that tag applied. Items that have a retention tag for which retention is disabled never expire. Because these items are still considered tagged items, the DPT does not apply to them. For example, if you want to troubleshoot retention tag settings, you can temporarily disable a retention tag to stop the Managed Folder Assistant from processing messages with that tag.

> **MORE INFO**   *REMOVE-RETENTIONPOLICYTAG*
>
> For more information about the *Remove-RetentionPolicyTag* cmdlet, see *http://technet .microsoft.com/en-us/library/dd335092.aspx*.

Quick Check

- What EMS command manually stops the Managed Folder Assistant?

Quick Check Answer

- *Stop-ManagedFolderAssistant*

Placing a Mailbox on Retention Hold

When users are temporarily out of the office and do not have access to email, you can apply retention to new messages. Depending on the retention policy, messages may be deleted or moved to a user's personal archive, but you can temporarily suspend such retention policies for a specified period by placing the mailbox on retention hold. When you place a mailbox on retention hold, you can specify a retention comment that informs the mailbox user (or another user authorized to access the mailbox) about the retention hold, including when the hold is scheduled to begin and end. Retention comments are displayed in supported Outlook clients. You can also localize the retention hold comment in the user's preferred language.

During long absences from work, users may accrue a large amount of email. Depending on the volume of email and the length of absence, it may take these users several weeks to sort through their messages. In such cases, consider the additional time it may take the users to catch up on their mail before removing mailboxes from retention hold. Also, placing a mailbox on retention hold does not affect how mailbox storage quotas are processed. Depending on the mailbox usage and applicable mailbox quotas, you should consider temporarily increasing the mailbox storage quota for users when they are on vacation or do not have access to email for an extended period.

> **MORE INFO** **CONFIGURING STORAGE QUOTAS**
>
> For more information about configuring mailbox storage quotas, see *http://technet .microsoft.com/en-us/library/aa998353.aspx*.

You can use the EMC or the EMS to place a mailbox on retention hold regardless of whether the mailbox has a retention policy or a managed folder mailbox policy applied to it.

To use the EMC, you access the Properties dialog box of the relevant mailbox and then access the Message Records Management dialog box from the Mailbox Settings tab. You can then enable retention hold and configure start and stop dates and times.

To configure retention hold through the EMS, you use the *Set-Mailbox* cmdlet to set the RetentionHoldEnabled parameter to $true. The StartDateForRetentionHold and EndDateForRetentionHold parameters of the same cmdlet let you specify when the retention hold starts and stops. You can release a retention hold by setting the RetentionHoldEnabled parameter to $false. For example, the following command enables retention hold for the Kim Akers mailbox and specifies retention start and stop dates:

```
Set-Mailbox –Identity "Kim Akers" –RetentionHoldEnabled $true –StartDateForRetentionHold
10-1-2011 –EndDateForRetentionHold 11-3-2011
```

You use the EMC to configure a retention hold and the EMS to release that retention hold in a practice session at the end of this chapter.

> **MORE INFO** **RETENTION HOLD**
>
> For more information about how to place a mailbox on retention hold, see *http://technet .microsoft.com/en-us/library/dd335168.aspx*.

Administrating Managed Folders

You can use the Exchange Server 2010 Managed Folders MRM feature to specify retention settings for default folders such as Inbox, Deleted Items, and Sent Items. In addition, you can create custom managed folders and specify their retention settings. Your users can classify messages for retention and move these messages to appropriate managed folders based on their retention requirements. You can define two types of managed folders:

- **Managed default folders** These are managed folder objects created for default folders, such as Inbox, Deleted Items, Sent Items, and so on. When you set up Exchange Server 2010, you create a set of managed default folders that are displayed on the Managed Default Folders tab in the EMC. Optionally, you can create additional folders for different sets of users.

- **Managed custom folders** These are managed folder objects you can use to create custom folders in a user's mailbox. Managed custom folders are created under a top-level folder called Managed Folders. Each mailbox that has managed custom folders requires an Exchange Server Enterprise client access license (CAL).

> **MORE INFO** **CLIENT ACCESS LICENSING**
>
> For more information about CAL on Windows Server 2008 R2, see *http://www.microsoft .com/windowsserver2008/en/us/client-licensing.aspx*.

Managed content settings specify the retention and journaling settings for a managed folder. You can configure settings for a specific message class (for example, email messages, calendar items, and tasks) or for all message classes. You can specify multiple managed content settings for different message classes. This lets you specify different retention settings for different types of items in the same folder.

These retention settings include a message class, whether retention is enabled for the specified message class, the retention age, and a retention action. The retention age specifies the period for which a message is retained in the mailbox. The retention action specifies the action to take after the item is past its retention age. For example, you can create a managed content setting for a managed default folder that moves all items to the Recovery Items folder after 100 days.

You can select from one of the following retention actions:

- **Move to the Deleted Items folder**
- **Move to a managed custom folder you have previously created**
- **Delete and allow recovery**   This moves items to the Recoverable Items folder. Deleted items are available for recovery from this folder until the specified deleted item retention time for the mailbox database or the user mailbox elapses.
- **Permanently delete**
- **Mark as past retention limit**   This marks items as expired after they reach their retention age. Items marked as expired are displayed by using strikethrough text in Microsoft Outlook 2010 and Microsoft Office Outlook 2007.

You can also specify whether the retention age is calculated from when a message is delivered to a mailbox or from when it is moved to the folder it currently resides in. For calendar items and recurring tasks, the retention age is calculated from the end date of the item. Detailed procedures for creating managed content settings are described later in this lesson, and you configure such settings in a practice exercise later in this chapter.

> **MORE INFO**   **RETENTION AGE**
>
> For more information about how the retention age is calculated, see *http://technet* *.microsoft.com/en-us/library/bb430780.aspx*.

Creating Managed Default Folders and Managed Custom Folders

Before you can create managed content settings, you must have at least one managed default folder or one managed custom folder to which you can apply these settings. A managed default folder is a mailbox folder (such as the Inbox folder) that appears in Office Outlook 2007 and Office 2010 by default and to which MRM has been applied. A managed custom folder is a managed folder that is created by an Exchange administrator and placed in a user mailbox for MRM purposes. To use the EMC to create a managed default folder, carry out the following procedure:

1. Open the EMC and expand the Console tree.
2. Under Organization Configuration, click Mailbox.
3. In the Actions pane, click New Managed Default Folder. This starts the New Managed Default Folder Wizard.
4. On the New Managed Default Folder page, shown in Figure 11-6, complete the following fields:
   - **Name**   This is the name of the managed folder object in Active Directory and does not change the standard name of the default folder (such as Inbox) that appears in user mailboxes. This name can be up to 65 characters in length.

- **Default Folder Type**   Select the type of default folder that you want to create (for example, Inbox) from the list provided.

- **Display The Following Comment When The Folder Is Viewed In Outlook**   A typical comment might be "Messages are removed from this folder after 120 days." The maximum length of this comment is 255 characters. Note that you can use the *Set-ManagedFolder* EMS cmdlet to configure comments localized to, for example, different countries.

- **Do Not Allow Users To Minimize This Comment In Outlook**   You should select this check box to prevent Outlook users from minimizing the comment that you entered in the preceding box.

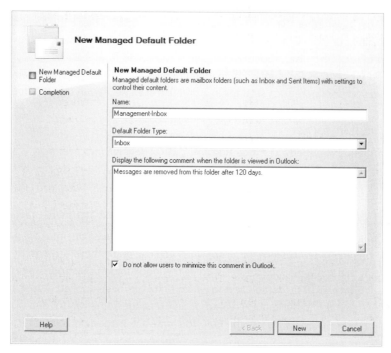

FIGURE 11-6 Completing the New Managed Default Folder page

5. Click New. On the Completion page, a status of Completed indicates that the wizard completed the task successfully. A status of Failed indicates that the task was not completed. If the task fails, review the summary for an explanation and then click Back to make any configuration changes required.

6. Click Finish.

The settings shown in Figure 11-6 create a folder of type Inbox named Management-Inbox. The comment "Messages are removed from the Inbox folder after 120 days." Is displayed on supported clients, and users are unable to minimize the comment in Outlook. Note that the retention period is determined by the settings of the default Inbox folder and cannot be configured using this procedure.

You can also use the EMS to create a managed default folder. The following command creates a managed default folder named Corporate-Inbox with the comment "Messages are removed from the Inbox folder after 120 days.":

```
New-ManagedFolder -Name "Corporate-Inbox" -DefaultFolderType Inbox -Comment "Messages
are removed from the Inbox folder after 120 days" -MustDisplayComment $true
```

Figure 11-7 shows the output from this command.

FIGURE 11-7 Creating a managed default folder using the EMS

EXAM TIP

The *New-ManagedFolder* cmdlet creates a managed folder but cannot be used to configure an existing one. You can use the *Set-ManagedFolder* cmdlet to configure an existing managed folder but not to create a new one.

The procedure to create a managed custom folder using the EMS is very similar to the procedure described earlier for creating a managed default folder, except that you click New Managed Custom Folder in the EMC Actions pane and start the New Managed Custom Folder Wizard. The New Managed Custom Folder page, shown in Figure 11-8, lets you configure the following settings:

- **Name** This is the name of the new managed custom folder object in Active Directory. It does not appear in users' mailboxes. This name can be up to 65 characters in length.
- **Display The Following Name When The Folder Is Viewed In Office Outlook** This is the name that users see when they view the folder in Outlook. By default, this is the same name as the one you enter in the Name box. This name can be up to 255 characters in length.
- **Storage Limit (KB) For This Folder And Its Subfolders** You can select this check box and specify the maximum size for the folder and its subfolders combined.
- **Display The Following Comment When The Folder Is Viewed In Outlook** A typical comment might be "The storage limit for this folder is 1 GB." The maximum length of this comment is 255 characters. Note that you can use the *Set-ManagedFolder* EMS cmdlet to configure comments localized to, for example, different countries.
- **Do Not Allow Users To Minimize This Comment In Outlook** You should select this check box to prevent Outlook users from minimizing the comment that you entered in the preceding box.

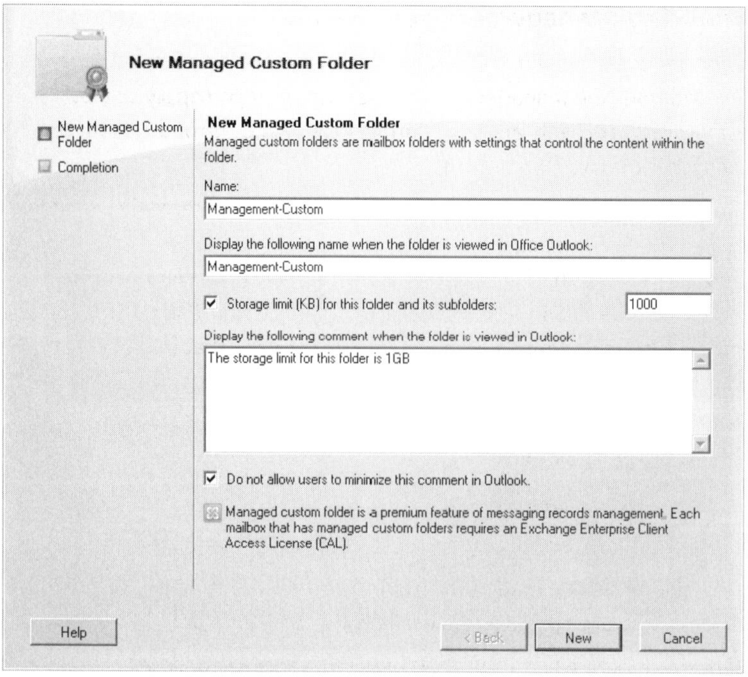

FIGURE 11-8 The New Managed Custom Folder page

As with managed default folders, you can use the *New-ManagedFolder* EMS cmdlet to create a managed custom folder, although different parameters are specified for the two types of folders. For example, the following command creates the managed custom folder Business Critical with a folder quota of 1.5 GB and enables a folder comment:

```
New-ManagedFolder -Name "Business Critical" -FolderName "Business Critical"
-StorageQuota 1.5GB -Comment "This is a managed folder with a 1.5GB storage limit."
-MustDisplayComment $true
```

Figure 11-9 shows the output from this command.

FIGURE 11-9 Creating a managed custom folder using the EMS

> **MORE INFO** **NEW-MANAGEDFOLDER**
>
> For more information about the *New-ManagedFolder* cmdlet, see *http://technet.microsoft .com/en-us/library/bb125245.aspx*.

Creating and Configuring Managed Content Settings

Managed content settings are used to define message retention settings and retention action for managed folders. For example, the managed content settings that you apply to a user's Inbox folder could specify that its contents are automatically deleted or moved to another folder after a specified number of days.

You can control message life span by controlling content retention and removing content that is no longer needed and by automatically copying important content to a separate storage location outside the mailbox. This is known as *journaling*. The journaling storage location can be any location that has a Simple Mail Transfer Protocol (SMTP) email address, including another Exchange mailbox. When an item is journaled, a label that indicates how the user classified the item is applied to it. Journaling is discussed in more detail in Lesson 2.

You can use the EMC or the EMS to create managed content settings and configure journaling. The procedure using the EMC is as follows:

1. Open the EMC and expand the Console tree.
2. Under Organization Configuration, click Mailbox.
3. In the Result pane, click either the Managed Default Folders tab or the Managed Custom Folders tab as appropriate. Click the managed folder you want to configure.
4. In the Actions pane, under the name of the folder you have selected, click New Managed Content settings to start the New Managed Content Settings Wizard.
5. On the Introduction page, shown in Figure 11-10, complete the following fields as appropriate:
   - Name Of The Managed Content Settings To Be Displayed In The Exchange Management Console
   - Message Type
   - Length Of Retention Period (Days)
   - Retention Period Starts
   - Action To Take At End Of Retention Period
6. Click Next. You can use journaling to automatically forward a copy of an item of the specified message type to another location. If you want to do this, select the Forward Copies To check box and complete the following fields on the Journaling page:
   - **Assign The Following Label To The Copy Of The Message**   You can browse for a suitable recipient.
   - **Format Of Copied Message Attached To Journal Report**   This can be Exchange Messaging Application Programming Interface Message Format or Outlook Message Format.
7. Click Next. On the New Managed Content Settings page, review your configuration settings. If you are satisfied, click New to create the managed content settings.
8. On the Completion page, review the status. If the status is Completed, click Finish to close the wizard. Otherwise, click Back to review your settings.

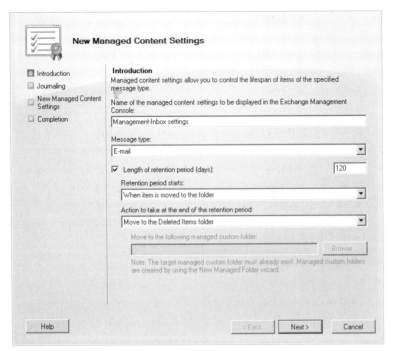

FIGURE 11-10 The Introduction page of the New Managed Content Settings Wizard

You can use the *New-ManagedContentSettings* EMS cmdlet to create managed content settings. For example, the following command creates managed content settings for the managed default folder Calendar with the name MyCalendarContentSettings, the message class CalendarItems, the age limit for retention 30 days, and the retention action Move to Deleted Items:

```
New-ManagedContentSettings -FolderName Calendar -MessageClass CalendarItems -Name
MyCalendarContentSettings -RetentionEnabled $true -RetentionAction MoveToDeletedItems
-AgeLimitForRetention 30
```

> **MORE INFO** **NEW-MANAGEDCONTENTSETTINGS**
>
> For more information about the *New-ManagedContentSettings* cmdlet, see *http://technet .microsoft.com/en-us/library/bb124565.aspx*.

As with creating managed content settings, you can reconfigure existing settings by using either the EMC or the EMS. To use the EMC to configure managed content settings, carry out the following procedure:

1. Open the EMC and expand the Console tree.
2. Under Organization Configuration, click Mailbox.

3. Click either the Managed Default Folders tab or the Managed Custom Folders tab (as appropriate) in the Result pane.

4. Expand the managed folder the contents of which you want to reconfigure. Click the managed content settings.

5. Click Properties under the name of the managed content settings in the Actions pane.

> **NOTE** **YOU CANNOT CREATE A NEW MANAGED FOLDER BY ACCESSING THIS PROPERTIES DIALOG BOX**
>
> You cannot create a new managed folder by using this procedure. If the managed folder does not exist, you need to use the New Managed Custom Folder Wizard or the *New-ManagedCustomFolder* EMS cmdlet (as described previously in this section) to create it.

6. Click the General tab, shown in Figure 11-11, and reconfigure managed content settings (for example, retention period). The settings configurable on the General tab are the same as those you specified when you configured managed content settings earlier, for example, Name, Message Type, Length Of Retention Period (Days), and so on.

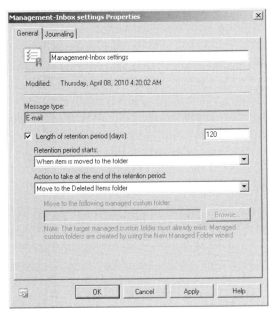

FIGURE 11-11 The General tab of the managed folder Properties dialog box

7. Click the Journaling tab. This lets you amend the journaling settings you configured earlier.

8. Click OK to confirm your changes and close the Properties dialog box. Note that if you decide not to amend any settings, you will get a warning to that effect.

You can also use the *Set-ManagedContentSettings* EMS cmdlet to configure managed content settings. The following command configures the managed content setting "Management-Inbox settings" to apply a retention age of 100 days, delete messages on expiration, and allow recovery.

```
Set-ManagedContentSettings -Identity "Management-Inbox settings" -RetentionEnabled
$true -AgeLimitForRetention 100 -RetentionAction DeleteAndAllowRecovery
```

EXAM TIP

The *Set-ManagedContentSettings* cmdlet amends managed content settings you have already configured but cannot be used to specify initial managed content settings for a managed folder. The *New-ManagedContentSettings* cmdlet specifies the initial managed content settings for a managed folder but cannot be used to reconfigure existing managed content settings.

Creating and Reconfiguring a Managed Folder Mailbox Policy

You can use managed folder mailbox policies to create linked groups of managed folders. When a managed folder mailbox policy is applied to users' mailboxes, all the managed folders that linked to the policy are deployed in a single operation. You can create as many managed folder mailbox policies as you need and add as many managed folders to each policy as you want. However, each user mailbox can be linked to only one managed folder mailbox policy.

If your organization has existing managed folders (including their corresponding managed content settings), you can add them to the managed folder mailbox policy as you create it. You can also add or remove managed folders from a managed folder mailbox policy anytime after the policy is created. After you assign a managed folder mailbox policy to a mailbox user, the managed folders and settings are applied to the mailbox when the Managed Folder Assistant (described earlier in this lesson) runs and processes the mailbox.

> **NOTE** **THE ENTIRE MAILBOX MANAGED DEFAULT FOLDER**
>
> Managed content settings that are applied to the Entire Mailbox folder control every folder in the mailbox except managed custom folders (and their subfolders) and managed default folders (and their subfolders). If a default folder in a mailbox is not linked to a managed folder mailbox policy, then the Entire Mailbox policy will apply to that default folder.

To use the EMC to create a managed folder mailbox policy, carry out the following procedure:

1. Open the EMC and expand the Console tree.
2. Under Organization Configuration, click Mailbox.
3. Click New Managed Folder Mailbox Policy in the Actions pane. This starts the New Managed Folder Mailbox Policy Wizard.

4. On the New Mailbox Policy page, shown in Figure 11-12, in the Managed Folder Mailbox Policy Name section, complete the Specify The Managed Folders That You Want To Link To This Policy field. You can click Add and use the Select Managed Folder dialog box to select the managed folders that you want to link to the policy, or you can select a managed folder from the list and then click the Remove button (the red cross) to remove it from the policy. Note that only one folder of a given default folder type (such as Inbox) can be linked to a managed folder mailbox policy.

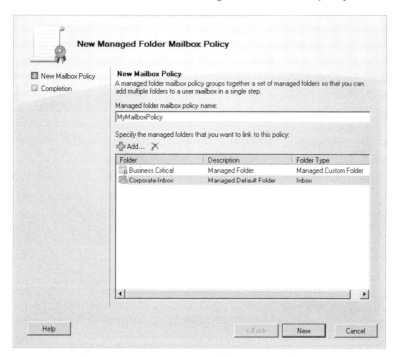

FIGURE 11-12 The New Mailbox Policy page of the New Managed Folder Mailbox Policy Wizard

5. On the Completion page, review the status. If the status is Completed, click Finish to close the wizard. Otherwise, click Back to review your settings.

You can use the *New-ManagedFolderMailboxPolicy* EMS cmdlet to create a managed folder mailbox policy. The following command creates the managed folder mailbox policy MyManagedFolderMailboxPolicy and links the Inbox managed default folder and the Business Critical managed customer folder to the policy:

```
New-ManagedFolderMailboxPolicy -Name "MyManagedFolderMailboxPolicy" -ManagedFolderLinks
Inbox,"Business Critical"
```

> **MORE INFO** **NEW-MANAGEDFOLDERMAILBOXPOLICY**
>
> For more information about the *New-ManagedFolderMailboxPolicy* cmdlet, see *http://technet.microsoft.com/en-us/library/aa996346.aspx*.

When you have created a managed folder mailbox policy, you might subsequently want to amend it. You can use both the EMC and the EMS to reconfigure managed folder mailbox policy settings. To use the EMC for this purpose, carry out the following procedure:

1. Open the EMC and expand the tree in the Console pane.

2. Under Organization Configuration, click Mailbox.

3. Click the Managed Folder Mailbox Policies tab in the Result pane, expand the appropriate managed folder, and then click the managed folder mailbox policy you want to configure.

4. In the Actions pane, click Properties under the name of the managed folder mailbox policy you want to configure. Note that the Properties dialog box lets you amend a policy. You cannot use this procedure to create one.

5. On the General tab, you can view or configure the following managed folder mailbox policy settings:

   ■ **Name**   This unlabeled box lets you view and, if required, modify the policy name.

   ■ **Modified**   This field displays the most recent date and time that the managed folder mailbox policy was modified. You cannot edit it.

   ■ **Managed Folders That Are Associated With This Policy**   You can add or remove folders with the same procedure that you used to specify folders when you set up the policy.

6. Click OK.

You can also use the EMS to configure managed folder mailbox policies. Note that you use the *Set-ManagedFolderMailboxPolicy* cmdlet to amend an existing policy. If you want to create a new policy, you need to use the *New-ManagedFolderMailboxPolicy* cmdlet. The following command adds the Calendar managed default folder to the managed folder mailbox policy MyMailboxPolicy:

```
Set-ManagedFolderMailboxPolicy -Identity MyMailboxPolicy -ManagedFolderLinks Calendar
```

> **MORE INFO**   *SET-MANAGEDFOLDERMAILBOXPOLICY*
>
> For more information about the *Set-ManagedFolderMailboxPolicy* cmdlet, see *http://technet.microsoft.com/en-us/library/bb124386.aspx*.

Applying a Managed Folder Mailbox Policy to Users

When you apply a managed folder mailbox policy to user mailboxes, all the managed folders linked to the policy are deployed in a single operation. As with retention policies, you can assign only one managed folder mailbox policy to a user mailbox. If you assigned a managed folder policy to a mailbox that already had a managed folder policy (or a retention policy) assigned, the new retention settings would override the existing settings.

To use the EMC to apply a managed folder mailbox policy to a user mailbox, carry out the following procedure:

1. Open the EMC and expand the Console tree.
2. Under Recipient Configuration, click Mailbox.
3. In the Result pane, click the user mailbox to which you want to apply the managed folder mailbox policy.
4. Click Properties in the Actions pane.
5. In the Properties dialog box, click the Mailbox Settings tab.
6. Click Messaging Records Management and then click Properties.
7. In the Messaging Records Management section, select the Managed Folder Mailbox Policy check box. Click Browse.
8. In the Select Managed Folder Mailbox Policy dialog box, select the managed folder mailbox policy that you want to apply to the mailbox and then click OK.
9. The policy you select appears in the Messaging Records Management dialog box, as shown in Figure 11-13. Click OK. Click OK again to close the Properties dialog box. If you see a Message box warning you that these settings are not compatible with Outlook 2007 or earlier, click OK to close the box.

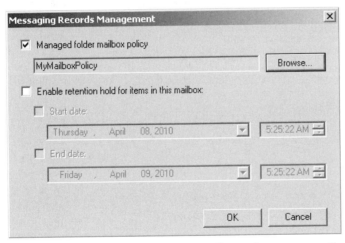

FIGURE 11-13 Applying a managed folder mailbox policy to a user mailbox

You can also use the *Set-Mailbox* EMS cmdlet to apply a managed folder mailbox policy to a user mailbox. The following command applies the mailbox policy MyManagedFolderMailboxPolicy to the Don Hall mailbox:

```
Set-Mailbox -Identity "Don Hall" -ManagedFolderMailboxPolicy
MyManagedFolderMailboxPolicy
```

Lesson Summary

- You can use retention tags to define mailbox retention settings. Retention tags include DPTs, RPTs, and personal tags.
- Retention policies let you group one or more retention tags in the same policy and apply that policy to individual user mailboxes or distribution groups.
- You can set retention hold to prevent retention settings from being applied when a user is unable to access email messages for an extended period.
- You can create managed default folders and managed custom folders and configure managed folder policies, which you can then apply to user mailboxes.
- Applying retention policies and managed folder policies to user mailboxes controls how those mailboxes operate in Outlook clients.

Lesson Review

You can use the following questions to test your knowledge of the information in Lesson 1, "Managing Records." The questions are also available on the companion CD if you prefer to review them in electronic form.

> **NOTE   ANSWERS**
>
> Answers to these questions and explanations of why each answer choice is correct or incorrect are located in the "Answers" section at the end of the book.

1. For which of the following default folders can you create RPTs? (Choose all that apply.)

    A. Deleted Items

    B. Junk E-mail

    C. Tasks

    D. Drafts

    E. Contacts

    F. Outbox

2. What EMS cmdlet would you use to create a default policy tag (DTP)?

    A. *New-RetentionPolicy*

    B. *Set-RetentionPolicy*

    C. *New-RetentionPolicyTag*

    D. *Set-RetentionPolicyTag*

3. Don Hall is a member of the mail-enabled distribution group Accountants. Which of the following commands applies the retention policy Accounting to the Don Hall mailbox? (Choose all that apply; each answer forms part of the solution.)

   A. *Set-Mailbox "Don Hall" -RetentionPolicy "Accounting"*

   B. *New-RetentionPolicy –Name "Accounting" -RetentionPolicyTagLinks "Tag-Don-Hall"*

   C. *Get-DistributionGroupMember -Identity "Accountants" | Set-Mailbox -RetentionPolicy "Accounting"*

   D. *New-RetentionPolicyTag "Tag-Don-Hall" -Type Personal -RetentionEnabled $true -AgeLimitForRetention 180 -RetentionAction MoveToArchive*

4. You want to create a default managed folder named Short-Stay of type Inbox. You want to display the message "Mail is deleted from this folder after 30 days." You do not want Outlook users to be able to minimize the message. What EMS command do you enter?

   A. New-ManagedFolder -Name "Short-Stay" -DefaultFolderType Inbox -Comment "Mail is deleted from this folder after 30 days." -MustDisplayComment $false

   B. New-ManagedFolder -Name "Short-Stay" -DefaultFolderType Calendar -Comment "Mail is deleted from this folder after 30 days." -MustDisplayComment $true

   C. Set-ManagedFolder -Name "Short-Stay" -DefaultFolderType Inbox -Comment "Mail is deleted from this folder after 30 days." -MustDisplayComment $true

   D. New-ManagedFolder -Name "Short-Stay" -DefaultFolderType Inbox -Comment "Mail is deleted from this folder after 30 days." -MustDisplayComment $true

5. You want to apply the managed folder mailbox policy TechnicalSupportPolicy to the Kim Akers mailbox. What command do you use?

   A. Set-Mailbox -Identity "Kim Akers" -ManagedFolderMailboxPolicy TechnicalSupportPolicy

   B. New-ManagedFolder -Name "Kim Akers" -DefaultFolderType Inbox

   C. Get-DistributionGroupMember -Identity TechnicalSupport | Set-Mailbox -RetentionPolicy "TechnicalSupportPolicy"

   D. Set-Mailbox "Kim Akers" -RetentionPolicy TechnicalSupportPolicy

Lesson 2: Implementing Compliance

Exchange Server 2010 provides several features that enable an administrator to capture, protect, modify, retain, and discover email messages in user mailboxes as these messages enter, flow through, and exit the Exchange organization. For example, organizations are typically required to keep data for a specific time and then remove that data to protect privacy. Exchange Server 2010 retention policies and MRM were previously discussed in Lesson 1, "Managing Records."

Organizations typically transmit sensitive and confidential information through email on a daily basis. Such organizations need to protect the privacy of individuals and the confidentiality of communications. You can implement privacy and confidentiality requirements by configuring *Information Rights Management (IRM)*. IRM permits your organization and your users to apply persistent protection to messages so that access is restricted to authorized users and permitted actions (such as forwarding, copying, and printing messages). Chapter 7 discussed IRM configuration in detail, and only a brief summary is therefore included in this lesson.

Rights Management Services (RMS) includes all the server and client technologies that are required to support IRM in an organization. In Chapter 7, you learned about the RMS prelicensing agent, and how to configure rights protection by using transport rules. In this lesson, you briefly revise how to apply an RMS template to messages sent to a specified SMTP address.

Chapter 7 also discussed transport rules. This lesson revisits transport rules and describes how you can use *transport protection rules* to apply messaging policies to email messages that flow through Hub Transport and Edge Transport servers.

Message classifications allow an organization to comply with email policies and regulatory responsibilities. When a message is classified, the message contains specific metadata that describes its intended use or audience. You will see how to configure message classifications and associate them with transport rules in this lesson.

Journaling, introduced in Lesson 1, helps an organization respond to legal, regulatory, and organizational compliance requirements by recording inbound and outbound email communications. Journal rules can be used to ensure that all messages that are sent to a specified email address are also stored is a journaling mailbox for compliance purposes. This lesson discusses how Microsoft Exchange Server 2010 helps secure journaled messages and implements journal rules that send messages to journaling mailboxes. It describes how you configure a journaling mailbox and an alternate journaling mailbox.

MailTips give your Outlook 2010 and OWA users information about their messages and recipients before they send an email. For example, it is not a good idea to send an important and confidential message to a recipient who is out of the office and have it sit in his or her mailbox for several weeks. It is a very bad idea to accidentally send a confidential message meant for a single recipient to everyone in the organization. You can improve confidentiality and compliance by configuring MailTips so that they can indicate when a recipient is sending automatic replies or when a message is being sent to a large number of people. This lesson discusses MailTips configuration.

This lesson also discusses *ethical walls*, which enable you to prohibit communication between specific groups in your own organization. It describes how you create an ethical wall for email communication by configuring a transport rule. This lesson discusses discovery searches, which are multimailbox searches that search mailboxes for content specified by defined criteria, and legal hold, which prevents the deletion of information such as email messages that might be required for litigation purposes.

After this lesson, you will be able to:

- Configure IRM and apply an RMS template.
- Implement journaling and apply a journaling rule to create a journaling mailbox.
- Create an alternate journaling mailbox.
- Configure MailTips.
- Configure ethical walls.
- Explain and configure discovery searches and legal hold.

Estimated lesson time: 50 minutes

Configuring IRM

Chapter 7 discussed Exchange Server 2010 IRM features in considerable detail. In summary, IRM provides persistent online and offline protection of email messages and attachments by applying the information protection technology AD RMS, also discussed in Chapter 7. IRM protection is configured by applying an AD RMS rights policy template. You can use policy templates to control permissions that recipients have on a message.

AD RMS Rights Policy Templates

Exchange 2010 ships with the Do Not Forward template. When this template is applied to a message, only the recipients addressed in the message can decrypt the message, and these recipients cannot forward the message to anyone else, copy content from the message, or print the message. You can create additional RMS templates on the AD RMS server in your organization (if installed) to meet your IRM protection requirements.

The following EMS command retrieves the list of active rights management services policy templates that are currently available to the Exchange Server 2010 server on which the command is run:

```
Get-RMSTemplate
```

MORE INFO   GET-RMSTEMPLATE

For more information about the *Get-RMSTemplate* EMS cmdlet, see *http://technet .microsoft.com/en-us/library/dd297960.aspx.*

Applying IRM Protection

IRM protection can be applied to messages manually by Outlook users. This process uses the IRM functionality in Outlook, but you can use Exchange to take actions (such as applying transport protection rules) that enforce your organization's messaging policy. OWA users can protect messages they send and view IRM-protected messages they receive.

In Outlook 2010, you can create Outlook protection rules that automatically IRM-protect messages. Outlook 2010 applies IRM protection when a user is composing a message. You can create transport protection rules on Hub Transport servers.

Configuring IRM Features and Testing IRM Configuration

As discussed in Chapter 7, you can use the EMS but not the EMC to configure IRM features. The *Set-IRMConfiguration* cmdlet is used to enable or disable IRM for internal messages and to enable or disable transport decryption, journal report decryption, IRM for Exchange Search, and IRM in OWA. The commands in this section were discussed in Chapter 7 but are repeated here for convenience.

The following command enables licensing and hence enables IRM features for messages sent to internal recipients (assuming that external licensing is currently disabled):

```
Set-IRMConfiguration -InternalLicensingEnabled $true
```

The following command enables licensing and hence enables IRM features for messages sent to external recipients if external licensing is currently disabled:

```
Set-IRMConfiguration -ExternalLicensingEnabled $true
```

Journal report decryption attaches a decrypted copy of an IRM-protected message to the journal report. The following command enables Journal report decryption if it is currently disabled:

```
Set-IRMConfiguration -JournalReportDecryptionEnabled $true
```

IRM features are enabled in OWA by default. The following command disables IRM features in OWA:

```
Set-IRMConfiguration -OWAEnabled $false
```

The following command enables IRM features in OWA if they have previously been disabled:

```
Set-IRMConfiguration -OWAEnabled $true
```

If transport decryption is mandatory, any message that cannot be decrypted is rejected, and a non-delivery report (NDR) is returned to the sender. The following command sets transport decryption to mandatory:

```
Set-IRMConfiguration -TransportDecryptionSetting mandatory
```

If transport decryption is disabled, no attempt is made to decrypt internal or external messages before delivery. The following command sets transport decryption to disabled:

```
Set-IRMConfiguration -TransportDecryptionSetting disabled
```

Setting transport decryption to optional provides a best effort approach to decryption. Messages are decrypted if possible but are delivered even if decryption fails. The following command sets transport decryption to optional:

```
Set-IRMConfiguration -TransportDecryptionSetting optional
```

> **MORE INFO**   *SET-IRMCONFIGURATION*
>
> For more information about the *Set-IRMConfiguration* EMS cmdlet, including the parameters that apply only to the Outlook Live service, see *http://technet.microsoft.com/ en-us/library/dd979792.aspx.*

If you want to view the current IRM configuration—either the default values before you configure it or the values after configuration—you enter the following command:

```
Get-IRMConfiguration | FL
```

The following command tests the IRM configuration for messages Kim Akers sends to Don Hall:

```
Test-IRMConfiguration -Sender KimAkers@adatum.com -Recipient DonHall@adatum.com
```

> **MORE INFO**   *TEST-IRMCONFIGURATION*
>
> For more information about the *Test-IRMConfiguration* EMS cmdlet, see *http://technet .microsoft.com/en-us/library/dd979798.aspx.*

Using Transport Protection Rules

Chapter 7 discussed transport protection rules. These are transport rules that implement messaging policies by inspecting message content, encrypting sensitive email content, and using rights management to control access. Transport protection rules apply an AD RMS rights policy template to protect messages through IRM.

You can use either the New Transport Rule Wizard in the EMC or the *New-TransportRule* EMS cmdlet to create a transport protection rule. To use the EMS to create a transport protection rule, your first step is to discover what rights management templates are available. The following command generates a list of available templates (note that this command does not list the pre-installed Do Not Forward template):

```
Get-RMSTemplate | FL
```

You then use a command that creates a transport protection rule. For example, if you wanted to create a rule named Protect-Confidential that IRM-protects messages that contain the word "Confidential" in the Subject field using the Do Not Forward template, you would use the following command:

```
New-TransportRule -Name "Protect-Confidential" -SubjectContainsWords "Confidential"
-ApplyRightsProtectionTemplate "Do Not Forward"
```

Protecting Outlook and OWA Messages

Outlook protection rules help an organization protect against the risk of information leakage by automatically applying IRM protection to messages. In Outlook 2010, messages are IRM-protected before they leave the Outlook client. This protection is also applied to any attachments using supported file formats. When you create Outlook protection rules on an Exchange Server 2010 server, these rules are automatically distributed to Outlook 2010 by Exchange Web Services.

You can use the EMS but not the EMC to create an Outlook protection rule. For example, the following command creates the Outlook protection rule MyProject. This rule protects messages sent to the TechnicalAuthors distribution group with the AD RMS template Protect-Confidential:

```
New-OutlookProtectionRule -Name "MyProject" -SentTo "TechnicalAuthors"
-ApplyRightsProtectionTemplate "Protect-Confidential"
```

You can use the *Get-OutlookProtectionRule* EMS cmdlet to obtain the configuration of an existing Outlook protection rule and the *Set-OutlookProtectionRule* EMS cmdlet to change that configuration. You can also use the *Remove-OutlookProtectionRule* EMS cmdlet to remove an Outlook protection rule. For example, the following command removes the MyProject Outlook protection rule:

```
Remove-OutlookProtectionRule -Identity "MyProject"
```

Enabling or Disabling IRM in OWA

You can use commands based on the *Set-IRMConfiguration* EMS cmdlet to enable or disable IRM in OWA for your entire Exchange Server 2010 organization. You can also enable or disable IRM for an OWA virtual directory using the *Set-OWAVirtualDirectory* cmdlet and setting the IRMEnabled parameter to $true (the default) or $false. Alternatively, you can enable or disable IRM for an OWA mailbox policy using the *Set-OWAMailboxPolicy* cmdlet and setting the IRMEnabled parameter to $true (the default) or $false.

The following command enables IRM in OWA for an entire Exchange Server 2010 organization:

```
Set-IRMConfiguration -OWAEnabled $true
```

The following command disables IRM in OWA for the virtual directory MyVirtualDirectory on Client Access server VAN-EX2:

```
Set-OWAVirtualDirectory -Identity VAN-EX2\MyVirtualDirectory -IRMEnabled $false
```

EXAM TIP

Note that the *Set-IRMConfiguration* cmdlet supports the OWAEnabled parameter, whereas the *Set-OWAVirtualDirectory* and *Set-OWAMailboxPolicy* cmdlets support the IRMEnabled parameter.

MORE INFO   *SET-IRMCONFIGURATION*, *SET-OWAVIRTUALDIRECTORY*, AND *SET-OWAMAILBOXPOLICY*

For more information about the *Set-IRMConfiguration* EMS cmdlet, see *http://technet .microsoft.com/en-us/library/dd979792.aspx*. For more information about the *Set-OWAVirtualDirectory* EMS cmdlet, see *http://technet.microsoft.com/en-us/library/ bb123515.aspx*. For more information about the *Set-OWAMailboxPolicy* EMS cmdlet, see *http://technet.microsoft.com/en-us/library/dd297989.aspx*.

Configuring Journaling

Journaling lets you record all communications in an organization, including email communications, for use in an email retention strategy. It enables organizations to maintain records of communications that occur when employees perform daily business tasks.

All Exchange Server 2010 email messages pass through at least one Hub Transport server. A journaling agent is a transport agent that processes messages on Hub Transport servers. It fires on the OnSubmittedMessage and OnRoutedMessage routing agent events.

MORE INFO   ROUTING AGENT EVENTS

For more information about routing agent events, see *http://msdn.microsoft.com/en-us/ library/microsoft.exchange.data.transport.routing.routingagent_events.aspx*.

Exchange 2010 provides the following journaling options:

- **Standard journaling**   Standard journaling, configured on a mailbox database, enables the journaling agent to journal all messages sent to and from mailboxes located on the specified database. To journal all messages to and from all recipients and senders, you need to configure journaling on all mailbox databases on all Mailbox servers in the organization.

- **Premium journaling** Premium journaling uses journal rules. You can, for example, use a journal rule to record all messages sent to a specific address and store these messages in a special journaling mailbox for compliance purposes. You can configure journal rules to match your organization's needs by journaling individual recipients or members of distribution groups. You must have an Exchange Enterprise CAL to use premium journaling.

When you enable standard journaling on a mailbox database, this information is saved in Active Directory and is read by the journaling agent. Journal rules configured using premium journaling are also saved in Active Directory and applied by the journaling agent.

Defining Journal Rule Scope and Recipients, and the Journaling Mailbox

Journal Rule Scope defines which messages are journaled by the journaling agent. You can target the journal rule to Internal, External, or Global recipients. These scopes are defined as follows:

- **Internal** Target messages are sent to recipients and received by senders inside an Exchange organization.
- **External** Target messages are sent to recipients and received from senders outside an Exchange organization.
- **Global** Target messages include all messages that pass through an organization's Hub Transport servers. These can include messages that may have already been processed by journal rules using the Internal and External scopes.

Journal Recipients specifies the SMTP address of the recipient you want to journal. The recipient can be an Exchange mailbox, a distribution group, or a contact. Typically, recipients may be subject to regulatory requirements or may be involved in legal proceedings. By specifying specific recipients or groups of recipients, you can configure a journaling environment that matches your organization's regulatory and legal requirements and hence minimize storage and other costs associated with retention of large amounts of data.

All messages sent to or from the journal recipients that you specify in a journaling rule are journaled (including all members of a distribution group if you specify this group as a recipient). If you do not specify a journaling recipient, all messages sent to or from recipients that match the journal rule scope are journaled.

Unified Messaging–Enabled Journal Recipients

Many organizations that implement journaling also use Unified Messaging (UM) to consolidate their email, voice mail, and fax infrastructure. You may not, however, want the journaling process to generate journal reports for messages generated by UM. You can decide whether to journal voice mail messages and missed call notification messages handled by an Exchange 2010 UM server or whether to skip such messages. However, messages that contain faxes generated by a UM server are always journaled, even if you configure a journal rule that specifies not to journal UM voice mail and missed call notification messages.

When you enable or disable the journaling of voice mail messages and missed call notification messages, your settings apply to all Hub Transport servers in your organization. You can use commands based on the *Set-TransportConfig* EMS cmdlet to enable or disable the journaling of voice mail messages and missed call notification messages. For example, the following command disables voice mail journaling on all Hub Transport servers:

```
Set-TransportConfig -VoicemailJournalingEnabled $false
```

For more information about the *Set-TransportConfig* EMS cmdlet, see *http://technet.microsoft.com/en-us/library/bb124151.aspx*.

Journaling mailbox specifies one or more mailboxes used for collecting journal reports. You can specify one journaling mailbox to collect messages for all the journal rules configured in the organization, or you can use different journaling mailboxes for different journal rules or sets of journal rules. How you configure the journaling mailbox depends on your organization's policies and regulatory and legal requirements.

Journaling mailboxes typically contain sensitive information, and you need to secure them. Messages that are part of legal proceedings must remain tamper-free before they are submitted to an investigatory authority. Because of this requirement, you should create policies that govern who can access the journaling mailboxes in your organization and limit access only to those individuals who have a direct access requirement. You will create and configure a journaling mailbox in the practice session later in this chapter.

Creating and Configuring Journal Rules

You can use commands based on the *New-JournalRule* EMS cmdlet to configure new journal rules. For example, the following command stores all messages sent to DonHall@adatum.com in the journaling mailbox "Don Hall Journal Mailbox":

```
New-JournalRule -Name "Don-Hall-Compliance" -JournalEmailAddress "Don Hall Journal
Mailbox" -Scope Global -Recipient DonHall@adatum.com -Enabled $True
```

The following command stores all messages sent to the distribution group BookAuthors@ contoso.com to the journaling mailbox "Authors Journal":

```
New-JournalRule -Name "Book-Authors-Journal" -JournalEmailAddress "Authors Journal"
-Scope Global -BookAuthors@contoso.com -Enabled $True
```

Note that in both cases, the Enabled parameter is optional. Journal rules are enabled by default unless the Enabled parameter is set to $false.

Replicating Journal Rules

Journal rules are stored in Active Directory and applied by all Hub Transport servers in an Exchange Server 2010 organization. If you create, modify, or remove a journal rule on a Hub Transport server, this change is replicated to all Active Directory servers in your organization. The Hub Transport servers then retrieve the updated journal rule configuration from the Active Directory servers. In this way, Exchange Server 2010 provides a consistent set of journal rules across the organization. All messages that pass in or through an Exchange Server 2010 organization are subject to the same journal rules. Journal rule replication depends on Active Directory replication.

Understanding Journal Reports

A journal report is the message that the journaling agent generates on a Hub Transport server when an email message matches a journal rule and is submitted to a journaling mailbox. Journal reports contain important message content and metadata. The original email message that matches the journal rule is included, unaltered as an attachment to the journal report. The body of a journal report contains information from the original message, such as the sender email address, message subject, message-ID, and recipient email addresses. This is the only journaling method supported by Exchange Server 2010 (and Exchange Server 2007) and is known as *envelope journaling*.

The information in a journal report is organized so that every value in each header field has its own line, which simplifies parsing. Exchange Server 2010 may generate more than one journal report for a single message. This depends on factors such as message bifurcation or distribution group expansion.

When the journaling agent journals a message, it tries to capture as much detail as possible. This information helps you determine the intent of the message, its recipients, and its senders. A journal report can tell you, for example, whether the recipients identified in the message are directly addressed in the To field or the Cc field or are included as part of a distribution list.

Journal report fields can be basic or extended. Basic journal report fields are listed and described in Table 11-1.

TABLE 11-1 Basic Journal Report Fields

FIELD	DESCRIPTION
Sender	Displays the SMTP address of the sender specified in the From header. If the message is sent on behalf of another sender, the field displays the address specified in the Sender header.
Subject	Displays the subject header value.
Message-ID	Displays the SMTP Message-ID.
Recipient	Displays the SMTP address of a recipient included in an email message when Exchange cannot determine the recipient addressing of that message. This occurs when messages are received from the Internet or from unauthenticated senders and when messages are received from legacy Exchange servers. Recipients added by transport rules or other transport agents are also listed in the Recipient field.

Extended journal report fields are listed and described in Table 11-2.

TABLE 11-2 Extended journal report fields

FIELD	DESCRIPTION
On-Behalf-Of	Displays the SMTP address of the mailbox from which the message appears if the Send On Behalf Of feature is specified by the sender.
To	Displays the SMTP address of a recipient included in the message envelope and in the To header field of the message.
Cc	Displays the SMTP address of a recipient included in the message envelope and in the Cc header field of the message.
Bcc	Displays the SMTP address of a recipient included in the message envelope and in the Bcc header field of the message.

> **NOTE   RECIPIENT ADDRESSES IN TO, CC, AND BCC FIELDS**
>
> The recipient address in a To, Cc, or Bcc field can be included directly by the sender or indirectly through distribution list expansion or if the message was forwarded to the recipient by another mailbox. To indicate whether the message went through distribution list expansion or was forwarded, the field may also contain one Expanded field or one Forwarded field, separated with commas. Expanded and Forwarded fields are described later in this lesson.

Whether extended journal report fields are populated depends on whether recipient addressing can be determined. If recipient addressing can be determined for a particular recipient, the recipient email address is inserted into the appropriate extended fields. In this case, the recipient email address is not inserted into the basic Recipient field.

If a message is submitted to a Hub Transport server by using any other method, such as anonymous submission from an Edge Transport server or submission from a server running Exchange Server 2003, Exchange cannot verify that the recipient addressing has not been tampered with. If recipient addressing cannot be verified, the recipient email address is inserted in the basic Recipient field and not into an extended To, Cc, or Bcc field.

For each recipient addressed on a message, one recipient journal report field is added. No recipient field contains more than one recipient email address, except for recipient fields that contain recipients expanded from a distribution group or that have received a message forwarded from another mailbox. For expanded or forwarded messages, the email address of the recipient that received final delivery of the message and the email address of the distribution group or mailbox that was originally addressed are included.

The Expanded field is provided as an addition to the To, Cc, and Bcc fields, preceded by a comma. The Field displays the SMTP address of the distribution group that contains either the recipient specified in the To, Cc, or Bcc field or the nested distribution lists that contain the specified recipient. The address displayed in this field is always the first distribution list to be expanded, regardless of how many nested distribution lists may be between the original parent distribution list and the expanded final recipient specified in the To, Cc, or Bcc field.

The Forwarded field is also an addition to the To, Cc, and Bcc fields and is preceded by a comma. Typically, this field displays the email address of a mailbox configured to forward email messages to the account specified in the To, Cc, or Bcc field. If a chain of forwarding mailboxes is configured, where each mailbox forwards messages to the next one, the first forwarding mailbox is displayed in the Forwarded field, and the SMTP address of the final, nonforwarding mailbox in the chain is displayed in the To, Cc, or Bcc field.

> **MORE INFO**   **JOURNAL REPORTS**
>
> For more information about journal reports, including examples of such reports, see *http://technet.microsoft.com/en-us/library/bb331962.aspx*.

Specifying a Journaling Mailbox Storage Quota

The size of a journaling mailbox can affect the delivery and availability of journal reports. When you configure a journaling mailbox to accept journal reports, you can decide to configure the maximum size of the journaling mailbox. You should consider the amount of data the mailbox needs to store, the hardware resources available, and the disaster recovery requirements for the server where the journaling mailbox is located. You must also consider what would occur if a journaling mailbox exceeded its configured mailbox quota.

You can configure the Prohibit Send And Receive At (MB) option for a storage quota on a journaling mailbox as you can with any other mailbox. The mailbox then accepts journal reports until it reaches the configured storage quota. When the prohibit send and receive storage quota is exceeded, the journaling mailbox stops accepting journal reports.

If a quota is exceeded, Exchange Server 2010 does not return journal reports to the original sender as it does with regular messages. It instead holds undelivered journal reports in a mail queue and tries to redeliver them until delivery is successful. Although this means that all journal reports generated are eventually delivered, it can generate excessively large mail queues on Hub Transport servers, especially in organizations with high messaging traffic.

Typically, you would configure the prohibit send and receive storage quota on journaling mailboxes to the maximum size that hardware resources and disaster recovery capabilities allow. However, if you decide to configure journaling mailboxes without storage quotas, take care to monitor your Mailbox servers to ensure that the size of a journaling mailbox does not exceed the available hardware resources or disaster recovery capabilities.

You specify a storage quota for a journaling mailbox in the same way as you do for any other mailbox. Chapter 3, "Exchange Mailboxes," described the procedures to do this. As a reminder, Figure 11-14 shows the Storage Quotas configuration box available from the Mailbox Settings tab of the Properties dialog box for the journaling mailbox Book-Authors-Journal with a Prohibit Send And Receive At (MB) setting of 1,024 (1 GB). Note that if you do not want to set any storage quotas for a journaling mailbox, which may often be the case, you need only clear the Use Mailbox Database Defaults on this configuration page.

Alternatively, you can use the *Set-Mailbox* EMS cmdlet. The following command configures the Prohibit Send And Receive At setting for the journaling mailbox Don-Hall-Journal-Mailbox to 500 MB:

```
Set-Mailbox -Identity "Don-Hall-Journal-Mailbox" -ProhibitSendReceiveQuota 524288000
```

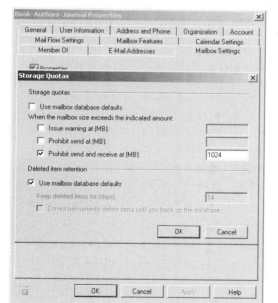

FIGURE 11-14 Configuring a storage quota

Configuring an Alternate Journaling Mailbox

If you do not want to allow rejected journal reports to collect in an email queue on a Hub Transport server when the journaling mailbox is unavailable, you can configure an alternate journaling mailbox to store those journal reports. The alternate journaling mailbox receives the NDRs generated when the journaling mailbox or the server on which it is located refuses delivery of the journal report or becomes unavailable. When the journaling mailbox becomes available again, you can use the Send Again feature of Microsoft Office Outlook to submit journal reports for delivery to the journaling mailbox.

Mailbox databases and journal rules may be configured to deliver journal reports to different journaling mailboxes. However, if you create an alternate journaling mailbox, all the journal reports that are rejected or cannot be delivered in your entire Exchange Server 2010 organization are delivered to the alternate journaling mailbox. Therefore, you must ensure that the alternate journaling mailbox and the Mailbox server on which it is located can support a large volume of journal reports.

It is important to monitor the alternate journaling mailbox to make sure that it does not become unavailable. You must also ensure that the use of an alternate journaling mailbox does not violate any laws or regulations that apply to your organization. If laws or regulations prohibit journal reports sent to different journaling mailboxes from being stored in the same alternate journaling mailbox, you may be unable to configure an alternate journaling mailbox. You need to discuss this with your legal representatives.

> **NOTE** **JOURNAL REPORTS ARE REDIRECTED ONLY AFTER THE ALTERNATE MAILBOX IS CONFIGURED**
> Journal reports that have already failed delivery before the alternate journaling mailbox is configured are not redirected.

You can use the *Set-TransportConfig* EMS cmdlet to configure an existing mailbox as an alternate journaling mailbox. You will configure an alternate journaling mailbox in the practice session later in this lesson.

EXAM TIP
You can use the *New-Mailbox* cmdlet to create a mailbox for use as an alternate journaling mailbox and then use the *Set-TransportConfig* cmdlet to configure it as an alternate journaling mailbox. You should not attempt to configure a mailbox you have already configured as a journaling mailbox (using the *New-JournalRule* cmdlet) as an alternate journaling mailbox.

Protecting Journal Reports

If journaling is configured, the journaling agent generates journal reports that contain message metadata, and the entire original message is attached to the journal report. It is important to protect the integrity of journal reports and the journaling mailbox and protect them from unauthorized access.

Exchange 2010 protects journal reports sent within an Exchange Server 2010 Organization by using secure links between Hub Transport servers and Mailbox servers. It sends the journal report as the Exchange recipient object, authenticates the session between the Hub Transport server and the Mailbox server, and accepts only secure, authenticated connections. This helps reduce the possibility of tampering with journal reports delivered to the journaling mailbox.

Also, you must implement access controls that ensure that the journaling mailbox is protected from unauthorized access. These controls should include recording and monitoring password changes to journaling mailbox user accounts, monitoring domain logons by such user accounts, and monitoring changes to mailbox permissions for journaling mailboxes. You will create and configure a journaling mailbox later in this chapter.

If there is a requirement to send journal reports to a recipient that does not reside in the same Exchange Server 2010 organization as the Hub Transport server, including recipients residing on another email system within your organization or to an external email system, the connections between the two email systems may not be automatically encrypted. However, you can use the following Exchange Server 2010 solutions to help protect journal reports sent to the third-party solution providers:

- Configure a mail-enabled contact that sends email messages to the SMTP address of the third-party solution and configure Exchange Server 2010 to send journal reports to that contact. Configure the contact to accept journal reports only from an Exchange recipient.
- Accept only email messages from the SMTP address of the Exchange contact.
- Require authentication on the receiving system.
- Configure Transport Layer Security (TLS) between the two systems.

> **MORE INFO** **TRANSPORT LAYER SECURITY**
>
> The TLS protocol provides secure communications over TCP/IP networks such as the Internet. It enables clients to authenticate servers or (optionally) servers to authenticate clients. It also provides a secure channel by encrypting communications. For more information, see *http://technet.microsoft.com/en-us/library/bb430753.aspx*.

Using MailTips

Exchange Server 2010 introduces the MailTips feature. MailTips gives your Outlook 2010 and OWA users information about their messages and recipients before they send them. For example, if a recipient has enabled an out-of-office reply, a user can use the automatic replies MailTip to read this reply before sending the message. If the recipient is on vacation for an extended period, the sender can decide whether to send the message now or wait for the recipient's return. MailTips also warn the sender if a recipient's mailbox is full or if the message that is about to be sent is large enough to fill it. The oversized message MailTip warns a sender if a message exceeds organizational size limits.

A MailTip can also warn you (and your users) whether a message is being sent to a large number of recipients. It is a common error, made even by experienced users, to reply to an email message that has been sent to a large number of recipients and to send the reply to all these recipients when it should go only to the original sender. Another situation that can occur is when a user has received a message on Bcc and replies to all, thus revealing that he or she was on the Bcc list. MailTips warn a sender if a message is being sent as reply-all-on-Bcc.

Sometimes, for various reasons, a message should be sent only to internal recipients. MailTips (by default) warn if a message is being sent to an external recipient or to a distribution group that contains external recipients. In the latter case, MailTips informs the sender how many internal recipients there are but does not identify them.

The moderated transport feature, new to Exchange Server 2010, can require that all email messages sent to specific recipients are approved by moderators. All messages sent to those recipients go through an approval process. The most common scenario is when messages are sent to large distribution groups. MailTips can warn users that they are sending emails to a moderated group. In this case, messages would be delayed pending moderator approval. MailTips can also warn users if they do not have permission to send to a mailbox or distribution group.

If someone leaves an organization, their email address might remain in the autocomplete list of Outlook users. MailTips can warn a sender that he or she is sending to a recipient that no longer exists. Prior to MailTips, the message would have bounced.

You can configure custom MailTips. These replace messages that might otherwise be sent as an automatic response, such as "This mailbox is not monitored" or "You will receive a response within 48 hours." Custom MailTips can be localized so that users can see them in their own language.

> **MORE INFO**   **MAILTIPS AND CLIENT-SIDE CONFIGURATION**
>
> For more information about MailTips, including client-side configuration and screenshots of MailTips on an Outlook 2010 client, see *http://blogs.msdn.com/outlook/archive/2009/08/12/introducing-mailtips.aspx*.

Configuring Organizational MailTips

Some client configuration of the MailTips feature is possible in Outlook 2010 or OWA. For example, an OWA user can turn the external recipient MailTips on or off by opening or closing the MailTips bar (click on the anchor icon). However, this lesson concentrates on server-side configuration implemented by an Exchange organization's administrator.

You can use the EMS but not the EMC to implement the following configurations:

- Enable or disable MailTips
- Configure the large audience size for your organization
- Enable or disable the external recipients MailTips

- Enable or disable MailTips that rely on mailbox data
- Enable or disable MailTips that rely on group metrics data

MailTips are enabled by default. The following command disables MailTips for an Exchange Server 2010 organization:

```
Set-OrganizationConfig -MailTipsAllTipsEnabled $false
```

The following command enables MailTips for an Exchange Server 2010 organization if the feature has previously been disabled:

```
Set-OrganizationConfig -MailTipsAllTipsEnabled $true
```

When senders address messages to more recipients than the number you specify, they are shown the large audience size MailTips. The large audience size is set to 25 by default. The following command configures the large audience size to 100:

```
Set-OrganizationConfig -MailTipsLargeAudienceThreshold 100
```

When the external recipients MailTips is enabled, senders are notified that the recipients of a message include one or more external recipient or a distribution group that contains external recipients. By default, the external recipients MailTips is disabled. The following command enables the external recipients MailTips:

```
Set-OrganizationConfig -MailTipsExternalRecipientsTipsEnabled $true
```

NOTE EXTERNAL RECIPIENTS AND GROUP METRICS

The external recipients MailTips relies on group metrics data. Therefore, if you enable the external recipients MailTips, you also need to ensure that MailTips that rely on group metrics data (as described later in this section) are enabled. These MailTips are enabled by default.

Mailbox data includes Out of Office and Mailbox Full information. By default, MailTips that rely on mailbox data are enabled. The following command disables MailTips that rely on mailbox data:

```
Set-OrganizationConfig -MailTipsMailboxSourcedTipsEnabled $false
```

Group metrics data consists of the membership count and external members count for all distribution groups and dynamic distribution groups. MailTips such as large audience size and external recipients rely on this data. By default, these MailTips are enabled. The following command disables MailTips that rely on group metrics data:

```
Set-OrganizationConfig -MailTipsGroupMetricsEnabled $false
```

MORE INFO SET-ORGANIZATIONCONFIG

For more information about the *Set-OrganizationConfig* EMS cmdlet, see *http://technet.microsoft.com/en-us/library/aa997443.aspx*.

Configuring Custom MailTips

Before you can use custom MailTips, you need to ensure that MailTips are enabled in your Exchange Server 2010 organization. Custom MailTips can include HTML links (hyperlinks), but scripts are not permitted. The length of a custom MailTips cannot exceed 250 characters. You can use the EMS but not the EMC to configure custom MailTips for recipients based on the following EMS cmdlets:

- *Set-Mailbox*
- *Set-MailContact*
- *Set-MailUser*
- *Set-DistributionGroup*
- *Set-DynamicDistributionGroup*
- *Set-MailPublicFolder*

Suppose, for example, that the response time service-level agreement (SLA) for your Help Desk is three hours and that the Help Desk mailbox is called CorporateAssistance. The following configures a custom MailTip for that mailbox to inform senders that they will receive a response within three hours:

```
Set-Mailbox -Identity "CorporateAssistance" -MailTip "A Corporate Assistance
representative will contact you within 3 hours."
```

Custom MailTips are also useful for recipients, such as distribution groups, whose display name could be misinterpreted. For example, assume that you have a distribution group called Marketing that is used for intradepartmental communications. The following command configures a MailTip that informs senders what the distribution group is used for and directs them to the correct address if they have a question or comment to submit to the Marketing Department:

```
Set-DistributionGroup -Identity Marketing -MailTip "This distribution group is used
for Marketing intra-departmental communications. If you want to contact a Marketing
representative, please e-mail MarketingRepresentatives@adatum.com."
```

Using Message Classifications

Message classifications are a feature of Exchange Server 2010, Office Outlook 2007, Outlook 2010, and OWA designed to help organizations comply with email policies and regulatory responsibilities. A classified message contains specific metadata that describes its intended use or audience of the message. An Outlook or OWA client can use this metadata to display a user-friendly description of the classification to senders and receivers of a classified message. In Exchange Server 2010, the Exchange Transport service acts on the metadata if a transport rule exists that meets criteria you have configured.

You can set the following Message classification fields:

- **Display name** This appears in the Permission menu in Outlook and OWA and is used by Outlook and OWA users to select the appropriate message classification before a message is sent. The display name is also displayed in the recipient description that appears in the InfoBar in an Outlook message.

- **Sender description** This explains to the sender what the message classification is intended to achieve. OWA and Outlook users use the sender description to select the appropriate message classification before a message is sent.
- **Recipient description** This explains to a recipient what the message classification is intended to achieve. OWA and Outlook users view the sender description when they receive a message that has this message classification.
- **Locale** This specifies a culture code to create a locale-specific version of the message classification.

After Outlook is enabled to accept the default message classifications, users can apply message classification to messages that they send. Senders see the sender description in the InfoBar in Outlook. You can use the EMS to customize the sender description for each message classification and locale.

The following message classifications are enabled by default in Exchange Server 2010— users cannot add these classifications to messages:

- **Attachment Removed** This notifies recipients when attachments have been removed from the message.
- **Originator Requested Alternate Recipient Mail** This notifies recipients that the message has been redirected.
- **Partner Mail** This notifies recipients that the message was encrypted and delivered through a secure connector.

By default, all message classifications are informational only and are not associated with any transport protection rules. They provide additional information about a message to message recipients, but the Microsoft Exchange Transport service does not take any special action on the message.

You can, however, create transport rules associated with message classifications. For example, you can configure a transport rule that checks all incoming messages for a specific message classification and direct that these messages be delivered to a designated recipient. You can also use the *New-TransportRule* EMS cmdlet or the New Transport Rule Wizard in the EMC to create a transport rule that is associated with a message classification. You will see how to create such a rule later in this lesson.

> **MORE INFO** **TRANSPORT RULES**
>
> For more information about transport rules, access *http://technet.microsoft.com/en-us/library/dd335050.aspx* and follow the links.

Message classifications can be separated into two classes based on how they are attached to a specific message:

- Manually added in Outlook or OWA by the sender of a message before the message is sent.
- Added as the result of a transport rule. For example, when the Attachment Filter agent removes an attachment from a message, the Attachment Removed message classification (ExAttachmentRemoved) is attached to the message.

Creating a Message Classification

You can use the *New-MessageClassification* EMS cmdlet to create a message classification. For example, the following command creates a message classification named SampleMessageClassification with the display name Sample Message Classification and the sender description "This is a sample message classification.":

```
New-MessageClassification -Name SampleMessageClassification -DisplayName "Sample Message
Classification" -SenderDescription "This is a sample message classification."
```

Figure 11-15 shows the output from this command.

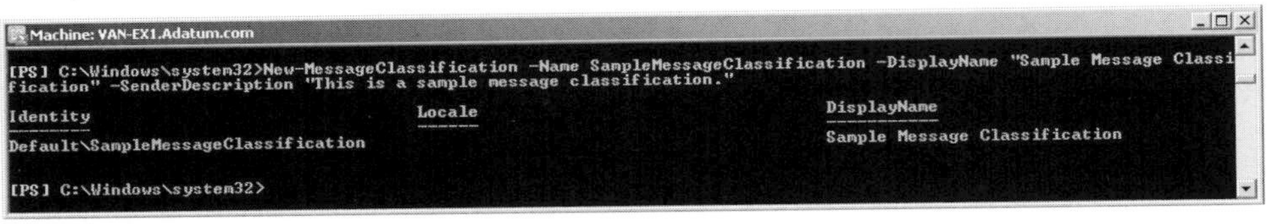

FIGURE 11-15 Creating a message classification

After you create a new message classification, you can specify it as a transport rule predicate. Before Outlook and OWA users can apply the message classification to messages, you need to update the end-user systems with the message classification Extensible Markup Language (XML) file created by the *Export-OutlookClassification.ps1* script file, which is located by default in the *C:\Program Files\Microsoft\Exchange Server\Scripts* directory.

Localizing Message Classifications

By default, a message classification is used for all locales. You can add new locales of the message classification by running the *New-MessageClassification* cmdlet and by specifying the default message classification identity that you want to localize. Sometimes, for example, you might need to use several different languages for message classifications. After you create the default message classification instance, you can create more message classification instances for different languages.

Each localized version of a specific message classification is implemented by a new message classification instance. The Locale parameter defines the locale for a particular message classification instance, such as es-ES (Spanish—Spain). The following command creates a locale-specific version of the existing message classification SampleMessageClassification:

```
New-MessageClassification -Identity SampleMessageClassification -Locale es-ES -DisplayName
"En Espanol" -SenderDescription "Esta es una clasificacion de mensajes muestra."
```

Figure 11-16 shows the locale-specific version of the message classification SampleMessageClassification.

FIGURE 11-16 Creating a locale-specific version of a message classification

You can also use a message classification instance to change the content of the sender description and recipient description to reflect differences in regulatory requirements for different jurisdictions. For example, health care–related companies that operate in the United States and in Europe may have to comply with Health Insurance Portability and Accountability Act (HIPAA) regulations in the United States but not in Europe. Therefore, the display of message classifications that are HIPAA specific should be enabled only for employees operating in the United States. You can set Read permission on classifications so that only appropriate users can view specific message classifications.

> **NOTE ACKNOWLEDGEMENT OF SOURCE**
>
> The example above was taken from Technet. It is an excellent example, and I cannot think of one nearly as good.

Configuring Message Classification Priority and Retention

Each message classification can be assigned a priority relative to other message classifications. This sets the precedence on a classification and determines how it is displayed to the recipient. The message classification with the highest precedence is shown first, and subsequent classifications with lesser precedence are displayed in order after it.

You set precedence by using the DisplayPrecedence parameter of the *Set-MessageClassification* EMS cmdlet. Valid input for the DisplayPrecedence parameter is Highest, Higher, High, MediumHigh, Medium (the default), MediumLow, Low, Lower, and Lowest.

You can also specify whether the message classification is retained when a recipient replies to or forwards the message by setting the RetainClassificationEnabled parameter of the *Set-MessageClassification* cmdlet to $true or $false. The following command changes the display precedence of the message classification SampleMessageClassification to MediumLow and specifies that the message classification should be retained if the message is forwarded or replied to:

```
Set-MessageClassification -Identity SampleMessageClassification -DisplayPrecedence
MediumLow -RetainClassificationEnabled $true
```

You can use the *Get-MessageClassification* EMS cmdlet to view the configuration of a message classification, such as follows:

```
Get-MessageClassification -Identity SampleMessageClassification | FL
```

Figure 11-17 shows the output from this command.

If you are using a default message classification and want to change one of its parameters, you can pipe the output of the *Get-MessageClassification* cmdlet into a *Set-MessageClassification* cmdlet. For example, the following command changes the priority of the default Attachment Removed message classification to Highest:

```
Get-MessageClassification -Identity ExAttachmentRemoved | Set-MessageClassification
-DisplayPrecedence Highest
```

```
[PS] C:\Windows\system32>Get-MessageClassification -Identity SampleMessageClassification | FL

ClassificationID          : f33feae3-fbff-4002-839c-01237b5b4d7e
DisplayName               : Sample Message Classification
DisplayPrecedence         : MediumLow
Identity                  : Default\SampleMessageClassification
IsDefault                 : True
Locale                    :
RecipientDescription      : This is a sample message classification.
RetainClassificationEnabled : True
SenderDescription         : This is a sample message classification.
UserDisplayEnabled        : True
Version                   : 1


[PS] C:\Windows\system32>
```

FIGURE 11-17 Viewing a message classification configuration

You can also use the New Transport Rule Wizard in the EMC to reconfigure a default message classification.

Configuring Read Access to Message Classifications

When you create a message classification and enable it on the computer on which Outlook or OWA runs, the new message classification will be present in the Permission menu of the client software. You can control read access for message classifications by configuring the Read permission on the message classifications that you export into the Classifications.xml file. By default, all message classifications are created with Read permission for any authenticated user.

In situations that require more restrictive access for message classifications, such as if a message is relevant to recipients in one locale but not another, the Read permission can be removed from a message classification object. You first use the *Get-MessageClassification* EMS cmdlet to access the message classification and then remove the AdPermission setting. For example, the following command removes Read access from a message classification instance named SampleMessageClassification for the user Kim Akers:

```
Get-MessageClassification -Identity SampleMessageClassification | -Remove AdPermission
-User "Kim Akers" -AccessRights GenericRead
```

The following command removes Read access from a message classification instance named SampleMessageClassification for a universal distribution group named Marketing:

```
Get-MessageClassification -Identity "SampleMessageClassification" | -Remove AdPermission
-User Marketing -AccessRights GenericRead
```

MORE INFORMATION **THE CLASSIFICATIONS.XML FILE**

For more information about how to create and use the Classifications.xml file, see *http://technet.microsoft.com/en-us/library/aa998271.aspx*. Note that the title of this link is "Deploy Message Classifications for Outlook 2007," but it also applies to Outlook 2010.

If you configure the Read permission on a message classification object, this does not affect whether the sender can use the message classification. Read permission on the message classification controls only whether the message classification is displayed in the Permission menu in Outlook and OWA.

> **MORE INFO** **GET-MESSAGECLASSIFICATION, GET-MESSAGECLASSIFICATION, AND *GET-MESSAGECLASSIFICATION***
>
> For more information about the *New-MessageClassification* EMS cmdlet, see *http://technet.microsoft.com/en-us/library/bb124400.aspx*. For more information about the *Set-MessageClassification* EMS cmdlet, see *http://technet.microsoft.com/en-us/library/bb125250.aspx*. For more information about the *Get-MessageClassification* EMS cmdlet, see *http://technet.microsoft.com/en-us/library/aa996911.aspx*.

Message Classifications and Transport Rules

After you create a message classification instance, you can associate a transport rule with the message classification. You use the *New-TransportRule* EMS cmdlet to create a transport rule and add the message classification as a condition. You can also use the EMC New Transport Rule Wizard to create a transport protection rule.

> **MORE INFO** **CREATING A TRANSPORT RULE USING THE EMC**
>
> For more information about how to use the New Transport Rule Wizard to create a transport rule, see *http://technet.microsoft.com/en-us/library/bb124737.aspx*.

If you use the *New-TransportRule* EMS cmdlet to create a transport rule, you can add a message classification as the result of this transport rule through the ApplyClassification parameter, which specifies a message classification to apply to the message. For example, the following command creates a transport rule that applies the message classification:Default\SampleMessageClassification to all messages sent from the user Kim Akers to the user Don Hall:

```
New-TransportRule -Name ClassificationTest -From "Kim Akers" -SentTo "Don Hall"
-ApplyClassification Default\SampleMessageClassification
```

Figure 11-18 shows the output of this command.

FIGURE 11-18 Creating a transport rule that applies a message classification

The HasClassification parameter specifies a message classification and enables you to create a transport rule that carries out a specified action only if a particular message classification is applied to the message. The ExceptIfHasClassification parameter also specifies a message classification, but in this case the action defined by the transport rule takes place if the classification is not applied to the message.

For example, the following command creates a transport rule that blocks messages between members of the Marketing distribution group and Finance distribution group that are not classified as Interdepartmental:

```
New-TransportRule BlockMessagesBetweenMarketingAndFinance -BetweenMemberOf1 Marketing
-BetweenMemberOf2 Finance -ExceptIfHasClassification Default\
Interdepartmental -RejectMessageReasonText "E-mail messages sent between the Marketing
department and the Finance department must be classified as Interdepartmental."
```

Figure 11-19 shows the output of this command. Note that for the above command to work, the Marketing and Finance distribution groups and the default instance of the Interdepartmental message classification must exist.

FIGURE 11-19 Using a message classification to determine whether a transport rule is applied

The New-TransportRule cmdlet also supports two Boolean parameters—that is, parameters that can take only the values $true or $false. The HasNoClassification parameter enables you to specify that a transport rule is applied to any message that has no message classification. Microsoft recommends that if you use this parameter, its argument should be $true. The ExceptIfHasNoClassification parameter enables you to specify that a transport rule is applied to any message that has any message classification. Table 11-3 summarizes the message classification parameters that the *New-TransportRule* EMS cmdlet supports.

TABLE 11-3 Message classification parameters in the *New-TransportRule* cmdlet

PARAMETER	ARGUMENT	DESCRIPTION
HasClassification	Message classification name	The rule is applied to messages with the specified classification.
ExceptIfHasClassification	Message classification name	The rule is applied to messages that do not have the specified classification.
HasNoClassification	$true or $false	If the parameter is used, the value should be set to $true. In this case, the rule is applied to messages that do not have any message classification.
ExceptIfHasNoClassification	$true or $false	If the value is true, the rule is applied to messages that have any message classification.

EXAM TIP

Take note of which of the parameters in Table 11-3 are Boolean and which take the name of a message classification as their argument.

Implementing a Discovery Search

A *discovery search* is a multimailbox search that returns email messages that meet specified conditions. By default, a discovery search will search all mailboxes in an Exchange Server 2010 organization. You can, however, specify the source mailboxes that you want to include in the search by using the SourceMailboxes parameter of the *New-MailboxSearch* EMS cmdlet.

Search results are saved in the mailbox Discovery Search Mailbox in a folder with the same name as the search. Exchange Server 2010 Setup creates a mailbox named Discovery Search Mailbox by default. Note that if you do not specify a search query, the entire content of all the specified mailboxes is copied to the target mailbox.

You can use the EMS or the Exchange Control Panel (ECP) in OWA to create a discovery search. This lesson concentrates on server-side configuration and the use of the *New-MailboxSearch* EMS cmdlet.

> **MORE INFO** **USING THE ECP TO CARRY OUT A DISCOVERY SEARCH**
>
> For more information about using the ECP to carry out a discovery search, see *http://help .outlook.com/en-us/140/ms.exch.ecp.newmailboxsearch.aspx*. A screenshot of this procedure in operation can be seen at *http://technet.microsoft.com/en-us/magazine/ 2009.07.exchangeqa.aspx*.

For example, you want to create the discovery search Adatum-ExchangeProject. The search should return email messages that contain the words "Adatum" and "Exchange project" and that are sent or received from January 1, 2011, through December 31, 2011. The search runs against all mailboxes on all Exchange 2010 Mailbox servers in the organization. Full logging is enabled for the search. This search includes items that cannot be indexed in Exchange Search. This last condition is specified by including the IncludeUnsearchableItems switch in the command. By default, such items are not included in search results. To create this search, you will enter the following command:

```
New-MailboxSearch -Name "Adatum-ExchangeProject" -StartDate "1/1/2011" -EndDate
"12/31/2011" -TargetMailbox "Discovery Search Mailbox" -SearchQuery '"Adatum" and
"Exchange project"'-MessageTypes Email -IncludeUnsearchableItems -LogLevel Full
```

You can use the –MessageTypes parameter to specify the message types to include in the search. Valid values can include one or more of the following:

- Email
- Meetings
- Tasks
- Notes

- Docs
- Journals
- Contacts
- Instant Messaging (IM)

If you do not specify a message type, all message types are included.

MORE INFO **NEW-MAILBOXSEARCH**

For more information about the *New-MailboxSearch* cmdlet, see *http://technet.microsoft .com/en-us/library/dd298064.aspx.*

Stopping, Restarting, or Removing a Discovery Search

You can stop, restart, or remove a discovery search from an OWA client or from an Exchange Server 2010 client at any time. On the OWA client, click My Organization, click Reporting, and then click Mailbox Searches. To stop a search, select the search and then click the Stop Search icon. To start a stopped search, select the search and then click the Restart Search icon. When a warning appears stating that the existing search will be removed from the target mailbox, click Yes. If you want to remove a search, select the search and click the Remove Search icon (red cross).

The following EMS command stops the discovery search Adatum-ExchangeProject:

```
Stop-MailboxSearch -Identity "Adatum-ExchangeProject"
```

The following EMS command starts the discovery search Adatum-ExchangeProject:

```
Start-MailboxSearch -Identity "Adatum-ExchangeProject"
```

The following EMS command removes the discovery search Adatum-ExchangeProject:

```
Remove-MailboxSearch -Identity "Adatum-ExchangeProject"
```

MORE INFO **STOP-MAILBOXSEARCH, START-MAILBOXSEARCH, AND *REMOVE-MAILBOXSEARCH***

For more information about the *Stop-MailboxSearch* EMS cmdlet, see *http://technet .microsoft.com/en-us/library/dd351075.aspx.* For more information about the *Start-MailboxSearch* EMS cmdlet, see *http://technet.microsoft.com/en-us/library/ dd351245.aspx.* For more information about the *Remove-MailboxSearch* EMS cmdlet, see *http://technet.microsoft.com/en-us/library/dd298130.aspx.*

Modifying a Discovery Search

You can use commands based on the *Set-MailboxSearch* EMS cmdlet to modify a discovery search. For example, the following command modifies the discovery search Adatum-ExchangeProject to search mailboxes belonging to members of the Accountants distribution group:

```
Set-MailboxSearch -Identity "Adatum-ExchangeProject " -SourceMailboxes "Accountants"
```

Placing a Mailbox on Legal Hold

Organizations are sometimes required to preserve electronically stored information such as email messages that could be relevant to litigation. An organization may decide preserve all email related to a specific topic or all email sent to or by selected individuals. Relying on individual users not to delete their email messages might not always work, and suspending automatic deletion mechanisms might result in a large volume of undeleted email. Manual archiving can increase administrative costs.

Exchange Server 2010 offers legal hold as a solution to this problem. Legal hold enables you to place users on hold and keep their mailbox items in an unaltered state. You can preserve mailbox items that may have been deleted by users or automatically by MRM. You can enable discovery searches of items placed on hold. Finally, legal hold is transparent to the user and does not affect user experience.

Legal hold uses the Recoverable Items folder (sometimes known as the dumpster). This folder is hidden from the default view of Outlook, OWA, and other email clients. Items in the Recoverable Items folder are retained for the deleted item retention period configured on the user's mailbox database. By default, the deleted item retention period is set to 14 days for mailbox databases.

Items are purged permanently from the Recoverable Items folder on a first-in, first-out basis when the folder's storage quota is exceeded or if the item has resided in the folder for a longer time than the deleted item retention period. Items in the Recoverable Items folder are not included when calculating a user's mailbox quota.

The Recoverable Items folder contains the following three subfolders that store deleted items in various states and thus facilitate legal hold:

- **Deletions** Items removed from the Deleted Items folder or hard-deleted from other folders are moved to this subfolder and are visible to the user when using the Recover Deleted Items tool in Outlook.

- **Purges** When a user deletes an item from the Recoverable Items folder the item is moved to the Purges folder. Items that exceed the deleted item retention period are also moved to the Purges folder. When the mailbox assistant processes the mailbox, items in the Purges folder are typically purged from the mailbox database. However, when you place the mailbox user on legal hold, the mailbox assistant does not purge items in this folder.

- **Versions** When a user who is placed on legal hold changes specific properties of a mailbox item, the original item is preserved to meet discovery obligations. A copy of the original mailbox item is created before the changed item is created, and this copy is saved in the Versions folder. This process is known as *copy on write*.

A legal hold preserves deleted mailbox items and records changes made to mailbox items. Deleted and changed items are returned in a discovery search. Legal hold is typically implemented for compliance purposes.

You use commands based on the Set-Mailbox EMS cmdlet to place a mailbox on legal hold or release a mailbox from legal hold. Note that it may take up to an hour before the legal hold takes effect.

The following command places the mailbox DonHall@adatum.com on legal hold:

```
Set-Mailbox DonHall@adatum.com -LitigationHoldEnabled $true
```

The following command removes the legal hold on the mailbox DonHall@adatum.com:

```
Set-Mailbox DonHall@adatum.com -LitigationHoldEnabled $false
```

MORE INFO **SET-MAILBOXSEARCH**

For more information about the *Set-MailboxSearch* EMS cmdlet, see *http://technet .microsoft.com/en-us/library/dd335145.aspx.*

Auditing Message Activity

Message tracking logs were discussed in Chapter 10, "Logging and Reports." The Tracking Log Explorer, described in detail in that chapter, provides a log of all message activity as messages are transferred to and from an Exchange server that has the Hub Transport server role, the Mailbox server role, or the Edge Transport server role installed. Message tracking logs can be used for message forensics, mail flow analysis, reporting, and troubleshooting. For compliance purposes, it is often important to track a message and discover whether it reached all recipients to which it was sent.

To briefly summarize the information given in Chapter 10, you can access the Tracking Log Explorer from the EMC Toolbox. By default, the RECEIVE EventID is enabled with a 10-minute interval specified. You can specify parameters such as Recipients, Sender, Server, and so on. If message subject logging is enabled, you can also specify Subject. The tool tracks messages defined by the parameters you specify. If your request highlights message tracking problems, you can select a symptom and obtain further information.

When the Tracking Log Explorer successfully completes a tracking request, a result file is generated. You can view the results of previous tracking requests by clicking Select A Result File To View on the Tracking Log Explorer left pane.

You can also use the EMS to, for example, locate messages with a RECEIVE EventID. The following command accesses messages with this EventID received between 5:37 AM and 5:47 AM on March 18, 2010:

```
Get-MessageTrackingLog -EventID RECEIVE -Start 3/18/2010 5:37:00 AM -End
3/18/2010 5:47:00 AM
```

Creating and Configuring Ethical Walls

An ethical wall is a zone of noncommunication between distinct departments of a business or organization that prevents conflicts of interest that might result in the inappropriate release of sensitive information. Exchange Server 2010 uses transport rules configured on Hub Transport servers to implement and configure ethical walls. Note that ethical walls configured in an Exchange organization are concerned only with email traffic and not with other methods of communication.

Typically, you implement an ethical wall by configuring a transport rule that rejects messages sent between specified senders and recipients, such as from one distribution group to another. When you create a transport rule to enforce an ethical wall, you either specify conditions to define which recipients and senders to prohibit from sending messages to each other or specify exceptions to narrow the scope of the transport rule. If you do not specify conditions or exceptions, the transport rule will block all messages sent to or from recipients or senders in your organization. Remember also that for transport rules to be applied to email messages, the messages must be routed by an Exchange Server 2010 Hub Transport server.

As discussed earlier in this lesson and in Chapter 7, you can create a transport rule (and hence implement an ethical wall) by using either the EMC or the EMS. The high-level procedure to use the Transport Rule Wizard in the EMC to create an ethical wall is as follows:

1. Start the New Transport Rule Wizard.

2. On the Introduction page, specify a name and (optionally) a description. Ensure that the Enable Rule check box is selected.

3. On the Conditions page in the Step 1. Select Condition(s) box, select one or more conditions. Typically, for an ethical wall, you would select Between Members Of Distribution List And Distribution List. For each condition, in the Step 2. Edit The Rule Description By Clicking An Underlined Value box, click each blue underlined word and supply the values to apply to the condition.

4. On the Actions page, in the Step 1. Select Actions box, select Send Bounce Message To Sender With Enhanced Status Code. This transport rule action deletes the message and returns an NDR to the sender of the message.

5. In the Step 2. Edit The Rule Description By Clicking An Underlined Value box, click each blue underlined word and supply the values to apply to the condition:

   - Specify the text to display in the Diagnostic Information For Administrators (the bounce message) section of the NDR returned to the sender of the rejected message.

   - Specify the delivery status notification (DSN) code you want to display in the Diagnostic Information For Administrators section of the NDR. Valid enhanced status code values are 5.7.1 and any value from 5.7.10 through 5.7.999.

   Figure 11-20 shows the completed Actions page.

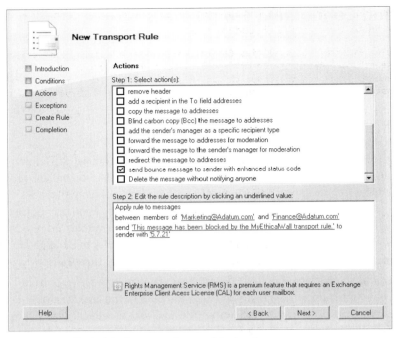

FIGURE 11-20 Typical Actions page for an ethical wall

6. Optionally, on the Exceptions page, select any exceptions you require and enter values for these exceptions using the same procedure that you used to enter values on the Conditions and Actions pages.

7. On the Create Rule page, review the Configuration Summary. If you are satisfied with the configuration of the new rule, click New.

8. When the status of the new rule is shown as Completed, click Finish.

You can also use the EMS to create an ethical wall. In this example, Trey Research wants to prevent members of its Finance distribution group and its Facilities distribution group from communicating. Trey's Exchange administrator, Don Hall, decides to implement an ethical wall between the two groups by using a transport rule.

The RejectMessage transport rule action blocks messages sent to a prohibited recipient and returns an NDR to the sender, so Don's procedure uses the RejectMessageReasonText parameter of the *New-TransportRule* EMS cmdlet to implement this action. Don decides to use the RejectMessageEnchancedStatusCode parameter and specify a custom DSN code 5.7.206. He then needs to associate this code with a custom DSN message. The DSN message appears in the user information section of the NDR. In this case, the default reason text "Delivery not authorized, message refused" is used in the RejectMessageReasonText parameter.

Don also decides to create an exception to this policy that allows members of the Managers distribution group, who may also belong to either of the two other groups, to communicate. He uses the ExceptIfFromMemberOf predicate to implement this exception.

The first command Don enters on a Trey Research Hub Transport server configures the ethical wall and defines the custom DSN code as follows:

```
New-TransportRule "Finance and Facilities Ethical Wall" -Enabled $true -BetweenMemberOf1
Finance@treyresearch.com -BetweenMemberOf2 Facilities@treyresearch.com
-ExceptIfFromMemberOf Managers@treyresearch.com -RejectMessageReasonText "Delivery not
authorized, message refused." -RejectionMessageEnhancedStatusCode 5.7.206
```

Don specifies the text that should be displayed when a message is returned with the custom DSN code by entering the following command:

```
New-SystemMessage -DsnCode 5.7.206 -Internal $true -Language En -Text "A message was
sent that violates Trey Research policy. Direct e-mail communication between the Finance
department and the Facilities department is prohibited unless the e-mail is sent by either
departmental manager. For more information, please contact Don Hall at System Support."
```

> **MORE INFO   DSN CODES**
>
> For more information about how Exchange Server 2010 associates a DSN code with a transport rule, see *http://technet.microsoft.com/en-us/library/bb123506.aspx*.

> **MORE INFO   NEW-SYSTEMMESSAGE**
>
> For more information about the *New-SystemMessage* EMS cmdlet, see *http://technet .microsoft.com/en-us/library/aa998878.aspx*.

Lesson Summary

- IRM permits your organization and your users to apply persistent protection to messages so that access is restricted to authorized users and permitted actions. IRM enables you to apply an RMS template to messages sent to a specified SMTP address.

- You can use transport protection rules to apply messaging policies to email messages that flow through Hub Transport and Edge Transport servers. Message classifications allow an organization to comply with email policies and regulatory responsibilities. You can associate message classifications with transport rules.

- Journaling helps an organization to respond to legal, regulatory, and organizational compliance requirements by recording inbound and outbound email communications. You can use journal rules to ensure that all messages that are sent to a specified email address are also stored in a journaling mailbox for compliance purposes. You can specify that if any journaling mailbox in an Exchange organization becomes unavailable, the subsequent NDRs are sent to an alternate journaling mailbox.

- MailTips give your Outlook 2010 and OWA users information about their messages and recipients before they send an email.

- Ethical walls enable you to prohibit communication between specific groups in your own organization. You can create an ethical wall for email communication by configuring a transport rule. Discovery search discovers items in multiple mailboxes based on search criteria. Legal hold retains items that would otherwise be deleted and records changes to such items. Items that have legal hold configured can be located using a discovery search even when they appear to the user to be deleted.

Lesson Review

You can use the following questions to test your knowledge of the information in Lesson 2, "Configuring Compliance." The questions are also available on the companion CD if you prefer to review them in electronic form.

> **NOTE ANSWERS**
>
> Answers to these questions and explanations of why each answer choice is correct or incorrect are located in the "Answers" section at the end of the book.

1. Which of the following commands disables IRM features in OWA for the entire Exchange organization?

   A. *Set-OWAMailboxPolicy –Identity Default –IRMEnabled $false*

   B. *Set-OWAVirtualDirectory –Identity VAN-EX2\MyVirtualDirectory –IRMEnabled $false*

   C. *Set-IRMConfiguration –TransportDecryptionSetting mandatory*

   D. *Set-IRMConfiguration –OWAEnabled $true*

2. You have created the mailbox KimAkers-Journaling and want to use it as a journaling mailbox. What command ensures that all mail sent to the KimAkers@adatum.com mailbox is also sent to this journaling mailbox for compliance purposes?

   A. *New-JournalRule -Name "Kim Akers" -JournalEmailAddress "Kim Akers Journal Mailbox" -Scope Global -Recipient KimAkers-Journaling @adatum.com -Enabled $True*

   B. *New-JournalRule -Name "KimAkers-Journaling" -JournalEmailAddress "Kim Akers Journal Mailbox" -Scope Global -Recipient KimAkers@adatum.com -Enabled $True*

   C. *New-OutlookProtectionRule -Name "KimAkers-Journaling" -SentTo "Kim Akers" -ApplyRightsProtectionTemplate "Protect-Confidential"*

   D. *Set-Mailbox -Identity "Kim Akers" -MailTip "Messages sent to this e-mail address are also stored in the mailbox KimAkers-Journaling for compliance purposes."*

3. What EMS cmdlet or cmdlets do you use to create a locale-specific version of an existing message classification?

   A. *Set-MessageClassification*

   B. *Get-MessageClassification*

   C. *New-MessageClassification*

   D. *Get-MessageClassification* –you pipe the output from a command using this cmdlet into a command using the *Set-MessageClassification* cmdlet.

4. Which of the following commands configures the existing mailbox MyJournalingMailbox@adatum.com as an alternate journaling mailbox?

   A. *Set-TransportConfig -JournalingReportNdrTo MyJournalingMailbox@adatum.com*

   B. *Set-Mailbox MyJournalingMailbox -AcceptMessagesOnlyFromSendersOrMembers "Microsoft Exchange" -RequireSenderAuthenticationEnabled $true*

   C. *Set-Mailbox –Identity "MyJournalingMailbox" -ProhibitSendReceiveQuota 524288000*

   D. *New-Mailbox -Name MyJournalingMailbox -UserPrincipalName OtherJournalingMailbox@adatum.com -Database MyMailboxDatabase -Password $password*

5. You want to create an ethical wall in your Exchange Server 2010 organization. Which of the following tools could you use? (Choose all that apply.)

   A. Set-TransportConfig

   B. New Transport Rule Wizard

   C. Set-IRMConfiguration

   D. New-OutlookProtectionRule

   E. New-TransportRule

   F. New Mailbox Wizard

PRACTICE **Creating Retention Tags and Applying a Retention Policy**

In this practice session, you will create a DPT, an RPT, and a personal tag and group them into a retention policy that you then apply to the Don Hall mailbox. Optionally, you will log on using the Don Hall account, access the Mailbox server using OWA, and observe the effects of this policy.

EXERCISE 1 Creating Retention Tags

In this exercise, you will create a DPT, an RPT, and a personal tag.

1. Log on to the VAN-EX1 Mailbox server using the Kim Akers account and open the EMS.

2. Create a DPT and set it as primary. When this tag is applied to a mailbox, items without an inherited or explicitly applied retention tag are deleted after 90 days but can be recovered from recoverable items. To create this tag, enter the following command:

```
New-RetentionPolicyTag "Tag-EXERCISE-DPT" -Type All -IsPrimary $true -Comment
"Items without a retention tag are deleted after 90 days but can be recovered
from recoverable items." -RetentionEnabled $true -AgeLimitForRetention
90 -RetentionAction DeleteAndAllowRecovery
```

Figure 11-21 shows some of the output from this command.

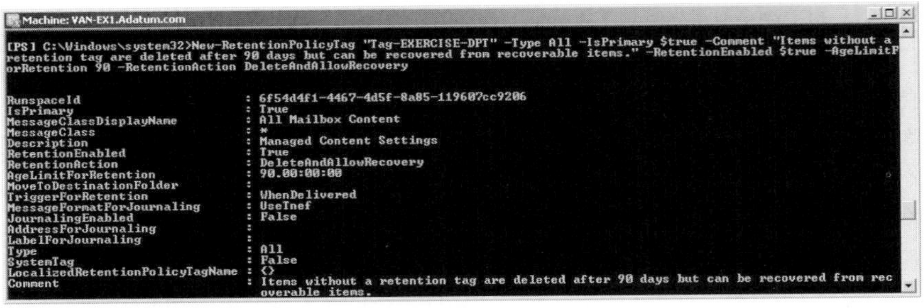

FIGURE 11-21 Creating the Tag-EXERCISE-DPT retention tag

3. Create an RPT for the default folder Deleted Items. When this tag is applied to a mailbox, items in the Deleted Items folder are permanently deleted after 30 days. To create this tag, enter the following command:

```
New-RetentionPolicyTag "Tag-EXERCISE-RPT" -Type "DeletedItems" -Comment "Deleted
Items purged after 30 days" -RetentionEnabled $true -AgeLimitForRetention
30 -RetentionAction PermanentlyDelete
```

Figure 11-22 shows some of the output from this command.

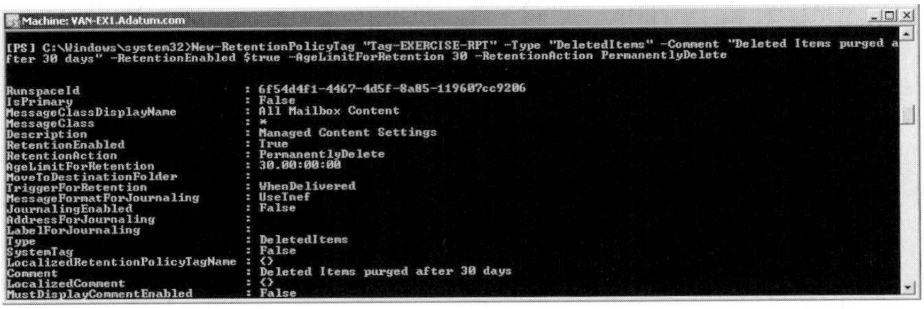

FIGURE 11-22 Creating the Tag-EXERCISE-RPT retention tag

4. Create a personal tag. Items to which this tag is applied are moved to the personal archive after 180 days. To create this tag, enter the following command:

```
New-RetentionPolicyTag "Tag-EXERCISE-Personal" -Type Personal -Comment "Tagged
messages are moved to the archive after 180 days." -RetentionEnabled $true
-AgeLimitForRetention 180 -RetentionAction MoveToArchive
```

Figure 11-23 shows some of the output from this command.

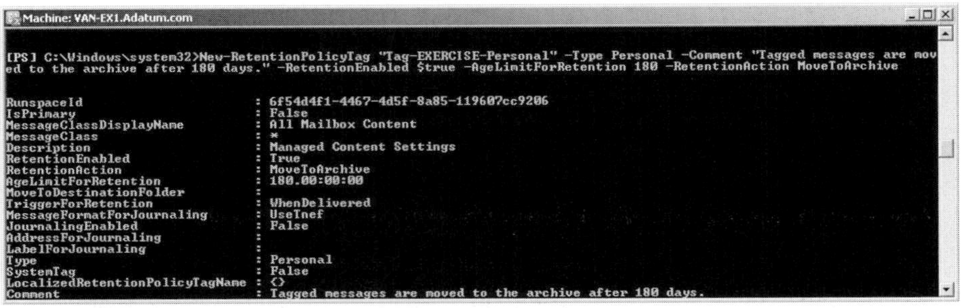

FIGURE 11-23 Creating the Tag-EXERCISE-Personal retention tag

EXERCISE 2 Creating a Retention Policy

In this exercise, you will group the tags you have created in Exercise 1 to create a retention policy and then apply this to the Don Hall mailbox. You need to have completed Exercise 1 before attempting this exercise.

1. If necessary, log on to the VAN-EX1 Mailbox server using the Kim Akers account and open the EMS.

2. Create the retention policy named Policy-EXERCISE. To create this policy, enter the following command:

```
New-RetentionPolicy –Name "Policy-EXERCISE" –RetentionPolicyTagLinks Tag-EXERCISE-
DPT,Tag-EXERCISE-RPT,Tag-EXERCISE-Personal
```

Figure 11-24 shows the output from this command.

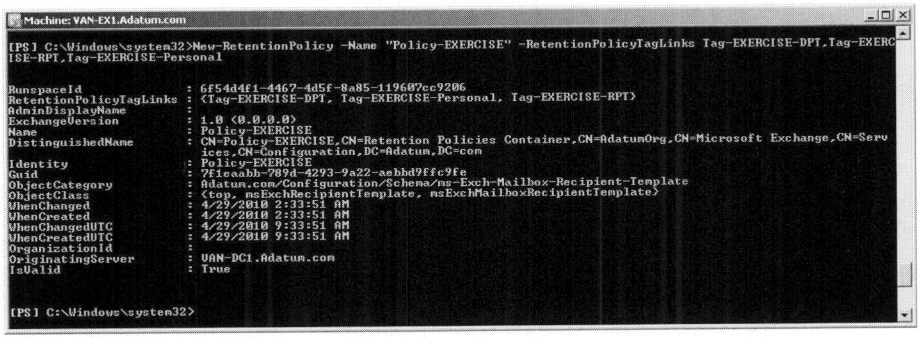

FIGURE 11-24 Creating the Policy-EXERCISE- retention policy

3. Apply the retention policy named Policy-EXERCISE to the Don Hall mailbox. To apply this policy, enter the following command:

```
Set-Mailbox "Don Hall" –RetentionPolicy "Policy-EXERCISE"
```

Note that there is no output from this last command. If it completes without error, the retention policy has been applied. You may be prompted with a Confirm statement, which informs you that versions of Outlook prior to Outlook 2007 do not support all the policy features. In this case, click Yes.

PRACTICE Configuring Retention Hold

Whether you use retention tags and policies or managed folders, the procedure to configure retention hold is the same. This practice uses the EMC to apply retention hold to the Don Hall mailbox and uses the EMS to reconfigure this retention hold and then to cancel it.

EXERCISE 1 Using the EMC to Apply Retention Hold to the Don Hall Mailbox

In this exercise, you will use the EMC to apply retention hold to the Don Hall mailbox. Note that the start and stop dates and times are given here only as an example. You should choose other dates and times that must be later than the time that you carry out the procedure.

The start date and time must be earlier than the stop date and time. Carry out the following procedure:

1. Log on to the VAN-EX1 Mailbox server using the Kim Akers account.

2. Open the EMC and expand the tree in the Console pane.

3. Under Recipient Configuration, click Mailbox.

4. In the Result pane, select the Don Hall mailbox.

5. In the Actions pane, click Properties.

6. Click the Mailbox Settings tab of the Don Hall Properties dialog box.

7. Click Messaging Records Management, as shown in Figure 11-25, and then click Properties.

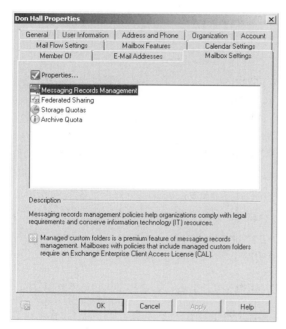

FIGURE 11-25 Selecting Messaging Records Management in the Mailbox Settings tab

8. In the Messaging Records Management dialog box, select Enable Retention Hold For Items In This Mailbox.

9. Select Start Date and specify a date and time when retention hold starts, such as Wednesday, May 05, 2010, at 8:08:15 AM.

10. Select Start Date and specify a date and time when retention hold ends, such as Friday, June 18, 2010, at 8:08:15 AM. Your Messaging Records Management dialog box should look similar to Figure 11-26.

11. Click OK to close the Messaging Records Management dialog box. Click OK again to close the Properties dialog box.

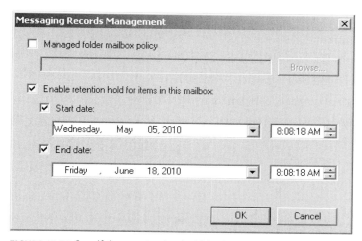

FIGURE 11-26 Specifying a retention hold in the Messaging Records Management dialog box

EXERCISE 2 Using the EMC to Release the Retention Hold on the Don Hall Mailbox

In this procedure, you decide that the retention hold you have configured on the Don Hall mailbox is not required. You use the EMS to disable it. You need to complete Exercise 1 before carrying out this procedure:

1. If necessary, log on to the VAN-EX1 Mailbox server using the Kim Akers account.
2. Open the EMS.
3. Enter the following command:

   ```
   Set-Mailbox "Don Hall" -RetentionHoldEnabled $false
   ```

   If the command runs successfully, it does not produce any output on the EMS Console but returns you to the prompt with no error messages.

PRACTICE Configuring a Journaling and an Alternate Journaling Mailbox

In this practice session, you will create a journaling mailbox and configure it. You will also create an alternate journaling mailbox that holds NDR messages if a journaling mailbox becomes unavailable.

EXERCISE 1 Creating and Configuring Mailbox for Use as a Journaling Mailbox Using the EMC

Before you carry out this exercise, you should create an OU named Journaling on the domain controller VAN-DC1. If you do not want to do this, you can still carry out the procedure but select an existing OU in Step 7. In the following procedure, you will create a mailbox for use as a journaling mailbox using the EMC:

1. If necessary, log on to the mailbox server VAN-EX1 with the Kim Akers account.
2. Open the EMC and expand the tree in the Console pane.

3. Click Recipient Configuration in the Console tree.

4. Click New Mailbox in the Actions pane. The New Mailbox Wizard starts.

5. Select User Mailbox on the Introduction page. Click Next.

6. Select New User on the User Type page. Click Next.

7. On the User Information page, complete the following fields:

   - Select the Specify The Organizational Unit Rather Than Using A Default One check box. Browse to the Journaling OU and click OK.

   - Leave the First Name, Initials, and Last Name boxes blank.

   - In the Name box, type **MyJournalingMailbox.**

   - In the User Logon Name (User Principal Name) box, type **MyJournalingMailbox.**

   - The User Logon Name (Pre-Windows 2000) should now contain the text MyJournalingMailbox. Do not change this.

   - In the Password box, type **Pa$$w0rd.**

   - In the Confirm Password, box type **Pa$$w0rd.**

   - Ensure that the User Must Change Password At Next Logon Check Box is not selected.

8. The User Information page should look like Figure 11-27. Click Next.

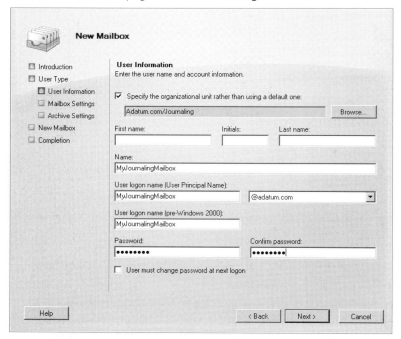

FIGURE 11-27 Configuring the User Information page

9. On the Mailbox Settings page, complete the following fields:

10. In the Alias box, type **MyJournalingMailbox.**

11. Check the Specify The Mailbox Database Rather Than Using A Database Automatically Selected check box. Click Browse, select a mailbox database, and click OK. In a production system, you would probably create a mailbox database (possibly called Journaling) before you carry out this procedure. Note that this step is optional and that the procedure still works if you accept the default mailbox database.

12. Select the Managed Folder Mailbox Policy check box. Click Browse and select a managed folder mailbox policy (if any exist), then click OK. Managed folder mailbox policies were discussed in Lesson 1.

13. Do not select the Exchange ActiveSync Mailbox Policy check box. Because journaling mailboxes are designed to be accessed using Microsoft Exchange ActiveSync, there is no need to specify this.

14. Your Mailbox Settings page should look similar to Figure 11-28. Click Next.

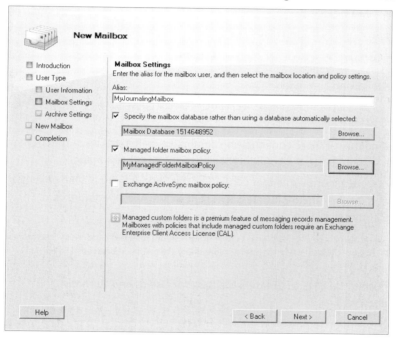

FIGURE 11-28 Configuring the Mailbox Settings page

15. On the Archive Settings page, do not select the Create An Archive Mailbox For This Account check box. Click Next.

16. On the New Mailbox page, review your configuration settings. To make any configuration changes, click Back. To create the journaling mailbox, click New. If you receive a warning that Outlook clients earlier than Outlook 2007 do not have all available client features, click Yes to close this box.

17. If the Completion page shows a status of Failed, click Back and review your settings. Otherwise, click Finish.

EXERCISE 2   Configuring a Mailbox as a Journaling Mailbox

In this exercise, you use the EMS to disable storage quota limits for the mailbox MyJournalingMailbox. You can also access the Properties dialog box for the mailbox through the EMC and configure storage quotas. Figure 11-4 earlier in this chapter shows the appropriate dialog boxes. You then configure the mailbox to accept messages only from the Microsoft Exchange recipient and to accept messages only from authenticated senders. Note that you cannot use the EMC to make these configuration changes. Finally, you create a journal rule that configures the mailbox as a journaling mailbox that stores messages sent to the Kim Akers mailbox. You need to have completed Exercise 1 before attempting this exercise. Carry out the following procedure:

1. If necessary, log on to the Mailbox server VAN-EX1 with the Kim Akers account and open the EMS.

2. Enter the following command:

   ```
   Set-Mailbox MyJournalingMailbox -UseDatabaseQuotaDefaults $false
   -IssueWarningQuota unlimited -ProhibitSendQuota unlimited
   -ProhibitSendReceiveQuota unlimited
   ```

3. Enter the following command:

   ```
   Set-Mailbox MyJournalingMailbox -AcceptMessagesOnlyFromSendersOrMembers "Microsoft
   Exchange" -RequireSenderAuthenticationEnabled $true
   ```

   Note that neither of these configuration commands generates an output. If they complete without error, the configuration changes have been made.

4. You now create a journal rule that configures the MyJournalingMailbox mailbox as a journaling mailbox that holds messages sent to KimAkers@adatum.com. Enter the following command:

   ```
   New-JournalRule -Name "Kim-Akers-Compliance" -JournalEmailAddress "MyJournaling-
   Mailbox" -Scope Global -Recipient KimAkers@adatum.com -Enabled $True
   ```

EXERCISE 3   Using the EMS to Create a Mailbox for Use as an Alternate Journaling Mailbox

You can also use a command based on the *New-Mailbox* EMS cmdlet to create a mailbox. You configure the mailbox you create in this exercise as an alternate journaling mailbox in Exercise 4. This exercise creates a mailbox named OtherJournalingMailbox with a user principal name OtherJournalingMailbox@adatum.com and a password *Pa$$w0rd* in the mailbox database Research. If this mailbox database does not exist on your test network, either create it or amend the command to use a mailbox database that does exist. To use the EMS to create a mailbox, carry out the following procedure:

1. If necessary, log on to the Mailbox server VAN-EX1 with the Kim Akers account and open the EMS.

2. Enter the following command:

   ```
   $password = Read-Host "Enter password" -AsSecureString
   ```

3. You are prompted for a password. Enter **Pa$$w0rd.**

4. Enter the following command:

```
New-Mailbox -Name OtherJournalingMailbox -UserPrincipalName
OtherJournalingMailbox@adatum.com -Database Research -Password $password
```

Figure 11-29 shows the result of these commands. Note that for security purposes, you cannot type a password directly into the *New-Mailbox* command.

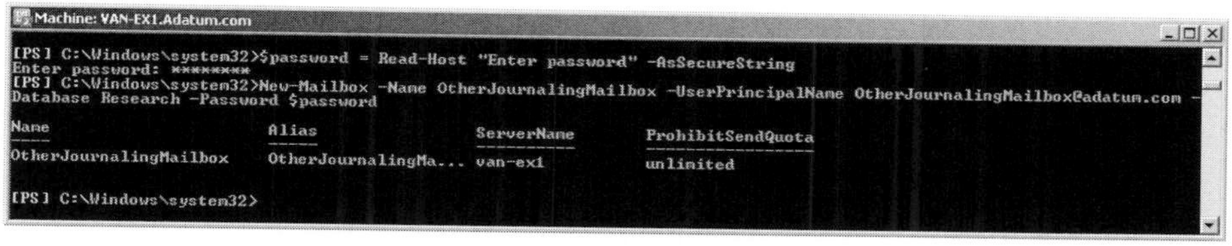

FIGURE 11-29 Creating a journaling mailbox using the EMS

EXERCISE 4   Configuring a Mailbox as an Alternate Journaling Mailbox

In this exercise, you configure the mailbox OtherJournalingMailbox you created in Lesson 3 as an alternate journaling mailbox. Carry out the following procedure:

1. If necessary, log on to the Mailbox server VAN-EX1 with the Kim Akers account and open the EMS.

2. Enter the following command:

```
Set-TransportConfig -JournalingReportNdrTo OtherJournalingMailbox@adatum.com
```

Note that this command does not generate an output. If it completes without error, the configuration change has been made.

> **MORE INFO   SET-TRANSPORTCONFIG**
>
> For more information about the *Set-TransportConfig* EMS cmdlet, see *http://technet.microsoft.com/en-us/library/bb124151.aspx*.

Chapter Review

To further practice and reinforce the skills you learned in this chapter, you can perform the following tasks:

- Review the chapter summary.
- Review the list of key terms introduced in this chapter.
- Complete the case scenarios. These scenarios set up real-world situations involving the topics of this chapter and ask you to create a solution.
- Complete the suggested practices.
- Take a practice test.

Chapter Summary

- You can apply retention policies that consist of one or more retention tags to configure retention settings for individual user mailboxes or distribution groups. You can also configure retention settings by creating managed folder policies and applying them to user mailboxes.
- You can set retention hold to prevent retention settings from being applied whether you use retention policies or managed folder policies to configure retention settings.
- IRM protects messages by restricting access to authorized users and permitted actions. IRM applies an RMS template to messages sent to a specified SMTP address. You can use transport protection rules to apply messaging policies.
- You can use message classifications and associate them with transport rules to enable your organization to comply with email policies and regulatory responsibilities. Journaling also helps an organization to respond to legal, regulatory, and organizational compliance requirements. You can configure mailboxes as journaling mailboxes by creating journal rules. Optionally, you can configure a mailbox as an alternate journaling mailbox.
- Ethical walls enable you to prohibit communication between specific groups in an organization. MailTips give your users information about their messages and recipients before they send an email. Discovery search searches multiple mailboxes for items that meet defined criteria. Legal hold prevents the deletion of items that might be required for legal purposes.

Key Terms

Do you know what these key terms mean?

- Default policy tag (DPT)
- Ethical wall
- Journaling

- Managed content settings
- Managed folder mailbox policy
- Personal tag
- Retention policy
- Retention policy tag (RPT)
- Retention tag

Case Scenarios

In the following case scenarios, you will apply what you've learned about subjects of this chapter. You can find answers to these questions in the "Answers " section at the end of this book.

Case Scenario 1: Configuring Retention Tags

Kim Akers is an Exchange Server 2010 administrator at Margie's Travel. She is tasked with creating retention policy tags for the Margie's Travel Exchange Server 2010 organization. Answer the following questions:

1. Kim needs to create an RPT named RPT-DeletedItems for the default folder Deleted Items. When this tag is applied to a mailbox, items in the Deleted Items folder are permanently deleted after 62 days. What EMS command does Kim use?

2. Kim needs to create a DPT named MT-Default that is applied to all default folders. When this tag is applied to a mailbox, items without an inherited or explicitly applied retention tag are moved to the Deleted Items folder after 270 days. What EMS command does Kim use?

3. Kim needs to create a personal tag named MT-PersonalArchive. Items to which the tag is applied are moved to the personal archive after 180 days. What EMS command does Kim use?

4. Because of a change in company policy, Kim needs to amend the RPT tag RPT-DeletedItems so that items in the Deleted Items folder are permanently deleted after 60 days. What EMS command does Kim use?

Case Scenario 2: Configuring MailTips

North Wind Traders has hired you as an Exchange Server 2010 administrator. You are tasked with implementing MailTips for the company. You discover that your predecessor has disabled MailTips for the entire North Wind Traders organization. Answer the following questions:

1. What command do you use to enable MailTips?

2. What command do you use to configure the large audience size as 30?

3. What command do you use to notify users that the recipients of a message include one or more external recipient or a distribution group that contains external recipients?

4. You discover that the previous command did not take effect. What is the likely reason for this, and what command can you use to correct the situation?

5. The response time SLA for the North Wind Traders Help Desk is two hours, and the Help Desk mailbox is called NWT-HelpDesk. What command configures a custom MailTip for that mailbox to inform senders that they will receive a response within two hours?

Suggested Practices

To help you master the examination objectives presented in this chapter, complete the following tasks.

Use Retention Policies and Managed Folder Policies

- **Practice 1**   Using retention tags and retention policies becomes much easier when you have done it a few times. Practice using retention tabs and policies and note the results you obtain. This will help you fully understand the procedure.

- **Practice 2**   As an experienced administrator, you may have used managed folders and managed folder policies before. Revise your knowledge of this topic and practice using the procedures.

Investigate the *New-TransportRule* EMS cmdlet

- **Practice 1**   In this chapter, you use this cmdlet to create transport rules associated with message configurations and to create ethical walls. The cmdlet supports a large number of parameters. You are not expected to remember them all, but you should read through the Technet link several times and try out the parameters relevant to this chapter or that you can use professionally.

Revise IRM

- **Practice 1**   Go back to Chapter 7 and revise IRM configuration, bearing in mind how RMS templates are used to configure IRM protection.

Create Message Classifications, MailTips, and Ethical Walls

- **Practice 1**   Practice creating these entities. All these tasks become easier with practice. Practice also assists understanding.

- **Practice 2**   Optionally, create a client computer on your network that can run Outlook 2010. You can use your domain controller for this purpose, but it is more realistic to create a virtual machine running a client operating system such as Microsoft

Windows 7 or Microsoft Windows Vista. Look at client-side configuration of message classification and the effect of MailTips on the client experience. Practice creating and using personal tags in Outlook.

Take a Practice Test

The practice tests on this book's companion CD offer many options. For example, you can test yourself on just one exam objective, or you can test yourself on all the 70-662 certification exam content. You can set up the test so that it closely simulates the experience of taking a certification exam, or you can set it up in study mode so that you can look at the correct answers and explanations after you answer each question.

> *MORE INFO* **PRACTICE TESTS**
>
> For details about all the practice test options available, see the "How to Use the Practice Tests" section in this book's Introduction.

CHAPTER 12

Message Integrity, Antivirus, and Anti-Spam

E mail communication is a mission-critical operation, and it is essential that organizations in today's business environment can guarantee that email messages come from who they say they come from and go to who they are supposed to go to (and nobody else). Confidential messages must be encrypted so that they can be read only by those entitled to read them and remain unread if intercepted by a malicious or unintended third party. All messages need to be tamperproof so that the recipient can guarantee that the message is as the sender sent it and has not been altered in any way.

Spam is a major problem. Unsolicited advertising and other types of junk mail, even if not malicious, can fill your users' Inboxes and waste a great deal of your organization's time. Possibly an even greater danger is posed by messages that are definitely malicious. Viruses, worms, and Trojan horses could corrupt your user's hard disks or steal their identities for fraudulent purposes. If unprotected, your organization could be put out of business by a virus attack.

This chapter discusses message integrity and confidentiality and authenticating message senders and recipients. It considers methods of identifying and filtering spam (although it is seldom possible to eradicate this nuisance completely). It looks at methods of blocking malicious email.

Exam objectives in this chapter:

- Configure message integrity.
- Configure anti-virus and anti-spam.

Lessons in this chapter:

Before You Begin

In order to complete the exercises in the practice session in this chapter, you need to have done the following:

- Installed the Windows Server 2008 R2 domain controller VAN-DC1 and the Windows Exchange 2010 Enterprise Mailbox, Hub Transport, and Client Access server VAN-EX1 as described in the Appendix, "Setup Instructions for Exchange Server 2010."

- Optionally installed the Windows Exchange 2010 server VAN-EX2 as described in the Appendix and reconfigured this as a stand-alone server with the Edge Transport server role. You can test all the commands in this chapter and complete the practice exercises on the Hub Transport server VAN-EX1. However, in a production network, many of the procedures described are performed on an Edge Transport server, and it is more realistic if you test them on a server with this role installed.

- Created the Kim Akers account with the password *Pa$$w0rd* in the Adatum.com domain. This account should be placed in the Domain Admins security group and be a member of the Organization Management role group.

- Created the Don Hall account with the password *Pa$$w0rd* in the Adatum.com domain. This account should be placed in the Backup Operators security group (so that it can be used to log on to the domain controller) and should be in the Marketing organizational unit.

- Created mailboxes for Kim Akers and Don Hall, accepting the default email address format for the email addresses.

 REAL WORLD

Ian McLean

Some users appear to have a death wish.

As an administrator, you may have come across the situation. Something nasty has slipped through the filter (it happens in even the most secure organizations), and users have received spam disguised as a message saying that their computers are at risk or a malicious email purporting to come from a bank telling them that their accounts will be closed unless they verify details, such as account number and password.

If an organization is to have any chance of surviving, it needs to train its users, even senior managers, never to respond to unsolicited email. However, some users will call in System Support just to make sure and then refuse to believe what they're told. Your advice to permanently delete the email is seldom accepted. Of course, they need to read it first. Then the problems begin. "But I do have an account with that bank," says one. "I certainly can't risk it being closed." You explain that if they respond to the email, they might still have an account with the bank, but they won't have any money in it.

Even more unfathomable is the user who does not have an account with the bank but feels the need to respond because the bank thinks he or she does. You explain that the message has been relayed to as many recipients as possible and that it doesn't actually come from the source it purports to come from. You need to remember that malicious email is probably the nearest that most decent people will come to the professional criminal, and most lack the experience and mind-set to understand what's happening.

Possibly the best reaction you're likely to get is from the user who accepts that the message is not what it purports to be and points out that it's your job to prevent this from happening. This is a good result. You could try to explain that block lists are by their nature retrospective and that a malicious sender is typically spotted when he or she has succeeded in getting a message through. You could list the many ways that highly intelligent and devious senders circumvent block lists and filters. You can explain that setting more stringent spam confidence level (SCL) policies could result in false positives and genuine, important messages being blocked. You can even point out that you are filtering 99 percent of malicious and nuisance mail and that only 1 percent is getting through. You're almost certainly wasting your time. Look humble and promise to try harder.

Life as an administrator is never easy. However, I hope better times are coming soon. It seems that a government minister in an oil-rich developing country is having problems moving money internationally and wants to put half a billion dollars into my bank account. Oh goody.

Lesson 1: Ensuring Message Integrity

Message integrity enables a user to be confident that the message he or she received is the same as the one that the sender sent and has not been tampered with. *Message confidentiality* means that the contents of a message are kept secret from an unintended listener, such as someone trying to eavesdrop on messages. *Message authentication* enables a user to be confident that he or she knows the identity of the other party in the communication and that message senders and recipients are who they purport to be.

To implement secure messaging, you need to be able to guarantee integrity, confidentiality, and authentication. It is possible to send a message in a tamperproof envelope but in clear text that anyone can read. It is possible to encrypt a message so that it cannot be read by an unintended user but fail to protect its integrity so that someone could delete part of it even if he or she could not read it. A message that is encrypted and tamperproof remains insecure if there is no method of confirming that it came from the sender that it purports to come from. Preferably, both sender and recipient should be authenticated so that not only can the recipient determine the message was sent by the identified sender but the sender can ensure that the message has been received by the identified recipient.

This lesson looks at methods of securing email communications both for internal email and messages sent between organizations.

After this lesson, you will be able to:

- Configure Secure/Multipurpose Internet Mail Extensions (S/MIME) for Outlook Web App (OWA).
- Use the Transport Layer Security (TLS) and Mutual Transport Layer Security (MTLS) protocols to provide encrypted communications and end-point authentication over network connections.
- Configure domain security.
- Manage permissions for Active Directory objects in Exchange.
- Explain how Active Directory Federation Services (AD FS) can be used to create a Rights Management Services (RMS) Federation.

Estimated lesson time: 45 minutes

Using S/MIME Extensions

Public key cryptography uses a mathematically related key pair—a secret private key and a published public key—to protect the authenticity of a message. It creates a digital signature of a message using the private key, which can be verified using the public key. It also allows protection of the confidentiality and integrity of a message by encrypting the message using the public key. The message can then be decrypted only by using the private key.

S/MIME is a standard for public key encryption and signing of MIME data. S/MIME provides authentication, message integrity and nonrepudiation of origin (using digital signatures), and privacy and data security (using encryption).

Before you can use S/MIME for public key cryptography, you need to obtain and install a certificate either from your organization's internal certificate authority (CA) or from a trusted third-party CA. An internal certificate can be used in-house only, as it is not trusted by external organizations. Typically, S/MIME clients require the installation of a certificate before permitting users to send encrypted messages.

OWA and S/MIME

A *public key infrastructure (PKI)* uses digital certificates to verify and authenticate the validity of each participant in an electronic transaction. You need to install Certificate Services on a member server in your organization to deploy a Windows PKI. A PKI enables your organization to publish its own certificates. Clients can request and receive certificates from a PKI on the internal network, and the PKI can renew or revoke certificates. Chapter 5, "Configuring Client Access"; Chapter 6 "Federated Sharing and Role-Based Access Control"; and Chapter 7, "Routing and Transport Rules" discuss the use of certificates.

OWA users can use S/MIME to encrypt outgoing messages and attachments so that only intended recipients who have a digital identification (a certificate) can read them. Users digitally sign a message, which enables its recipients to verify the identity of the sender and that the message has not been tampered with.

Users must have a digital ID and must install the S/MIME control for OWA before they can send encrypted and digitally signed messages or read encrypted messages using the OWA client. The S/MIME control is necessary to verify the signature on a digitally signed message. It is installed on a client computer by using the SMIME tab in Options. When they use S/MIME, users have access to features that are not otherwise available in OWA. They can, for example, do the following:

- Attach messages to other messages
- Paste images into messages
- Attach multiple files in a single operation

However, if the S/MIME control is installed in OWA, WebReady document viewing works in only clear-signed messages, not in encrypted messages or opaque-signed messages. When certain content types are sent from Outlook as S/MIME messages, they are not displayed in OWA. In such cases, OWA displays a banner in the message header. When a user opens a folder in another mailbox or uses explicit sign-in to open another user's mailbox, most S/MIME features are not available. In such cases, the only S/MIME feature that is available is verification of digital signatures.

> **MORE INFO** **WEBREADY DOCUMENT VIEWING**
>
> For more information about WebReady document viewing, see *http://technet.microsoft .com/en-us/library/aa995967.aspx.*

Enabling and Disabling S/MIME in OWA

You can use the Exchange Management Console (EMC) or the Exchange Management Shell (EMS) to enable or disable S/MIME in OWA. To use the EMC, carry out the following procedure:

1. Open the EMC and expand the tree in the Console pane.
2. In the console tree, click Client Access under Server Configuration.
3. At the top of the Result pane, click the server that hosts the OWA virtual directory.
4. On the Outlook Web App tab under the server name, click Owa (Default Web Site).
5. In the Actions pane under Owa (Default Web Site), click Properties.
6. On the Owa (Default Web Site) Properties dialog box, click the Segmentation tab.
7. In the Segmentation window, click the SMime, as shown in Figure 12-1.

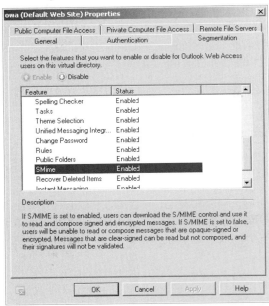

FIGURE 12-1 Selecting the SMime feature on the Segmentation tab

8. Click Enable or Disable as appropriate.
9. Click OK to save your changes and close the Properties dialog box.

By default, S/MIME is enabled. To use the EMS to disable S/MIME on the OWA virtual directory in the default Internet Information Services (IIS) website on the local server, enter the following command:

```
Set-OWAVirtualDirectory -Identity "owa (Default Web Site)" -SMimeEnabled $false
```

To enable S/MIME when it has previously been disabled, enter the following command:

```
Set-OWAVirtualDirectory -Identity "owa (Default Web Site)" -SMimeEnabled $true
```

Neither of the previously listed EMS commands generates an output. If the command completes without error, the change has been made.

> **MORE INFO** **SET-OWAVIRTUALDIRECTORY**
>
> For more information about the *Set-OwaVirtualDirectory* EMS cmdlet, see *http://technet .microsoft.com/en-us/library/bb123515.aspx.*

Managing S/MIME for OWA

You manage S/MIME for OWA by using the Regedit utility to edit the registry on an Exchange Server 2010 Client Access server. Changes are made on a per-server basis, and if you have more than one Client Access server and you need the same S/MIME behavior on all such servers, you need to make the same changes on each server. Changes to the S/MIME settings in the registry take effect immediately. Users do not need to sign out or to restart any services.

The registry settings that control S/MIME behavior on a Client Access server can be found by accessing the following registry key:

```
HKLM\System\CurrentControlSet\Services\MSExchange OWA\SMIME
```

As shown in Figure 12-2, the settings that control S/MIME are not in the registry by default, and you need to add them. Table 12-1 shows some of the settings you can use. This list is not exclusive.

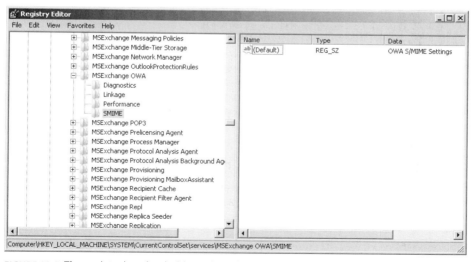

FIGURE 12-2 The registry key that holds settings that control S/MIME behavior

TABLE 12-1 Settings that control S/MIME behavior

NAME AND TYPE	VALUES	EXPLANATION
CheckCRLOnSend (DWORD)	1=True, 0=False (default).	If a certificate revocation list (CRL) distribution point in a sender's certificate chain cannot be accessed during revocation verification when sending signed or encrypted email, OWA will indicate a failure and prevent the email message from being sent when CheckCRLonSend is set to true.
DLExpansionTimeout (DWORD)	A value in milliseconds. The default is 60000 (60 seconds); the range is 0 through 2147483647.	This attribute controls how long OWA waits for a distribution list in Active Directory to expand when sending encrypted email before the operation fails. A zero setting disables the ability to send encrypted email to distribution lists. When this parameter is set to its maximum value, OWA waits until the distribution list is expanded regardless of how long expansion takes.
UseSecondaryProxiesWhenFindingCertificates (DWORD)	1=True (default), 0=False.	OWA matches a certificate in Active Directory for a recipient when sending encrypted email. The certificate subject or subject alternative name can contain a Simple Mail Transfer Protocol (SMTP) address as one of its values. If the value of this parameter is set to true, OWA accepts certificates that do not match the primary SMTP address of the recipient as valid. If the value is set to false, OWA accepts only certificates that match the primary SMTP address of the recipient as valid.
CRLConnectionTimeout (DWORD)	A value in milliseconds. The default is 60000 (60 seconds); the range is 5000 through 2147483647.	This setting specifies the time that OWA waits while connecting to retrieve a single CRL as part of a certificate validation operation. If the CRL is not retrieved before the time expires, the operation fails. If the setting is less than 5000, the default value (60000) is used. If the maximum value is specified, the connection does not time-out.

Setting	Value	Description
CRLRetrievalTimeout (DWORD)	A value in milliseconds. The default is 10000 (10 seconds); the range is 0 through 2147483647.	This setting specifies the time that OWA waits to retrieve all CRLs when validating a certificate. If all CRLs are not retrieved before the specified time expires, the operation fails.
Disable CRL Check (DWORD)	1=True, 0=False (default).	If true this setting prevents CRLs from being checked while certificates are being validated. Disabling CRL checking can decrease the time it takes to validate signatures. However, it shows revoked email messages signed with revoked certificates as valid instead of not valid.
AlwaysSign (DWORD)	1=True, 0=False (default).	If true this setting requires users to digitally sign email messages when they use OWA with the S/MIME control. The OWA Options page and the Message Options dialog box show the "Send signed e-mail" option as selected.
AlwaysEncrypt (DWORD)	1=True, 0=False (default).	If true this setting requires users to encrypt email when they use OWA with the S/MIME control. The OWA Options page and the Message Options dialog box show the "Send encrypted e-mail" option as selected.
ClearSign (DWORD)	1=True (default), 0=False.	If true this setting requires any digitally signed email message that is sent from OWA to be clear-signed. If false this setting causes OWA to use an opaque signature.
IncludeCertificateChainWithoutRootCertificate (DWORD)	1=True, 0=False (default).	If this setting is true, signed or encrypted email will include the full certificate chain, except for the root certificate. By default, OWA includes only the signing and encrypting certificates and not their corresponding certificate chains when sending signed or encrypted email.

MORE INFO **MANAGING S/MIME FOR OWA**

For more information about managing S/MIME for OWA, including additional registry settings you can add to the registry on Client Access servers, see *http://technet.microsoft .com/en-us/library/bb738151.aspx*.

NOTE **CLEAR AND OPAQUE-SIGNED EMAIL MESSAGES**

Clear-signed email messages are larger than opaque-signed (encrypted) messages, but they can be opened and read using most email clients, including clients that do not support S/MIME.

CAUTION

Edits to the registry take effect immediately without requiring confirmation. Take care when editing the registry.

MORE INFO **OWA SECURITY**

For more information about OWA security, including other methods of authentication, see *http://technet.microsoft.com/en-us/library/bb124507.aspx*.

MORE INFO **UNDERSTANDING S/MIME**

For general information about S/MIME, see *http://technet.microsoft.com/en-us/library/ aa995740(EXCHG.65).aspx*.

Using TLS and MTLS

The TLS and MTLS protocols, introduced in Chapter 7, provide encrypted communications and end-point authentication over network connections such as Internet connections. Server-to-server connections (for example, connections between SMTP servers on an organizational internetwork or the Internet) rely on MTLS for mutual authentication. On an MTLS connection, the server originating a message and the server receiving it exchange certificates from a mutually trusted CA. The certificates prove the identity of each server to the other.

The TLS protocol provides secure web communications on the Internet or intranets. It enables clients to authenticate servers and (optionally) servers to authenticate clients. It provides a secure channel by encrypting communications. However, when TLS is deployed, it typically provides only confidentiality in the form of encryption. Sometimes no authentication occurs between the sender and the receiver, and sometimes only the receiving server is authenticated. For example, the Secure Sockets Layer (SSL) protocol, which is the Hypertext Transfer Protocol (HTTP) implementation of TLS, authenticates only the receiving server.

When using MTLS authentication, on the other hand, each server verifies the identity of the other server by validating a certificate provided by that server. When messages are received from external domains over verified connections in an Exchange Server 2010 environment, Microsoft Outlook displays a Domain Secured icon. MTLS is a manageable technology for implementing the various features required for domain security, such as certificate management, connector functionality, and Outlook client behavior.

In Exchange 2010, Setup creates a self-signed certificate, and TLS is enabled by default. This enables any sending system to encrypt the inbound SMTP session. Exchange Server 2010 also attempts to use TLS for all remote connections by default. All traffic between Edge Transport servers and Hub Transport servers is authenticated and encrypted using MTLS.

Exchange Server 2010 uses direct trust to authenticate the certificates. Active Directory is considered a trusted storage mechanism, and the certificate is validated because it is present in Active Directory or Active Directory Lightweight Directory Services (AD LDS). When direct trust is used, it does not matter whether the certificate is self-signed or signed by a CA. When you subscribe an Edge Transport server to the Exchange organization, the Edge subscription publishes the Edge Transport server certificate in Active Directory for the Hub Transport servers to validate. The Microsoft Exchange EdgeSync service updates AD LDS with the set of Hub Transport server certificates for the Edge Transport server to validate.

> **MORE INFO**   **EDGE SUBSCRIPTIONS AND THE EDGESYNC SYNCHRONIZATION PROCESS**
>
> For more information about Edge subscriptions and the EdgeSync synchronization process, see *http://technet.microsoft.com/en-us/library/aa997438.aspx.*

Chapter 5 introduced certificates and the Active Directory Certificate Services role. TLS and MTLS require a certificate for authentication of inbound connections to a front-end server (for example, an Edge Transport server) and for outbound connections from the Front End Server. The certificate is provided by the server in response to authentication challenges from clients or servers that send messages to this server. Each Edge Transport server must have a certificate for MTLS communication with other servers on the network, in particular Hub Transport servers.

Inbound Anonymous TLS Certificates

Inbound anonymous TLS certificates can authenticate SMTP sessions between Edge Transport servers and Hub Transport servers. They can also be used to encrypt SMTP sessions between Hub Transport servers. In the latter case, where anonymous TLS and the public keys from certificates are used to encrypt the session between Hub Transport servers, the Kerberos protocol is used for authentication. When an SMTP session is established, the receiving server initiates a certificate selection process to determine which certificate to use in the TLS negotiation. The sending server also performs a certificate selection process.

Inbound STARTTLS Certificates

An inbound STARTTLS certificate is selected whenever SMTP hosts request TLS security when communicating with Edge Transport servers. The requesting host may be any SMTP host other than the Edge Transport server. Note that SMTP hosts other than Edge Transport servers requesting TLS security is a feature of the domain security scenario. Domain security is discussed later in this lesson.

An inbound STARTTLS certificate is also used when SMTP clients, such as Microsoft Outlook Express, request TLS security when communicating with Hub Transport servers and when Internet-facing Hub Transport servers request TLS security with Edge Transport servers. When an SMTP session is established, the receiving server initiates a certificate selection process to determine which certificate to use in the TLS negotiation.

Outbound Anonymous TLS Certificates

An outbound anonymous TLS certificate is selected for authentication during an SMTP session between an Edge Transport server and a Hub Transport server. This type of certificate is also used to encrypt SMTP sessions between Hub Transport servers by using public keys. When an SMTP session is established, the receiving server initiates a certificate selection process to determine the outbound anonymous TLS certificate to use in the TLS negotiation. The receiving server also performs a certificate selection process, as described in the previous sections of this lesson.

Implementing Domain Security

Domain security provides a lower-cost alternative to S/MIME or other message-level security solutions. The domain security feature provides a method of managing secured message paths between business partners over the Internet. After secured message paths are configured, messages that have successfully traveled over these paths from authenticated senders are displayed to users as domain secured in the Outlook and OWA interfaces.

Domain security uses MTLS authentication to provide session-based authentication and encryption. MTLS authentication differs from a typical TLS implementation. When TLS is implemented, the client verifies that the connection securely connects to the intended server by validating the server's certificate. The client authenticates the server before transmitting data. However, the server does not authenticate the session with the client. When MTLS authentication is used, each server verifies the connection with the other server by validating a certificate provided by that other server—in other words, both the message sender and the message recipient are validated.

Exchange Server 2010 provides a set of cmdlets that create, request, and manage TLS certificates. By default, TLS certificates are self-signed. That is, they are signed by their own creator. In Exchange Server 2010, self-signed certificates are created on the Exchange server by using the Microsoft Windows Cryptography Application Programming Interface. Self-signed certificates are considered less trustworthy than certificates generated by PKI or a trusted third-party CA and are typically used for internal mail only. However, you can use self-signed certificates to secure email messages from your organization to another Exchange Server 2010 organization if the receiving organization agrees to install your self-signed certificates in the trusted root certificate store in each of its inbound Edge Transport servers. In this case, the self-signed certificates are trusted explicitly.

> **MORE INFO** **TRUSTED CERTIFICATES AND DOMAIN SECURITY**
>
> For more information about trusted certificates and domain security, see *http://technet .microsoft.com/en-us/library/bb124817.aspx*.

Configuring Domain Security

To secure email messages that traverse the Internet, you would typically generate TLS certificates with a PKI or obtain them from a third-party CA. Suppose, for example, that you are an Exchange administrator at the Adatum Corporation and you want to configure Adatum's Exchange Server 2010 organization to exchange domain-secured email with its partner organization, NorthWind Traders. You want to ensure that all email messages sent to and received from NorthWind Traders are protected with MTLS, and you want to configure domain security functionality so that all mail between the Adatum Corporation and NorthWind Traders is rejected if mutual TLS cannot be used.

Adatum has an internal PKI that generates certificates. The PKI's root certificate has been signed by a trusted third-party CA. NorthWind Traders uses the same third-party

CA to generate its certificates. Therefore, both organizations trust the other's root CA. By default, the public third-party CA is one of the trusted root certificates in the Microsoft Windows certificate store in the adatum.com domain. Therefore, any client that includes the same third-party CA in its trusted root store and that connects to Adatum can authenticate to the certificate presented by Adatum.

The Edge Transport server VAN-EX2.adatum.com requires a certificate. You therefore generate a base64-encoded PKCS#10 certificate request on that server by entering the following commands:

```
$Data1 = New-ExchangeCertificate -GenerateRequest -FriendlyName "Internet certificate
for VAN-EX2" -SubjectName "DC=com,DC=Adatum,CN=VAN-EX2.adatum.com" -DomainName mail
.adatum.com
Set-Content -Path "C:\Certificates\VAN-EX2-request.req" -Value $Data1
```

Figure 12-3 shows these commands. Note that the folder C:\Certificates must exist on VAN-EX2; otherwise, the second command returns an error.

FIGURE 12-3 Generating a certificate request

MORE INFO   **NEW-EXCHANGECERTIFICATE**

For more information about the *New-ExchangeCertificate* EMS cmdlet, see *http://technet .microsoft.com/en-us/library/aa998327.aspx*.

MORE INFO   **GENERATING A CERTIFICATE REQUEST**

For more information about how to create a certificate request, see *http://technet .microsoft.com/en-us/library/ee861120.aspx*.

Your next step is to import the certificate and enable it in the trusted certificate store on the Edge Transport server. Note that you should not use the Certificate Manager snap-in in the Microsoft Management Console (MMC) to import the certificates for TLS on an Exchange server because this does not bind the request created in this procedure to the issued certificate. You can use the *Import-ExchangeCertificate* EMS cmdlet to import an existing certificate and private key from a Personal Information Exchange Syntax Standard (PKCS) #12 (.pfx or .p12) file to the certificate store on the local Edge Transport server. PKCS #12 is a file format used to store certificates with corresponding private keys protected with a password. The following command imports and enables the certificate by piping the certificate into the *Enable-ExchangeCertificate* EMS cmdlet and starts the SMTP service on the Edge Transport server:

```
Import-ExchangeCertificate -FileData ([Byte[]]$(Get-Content -Path C:\Certificates\
VAN-EX2-certificate.pfx -Encoding Byte -ReadCount 0)) | Enable-ExchangeCertificate
-Services SMTP
```

Note that the VAN-EX2-certificate.pfx file must exist in the path specified; otherwise, the command returns an error.

> **MORE INFO** **IMPORT-EXCHANGECERTIFICATE AND ENABLE-EXCHANGECERTIFICATE**
>
> For more information about the *Import-ExchangeCertificate* EMS cmdlet, see *http://technet.microsoft.com/en-us/library/bb124424.aspx*. For more information about the *Enable-ExchangeCertificate* EMS cmdlet, see *http://technet.microsoft.com/en-us/library/aa997231.aspx*.

You next need to configure outbound domain security and verify your settings. Note that because the changes that you make in outbound domain security are global, you must make these changes on an internal Exchange Server 2010 server (for example, a Hub Transport server). The configuration changes you make are replicated to Edge Transport servers by using the Microsoft Exchange EdgeSync service. The following command specifies the domain to which you want to send domain-secured email (in this case northwindtraders.com):

```
Set-TransportConfig -TLSSendDomainSecureList northwindtraders.com
```

You then use the *Set-SendConnector* EMS cmdlet to set the DomainSecureEnabled property on the Send connector that sends email to this domain. For a Send connector named Internet and configured for Internet connection, you enter the following command:

```
Set-SendConnector Internet -DomainSecureEnabled:$true
```

Neither of these two commands generates an output. If they complete without error, you have specified a target domain and enabled domain security on the Send connector. Note that an appropriately configured Send connector named Internet must exist for the second command to be successful.

The final step in configuring outbound domain security is to check that the Send connector you are using to send domain-secured email routes mail using the Domain Name System (DNS) and that the fully qualified domain name (FQDN) of the Send connector matches either the Subject Name or the Subject Alternative Name of certificates that you are using for domain security. To verify the Send connector settings, enter the following command:

```
Get-SendConnector Internet | FL Name,DNSRoutingEnabled,FQDN,DomainSecureEnabled
```

Figure 12-4 shows the output of this command. Note that the Fqdn value is shown as blank. The default value of the Fqdn parameter is $null, which indicates that the actual default FQDN value is the FQDN of the Edge Transport server that contains the Send connector.

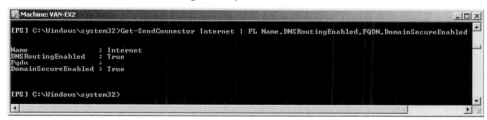

FIGURE 12-4 Verifying the Send connector settings

Quick Check

1. Which EMS cmdlet enables you to import an existing certificate and private key
   from a PKCS #12 file to the certificate store on the local Edge Transport server?

2. Which EMS cmdlet enables the imported certificate?

Quick Check Answers

1. *Import-ExchangeCertificate*

2. *Enable-ExchangeCertificate*

When you have configured and verified outbound domain security, you next need to
configure inbound domain security. To do this, you use the *Set-TransportConfig* EMS cmdlet
to specify the domain from which you want to receive domain-secured email and, on the
Edge Transport server, enable domain security on the Receive connector from which you want
to receive domain-secured email. Because domain security requires MTLS authentication, you
must also enable TLS on the Receive connector. To specify the domain from which you want
to receive domain-secured email, you run the following command on an internal Exchange
Server 2010 server (for example, a Hub Transport server):

```
Set-TransportConfig -TLSReceiveDomainSecureList northwindtraders.com
```

Figure 12-5 shows this command entered on the VAN-EX1 Hub Transport server.

FIGURE 12-5 Specifying the domain from which your organization receives domain-secured email

You need to configure the Receive connector on each Edge Transport server that accepts
mail from the domain from which you want to receive domain-secured email—in the
example given, the VAN-EX2.adatum.com Edge Transport server. Assuming that the Adatum
environment is configured to have a single Internet Receive connector, with an Identity
parameter value of Internet on this Edge Transport server, you enable domain security
and TLS by running the following command on the Edge Transport server:

```
Set-ReceiveConnector Internet -DomainSecureEnabled $true -AuthMechanism TLS
```

This command generates no output. If it completes without error, you have enabled domain security on the specified Receive connector.

MORE INFO **SET-RECEIVECONNECTOR**

For more information about the *Set-ReceiveConnector* EMS cmdlet, see *http://technet .microsoft.com/en-us/library/bb125140.aspx.*

MORE INFO **DOMAIN SECURITY**

For more information about using MTLS to send secure email between domains, see *http://technet.microsoft.com/en-us/library/bb124392.aspx.*

 EXAM TIP

The *Enable-ServiceEmailChannel* cmdlet allows you to enable the .NET service channel for a specific user. It does not enable domain security or use TLS or MTLS to send secure email between domains.

Testing Domain-Secured Mail Flow

After you configure domain-secured email, you can test the connection by reviewing performance counters and protocol logs. Protocol logs were discussed in Chapter 10, "Logging and Reports," and the Exchange Server Performance Monitor and the Performance Logs and Alerts tool were discussed in Chapter 9, "Monitoring Exchange Server 2010." Messages that have successfully authenticated over the domain-secured mail flow path are displayed in Outlook as domain-secured messages.

You can review the send and receive protocol logs to determine whether TLS negotiation has been successful. You should set the protocol logging level to Verbose on the connectors that your organization uses to send and receive domain-secured email. You need to enter the following command on all Edge Transport servers involved in domain security:

```
Set-ReceiveConnector Internet -ProtocolLoggingLevel Verbose
```

To enable protocol logging on the Send connector, you need to enter the following command on an internal Exchange server, such as a Hub Transport server:

```
Set-SendConnector Internet -ProtocolLoggingLevel Verbose
```

Neither of these two commands generates an output. If they complete without error, you have successfully enabled protocol logging on the specified Receive and Send connectors.

MORE INFO **SET-RECEIVECONNECTOR AND SET-SENDCONNECTOR**

For more information about the *Set-ReceiveConnector* EMS cmdlet, see *http://technet .microsoft.com/en-us/library/bb125140.aspx.* For more information about the *Set-SendConnector* EMS cmdlet, see *http://technet.microsoft.com/en-us/library/aa998294.aspx.*

You can use the following performance counters under the MSExchange Secure Mail Transport object in Exchange Server Performance Monitor to monitor domain security:

- Domain-Secured Messages Received
- Domain-Secured Messages Sent
- Domain-Secured Outbound Session Failures

Figure 12-6 shows these counters.

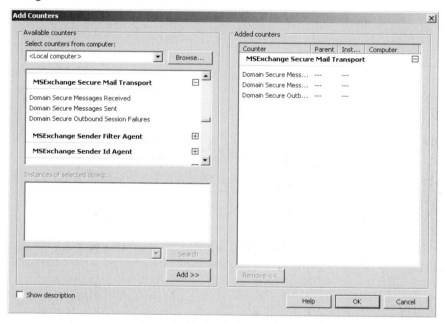

FIGURE 12-6 Counters associated with the MSExchange Secure Mail Transport object

A counter log file for domain-secured mail flow that logs the values of these counters using the Performance Logs and Alerts MMC snap-in helps you monitor the number of messages sent and received and also to monitor failed MTLS sessions.

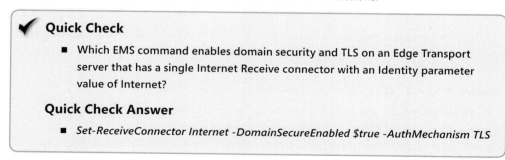

✔ Quick Check

- Which EMS command enables domain security and TLS on an Edge Transport server that has a single Internet Receive connector with an Identity parameter value of Internet?

Quick Check Answer

- *Set-ReceiveConnector Internet -DomainSecureEnabled $true -AuthMechanism TLS*

Configuring Permissions on Active Directory Objects

You can perform functions (for example, allowing one user to send on behalf of another) and alter Exchange Server 2010 behavior by configuring the permissions on Active Directory objects, such as user mailboxes, distribution groups, Send connectors, and Receive connectors. In Chapter 11, "Managing Records and Compliance," you saw how you could control read access for message classifications by denying Read permission to a message classification instance for a user mailbox or distribution group.

Adding and Denying Active Directory Permissions

You can use the *Add-ADPermission* EMS cmdlet to add an Active Directory permission and the *Remove-ADPermission* EMS cmdlet to remove such a permission. For example, the following command grants Kim Akers the Send As permission to the Don Hall mailbox, allowing Kim to send mail as Don:

```
Add-ADPermission –Identity "Don Hall" –User "Kim Akers" –AccessRights ExtendedRight
–ExtendedRights "send as" | FL
```

The command is piped into the PowerShell Format-List function so that its output can be seen in more detail. Figure 12-7 shows this output.

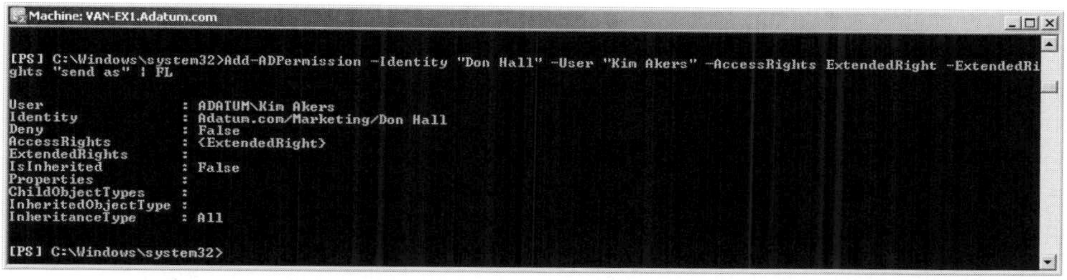

FIGURE 12-7 Granting Kim Akers permission to send as Don Hall

The identity parameter specifies the Active Directory object to which permissions are being granted (or from which they are being removed). It could, for example, identify a mailbox, a Receive connector, or a Send connector. If the Active Directory object has an owner, you can use the Owner parameter to identify this. The User parameter specifies the user or group to which the permissions are granted. The AccessRights parameter specifies the rights needed to perform the operation. Valid values include the following:

- CreateChild
- DeleteChild
- ListChildren
- Self
- ReadProperty
- WriteProperty
- DeleteTree
- ListObject

- ExtendedRight
- Delete
- ReadControl
- GenericExecute
- GenericWrite
- GenericRead
- WriteDacl
- WriteOwner
- GenericAll
- Synchronize
- AccessSystemSecurity

The AccessRights parameter can take the argument ExtendedRight as specified in the above list. You can specify the extended rights, such as Send As, ms-Exch-SMTP-Submit, ms-Exch-SMTP-Accept-Any-Recipient, and ms-Exch-Bypass-Anti-Spam, by using the ExtendedRights parameter. For example, the following command configures the Receive connector MyReceiveConnector to accept anonymous SMTP messages and bypass the spam filter:

```
Add-ADPermission "MyReceiveConnector" -User "NT AUTHORITY\ANONYMOUS LOGON" -AccessRights
ExtendedRight -ExtendedRights ms-Exch-SMTP-Submit,ms-Exch-SMTP-Accept-Any-Recipient,
ms-Exch-Bypass-Anti-Spam
```

Note that the Receive connector MyReceiveConnector must exist on the server on which the command runs; otherwise, the command returns an error. Note also that you would not configure a Receive connector in this way unless you had another mechanism in place for blocking unsolicited email.

You can use the Deny switch to deny a permission to an Active Directory object. For example, the following command denies the Send As permission on the Don Hall mailbox to the user Kim Akers:

```
Add-ADPermission -Identity "Don Hall" -User "Kim Akers" -Deny -AccessRights
ExtendedRight -ExtendedRights "send as"
```

EXAM TIP

Bear in mind that denying a permission is not the same as removing it. If an Active Directory permission is removed, the user no longer has the permission granted through this mechanism but may have the permission because of, for example, membership of a distribution group that has been allocated that permission. If a permission is denied to a user, the user cannot be allocated this permission through a group membership. The Deny setting overrides any allocation of the denied permission by any other means.

MORE INFO   ADD-ADPERMISSION

For more information about the *Add-ADPermission* EMS cmdlet, see *http://technet .microsoft.com/en-us/library/bb124403.aspx*.

Removing a Permission and Obtaining Permission Details

You can remove a permission by using a command based on the *Remove-ADPermission* EMS cmdlet. For example, the following command removes the permissions that enable the Receive connector MyReceiveConnector to accept anonymous SMTP messages and bypass the spam filter:

```
Remove-ADPermission "MyReceiveConnector" -User "NT AUTHORITY\ANONYMOUS LOGON"
-AccessRights ExtendedRight -ExtendedRights ms-Exch-SMTP-Submit,ms-Exch-SMTP-Accept-Any
-Recipient,ms-Exch-Bypass-Anti-Spam
```

Figure 12-8 shows the output from this command. You need to confirm your action unless you set the Confirm parameter to false in the command by using the syntax –Confirm:$false.

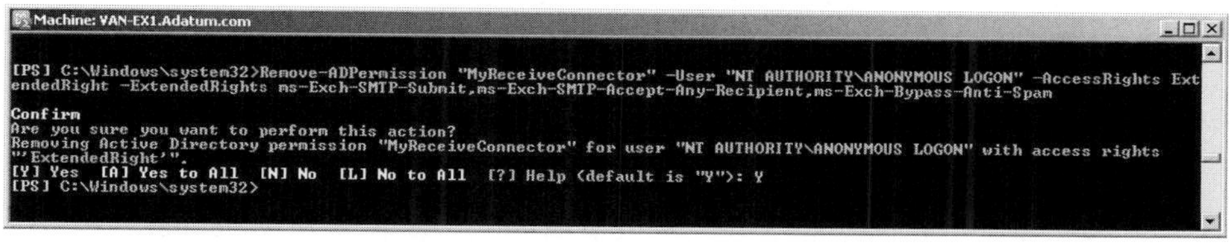

FIGURE 12-8 Removing Active Directory permissions

You can discover the Active Directory permissions that have been set on an object by using a command based on the *Get-ADPermission* EMS cmdlet. For example, the following command lists the permissions set on the Don Hall mailbox:

```
Get-ADPermission -Identity "Don Hall" | FL > C:\"Don Hall Permissions"
```

This command generates a large volume of information, and its output has therefore been redirected into a text file named "Don Hall Permissions." Figure 12-9 shows a portion of this text file.

FIGURE 12-9 Some of the permissions set on the Don Hall mailbox object

Quick Check

- Which EMS command configures the Receive connector MyReceiveConnector
  to accept anonymous SMTP messages and bypass the spam filter?

Quick Check Answer

- *Add-ADPermission "MyReceiveConnector" -User "NT AUTHORITY\ANONYMOUS
  LOGON" -AccessRights ExtendedRight -ExtendedRights ms-Exch-SMTP-Submit,
  ms-Exch-SMTP-Accept-Any-Recipient,ms-Exch-Bypass-Anti-Spam*

Rights Management Services Federation

In Chapter 7, you looked at Active Directory Rights Management Services (AD RMS), and saw
how Information Rights Management (IRM) makes use of AD RMS. AD RMS can be used in a
federated environment, where a user from an organization that is part of the federation can
access and decrypt messages sent by a user in another organization that are protected using
an RMS template either through IRM or through a transport protection rule, where the other
organization is also a member of the federation. The user in the first organization does not
need to log on to the second organization's domain or provide additional credentials in order
to gain access to this protected traffic. The technology that provides this facility is AD FS.

AD FS is a single sign-on (SSO) technology that is often described as a limited trust
relationship. The AD FS service provides external support for the internal identity and access
services that Active Directory Directory Services (AD DS) requires and extends the authority of
your internal network to external networks. In other words, AD FS lets you use the credentials
required to log on to your own organization to access information (both protected files
and protected email) held in another organization that is part of the same federation. In this
section, you learn how AD FS authenticates a user, how you install and configure the service,
and how you manage the trusts and certificates it requires.

Understanding AD FS

AD FS allows users of external web-based applications (for example, OWA) to access and
authenticate through a browser. It relies on the internal authentication store of the user's
own domain to authenticate a client and does not have a store of its own. It also relies
on the original authentication that clients perform in their own networks and passes this
authentication to web applications that are AD FS enabled. AD FS federates a user's internal
AD DS identity and submits it to external networks. Users need to authenticate only once.

For example, David Hamilton, Nancy Anderson, and Jeff Hay buy supplies for Wingtip Toys from World Wide Importers, an organization with which their company has a long-standing relationship. David, Nancy, and Jeff need to log on to web applications at World Wide Importers. Employees at World Wide Importers need to be able to add David, Nancy, and Jeff to distribution lists that otherwise contain only World Wide Importers employees and send David, Nancy, and Jeff email messages that have their content protected by an RMS template.

World Wide Importers have user name and password policies that are different from those at Wingtip Toys. If no federation mechanism were in place, David, Nancy, and Jeff would need to log on to the World Wide Importers domain as if they were employees and remember two sets of login names and passwords, which regularly change. AD FS allows Wingtip Toys and World Wide Importers to set up a partnership so that David, Nancy, and Jeff can log on to these web applications and decrypt protected World Wide Importers internal email messages using their Wingtip Toys credentials. They are not required to log in twice and remember two user names and two passwords in order to do their job.

Unlike forest trusts, AD FS does not use Lightweight Directory Application Protocol (LDAP) ports but rather the common HTTP ports, specifically port 443, so that all AD FS trust communications can be secured and encrypted. AD FS relies on Active Directory Certificate Services (AD CS) to manage certificates for each server in the AD FS implementation. AD FS can extend AD RMS deployment and provide federation services for intellectual property management between partners.

AD FS provides extensions to internal forests and enables your organization to create partnerships without needing to open any additional ports on its firewall. It relies on each partner's internal AD DS directory to provide authentication for extranet or perimeter services. When a user attempts to authenticate to an application integrated to AD FS, the AD FS engine polls the internal directory for authentication data. Users who have access provided through the internal directory are granted access to the external application. This means that each partner needs to manage authentication data only in its internal network. The federation services of AD FS do all the rest.

Forming Business-to-Business Partnerships

You can use AD FS and RMS Federation to form business-to-business (B2B) partnerships. In this arrangement, partners can be account or resource organizations (or both). These can be described as follows:

- **Account organizations**   Manage the accounts used to access shared resources and decrypt protected email messages in SSO scenarios. Account organizations join partnerships created by resource organizations and access resources (including email) in these organizations.

- **Resource organizations**   Form the partnerships in SSO scenarios. An organization that has resources (such as a collaboration website) can use AD FS to simplify the authentication process to these resources by forming partnerships that account organizations then join. The organization that initially forms the partnership is deemed the resource organization because it hosts the shared resources in its perimeter network.

In the example given earlier, David, Nancy, and Jeff are logged on to the Wingtip Toys forest and can access web applications and protected email messages at World Wide Importers without needing to supply additional credentials. In this case, Wingtip Toys is the account organization (or account partner), and World Wide Importers is the resource organization (or resource partner).

AD FS uses claims, cookies, and certificates to implement a federated B2B partnership.

Using Claims in AD FS

A claim is a statement that the federation server makes about a user or client. Claims are stored as AD DS attributes that each partner in an AD FS relationship attaches to its user accounts. They can be based on several different values, such as user names, certificate keys, membership of security groups, and so on. Claims are included in the signed security token that AD FS sends to the web application and are used for authorization. They can be based on user identity (the identity claim type) or on security group membership (the group claim type). Claims can also be based on custom information (the custom claim type), such as a custom identification number (for example, employee number or bank account number).

> **MORE INFO   AD FS CLAIMS**
>
> For more information on AD FS claims, see *http://technet.microsoft.com/en-us/library/cc730612.aspx*.

Using Cookies in AD FS

User browsers hold cookies that are generated during web sessions authenticated through AD FS. AD FS uses authentication cookies, account partner cookies, and sign-out cookies. When a user is authenticated through AD FS, an authentication cookie is placed within the user's browser to support SSO for additional authentications. This cookie includes all the claims for the user. It is a session cookie and is erased after the session is closed.

The AD FS process writes an account partner cookie when a client announces its account partner membership during authentication, so it does not need to perform partner discovery again the next time the client authenticates. An account partner cookie is long-lived and persistent.

Each time the federation service assigns a token, it adds the resource partner or target server linked to the token to a sign-out cookie. The authentication process uses sign-out cookies for various purposes, such as for cleanup operations at the end of a user session. A sign-out cookie is a session cookie and is erased after the session is closed.

> **MORE INFO   AD FS COOKIES**
>
> For more information on AD FS cookies, see *http://technet.microsoft.com/en-us/library/cc770382.aspx*.

Using Certificates in AD FS

AD FS communications must be encrypted at all times, and this requires several certificate types. The type of certificate required by the role depends on its purpose.

A federation server requires both a server authentication certificate and a token-signing certificate. In addition, the trust policy requires a verification certificate. The server authentication certificate is an SSL authentication certificate that is typically requested and installed through IIS Manager.

A token-signing certificate is made up of a private key and a public key pair. When a federation server generates a security token, it digitally signs the token with its token-signing certificate. A verification certificate is used during the verification process that takes place between servers when there is more than one federation server in a deployment. It contains only the public key of the token-signing certificate.

A federation service proxy requires a server authentication certificate to support SSL-encrypted communications with web clients. It also needs a client authentication certificate (known as a federation service proxy certificate) to authenticate the federation server during communications. Both private and public keys for this certificate are stored on the proxy. The public key is also stored on the federation server and in the trust policy. A web server hosting the AD FS web agent also requires a server authentication certificate to secure its communications with web clients, typically federation servers.

> **NOTE** **CERTIFICATES AND OUTWARD-FACING ROLES**
>
> Many AD FS roles are outward facing. Therefore, your certificates should be from a trusted CA. If you use Active Directory–generated certificates, you need to modify the Trusted CA store on each web client. AD FS relies on AD CS to manage these certificates.

> **MORE INFO** **AD FS CERTIFICATES**
>
> For more information on AD FS certificates, see *http://technet.microsoft.com/en-us/library/cc730660.aspx*.

 Quick Check

- Which claim types does AD FS support?

Quick Check Answer

- AD FS supports three claim types:
  - Identity claims. These can be user principal name, email address, or common name.
  - Group claims. These consist of membership in specific distribution or security groups in AD DS.
  - Custom claims. These can include custom information, such as a user's bank account number.

AD FS Role Services

Federated identity is the process of authenticating a user's credentials across multiple information technology systems and organizations. Identity federation enables users in one domain to securely access data or systems of another domain by using SSO. AD FS relies on the following role services to support identity federation:

- **Federation Service**   A server running the federation service (a federation server) routes authentication requests to the appropriate source directory to generate security tokens for the user requesting access. Servers that share a trust policy use this service.

- **Federation Service Proxy**   A federation server relies on a proxy server located in the perimeter network to obtain authentication requests from a user. The proxy collects authentication information from the user's browser through the WS-Federation Passive Requestor Profile and passes it on to the federation service.

- **Windows Token-Based Agent**   A Windows token-based agent converts an AD FS security token into an impersonation-level Windows NT access token that is recognized by applications that rely on Windows authentication rather than web-based authentication.

- **Claims-Aware Agent**   A claims-aware agent on a web server initiates queries of security token claims to the federation service. Each claim is used to grant or deny access to a given application. For example, ASP.NET applications that examine the various claims contained in the user's AD FS security token are claims-aware applications, as is AD RMS.

> **MORE INFO   AD FS**
>
> For more information about AD FS and the enhancements introduced by Windows Server 2008, access *http://technet.microsoft.com/en-us/library/cc534990.aspx* and follow the links.

AD FS Configurations

AD FS supports three configurations (or architectural designs) depending on the type of B2B partnership you need to establish. Each supports a particular partnership scenario. These architectural designs are as follows:

- **Federated Web SSO**   This deployment scenario typically spans several firewalls. It links applications contained within an extranet in a resource organization to the internal directory stores of account organizations. The federation trust is the only trust used in this model. A federation trust is a one-way trust from the resource organization to the account organization(s).

> **MORE INFO   Federation trusts**
>
> For more information about federation trusts, see *http://technet.microsoft.com/en-us/library/cc770993.aspx*.

- **Web SSO**   This is deployed when all users of an extranet application are external. It allows users to authenticate using SSO to multiple web applications. It relies on multihomed web servers that are connected to both the internal and the external network and that are part of the AS DS domain. The Federation Service Proxy is also multihomed to provide access to both the external and the internal network.

- **Federated Web SSO with Forest Trust**   In this model, a forest trust is established between an external forest in the perimeter network and an internal forest. A federation trust is also established between the resource federation server located within the perimeter and the account federation server located in the internal network. Internal users have access to the applications from both the internal network and the Internet, whereas external users have access to the applications only from the Internet.

The most common scenarios are Web SSO and Federated Web SSO. Ideally, all members of an identity federation deployment have their own AD DS directory and act as account organizations to simplify the deployment strategy.

AD FS Authentication

When an AD FS partnership is in place, users can log on transparently to external web applications included in the partnership. In a typical AD FS email scenario, a user receives and attempts to open a protected email message across an extranet. AD FS automatically provisions the user's credentials and outlines the claims included in the user's AD DS account attributes. Figure 12-10 illustrates the process.

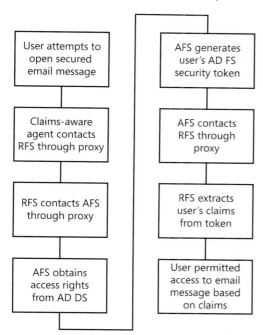

FIGURE 12-10 AD FS authentication

A more detailed high-level description of the process is as follows:

1. A user attempts to open a protected email message in an extranet.

2. The claims-aware agent on the Exchange server contacts a resource federation server (RFS) in the resource organization through a federation service proxy (FSP).

3. The RFS accesses an account federation server (AFS) in the account organization's internal network, again through a proxy, to identify the user's access rights.

4. The AFS obtains access rights from AD DS through an LDAP query. These access rights are listed in the form of claims linked to the user's account object in AD DS.

5. The AFS generates the user's AD FS security token. This includes the claims linked in the user's AD DS account. Security tokens also identify the user and include the AFS digital certificate.

6. The AFS contacts the RFS through the proxy server and sends the security token.

7. The RFS decrypts the token and extracts the user's claims. It filters them depending on the access requirements of the protected message and generates a signed security token. The signature for the token is based either on the RFS digital certificate or on a Kerberos session key.

8. The signed security token is sent to the Exchange server in the resource organization's extranet. The claims-aware agent decrypts the token and grants access to the protected message based on the claims in the token. A local authentication cookie is generated in the user's browser so that the process is not repeated if the user needs to authenticate again during this session.

MORE INFO **FEDERATING RMS**

For more information about RMS Federation, see *http://technet.microsoft.com/en-us/ library/ee256071(WS.10).aspx.*

 Quick Check

1. What are the four role services and features that make up the AD FS server role?

2. What are the three AD FS architectural designs?

Quick Check Answers

1. AD FS includes the following role services:

   ■ The federation service provides the core AD FS functionality. It manages resource access, claims filtering, and security token generation.

   ■ The federation service proxy is an Internet relay that passes requests on to internal federation service servers.

- The Windows token-based agent supports the integration of Windows applications to AD FS processes.

- The claims-aware agent supports the integration of web applications with AD FS processes.

2. AD FS supports three architectural designs: Federated Web Single-Sign-On, Web SSO, and Federated Web SSO with Forest Trust.

Configuring AD FS

Servers in an AD FS relationship rely on certificates to create a chain of trust and ensure that all traffic transported over the relationship is encrypted at all times. To ensure that the chain of trust is valid and trusted in all locations, you can obtain certificates from a trusted third-party CA or through the creation of a linked implementation of AD CS that uses a trusted third-party CA as its root.

When you deploy AD FS, you need to configure AD FS–aware applications, trust policies between partner organizations, and claims for your users and groups. After you install and deploy AD FS, you need to carry out the following configuration tasks:

- Configure the web service on each AD FS server to use SSL/TLS encryption on the website that hosts the AD FS service.

- Configure IIS on servers that host claims-aware applications.

- Export certificates from each server and import them on the other servers in the relationship.

- Create and configure the claims-aware applications you are hosting.

- On the federation servers in both account and resource organizations, configure the trust policy, create claims for users, and configure the AD DS account store for identity federation. In a resource organization, you also then enable the claims-aware applications.

- Create the federation trust to enable identity federation by exporting the trust policy from the account organization and importing it into the resource organization, creating and configuring a claim mapping in the resource organization, and exporting the partner policy from the resource organization so that you can import it into the account organization.

Much of the configuration process involves certificate mapping from one server to another. You need to be able to access the certificate revocation lists (CRLs) for each certificate. CRLs indicate to a member of a trust chain whether a certificate is valid.

In AD FS, CRL checking is enabled by default. Typically, CRL checking is performed for security token signatures, but it is good practice to rely on it for all digital signatures.

Creating Transport Rules

Chapter 5 discussed transport rules and introduced the EMC Transport Rules Wizard and the *New-TransportRule* EMS cmdlet. You saw how to create a new transport rule and how to use a transport protection rule that applies an RMS template. In Chapter 11, you saw how to associate transport rules with message classifications and to use transport rules to create ethical walls. In Lesson 2, "Managing Anti-Spam and Antivirus Countermeasures," you will see how to configure edge transport rules on an Edge Transport server.

Transport rules allow organizational message policies to be applied to email messages that pass through Hub and Edge transport servers. You use transport rules to manage communication within an organization and communication from the organization to the rest of the world. They can filter internal communication and perform actions based on message properties such as sender, receiver, message content, and classification.

Transport rules are made up of conditions, exceptions, and actions. It is possible that a message may meet the conditions of multiple transport rules. Conditions determine to which messages a transport rule is applied. Transport rules without any conditions are applied to all messages, unless those messages meet a configured exception. Conditions can include, for example, messages received from or sent to a specified mailbox or distribution list or received from or sent to users inside or users outside the organization.

You use exceptions to exempt messages that match a transport rule's conditions from the transport rule's actions. Unlike conditions, where every specified condition must be met for a rule to apply, only one exception condition must be met for the message to be exempted from the rule. Exceptions can include, for example, "except when messages are received from or sent to a specified mailbox or distribution list" or "except when received from or sent to users inside or users outside the organization." You can also configure a transport rule to apply to all email messages except when any of the recipients in the To or Cc fields are in a list of specified mailboxes or in a specified distribution list.

Actions are applied to messages that meet transport rule conditions and where the action is not blocked by any exceptions. They can, for example, include logging an event with a specified message (used for debugging), applying a message classification, copying the message to a specified address (used for journaling), and setting the spam confidence level (SCL) to a specified value.

For example, the following command applies a message classification named ManagementCommunication to all messages sent by members of the distribution group Managers to one or more members of the group AllEmployees, except when the message title contains the words "Holiday Photos":

```
New-TransportRule -Name "ManagerMessage" -FromMemberOf "Management"
-SentToMemberOf "AllEmployees" -ApplyClassification "ManagementCommunication"
-ExceptIfSubjectContainsWords "Holiday Photos"
```

IRM permits your organization and your users to apply persistent protection to messages so that access is restricted to authorized users and permitted actions. The following transport protection rule implements privacy and confidentiality requirements by automatically configuring IRM using the default Do Not Forward RMS template:

```
New-TransportRule -Name "Protect-Secrecy" -SubjectContainsWords "Top Secret"
-ApplyRightsProtectionTemplate "Do Not Forward"
```

Chapter 7 discusses IRM. Chapter 11 discusses journaling and message classification. Chapter 5 provides more comprehensive lists of transport rule conditions, exceptions, and actions. Lesson 2 of this chapter discusses SCLs.

Lesson Summary

- To implement secure messaging, you need to be able to guarantee integrity, confidentiality, and authentication.

- S/MIME is a standard for public key encryption and signing of MIME data. It provides authentication, message integrity and nonrepudiation of origin (using digital signatures), and privacy and data security (using encryption).

- TLS and MTLS protocols provide encrypted communications and end-point authentication over network connections such as Internet connections.

- Domain security provides a method of managing secured message paths between business partners over the Internet.

- You can perform functions and alter Exchange Server 2010 behavior by configuring the permissions on Active Directory objects such as user mailboxes, distribution groups, Send connectors, and Receive connectors.

- AD FS lets you use the credentials required to log on to your own organization to access information (both protected files and protected email) held in another organization that is part of the same federation.

Lesson Review

You can use the following questions to test your knowledge of the information in Lesson 1, "Ensuring Message Integrity." The questions are also available on the companion CD if you prefer to review them in electronic form.

Configuring Message Compliance and Security

1. You want to use the MTLS protocol to secure email messages over the Internet between your organization and the contoso.com domain. Your Edge Transport server DEN-Edge1 has a Send and a Receive connector both named Internet and both configured for Internet communications. Your organization also contains a Hub Transport server, DEN-Hub1. Which command specifies the domain (contoso.com) to which you want to send domain-secured email, and which server should you run it on? Which command enables domain security on the Internet Send connector, and which server should you run it on? (Choose 2; each answer forms part of the solution.)

   A. Run the command *Set-SendConnector Internet -DomainSecureEnabled:$true on DEN-Hub1*

   B. Run the command *Set-SendConnector Internet -DomainSecureEnabled:$true on DEN-Edge1*

   C. Run the command *Set-TransportConfig -TLSSendDomainSecureList contoso.com on DEN-Hub1*

   D. Run the command *Set-TransportConfig -TLSSendDomainSecureList contoso.com on DEN-Edge1*

   E. Run the command *Set-SendConnector Internet -ProtocolLoggingLevel Verbose on DEN-Hub1*

   F. Run the command *Set-SendConnector Internet -ProtocolLoggingLevel Verbose on DEN-Edge1*

2. What protocol mandates the authentication of both the receiving and the sending server and encrypts email messages?

   A. Standard TLS

   B. SSL

   C. HTTP

   D. MTLS

3. What command disables S/MIME on the OWA virtual directory in the default IIS website on the server on which it is entered?

   A. *Set-OWAVirtualDirectory -Identity "owa (Default Web Site)" -SMimeEnabled $false*

   B. *Set-OWAVirtualDirectory -Identity "owa (Default Web Site)" -SMimeEnabled $true*

   C. *Remove-OWAVirtualDirectory -Identity "owa (Default Web Site)"*

   D. *Get-OWAVirtualDirectory -Identity "owa (Default Web Site)"*

4. What service specifically enables you to deploy AD RMS with identity federation support?

   A. AD DS

   B. AD CS

   C. AD FS

   D. AD LDS

5. What EMS command specifically prevents Kim Akers from sending mail as Don Hall, no matter what Send As permissions Kim is granted by virtue of group membership?

   A. *Add-ADPermission -Identity "Don Hall" -User "Kim Akers" -AccessRights ExtendedRight -ExtendedRights "send as"*

   B. *Add-ADPermission -Identity "Don Hall" -User "Kim Akers" –Deny -AccessRights ExtendedRight -ExtendedRights "send as"*

   C. *Remove-ADPermission -Identity "Don Hall" -User "Kim Akers" -AccessRights ExtendedRight -ExtendedRights "send as"*

   D. *Remove-ADPermission -Identity "Don Hall" -User "Kim Akers" –Deny -AccessRights ExtendedRight -ExtendedRights "send as"*

Lesson 2: Managing Anti-Spam and Antivirus Countermeasures

This lesson discusses antivirus and anti-spam countermeasures including the use of the SCL setting and the use of edge transport rules to manage viruses. It considers anti-spam stamps and the *phishing confidence level (PCL)*. It looks at Sender Identity (ID), *block lists*, and *allow lists*. The lesson discusses Sender Policy Framework (SPF) records, the *sender reputation list (SRL)*, and the configuration of anti-spam agents.

Quarantined messages are placed in the spam quarantine mailbox, and this lesson looks at how you specify this mailbox. The lesson also considers how you manage updates for content filters. If you choose to use file-level antivirus scanners, you can avoid the problems associated with such software by configuring exclusions. The lesson looks at directory, process, and file exclusions.

You can configure Exchange Server 2010 to deal with spam and viruses on both Edge Transport and Hub Transport servers. In the production environment, you would typically block spam and viruses (as much as possible) on a perimeter network. Your Edge Transport servers are the first to receive external email, and it is on these servers that you should discard communication that is harmful to your organization's health. Cleaning your email traffic flow before it reaches the internal network is a superior strategy to relying on mail filters and antivirus software installed on desktop computers.

Although you can configure a Hub Transport server to deal with spam and viruses—and you may have to if you suspect that some of these are internally generated—not all the available anti-spam and antivirus transport agents function on a Hub Transport server. Installing one or more Edge Transport servers in a production organization typically results in a significant reduction virus and spam messages delivered to user mailboxes.

After this lesson, you will be able to:
- Identify transport agents on a Hub Transport server.
- Configure the antivirus and anti-spam system.
- Modify spam settings.
- Use edge transport rules and attachment filtering to combat viruses.
- Configure file-level antivirus software.

Estimated lesson time: 50 minutes

Configuring Anti-Spam Features

In Exchange Server 2010, incoming messages pass through a series of transport agents before they are forwarded to user mailboxes. Each of these transport agents concentrates on a different aspect of the incoming message, such as the Internet Protocol (IP) address of the SMTP server where the message originates, the sender's address, or the likelihood that the message is actually spam. The following built-in transport agents are installed by default on an Edge Transport server:

- Connection Filtering agent
- Address Rewriting Inbound agent
- Edge Rule agent
- Content Filter agent
- Sender ID agent
- Sender Filter agent
- Recipient Filter agent
- Protocol Analysis agent
- Attachment Filtering agent
- Address Rewriting Outbound agent

You can view the transport agents in the order in which they are applied by entering the following EMS command:

```
Get-TransportAgent
```

If the Microsoft Exchange Transport service is running and at least one message has been sent through the system, the following command shows all the enabled transport agents—and the SMTP events on which they are registered—that have encountered messages in the transport pipeline between the time when the Microsoft Exchange Transport service was started and the time when the command runs:

```
Get-TransportPipeline
```

Only the transport agents that encountered a message are displayed using this command.

> **MORE INFO** **TRANSPORT AGENTS**
>
> For more information about transport agents, see *http://technet.microsoft.com/en-us/library/bb125012.aspx*.

Connection Filtering

You can enable the Connection Filter anti-spam agent and its associated connection filtering features on an Edge Transport server. The agent filters all messages that come through all Receive connectors on that server. Only messages that come from nonauthenticated external sources—that is, anonymous Internet sources—are filtered.

The Connection Filter agent enables the following features:

- IP block list
- IP allow list

- IP block list providers
- IP allow list providers

Each of these features can be enabled or disabled separately. By default, the Connection Filter agent is enabled on Edge Transport servers. To disable connection filtering using the IP allow list, you enter the following EMS command:

```
Set-IPAllowListConfig -Enabled $false
```

To enable connection filtering using the IP allow list (assuming it has been previously disabled), you enter the following EMS command:

```
Set-IPAllowListConfig -Enabled $true
```

To remove an IP allow list provider (for example, treyresearch.com) from connection filtering configuration, enter the following EMS command:

```
Remove-IPAllowListProvider -Identity treyresearch.com
```

To disable connection filtering using the IP block list, you enter the following EMS command:

```
Set-IPBlockListConfig -Enabled $false
```

To configure the Connection Filter agent to block an IP address if any IP address status codes are returned by the IP block list provider fabricam.com, you enter the following EMS command:

```
Set-IPBlockListProvider -Identity fafricam.com -AnyMatch $true
```

You can also disable connection filtering entirely by disabling the Connection Filtering agent using the following command (note that you need to confirm this action unless you use the –Confirm:$false switch):

```
Disable-TransportAgent -Identity "Connection Filtering agent"
```

> **MORE INFO**   **ENABLING AND DISABLING CONNECTION FILTERING**
>
> For more information about enabling and disabling connection filtering, see *http://technet .microsoft.com/en-us/library/bb124376.aspx*. Note that this link also describes how you can use the EMC for this purpose.

Managing Allow Lists and Block Lists

When an incoming message arrives on an Edge Transport server and connection filtering is enabled, the IP address of the SMTP server that sent the message is compared against IP allow and block lists. Action is then taken, as shown in Table 12-2.

TABLE 12-2 Allow and Block List actions

LIST CONDITION	ACTION
The forwarding SMTP server's IP address is on the allow list	The message is forwarded to the Exchange organization.
The SMTP server's IP address is on the block list.	The message is dropped.
The SMTP server's IP address is not on either list.	The message passes through other anti-spam agents on the configured server.

IP block and allow lists are also known as blacklists and whitelists, respectively. Block lists are also known as real-time block lists (RBLs) because they are queried each time mail arrives from a new IP address. They can be configured by adding entries as the need arises. You can also subscribe to IP block and allow list providers. In particular, third-party IP block list providers are typically used by Exchange Server 2010 organizations. This allows a third-party organization to keep your list of the IP addresses of malware senders up to date. IP block list providers generate their lists based on spam reports and the spam that they have received from SMTP servers located on the Internet.

Messages received from SMTP servers on the block list will always be discarded, even if they also appear on the allow list. The only way to receive email from an SMTP server on a block list is to remove it from the block list. If you added the IP address to the block list during configuration, you can remove it. If, on the other hand, it is obtained from a block list provider, you may need to intercede with the block list provider.

You can add IP addresses, IP subnets, or IP address ranges to the IP allow list. Email messages from these sources will not be blocked by connection filtering. You can also specify a list of IP allow list providers. These providers supply IP addresses for your IP allow list.

The following EMS command adds the IP address 10.20.0.123 to the IP allow list:

```
Add-IPAllowListEntry -IPAddress 10.20.0.123
```

Note that the Microsoft Exchange Transport service must be running on the local Edge Transport server. Also, this command requires confirmation unless the –Confirm switch is used. The following EMS command adds the IP address 10.20.0.125 to the IP allow list and configures it to expire on February 2, 2011, at 11:00 AM:

```
Add-IPAllowListEntry -IPAddress 10.20.0.125 -ExpirationTime "2/2/2011 11:00"
```

EXAM TIP

In Exchange Server 2010, you can configure expiry for both IP allow and IP block lists. In Exchange Server 2007, you could configure this only for IP block lists.

The following EMS command adds the IP subnet 10.30.1.1/25 to the IP allow list:

```
Add-IPAllowListEntry -IPRange 10.30.1.1/25
```

The following EMS command adds the IP range 10.20.20.100 through 10.20.20.200 to the IP allow list:

```
Add-IPAllowListEntry -IPRange 10.20.20.100-10.20.20.200
```

To remove an address from the IP allow list, you need to specify its ID. The most straightforward way of accomplishing this is to pipe the output of the *Get-IPAllowListEntry* EMS cmdlet to the *Remove-IPAllowListEntry* EMS cmdlet. For example, the following command removes the IP address 10.20.0.123 from the IP allow list:

```
Get-IPAllowListEntry -IPAddress 10.20.0.123 | Remove-IPAllowListEntry
```

You can use the IP allow list providers feature to determine whether the Messaging server that initiated a connection is a host that can be relied on not to send spam. The Connection Filter agent queries the specified IP allow list provider services to determine if the source IP address of the message is on the IP allow list.

The following EMS command adds a new IP allow list provider called Trey Research Provider:

```
Add-IPAllowListProvider -Name "Trey Research Provider" -LookupDomain "treyresearch.com"
-AnyMatch $true
```

Figure 12-11 shows the output from this command.

FIGURE 12-11 Adding an IP allow list provider

You can specify an order of preference for allow list providers. The following EMS command configures the same IP allow list provider to be the top preferred provider:

```
Set-IPAllowListProvider "Trey Research Provider" -Priority 1
```

The following EMS command removes the IP allow list provider Trey Research Provider (note that this command requires confirmation):

```
Remove-IPAllowListProvider -Identity "Trey Research Provider"
```

> **MORE INFO**   **CONFIGURING IP ALLOW LISTS AND IP ALLOW LIST PROVIDERS**
>
> For more information about configuring IP allow lists, see *http://technet.microsoft.com/en-us/library/bb125225.aspx*. For more information about configuring IP allow list providers, see *http://technet.microsoft.com/en-us/library/bb123964.aspx*. Both of these links give details on how you can use the EMC to perform the same tasks.

You can add IP addresses, ranges, and subnets to an IP block list in the same way as you can to an allow list. However, you would typically use a commercial IP block list provider to manage your block list. The list of malware sources is lengthy and changes frequently. The following EMS command adds the IP address 10.50.4.127 to a block list:

```
Add-IPBlockListEntry -IPAddress 10.50.4.127
```

The following EMS command adds the IP subnet 10.0.100.1/24 to the IP block list:

```
Add-IPBlockListEntry -IPRange 10.0.100.1/24
```

The following EMS command adds the IP range 10.40.150.120 through 10.40.150.179 to the IP block list:

```
Add-IPBlockListEntry -IPRange 10.40.150.120-10.40.150.179
```

As with allow lists, the easiest way to remove an address from the IP block list is to pipe the output of the *Get-IPBlockListEntry* EMS cmdlet to the *Remove-IPBlockListEntry* EMS cmdlet. For example, the following EMS command removes the IP address 10.50.4.127 from the IP allow list:

```
Get-IPBlockListEntry -IPAddress 10.59.4.127 | Remove-IPBlockListEntry
```

If you want to remove a range, specify an IP address that is within that range for the IPAddress parameter of the *Get-IPBlockListEntry* cmdlet. The following EMS command removes the subnet 10.0.100.1/24:

```
Get-IPBlockListEntry -IPAddress 10.0.100.1 | Remove-IPBlockListEntry
```

If the IP block list providers feature is enabled on a computer, the Connection Filter agent queries the specified IP block list provider services to determine if the Messaging server that initiated the connection is a host that is known to send spam. By default, this anti-spam feature is only available on Edge Transport servers. The following EMS command adds a new IP block list provider called "Trey Block List Provider" and configures it to use bitmask matching for 127.0.0.1 (block messages from IP addresses that are on the block list):

```
Add-IPBlockListProvider -Name "Trey Block List Provider" -LookupDomain treyresearch.com
-BitMaskMatch 127.0.0.1
```

Figure 12-12 shows the output from this command.

FIGURE 12-12 Adding an IP block list provider

The following EMS command configures the Trey Block List Provider service to use a custom rejection response:

```
Set-IPBlockListProvider "Trey Block List Provider" -RejectionResponse "Your message was
rejected because the IP address of the server sending your message is in the block list
of the Trey Block List Provider service."
```

> **MORE INFO** **CONFIGURING IP BLOCK LISTS AND IP BLOCK LIST PROVIDERS**
>
> For more information about configuring IP block lists, see *http://technet.microsoft.com/en-us/library/dd351199.aspx*. For more information about configuring IP block list providers, see *http://technet.microsoft.com/en-us/library/dd351199.aspx*. Both of these links give details of how you can use the EMC to perform the same tasks.

Content Filtering

Content filtering uses algorithms to assess the contents of a message and provide a rating that indicates how likely the message is to be spam. How the message is then treated depends on the threshold values that you set. You can configure Exchange to drop any message that has even a minimal likelihood of being spam, you can configure Exchange to reject only those messages that are very likely to be spam, or (typically) you can choose settings that filter out most spam but avoid false positives—that is, filtering out valid messages that are not spam.

The search algorithms look for patterns within messages rather than merely looking for specific words. These algorithms are updated on a regular basis because spammers are continually attempting to get around detection software.

Content filtering is enabled by default on an Edge Transport server only for inbound, unauthenticated messages from the Internet, which are then handled as external messages. The following EMC command disables content filtering:

```
Set-ContentFilterConfig -Enabled $false
```

The following EMC command enables content filtering if it has previously been disabled:

```
Set-ContentFilterConfig -Enabled $true
```

You can enable or disable content filtering specifically for internal and external messages. By default, content filtering is enabled for external messages and disabled for internal messages.

The following EMS command disables content filtering for external messages:

```
Set-ContentFilterConfig -ExternalMailEnabled $false
```

The following EMS command enables content filtering for internal messages:

```
Set-ContentFilterConfig -InternalMailEnabled $true
```

However, you should not (as a best practice) filter messages from trusted partners or from inside your organization. When you run anti-spam filters, there is always a risk that the filters detect false positives. To reduce the risk of mishandling legitimate email messages, you should enable anti-spam agents to run only on messages from potentially untrusted and unknown sources.

You can use the *Set-ContentFilterConfig*, *Add-ContentFilterPhrase*, and *Remove-ContentFilterPhrase* EMS cmdlets to modify your content filtering settings. For example, you might want to block all email messages whose subject lines contain the words "lose weight" or "earn extra cash." On the other hand, if you work for an organization that, for example, manufactures bicycles, you might want to allow email messages whose subject lines contain words such as "bicycle," "chain," "wheel," "handlebars," and so on.

You can use the *Add-ContentFilterPhrase* cmdlet to add both allowed and blocked words and phrases. The value of the Influence parameter determines if the word or phrase is allowed or blocked. For example, the following EMS commands allow all messages that contain the word "bicycle" and block all messages that contain the phrase "earn extra cash":

```
Add-ContentFilterPhrase -Phrase "bicycle" -Influence GoodWord
Add-ContentFilterPhrase -Phrase "earn extra cash" -Influence BadWord
```

Figures 12-13 and 12-14 show the output from these commands.

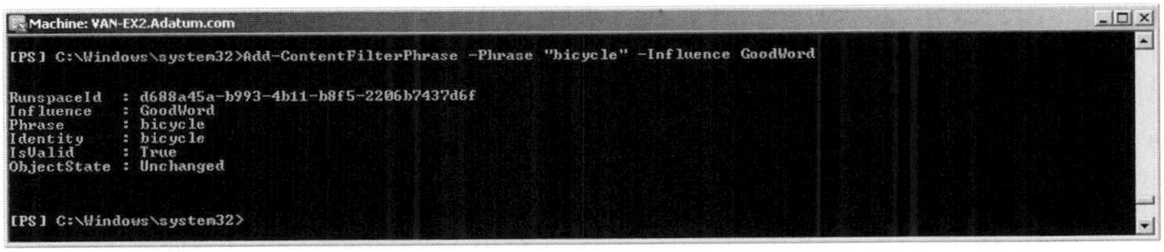

FIGURE 12-13 Adding an allowed word

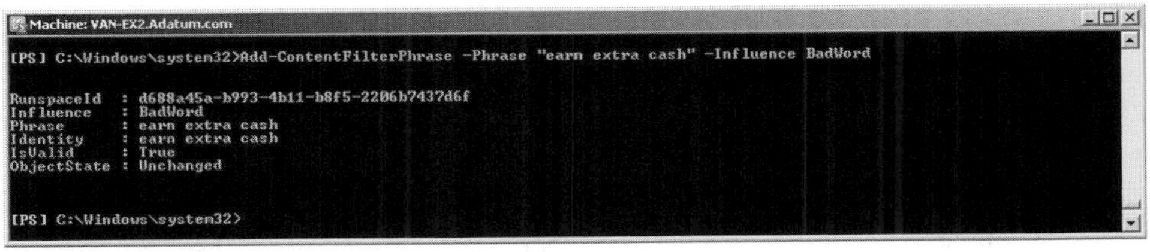

FIGURE 12-14 Adding a blocked phrase

Sometimes you do not want to apply content filtering to email messages sent to a specific recipient or received from a specific sender. You can use the *Set-ContentFilterConfig* EMS cmdlet to configure both recipient and sender exceptions. For example, the following EMS command creates an exception for the recipient KimAkers@adatum.com so that messages sent to this recipient are not checked by the content filter agent:

```
Set-ContentFilterConfig -BypassedRecipients KimAkers@adatum.com
```

The following EMS command creates an exception for the senders PatrickHines@fabrikam.com and RussellKing@fabricam.com so that messages received from these senders are not checked by the content filter agent:

```
Set-ContentFilterConfig -BypassedSenders PatrickHines@fabrikam.com,
RussellKing@fabricam.com
```

You can also bypass content filtering for all messages received from specific domains. The following EMS command creates an exception for the domain contoso.com so that messages received from this domain are not checked by the content filter agent:

```
Set-ContentFilterConfig -BypassedSenderDomains contoso.com
```

The following EMS command creates an exception for the domain fabricam.com and all its subdomains and for the domain treyresearch.com:

```
Set-ContentFilterConfig -BypassedSenderDomains *.fabrikam.com,treyresearch.com
```

After analyzing the content of a message, the content filter assigns an SCL rating to the message. How those messages are treated depends on the configuration. You can use the *Set-ContentFilterConfig* EMS cmdlet to configure SCL thresholds and actions. The Delete action takes precedence over the Reject action, and the Reject action takes precedence over the Quarantine action. Therefore, the SCL threshold for the Delete action must be greater than the SCL threshold for the Reject action, which in turn should be greater than the SCL threshold for the Quarantine action.

For example, you may want messages that have an SCL rating of 5 or 6 to be forwarded to the quarantine mailbox, messages that have an SCL rating of 7 or 8 to be rejected, and messages with an SCL rating of 9 to be deleted. The difference between rejection and deletion is that the sender is informed when a message is rejected. In the case of deletion, the sender receives no response.

The following EMS commands enable the Delete action and set the corresponding SCL threshold to 9, enable the Reject action and set the corresponding SCL threshold to 7, and enable the Quarantine action and set the corresponding SCL threshold to 5:

```
Set-ContentFilterConfig -SCLDeleteEnabled $true -SCLDeleteThreshold 9
Set-ContentFilterConfig -SCLRejectEnabled $true -SCLRejectThreshold 7
Set-ContentFilterConfig -SCLQuarantineEnabled $true -SCLQuarantineThreshold 5
```

Note that the command to enable the Quarantine action works only if a quarantine mailbox has been specified, as described in the next section of this lesson. If you enable the Reject action, you can customize the response sent to the message originator when a message is rejected. The following EMS command configures the content filter agent to send the rejection response "Your message has been rejected because it was judged to be spam":

```
Set-ContentFilterConfig -RejectionResponse "Your message has been rejected because it
was judged to be spam."
```

Specifying a Quarantine Mailbox

If you enable message quarantine, you need to specify a quarantine mailbox. This is a specially created mailbox to which all messages that meet the SCL quarantine levels are forwarded. You should place the quarantine mailbox in a separate mailbox database. If you are going to use quarantine, you need to ensure that someone checks the quarantine mailbox on a regular basis to see how much legitimate email and how much spam it contains. By assessing the contents of the quarantine mailbox, you can determine whether your SCL levels are correctly configured. You can also, when appropriate, release legitimate messages to their intended recipients by using the Send Again feature in Microsoft Office Outlook.

You can use the EMS but not the EMC to specify a quarantine mailbox. The following EMS command sends all messages that meet the spam quarantine SCL level to spamquarantine @adatum.com:

```
Set-ContentFilterConfig -QuarantineMailbox spamquarantine@adatum.com
```

The following EMS command ensures that all incoming messages that have an SCL rating of 5 or higher are forwarded to the mailbox spamquarantine@adatum.com (unless other settings result in messages with higher SCLs being rejected or deleted):

```
Set-ContentFilterConfig -SCLQuarantineEnabled $true -SCLQuarantineThreshold
5 -QuarantineMailbox spamquarantine@adatum.com
```

 Quick Check

- What EMS command allows email messages whose subject lines contain the word "handlebars"?

Quick Check Answer

- *Add-ContentFilterPhrase -Phrase "handlebars" -Influence GoodWord*

Recipient Filtering

Recipient filtering allows you to block messages based on whom they are sent to. This technology is most often used to block messages sent to recipients that are not listed in the global address list (GAL). Some spammers send messages to common names at a particular address, hoping to get a hit. If recipient filtering is enabled, messages will be forwarded from an Edge Transport server to an internal Hub Transport server only if the recipient is listed in the GAL. GAL information is stored within the Active Directory Application Mode directory service. If this setting is not enabled, the Hub Transport server will reject the invalid address.

When recipient filtering is enabled on a server, it filters all messages that come through all Receive connectors on that server. Recipient filtering is enabled by default on an Edge Transport server for inbound messages that come from the Internet but are not authenticated.

The following EMS command disables recipient filtering:

```
Set-RecipientFilterConfig -Enabled $false
```

You can use the *Set-RecipientFilterConfig* EMS cmdlet to manage recipient filtering. For example, the following EMS cmdlet configures the recipient filter agent to block recipients on the Recipients block list:

```
Set-RecipientFilterConfig -BlockListEnabled $true
```

You can use the BlockedRecipients parameter of the *Set-RecipientFilterConfig* EMS cmdlet to add SMTP addresses to the Recipient block list. If you want to specify multiple SMTP addresses, you can separate them with commas. The following EMS command adds the email addresses CEO@adatum.com and Comptroller@adatum.com to the Recipient block list:

```
Set-RecipientFilterConfig -BlockedRecipients CEO@adatum.com,Comptroller@adatum.com
```

However, you need to be careful when using this type of command. The SMTP addresses that you specify replace the existing list of SMTP addresses. To preserve the existing list, you can use a temporary Shell variable to add an address to the Recipient block list. The following set of EMS commands uses the temporary variable $Listing to hold the current list of SMTP addresses. You add the new address temp@adatum.com to the variable so that the existing addresses are retained and the new address is added when the variable is applied to the Recipient block list:

```
$Listing = Get-RecipientFilterConfig
$Listing.BlockedRecipients += "temp@adatum.com"
Set-RecipientFilterConfig -BlockedRecipients $Listing.BlockedRecipients
```

The following EMS command blocks messages to recipients that do not exist in your organization:

```
Set-RecipientFilterConfig -RecipientValidationEnabled $true
```

Sender Filtering and Sender ID

The Sender Filter agent is an anti-spam filter that is enabled by default on Edge Transport
servers. The agent relies on the MAIL FROM: SMTP header to determine what action, if any,
to take on an inbound email message. When sender filtering functionality is enabled on an
Edge Transport server, it filters all messages that come through all Receive connectors on
that computer. You use sender filtering to drop messages on the basis of the sender's email
address.

Sender filtering can be configured for a specific sender address or the sender's domain.
For example, you can filter the sender address KimAkers@adatum.com or filter all email
messages that come from the @adatum.com domain. Sender filtering is often used to
block incoming email from email domains that provide free addresses. It is also possible
to configure the blocked senders list to automatically block messages that have no sender
information.

The following EMS command disables sender filtering:

```
Set-SenderFilterConfig -Enabled $false
```

The following EMS command enables sender filtering if it has previously been disabled:

```
Set-SenderFilterConfig -Enabled $false
```

You use the *Set-SenderFilterConfig* cmdlet to manage sender filtering. You can configure
two actions for messages whose sender appears on the blocked senders list. These actions are
the following:

- **Reject Message**   The message is deleted.
- **Stamp Message with Blocked Sender and Continue Processing**   The message's
  metadata is modified to indicate that the message has come from a blocked sender.

The following EMS command configures the Sender Filter agent to block messages from
the specific email addresses KimAkers@adatum.com and DonHall@adatum.com:

```
Set-SenderFilterConfig -BlockedSenders KimAkers@adatum.com,DonHall@adatum.com
```

The following EMS command configures the Sender Filter agent to block messages from
the specific domain treyresearch.com:

```
Set-SenderFilterConfig -BlockedDomains treyresearch.com
```

The following EMS command configures the Sender Filter agent to block messages from the northwindtraders.com domain and all its subdomains:

```
Set-SenderFilterConfig -BlockedDomainsAndSubdomains *.northwindtraders.com
```

The values that you specify by using the parameters such as BlockedSenders, BlockedDomains, and BlockedDomainsAndSubdomains replace the existing list of blocked senders. To preserve the existing list, you can use a temporary Shell variable to add an address or domain to the blocked senders list. The following EMS commands use the temporary variable $Listing to add the sender ChenYang@adatum.com and the domain tailspintoys.com to the blocked senders list:

```
$Listing = Get-SenderFilterConfig
$Listing.BlockedSenders += "ChenYang@adatum.com"
$Listing.BlockedDomains += "tailspintoys.com"
Set-SenderFilterConfig -BlockedSenders $Listing.BlockedSenders -BlockedDomains $Listing.
BlockedDomains
```

The following EMS command configures the Sender Filter agent to block messages that do not specify a sender in the MAIL FROM: SMTP header:

```
Set-SenderFilterConfig -BlankSenderBlockingEnabled $true
```

> **MORE INFO** **ENABLING, DISABLING, AND CONFIGURING SENDER FILTERING**
>
> For more information about enabling, disabling, and configuring sender filtering, see *http://technet.microsoft.com/en-us/library/bb125187.aspx* and *http://technet.microsoft .com/en-us/library/bb125179.aspx*. These links also give information about how to use the EMC to perform the same tasks.

 Quick Check

1. Which filtering technology blocks incoming messages going to internal distribution lists?
2. Which filtering technology blocks messages from a specific sender?

Quick Check Answers

1. Recipient filtering.
2. Sender filtering.

The Sender ID agent is an anti-spam agent enabled on Edge Transport servers. The agent relies on the RECEIVED SMTP header and queries the sending system's DNS service to determine what action, if any, to take on an inbound message.

Sender ID is designed to combat spoofing, which is the impersonation of a sender and a domain. A spoofed email is a message that has a modified sending address and appears as if it originates from a sender other than its actual sender. Spoofed mails typically contain a From address that purports to be from a reputable organization.

When you enable Sender ID in Exchange Server 2010, each message contains a Sender ID status in the metadata of the message. When an email message is received, the Edge Transport server queries the sender's DNS server to verify that the IP address from which the message was received is authorized to send messages for the domain that is specified in the message headers. The IP address of the authorized sending server is referred to as the Purported Responsible Address (PRA).

The Sender ID Federation, Sender Policy Framework Records, and Phishing Confidence Level Ratings

Domain administrators publish SPF records on their DNS servers. SPF records identify authorized outbound email servers. If an SPF record is configured on the sender's DNS server, the Edge Transport server parses the SPF record and determines whether the IP address from which the message was received is authorized to send email on behalf of the domain specified in the message.

A very large proportion of phishing (identity theft) scams come from spoofed domains that have spoofed sender email addresses. The Sender ID Federation is an industry initiative to counter spoofed domains by publishing SPF records. This enables suspected phishing sites to be identified through PCL ratings, which are used by, for example, the phishing filter built into Microsoft Internet Explorer.

The Edge Transport server updates the message metadata with the Sender ID status based on the SPF record. After the Edge Transport server updates the message metadata, it delivers the message as normal.

The Sender ID evaluation process generates a Sender ID status for the message, which used to evaluate the SCL rating. This status can be set to one of the following values:

- **Pass** Both the IP address and PRA passed the Sender ID verification check.
- **Neutral** The published Sender ID data is inconclusive.
- **Soft fail** The IP address for the PRA may not be permitted.
- **Fail** The IP Address is not permitted, no PRA is found in the incoming mail, or the sending domain does not exist.
- **None** No published SPF data exists in the sender's DNS.
- **TempError** A temporary DNS failure occurred (for example, an unavailable DNS server).
- **PermError** The DNS record is invalid. For example, there is an error in the record format.

The Sender ID status is added to the message metadata and is later converted to a Messaging Application Program Interface (MAPI) property. The junk email filter in Office Outlook uses the MAPI property during the generation of the SCL value.

The Sender ID evaluation process may reveal instances where the From IP address is missing. If the From IP address is missing, the Sender ID status cannot be set. In this case, Exchange Server 2010 continues to process the message without including a Sender ID status on the message. The message is not discarded or rejected, but an application event is logged.

You can define how an Edge Transport server handles messages that are identified as spoofed mail and how it handles messages when a DNS server cannot be reached. The available options include the following:

- **Delete**   This option deletes the message without informing the sending system of the deletion. Instead, the Edge Transport server sends a fake OK SMTP command to the sending server and then deletes the message. Because the sending server assumes the message was sent, it does not retry sending the message.
- **Reject**   The message is rejected, and an SMTP error response is returned to the sending server. The error response is a 5xx-level protocol response with text that corresponds to the Sender ID status.
- **Stamp the status**   All inbound messages to your organization have the Sender ID status included in the metadata of the message. This is the default action.

The effectiveness of Sender ID in combating spoofing depends on specific DNS data. The more organizations that update their Internet-facing DNS servers by using an SPF record, the more effectively Sender ID identifies spoofed email messages. To support the Sender ID infrastructure, you need to update your Internet-facing DNS data by creating an SPF record and hosting the SPF record on your public DNS servers.

> **MORE INFO   CREATING AND DEPLOYING SPF RECORDS**
>
> For more information about how to create and deploy SPF records, access *http://www .microsoft.com/mscorp/safety/technologies/senderid/default.mspx* and follow the links.

You use the *Set-SenderIDConfig* cmdlet to configure Sender ID options and actions. You may, for example, want to exclude specific recipients and sender domains from Sender ID filtering, configure actions for messages that are spoofed, and configure actions for transient failures.

For example, the following EMS command configures the Sender ID agent to reject any messages that were spoofed—these are messages where the IP address of the sending server is not listed as an authoritative SMTP sending server in the DNS SPF record for the sending domain:

```
Set-SenderIDConfig -SpoofedDomainAction Reject
```

You can also configure Sender ID action for transient errors. For example, it is considered a transient error if a DNS server is unavailable when Exchange attempts to verify the Sender ID for a sending domain. The following EMS command configures the Sender ID agent to stamp the messages for which the Sender ID status cannot be determined because of a temporary error—the message is processed by other anti-spam agents, and the Content Filter agent uses the mark when determining the SCL value for the message:

```
Set-SenderIDConfig -TempErrorAction StampStatus
```

You can set exceptions so that messages sent to a specific recipient or received from a specific sender domain bypass the Sender ID check. For example, the following EMS command configures the Sender ID agent to bypass the Sender ID check for the recipients KimAkers@adatum.com and DonHall@adatum.com:

```
Set-SenderIDConfig -BypassedRecipients KimAkers@adatum.com,DonHall@adatum.com
```

The following EMS command configures the Sender ID agent to bypass the Sender ID check for messages that are received from the domain northwindtraders.com:

```
Set-SenderIDConfig -BypassedSenderDomains northwindtraders.com
```

However, the values that you specify by using the BypassedRecipients and BypassedSenderDomains parameters replace the existing exceptions. To preserve the existing listing of recipients or sender domains, you can use a temporary Shell variable to add a recipient or domain to the exceptions list. The following EMS commands use the temporary variable $Listing to add the domain treyresearch.com to the list of domains for which you want to bypass Sender ID check:

```
$Listing = Get-SenderIDConfig
$Listing.BypassedSenderDomains += "treyresearch.com"
Set-SenderIDConfig -BypassedSenderDomains $Listing.BypassedSenderDomains
```

MORE INFO   **SENDER ID AND SENDER ID CONFIGURATION**

For general information about Sender ID, see *http://technet.microsoft.com/en-us/library/ aa996295.aspx*. For more information about Sender ID configuration, including the (limited) tasks for which you can use the EMC, see *http://technet.microsoft.com/en-us/ library/bb125259.aspx*.

MORE INFO   **ANTI-SPAM STAMPS**

Sender ID, SCL, and PCL are also types of anti-spam stamps. You can use anti-spam stamps as diagnostic tools to determine what actions to take on false positives and on suspected spam messages that individuals receive in their mailboxes. You can view anti-spam stamps in Office Outlook, and you can generate an anti-spam report. For more information, see *http://technet.microsoft.com/en-us/library/aa996878.aspx*.

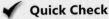
Sender Reputation

Sender reputation is used on Edge Transport servers to block messages according to various sender characteristics. It relies on these characteristics to determine the action to take on an inbound message. By default, sender reputation processing is enabled on an Edge Transport server for inbound messages that come from the Internet and are not authenticated. Such messages are handled as external messages. The following EMS command disables sender reputation for all messages:

```
Set-SenderReputationConfig -Enabled $false
```

The following EMS command disables sender reputation specifically for external messages:

```
Set-SenderReputationConfig -ExternalMailEnabled $false
```

By default, sender reputation is disabled for internal messages. The following EMS command enables sender reputation for internal messages:

```
Set-SenderReputationConfig -InternalMailEnabled $true
```

An SRL is calculated from the following statistics:

■ **Analysis of SCL ratings on messages from a particular sender**   When the Content Filter agent processes a message, it assigns an SCL rating to the message. Sender reputation calculates statistics about a sender according to the ratio between previous messages from that sender that had a low SCL rating and previous messages from the same source that had a high SCL rating. In addition, the number of messages with a high SCL rating sent in the past day is applied to the overall SRL.

■ **Reverse DNS lookup**   Sender reputation verifies that the originating IP address from which the sender transmitted the message matches the registered domain name that the sender submits in the HELO or EHLO SMTP command by performing reverse DNS query and submitting the originating IP address to DNS. Sender reputation compares the domain name returned by DNS to the domain name that the sender submitted in the HELO/EHLO SMTP command. If the domain names do not match, the sender is likely to be a spammer, and the overall SRL rating for the sender is adjusted upward.

■ **HELO/EHLO analysis**   The HELO and EHLO SMTP commands provide the domain name or IP address of the sending SMTP server to the receiving SMTP server. Spammers may attempt to forge the HELO/EHLO statement, and analysis of this statement on a per-sender basis may indicate that the sender is likely to be a spammer. For example, a sender that provides many different unique HELO/EHLO statements in a specific time period is more likely to be a spammer, as is a sender who consistently provides an IP address in the HELO statement that does not match the originating IP address as determined by the Connection Filter agent.

- **Sender open proxy test**   An open proxy is a proxy server that accepts connection requests and forwards the traffic as if it originated from the local host. Proxy servers relay Transmission Control Protocol traffic through firewalls to provide user applications transparent access across the firewall. Proxies can also be used to permit multiple hosts to share a single Internet connection. Proxies are usually set up so that only trusted hosts inside the firewall can cross through the proxies. However, open proxies can exist because of misconfiguration or malicious Trojan horse programs and can provide a method for malicious users to hide their true identities and launch denial-of-service attacks or send spam. When sender reputation performs an open proxy test, it generates an SMTP request in an attempt to connect back to the Edge Transport server from the open proxy. If an SMTP request is received from the proxy, sender reputation verifies that the proxy is an open proxy and updates the open proxy test statistic for that sender.

Sender reputation weighs each of these statistics and calculates an SRL for each sender. The SRL is a number from 0 through 9 that predicts the probability that a specific sender is a spammer or other type of malicious user. A value of 0 indicates that the sender is most unlikely to be a spammer; a value of 9 indicates that the sender very likely is a spammer.

The following EMS command configures sender reputation to perform an open proxy test for determining sender confidence:

```
Set-SenderReputationConfig -OpenProxyDetectionEnabled $true
```

The following EMS command configures sender reputation to add the IP addresses of hosts that fail the open proxy test to the IP block list:

```
Set-SenderReputationConfig -SenderBlockingEnabled $true -OpenProxyDetectionEnabled $true
```

Sender reputation is used to add SMTP servers to the IP block list for a limited duration based on the characteristics of the messages sent. You can configure an SRL block threshold at which sender reputation issues a request to the Sender Filter agent to block the sender from sending a message into your organization. A blocked sender is added to the blocked senders list for a configurable time period. The following EMS command sets the SRL block threshold to 5 (it is 7 by default) and configures sender reputation to add offending senders to the IP block list for 48 hours:

```
Set-SenderReputationConfig -SenderBlockingEnabled $true -SrlBlockThreshold
5 -SenderBlockingPeriod 48
```

The following options are available for blocked messages:

- Accept and mark as a blocked sender
- Delete and archive
- Reject

If a sender is included in the Microsoft block list or Microsoft IP Reputation Service sender reputation issues, an immediate request is made to the Sender Filter agent to block the sender. To take advantage of this functionality, you must enable the Microsoft Exchange Anti-Spam Update Service. By default, an Edge Transport server sets an SRL of 0 for senders that have not been analyzed. After a sender has sent 20 or more messages, sender reputation calculates an SRL that is based on the statistics returned by analyzing these messages.

MORE INFO   **SENDER REPUTATION**

For general information about sender reputation, see *http://technet.microsoft.com/en-us/ library/bb124512.aspx*.

MORE INFO   **ENABLING, DISABLING, AND CONFIGURING SENDER REPUTATION**

For more information about enabling, disabling, and configuring sender reputation, see *http://technet.microsoft.com/en-us/library/bb125186.aspx* and *http://technet.microsoft .com/en-us/library/aa998542.aspx*. These links also describe how you can use the EMC to carry out some configuration tasks.

Microsoft Update for Anti-Spam Services

Exchange 2010 offers additional services to help keep anti-spam components up to date through the Microsoft Update infrastructure. Microsoft Exchange 2010 Standard Anti-Spam Filter Updates offer anti-spam updates every two weeks.

The Microsoft Forefront Protection 2010 for Exchange Server Anti-Spam Update service is a premium service that updates the content filter daily via Microsoft Update. In addition, this service includes available spam signature and IP Reputation Service updates on an as-needed basis up to several times a day. Spam signature updates identify the most recent spam campaigns. IP Reputation Service updates provide sender reputation information about IP addresses that are known to send spam.

To ensure that Forefront Protection 2010 for Exchange Server stays up to date, you run the Enable Anti-Spam Updates Wizard, as shown in Figure 12-15. To use Microsoft Update to update the Forefront Protection 2010 for Exchange Server anti-spam definitions automatically, you select the Use Microsoft Update To Help Keep Your Exchange Server Up-To-Date With Anti-Spam Definition Updates check box.

You can also ensure that spam signature updates are downloaded automatically by selecting Automatic under Enable Anti-Spam Updates and selecting the Spam Signature Updates check box. You can ensure that the Edge Transport server is kept up to date with information about IP addresses that are known to forward spam by selecting Automatic under Enable Anti-Spam Updates and selecting IP Reputation Updates. Both of these options exist independently of updating Forefront Protection 2010 for Exchange Server's anti-spam definitions using Microsoft Update.

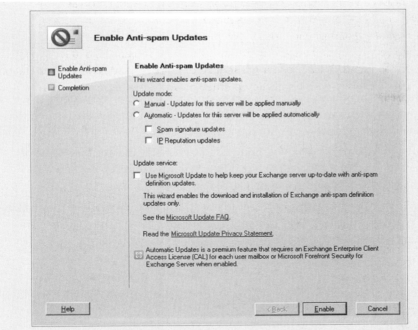

FIGURE 12-15 Enabling anti-spam updates for Forefront Protection 2010 for Exchange Server

The Manual — Updates For This Server Will Be Applied Manually option allows you to manually apply updates. This option also exists independently of updating Forefront Protection 2010 for Exchange Server's anti-spam definitions using Microsoft Update.

Configuring Antivirus Features

Spam can be a considerable nuisance, and an email system clogged with excessive spam can be virtually useless. However, virus attacks are arguably a greater and more sinister threat. Spam mail can be malicious—for example, it can include attachments that install a virus, it can induce the unwary to access a phishing site, or it can initiate some other scam that persuades a victim to reveal passwords or banking details. However, the vast majority of spammers want to sell their goods and services, not put you out of business. A virus can destroy an entire system or can lurk silently in the background, stealing your users' confidential details.

You can combat viruses such as worms, Trojan horses, and other malware by the application of attachment filtering and the use of edge transport rules. You can also use Microsoft Forefront Protection 2010 for Exchange Server and file-level antivirus scanning software.

Attachment Filtering

Attachment filtering applies filters at the server level to control the attachments your users receive. Remember that attachment filters can be configured only on a per-server basis. If your organization has multiple Edge Transport servers, you need to add the same attachment filter to all Edge Transport servers.

Many attachments can potentially contain viruses or other inappropriate material that could cause significant damage. You can use the following types of attachment filtering to control attachments that enter or leave your organization:

- **File name or file name extension filtering**   You can specify the exact file name or file name extension to be filtered. An exact file name filter could be, for example, TrojanHorse.exe. A file name extension filter could be, for example, *.exe.

- **File MIME content type filtering**   You can filter attachments by specifying the MIME content type to be filtered. MIME content types indicate, for example, whether the attachment is a JPEG image, an executable file, a Microsoft Word file, or some other file type.

The following EMS command lists all the file name extensions and content types that attachment filtering can filter:

```
Get-AttachmentFilterEntry | FL
```

If an attachment matches your filter criteria, you can specify that one of the following actions is performed on the attachment:

- **Strip attachment but allow message through**   This is the default setting. The attachment is removed, but the email message and any other attachments that do not match the filter are allowed through. If an attachment is removed, it is replaced with a text file that explains why it was removed.

- **Block whole message and attachment**   The attachment, together with its whole email message, is blocked from entering the messaging system. The sender receives a delivery status notification (DSN) message that indicates that the message contains an unacceptable attachment file name.

- **Silently delete message and attachment**   The attachment, together with its whole email message, is blocked from entering the messaging system. Neither the sender nor the recipient receives notification.

It is not a good idea to remove attachments from digitally signed, encrypted, or rights-protected email messages. If you remove attachments from such messages, you invalidate the digitally signed messages and make encrypted and rights-protected messages unreadable. If such a message includes a suspect attachment, you need to block or silently delete the message and attachment.

By default, the Attachment Filter agent is enabled on an Edge Transport server. The following EMS command disables the Attachment Filter agent on the Edge Transport server on which it is entered:

```
Disable-TransportAgent -Identity "Attachment Filter agent"
```

The following EMS command enables the Attachment Filter agent if it has previously been disabled:

```
Enable-TransportAgent -Identity "Attachment Filter agent"
```

You can configure an attachment filter entry to filter attachments by attachment content type or by attachment file name. In Exchange Server 2010, you can configure multiple attachment filters on an Edge Transport server. The following EMS command filters all JPEG images on the Edge Transport server on which it is entered:

```
Add-AttachmentFilterEntry -Name image/jpeg -Type ContentType
```

The following EMS command filters all email attachments that have the file name extension *.exe* on the Edge Transport server on which it is entered:

```
Add-AttachmentFilterEntry -Name *.exe -Type FileName
```

You can use commands based on the *Set-AttachmentFilterListConfig* EMS cmdlet to configure attachment filtering on an Edge Transport server. For example, the following EMS command sets the Attachment Filter agent to reject messages that have prohibited attachments and configures a custom response for rejected messages:

```
Set-AttachmentFilterListConfig -Action -Reject -RejectResponse "A prohibited attachment
was included in your e-mail message. Please remove the attachment and send your
message again."
```

Using Forefront Protection 2010 for Exchange Server

The file-filtering functionality provided by Microsoft Forefront Protection 2010 for Exchange Server includes advanced features that are unavailable in the default Attachment Filter agent. For example, Forefront can scan files that contain other files (container files) for offending file types. Forefront can scan the following container files and act on embedded files:

- PKZip (.zip)
- GNU Zip (.gzip)
- Self-extracting compressed file archives (.zip)
- Compressed files (.zip)
- Java archive (.jar)
- TNEF (winmail.dat)
- Structured storage (.doc, .xls, .ppt, and others)
- MIME (.eml)
- SMIME (.eml)
- UUEncode (.uue)
- UNIX tape archive (.tar)
- RAR archive (.rar)
- MACBinary (.bin)

Forefront also enables you to filter files by file size. In addition, you can configure Forefront to quarantine filtered files or to send email notifications based on file filter matches.

MORE INFO   **FOREFRONT PROTECTION 2010 FOR EXCHANGE SERVER**

For more information about Forefront Protection 2010 for Exchange Server, see *http://technet.microsoft.com/en-us/library/cc482977.aspx*.

Using Edge Transport Rules

You can use the Edge Rules agent and edge transport rules in Microsoft Exchange Server 2010 to help protect your organization from viruses. Transport rules were introduced in Chapter 5.

Antivirus vendors and administrators respond to virus threats as quickly as possible, but there is inevitably a gap between the time that a virus threat appears and the time that a solution is available. This gap, during which a virus threat remains unknown and unresolved, is called a *zero-day virus threat*. Transport rules on Edge Transport servers help you manage and control zero-day virus threats in addition to preexisting or ongoing virus threats.

Most viruses contain unique characteristics that identify them, such as a specific email address in the From message header field, a specific subject, or an attachment. You can configure transport rules to identify potentially harmful messages by these unique characteristics and perform a specific action on them. Available actions include sending the message to a quarantine mailbox, deleting it completely, or adding a warning to the subject line. If you can identify an infected message on an Edge Transport server and either reject or delete it, you do not incur the cost (and risk) of storing the message on your internal servers or of scanning the message internally for viruses.

Edge transport rules are used to control the flow of messages that are sent to or received from the Internet. They help protect corporate network resources and data by applying an action to messages that meet specified conditions. These rules are configured for each server.

Edge transport rule conditions are based on data, such as specific words or text patterns in the message subject, body, header, or From address; the SCL; or attachment type. Actions determine how the message is processed when a specified condition is true. Possible actions include the quarantine of a message, dropping or rejecting a message, appending additional recipients, or logging an event. Optional exceptions exempt particular messages from having an action applied.

When you create a transport rule to identify virus threats, you need to examine the reports published about the virus and look for characteristics that identify the virus and that could be used in a transport rule. You also need to ensure that these characteristics do not match any content that may exist in legitimate messages. The following list describes some unique characteristics that a virus may contain:

- A limited number of identifiable strings in the subject or message body
- A specific email address in either the From header field or the To header field
- A message header field that has a specific value

Edge transport rule conditions and exceptions consist of predicates that instruct the Edge Rules agent on an Edge Transport server to examine a specific part of an email message, such as sender, recipients, subject, other message headers, and the message body, to determine whether the rule should be applied to that message.

The Edge Rules agent inspects message properties for specified predicate values. To assign a value to a predicate, you must determine the predicate property. The following predicate properties are available as parameters of the *New-TransportRule* and *Set-TransportRule* EMS cmdlets:

- **SubjectContains**   Matches messages that contain the specified words in the Subject field
- **SubjectOrBodyContains**   Matches messages that contain the specified words in the Subject field or message body
- **HeaderContains**   Matches messages where the value of the specified message header contains the specified words
- **FromAddressContains**   Matches messages that contain the specified words in the From field
- **AnyOfRecipientAddressContains**   Matches messages that contain the specified words in the To, Cc, or Bcc fields of the message
- **SubjectMatches**   Matches messages where text patterns in the Subject field match a specified regular expression
- **SubjectOrBodyMatches**   Matches messages where text patterns in the Subject field or message body match a specified regular expression
- **HeaderMatches**   Matches messages where the specified message header field contains text patterns that match a specified regular expression
- **FromAddressMatches**   Matches messages that contain text patterns in the From field of the messages that match a specified regular expression
- **AnyOfRecipientAddressMatches**   Matches messages where text patterns in the To, Cc, or Bcc fields of the message match a specified regular expression
- **SclOver**   Matches messages with an SCL equal to or greater than the value specified
- **AttachmentSizeOver**   Matches messages that contain attachments larger than the specified value
- **FromScope**   Matches messages that are sent from the specified (external) address scope

> **MORE INFO   TRANSPORT RULE PREDICATES**
>
> For more information about transport rule predicates used on both Edge Transport and Hub Transport servers, see *http://technet.microsoft.com/en-us/library/dd638183.aspx*.

After you identify the unique characteristics of a virus, you can create a transport rule to perform actions on it, such as delete, reject, or quarantine. Take care, however. If you decide to delete or reject a message, you cannot retrieve it. If you want to prevent the message from being delivered but do not want to irretrievably delete it, configure the rule to deliver the message to a quarantine mailbox.

The following actions are available as parameters of the *New-TransportRule* and *Set-TransportRule* EMS cmdlets on Edge Transport servers:

- **LogEvent**   Inserts an event into the Application log of the local Hub Transport server
- **PrependSubject**   Prepends a string to the start of the email message subject field
- **SetScl**   Configures the SCL on an email message
- **SetHeader**   Creates a new message header field or modifies an existing message header field
- **RemoveHeader**   Removes the specified message header field from an email message
- **AddToRecipient**   Adds one or more email addresses to the To address list of the email message. The original recipients can see the additional address.
- **CopyTo**   Adds one or more email addresses to the Cc field of the email message. The original recipients can see the original address.
- **BlindCopyTo**   Adds one or more email addresses to the Bcc address list of the email message. The original recipients are not notified and cannot see the additional address.
- **Disconnect**   Ends the connection between the sending server and the Edge Transport server without generating a non-delivery report message
- **RedirectMessage**   Redirects the email message to one or more email addresses specified by the administrator. The message is not delivered to the original recipient, and no notification is provided to the recipient or the sender.
- **Quarantine**   Redirects the email message to the spam quarantine mailbox
- **SmtpRejectMessage**   Deletes the email message and sends a notification to the sender. The recipients do not receive the message or notification. This action enables you to specify a specific DSN code.
- **DeleteMessage**   Deletes the email message without sending a notification to either the recipient or the sender

For example, the following EMS command creates an edge transport rule that sets an SCL level of 7 on any message from the sender NoReply@treyresearch.com where the subject contains the words "lower prices" unless the subject also contains the word "bicycle":

```
New-TransportRule -Name "SpamDetection" -From "NoReply@treyresearch.com"
-SubjectContains "lower prices" -SetScl 7 ExceptIfSubjectContainsWords "bicycle"
```

> **MORE INFO**   **TRANSPORT RULE ACTIONS**
>
> For more information about transport rule actions used on both Edge Transport and Hub Transport servers, see *http://technet.microsoft.com/en-us/library/aa998315.aspx*.

Implementing File-Level Antivirus Scanning

Implementing file-level antivirus scanning can help enhance the security and health of your Exchange Server 2010 organization. However, you need to take care that the file-level scanner you use is correctly configured. Badly configured file-level scanners can cause problems in Exchange Server 2010. You can use two types of file-level scanners:

- **Memory-resident file-level scanners**   The antivirus software is loaded in memory at all times and checks all the files that are used on the hard disk and in computer memory.

- **On-demand file-level scanners**   You can configure the antivirus software to scan files on a hard disk manually or at scheduled intervals. Some antivirus software packages start an on-demand scan automatically after virus signatures are updated to ensure that all files are scanned with the latest signatures.

Potential Problems Related to File-Level Scanners

A number of problems may occur when you use file-level scanners with Exchange Server 2010. For example, a scanner may scan a file when the file is being used. This can cause the scanner to lock or quarantine the file. In particular, a file-level scanner could lock an Exchange log or a database file while Exchange tries to use it, resulting in a severe failure.

You should also be aware that file-level scanners do not provide protection against some email viruses, such as backdoor Trojan horse viruses. An example of this is the Storm Worm, which propagated itself through email messages. The worm joined the infected computer to a network of similarly compromised machines, known as a *botnet,* which could then be remotely controlled by an attacker and used to send spam email messages in periodic bursts.

> **MORE INFO   THE STORM WORM**
>
> For more information about the Storm Worm, see *http://blogs.technet.com/b/antimalware/archive/2007/09/20/storm-drain.aspx.*

When you deploy file-level scanners on Exchange Server 2010 servers, you can avoid many of the associated problems by ensuring that the appropriate exclusions, such as directory exclusions, process exclusions, and file name extension exclusions, are in place for both memory-resident and file-level scanning.

Directory Exclusions

You must exclude specific directories on each Exchange Server 2010 server or server role on which you run a file-level antivirus scanner. On a Mailbox server, you should exclude the following:

- **Exchange databases, checkpoint files, and log files**   These are located by default in subfolders of the %ExchangeInstallPath%\Mailbox folder. You can obtain the directory location using the EMS. For example, the following command determines the location of mailbox databases, transaction logs, and checkpoint files on the Mailbox server VAN-EX1:

```
Get-MailboxDatabase -server VAN-EX1 | FL *path*
```

Figure 12-16 shows the output from this command.

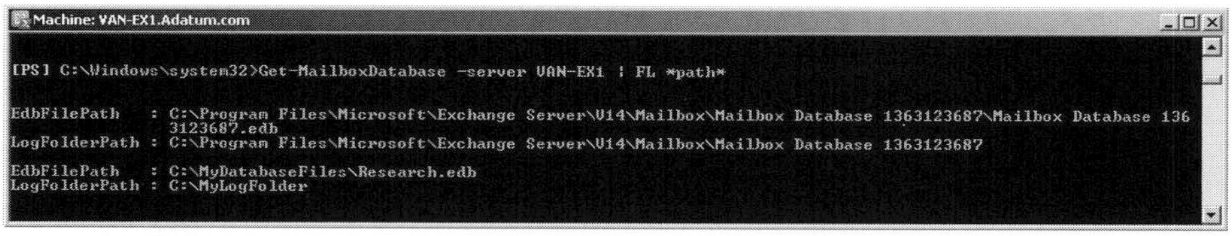

FIGURE 12-16 Discovering the location of mailbox databases, transaction logs, and checkpoint files

- **Database content indexes**   These are located by default in the same folder as the database file.

- **Group Metrics files**   These are located by default in the %ExchangeInstallPath%\ GroupMetrics folder.

- **General log files**   These include, for example, message tracking and calendar repair log files. These files are located by default in subfolders in the %ExchangeInstallPath%\ TransportRoles\Logs folder and %ExchangeInstallPath%\Logging folder. The following command determines the log paths being used on the Mailbox server VAN-EX1:

```
Get-MailboxServer -Identity VAN-EX1 | FL *path*
```

Figure 12-17 shows the output from this command.

FIGURE 12-17 Discovering the location of log paths

- **IIS system files**   These are located in the %SystemRoot%\System32\Inetsrv folder.

- **Offline address book files**   These are located by default in subfolders in the %ExchangeInstallPath%\ExchangeOAB folder.

- **Temporary folder used with offline maintenance utilities such as Eseutil.exe**   This is the folder location from which you run the .exe file. You can configure where you perform the operation when you run the utility.

- **The Mailbox database temporary folder**   This is located at %ExchangeInstallPath%\ Mailbox\MDBTEMP.

- **Exchange-aware antivirus program folders.**

If the Mailbox server is a member of a database availability group (DAG), you should also exclude the quorum disk and the %Winnt%\Cluster folder. If the server is a witness server, you should exclude the witness directory files. These are located on another server in the environment—typically a Hub Transport server—by default in \\%SystemDrive%:\ DAGFileShareWitnesses\<DAGFQDN> and default share (<DAGFQDN>) on that server.

> **MORE INFO** **DAGs AND WITNESS SERVERS**
>
> For more information about DAGs and witness servers, see *http://technet.microsoft.com/ en-us/library/dd298065.aspx*.

On a Hub Transport server, you should exclude the following:

- **Pickup and Replay message directory folders**   These folders are located by default in the %ExchangeInstallPath%\TransportRoles folder. To determine the paths being used on, for example, the Hub Transport server DEN-EX1, you run the following command:

```
Get-TransportServer -Identity DEN-EX1 | FL *dir*path*
```

- **General log files**   These include, for example, message tracking and connectivity logs. These files are located by default in subfolders under the %ExchangeInstallPath%\ TransportRoles\Logs folder. The following command would, for example, determine the log paths being used on the Transport server DEN-EX2:

```
Get-TransportServer -Identity DEN-EX2| FL *logpath*,*tracingpath*
```

- **The Transport Server role Sender Reputation database, checkpoint, and log files**   These are located by default in the %ExchangeInstallPath%\TransportRoles\ Data\SenderReputation folder.
- **The Transport Server role IP filter database, checkpoint, and log files**   These are located by default in the %ExchangeInstallPath%\TransportRoles\Data\IpFilter folder.
- **The Transport Server role queue database, checkpoint, and log files**   These are located by default in the %ExchangeInstallPath%\TransportRoles\Data\Queue folder.
- **The temporary folders used to perform content and object linking and embedding (OLE) conversions**   By default, content conversions are performed in the Exchange server's TMP folder, and OLE conversions are performed in the %ExchangeInstallPath%\Working\OleConvertor folder.
- **Exchange-aware antivirus program folders.**

On an Edge Transport server, you should exclude the following:

- **General log files**   These can include, for example, message tracking log files. These files are located by default in subfolders in the %ExchangeInstallPath%\TransportRoles\ Logs folder. To determine the log paths being used on the Edge Transport server VAN-EX2, for example, you run the following EMS command:

```
Get-TransportServer -Identity VAN-EX2 | FL *logpath*,*tracingpath*
```

- **Pickup and Replay message folders**   These are located by default in the %ExchangeInstallPath%\TransportRoles folder. To determine the log paths being used on the Edge Transport server VAN-EX2, for example, you run the following command:

```
Get-TransportServer -Identity VAN-EX2 | FL *dir*path*
```

- **AD LDS database and log files**   These are located by default in the %ExchangeInstallPath%\TransportRoles\Data\Adam folder.
- **Transport Server role queue database, checkpoint, and log files**   These are located by default in the %ExchangeInstallPath%\TransportRoles\Data\Queue folder.
- **Transport Server role IP filter database, checkpoint, and log files**   These are located by default in the %ExchangeInstallPath%\TransportRoles\Data\IpFilter folder.
- **Transport Server role Sender Reputation database, checkpoint, and log files**   These are located by default in the %ExchangeInstallPath%\TransportRoles\Data\SenderReputation folder.
- **The temporary folders that are used to perform content and OLE conversions**   By default, content conversions are performed in the Exchange server's TMP folder, and OLE conversions are performed in the %ExchangeInstallPath%\Working\OleConvertor folder.
- **Exchange-aware antivirus program folders.**

On a Client Access server, you should exclude the following:

- **The compression folder used with OWA**   On servers running IIS 7.0, the compression folder is located by default at %SystemDrive%\inetpub\temp\IIS Temporary Compressed Files. On servers running IIS 6.0, the compression folder is located by default at %systemroot%\IIS Temporary Compressed Files.
- **IIS system files in the %SystemRoot%\System32\Inetsrv folder.**
- **The Internet-related files stored in subfolders of the %ExchangeInstallPath%\ClientAccess folder.**
- **Folders on servers that have protocol logging enabled for POP3 or IMAP4**   The POP3 folder %ExchangeInstallPath%\Logging\POP3 and the IMAP4 folder: %ExchangeInstallPath%\Logging\IMAP4.
- **The folder Inetpub\logs\logfiles\w3svc.**
- **The temporary folders that are used to perform content and OLE conversions**   By default, content conversions are performed in the Exchange server's TMP folder, and OLE conversions are performed in the %ExchangeInstallPath%\Working\OleConvertor folder.

On a Unified Messaging server, you should exclude the following:

- **Grammar files for different locales**   These could include, for example, en-EN and es-ES. By default, these files are stored in subfolders of the %ExchangeInstallPath%\UnifiedMessaging\grammars folder.

- **Voice mail files temporarily stored in the %ExchangeInstallPath%\UnifiedMessaging\ voicemail folder.**

- **Voice prompts, greetings, and informational message files**   These are stored by default in the subfolders of the %ExchangeInstallPath%\UnifiedMessaging\Prompts folder.

- **Temporary files generated by unified messaging**   These are stored by default in the %ExchangeInstallPath%\UnifiedMessaging\temp folder.

On a server running Microsoft Forefront Protection 2010 for Exchange Server, you should exclude the following:

- **The Forefront installation folder**   By default, this is %Program Files%\Microsoft Forefront Security\Exchange Server.

- **Quarantined files**   These are stored by default in the %Program Files%\Microsoft Forefront Security\Exchange Server\Data\Quarantine folder.

- **Archived messages**   These are stored by default in the %Program Files%\Microsoft Forefront Security\Exchange Server\Data\Archive folder.

- **Antivirus engine files**   These are stored by default in the subfolders of %Program Files%\Microsoft Forefront Security\Exchange Server\Data\Engines\x86 folder.

- **Configuration files**   These are stored by default in the %Program Files%\Microsoft Forefront Security\Exchange Server\Data folder.

EXAM TIP

The topic of exclusions configured on file-level virus scanning software inevitably involves lists of exclusions. Treat these lists as a reference. Read through them a few times but do not attempt to memorize them. Know that you need to configure directory, file, and process exclusions.

Process Exclusions

If a file-level scanner supports the scanning of processes and the incorrect processes are scanned, this can adversely affect Exchange operation. You should exclude the following processes from file-level scanners:

- Cdb.exe

- Cidaemon.exe

- Cluster.exe

- Dsamain.exe

- EdgeCredentialSvc.exe

- EdgeTransport.exe

- ExFBA.exe

- GalGrammarGenerator.exe

- Inetinfo.exe

- Mad.exe
- Microsoft.Exchange.AddressBook.Service.exe
- Microsoft.Exchange.AntispamUpdateSvc.exe
- Microsoft.Exchange.ContentFilter.Wrapper.exe
- Microsoft.Exchange.EdgeSyncSvc.exe
- Microsoft.Exchange.Imap4.exe
- Microsoft.Exchange.Imap4service.exe
- Microsoft.Exchange.Infoworker.Assistants.exe
- Microsoft.Exchange.Monitoring.exe
- Microsoft.Exchange.Pop3.exe
- Microsoft.Exchange.Pop3service.exe
- Microsoft.Exchange.ProtectedServiceHost.exe
- Microsoft.Exchange.RPCClientAccess.Service.exe
- Microsoft.Exchange.Search.Exsearch.exe
- Microsoft.Exchange.Servicehost.exe
- MSExchangeASTopologyService.exe
- MSExchangeFDS.exe
- MSExchangeMailboxAssistants.exe
- MSExchangeMailboxReplication.exe
- MSExchangeMailSubmission.exe
- MSExchangeRepl.exe
- MSExchangeTransport.exe
- MSExchangeTransportLogSearch.exe
- MSExchangeThrottling.exe
- Msftefd.exe
- Msftesql.exe
- OleConverter.exe
- Powershell.exe
- SESWorker.exe
- SpeechService.exe
- Store.exe
- TranscodingService.exe
- UmService.exe
- UmWorkerProcess.exe
- W3wp.exe

If you are deploying Forefront Protection for Exchange Server, you should also exclude the following processes:

- Adonavsvc.exe
- FscController.exe
- FscDiag.exe
- FscExec.exe
- FscImc.exe
- FscManualScanner.exe
- FscMonitor.exe
- FscRealtimeScanner.exe
- FscStatsServ.exe
- FscTransportScanner.exe
- FscUtility.exe
- FsEmailPickup.exe
- FssaClient.exe
- GetEngineFiles.exe
- PerfmonitorSetup.exe
- ScanEngineTest.exe
- SemSetup.exe
- File name extension exclusions

Sometimes directory exclusions fail or files are moved from their default locations. Therefore, in addition to excluding directories and processes, you should exclude the following Exchange-specific file name extensions:

- Application-related extensions, for example, .config, .dia, and .wsb
- Database-related extensions, for example, .chk, .log, .edb, .jrs, and .que
- Offline address book–related extensions (.lzx)
- Content Index–related extensions, for example, .ci, .wid, .dir, .000, .001, and .002
- Unified Messaging–related extensions, for example, .cfg and .grxml
- GroupMetrics extensions, for example, .dsc, .bin, and .xml
- Forefront Protection 2010 for Exchange Server–related extensions, for example, .avc, .dt, .lst, .cab, .fdb, .mdb, .cfg, .fdm, .ppl, .config, .ide, .set, .da1, .key, .v3d, .dat, .klb, .vdb, .def, .kli, and .vdm

Note that the file name extensions listed for Forefront Protection 2010 for Exchange Server are the signature files from various antivirus directory engines. Additional file name extensions may be added in the future as third-party antivirus vendors update their antivirus signature files.

Lesson Summary

- When an incoming message arrives on an Edge Transport server and connection filtering is enabled, the IP address of the SMTP server that sent the message is compared against IP allow and IP block lists.

- Content filtering uses algorithms to assess the contents of a message and provide a rating (the SCL) that indicates how likely the message is to be spam. You can delete, reject, or quarantine a message depending on its SCL rating. If you use message quarantine, you need to specify a quarantine mailbox.

- Recipient filtering allows you to block messages based on whom they are sent to. This technology is most often used to block messages sent to recipients that are not listed in the GAL.

- The Sender ID agent is an anti-spam agent enabled on Edge Transport servers. The agent queries the sending system's DNS service to determine what action, if any, to take on an inbound message. Sender ID is designed to combat spoofing, which is the impersonation of a sender and a domain.

- Sender reputation and SRL values are used on Edge Transport servers to block messages according to various sender characteristics.

- Many attachments can potentially contain viruses or other inappropriate material that could cause significant damage. You can use attachment filtering to control attachments that enter or leave your organization.

- You can use the Edge Rules agent and edge transport rules to help protect your organization from viruses. Implementing file-level antivirus scanning can also help enhance the security and health of your Exchange organization.

Lesson Review

You can use the following questions to test your knowledge of the information in Lesson 2, "Managing Anti-Spam and Antivirus Countermeasures." The questions are also available on the companion CD if you prefer to review them in electronic form.

> **NOTE ANSWERS**
>
> Answers to these questions and explanations of why each answer choice is correct or incorrect are located in the "Answers" section at the end of the book.

1. What EMS command disables connection filtering using the IP allow list on a Hub Transport server but does not affect connection filtering using the IP block list?

   A. *Remove-IPAllowListProvider –Identity contoso.com*

   B. *Set-IPBlockListConfig -Enabled $false*

   C. *Set-IPAllowListConfig -Enabled $false*

   D. *Disable-TransportAgent -Identity "Connection Filtering agent"*

2. What EMS command removes the IP address 10.100.20.45 from the IP allow list?
   A. *Remove-IPAllowListEntry –Identity 10.100.20.45*
   B. *Get-IPAllowListEntry -IPAddress 10.100.20.45 | Remove-IPAllowListEntry*
   C. *Remove-IPAllowListEntry –IPAddress 10.100.20.45*
   D. *Get-IPAllowBlockEntry -IPAddress 10.100.20.45 | Remove-IPBlockListEntry*

3. You do not want to apply content filtering to email messages received from KimAkers@contoso.com. What EMS command configures content filtering to bypass only this sender?
   A. *Set-ContentFilterConfig -BypassedSenders KimAkers@contoso.com*
   B. *Set-ContentFilterConfig -BypassedRecipients KimAkers@contoso.com*
   C. *Set-ContentFilterConfig -BypassedSenderDomains contoso.com*
   D. *Set-ContentFilterConfig -BypassedSenderDomains KimAkers@contoso.com*

4. An Edge Transport server is evaluating the Sender ID for an email message. What Sender ID status value is set if no published SPF data exists in the sender's DNS?
   A. Pass
   B. Fail
   C. None
   D. TempError

5. What EMS command filters all email attachments that have the file name extension .vba?
   A. *Add-AttachmentFilterEntry -Name *.vba -Type ContentType*
   B. *Add-AttachmentFilterEntry -Identity *.vba -Type ContentType*
   C. *Add-AttachmentFilterEntry -Identity *.vba -Type FileName*
   D. *Add-AttachmentFilterEntry -Name *.vba -Type FileName*

PRACTICE Configuring, Disabling, and Enabling S/MIME

In this practice session, you will use the registry editor to configure S/MIME for OWA and the EMS to disable and then enable it. Note that it is not essential to disable and enable S/MIME for OWA after reconfiguring the registry settings, but it is good practice to do so.

EXERCISE 1 Managing S/MIME for OWA

In this exercise, you will manage S/MIME for OWA by using the Regedit utility to edit the registry on the Exchange Server 2010 Client Access server VAN-EX1. You specify the time that OWA waits while connecting to retrieve a single CRL as part of a certificate validation operation. You specify the time that OWA waits to retrieve all CRLs when validating a certificate.

You require that any digitally signed email message that is sent from OWA be clear-signed. Carry out the following procedure:

1. Log on to the Client Access server VAN-EX1 using the Kim Akers account.

2. In the Run box, enter regedit.

3. Navigate to the following registry key:

    HKLM\System\CurrentControlSet\Services\MSExchange OWA\SMIME

4. Right-click the MIME key and click New, as shown in Figure 12-18.

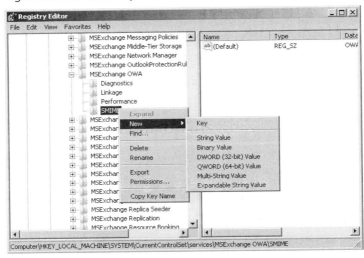

FIGURE 12-18 Adding an additional key to a registry key

5. Click Key.

6. In the new key under SMIME, enter **CRLConnectionTimeout,** as shown in Figure 12-19.

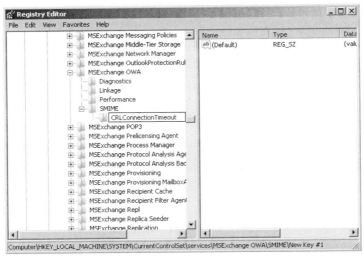

FIGURE 12-19 Naming the new registry key

7. Right-click the CRLConnectionTimeout key and click New.

8. Click DWORD (32-Bit) Value.

9. Type **120000,** as shown in Figure 12-20. This specifies that OWA waits a maximum of 120 seconds while connecting to retrieve a single CRL as part of a certificate validation operation before the operation fails. Press Enter.

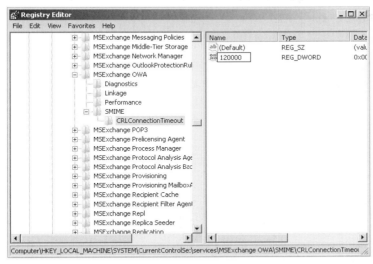

FIGURE 12-20 Setting the value of the CRLConnectionTimeout key to 120000

10. Right-click the MIME key and click New.

11. Click Key.

12. In the new key under SMIME, enter **CRLRetrievalTimeout,** as shown in Figure 12-21.

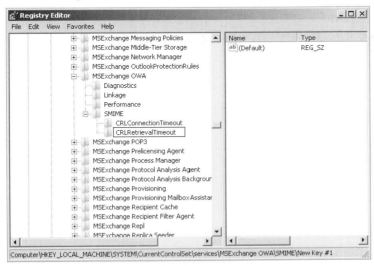

FIGURE 12-21 Naming the CRLRetrievalTimeout registry key

13. Right-click the CRLRetrievalTimeout key and click New.

14. Click DWORD (32-Bit) Value.

15. Type **20000** to specify that OWA waits a maximum of 20 seconds to retrieve all CRLs when validating a certificate. Press Enter.

16. Right-click the MIME key and click New.

17. Click Key.

18. In the new key under SMIME, enter **ClearSign,** as shown in Figure 12-22.

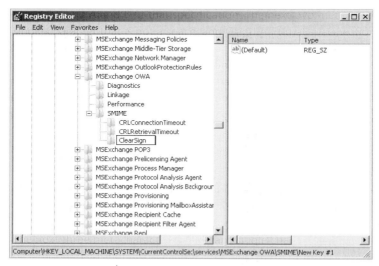

FIGURE 12-22 Naming the ClearSign registry key

19. Right-click the ClearSign key and click New.

20. Click DWORD (32-Bit) Value.

21. Type 1 to require that any digitally signed email message that is sent from OWA is clear-signed. Press Enter.

22. Close the registry editor.

EXERCISE 2 Disabling and Enabling S/MIME for OWA

By default, S/MIME is enabled. In this exercise, you use the EMS to disable S/MIME on the OWA virtual directory in the default IIS website on the Client Access server VAN-EX1. You then enable S/MIME on the same website. You should perform this exercise after you have completed Exercise 1. Carry out the following procedure:

1. If necessary, log on to the Client Access server VAN-EX1 using the Kim Akers account.

2. Start the EMS.

3. Enter the following EMS command:

```
Set-OWAVirtualDirectory -Identity "owa (Default Web Site)" -SMimeEnabled $false
```

4. Enter the following EMS command:

```
Set-OWAVirtualDirectory -Identity "owa (Default Web Site)" -SMimeEnabled $true
```

PRACTICE   Configuring the Sender Filtering Agent

In this practice session, you will configure the Sender Filtering agent to block email from specific senders and specific domains. You will add a sender to a list of blocked senders without deleting the current list, and you will configure the Sender Filter agent to block messages that do not specify a sender in the MAIL FROM: SMTP header.

EXERCISE 1   Block Email from Specific Senders and Specific Domains

In this exercise, you will specify individual senders, a domain, and a domain, including its subdomains. Carry out the following procedure:

1. Log on to the Edge Transport server VAN-EX2 using the Local Administrator account and start the EMS.

2. To configure the Sender Filter agent to block messages from the specific email addresses JasonCarlson@contoso.com and PatrickHinesl@contoso.com, enter the following command:

```
Set-SenderFilterConfig -BlockedSenders
JasonCarlson@contoso.com,PatrickHinesl@contoso.com
```

3. To configure the Sender Filter agent to block messages from the specific domain fabricam.com, enter the following command:

```
Set-SenderFilterConfig -BlockedDomains fabricam.com
```

4. To configure the Sender Filter agent to block messages from the treyresearch.com domain and all its subdomains, enter the following command:

```
Set-SenderFilterConfig -BlockedDomainsAndSubdomains treyresearch.com
```

As shown in Figure 12-23, these Sender Filter configuration commands do not generate an output. If the commands complete without error, the configuration changes have been made.

FIGURE 12-23 Sender Filter configuration commands

EXERCISE 2 Add a Sender to a List of Blocked Senders

In this exercise, you will add a sender to a list of blocked senders without removing the current blocked senders from the list. When you specify values by using parameters such as BlockedSenders, BlockedDomains, and BlockedDomainsAndSubdomains, these replace the existing list of blocked senders. To preserve the existing list, you can use a temporary Shell variable to add an address or a domain to the blocked senders list. The following exercise uses the temporary variable $ExerciseListing to add the sender ChenYang@fabricam.com to the blocked senders list. You should perform this exercise after you have completed Exercise 1. Carry out the following procedure:

1. If necessary, log on to the Edge Transport server VAN-EX2 using the Local Administrator account and start the EMS.

2. Place the existing Sender Filter list in the variable $ExerciseListing by entering the following command:

    ```
    $ExerciseListing = Get-SenderFilterConfig
    ```

3. Add the sender ChenYang@fabricam.com to the variable $ExerciseListing by entering the following command:

    ```
    $ExerciseListing.BlockedSenders += "ChenYang@fabricam.com"
    ```

4. Use the variable $ExerciseListing to update the Sender Filter list by entering the following command:

    ```
    Set-SenderFilterConfig -BlockedSenders $ExerciseListing.BlockedSenders
    ```

    As shown in Figure 12-24, the Sender Filter configuration commands to update the Sender Filter list do not generate an output. If the commands complete without error, the configuration change has been made.

FIGURE 12-24 Updating a Sender Filter list

EXERCISE 3 Configure the Sender Filter Agent to Block Messages That Do Not Specify a Sender in the MAIL FROM: SMTP Header

In this exercise, you will configure the Sender Filter agent to block messages that do not specify a sender in the MAIL FROM: SMTP header. Messages that meet this condition are likely to be spam. You should perform this exercise after you have completed Exercises 1 and 2. Carry out the following procedure:

1. If necessary, log on to the Edge Transport server VAN-EX2 using the Local Administrator account and start the EMS.

2. Configure the Sender Filter agent to block messages that do not specify a sender in the MAIL FROM: SMTP header by entering the following command:

```
Set-SenderFilterConfig -BlankSenderBlockingEnabled $true
```

The command to configure the Sender Filter agent to block messages that do not specify a sender in the MAIL FROM: SMTP header does not generate an output. If the command completes without error, the configuration change has been made.

Chapter Review

To further practice and reinforce the skills you learned in this chapter, you can perform the following tasks:

- Review the chapter summary.
- Review the list of key terms introduced in this chapter.
- Complete the case scenarios. These scenarios set up real-world situations involving the topics of this chapter and ask you to create a solution.
- Complete the suggested practices.
- Take a practice test.

Chapter Summary

- Various protocols and standards such as S/MIME, LTS, and MTLS guarantee the integrity, confidentiality, or authentication (or all three) of email communications.
- You can configure permissions on Active Directory objects such as user mailboxes, distribution groups, Send connectors, and Receive connectors. The AD FS protocol works with AD RMS to provide RMS Federation.
- IP allow lists, IP block lists, SCL ratings, recipient filtering, Sender ID, SRL values, and PCL ratings can all be configured to help filter spam and identify phishing sites and spoofed email.
- Attachment filtering, edge transport rules, and file-level virus scanning can detect viruses and other malware and prevent them from entering your email organization.

Key Terms

Do you know what these key terms mean?

- Allow list
- Block list
- Message
- Message confidentiality
- Message integrity
- Phishing confidence level (PCL)
- Public key infrastructure (PKI)
- Sender reputation level (SRL)
- Spam confidence level (SCL)

Case Scenarios

In the following case scenarios, you apply what you've learned about subjects covered in this chapter. You can find answers to these questions in the "Answers" section at the end of this book.

Case Scenario 1: Configuring Domain Security

You are the Exchange Administrator at Tailspin Toys. You want to configure Tailspin Toys' Exchange Server 2010 organization to exchange domain-secured email with its partner organization, Trey Research. You want to ensure that all email messages sent to and received from Trey Research are protected with MTLS and to configure domain security functionality so that all mail between the Tailspin Toys and Trey Research is rejected if MTLS cannot be used.

Tailspin Toys has an internal PKI that generates certificates. The PKI's root certificate has been signed by a trusted third-party CA. Trey Research uses the same third-party CA to generate its certificates. Therefore, both organizations trust the other's root CA. Answer the following questions:

1. The Edge Transport server TST-EX2.tailspintoys.com requires a certificate. You create the folder C:\Certificates on that server. What EMS commands do you enter to generate a base64-encoded PKCS#10 certificate request?

2. You next want to import the certificate and enable it in the trusted certificate store on the TST-EX2 Edge Transport server. The TST-EX2-certificate.pfx file exists in the path C:\Certificates on that server. Which EMS command imports the certificate?

3. You now need to specify treyresearch.com as the domain to which you want to send domain-secured email. Which EMS command do you run on a Hub Transport server in the tailspintoys.com domain?

4. You need to set the DomainSecureEnabled property on the Send connector that sends email to the target domain. For a Send connector named Internet and configured for Internet connection, which EMS command do you run on a Hub Transport server in the tailspintoys.com domain?

Case Scenario 2: Configuring Anti-Spam Settings

The Bicycle Manufacturing division at Tailspin Toys has recently implemented an email organization based on Exchange Server 2010. The division's previous email system received large volumes of spam email that made it difficult to locate and respond to legitimate messages. Management has hired you as a consultant, and the technical director wants to know how best to intercept spam at the peripheral network and stop it from getting to internal servers. Answer the following questions:

1. What technology should be used to block email from SMTP servers that repeatedly send spam to the organization?

2. How can they ensure that mail from their partner trading organization, NorthWind Traders, is never blocked, even if some of the messages from that organization are of a commercial nature?

3. How can they ensure that messages from the Internet whose subjects contain phrases such as "lose weight" or "earn extra cash" are blocked, whereas messages whose subjects contain the word "bicycle" are never blocked?

Suggested Practices

To help you master the examination objectives presented in this chapter, complete the following tasks.

Find Out More about S/MME and OWA Security

- **Practice 1** Follow the links given in this chapter to learn more about S/MIME and other methods of implementing OWA security.

- **Practice 2** Use the registry editor to configure S/MIME. Many administrators are wary of this valuable and powerful tool—quite rightly so, because careless registry editing can damage your infrastructure. Nevertheless, as a professional, you should be competent and confident when editing the registry. Practice on your test network, where, if you do something wrong, only you will know about it.

Learn More about Certificates, CAs, and PKIs

- **Practice 1** The use of certificates is central to almost all network security considerations. Follow the links given in this chapter and search the Internet for security information. If you are confident about obtaining and using security certificates, your knowledge could help you in the examination and almost certainly will help you in your career.

Learn How to Manage Active Directory Permissions on Exchange Objects

- **Practice 1** You can perform a wide range of configuration tasks (not merely configuring Send As permission as used as an example in this chapter) by working with Active Directory permissions. Follow the links given in this chapter to learn more about this topic.

Learn More about Anti-Spam Configuration

- **Practice 1** This is a moving target. Spammers and senders of other malware appear to have an unlimited supply of low cunning, and the measures to counter this problem grow more sophisticated on a daily basis. Almost every technical computer magazine you read will have articles about this. As a professional, it is your job to stay up to date (nobody said this was easy).

- **Practice 2**   Read as much as you can about phishing, spoofing, and other techniques used by malicious and criminal persons to harm and steal from your users. Learn how electronic messaging systems can be attacked and how these attacks can be countered.

Learn More about Federation

- **Practice 1**   This is an important topic. Single sign-on systems are becoming more and more important as organizations combine, both in the business and the public service environments, to create nationwide and worldwide information networks.

Take a Practice Test

The practice tests on this book's companion CD offer many options. For example, you can test yourself on just one exam objective, or you can test yourself on all the 70-662 certification exam content. You can set up the test so that it closely simulates the experience of taking a certification exam, or you can set it up in study mode so that you can look at the correct answers and explanations after you answer each question.

> **MORE INFO   PRACTICE TESTS**
>
> For details about all the practice test options available, see the "How to Use the Practice Tests" section in this book's Introduction.

CHAPTER 13

Exchange High-Availability Solutions

Think for a moment how many minutes or hours your organization could survive during the middle of the day without Mailbox, Client Access, or Hub Transport servers. In this chapter, you will learn how to ensure that all critical roles in your Exchange Server 2010 infrastructure remain available even when one of the servers hosting those roles fails completely. You will learn about the new database availability group and client access array features, how to make public folders highly available, and what you need to do to ensure that message transport continues to function even if one of your message Transport Servers does not.

Exam objectives in this chapter:

- Create and configure the Database Availability Group (DAG).
- Configure public folders for high availability.
- Configure high availability for non–mailbox servers.

Lessons in this chapter:

Before You Begin

In order to complete the exercises in the practice sessions in this chapter, you need to have done the following:

- Installed servers VAN-DC, VAN-EX1, and VAN-EX2, as described in the Appendix
- Have completed Exercise 4 of Chapter 4, "Distribution Groups and Public Folders."

REAL WORLD

Orin Thomas

When I started out in information technology working at a large Australian university, it wasn't unusual for the university email service to go offline for a couple of hours every few months. Sure, at the Help desk, I would need to field a number of calls from people wondering what was up, but back then average people were fairly understanding when they didn't have access to their email. This might have been because, to most of them, work-related email was recent. For most organizations in the mid-1990s, messaging had not become a critical part of daily work flow. Today, if you were to announce to a large organization that email would be unavailable for most of the afternoon, your colleagues would go into conniptions. If you are careful in the way you deploy Exchange, there will be very few things that stop the people you work with from being able to access their email when they need it rather than having to wait a couple of hours like my colleagues at the university had to back in the 1990s.

Lesson 1: Managing Database Availability Groups

Database availability groups (DAGs) provide a high-availability solution without the complexities involved in deploying failover clustering and a Storage Area Network. In its simplest form, DAGs are collections of servers that can host up-to-date replicated copies of each other's mailbox databases that automatically failover without requiring complicated cluster configuration. In this lesson, you will learn how to create a DAG, add servers to the DAG, add and remove mailbox database copies, and configure database copy lag and failover priority.

> **After this lesson, you will be able to:**
> - Create a DAG.
> - Configure a file share witness.
> - Add and remove servers from a DAG.
> - Add and remove database copies.
> - Manage replication latency.
> - Set up a lagged mailbox copy.
> - Configure failover priority.
>
> **Estimated lesson time: 40 minutes**

DAGs

A DAG is a collection of up to 16 Exchange Server 2010 Mailbox servers that provide automatic mailbox database failover in the event of database, server, or network failure. DAGs provide Exchange Mailbox servers with high availability without requiring the expense or complexity of a Storage Area Network. Any server in a DAG can host a copy of a mailbox database from any other server in the DAG. DAGs allow for incremental deployment, which means that you can change which servers are members of a DAG or which mailbox databases are being replicated without having to re-create the DAG.

The Active Manager is the internal Exchange 2010 component responsible for managing switchovers and failovers and runs on every server in a DAG. The Active Manager detects failures of local resources and initiates failover. Active Manager also forwards information to Client Access servers so that these servers are aware which server in a DAG hosts the active copy a specific mailbox database. Exchange administrators do not need to directly interact with the Active Manager in order to manage DAGs.

> **MORE INFO** **UNDERSTANDING DAGs**
>
> To learn more about DAGs, consult the following reference on TechNet: *http://technet .microsoft.com/en-us/library/dd979799.aspx*.

Create DAGs

The DAG itself is a collection of up to 16 Exchange Server 2010 Mailbox servers where there is less than a 250-millisecond (ms) round-trip delay between any two servers. An Exchange Server 2010 organization can host multiple DAGs, but a server can be a member of only one DAG. You must create a DAG in the Exchange organization before you add members to the DAG.

To create a new DAG using the Exchange Management Console (EMC), perform the following general steps:

1. Select the Organization Configuration\Mailbox node in the EMC and then click on New Database Availability Group on the Actions pane. This will launch the New Database Availability Group dialog box.

2. On the New Database Availability Group page, shown in Figure 13-1, enter a name for the DAG, the fully qualified domain name of the witness server, and the directory on the witness server that will be used to store witness data. Click New.

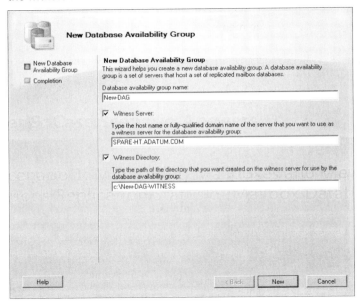

FIGURE 13-1 New DAG Wizard

A DAG name must be unique within the organization and can be up to 15 characters. You can assign an Internet Protocol version 4 (IPv4) or an IPv6 address to the DAG when using the Exchange Management Shell (EMS) or have those addresses assigned automatically through DHCP, which is the default when you use the EMC to create the DAG. To create a DAG using the EMS, use the *New-DatabaseAvailabilityGroup* cmdlet. For example, to create a new DAG named DAG-ALPHA with the virtual IP address 10.10.0.100 using the witness server ht.adatum.com and the directory c:\witness, issue the following command:

```
New-DatabaseAvailabilityGroup —Name DAG-ALPHA —DatabaseAvailabilityGroupIpAddresses
10.10.0.100 —WitnessServer 'ht.adatum.com' —WitnessDirectory 'c:\witness'
```

The witness server should be a Hub Transport server that does not have the Mailbox role installed. It is possible to configure other servers to function as DAG witnesses, and although you do this in the exercise at the end of the chapter, Microsoft does not recommend this alternate configuration. Witness servers should have the following properties:

- Witness server cannot be a member of a DAG.

- Witness server must be a member of the same Active Directory forest as the DAG.

- Though a single server can function as a witness for multiple DAGs, each DAG must have a unique witness directory.

- If the witness server is not an Exchange Server 2010 server, it is necessary to add the Exchange Trusted Subsystem universal security group to the local Administrators group on the witness server.

If you do not specify a witness server during DAG creation, the DAG creation process will search for a Hub Transport server that does not have the Mailbox server role installed and will automatically create the default directory and share, configuring it as the witness server. You can remove a DAG only if the DAG has no members.

> **MORE INFO**   **CREATE A DAG**
>
> To learn more about creating DAGs, consult the following link on TechNet: *http://technet .microsoft.com/en-us/library/dd351172.aspx*.

Add and Remove Servers from DAGs

Once a DAG exists, you are able to add Exchange Server 2010 Mailbox servers. You can add a maximum of 16 Mailbox servers to a DAG. Adding a server to a DAG automatically installs the Windows Failover Clustering feature. You can add a server to a DAG only if the server's IPv4 address information includes a default gateway address.

A server must be running one of the following operating systems:

- Windows Server 2008 with Service Pack 2 Enterprise edition or Datacenter edition

- Windows Server 2008 R2 Enterprise edition or Datacenter edition

The Enterprise or Datacenter editions are required because these operating systems support the Windows Failover Clustering feature. The Standard editions of Windows Server 2008 and Windows Server 2008 R2 do not support the Windows Failover Clustering feature. All servers in the DAG must be running the same operating system. This means that you can have all DAG members running Windows Server 2008 R2 or Windows Server 2008 with Service Pack 2, but you are unable to have a mixture of these operating systems.

Perform the following general steps to add a Mailbox server to a DAG:

1. Select the Organization Configuration\Mailbox node in the EMC.

2. On the middle pane, select the Database Availability Groups tab and then select the DAG to which you wish to add Mailbox servers. On the Actions pane, click on Manage Database Availability Group.

3. In the Manage Database Availability Group Membership dialog box, click Add. In the Select Mailbox server dialog box, select the Mailbox server that you wish to add to the DAG and then click OK.

You can also use this dialog box to remove servers from a DAG. Instead of clicking add, select the server that you want to remove from the DAG and then click on the red X icon to remove it. While you can add and remove DAG members at any time, you can remove a server from a DAG only if there are no mailbox database copies hosted on the server.

Use the *Add-DatabaseAvailabilityGroupsServer* cmdlet to add a Mailbox server to a DAG. For example, to add the server MBX-ALPHA to DAG DAG-ONE, issue the following command:

```
Add-DatabaseAvailabilityGroupServer –Identity DAG-ONE –MailboxServer MBX-ALPHA
```

Use the *Remove-DatabaseAvailabilityGroupServer* cmdlet to remove a Mailbox server from a DAG. For example, to remove the server MBX-BETA from DAG DAG-ONE, issue the following command:

```
RemoveDatabaseAvailabilityGroupServer –Identity DAG-ONE –MailboxServer MBX-BETA
```

> **MORE INFO** **MANAGE DAG GROUP MEMBERSHIP**
>
> To learn more about adding and removing servers from DAGs, consult the following link on TechNet: *http://technet.microsoft.com/en-us/library/dd351278.aspx*.

 Quick Check

- What is the maximum round-trip latency, in milliseconds, between any two servers in a DAG?

Quick Check Answer

- The maximum round-trip latency between any two servers in a DAG is 250 ms.

Mailbox Database Copies

A mailbox database copy is a copy of an existing mailbox database that Exchange Server 2010 keeps up to date through continuous replication. Once you have created a DAG and added Mailbox servers as members, you are able configure mailbox database copies. There are several conditions when configuring mailbox database copies. These conditions include the following:

- The mailbox database copy that you are creating must be of a mailbox database that already exists on a server within the DAG.
- You can create a mailbox database copy of only a mailbox database that is in the same DAG. You cannot create a mailbox database copy of a mailbox that is in a different DAG.

- The active copy of the mailbox database that you are creating a copy of must be mounted.
- Circular logging must not be enabled for the source mailbox database. You can reenable circular logging after you have added the mailbox database copy.
- DAGs do not support database copies where the round-trip network latency between Mailbox servers exceeds 250 ms.
- A single Mailbox server cannot host more than one instance of a specific mailbox database copy.
- All mailbox database copies must use the same path. For example, if the first mailbox database uses the path e:\mbx-db-one, all subsequent mailbox database copies must also use the path e:\mbx-db-one. If volume E does not exist on a member server within the DAG, it will not be able to host a copy of that mailbox database.

To create a mailbox database copy, perform the following general steps:

1. Select the Organization Configuration\Mailbox node from within the EMC. In the middle pane, select the database for which you wish to create a database copy.

2. On the Actions pane, click on Add Mailbox Database Copy. This will open the Add Mailbox Database Copy Wizard.

3. The Add Mailbox Database Copy dialog box, shown in Figure 13-2, will display the servers that host copies of the database. Click the Browse button to select a server within the DAG to which you will add the copy.

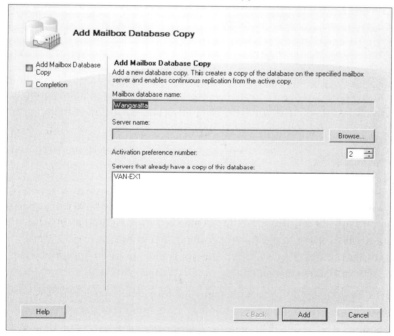

FIGURE 13-2 Add Mailbox Database Copy

4. Select an Activation Preference number and then click Add. Click Finish to close the Add Mailbox Database Copy Wizard.

You can add mailbox database copies by using the *Add-MailboxDatabaseCopy* cmdlet. For example, to add a mailbox database copy of an existing mailbox database named Wangaratta to DAG member MBX2, with an activation preference of 2, issue the following command:

```
Add-MailboxDatabaseCopy -Identity 'Wangaratta' -MailboxServer 'MBX2'
-ActivationPreference '2'
```

To remove a mailbox database copy, either select the database copy in the EMC and click Remove on the Actions pane or use the *Remove-MailboxDatabaseCopy* cmdlet. You cannot use these methods to remove the last copy of a mailbox database, which you must delete using the *Remove-MailboxDatabase* cmdlet.

You cannot create a database copy of a public folder database. You use public folder replication to provide redundancy for public folders. You will learn about public folder replication in Lesson 2, "Highly Available Public Folders."

> **MORE INFO** **MAILBOX DATABASE COPIES**
>
> To learn more about mailbox database copies, consult the following link on TechNet: *http://technet.microsoft.com/en-us/library/dd335158.aspx.*

Activating, Suspending, and Resuming Mailbox Database Copies

You can make a passive database copy active by performing switchover. You might want to perform switchover when you need to perform maintenance on the Mailbox server that hosts the active copy of the database, such as when it is necessary to reboot the server after installing a service pack or a software update.

When you activate a passive copy, you have the option of using the override mount dial list. Using the override mount dial settings allows you to specify the conditions under which the new activation occurs. If you use None, the default setting of Best Availability is used. The options that you can select from are as follows:

- **Lossless** When you choose this setting, the passive database will not become the active database until all the logs that were generated on the current active copy are copied to the copy you are attempting to make active.
- **Good Availability** The database becomes active as long as the copy queue length is less than or equal to six. In the event that the copy queue length is greater than six, Exchange will attempt to replicate remaining logs to the passive copy prior to mounting the database. The copy queue length is the number of logs that the passive copy needs to replicate to become up to date.
- **Best Effort** The passive copy becomes active automatically, regardless of the copy queue length. Using this option can result in a large amount of data loss.
- **Best Availability** The database will become active as long as the copy queue length is less than or equal to 12. If the copy queue length is greater than 12, Exchange attempts to replicate remaining logs before making the database active.

To make a passive mailbox database copy active, perform the following general steps:

1. Select the Organization Configuration\Mailbox node within the EMC.

2. In the middle pane, select the Database Management tab. Select the database and then the database copy that you want to activate. Click on Activate Database on the Actions pane.

3. In the Activate Database Copy dialog box, choose the Override Mount Dial settings option. If you choose None, the default Best Availability setting is used. Click OK.

You can activate a passive mailbox database copy from the EMS using the *Move-ActiveMailboxDatabase* cmdlet. If you do not specify a setting for the MountDialOverride parameter, it uses the Lossless setting. For example, to activate database SydneyMBX on server VAN-MBX, issue the following command:

```
Move-ActiveMailboxDatabase SydnyMBX -ActivateOnServer VAN-MBX
```

Just as there are reasons where you need to transfer the active copy of a database to another database in the DAG, there may be times when you need to suspend continuous replication for a passive database copy. You cannot suspend the active mailbox database copy. If you want to perform maintenance on the server hosting the active mailbox database copy, activate a passive copy hosted on another server and then suspend the now passive mailbox database copy. To suspend a mailbox database copy, select the database copy that you wish to pause and then click Suspend Database Copy. A dialog box will prompt you to provide a comment and to confirm your wish to suspend replication. To resume a suspended database copy, select the copy and then click Resume Database Copy on the Actions pane. You will be asked to confirm the resumption, and Exchange will display the message entered when the database copy was suspended. To suspend a passive mailbox database copy, use the *Suspend-MailboxDatabaseCopy* cmdlet. For example, to suspend the passive mailbox database named DB-ALPHA on server VAN-MBX, issue the following command:

```
Suspend-MailboxDatabaseCopy -Identity DB-ALPHA\VAN-MBX
```

To resume a suspended passive mailbox database copy, use the *Resume-MailboxDatabaseCopy* cmdlet. For example, to resume the suspended passive mailbox database named DB-ALPHA hosted on server VAN-MBX, issue the following command:

```
Resume-MailboxDatabaseCopy -Identity DB-ALPHA\VAN-MBX
```

> **MORE INFO**   **SUSPENDING AND RESUMING MAILBOX DATABASE COPIES**
>
> To learn more about suspending or resuming mailbox database copies, consult the following link on TechNet: *http://technet.microsoft.com/en-us/library/dd298159.aspx*.

Seeding Database Copies

Updating a mailbox database copy, also known as *seeding,* is the process by which a copy of a mailbox database is added to a Mailbox server. By default, a new database copy is populated from the currently active mailbox database copy. Automatic seeding usually occurs when you create a new mailbox database copy, though there may be reasons why you want to postpone automatic seeding and seed from a passive database copy instead. For example, your organization has three servers that are members of a DAG: two in the city of Melbourne and one in the city of Darwin. You add a second DAG member server in Darwin. You want to create a new mailbox database copy on this new DAG member of a large database that is currently active on one of the Melbourne servers and where there is a copy of the database on the original server in Darwin. Through the process of seeding, you can have the new mailbox database copy populated from the passive copy on the original server in Darwin rather than having it populated by transferring the entire mailbox database over the WAN link from Melbourne.

To update or seed a mailbox database copy from a source other than the active database, perform the following general steps:

1. Select the Organization Configuration\Mailbox node within the EMC.

2. In the middle pane, select the Database Copies tab. Choose the database copy that you want to update and select Update Database Copy. It is not possible to update a database copy that is already up to date.

3. In the Update Database Copy dialog box, shown in Figure 13-3, select the source server that hosts the copy of the database that you wish to use to seed the database copy. The default seed will be the active copy of the mailbox database.

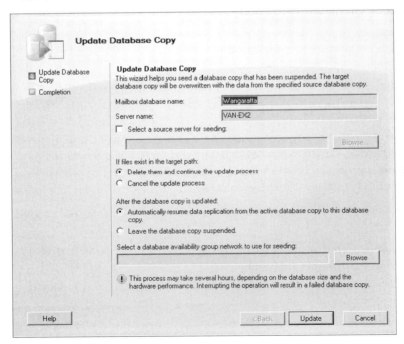

FIGURE 13-3 Update database copy

You can use the *Update-MailboxDatabaseCopy* cmdlet to update/seed a mailbox database copy. For example, to seed a copy of a database named Accounting hosted on server Darwin-2 from a passive copy of the database hosted on server Darwin-1, issue the following command:

```
Update-MailboxDatabaseCopy -Identity Accounting\Darwin-2 -SourceServer Darwin-1
```

> **MORE INFO** **SEEDING/UPDATING DATABASE COPIES**
>
> To learn more about seeding/updating mailbox database copies, consult the following link on TechNet: *http://technet.microsoft.com/en-us/library/dd351100.aspx.*

Lagged Mailbox Database Copies

A lagged mailbox database copy is a mailbox database copy that reflects the state of the active mailbox database copy up to 14 days previously. You can leverage lagged mailbox database copies to recover corrupt data without having to restore from backup. The two important concepts in configuring lagged mailbox database copies are replay lag time and truncation lag time. These work as follows:

- **Replay Lag Time**   The length of time to delay the replay of logs against the passive database copy. The replay lag timer begins when a log file successfully replicates to the passive copy. The maximum replay lag time is 14 days.
- **Truncation Lag Time**   The length of time a transaction log should be kept after the log has been replayed to the mailbox database copy. The truncation lag timer starts after the transaction log has been successfully replayed to the copy of the database. Delaying the truncation of log files from the database copy allows you to recover from failures that impact on the log files for the active database copy. The maximum allowable setting is 14 days.

To create a lagged mailbox database copy, use the *Add-MailboxDatabaseCopy* cmdlet with the ReplayLagTime and TruncationLagTime parameters. For example, to add a copy of a mailbox database named DB-ALPHA to mailbox DAG member VAN-EX1 with a lag time of 14 days and a truncation lag time of 7 days, issue the following command:

```
Add-MailboxDatabaseCopy -Identity DB-ALPHA -MailboxServer VAN-EX1 -ReplayLagTime
14.00:00:00 -TruncationLagTime 7.00:00:00
```

You can use the *Set-MailboxDatabaseCopy* cmdlet to modify replay lag time and log truncation lag time. For example, to reconfigure mailbox database DB-BETA, which is hosted on server VAN-EX2 with a replay lag time of 10 days and a log truncation lag time of 5 days, issue the following command:

```
Set-MailboxDatabaseCopy -Identity DB-BETA\VAN-EX2 -ReplayLagTime 10.00:00:00
-TruncationLagTime 5.00:00:0
```

When you choose to activate a lagged database copy, you can either replay all log files and make the lagged copy up to date or choose to replay log files up to a specific point in time. Replaying to a specific point in time requires that you manually manipulate log files using the eseutil.exe utility. The amount of time that it takes to activate a lagged copy is dependent on the number of log files that you need to replay. Microsoft suggests a minimum estimate of two logs per second per database.

> **MORE INFO** **ACTIVATING LAGGED MAILBOX COPIES**
>
> To learn more about activating lagged mailbox database copies, consult the following link on TechNet: *http://technet.microsoft.com/en-us/library/dd979786.aspx*.

Failover Priority

The activation preference number for a mailbox database copy, shown in Figure 13-4, indicates the order in which passive mailbox database copies will activate in the event that a failure occurs with the active mailbox database copy. You can configure the activation preference number on the general tab of the passive database copy's properties dialog box. You can also configure the activation priority when you create the mailbox database copy or by using the *Set-MailboxDatabaseCopy* cmdlet with the ActivationPreference parameter.

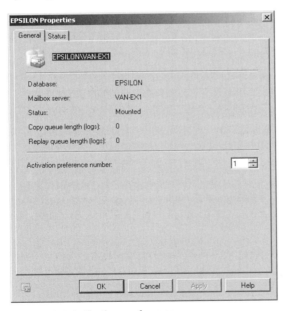

FIGURE 13-4 Activation preference

Lesson Summary

- A DAG consists of up to 16 servers running the same operating system that are members of the same Active Directory forest where there is less than a 250-ms round-trip delay between members.

- The DAG witness should be a Hub Transport server that does not have the Mailbox server role installed.

- You can add a server to a DAG using the *Add-DatabaseAvailabilityGroupServer* cmdlet.

- You add a mailbox database copy to a server in a DAG using the *Add-MailboxDatabaseCopy* cmdlet. Only one copy of a specific mailbox database can be stored on a server.

- You can configure database copy lag and truncation log delay using the *Set-MailboxDatabaseCopy* cmdlet.

- You activate a mailbox database copy using the *Move-ActiveMailboxDatabase* cmdlet.

EXAM TIP

Remember which EMS cmdlets you can use to manipulate DAGs.

Lesson Review

You can use the following questions to test your knowledge of the information in Lesson 1, "Managing Database Availability Groups." The questions are also available on the companion CD if you prefer to review them in electronic form.

NOTE   ANSWERS

Answers to these questions and explanations of why each answer choice is correct or incorrect are located in the "Answers" section at the end of the book.

1. Which of the following EMS cmdlets can you use to configure an alternate witness server and alternate witness directory for an existing DAG?

   A. *Set-DatabaseAvailabilityGroup*

   B. *Add-DatabaseAvailabilityGroupServer*

   C. *New-DatabaseAvailabilityGroup*

   D. *Set-MailboxDatabaseCopy*

2. You are in the process of planning a DAG for the Mailbox servers in your organization. You have four servers that could possibly function as the witness server for the DAG. These servers each hold a single Exchange Server 2010 role and are configured as follows:

   - VAN-MBX: Mailbox server

   - VAN-CAS: Client Access server

   - VAN-HT: Hub Transport server

   - VAH-ET: Edge Transport server

3. VAN-MBX, VAN-CAS, and VAN-HT are members of the same Active Directory domain as the servers that will participate in the DAG. Which of the servers should you choose to act as the DAG witness server?

   A. VAN-MBX

   B. VAN-CAS

   C. VAN-HT

   D. VAN-ET

4. You have just built a new Exchange Server 2010 Mailbox server and have added this server to an existing DAG. You want to populate this Mailbox server with copies of mailbox databases that are hosted on other servers in the DAG. Which of the following EMS cmdlets can you use to accomplish this goal?

   A. *Set-MailboxDatabaseCopy*

   B. *Add-DatabaseAvailabilityGroupServer*

   C. *Set-DatabaseAvailabilityGroup*

   D. *Add-MailboxDatabaseCopy*

5. Which of the following EMS cmdlets can you use to configure the replay lag time and activation preference for an existing mailbox database copy?

   A. *Add-MailboxDatabaseCopy*

   B. *Set-MailboxDatabaseCopy*

   C. *Set-DatabaseAvailabilityGroup*

   D. *Resume-MailboxDatabaseCopy*

6. Which of the following EMS cmdlets can you use to configure the failover priority of a group of existing mailbox database copies in a DAG?

   A. *Set-DatabaseAvailabilityGroup*

   B. *Add-DatabaseAvailabilityGroupServer*

   C. *Set-MailboxDatabaseCopy*

   D. *Set-DatabaseAvailabilityGroupNetwork*

Lesson 2: Highly Available Public Folders

As you cannot make public folders members of a DAG, the key to making them highly available is to use public folder replicas. A public folder replica is a copy of an existing public folder hosted on separate Exchange Server 2010 Mailbox servers. These replicas stay up to date through periodic replication. In this lesson, you will learn how to add and remove public folder replicas, how you can modify the replication interval, and what steps you need to take to successfully back up and restore public folders.

After this lesson, you will be able to:

- Add and remove public folder replicas.
- Configure public folder schedules.
- Back up and restore public folder data.

Estimated lesson time: 30 minutes

Public Folder Replicas

Public folder replication is the method through which you can make public folder content highly available. Public folder replication replicates public folder content and the public folder hierarchy to other public folder databases. In the event that a Mailbox server hosting a public folder fails, clients will automatically redirect to the closest public folder replica. It is important to remember that although you can put a public folder database on a Mailbox server that is a member of a DAG, public folders cannot leverage the DAG replication process to replicate content.

Public folder content and the public folder hierarchy replicate independently of each other. Every public folder database stores a copy of the hierarchy, including information about which public folder databases host content replicas of specific folders. Hierarchy replication occurs automatically when you modify a folder name, a replica list, a folder's position in the public folder tree, or folder permissions. A content replica is a copy of a folder that includes all that folder's content. Content replicas replicate only to the public folder databases that you choose. For example, you have public folder databases on three Mailbox servers. Each of those three public folder databases will have a copy of the public folder hierarchy, and this copy of the public folder hierarchy updates when changes occur. You decide to configure a public folder so that a replica is hosted on both the first and the third Mailbox servers. In this case, unlike the public folder hierarchy data, only the first and third servers will host the actual public folder content. Each public folder replica replicates according to a configured schedule that usually sets at the public folder database level. You will learn about configuring replication schedules later in this lesson.

To configure a public folder to replicate to a public folder database hosted on another Mailbox server, perform the following general steps:

1. From the Toolbox node of the EMC, open the Public Folder Management Console.

2. In the Public Folder Management Console, select the parent node of the folder that you wish to configure to replicate.

3. Click on the desired folder in the middle pane and then click on Properties on the Actions pane and then click on the Replication tab.

4. The Replication tab will display the current host public folder databases. Click on the Add button. In the Select Public Folder Database dialog box, shown in Figure 13-5, select the additional public folder databases to which you want the public folder to replicate and then click OK.

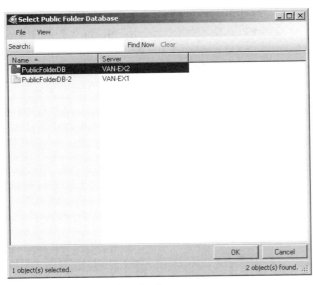

FIGURE 13-5 Select Replica databases

You can use the *Set-PublicFolder* cmdlet with the Replicas parameter to specify on which public folder databases the replica should reside. You need to include the current public folder database as well as any additional public folder databases when choosing to add replicas. For example, to configure the public folder ExamplePF, already present on database PublicFolderDB, to have a new replica on PublicFolderDB-2, issue the following command:

```
Set-PublicFolder –Identity '\ExamplePF' –Replicas 'PublicFolderDB','PublicFolderDB-2'
```

To remove a public folder replica, change the list of public folder databases after the Replicas parameter. For example, if public folder ExamplePF has replicas on public folder databases PublicFolderDB and PublicFolderDB-2 and you want to remove the replica from database PublicFolderDB, issue the following command:

```
Set-PublicFolder –Identity '\ExamplePF' –Replicas'PublicFolderDB-2'
```

You can suspend public folder replication by issuing the *Suspend-PublicFolderReplication* cmdlet. Suspending public folder replication applies only to content replication, and public folder hierarchy data will continue to replicate. You can resume public folder replication by issuing the *Resume-PublicFolderReplication* cmdlet. You can trigger an update of the public folder hierarchy by using the *Update-PublicFolderHierarchy* cmdlet. For example, to update the public folder hierarchy on server VAN-EX1, issue the following command:

```
Update-PublicFolderHierarchy -Server 'VAN-EX1'
```

You can trigger the update of a particular replica by using the *Update-PublicFolder* cmdlet or by right-clicking on the replica in the middle pane in the Public Folder Management Console and then clicking on Update Content.

> **MORE INFO   PUBLIC FOLDER REPLICATION**
>
> To learn more about public folder replication, consult the following TechNet article: *http://technet.microsoft.com/en-us/library/bb629523.aspx.*

Replication Schedules

Replication schedules determine how often Exchange updates a specific public folder replica. Exchange Server 2010 public folders do not support continuous replication and replicate on only a periodic basis. The default settings have content replication occurring every 15 minutes. You can configure replication schedules on the level of the public folder database or on the level of the individual public folder. Schedules that you configure on the public folder replica level override those that you configure at the public folder database level. If you are using the EMC, you can configure the replication period by editing the settings on the Replication tab of a public folder database's properties dialog box. The replication periods that you can set using the drop-down menu are as follows:

- Always Run
- Never Run
- Run Every Hour
- Run Every 2 Hours
- Run Every 4 Hours
- Use Custom Schedule

When you choose a custom schedule, you block out the times that replication can occur during the week. For example, by using a custom schedule, you can configure public folder replication to occur during off-peak periods or only during specific times of the day. When you configure the replication interval to Always Run or Use Custom Schedule, you need to set a replication period. The replication period determines how often updates occur during the scheduled replication windows. Figure 13-6 shows replication schedule set to Always Run, and updates will occur every 15 minutes.

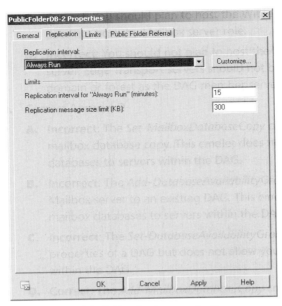

FIGURE 13-6 Public folder database replication

You can also configure public folder database replication by using the *Set-PublicFolderDatabase* cmdlet with the ReplicationPeriod and ReplicationSchedule parameters. When using the Replication Schedule parameter, you can configure specific times or choose the Always option, in which case replication occurs according to the set period. For example, to set replication to occur every 20 minutes on a public folder database named PF-DB-ALPHA, issue the following command:

```
Set-PublicFolderDatabase -ReplicationPeriod '20' -ReplicationSchedule 'Always' -Identity
'PF-DB-ALPHA'
```

If you want to have different replication schedules for individual public folders, you can configure how public folder replication occurs at the public folder replica level. Configuring a replication schedule at this level overrides the replication schedule configured at the public folder database level. To configure a replication schedule at the public folder level, edit the settings on the Replication tab of a specific public folder replica's properties. To edit these settings, you must ensure that you disable the Use Public Folder Database Replication Schedule option. You can then configure the same replication intervals that are available for public folder database replication. Figure 13-7 shows a replication scheduled once every hour and a replica age limit of 30 days.

If you are using the EMS, you can configure public folder replication using the *Set-PublicFolder* cmdlet with the ReplicationShedule and UseDatabaseReplicationSchedule parameters. To configure the public folder named ExampleReplica hosted on server van-ex1. adatum.com to Always Replicate, use the following command:

```
Set-PublicFolder -Identity "\ExampleReplica' -Server 'Van-ex1.adatum.com'
-UseDatabaseReplicationSchedule $false -ReplicationSchedule 'Always'
```

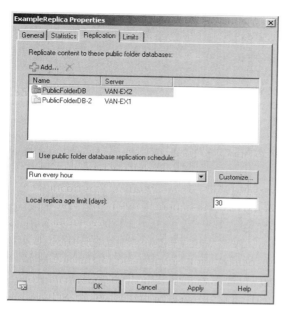

FIGURE 13-7 Public folder replication

MORE INFO **PUBLIC FOLDER REPLICATION**

To learn more about public folder replication, consult the following TechNet article:
http://technet.microsoft.com/en-us/library/bb691120.aspx.

 Quick Check

- Which cmdlet should you use to configure a public folder's replication schedule without modifying the replication schedule of the public folder database that hosts the public folder?

Quick Check Answer

- The *Set-PublicFolder* cmdlet allows you to modify the replication schedule of a public folder without modifying the replication schedule of the public folder database.

Public Folder Backup and Restore

You can back up public folders as a part of the normal Windows Server Backup process. You will learn more about the backup and restore process in Chapter 14, "Exchange Disaster Recovery." Performing a full server backup with Windows Server Backup backs up all public folder database and transaction log files.

Performing public folder database recovery is different from performing mailbox database recovery. When you recover a public folder, you can use recovery mode to mount the folder, extracting items from the mounted recovery database and merging them back into the appropriate mailbox database. You cannot mount public folder databases as recovery databases, and you need to overwrite the existing database with the contents of the public folder database that you are recovering from backup. You accomplish this by enabling the This Database Can Be Overwritten By A Restore option for the public folder database prior to overwriting it with the restored files. You can configure this option by editing the database properties, as shown in Figure 13-8, or by using the *Set-PublicFolderDatabase* cmdlet with the AllowFileRestore parameter set to $true.

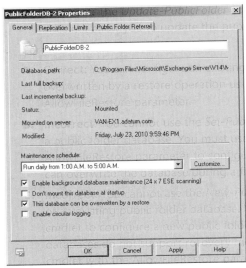

FIGURE 13-8 Overwrite database with restore

The most common form of public folder recovery is the recovery of individual public folders that have been deleted where that deletion has replicated to other public folder databases. You can recover specific deleted public folders using Outlook as long as the deleted public folder is within the retention period. You can configure the retention period for a public folder database using the *Set-PublicFolderDatabase* cmdlet or through the EMC by editing the properties of the public folder database and configuring the setting on the Limits tab, as shown in Figure 13-9. The default deleted item retention period for public folder databases is 14 days.

To recover a deleted public folder using Outlook, perform the following general steps:

1. Log on using an account that has full control over the public folders to be recovered.

2. Access the Public Folders node in Outlook. Select the parent node of the node that contained the deleted public folder.

3. On the Tools menu, select Recover Deleted Items. This launches the Recover Deleted Items dialog box.

4. Select the public folders that you wish to recover and then click the Recover Selected Items button.

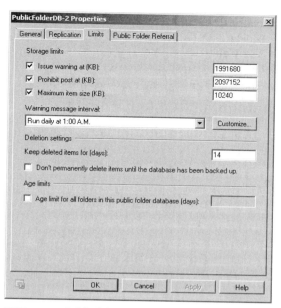

FIGURE 13-9 Public folder database limits

EXAM TIP

Remember that you cannot use DAGs to ensure that public folders are highly available.

Lesson Summary

- A public folder replica is a copy of a public folder hosted on another public folder database.
- Use the *Set-PublicFolder* cmdlet to configure the public folder databases to which public folder replica replicates. You can use this method to add and remove replicas.
- You can configure public folder schedules using the *Set-PublicFolder* cmdlet.
- You cannot create a new public folder database and set them to recovery mode as you can with mailbox databases.
- You can recover recently deleted public folders using Outlook as long as the public folder was deleted within the configured retention period.
- You can configure a public folder database to be overwritten by a restore operation if you wish to overwrite the contents of the public folder database with a backup.

Lesson Review

You can use the following questions to test your knowledge of the information in Lesson 2, "Highly Available Public Folders." The questions are also available on the companion CD if you prefer to review them in electronic form.

1. Which of the following EMS cmdlets can you use to configure an existing public folder so that replicates to two other public folder databases within your organization?

    A. Get-PublicFolder

    B. New-PublicFolder

    C. Set-PublicFolder

    D. Remove-PublicFolder

2. Which of the following EMS cmdlets can you use to remove a replica of a mail-enabled public folder from a specific public folder database?

    A. Set-PublicFolder

    B. Remove-PublicFolder

    C. Set-MailPublicFolder

    D. Disable-MailPublicFolder

3. Which of the following cmdlets can you use to configure a public folder's replication schedule?

    A. Update-PublicFolder

    B. Update-PublicFolderHierarchy

    C. Set-PublicFolder

    D. Set-MailPublicFolder

4. You have deployed a new public folder database on a Mailbox server. Which of the following cmdlets can you use to update the list of folders that will be available on this new public folder database?

    A. Set-PublicFolderDatabase

    B. Update-PublicFolderHierarchy

    C. Get-PublicFolder

    D. Update-PublicFolder

5. Which EMS cmdlet can you use to configure an existing public folder database so that it can be overwritten by a restore operation?

    A. Set-PublicFolderDatabase

    B. Set-PublicFolder

    C. New-PublicFolderDatabase

    D. New-PublicFolder

Lesson 3: High Availability for Other Exchange Roles

Although DAGs are the headline feature for Exchange, you need to take steps to ensure that servers offering other Exchange roles, such as the Hub Transport, Client Access, and Edge Transport servers, will also be available to the Exchange organization in the event that a server suffers complete failure. As you will remember from reading earlier chapters, having a Mailbox server in a site also requires that you have a Client Access server and a Hub Transport server in the same site. Even if you have a DAG deployed, you will still need other server roles to be highly available if you want to ensure that messages flow in the event of server failure. In this lesson, you will learn what steps you need to take to make Client Access servers, Hub Transport servers, and Edge Transport servers highly available.

> **After this lesson, you will be able to:**
> - Configure a client access server array.
> - Ensure that Hub Transport servers are highly available.
> - Configure Edge Transport server redundancy.
>
> **Estimated lesson time: 15 minutes**

Configuring Network Load Balancing

Client Access servers and Edge Transport servers can leverage network load balancing (NLB) as a part of their high-availability strategy. NLB distributes traffic between multiple hosts based on each host's current load. Each new client is directed to the host under the least load. It is also possible to configure NLB to send traffic proportionally to hosts within the cluster. For example, in a cluster with four hosts, you could configure an NLB cluster to send 40 percent of incoming traffic to one host and split the remaining 60 percent across the other three hosts. When considering high availability for Client Access servers and Edge Transport servers, you have the option of using the NLB feature available in Windows Server 2008 and Windows Server 2008 R2. All editions of Windows Server 2008 and Windows Server 2008 R2 support NLB.

You can add and remove nodes to NLB clusters easily by using the Network Load Balancing Manager console. NLB clusters reconfigure themselves automatically when you add a new node or remove a node or a node in the cluster fails. Each node in an NLB cluster sends a message to all other nodes after a second, informing them of its status. The term for this message is "heartbeat." When a node fails to transmit five consecutive heartbeat messages, the other nodes in the cluster alter the configuration of the cluster, excluding the failed node. The term for the reconfiguration process is "convergence." Convergence also occurs when the heartbeat of a previously absent node is again detected by other nodes in the cluster. You can take an existing node in an NLB cluster offline for maintenance and then return it to service without having to reconfigure the cluster manually because the removal and addition process occurs automatically.

You cannot configure a Client Access server that also hosts a DAG to be a part of a Windows NLB cluster, as you cannot use both NLB and Windows Failover Clustering concurrently. You must install the NLB feature on each node before creating an NLB cluster. NLB detects server failure but not application failure, so it is possible that clients can be directed to a node on which a Client Access server component has failed.

Configuring NLB Cluster Operation Mode

The cluster operation mode determines how you configure the cluster's network address and how that address relates to the existing network adapter addresses. You can configure the operation mode of an NLB cluster by editing the cluster properties, as shown in Figure 13-10. All nodes within a cluster must use the same cluster operations mode. This tab also displays the virtual MAC address assigned to the cluster by using this dialog box.

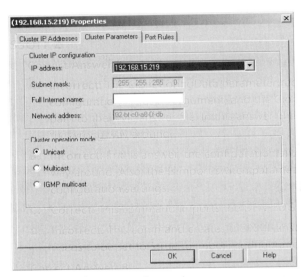

FIGURE 13-10 Cluster operation mode

The cluster operations modes—and the differences between them—are as follows:

- **Unicast Mode** When an NLB cluster is configured to work in the unicast cluster operation mode, all nodes in the cluster use the MAC address assigned to the virtual network adapter. NLB substitutes the cluster MAC address for the physical MAC address of a network card. If your network adapter does not support this substitution, you must replace it. When nodes in a cluster have only a single network card, this limits communication between nodes but does not pose a problem for hosts outside the cluster. Unicast mode works better when each node in the NLB cluster has two network adapters. The network adapter assigned the virtual MAC address is used with the cluster; the second network adapter facilitates management and internode communication. Use two network adapters if you choose unicast mode and use one node to manage others.

- **Multicast Mode**   Multicast mode is a suitable solution when each node in the cluster has a single network adapter. The cluster MAC address is a multicast address. The cluster IP address resolves to the multicast MAC address. Each node in the cluster can use its network adapter's MAC address for management and internode communication. You can use multicast mode only if your network hardware supports multicast MAC addressing.

- **IGMP Multicast Mode**   This version of multicast uses Internet Group Membership Protocol (IGMP) for communication, which improves network traffic because traffic for an NLB cluster passes only to those switch ports the cluster uses, not to all switch ports. The properties of IGMP multicast mode are otherwise identical to those of multicast mode.

Configuring NLB Port Rules

Port rules, shown in Figure 13-11, control, on a port-by-port basis, how network traffic is treated by an NLB cluster. By default, the cluster balances all traffic received on the cluster IP address across all nodes. You can modify this so that only specific traffic, designated by port, received on the cluster IP address is balanced. The cluster drops any traffic that does not match a port rule. You can also configure the cluster to forward traffic to a specific node rather than to all nodes, enabling the cluster to balance some traffic but not all traffic. You accomplish this by configuring the port rule's filtering mode. The options are multiple host or single host.

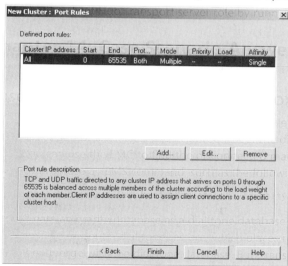

FIGURE 13-11 Port rules

When you configure a rule to use the multiple host filtering mode, you can also configure the rule's affinity property. The affinity property determines where the cluster will send subsequent client traffic after the initial client request. If you set the affinity property to Single, the cluster will tie all client traffic during a session to a single node. The default port rule, shown in Figure 13-12, uses the Single affinity setting. When you set a rule's affinity property to None, the cluster will not bind a client session to any particular node. When you set a rule's affinity property to Network, a client session will be directed to cluster nodes located on a specific TCP/IP subnet. It is not necessary to configure the affinity for a single host rule because that rule already ties traffic to a single node in the cluster.

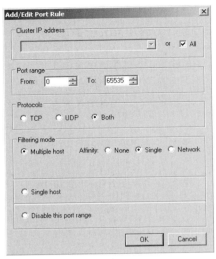

FIGURE 13-12 Port rules

You can edit the load placed on each node by editing port rules on each node of the cluster. Editing the load changes the load from balanced between all nodes to preferring one node or several nodes over other nodes. Do this when the hardware or one or more nodes have greater capacity than other nodes. You configure port rules in the practice at the end of this lesson.

When you need to perform maintenance on a node in an NLB cluster, you can use the Drain function to stop new connections to the node without disrupting existing connections. When all existing connections have finished, you can then take the cluster offline for maintenance. You can drain a node by right-clicking it from within Network Load Balancing Manager, clicking Control Ports, and then clicking Drain.

> **MORE INFO** **NLB**
>
> To learn more about NLB on Windows Server 2008 R2, consult the following document on TechNet: *http://technet.microsoft.com/en-us/library/cc770558.aspx*.

Client Access Arrays

Client access arrays, sometimes called client access server arrays, are collections of load-balanced Client Access servers. If one Client Access server in a client access array fails, client traffic will automatically be redirected to other Client Access servers in the array. Client access arrays work on a per-site basis. A single client access array cannot span multiple sites. Client access arrays can use Windows NLB or a hardware NLB solution. If you are using a Windows NLB, you will be limited to eight nodes in the array and will not be able to also configure the server hosting the Client Access server role as a part of a DAG.

To create a client access array, perform the following general steps:

1. Configure load balancing for your Client Access servers. You can use Windows NLB or a hardware NLB solution. Ensure that your load-balancing array balances TCP port 135 and UDP and TCP ports 6005 through 65535.

2. Configure a new DNS record that points to the virtual IP address that you will use for the client access array.

3. Use the *New-ClientAccessArray* cmdlet to create the client access array. For example, if you created a DNS record for casarray.adatum.com and you have configured load balancing for Client Access servers in the Wangaratta site, use the following command to create a client access array:

```
New-ClientAccessArray -Name 'Wangaratta Array' -Fqdn 'casarray.adatum.com' -Site
'Wangaratta'
```

4. Configure existing mailbox databases in the site to use the new CAS array with the *Set-MailboxDatabase* cmdlet and the RpcClientAccessServer parameter. For example, to configure MBX-DB-1 to use casarray.adatum.com, issue the following command:

```
Set-MailboxDatabase MBX-DB-1 -RpcClientAccessServer 'casarray.adatum.com'
```

> **MORE INFO**   **CLIENT ACCESS ARRAYS**
>
> To learn more about client access arrays, consult the following document on TechNet:
> *http://technet.microsoft.com/en-us/library/dd351149.aspx.*

 Quick Check

- What type of load balancing must you use if you want to create a client access array using two servers that also host the mailbox role?

Quick Check Answer

- You will need to use a hardware NLB solution, as Windows Network Load Balancing cannot be used on the same server as Windows Failover Clustering.

Transport Server High Availability

To ensure that Hub Transport servers are highly available, deploy multiple Hub Transport servers in each site. Deploying multiple Hub Transport servers provides server redundancy, as messages will automatically reroute in the event that a Hub Transport server fails. When you deploy an extra Hub Transport server on a site, you do not need to perform any additional configuration, as configuration data automatically replicates through Active Directory.

There are two methods through which you can make Edge Transport servers highly available. You can load-balance Edge Transport servers using NLB, or you can configure multiple MX records in the external DNS namespace.

As Windows NLB requires that hosts be members of the same Active Directory domain and that you deploy Edge Transport servers on perimeter networks, most Edge Transport server load-balancing solutions use hardware load balancing. You may need to use a NLB solution if you have multiple Edge Transport servers but have only one public IPv4 address available for incoming Simple Mail Transfer Protocol (SMTP) traffic. In this situation, you would assign the public IPv4 address as the NLB virtual address, allowing requests to be spread across Edge Transport servers with private IP addresses on the perimeter network.

Configuring multiple MX records in the external DNS zone uses the SMTP protocol's natural high-availability features. When an external SMTP server needs to send a message to a specific mail domain, it runs a query against the target domain's zone looking for MX records. If the SMTP server is unable to deliver mail to the first address returned by the MX record query, the SMTP server then attempts delivery to other addresses returned by the query.

> **MORE INFO** **HIGH AVAILABILITY AND SITE RESILIENCE**
>
> To learn more about high availability for non–Mailbox server roles, consult the following document on TechNet: *http://technet.microsoft.com/en-us/library/dd638137.aspx*.

> **EXAM TIP**
>
> Remember that you need to add additional Hub Transport servers to a site only to provide high availability; it is not necessary to configure NLB.

Lesson Summary

- Windows Network Load Balancing can be used to load-balance Client Access servers and Edge Transport servers.
- You need to configure NLB before creating a client access array.
- A client access array is a collection of load-balanced Client Access servers that are located in the same Active Directory site.
- You can make Hub Transport servers highly available by adding additional Hub Transport servers to a site.
- You can make Edge Transport servers highly available either by using a NLB solution or by configuring multiple MX records.

Lesson Review

You can use the following questions to test your knowledge of the information in Lesson 3, "High Availability for Other Exchange Roles." The questions are also available on the companion CD if you prefer to review them in electronic form.

> **NOTE** **ANSWERS**
>
> Answers to these questions and explanations of why each answer choice is correct or incorrect are located in the "Answers" section at the end of the book.

1. Your organization has five sites. There are two Client Access servers on each site. The round-trip delay between any two Client Access servers in the organization is less than 100 ms. You want to deploy the minimum number of Client Access arrays while ensuring that each Client Access server in the organization is a member of a client access array. How many client access arrays should you configure?

   A. 1

   B. 2

   C. 4

   D. 5

2. Your organization has three Edge Transport servers located on the perimeter network. Your organization has two Hub Transport servers located on the internal Active Directory site that borders the perimeter network. How many individual EdgeSync subscriptions should you configure to ensure that any Edge Transport server can be used to route messages to the Internet in the event that any two Edge Transport servers fail?

   A. One

   B. Two

   C. Three

   D. Six

3. Your organization has three sites. Each site has a separate Hub Transport, Mailbox, and Client Access server. You want to ensure that clients are able to access their mailboxes through Outlook Web App (OWA) in the event that one of the Client Access servers in the organization fails. Which of the following strategies could you pursue to accomplish this goal while ensuring that a minimum number of extra servers is deployed? (Choose 2; each answer forms part of the solution.)

   A. Add an additional Client Access server at each site

   B. Configure a client access server array at each site

   C. Configure a DAG at each site

   D. Add an additional Hub Transport server at each site

4. Your Exchange Server 2010 organization has three sites. Each site currently has one Hub Transport server. Which of the following strategies could you pursue to ensure that each site has mail delivered properly in the event that one Hub Transport server fails?

   A. Add all three Hub Transport servers to a DAG.

   B. Add all three Hub Transport servers to a client access server array.

   C. Add an additional Hub Transport server in each site.

   D. Add all three Hub Transport servers to an NLB array.

5. Which of the following high-availability strategies could you use with three Edge Transport servers located on your organization's perimeter network? (Choose 2; each answer forms part of the solution.)

   A. DAG

   B. Client access server array

   C. DNS round-robin

   D. NLB

PRACTICE   **DAGs and Public Folder Replication**

In this set of exercises, you will configure a DAG, perform manual failover, and then test automatic failover.

EXERCISE 1   Create a DAG

In this exercise, you will create a DAG and add servers VAN-EX1 and VAN-EX2 to this group. You will use VAN-DC as the witness for the DAG. In real-life situations, you would choose to use an existing Hub Transport server as a witness server. To complete this exercise, perform the following steps:

1. Log on to server VAN-EX1 with the Kim Akers user account and issue the following command from an elevated command prompt:

   ```
   Netsh interface ipv4 set address "Local Area Connection" static 10.10.0.20
   255.255.255.0 10.10.0.1
   ```

2. Log on to server VAN-EX2 with the Kim Akers user account and issue the following command from an elevated command prompt:

   ```
   Netsh interface ipv4 set address "Local Area Connection" static 10.10.0.21
   255.255.255.0 10.10.0.1
   ```

3. On server VAN-EX1, open Active Directory Users And Computers. Add the Exchange Trusted Subsystem group to the Builtin\Administrators group, as shown in Figure 13-13.

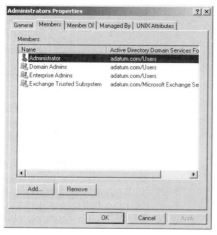

FIGURE 13-13 Add Exchange Trusted Subsystem to Builtin\Administrators

4. Open the EMC. In the Organization Configuration\Mailbox node, click on New Mailbox Database on the Actions pane.

5. On the first page of the New Mailbox Database Wizard, enter the Mailbox Database Name as EPSILON and set the server as VAN-EX1.

6. On the Set Paths page, accept the default settings and then click Next. Click New and then click Finish to complete the New Mailbox Database Wizard.

7. When the Organization Configuration\Mailbox node is selected, click on New Database Availability Group on the Actions pane. This will start the New Database Availability Group Wizard. Enter the Database Availability Group name as DAG-ONE. Enter the Witness Server as VAN-DC and enter the Witness Directory as c:\DAG-WIT, as shown in Figure 13-14. Click New and then click Finish. If you are presented with a warning about VAN-DC not being part of the Exchange Server security group, click OK.

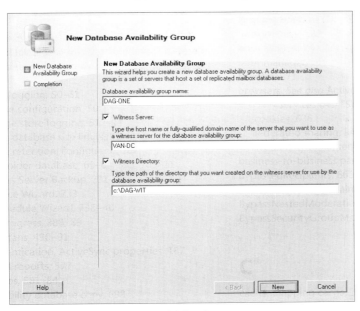

FIGURE 13-14 New Database Availability Group

8. Click on the Organization Configuration\Mailbox node and then click on the Database Availability Groups tab. Click on DAG-ONE and then on the Actions pane click on Manage Database Availability Group Membership.

9. On the Manage Database Availability Group Membership page, click Add. In the Select Mailbox server dialog box, select both VAN-EX1 and VAN-EX2 and then click OK. Verify that the Manage Database Availability Group Membership matches Figure 13-15 and then click Manage.

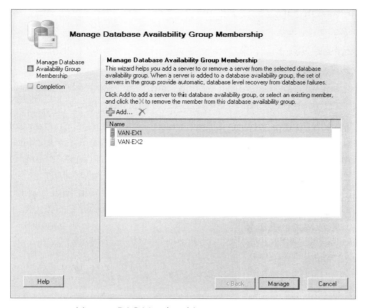

FIGURE 13-15 Manage DAG Membership

10. Click on Organization Configuration\Mailbox, click on the Database Management tab, and then click on EPSILON. On the Actions pane, click on Add Mailbox Database Copy

11. In the Add Mailbox Database Copy Wizard, click Browse. Click on VAN-EX2 and then click OK. Verify that the Add Mailbox Database Copy Wizard matches Figure 13-16 and then click Add. When the wizard completes, click Finish.

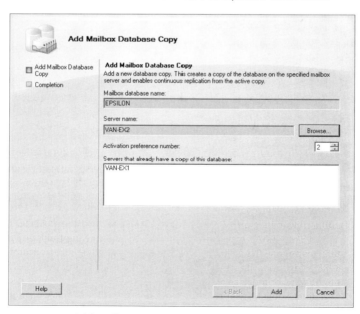

FIGURE 13-16 Add mailbox database copy

EXERCISE 2   Perform Manual Failover of a DAG

In this exercise, you will activate the passive copy of a mailbox database. To complete this exercise, perform the following steps:

1. Ensure that you are logged on to server VAN-EX1 with the Kim Akers user account.

2. In the EMC, click on the Organization Configuration\Mailbox node, click on the Database Management tab, and then click on mailbox database EPSILON.

3. Verify that the status of Mailbox Database EPSILON is set to Mounted on server VAN-EX1 and Healthy on server VAN-EX2.

4. Click on the copy of EPSILON that is Healthy. On the Actions pane, click Activate Database Copy.

5. In the Activate Database Copy dialog box, use the drop-down menu to select Best Availability and then click OK.

6. Click Refresh on the Actions pane and verify that the copy of EPSILON on server VAN-EX2 is set to Mounted and verify that the copy of EPSILON on VAN-EX1 is set to Healthy.

EXERCISE 3   Perform Failover of a DAG

In this exercise, you will demonstrate the automatic failover process. To complete this exercise, perform the following steps:

1. On server VAN-EX1, keep the EMC open so that you can view the status of the EPSILON database.

2. Log on to server VAN-EX2 using the Kim Akers account. Shut down the server.

3. Verify that the status of database EPSILON on Mailbox server VAN-EX1 is set to Mounted and that the status of database EPSILON on Mailbox server VAN-EX2 is set to ServiceDown.

4. Start server VAN-EX2. When the server has started, verify that the status of mailbox database EPSILON on server VAN-EX2 returns to Healthy.

EXERCISE 4   Configure Highly Available Public Folders

In this exercise, you will configure public folder replication. This exercise requires that you have completed practice Exercise 4 in Chapter 4, "Distribution Groups and Public Folders." To complete this exercise, perform the following steps:

1. If you have not done so already, log on to server VAN-EX1 using the Kim Akers user account.

2. Open the EMS and issue the following command:

```
Get-PublicFolderDatabase
```

3. Verify that the only public folder database present in the organization is PublicFolderDB, which is mounted on server VAN-EX2.

> **WARNING EXISTING PUBLIC FOLDER DATABASE**
>
> Although no public folder databases have been created on server VAN-EX1 during the end-of-chapter exercises, you may have created a public database when reading through the examples in Chapters 2 or 4. If there is a public folder database present on server VAN-EX1, you should remove this public folder database before proceeding to the next step.

4. Issue the following command to create a new public folder database on server VAN-EX1:

   ```
   New-PublicFolderDatabase PublicFolderDB-2 -Server VAN-EX1
   ```

5. Mount the newly created public folder database by running the following command:

   ```
   Mount-Database PublicFolderDB-2
   ```

6. Open the EMC. In the Toolbox node, open the Public Folder Management Console. Ensure that the Public Folder Management Console connects to server van-ex1 .adatum.com.

7. In the Public Folder Management Console, click on the Default Public Folders node. On the Actions pane, click New Public Folder.

8. Enter the public folder name **ExampleReplica** and then click New. Click Finish to dismiss the New Public Folder dialog box.

9. Right-click on the ExampleReplica public folder and then click Properties. On the Replication tab, click Add. In the Select Public Folder Database dialog box, click on PublicFolderDB on server VAN-EX2 and click OK.

10. Verify that the properties of public folder ExampleReplica match those shown in Figure 13-17 and then click OK.

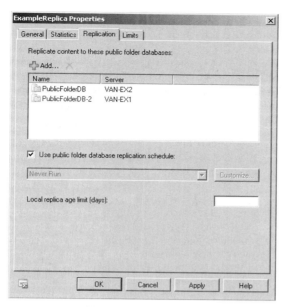

FIGURE 13-17 Public folder replicas

11. Click on the Public Folders –van-ex1.adatum.com node. On the Actions pane, click Connect To Server. Click Browse. In the Select Public Folder Servers dialog box, click on VAN-EX2, click on OK, and then click on Connect.

12. In the Default Public Folder node, verify that the ExampleReplica public folder is present on VAN-EX2.

Chapter Review

To further practice and reinforce the skills you learned in this chapter, you can perform the following tasks:

- Review the chapter summary.
- Review the list of key terms introduced in this chapter.
- Complete the case scenarios. These scenarios set up real-world situations involving the topics of this chapter and ask you to create a solution.
- Complete the suggested practices.
- Take a practice test.

Chapter Summary

- DAGs are collections of Mailbox servers that provide mailbox database failover.
- You can have a maximum of 16 servers in a DAG.
- Mailbox database copies can be configured with a lag time of up to 14 days.
- Public folders are made highly available through public folder replication.
- Public folders cannot leverage DAGs for high availability.
- Client access arrays provide high availability for Client Access servers.

Key Terms

Do you know what these key terms mean?

- Client access array
- Content replica
- Database availability group
- Lagged database copy

Case Scenarios

In the following case scenarios, you will apply what you've learned about subjects of this chapter. You can find answers to these questions in the "Answers" section at the end of this book.

Case Scenario 1: Database Availability Groups at ProseWare

You are in the process of migrating Proseware from their existing Exchange high-availability solution to a solution based on Exchange Server 2010 DAGs.

You want to configure mailbox databases on server VAN-LAG. With these facts in mind, answer the following questions:

1. Which EMS cmdlet should be used to create a new DAG?
2. Which EMS cmdlet should you use to add server VAN-LAG to the DAG?
3. Which EMS cmdlet should you use to create a database copy of an existing database hosted on a DAG member?

Case Scenario 2: High Availability at Contoso

You have just completed the deployment of a DAG at Contoso. You must now provide high-availability solutions to other Exchange server 2010 roles at the organization. One of the first issues you must deal with involves three Client Access servers at the Melbourne site. At present, one Client Access server appears to be taking a disproportionate amount of the client load. You need to ensure that the client load is distributed more equitably and that clients will retain connectivity in the even that a Client Access server fails. At present, there is a single Edge Transport server. You need to ensure that mail can flow to and from the Internet in the event that this server suffers hardware failure. Although a DAG exists at Contoso, there is only one public folder database. Management is concerned that the important information hosted within public folders be accessible in the event that the server hosting this public folder database fails. With these facts in mind, answer the following questions:

1. What steps can you take to make the Edge Transport server highly available?
2. What steps can you take to prepare the Client Access servers prior to configuring a client access array in the Melbourne site?
3. What steps can you take to make public folders at Contoso highly available?

Suggested Practices

To help you successfully master the exam objectives presented in this chapter, complete the following tasks.

Extending Database Availability Groups

To further expand your knowledge of DAGs, perform the following exercises:

- **Practice 1**   Add an additional server to the DAG that you created in the exercise at the end of the chapter.
- **Practice 2**   Configure an existing mailbox database to be present on all three servers on the DAG. Configure a lag of 24 hours for this DAG.

Highly Available Public Folders

To further expand your knowledge of public folder replication, perform the following exercises:

- **Practice 1** Configure a new replication schedule for the public folders that you configured to replicate in the exercise at the end of the chapter.
- **Practice 2** Post a message to a public folder and then track the message.

High Availability for Other Exchange Roles

To further expand your knowledge of high availability for other Exchange roles, perform the following exercises:

- **Practice 1** Configure NLB on VAN-EX1 and VAN-EX2.
- **Practice 2** Configure a client access array for Default-First-Site-Name site.

Take a Practice Test

The practice tests on this book's companion CD offer many options. For example, you can test yourself on just one exam objective, or you can test yourself on all the 70-680 certification exam content. You can set up the test so that it closely simulates the experience of taking a certification exam, or you can set it up in study mode so that you can look at the correct answers and explanations after you answer each question.

> **MORE INFO** **PRACTICE TESTS**
>
> For details about all the practice test options available, see the "How to Use the Practice Tests" section in this book's Introduction.

CHAPTER 14

Exchange Disaster Recovery

Exchange Server 2010 has different units of backup and recovery than do other types of Windows servers. You can work with files and drives, but you also work with the information store and the databases it contains. In Exchange Server 2010, databases are the smallest items of backup, and mailboxes are the smallest items of recovery. In this chapter, you will consider how you implement backup and restore plans in Exchange Server 2010 and how you can recover from disasters such as the loss of Exchange data and the loss of Exchange server roles.

Exam objectives in this chapter:
- Perform backup and restore of data.
- Back up and recover server roles.

Lessons in this chapter:

Before You Begin

In order to complete the exercises in the practice session in this chapter, you need to have done the following:

- Installed the Windows Server 2008 R2 domain controller VAN-DC1 and the Windows Exchange 2010 Enterprise Mailbox, Hub Transport, and Client Access server VAN-EX1, as described in the Appendix, "Setup Instructions for Exchange Server 2010."

- Optionally installed the Windows Exchange 2010 Enterprise server VAN-EX2 as a member server in the Adatum.com domain as described in the Appendix and configured this server with the Hub Transport server role. This enables you to carry out the optional practice session "Recovering a Hub Transport Server" in this chapter.

- Created the Kim Akers account with the password *Pa$$w0rd* in the Adatum.com domain. This account should be placed in the Domain Admins security group and be a member of the Organization Management role group.

- Created the Don Hall account with the password *Pa$$w0rd* in the Adatum.com domain. This account should be placed in the Backup Operators security group (so it can be used to log on to the domain controller) and should be in the Marketing organizational unit.
- Created mailboxes for Kim Akers and Don Hall, accepting the default email address format for the email addresses.

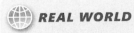

REAL WORLD

Ian McLean

Why is a backup plan and (possibly more so) a recovery plan more important for Exchange servers than it is for any other type of server? What is so special about Exchange that makes downtime even less acceptable than it is on, for example, a file server? The answer lies in user expectation. Your users are accustomed to email being almost instantaneous and constantly available. It is what they expect and require.

If a Client Access server crashes and you do not have failover facilities and the ability to recover lost information, your users cannot remotely access messages, calendars, address lists, and so on. If a Mailbox server crashes and no recovery plan is in place, every user on that server could lose days, weeks, or months of work. If a Transport server crashes and you do not have a recovery strategy in place, messages will not be properly routed and delivered. Even if you can recover the lost information on such servers, can you do it quickly enough? Can you recover information right up to the point of failure and not merely to the last backup?

You need to ensure continuous and (as far as possible) uninterrupted access to Exchange servers, their functionality, and the information they hold. You need to ensure that your Exchange organization meets your users' availability expectations, and a key element in so doing is a sound backup and recovery plan.

Lesson 1: Backup and Recover Exchange Data

In this lesson, you look at backing up Exchange server and creating a backup schedule. You consider the use of the recovery database (RDB) and dial tone restores that use mailbox merge. The lesson discusses how you deal with disconnected mailboxes and configure deleted mailbox retention and deleted item retention periods. Finally, the lesson outlines the various high-availability techniques you can use on Mailbox servers to reduce downtime and avoid having to restore from backups.

After this lesson, you will be able to:

- Perform manual Exchange backups and define a backup schedule.
- Restore data to its original location using the Windows Server Backup utility.
- Restore a single database to an alternate location.
- Create a RDB and use the RDB and mailbox merge to recover a single database.
- Restore a recovered mailbox or specified items within a mailbox that have been recovered from backup and moved to an RDB.
- Use the dial tone portability feature to perform dial tone restores.
- Restore a disconnected mailbox and configure the mailbox retention and item retention periods.

Estimated lesson time: 50 minutes

Using Windows Server Backup

Exchange Server 2010 provides high availability and site resilience features that enable you to deploy redundant, highly available mailbox databases. However, redundancy and fault tolerance cannot protect against every possible failure or disaster. You need to create and implement a backup and recovery plan that ensures the protection of critical data in your Exchange organization. You need to understand how data can be protected and determine the data protection strategy that best suits your organization's needs.

Backup Technologies Supported by Exchange Server 2010

Unlike Exchange Server 2007 and Exchange Server 2003, Exchange Server 2010 does not support the Extensible Storage Engine streaming Application Programming Interfaces for backup and restore of program files or data. Exchange Server 2010 supports only Volume Shadow Copy Service (VSS)–based backups and includes a plug-in for Windows Server Backup that enables you to make VSS-based backups of Exchange data.

To back up and restore Exchange Server 2010, you must use an Exchange-aware application that supports the VSS writer for Exchange 2010, such as Windows Server Backup (with the VSS plug-in), Microsoft System Center Data Protection Manager, or a third-party Exchange-aware VSS-based application.

You can use the VSS plug-in that ships with Exchange Server 2010 to back up volumes containing active mailbox database copies or stand-alone (nonreplicated) mailbox databases. You cannot use this plug-in to back up volumes that contain passive mailbox database copies. You need either Microsoft System Center Data Protection Manager or a third-party Exchange-aware VSS-based application to back up passive mailbox database copies.

If, however, you use either of these methods to back up a passive mailbox database copy, you cannot perform a VSS restore directly to a passive mailbox database copy. You can instead perform a VSS restore to an alternate location, suspend replication to the passive copy, and copy the database and log files from the alternate location to the location of the passive database copy in the file system.

The VSS plug-in is implemented by an executable file named WSBExchange.exe and runs as a service named Microsoft Exchange Server Extension for Windows Server Backup (WSBExchange). It is automatically installed on all Exchange 2010 Mailbox servers and configured by default for manual startup. To use the plug-in, you must have the Windows Server Backup feature installed. The command-line tool WBAdmin.exe is also installed at the same time, and you can run this tool from the command prompt.

Using Windows Server Backup to Perform an Exchange Backup

You can use Windows Server Backup on an Exchange Server 2010 server running the Windows Server 2008 or Windows Server 2008 R2 operating system to back up and restore your Exchange databases. During the backup operation, the Exchange data files are checked for consistency to ensure that they can be used for recovery. Windows Server Backup runs the consistency check on the snapshot taken for the backup.

Manual backups taken with Windows Server Backup take place at the volume level. You should consider which volumes you want to back up and whether backups will include system state recovery data, application data, or both. To back up a database and its log stream, you need to back up the entire volume containing the database and logs. Windows Server Backup with the VSS plug-in runs locally on the server being backed up and cannot be used directly to take remote VSS backups. You can, however, use Terminal Services or Remote Desktop Services to remotely manage backups. The manual backup can be written to a local drive, DVD media, or a remote network share. You require a separate, dedicated hard disk or storage system to run scheduled backups. After you configure a disk for scheduled backups, Windows Server Backup automatically manages disk usage and reuses the space of older backups when creating new backups.

When you create or schedule backups, you will need to specify the volumes that you want to include. You also need to specify a storage location for backups. If you use an internal hard disk for storing backups, this limits how much of your system you can restore. You can recover the data from a volume, but you cannot rebuild the entire disk structure.

If you use an external hard disk for storing backups, the disk is dedicated to backup storage and is not be visible in Windows Explorer. The external, dedicated disk or disk system is formatted, removing any existing data. If you use a remote shared folder to store backups, your backup will be overwritten each time you create a new backup. You should not choose this option if you want to store multiple backups for each server. If you use removable media or DVDs for storing backups, you can recover only entire volumes, not applications or individual files. The media you use must be at least 1 GB in size.

You perform a manual backup using Windows Server Backup locally on a computer running Exchange Server 2010 in a practice session exercise later in this lesson. The Windows Server Backup feature must be installed on the local computer. The high-level procedure to perform such a backup is as follows:

1. Start Windows Server Backup and click Backup Once on the Actions pane to start the Backup Once Wizard.

2. Select Different Options on the Backup Options page and then select the type of backup that you want on the Select Backup Configuration page. You can choose to back up selected volumes. You can also choose whether to back up system state data or perform a bare metal backup. Note that volumes that contain operating system components must be included.

3. Select the location where you want to store the backup on the Specify Destination Type page. If you select Remote Shared Folder, you need to specify a UNC path for the backup files.

4. If necessary, select VSS Full Backup on the Specify Advanced Options page.

5. Click Backup on the Confirmation page. Click Close when the backup is complete.

If the server that hosts the data you want to back up is a member of a database availability group (DAG) and holds both active and passive database copies, you must disable the Microsoft Exchange Replication service VSS writer; otherwise, the backup operation will fail. Disabling this service requires that you edit the registry on the local computer as follows:

1. Start the Registry Editor (Regedit.exe).

2. Navigate to HKEY_LOCAL_MACHINE\Software\Microsoft\ExchangeServer\v14\Replay\ Parameters.

3. Add a new DWORD value named EnableVSSWriter. Set its value to 0.

4. Close the Registry Editor and restart the Microsoft Exchange Replication service.

Using Windows Server Backup to Perform an Exchange Recovery

Windows Server Backup can recover an Exchange database to the point of failure by restoring the most recent normal (full) backup and then applying each incremental backup in order. The following procedure uses Windows Server Backup to perform a recovery:

1. Click Recover on the Windows Server Backup Actions pane to start the Recovery Wizard.

2. If the data being recovered was backed up from the server on which Windows Server Backup is running, select This Server (ServerName) on the Getting Started page. Otherwise, select A Backup Stored On Another Location.

3. If you are recovering from the local computer and there are multiple backups, select the location of the backup on the drop-down list on the Select Backup Location page.

4. If you are recovering data from another computer, specify that the backup you want to restore is on a remote shared folder on the Specify Location Type page, shown in Figure 14-1. You can then specify location-specific settings by typing the path to the folder that contains the backup on the Specify Remote Folder page, as shown in Figure 14-2. If you are recovering from a local drive, select the location of the backup from the drop-down list on the Select Backup Location page.

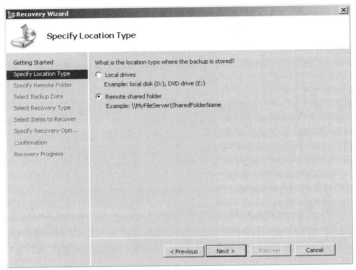

FIGURE 14-1 The Specify Location Type page

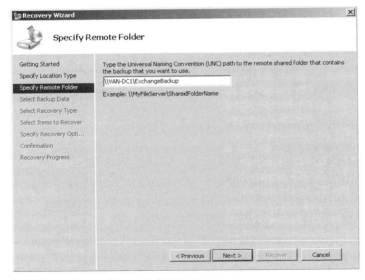

FIGURE 14-2 The Backup Location page

5. If more than one backup exists, select the date and time of the backup that you want to recover on the Select Backup Date page, shown in Figure 14-3.

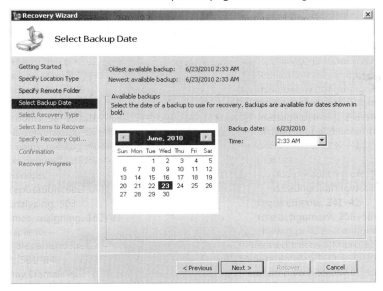

FIGURE 14-3 The Select Backup Date page

6. Select from the options available on the Select Recovery Type page, shown in Figure 14-4, depending on what you want to restore. If, for example, you want to restore a backed-up database, select Applications. If you want to recover certificates, logs, or users, select Files And Folders.

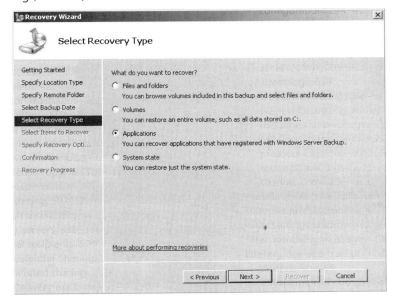

FIGURE 14-4 The Select Recovery Type page

7. If you select Applications, verify that Exchange is selected in the Applications field on the Select Application page. Click View Details to view the application components of the backups. If you are recovering the most recent backup, the Do Not Perform A Roll-Forward Recovery Of The Application Database check box displays. Select this check box if you want to prevent Windows Server Backup from rolling forward the database being recovered.

8. On the Specify Recovery Options page, select where you want to recover the data. You can select Recover To Original Location to recover backed-up data to its original location. This option is available if you are restoring one or more databases and results in all backed-up databases being restored to their original location. Alternatively, you can select Recover To Another Location and specify the alternate location. If you use this option, you can restore a single database or multiple databases into a custom location. After being restored, the data files can then be moved into an RDB and moved back to their original location using mailbox merge.

> **NOTE DIRTY AND CLEAN SHUTDOWN STATES**
>
> When you restore a database to an alternate location, the restored database is in what is known as a dirty shutdown state and cannot be mounted. You can bring a database into a clean shutdown state by using Exchange Server Database Utilities (Eseutil.exe). If you are restoring to the original location, you can mount the restored database without needing to use Eseutil.exe to bring it into a clean shutdown state.

9. Review your recovery settings on the Confirmation page and then click Recover.

10. Click Close when the recovery operation has completed.

If you use Windows Server Backup to restore data, you can restore Exchange data to its original location or to an alternate location. If you restore the data to its original location, Windows Server Backup and the plug-in automatically handle the recovery process, including dismounting any existing databases and replaying logs into the recovered database. Although the restore process does not directly support the RDB, if you restore to an alternate location, you can manually move a restored data from that alternate location into the RDB if you need to do so.

Creating an Exchange Server Disaster Recovery Plan

Backup and recovery are particularly important in an Exchange organization, where data loss is seldom acceptable and failover and fast recovery is required to meet Service Level Agreements and user expectations. As an Exchange administrator, you need to create, test, and document a detailed backup and recovery plan. You need take a close look at the overall architecture of your Exchange organization and make any changes required to ensure that the architecture meets availability and recoverability expectations.

Backup and Recovery Plan Considerations

You need to decide on the number of Exchange servers running specific Exchange Server roles in your organization. Do you need additional servers to ensure high availability? Do you need additional servers to improve performance? Do you need additional servers because your organization spans several geographic areas?

You need to decide the number of databases held on each Exchange server and how the groups are organized. Should you create databases for each department or division or for different business functions in your organization? Are separate databases required for public folders and other types of data?

When you have reviewed the architecture of your Exchange organization and implemented any necessary changes or changes that you can convince senior management are necessary, you need to create a backup and recovery plan to support your organization. You should decide what data you need to back up, how often you should back up this data, and what types of backup you should use. You need to plan your restore policy with considerable care and test that it works by carrying out trial restores.

You need to judge the importance of any mailbox or public folder database you intend to include in your backup plan. For critical data, such as a departmental mailbox database, you should plan redundant backup sets that extend through several backup periods. For less important data, such as public folders that hold nonessential documents, you can use a less complex plan, although you still need to ensure that you back up the data regularly and that you can recover the data easily.

One of the most important considerations is how quickly you need to recover the data. To get critical data, such as the primary mailbox database, back online swiftly, you might need to amend your backup plan. You could for example create multiple mailbox databases and place them in different availability groups. You can then recover individual databases or individual servers as the situation warrants.

What equipment is available to perform backups? To perform timely backups, you might need several backup devices and several sets of backup media. Backup hardware can include tape drives, tape library systems, storage arrays, and removable disk drives. You need to decide on the best time to carry out backups. If you schedule backups for when the system use is as low as possible, this speeds up the backup process, but this is not always possible.

You need to determine who is responsible for the backup and recovery plan. There needs to be a primary contact. This person (probably you) could also be responsible for performing the backups. However, several people need to be able to perform a restore, and at least one responsible person needs to be available at any given time. If data is corrupted and a restore operation is required, it is required immediately. The backup and restore plan and all the procedures need to be documented. If, in the worst-case scenario, your entire technical support team is struck with a mystery illness, the consultants that management brings in would need to have clear instructions.

Typically, you need to store backups off-site. A natural disaster, such as a major fire or an earthquake, could destroy both your system and your in-house backups. Storing backups off-site lets you recover your Exchange Server infrastructure, provided that your off-site storage location also includes copies of all the software you need to recover Exchange Server.

Choosing Backup Options

You can perform backups with Exchange services running (online backups) or with Exchange services stopped (offline backups). With online backups, you can archive the following:

- System State data, including Exchange configuration data
- Exchange user data
- Files and folders that contain Windows and Exchange files

Offline backups cannot archive Exchange configuration or user data and can archive only the following:

- System State data
- Files and folders containing Windows and Exchange files

You can perform the following types of backup with Exchange Server 2010:

- **Normal/full backups**   These back up all selected Exchange data, including databases and current transaction logs. A full backup indicates that you have performed a complete backup, and Exchange Server 2010 clears the transaction logs.

- **Copy backups**   These back up all selected Exchange data, including related databases and current transaction logs. A copy backup does not clear the log files.

- **Differential backups**   These backup any data that has changed since the last normal backup by backing up transaction log files and not actual databases. A differential backup does not clear the log files. To recover Exchange Server, you apply the most recent normal backup and the most recent differential backup.

- **Incremental backups**   These backup any data that has changed since the last normal backup or incremental backup by backing up transaction log files and not the actual databases. An incremental backup clears the log files after it completes. To recover Exchange Server, you apply the most recent full backup and then apply each incremental backup in order.

In your backup plan, you could, for example, perform full backups on a weekly basis and supplement them with more frequent differential or incremental backups. You might also want to create a regular copy backup to removable media for off-site storage and archiving.

Scheduling Backups

You can create a backup plan by scheduling backups. Windows Server Backup lets you schedule full or incremental backups so that they occur one or more times per day. You can configure backup jobs that perform manual backups and schedule these using Windows Task Scheduler. An expected update to Windows Server Backup will allow you to create multiple master schedules for any day of the week or month. When you implement this update, which may be available by the time you read this book, you will be able to configure separate schedules for full and incremental backups on the same server.

The high-level procedure to create a backup schedule using Windows Server Backup is as follows:

1. Click Backup Schedule on the Windows Server Backup Actions pane to start the Backup Schedule Wizard.

2. Read the information on the Getting Started page.

3. Select Full Server or Custom on the Backup Configuration page. If you select Custom, you can choose the items you want to back up in the same way as you do for a manual backup. You will perform a manual backup in a practice exercise later in this chapter.

4. On the Specify Backup Time page, shown in Figure 14-5, you can choose to backup once per day or more than once per day and choose your backup time or times.

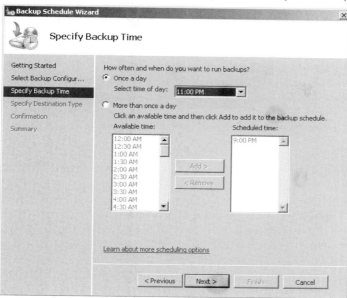

FIGURE 14-5 The Specify Backup Time page

5. On the Specify Destination Type page, shown in Figure 14-6, you can specify whether to back up to a hard disk, a volume, or a network share. If you specify an external hard disk, this disk is dedicated to backup, and any non-backup data it contains will be deleted. If you specify more than one hard disk, the backup uses each of them in turn.

6. If you choose a remote shared folder as your backup destination, you receive a warning that backups will overwrite any previous backups. On the Specify Remote Shared Folder page, shown in Figure 14-7, you can specify the UNC path to the shared folder. Note that only the Inherit Access Control option is available for scheduled backups.

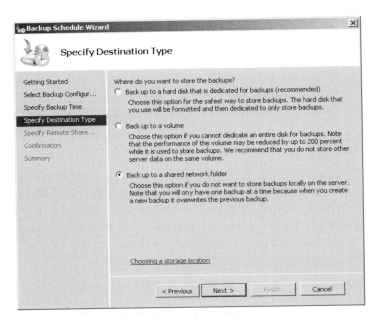

FIGURE 14-6 The Specify Destination Type page

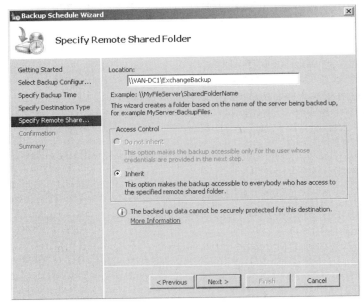

FIGURE 14-7 The Specify Remote Shared Folder page

7. If prompted, provide a user name and password and then click Finish on the Confirmation page.

Recovering Exchange Server

Earlier in this lesson, you saw how to recover lost or corrupted Exchange data by using Windows Server Backup to recover Exchange databases to either their original or another location. However, this is not always the most appropriate procedure. In the worst possible case, an entire server has failed through a crashed Windows Server operating system and needs to be recovered. At the opposite end of the scale, a single mailbox is corrupted and needs to be restored.

Performing a Full Server Recovery

If you need to recover a full server because of corrupted or missing system files, you can use the Windows Server 2008 startup repair features. The startup repair process can also recover from certain types of boot failures that involve the boot manager. If the boot manager itself is corrupt and you cannot start the server as a result, you can use the Windows Server 2008 or Windows Server 2008 R2 installation disc or a recovery partition to restore the boot manager and enable startup.

If startup repair fails and you are not able to start the server, you can attempt to recover the server from a backup using the following procedure:

1. Insert the Windows disc into the DVD drive and turn on the computer. If needed, press the required key to boot from the disk. The Install Windows Wizard appears.

2. Specify the language settings and click Next.

3. Click Repair Your Computer. Setup searches the hard disk drives for an existing Windows installation and then displays the results in the System Recovery Options Wizard. If you are recovering the operating system onto separate hardware, the list should be empty, and there should be no operating system on the computer. Click Next.

4. Click Windows Complete PC Restore on the System Recovery Options page. This starts the Windows Complete PC Restore Wizard.

5. Either click Use The Latest Available Backup (Recommended) or click Restore A Different Backup and then click Next.

6. If you choose to restore a different backup, do one of the following on the Select The Location Of The Backup page:

   - Click the computer that contains the backup that you want to use and then click Next. On the Select The Backup To Restore page, click the backup that you want to use and then click Next.

   - To browse for a backup on the network, click Advanced and then click Next. Browse the network to select the backup to restore and then click Next.

7. On the Choose How To Restore The Backup page, you can optionally perform the following tasks:

   - Select the Format And Repartition Disks check box to delete existing partitions and reformat the destination disks to be the same as the backup.

- Click the Exclude Disks button and then select the check boxes associated with any disks that you want to exclude from being formatted and partitioned. The disk that contains the backup that you are using is automatically excluded.

- Click Install Drivers to install device drivers for the hardware to which you are recovering.

- Click Advanced to specify whether the computer is restarted and the disks are checked for errors immediately after the recovery operation is completed.

8. Click Next.

9. On the Confirmation page, review the details for the restoration and then click Finish. The Windows Complete PC Restore Wizard will then perform the restore, depending on the options you have selected.

Using an RDB

An RDB is a special kind of mailbox database that allows you to mount a restored mailbox database and extract data from the restored database as part of a recovery operation. This lets you recover data from a backup or copy of a database without disturbing user access to current data. You can use the *Restore-Mailbox* Exchange Management Shell (EMS) cmdlet to extract data from an RDB. An example of this is given later in this section. After extraction, the data can be exported to a folder or merged into an existing mailbox. Mounting recovered data as an RDB lets you restore individual mailboxes or individual items in a mailbox.

EXAM TIP

If you restore to the original location, you need to restore all the databases you have backed up. If you restore to an alternate location, you can restore a single database. This can significantly reduce the recovery time when only a single database or an item in that database needs to be recovered.

A database and log files can be restored to any disk location. Exchange analyzes the restored data and replays the transaction logs to bring the databases up to date. You can then configure an RDB to point to the recovered database files.

Before you can move a recovered or restored mailbox database into an RDB and then extract data from the recovered database, you first need to create an RDB for this purpose. You use the *New-MailboxDatabase* EMS cmdlet to create an RDB. You cannot use the EMS for this purpose. For example, the following command creates the recovery database RecoverDB on the Mailbox server VAN-EX1:

```
New-MailboxDatabase -Recovery -Name RecoverDB -Server VAN-EX1
```

Figure 14-8 shows the output from this command.

FIGURE 14-8 Creating a recovery database

You need to bear the following information in mind when working with RDBs:

■ You cannot use an RDB to insert mail into or remove mail from the messaging system. All client protocol access to an RDB (including Simple Mail Transfer Protocol, Post Office Protocol version 3, and Internet Message Access Protocol version 4) is blocked.

■ RDB mailboxes cannot be connected to user accounts. If you need to permit user access to the data in an RDB mailbox, you need to merge this mailbox into an existing mailbox or export it to a folder.

■ Client access to Messaging Application Programming Interface (MAPI) using Microsoft Office Outlook or Outlook Web App (OWA) is blocked. MAPI access to an RDB is available only to recovery tools and applications.

■ An RDB cannot be deleted by the system during the recovery process.

■ A recovered database mounted as an RDB is not tied to the original mailbox database in any way.

■ Circular logging cannot be enabled for RDBs.

■ Online maintenance is not performed on RDBs.

■ You cannot use an RDB to recover public folder data.

■ You cannot create mailbox database copies of an RDB.

■ You can mount only one RDB on a Mailbox server at any time.

■ The use of an RDB does not count against the 100-database limit on a Mailbox server.

An RDB can be used to recover Exchange Server 2010 mailbox databases only. Mailbox databases from previous versions of Exchange are not supported, and the target mailbox used for data merges and extraction must be in the same Active Directory forest as the database mounted in the RDB. An RDB can be used to recover data in the following scenarios:

■ **Same-server dial tone recovery**   You can perform a recovery from an RDB as part of a dial tone recovery operation after the original database has been restored from backup. Dial tone recovery is discussed later in this lesson.

■ **Alternate-server dial tone recovery**   You can use an alternate server to host a dial tone database and recover data from an RDB after the original database has been restored from backup.

- **Mailbox recovery**   You can recover an individual mailbox from backup after its deleted mailbox retention period has elapsed. You then extract data from the restored mailbox and copy it to a target folder or merge it with another mailbox.
- **Specific item recovery**   You can restore data that has been deleted or purged from a mailbox from backup.

EXAM TIP

You should not use an RDB when you are recovering public folder content, when you need to restore entire servers, when you need to restore multiple databases, or when you need to change or rebuild your Active Directory topology.

Before you can restore Exchange data using an RDB, the RDB must exist and the database and log files containing the recovered data must be copied into the RDB folder structure. The database must be in a clean shutdown state. All databases restored to an alternate restore location are in a dirty shutdown state by default, and you need to use the Eseutil utility in recover mode (for example, eseutil /r E00, where E00 is the log file prefix) to put the database in a clean shutdown state before moving the restored database data into an RDB.

When you have moved the restored database into an RDB, you can mount the RDB and merge its contents into the database you want to restore. You merge the databases by exporting the data from the RDB and importing it into the original database one mailbox at a time using the *Restore-Mailbox* EMS cmdlet. For example, the following command merges the contents of the RDB RecoverDB into the mailbox database MyDatabase:

```
Get-Mailbox –Database MyDatabase | Restore-Mailbox –RecoveryDatabase RecoverDB
```

EXAM TIP

You need to use the Eseutil utility if you want to put a mailbox database in a clean shutdown state. You can use the Isinteg utility to repair a mailbox database but not to bring a mailbox database that is in a dirty shutdown state into a clean shutdown state. No EMS cmdlet can be used to put a mailbox database in a clean shutdown state.

You can also recover a single mailbox or specified messages within a mailbox by using the *Restore-Mailbox* cmdlet. For example, you are recovering the DonHall mailbox from a recovery database named RecoverDB. The following command recovers all messages located in the Inbox folder of the DonHall mailbox that contain the word "Marketing" in the subject and places them in the DonMarketing folder of the KimAkers mailbox:

```
Restore-Mailbox –Identity DonHall –RecoveryDatabase RecoverDB –SubjectKeywords
"Marketing" –IncludeFolders \Inbox –RecoveryMailbox KimAkers –TargetFolder DonMarketing
```

EXAM TIP

The recovery database replaces the recovery storage group found in previous versions of Exchange.

> **MORE INFO** ***RESTORE-MAILBOX* AND *NEW-MAILBOXDATABASE***
>
> For more information about the *Restore-Mailbox* EMS cmdlet, see *http://technet.microsoft.com/en-us/library/bb125218.aspx*. For more information about the *New-MailboxDatabase* EMS cmdlet, see *http://technet.microsoft.com/en-us/library/aa997976.aspx*.

Database Portability

Database portability enables you to move and mount an Exchange 2010 mailbox database on any other Exchange 2010 Mailbox server in the same organization. If you make use of database portability, you can improve reliability by removing several manual steps from the recovery processes. In addition, database portability reduces the overall recovery times for various failure scenarios. Only Exchange 2010 mailbox databases are portable. Public folder databases are not, and neither are mailbox databases from previous versions of Exchange. The preferred way to move public folder data between servers is to use public folder replication.

To move a mailbox database using database portability, you first need to ensure that the database is in the clean shutdown state. You can then use a command based on the *New-MailboxDatabase* EMS cmdlet to create a database on the new server. For example, the following command creates a database called MyNewDatabase on the Mailbox server VAN-EX2:

```
New-MailboxDatabase -Name MyNewDatabase -Server VAN-EX2 -EdbFilePath
C:\Databases\MyNewDatabase\MyNewDatabase.edb -LogFolderPath C:\Databases\MyNewDatabase
```

Figure 14-9 shows the output from this command.

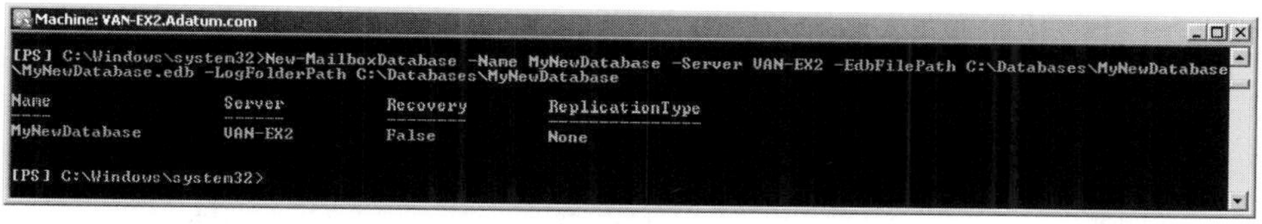

FIGURE 14-9 Creating a new database on server VAN-EX2

The next step is to set the This Database Can Be Over Written By Restore attribute using a command based on the *Set-MailboxDatabase* EMS cmdlet:

```
Set-MailboxDatabase MyNewDatabase -AllowFileRestore:$true
```

The database files (.edb file, log files, and Exchange Search catalog) can now be moved to the appropriate location and the new database mounted:

```
Mount-Database MyNewDatabase
```

The final step is to modify the user account settings so that the user accounts point to the mailbox on the new Mailbox server. For example, the following command moves all the users (but not the system mailboxes) from the old database MyOldDatabase to the new database MyNewDatabase:

```
Get-Mailbox -Database MyOldDatabase | where {$_ObjectClass -NotMatch
'(SystemAttendantMailbox|ExOleDbSystemMailbox)'} | Set-Mailbox -Database MyNewDatabase
```

After Active Directory replication occurs, all users can access their mailboxes on the new Exchange server. Microsoft Outlook 2010, Office Outlook 2007, and Windows Mobile 6.1 (and later) clients are redirected via the Autodiscover service, OWA users are automatically redirected, and (if the server name has changed) older Outlook clients need to be manually configured to point to the new server.

Dial Tone Portability

Dial tone portability enables a user to have a mailbox in a dial tone database for sending and receiving email while his or her original mailbox is being restored or repaired and thus provides a business continuity solution. The dial tone database can be on the same Exchange 2010 Mailbox server or on any other Exchange 2010 Mailbox server in the same Exchange organization. Clients that support Autodiscover, such as Microsoft Outlook 2010 or Office Outlook 2007, are automatically redirected to the new server without the need to manually update the user's desktop profile. After the original mailbox data has been restored, you can merge the recovered mailbox and the mailbox in the dial tone database into a single, up-to-date mailbox.

A recovery process using dial tone portability is called a *dial tone recovery*. A dial tone recovery involves creating an empty database on a Mailbox server to replace a failed database. This empty database, referred to as a dial tone database, allows users to send and receive email while the failed database is recovered and moved into an RDB. Note that dial tone restores are necessary only when the original database is offline when restoration occurs and service to users has been interrupted. After the failed database is recovered and moved into the RDB, the data from the RDB is merged into the dial tone database, which is now operating as the recovered production database.

The procedure to carry out a dial tone recovery of a mailbox database is as follows:

1. Save any noncorrupted files that exist on the database being recovered. These may be required for further recovery operations.

2. Create a dial tone database. For example, the following EMS command creates a dial tone database named MyDialToneDB on the Mailbox server VAN-EX1:

   ```
   New-MailboxDatabase -Name MyDialToneDB -Server VAN-EX1 -EdbFilePath C:\DialTone\
   MyDialToneDB.edb
   ```

3. Transfer the user mailboxes hosted on the database being recovered (for example, MyOriginalDB), as shown in the following example:

   ```
   Get-Mailbox -Database MyOriginalDB | Set-Mailbox -Database MyDialToneDB
   ```

4. Mount the dial tone database, as shown in the following example:

   ```
   Mount-Database -Identity MyDialToneDB
   ```

5. Create an RDB (for example, RecoverDB). Restore the database and log files containing the data you want to recover to an alternate location and copy them into the RDB. The procedure to create an RDB was described earlier in this lesson.

6. After you copy the data to the RDB but before mounting the restored database, copy any log files from the failed database to the RDB log folder so that they can be played against the restored database.

7. Mount the RDB and then dismount it:

   ```
   Mount-Database -Identity RecoverDB

   Dismount-Database -Identity RecoverDB
   ```

8. Move the current database and log files within the RDB folder to a safe location to prepare for swapping the recovered database with the dial tone database.

9. Dismount the dial tone database, as shown in the following example. Note that your users experience an interruption in service between the time you dismount this database and the time you mount it again:

   ```
   Dismount-Database -Identity MyDialToneDB
   ```

10. Move the database and log files from the dial tone database folder into the RDB folder.

11. Move the database and log files from the safe location containing the recovered database into the dial tone database folder and then mount the database:

    ```
    Mount-Database -Identity MyDialToneDB
    ```

    The dial tone database is now operating as the recovered production database, and service to the user is resumed. However, to ensure that recovery is as complete as possible, the contents of the RDB need to be merged with the contents of the dial tone database.

12. Mount the RDB:

    ```
    Mount-Database -Identity RecoverDB
    ```

13. Merge the databases by exporting the data from the RDB and importing it into the recovered database:

    ```
    Get-Mailbox -Database MyDialToneDB | Restore-Mailbox -RecoveryDatabase RecoverDB
    ```

14. After the restore operation is complete, dismount and remove the RDB:

    ```
    Dismount-Database -Identity RecoverDB

    Remove-MailboxDatabase -Identity RecoverDB
    ```

Recovering a Mailbox within the Deleted Mailbox Retention Period

Deleted mailbox retention enables you to recover mailboxes after they have been removed (or disconnected) without needing to restore them from backup. By default, Exchange Server 2010 retains disconnected mailboxes for 30 days after deletion, and mailbox recovery must occur during this retention period. You recover a deleted mailbox within the retention period by using either the EMS or the Exchange Management Console (EMC).

To list the deleted (or disconnected) mailboxes in the Recoverable Items folder (or dumpster) on, for example, the Mailbox server VAN-EX1 and the dates on which they were deleted, enter the following EMS command:

```
Get-MailboxStatistics -Server VAN-EX1 | where {$_DisconnectDate -ne $null} | select
DisplayName,DisconnectDate
```

If you do not specify the Server parameter, the command will list the disconnected mailboxes on the Mailbox server on which it runs. Note that this command returns statistics only for those mailboxes where the user has logged on at least once to the Exchange organization. A mailbox can also be disconnected but not yet marked as disconnected. You can use the *Clean-MailboxDatabase* cmdlet to scan Active Directory for such mailboxes in the Microsoft Exchange mailbox database and update the status of those mailboxes in the Exchange mailbox store.

> **MORE INFO** **GET-MAILBOXSTATISTICS AND CLEAN-MAILBOXDATABASE**
>
> For more information about the *Get-MailboxStatistics* EMS cmdlet, see *http://technet .microsoft.com/en-us/library/bb124612.aspx*. For more information about the *Clean-MailboxDatabase* EMS cmdlet, see *http://technet.microsoft.com/en-us/library/ bb124076.aspx*.

Connecting a Mailbox

You recover a disconnected a mailbox by connecting it to a user account. In this example, the account Paul West exists in Active Directory but does not have an associated mailbox. You can check whether this user account exists and is not disabled by entering the following EMS command:

```
Get-User "Paul West" | FL
```

Figure 14-10 shows some of the output from this command.

To reconnect a disconnected mailbox in the Research mailbox database to user Paul West when the user object exists in Active Directory Directory Service and has no associated mailbox, run the following command:

```
Connect-Mailbox -Database "Mailbox Database 1514648952" -Identity "Paul West" -User
"Paul West"
```

FIGURE 14-10 Details of the Paul West account in Active Directory

Note that if you want to try running this command, you must first create a mailbox for the user Paul West in your default mailbox database (which might not be called Mailbox Database 1514648952) and then disable this mailbox.

If you have a number of disconnected mailboxes in a mailbox database, you can attempt to reconnect all of them with a single command, such as the following:

```
Get-MailboxStatistics -Database "Mailbox Database 1514648952" | where {$_.disconnectdate
-ne $null} | ForEach {Connect-Mailbox -Id $_mailboxguid -Database "Mailbox Database
1363123687"}
```

This command works for disconnected mailboxes that have equivalent Active Directory user accounts that are not already associated with mailboxes.

> **MORE INFO** **CONNECT-MAILBOX**
>
> For more information about the *Connect-Mailbox* EMS cmdlet, see *http://technet.microsoft .com/en-us/library/aa997878.aspx.*

You can also use the EMC to connect a disconnected mailbox. A user account that does not have an associated mailbox needs to exist in Active Directory so that you can connect the mailbox to it. In the EMC, expand Recipient Configuration and click Disconnected Mailbox in the Console tree. If required, click Connect To Server on the Actions pane to specify the Mailbox server that holds the disconnected mailbox. Right-click the mailbox you want to connect and click Connect, as shown in Figure 14-11. Follow the steps in the Connect Mailbox Wizard. Note that in order to replicate this figure, you need to create and disable mailboxes for Mark Harrington and Angela Barbariol.

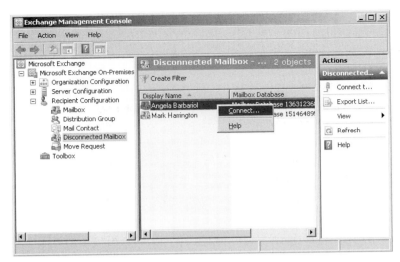

FIGURE 14-11 Connecting a mailbox using the EMS

Configuring the Deleted Mailbox Retention Period

Disconnected mailboxes are retained for 30 days by default and can be recovered at any point during this 30-day period by associating them with an Active Directory user account. You can use the EMS but not the EMC to configure the deleted mailbox retention period. If, for example, you wanted to change the deleted mailbox retention time to 20 days for mailboxes in the database Mailbox Database 1514648952, you would enter the following EMS command:

```
Set-MailboxDatabase -Identity "Mailbox Database 1514648952" -MailboxRetention
20.00:00:00
```

EXAM TIP

Note the format for retention periods. If you see an answer in the examination that, for example, gives a deleted mailbox retention setting of 15.00.00.00 or 30:00:00:00, that answer is wrong.

Recovering Single Items

Exchange Server 2010 introduces single item recovery functionality and the Recoverable Items folder, which was formerly known as the dumpster in Exchange 2007. The same name is used in some Technet articles about Exchange Server 2010, but the correct name is the Recoverable Items folder.

Single item recovery functionality helps you ensure that deleted and modified items are preserved and that deleted and modified items can be recovered easily in compliance cases.

This was discussed in Chapter 11, "Managing Records and Compliance." Single item recovery helps you reduce the risks associated with email and other communications and makes it easier to keep what you need to comply with company policy, government regulations, or legal needs.

Single item recovery provides the following features:

- The Recoverable Items folder is given a quota to help prevent potential denial-of-service attacks during which a malicious user places large amounts of data in this folder.

- All items in a user's Recoverable Items folder are indexed and searchable using the discovery cmdlets discussed in Chapter 11.

- All items in the Recoverable Items folder are moved when a move request is implemented.

In Exchange Server 2010, items are retained when the single item recovery feature is enabled for a mailbox, even if end users purge these items from their Recoverable Items folders. The Recoverable Items folder contains the following subfolders (note that items placed in these folders do not count toward the mailbox quota):

- **Purges** All items that the user hard-deletes are moved to this folder whenever either legal hold or single item recovery is enabled. This folder is invisible to the end user.

- **Deletions** All items that the user soft-deletes from the Deleted Items folder within the user mailbox are moved to this folder, which is exposed when a user accesses the Recover Deleted Items feature in Microsoft Outlook.

- **Versions** Original and modified copies of an item are placed in this folder when either legal hold or single item recovery is enabled. This folder is invisible to the end user.

Although the Purges and Versions subfolders of the Recoverable Items folder are inaccessible to the end user, they can be accessed by an administrator or a user who is a member of the Discovery Management role group and carries out a multi-mailbox or a discovery search.

Whether single item recovery is disabled or enabled, Messaging Policy and Compliance automatically purges items from the Recoverable Items folder after 14 days by default—except for calendar items that are purged after 120 days. Also, soft-deleted items are stored in the Recoverable Items folder whether single item recovery is disabled or enabled.

If single item recovery is enabled, modified and stored hard-deleted items are stored in the Recoverable Items folder, and the user cannot purge items from this folder. If, on the other hand, single item recovery is disabled, modified and stored hard-deleted items are not stored in the Recoverable Items folder, and the user can purge items from this folder.

> **MORE INFO** **DISCOVERY MANAGEMENT ROLE GROUP**
>
> For more information about the Discovery Management role group, see *http://technet .microsoft.com/en-us/library/dd351080.aspx*.

Recoverable Items Mailbox Quota

When an item is moved to the Recoverable Items folder, the size of the item is subtracted from the parent mailbox quota and added to the size of the Recoverable Items folder. The Recoverable Items folder has a configurable soft limit default of 20 GB and a hard limit default of 30 GB. You are notified via an event log and a Microsoft System Center Operations Manager alert when the Recoverable Items folder reaches its soft and hard limit defaults. This alert fires when the soft and hard limit defaults are reached and then once every day after that. Note that when legal hold is enabled, records management purging of recoverable items stops.

Configuring Single Item Recovery

You can use commands based on the *Set-Mailbox* EMS cmdlet to configure single item recovery settings on a mailbox and commands based on the *Set-MailboxDatabase* EMS cmdlet to configure single item recovery settings on a mailbox database. Note that these values are ignored when legal hold (discussed in Chapter 11) is enabled.

For example, the following command sets the Recovery Items folder quota limit at which a warning event is entered in Event Viewer to 10 GB for the Don Hall Mailbox:

```
Set-Mailbox -Identity "Don Hall" -RecoverableItemsWarningQuota 10GB
```

The following EMS command sets the hard limit for the Recovery Items folder in the Don Hall Mailbox to 20 GB:

```
Set-Mailbox -Identity "Don Hall" -RecoverableItemsQuota 20GB
```

The following EMS command sets the hard limit quota for the Recovery Items folder for all mailboxes that reside on the Research mailbox database to 25 GB:

```
Set-MailboxDatabase -Identity Research -RecoverableItemsQuota 25GB
```

Note that if you want to set Recovery Items folder quotas at a database level rather than the quotas that are set at the mailbox level, you need to use the *Set-Mailbox* EMS cmdlet to set the UseDatabaseQuotaDefaults parameter to $true on the user's mailbox.

Configuring the Deleted Item Retention Period

Deleted items such as email messages can be retrieved by the user during a configurable deleted item retention period, by default 14 days (120 days for calendar items), after which they need to be restored from backup. Note that the deleted item retention period is not the same as the deleted mailbox retention period. If, for example, you wanted to change the deleted item retention period to seven days for all mailboxes in the database Mailbox Database 1514648952, you would enter the following EMS command:

```
Set-MailboxDatabase -Identity "Mailbox Database 1514648952" -DeletedItemRetention
7.00:00:00
```

Using Exchange Native Data Protection

Exchange Server 2010 includes several new features that can provide native data protection and eliminates the need to restore data from backup. The high-availability features described in Chapter 13, "Exchange High-Availability Solutions," minimize downtime and data loss in the event of a disaster. By combining these features with other built-in features, such as legal hold, described in Chapter 11, you can reduce your Exchange organization's dependency on traditional point-in-time backups. Depending on organizational requirements, it is likely that an Exchange Server 2010 environment with at least three mailbox database copies can provide lower total cost of ownership than an organization that depends on backups for disaster recovery.

Native Data Protection Features

In the event of a hardware or software failure, multiple database copies in a DAG enable high availability with fast failover and no data loss. This eliminates end-user downtime, which represents a significant cost when recovering from a past point-in-time backup to disk or tape. DAGs can be extended to multiple sites and can provide resilience against failures in large organizations.

The Recoverable Items folder introduced in Exchange 2010 and the hold policy that can be applied to it makes it possible to retain all deleted and modified data for a specified period of time, and recovery of these items is easier and faster. This enables end users to recover accidentally deleted items themselves, thereby reducing the administrative costs associated with single item recovery.

The archiving, multi-mailbox search, and message retention features introduced by Exchange Server 2010 can efficiently preserve data in a manner that makes it accessible to the end user for extended periods of time. This eliminates expensive restores from tape or optical media and enables clients such as Microsoft Outlook and OWA access to older data.

Point-in-time copies of mailbox data may be one of your organizational requirements. Exchange Server 2010 lets you create a lagged copy in a DAG environment. This can be useful if logical corruption occurs and this replicates across the databases in the DAG, resulting in a need to return to a previous point in time. Lagged copies can also be useful if an administrator accidentally deletes mailboxes or user data. Recovery from a lagged copy can be faster than restoring from a backup because lagged copies do not require a copy process from the backup server to the Exchange server.

Log Truncation without Backups

At the end of a successful full or incremental backup, Exchange truncates those transaction log files that are no longer needed for database recovery. If full or incremental backups are not taken, log truncation does not occur. You can enable circular logging for your replicated databases to prevent a buildup of log files. If you combine circular logging with continuous replication, this creates a type of circular logging called *continuous replication circular logging (CRCL)*, which differs from Extensible Storage Engine (ESE) circular logging. ESE circular logging is performed and managed by the Microsoft Exchange Information Store service, whereas CRCL is performed and managed by the Microsoft Exchange Replication Service.

ESE circular logging does not generate additional log files and instead overwrites the current log file when needed. However, in a continuous replication environment, log files are needed for log shipping and replay. As a result, when you enable CRCL, the current log file is not overwritten, and closed log files are generated for the log shipping and replay process. The Microsoft Exchange Replication Service manages CRCL so that log continuity is maintained, and logs are not deleted if they are still needed for replication.

Lesson Summary

- Windows Server Backup lets you backup and restore some or all of the Exchange data on a Mailbox server.
- If you restore databases to their original location, you need to restore all the databases on a server.
- You can restore a single database to an alternate location and recover it using an RDB.
- If a database is corrupt and offline, you can minimize user downtime by carrying out a dial tone restore.
- You can reconnect a disconnected mailbox within the deleted mailbox retention time without needing to restore from backup.
- Users can retrieve deleted items in a mailbox within the deleted item retention time.

Lesson Review

You can use the following questions to test your knowledge of the information in Lesson 1, "Backup and Recover Exchange Data." The questions are also available on the companion CD if you prefer to review them in electronic form.

1. You are performing a dial tone recovery and need to merge the data in the RDB MyRecovery with the data in the recovered database RecovereyDB. What EMS command do you enter to do this?

   A. Get-Mailbox -Database MyRecovery | Restore-Mailbox -RecoveryDatabase RecoveryDB

   B. Restore-Mailbox -RecoveryDatabase RecoveryDB | Get-Mailbox -Database MyRecovery

   C. Get-Mailbox -Database RecoveryDB | Restore-Mailbox -RecoveryDatabase MyRecovery

   D. Restore-Mailbox -RecoveryDatabase MyRecovery | Get-Mailbox -Database MyRecoveryDB

2. You want to configure the mailbox retention period for all mailboxes in the mailbox database Research to be 24 days. What command do you enter?

   A. Set-MailboxDatabase –Identity "Research" -MailboxRetention 24:00:00:00

   B. Set-MailboxDatabase –Identity "Research" –DeletedItemRetention 24:00:00:00

   C. Set-MailboxDatabase –Identity "Research" -MailboxRetention 24.00:00:00

   D. Set-MailboxDatabase –Identity "Research" –DeletedItemRetention 24.00:00:00

3. What utility or EMS cmdlet can you use to repair a mailbox database and to bring a mailbox database that is in a dirty shutdown state into a clean shutdown state?

   A. Eseutil

   B. Isinteg

   C. Get-MaiboxDatabase

   D. Mount-Database

4. Some items in a mailbox database have been accidentally deleted, although the database has not been corrupted and is still online. The Mailbox server holds another four databases that have not been affected in any way and are operating normally. You want to restore the first database from backup. What actions should you take? (Choose all that apply.)

   A. Create an empty database to use as a dial tone recovery database.

   B. Create an RDB (if one does not already exist).

   C. Perform a recovery using Windows Server Backup and select Recover To Original Location.

   D. Perform a recovery using Windows Server Backup and select Recover To Another Location.

5. You want to move all the user mailboxes but not the system mailboxes from the database OldDatabase to the new database NewDatabase. What EMS command do you enter?

   A. *Get-MailboxStatistics -Database OldDatabase | where {$_ObjectClass -NotMatch '(SystemAttendantMailbox|ExOleDbSystemMailbox)'} | Set-Mailbox -Database NewDatabase*

   B. *Set-Mailbox -Database OldDatabase | where {$_ObjectClass -NotMatch '(SystemAttendantMailbox|ExOleDbSystemMailbox)'} | Get-Mailbox -Database NewDatabase*

   C. *Get-Mailbox -Database NewDatabase | where {$_ObjectClass -NotMatch '(SystemAttendantMailbox|ExOleDbSystemMailbox)'} | Set-Mailbox -Database OldDatabase*

   D. *Get-Mailbox -Database OldDatabase | where {$_ObjectClass -NotMatch '(SystemAttendantMailbox|ExOleDbSystemMailbox)'} | Set-Mailbox -Database NewDatabase*

Lesson 2: Recovering Exchange Roles

Lesson 1 discussed the recovery of Exchange databases and mailboxes located on Mailbox servers. However, you might need to restore the Mailbox server role itself or restore servers that have other server roles installed, and you need to design your recovery plan depending on the roles installed on an Exchange Server 2010 server.

Exchange Server 2010 configuration data is stored in Active Directory (except for servers with the Edge Transport server role), and you can fully restore some server roles, such as Hub Transport server, by running Exchange Setup in the Recoverserver mode using the following command:

```
Setup /m:Recoverserver
```

With other roles, such as Mailbox server, this command restores the Exchange configuration, but you need to recover critical Exchange data from backup. This lesson looks at the various Exchange server roles and how you should plan to recover each role.

> **After this lesson, you will be able to:**
> - Recover a Hub Transport server.
> - Recover a Client Access server.
> - Recover a Mailbox server.
> - Recover an Edge Transport server.
>
> **Estimated lesson time: 30 minutes**

Creating a Disaster Recovery Plan Based on Exchange Roles

Before considering the recovery of Exchange server roles, it is important to remember that certain types of hardware failure do not require a server recovery process. If, for example, a server's processor, motherboard, or power supply fails, recovery often requires only the replacement the failed components and a server reboot. It might be necessary to go through the Windows Product Activation process again because of the hardware changes and to install new hardware device drivers, but in general you need to go through the server recovery process only when all the data on your storage devices has been lost or is irretrievably corrupted.

The Exchange Server 2010 Setup routine, discussed in Chapter 1, "Installing Exchange Server 2010," includes a Recoverserver mode that is used for recovering a server or moving a server to new hardware while maintaining the same server name. When you run Setup in this mode, it reads configuration data from Active Directory for a server with the same name as the server from which you are running Setup. Note that the Recoverserver mode does not migrate locally stored custom settings or databases, only settings stored in Active Directory.

You can use a basic set of recovery steps for all server roles, except for Edge Transport server. Edge Transport servers are stand-alone and are not part of a domain. They therefore do not have configuration data associated with a computer account.

Before you run Setup in Recoverserver mode to recover a server role to a replacement computer (or to the same computer with its system hard disk reformatted), you need to take the following steps:

- **Reset the Active Directory computer account** This allows you to join a replacement computer to the domain. Take care not to delete the failed server's computer account because this would result in the loss of all Exchange configuration data stored with the computer account. Resetting the account enables you to join the replacement server to the domain but does not delete configuration data.

- **Install the operating system** You need to install Windows Server 2008 SP2 (64-bit) or Windows Server 2008 R2 on the replacement server specifying exactly the same volume and operating system configuration as you used in the server you are recovering. The operating system you install must be exactly the same as the operating system that was installed on the failed server.

- **Specify the replacement server name** The replacement server must be assigned precisely the same name as that of the failed server.

- **Configure the replacement server to host the relevant Exchange Server 2010 server role or roles** You need to install specific roles, role services, prerequisite components, and features on the replacement server prior to attempting to deploy specific Exchange server roles. This is discussed in Chapter 1.

- **Join the replacement server to the domain**

When you have gone through the preliminary steps listed, you run Exchange Setup in Recoverserver mode, as described previously in this lesson. This extracts the configuration data that is associated with the failed server's Active Directory computer account and applies that data as part of the recovery process.

> **MORE INFO** **RECOVERING AN EXCHANGE SERVER**
>
> For more information about recovering an Exchange server, see *http://technet.microsoft .com/en-us/library/dd876880.aspx*.

Recovering a Hub Transport Server

Typically, you can restore a server running the Hub Transport server role almost completely by running Exchange Setup in Recoverserver mode. Hub Transport servers store all essential configuration data in Active Directory in addition to some limited configuration data stored in the registry. You can back up the registry by performing a System State data backup and if necessary restore it with a System State data restore.

The only items that will not be restored by using Recoverserver mode on a Hub Transport server are message queues stored in database files and any message tracking, protocol, and connectivity logs you enabled on the failed server. Queues store messages currently being processed, and because of their transient nature, they use circular logging and are not backed up. Logs are used primarily for historical reference and troubleshooting.

Queues and logs are typically not essential to restoring Hub Transport server functionality. If, however, you want to recover a particularly important message, you can mount the message queue databases, located in the C:\Program Files\Microsoft\Exchange Server\ TransportRoles\data\Queue directory on an alternate Hub Transport server, assuming of course that this data was not lost when the server failed. In general, however, it is easier to look for a copy of a sent message in a user's Outbox or ask the sender to retransmit it.

Recovering a Client Access Server

You can restore a failed server running the Client Access server role to its initial default state by running Exchange Setup in Recoverserver mode. Any changes you have made to Hypertext Transfer Protocol (HTTP) virtual servers running on the Client Access server are, however, not restored because changes to these virtual servers are stored in Internet Information Server (IIS) configuration data.

Restoring the IIS configuration data from backup to recover the custom settings can generate errors on the Client Access server if the IIS configuration data and the recovered Active Directory settings are not exactly in synchronization. This procedure is not therefore recommended.

Client Access servers store some configuration data in the registry that you can restore if you have backed up System State data. However, this configuration data is limited.

Many organizations do not apply customizations to their Client Access servers, in which case running Exchange Setup in Recoverserver mode restores the server role. If, however, your organization does customize a Client Access server, you need to take the following precautions to enable you to recover the server role in the vent of failure:

- **Keep a log of all customizations that you make to the original Client Access server**   This information is required for server role recovery because some configuration settings are not associated with the computer account in Active Directory.

- **Take a note of the server's volume configuration**   The recovery process requires that the recovered server's volume configuration matches that of the failed server.

- **Ensure you have a valid Secure Sockets Layer (SSL) certificate**   You can reapply for an SSL certificate from an enterprise certification authority (CA) server in your domain through the Internet Information Services (IIS) console. If, however, you obtained the server's SSL certificate from a trusted third-party authority, you should store a copy of this certificate somewhere secure. Many organizations keep purchased certificates in a safe after they have been installed.

- **Keep a record of your custom virtual directories**   If a Client Access server uses custom virtual directories to, for example, publish custom offline address books, you need to re-create these manually when the server is recovered.

- **Apply customization changes after you have performed the recovery process**
  Otherwise, it is possible that these configuration changes will be overwritten by that
  process.

If a significant amount of customization has occurred you may find it easier to run
Exchange Setup and restore your Client Access server by building a new server with a new
name. However, if, as is more typical, little or no customization has been carried out, you can
restore the failed server with the same name by running Exchange Setup in Recoverserver
mode. If you choose the second alternative, you then need to apply the same customizations
that you had on the failed server by re-creating additional websites and virtual directories as
necessary. You restart IIS to apply the setting changes.

Quick Check
  - You are recovering a Hub Transport server. What elements can you not recover by
    running Exchange Setup in Recoverserver mode?

Quick Check Answer
  - You cannot recover message queues stored in database files and any message
    tracking, protocol, and connectivity logs that were enabled on the failed server.

Recovering a Mailbox Server

You cannot fully restore the Mailbox Server role by running the Exchange Setup program
in Recoverserver mode but must, in addition, restore the Mailbox server from a backup
that includes the necessary Exchange data and the System State data. Mailbox servers store
Exchange mailbox and public folder database files together with Exchange transaction log
files specific to each database. You need to back up these files with an Exchange-aware
backup application, such as Windows Server Backup.

If available replicas exist, you can rebuild replicated public folder data through the normal
replication process. Mailbox servers also store full-text indexing information specific to each
mailbox database, but you do not back up or restore full-text indexes because you need
instead to rebuild them. Other types of Exchange databases on Mailbox servers include free/
busy information and the offline address book. This information is rebuilt through automated
maintenance and then replicated.

To recover the Mailbox server role, you first use Exchange Setup in Recoverserver mode
to extract the original Mailbox server's configuration data from Active Directory. The volume
configuration of the replacement server must be exactly the same as that of the failed
server. Mailbox servers are particularly sensitive to any configuration differences, and you
need to document the exact configuration of the server's storage devices and volumes. If
this configuration is not precisely reproduced, you are likely to encounter problems when
attempting to restore mailbox and storage group data.

EXAM TIP

Exchange Server 2007 uses cluster continuous replication (CCR) or a single copy cluster configuration to provide failover protection and high availability for Mailbox servers. If you need to recover a clustered Mailbox server in Exchange Server 2007, you re-create the failed cluster node and then run Exchange Setup with the RecoverCMS switch to install the passive Mailbox server role on the computer. However, Exchange Server 2010 uses DAGs and mailbox database copies to implement the same functionality. If you see an answer in the examination that features CCR or the RecoverCMS switch, that answer is likely to be wrong.

MORE INFO DISCONTINUED FEATURES

For more information about features such as CCR that are discontinued in Exchange Server 2010, see *http://technet.microsoft.com/en-us/library/aa998911.aspx*.

 Quick Check

- You are recovering a Client Access server. What elements can you not recover by running Exchange Setup in Recoverserver mode?

Quick Check Answer

- You cannot recover any changes you have made to HTTP virtual servers running on the Client Access server by running Exchange Setup in Recoverserver mode. Also, you need to ensure that you have a valid SSL certificate.

Recovering a Member Server in a DAG

If a member of a DAG fails and you want to replace it, you need to remove any database copies that were held on the failed server from the DAG. You also remove the configuration of the failed server from the DAG. You then reset the failed server's computer account and use Exchange Setup in Recoverserver mode to perform the server recovery operation in the same way as you do for any failed Mailbox server.

The original Exchange files and services are then installed on the server, and the roles and settings that were stored in Active Directory are applied to the server. You add the recovered server to the DAG and reconfigure the mailbox database copies. The step-by-step procedure to recover a failed DAG member server is as follows:

1. Retrieve any replay lag or truncation lag settings for any mailbox database copies that exist on the failed server by entering an EMS command based on the *Get-MailboxDatabase* cmdlet:

   ```
   Get-MailboxDatabase Research | FL *lag*
   ```

Figure 14-12 shows the output of this command. Note that in this case, both the replay lag and the truncation lag times are zero.

FIGURE 14-12 Listing the replay lag and truncation lag for a mailbox database copy

2. Remove any mailbox database copies that exist on the failed server by entering an EMS command based on the *Remove-MailboxDatabaseCopy* cmdlet:

   ```
   Remove-MailboxDatabaseCopy Research\VAN-EX1
   ```

3. Remove the failed server's configuration from the DAG by entering an EMS command based on the *Remove-DatabaseAvailabilityGroupServer* cmdlet:

   ```
   Remove-DatabaseAvailabilityGroupServer -Identity Research -MailboxServer VAN-EX1
   ```

4. Reset the server's computer account in Active Directory.

5. Install exactly the same operating system on the replacement server that was installed in the failed server. Ensure that the computer names are also identical.

6. Insert the original Exchange Server 2010 setup media into the replacement server. Open a Command Prompt window, access the volume that holds the setup media, and enter the following command:

   ```
   Setup /m:Recoverserver
   ```

7. When the Setup recovery process is complete, add the recovered server to the DAG by entering an EMS command based on the *Add-DatabaseAvailabilityGroupServer* cmdlet:

   ```
   Add-DatabaseAvailabilityGroupServer -Identity MyDAG -MailboxServer VAN-EX1
   ```

8. Reconfigure mailbox database copies by entering one or more EMS commands based on the *Add-MailboxDatabaseCopy* cmdlet. If any of the database copies being added previously had replay lag or truncation lag times greater than zero, you can use the ReplayLagTime and TruncationLagTime parameters of this cmdlet to reconfigure those settings:

   ```
   Add-MailboxDatabaseCopy -Identity Research -MailboxServer VAN-EX1

   Add-MailboxDatabaseCopy -Identity Marketing -MailboxServer VAN-EX1 -ReplayLagTime
   2.00:00:00

   Add-MailboxDatabaseCopy -Identity Sales -MailboxServer VAN-EX1 -ReplayLagTime
   2.00:00:00 -TruncationLagTime 1.00:00:00
   ```

Recovering a Unified Messaging Server

Like the Hub Transport server role, the Unified Messaging server role stores its essential configuration data in Active Directory and some limited configuration data in the registry. You can restore a Unified Messaging server to its initial default state by running the Exchange Setup program in Recoverserver mode. If necessary, you can restore registry settings from a System State data backup.

Queues and logs are not essential to restoring Unified Messaging server functionality. You can mount message queues on a new server if you can recover them from a failed server. You can also restore custom audio files used for prompts automatically through replication if you have other Unified Messaging servers in the organization.

Recovering an Edge Transport Server

The Edge Transport server role is installed on a stand-alone server. Edge Transport servers store configuration data, queues, replicated data from Active Directory, and any logs, such as message tracking, protocol, and connectivity logs, that have been enabled. These servers also store some configuration data in the registry.

Replicated data from Active Directory is stored in Active Directory Application Mode. Queues store messages that are being processed, and logs are used primarily for historical reference and troubleshooting. Replicated data, queues, and logs are not essential to restoring Edge Transport server functionality. Replicated data can be resynchronized as necessary, and both queues and logs are created automatically as necessary.

If you have applied custom settings to an Edge Transport server (for example, for content filtering), you can create a backup of the configuration through cloning.

Cloning Edge Transport Server Configurations

Edge Transport server settings are configured by information from the web (for example, anti-spam updates) or are replicated from Active Directory through the EdgeSync process. If you have not modified or customized these settings, you do not need to back up Edge Transport server data. In this case, you can fully recover edge transport services by setting up a new Edge Transport server. If, however, you modify or customize settings, you need to clone the configuration to capture your changes.

Two scripts exist in the C:\Program Files\Microsoft\Exchange Server\Scripts directory on an Edge Transport server. When you run the ExportEdgeConfig.ps1 script, Exchange exports all user-configured settings and stores the data in an extensible markup language (XML) file. When you copy this XML file (or a backup of the XML file) to a new Edge Transport server and run the ImportEdgeConfig.ps1 script, Exchange imports the user-configured settings saved in the in the XML file.

Creating the Configuration XML File

The step-by-step procedure to create the configuration XML file is as follows:

1. Copy the ExportEdgeConfig.ps1 script from the C:\Program Files\Microsoft\Exchange Server\Scripts directory to the root folder of your user profile on the source Edge Transport server.

2. Export the server configuration data by using the ExportEdgeConfig.ps1 script on the source server. To do this, you enter an EMS command with the following syntax:

   ```
   ./ExportEdgeConfig -CloneConfigData:"<path of the XML file to be created>"
   ```

3. The confirmation message "Edge configuration data is exported successfully to: <path of the XML file to be created>" appears. Copy the XML file to the target server.

Creating an XML Answer File and Importing Configuration Settings

The ImportEdgeConfig.ps1 script checks the XML file to see whether the server-specific settings are valid for the target Edge Transport server. If any settings need to be modified, the script writes the invalid settings to an XML answer file that you can use to modify the target server information in the XML configuration file. During the import configuration step, the script imports the user-configured settings and data stored in the XML file. The step-by-step procedure to validate a configuration file and create an answer file is as follows:

1. Copy the ImportEdgeConfig.ps1 script from the C:\Program Files\Microsoft\Exchange Server\Scripts directory to the root folder of your user profile on the target Edge Transport server.

2. Validate the configuration file and create an answer file that enables you to modify any settings that are listed as invalid on the target server by using the ImportEdgeConfig .ps1 script. To do this, enter an EMS command with the following syntax:

   ```
   ./ImportEdgeConfig -CloneConfigData:"<path of the XML file you have copied from
   the source server>" -IsImport $false -CloneConfigAnswer:"<path of the XML answer
   file used to configure server-specific settings>"
   ```

3. The confirmation message "Answer file is successfully created" appears. Open the answer file and modify any settings that are invalid for the target server. If no modifications are required, the answer file will have no entries. Save your changes.

When you have created an answer file and made any required modifications, you then import the configuration settings in the XML file you copied from the source server, modified by the settings in the answer file. To do this, enter an EMS command with the following syntax:

```
./ImportEdgeConfig -CloneConfigData:"<path of the XML file you have copied from the
source server>" -IsImport $true -CloneConfigAnswer:"<path of the XML answer file used to
configure server-specific settings>"
```

The confirmation message "Importing Edge configuration information succeeded" appears.

> **MORE INFO EDGE TRANSPORT SERVER CLONED CONFIGURATION**
>
> For more information about cloning Edge Transport server configurations, see *http:// technet.microsoft.com/en-us/library/aa998622.aspx*.

Lesson Summary

- You can recover Hub Transport servers, Client Access servers, and Unified Messaging servers almost completely by running Setup on the Exchange Server 2010 installation media in Recoverserver mode.

- You can recover the Mailbox server role by running Setup on the Exchange Server 2010 installation media in Recoverserver mode, but you also need to restore the Exchange databases from backup.

- If a Mailbox server is part of a DAG, you need to delete the server configuration and the associated database replicas from the DAG before recovering the server. You join the recovered server to the DAG and reconfigure the database replicas.

- You cannot recover the Edge Transport server role by running Setup on the Exchange Server 2010 installation media in Recoverserver mode. To provide backup support for custom settings on an Edge Transport server, you need to clone the server.

Lesson Review

You can use the following questions to test your knowledge of the information in Lesson 2, "Recovering Exchange Roles." The questions are also available on the companion CD if you prefer to review them in electronic form.

> **NOTE ANSWERS**
>
> Answers to these questions and explanations of why each answer choice is correct or incorrect are located in the "Answers" section at the end of the book.

1. You are cloning the configuration of Edge Transport server DEN-EDGE1 on server DEN-EDGE2. You generate the XML configuration file MyEdgeConfig.xml on DEN-EDGE1 and copy it into the C:\Cloning directory on DEN-EDGE2. You generate the answer file MyEdgeAnswer.xml in the C:\Cloning directory on DEN-EDGE2 and modify settings in that answer file that are invalid for the target server DEN-EDGE2. You have copied the ImportEdgeConfig.ps1 script into the appropriate directory. What EMS command do you run on DEN-EDGE2 to import the DEN-EDGE1 configuration settings?

    A. ./ImportEdgeConfig –CloneConfigData: "C:\Cloning\MyEdgeAnswer.xml" -IsImport $true -CloneConfigAnswer: "C:\Cloning\MyEdgeConfig.xml"

    B. ./ImportEdgeConfig –CloneConfigData: "C:\Cloning\MyEdgeAnswer.xml" -IsImport $false -CloneConfigAnswer: "C:\Cloning\MyEdgeConfig.xml"

    C. ./ImportEdgeConfig –CloneConfigData: "C:\Cloning\MyEdgeConfig.xml" -IsImport $true -CloneConfigAnswer: "C:\Cloning\MyEdgeAnswer.xml"

    D. ./ImportEdgeConfig –CloneConfigData: "C:\Cloning\MyEdgeConfig.xml" -IsImport $false -CloneConfigAnswer: "C:\Cloning\MyEdgeAnswer.xml"

2. You are recovering the Hub Transport server role on a replacement server. Which of the following procedures do you use?

    A. Insert the media containing the operating system that was installed on the failed server into the replacement server. Open the Command Prompt window and navigate to the directory that contains the installation media. Enter the *Setup /m:Recoverserver* command in the Command Prompt window.

    B. Insert the media containing the edition of Exchange Server 2010 that was installed on the failed server into the replacement server. Open the Command Prompt window and navigate to the directory that contains the installation media. Enter the *Setup /m:Recoverserver* command in the Command Prompt window.

    C. Insert the media containing the operating system that was installed on the failed server into the replacement server. Open the Command Prompt window and navigate to the directory that contains the installation media. Enter the *Setup /RecoverCMS* command in the Command Prompt window.

    D. Insert the media containing the edition of Exchange Server 2010 that was installed on the failed server into the replacement server. Open the Command Prompt window and navigate to the directory that contains the installation media. Enter the *Setup /RecoverCMS* command in the Command Prompt window.

3. You have recovered a member server named VAN-EX1 in a DAG and need to reconfigure a mailbox database copy of the Research database. You know that this mailbox database copy previously had replay lag time of two days and a truncation

lag time of three days. What EMS command do you enter to reconfigure this mailbox database copy?

    A. *Add-MailboxDatabaseCopy -Identity Research -MailboxServer VAN-EX1 -ReplayLagTime 2.00:00:00 -TruncationLagTime 3.00:00:00*

    B. *Add-MailboxDatabaseCopy -Identity Research -MailboxServer VAN-EX1 -ReplayLagTime 2:00:00:00 -TruncationLagTime 3:00:00:00*

    C. *Add-MailboxDatabaseCopy -Identity Research -MailboxServer VAN-EX1 -ReplayLagTime 2.00.00.00 -TruncationLagTime 3.00.00.00*

    D. *Add-MailboxDatabaseCopy -Identity Research -MailboxServer VAN-EX1 -ReplayLagTime 3.00:00:00 -TruncationLagTime 2.00:00:00*

4. The configuration for which server role is not stored in Active Directory and cannot be recovered by using the *Setup /m:RecoverServer* command?

    A. Edge Transport

    B. Client Access

    C. Mailbox

    D. Hub Transport

PRACTICE   **Using Windows Server Backup**

In this practice session, you install Windows Server Backup on the Mailbox server VAN-EX1 and carry out a manual full backup.

EXERCISE 1   **Installing Windows Server Backup**

Typically, Windows Server Backup is not installed by default on a Mailbox server. If Windows Server Backup has already been installed on your VAN-EX1 Mailbox server, you do not need to carry out this exercise. To install Windows Server Backup, carry out the following procedure:

1. Log on to the Mailbox server VAN-EX1 using the Kim Akers account.

2. Click Start and then click Server Manager.

3. Click Features and then click Add Features.

4. In the Add Features Wizard, expand Windows Server Backup Features and select Windows Server Backup and Command Line Utilities, as shown in Figure 14-13.

5. Click Next. On the Confirm Installation Selections page, click Install.

6. Installation proceeds. When it is complete, the Installation Results page, shown in Figure 14-14, appears. Note that Windows Automatic Updating cannot be enabled on your isolated test network. You would enable this feature on a production network.

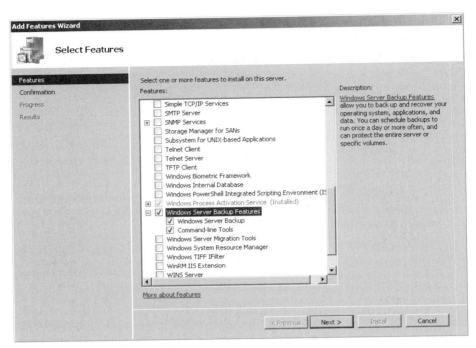

FIGURE 14-13 The Add Features Wizard

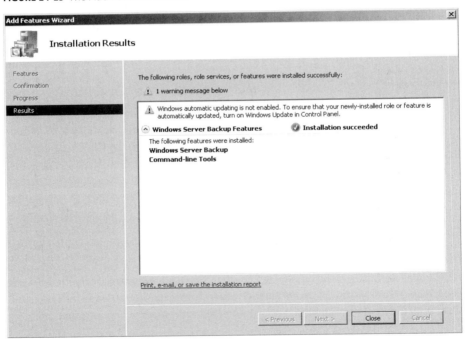

FIGURE 14-14 The Installation Results page

7. Click Close.

EXERCISE 2 Backing Up Exchange Server

In this exercise, you use Windows Server Backup to perform a manual full backup of Mailbox server VAN-EX1. Windows Server Backup needs to be installed on VAN-EX1 before you proceed with this exercise. You can choose to backup to a DVD drive, an internal or an external hard disk, or a network share. Carry out the following procedure:

1. Log on to the Mailbox server VAN-EX1 using the Kim Akers account.

2. Click Start, click Administrative Tools, and then click Windows Server Backup.

3. On the Actions pane of the Windows Server Backup dialog box, shown in Figure 14-15, click Backup Once. This starts the Backup Once Wizard.

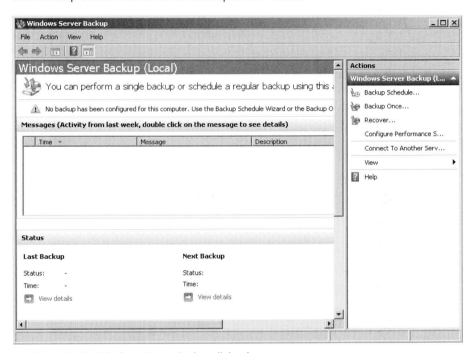

FIGURE 14-15 the Windows Server Backup dialog box

4. Select Different Options on the Backup Options page, shown in Figure 14-16. Click Next.

5. On the Select Backup Configuration page, select Custom, as shown in Figure 14-17. Click Next.

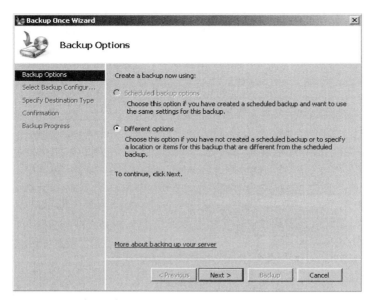

FIGURE 14-16 The Backup Options page

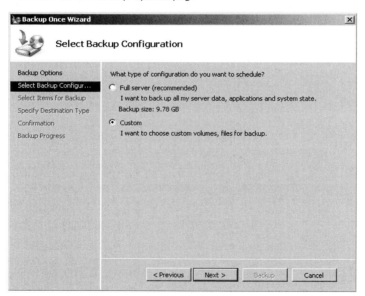

FIGURE 14-17 The Select Backup Configuration page

6. On the Select Items For Backup page, click Add Items. On the Select Items page, select the items you want to back up—for example, Local Disk (C:)—as shown in Figure 14-18. Click OK.

7. Click Next on the Select Items For Backup page.

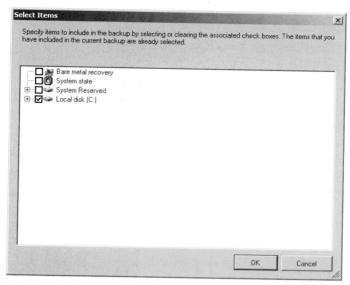

FIGURE 14-18 The Select Items For Backup page

8. Select the location where you want to store the backup on the Specify Destination Type page, shown in Figure 14-19. Click Next.

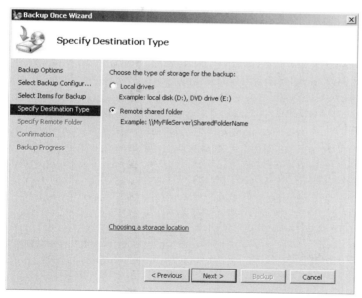

FIGURE 14-19 The Specify Destination Type page

9. If you select Remote Shared Folder, you need to specify a UNC path for the backup files and then select Inherit if you want the backup to be accessible by everyone who has access to the remote folder. Alternatively, select Do Not Inherit if you want the

backup to be accessed by specifying predefined user credentials. These settings are available on the Specify Remote Folder page, shown in Figure 14-20. Click Next.

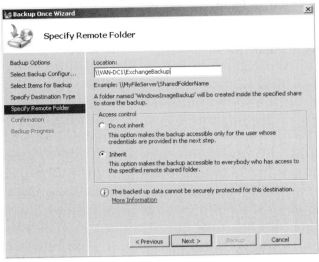

FIGURE 14-20 The Specify Remote Folder page

10. If required, select VSS Full Backup on the Specify Advanced Options page and click Next. If you back up to a network share, this option is already selected, and this step is not required.

11. Click Backup on the Confirmation page. Click Close on the Backup Progress page, shown in Figure 14-21, when the backup is complete. If you want to, you can click Close before backup completes, and backup will proceed in the background while you perform other tasks.

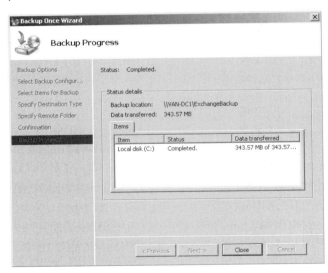

FIGURE 14-21 The Backup Progress page

In this optional practice session, you will format the hard disk on the Hub Transport server VAN-EX2 and then recover the server.

EXERCISE   **Recovering Hub Transport Server VAN-EX2**

In this exercise, you will reformat the hard disk on server VAN-EX2. If you are using a virtual computer to host this server, you should not delete this computer, as this would remove its account from Active Directory. Carry out the following procedure:

1. Log on to the Hub Transport server VAN-EX2 using the Kim Akers account.

2. Format the hard disk drive on VAN-EX1 that contains the operating system.

3. Log on to the domain controller VAN-DC1 using the Kim Akers account and open Active Directory Users And Computers.

4. Expand Adatum.com, click Computers, and then right-click VAN-EX2, as shown in Figure 14-22.

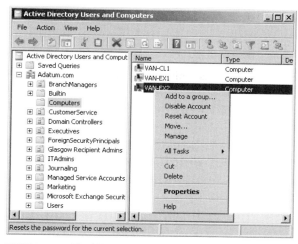

FIGURE 14-22 The VAN-EX2 computer account

5. Reset the VAN-EX2 computer account.

6. Install Windows Server 2008 R2 on the newly formatted computer, as described in the Appendix. Ensure that you use the same installation media and install exactly the same operating system that you installed when you originally set up the server.

7. Assign the computer the name VAN-EX2 and join it to the Adatum.com domain.

8. Log on to the member server VAN-EX2 using the Kim Akers account.

9. Remove the operating system installation media and insert the installation media you used to install Exchange Server 2010 Enterprise when you originally set up the computer.

10. If an Autorun box appears, close it.

11. Open the Command Prompt window and access the volume on the computer that holds the installation media.

12. Enter the following command:

    ```
    Setup /m:RecoverServer
    ```

13. When the recover routine completes, open the EMC on VAN-EX2.

14. On the Console pane, expand Server Configuration. Check that the Hub Transport server role is installed.

Chapter Review

To further practice and reinforce the skills you learned in this chapter, you can perform the following tasks:

- Review the chapter summary.
- Review the list of key terms introduced in this chapter.
- Complete the case scenarios. These scenarios set up real-world situations involving the topics of this chapter and ask you to create a solution.
- Complete the suggested practices.
- Take a practice test.

Chapter Summary

- Windows Server Backup is Exchange aware and lets you perform a VSS backup and restore Exchange data.
- You can restore all mailbox databases to an original location or one or more selected databases to an alternate location. You can move restored data to an RDB for recovery. Dial tone recovery minimizes user downtime when a corrupted database cannot be mounted.
- You can reconnect a disconnected mailbox within the deleted mailbox retention time, and users can retrieve deleted items in a mailbox within the deleted item retention time without needing to restore from backup.
- You can recover Hub Transport servers, Client Access servers, and Unified Messaging servers by running Setup in Recoverserver mode. Recovering a Mailbox server also requires restoring data from backup. You can implement failover support for Edge Transport servers through cloning.

Key Terms

Do you know what these key terms mean?

- Copy backup
- Database availability group (DAG)
- Deleted item retention time
- Deleted mailbox retention time
- Differential backup
- Edge server cloning
- Full backup
- Incremental backup
- Point-in-time backup

- Recoverserver mode
- Volume Shadow Copy Service (VSS)

Case Scenarios

In the following case scenarios, you apply what you've learned about subjects covered in this chapter. You can find answers to these questions in the "Answers" section at the end of this book.

Case Scenario 1: Recovering Mailbox Data

You are the senior Exchange Administrator at Margie's Travel. All the company's Exchange servers run Exchange Server 2010 Enterprise edition and Windows Server 2008 R2 Enterprise operating systems. Answer the following questions:

1. The mailbox for the user Don Hall has become disconnected, possibly because of an error by one of your junior administrators. This happened at some time in the past few hours. You determine that the user account still exists in Active Directory. You know that the mailbox was in the mailbox database named Marketing. How do you restore the email service to this user?

2. The mailbox database named Accounting has become corrupt and cannot be mounted. Members of the Accounting Department cannot currently receive or send email messages. How can you minimize disruption of service experienced by these users?

Case Scenario 2: Restoring a Client Access Server

You are the senior Exchange Administrator at Tailspin Toys. All the company's Exchange servers run Exchange Server 2010 Enterprise edition and the Windows Server 2008 R2 Enterprise operating system. Your single Client Access server has crashed, and you need to restore it. Answer the following questions:

1. You restore the failed server running the Client Access server role to its initial default state by running Exchange Setup in Recoverserver mode. What custom configurations are not restored by this procedure?

2. Where are these changes stored?

3. What type of certificate needs to be installed on the recovered Client Access server?

Suggested Practices

To help you master the examination objectives presented in this chapter, complete the following tasks.

Carry Out a Trial Restore

- **Practice 1** Perform a manual full server backup and restore all your Exchange data to its original location. Note that you would not normally do this on a production system, on which you would typically create a trial network in a different Active Directory forest for trial restores.

Implement Scheduled Backups

- **Practice 1** Create a backup plan and implement a backup schedule that creates full and incremental backups as dictated by that plan. Check the times and dates of your backup files to ensure that backups are being created according to the schedule.

Restore a Single Database

- **Practice 1** Restore a single database to an alternate location and move the restored data into an RDB. You can restore a database that has lost data but is still online, or you can perform a dial tone restore of an offline database. Merge the data in the RDB with the data in the database you want to recover.

Reconnect a Mailbox

- **Practice 1** Disconnect a user mailbox and reconnect it within the mailbox retention period. Use both the EMC and the EMS to carry out this task.

Recover a Client Access Server

- **Practice 1** Create a Client Access server in the Adatum.com domain and obtain a self-signed SSL certificate from the Adatum.com CA (if VAN-DC1 does not have the Enterprise CA role installed, then install it). Format the Client Access server's system hard disk and then recover this server role. Reapply for the SSL certificate.

Clone an Edge Transport Server (Optional)

- **Practice 1** Optionally, create two Edge Transport servers on your test network and apply some custom configuration settings on one of them. Clone these settings to the second Edge Transport server.

Take a Practice Test

The practice tests on this book's companion CD offer many options. For example, you can test yourself on just one exam objective, or you can test yourself on all the 70-662 certification exam content. You can set up the test so that it closely simulates the experience of taking a certification exam, or you can set it up in study mode so that you can look at the correct answers and explanations after you answer each question.

> **MORE INFO PRACTICE TESTS**
>
> For details about all the practice test options available, see the "How to Use the Practice Tests" section in this book's Introduction.

Setup Instructions for Exchange Server 2010

This set of exercises contains abbreviated instructions for setting up VAN-DC, VAN-EX1, and VAN-EX2 computers used in the practice exercises in all chapters of this Training Kit except Chapter 1, "Installing Exchange Server 2010." To perform these exercises, first install Windows Server 2008 R2 Enterprise edition using the default configuration, setting the administrator password to *Pa$$w0rd*.

EXERCISE 1   Prepare a computer to function as a Windows Server 2008 R2 domain controller in an Exchange environment

1. Log on to the first computer that you have installed Windows Server 2008 R2 on using the Administrator account and the password *Pa$$w0rd*.

2. Open an elevated command prompt and issue the following commands:

   ```
   Netsh interface ipv4 set address "Local Area Connection" static 10.10.0.10
   ```

3. Enter the following command:

   ```
   netdom renamecomputer %computername% /newname:VAN-DC
   ```

4. Restart the computer and log back on using the Administrator account.

5. Click Start. In the Search Programs and Files Textbox, type the following:

   ```
   Dcpromo
   ```

6. When the Active Directory Domain Services Installation Wizard starts, click Next twice.

7. On the Choose A Deployment Configuration page, choose Create A New Domain In A New Forest and then click Next.

8. On the Name The Forest Root Domain, enter **Adatum.com** and then click Next.

9. On the Forest Functional Level page, set the Forest Functional Level to Windows Server 2008 and then click Next.

10. On the Set Domain Functional Level page, ensure that Windows Server 2008 is set and then click Next.

11. On the Additional Domain Controller Options page, ensure that the DNS server option is checked and then click Next. When presented with the warning describing that the delegation for the DNS server cannot be created, click Yes when asked if you want to continue.

12. Accept the default settings for the Database, Log Files, and SYSVOL locations and click Next.

13. In the Directory Services Restore Mode Administrator Password dialog box, enter the password **Pa$$w0rd** twice and then click Next.

14. On the Summary page, click Next to begin the installation of Active Directory Domain Services on computer VAN-DC. When the wizard completes, click Finish. When prompted, click Restart Now to reboot computer VAN-DC.

EXERCISE 2 **Prepare Active Directory for the installation of Exchange**

1. Log on to server VAN-DC using the Administrator account.

2. Using Active Directory Users and Computers, create a user account named Kim_Akers in the Users container and assign the account the password *Pa$$w0rd*. Configure the password to never expire. Add this user account to the Enterprise Admins, Domain Admins, and Schema Admins groups.

3. Open an elevated command prompt and navigate to the directory that contains the Exchange Server 2010 setup files.

4. In the elevated command prompt, run the following command:

```
Setup /PrepareSchema
```

5. Ensure that you do not press a key unless you want to cancel the process. Setup will begin to extend the Active Directory Domain Services schema.

6. Run the following command and ensure that you do not press any keys until Active Directory preparation completes:

```
Setup /PrepareAD /OrganizationName:AdatumOrg
```

7. Add the Kim Akers user account that you created earlier to the Organization Management group in the Microsoft Exchange Security Groups container.

8. From the elevated command prompt, run the following command:

```
Setup /PrepareAllDomains
```

9. When this command completes, verify that the Microsoft Exchange System Objects container has been created and that the Exchange Install Domain Servers security group is located within this container.

10. Open the DNS Console and create a reverse lookup zone for the subnet 10.10.0.x.

EXERCISE 3   Preparing a computer and joining it to the domain

1. Ensure that computer VAN-DC is powered on and connected to the network or virtual network to which the second computer is connected.

2. Log on to the second computer that you have installed Windows Server 2008 R2 on using the Administrator account and the password *Pa$$w0rd*.

3. Open an elevated command prompt and issue the following commands:

    ```
    Netsh interface ipv4 set address "Local Area Connection" static 10.10.0.20
    ```

    ```
    Netsh interface ipv4 set dnsservers "Local Area Connection" static 10.10.0.10
    primary
    ```

4. Enter the following command:

    ```
    netdom renamecomputer %computername% /newname:VAN-EX1
    ```

5. Restart the computer and then log on again using the Administrator account.

6. From an elevated command prompt, issue the following command:

    ```
    netdom join VAN-EX1 /domain:adatum
    ```

7. Restart the computer. When the computer restarts, log on as adatum\Administrator.

8. Transfer the Office System Converter: Microsoft Filter Pack x64 installation file to VAN-EX1. Double-click on this installation file to commence installation. Click Next in the dialog box and accept the license terms, and then the filter pack will install.

9. Open an elevated PowerShell session and then enter the following commands:

    ```
    Import-Module ServerManager
    ```

    ```
    Add-WindowsFeature NET-Framework,RSAT-ADDS,Web-Server,Web-Basic-Auth,
    Web-Windows-Auth,Web-Metabase,Web-Net-Ext,Web-Lgcy-Mgmt-Console,
    WAS-Process-Model,RSAT-Web-Server,Web-ISAPI-Ext,Web-Digest-Auth,
    Web-Dyn-Compression,NET-HTTP-Activation,RPC-Over-HTTP-Proxy
    ```

10. Restart computer VAN-EX1 and log on using the Adatum\Administrator account:

    ```
    Import-Module ServerManager
    ```

    ```
    Set-Service -Name NetTcpPortSharing -StartupType Automatic
    ```

EXERCISE 4   Install Exchange Server 2010 in the default configuration

1. Log on to computer VAN-EX1 with the Adatum\Kim_Akers user account.

2. Use Windows Explorer to navigate to the location of the Exchange installation files. Run Setup.exe. When prompted, click Yes in the User Account Control dialog box.

3. On the splash screen, click on Step 3: Choose Exchange Language Option. Click on the Install Only Languages From The DVD option.

4. Click on Step 4: Install Microsoft Exchange. On the Introduction page, click Next.

5. On the License Agreement page, click on I Accept The Terms In The License Agreement and then click Next.

6. On the Error Reporting page, ensure that No is selected and then click Next.

7. On the Exchange Server 2010 Setup page, ensure that Typical Exchange Server Installation is selected and then click Next.

8. On the Client Settings page, select No when asked whether you have client computers running Outlook 2003 or Entourage and then click Next.

9. On the Configure Client Access Server External Domain page, ensure that The Client Access Server Role Will Be Internet Facing option is not selected and then click Next.

10. On the Customer Experience Improvement Program page, select I Don't Wish To Join The Program At This Time and then click Next.

11. The readiness checks will now run. Verify that all readiness checks complete successfully and then click Install.

12. When setup completes, verify that all stages of the setup are marked as Completed. Click on View Setup Log to view the Exchange setup log in Notepad. Review the contents of this log by clicking on View Setup and then close the log. Click Finish.

13. On the Exchange Server Setup splash screen, click Close.

EXERCISE 5   Preparing a second computer and joining it to the domain

1. Ensure that computer VAN-DC is powered on and connected to the network or virtual network to which the second computer is connected.

2. Log on to the second computer that you have installed Windows Server 2008 R2 on using the Administrator account and the password *Pa$$w0rd*.

3. Open an elevated command prompt and issue the following commands:

   ```
   Netsh interface ipv4 set address "Local Area Connection" static 10.10.0.21

   Netsh interface ipv4 set dnsservers "Local Area Connection" static 10.10.0.10
   primary
   ```

4. Enter the following command:

   ```
   netdom renamecomputer %computername% /newname:VAN-EX2
   ```

5. Restart the computer and then log on again using the Administrator account.

6. From an elevated command prompt, issue the following command:

   ```
   netdom join VAN-EX2 /domain:adatum
   ```

7. Restart the computer. When the computer restarts, log on as adatum\Administrator.

8. Transfer the Office System Converter: Microsoft Filter Pack x64 installation file to VAN-EX1. Double-click on this installation file to commence installation. Click Next in the dialog box and accept the license terms, and then the filter pack will install.

9. Open an elevated PowerShell session and then enter the following commands:

```
Import-Module ServerManager

Add-WindowsFeature NET-Framework,RSAT-ADDS,Web-Server,Web-Basic-Auth,
Web-Windows-Auth,Web-Metabase,Web-Net-Ext,Web-Lgcy-Mgmt-Console,
WAS-Process-Model,RSAT-Web-Server,Web-ISAPI-Ext,Web-Digest-Auth,
Web-Dyn-Compression,NET-HTTP-Activation,RPC-Over-HTTP-Proxy
```

10. Restart computer VAN-EX2 and log on using the Adatum\Administrator account:

```
Import-Module ServerManager

Set-Service -Name NetTcpPortSharing -StartupType Automatic
```

11. Use the Server Manager Console to add the Adatum\Kim_Akers user account to the local Administrators group on VAN-EX2.

12. Shut down the server.

EXERCISE 6   Install Exchange Server 2010 on VAN EX2 in the default configuration

1. Log on to computer VAN-EX2 with the Adatum\Kim_Akers user account.

2. Use Windows Explorer to navigate to the location of the Exchange installation files. Run Setup.exe. When prompted, click Yes in the User Account Control dialog box.

3. On the splash screen, click on Step 3: Choose Exchange Language Option. Click on the Install Only Languages From The DVD option.

4. Click on Step 4: Install Microsoft Exchange. On the Introduction page, click Next.

5. On the License Agreement Page, click on I Accept The Terms In The License Agreement and then click Next.

6. On the Error Reporting page, ensure that No is selected and then click Next.

7. On the Exchange Server 2010 Setup page, ensure that Typical Exchange Server Installation is selected and then click Next.

8. On the Configure Client Access Server External Domain page, ensure that The Client Access Server Role Will Be Internet Facing option is not selected and then click Next.

9. On the Customer Experience Improvement Program page, select I Don't Wish To Join The Program At This Time and then click Next.

10. The readiness checks will now run. Verify that all readiness checks complete successfully and then click Install.

11. When setup completes, verify that all stages of the setup are marked as Completed. Click on View Setup Log to view the Exchange setup log in Notepad. Review the contents of this log by clicking on View Setup and then close the log. Click Finish.

EXERCISE 7   Create an Exchange mailbox for the Kim Akers user account

1. Log on to computer VAN-EX1 with the Adatum\Kim_Akers user account.

2. Open Exchange Management Shell.

3. Issue the following command:

```
New-MailboxDatabase -Server 'VAN-EX1' -Name 'MBX-DB-ALPHA' -EdbFilePath
'c:\Program Files\Microsoft\Exchange Server\V14\Mailbox\MBX-DB-ALPHA\MBX-DB-ALPHA
.edb' -LogFolderPath 'c:\Program Files\Microsoft\Exchange Server\V14\Mailbox\
MBX-DB-ALPHA'
```

4. Verify whether the Kim Akers user account has an associated mailbox. If the account does not have an associated mailbox, issue the following command:

```
Enable-Mailbox -Identity 'adatum.com/Users/Kim Akers' -Alias 'Kim_Akers' -Database
'MBX-DB-ALPHA'
```

Answers

Chapter 1: Lesson Review Answers

Lesson 1

1. **Correct Answer: B**
   - **A.** **Incorrect:** It is not necessary to run *Setup /PrepareLegacyExchangePermissions* if your organization has an existing Exchange Server 2010 deployment.
   - **B.** **Correct:** It is necessary to run *Setup /PrepareLegacyExchangePermissions* only if your organization has an existing Exchange Server 2003 organization.
   - **C.** **Incorrect:** It is not necessary to run *Setup /PrepareLegacyExchangePermissions* if your organization has an existing Exchange Server 2007 deployment.
   - **D.** **Incorrect:** It is not necessary to run *Setup /PrepareLegacyExchangePermissions* if your organization has not previously deployed Exchange.

2. **Correct Answer: C**
   - **A.** **Incorrect:** You should not upgrade the domain controllers to Windows Server 2008, as this would require unnecessary administrative effort. Applying a service pack will prepare the site for the deployment of Exchange Server 2010.
   - **B.** **Incorrect:** You should not upgrade the domain controllers to Windows Server 2008 R2. Applying a service pack will prepare the site for the deployment of Exchange Server 2010.
   - **C.** **Correct:** Prior to deploying Exchange Server 2010 to a site, you should ensure that the global catalog server at the site is running the Windows Server 2003 Service Pack 1 operating system or later.
   - **D.** **Incorrect:** You should not upgrade the domain controllers to Windows Server 2008 R2. Applying a service pack will prepare the site for the deployment of Exchange Server 2010.

3. **Correct Answer: D**
   - **A.** **Incorrect:** Servers that have Exchange Server 2003 installed must have Exchange Server 2003 Service Pack 2 applied to allow for coexistence with Exchange Server 2010.
   - **B.** **Incorrect:** It is not necessary to upgrade the host platform to Windows Server 2008 to allow for coexistence with Exchange Server 2010. Exchange Server 2003 cannot be installed on Windows Server 2008.
   - **C.** **Incorrect:** It is not necessary to upgrade the host platform to Windows Server 2008 to allow for coexistence with Exchange Server 2010.
   - **D.** **Correct:** Servers that have Exchange Server 2003 installed must have Exchange Server 2003 Service Pack 2 applied to allow for coexistence with Exchange Server 2010.

4. **Correct Answer: A**

   A. **Correct:** You suppress minor link state updates by editing the registry on every Exchange Server 2003.

   B. **Incorrect:** You cannot suppress minor link state updates by using Exchange Management Console.

   C. **Incorrect:** You cannot suppress minor link state updates by using Exchange Management Shell.

   D. **Incorrect:** Although you can use Exchange System Manager to manage an Exchange Server 2003 organization, you cannot use this tool to suppress minor link state updates.

5. **Correct Answer: A**

   A. **Correct:** You can use the *command dsquery server –hasfsmo schema* command to determine which computer holds the Schema Master role.

   B. **Incorrect:** You cannot use the dsget command-line utility to determine which computer in the organization hosts the Schema Master role. Dsget provides information about specific objects but does not query Active Directory for information about specific FSMO roles.

   C. **Incorrect:** The dsadd utility is used to add objects to Active Directory. It cannot be used to determine which computer holds the Schema Master role.

   D. **Incorrect:** The dsmod utility is used to modify objects in Active Directory. You cannot use this utility to determine which computer holds the Schema Master role.

Lesson 2

1. **Correct Answers: A and C**

   A. **Correct:** The Office System Converter: Microsoft Filter Pack is used with the Mailbox and Hub Transport roles.

   B. **Incorrect:** The Client Access role does not utilize the Office System Converter: Microsoft Filter Pack.

   C. **Correct:** The Office System Converter: Microsoft Filter Pack is used with the Mailbox and Hub Transport roles.

   D. **Incorrect:** The Edge Transport role does not utilize the Office System Converter: Microsoft Filter Pack.

2. **Correct Answer: B**

   A. **Incorrect:** You cannot install Exchange Server 2010 on computers running the Windows Server 2003 or Windows Server 2003 R2 operating system.

   B. **Correct:** You can install Exchange Server 2010 on a computer running Windows Server 2008 Standard edition as long as it is the x64 version and has Service Pack 2 installed.

   C. **Incorrect:** You cannot install Exchange Server 2010 on a computer running an x86 version of Windows Server 2008.

   D. **Incorrect:** You cannot install Exchange Server 2010 on computers running the Windows Server 2003 or Windows Server 2003 R2 operating system.

3. **Correct Answer: C**

   A. **Incorrect:** It is not necessary to install Silverlight 3 to install the Hub Transport server role.

   B. **Incorrect:** It is not necessary to install Microsoft Data Engine (MSDE) to install the Hub Transport server role. MSDE has been replaced by the Windows Internal Database feature on computers running Windows Server 2008.

   C. **Correct:** You should ensure that the Office System Converter: Microsoft Filter Pack component is installed on a computer running the Windows Server 2008 R2 Enterprise Edition (x64) operating system.

   D. **Incorrect:** The Microsoft Office Outlook Connector 12.1 or later is used to allow users of Microsoft Office Outlook to access Microsoft Windows Live Hotmail or Microsoft Office Live Mail accounts. It is not necessary to install this component to support the Hub Transport server role.

4. **Correct Answers: A and C**

   A. **Correct:** You need to install the .NET Framework feature to support Exchange Server 2010.

   B. **Incorrect:** You do not need to add the SMTP feature to support Exchange Server 2010.

   C. **Correct:** You need to ensure that the Net.Tcp Port Sharing service is set to start automatically to support Exchange Server 2010.

   D. **Incorrect:** You do not need to configure the SNMP Trap service to support Exchange Server 2010.

Lesson 3

1. **Correct Answer: C**

   A. **Incorrect:** *Setup.com /PrepareTopology* is used to prepare Active Directory. The command cannot be used to allow a user who is a member of the Delegated Setup role to install Exchange Server 2010.

   B. **Incorrect:** The *Setup.com /RemoveProvisionedServer:SYD-MBX02* command.

   C. **Correct:** You must run the *Setup /NewProvisionedServer:SYD-MBX02* command to provision SYD-MBX02 so that it can be setup by a user who is a member of the Delegated Setup role group.

   D. **Incorrect:** You do not use the *Setup.com /mide:install* command to provision a server to allow a user who is a member of the Delegated Setup role to install Exchange Server 2010.

2. **Correct Answers: A, C, and D**

   A. **Correct:** You need to deploy the Hub Transport and Mailbox server roles to ensure that mail flow at each branch office site functions correctly.

   B. **Incorrect:** You do not need to deploy the Edge Transport server role at each site to ensure that mail flow or client access at each branch office site functions correctly.

   C. **Correct:** You need to deploy the Hub Transport and Mailbox server roles to ensure that mail flow at each branch office site functions correctly.

D. Correct: You need to deploy the Client Access server role at each site to ensure that client access at each branch office site functions correctly.

3. **Correct Answer: A**

    A. Correct: You can use the command *setup.com /mode:Install /role:HT,M* to install the Mailbox and Hub Transport server roles on an appropriately configured Windows Server 2008 R2 host.

    B. Incorrect: The command *setup.com /mode:Uninstall /role:HT,M* removes the Hub Transport and Mailbox server roles from a computer running Exchange Server 2010.

    C. Incorrect: The command *setup.com /mode:install /role:C,M* installs the Client Access and Mailbox server roles. It does not install the Hub Transport server role as specified in the question text.

    D. Incorrect: The command *setup.com /mode:Uninstall /role:C,M* removes the Client Access and Mailbox server roles from a computer running Exchange Server 2010.

4. **Correct Answer: D**

    A. Incorrect: You should not use the command *Setup.com /mode:Install /role:Mailbox*, as this will attempt to install the Mailbox server role on a computer that already has this role.

    B. Incorrect: You should not use the command *Setup.com /mode:Uninstall /role:Mailbox*, as this will remove the Mailbox server role when you wanted to retain this role on the branch office server.

    C. Incorrect: You should not use the command *Setup.com /mode:Install / role:ClientAccess,HubTransport*, as this command attempts to install the Client Access and Hub Transport server roles rather than remove these roles as specified in the question text.

    D. Correct: The command *Setup.com /mode:Uninstall /role:ClientAccess,HubTransport* removes the Client Access and Hub Transport server roles from an existing computer running Exchange Server 2010.

5. **Correct Answer: C**

    A. Incorrect: The *Test-SystemHealth* cmdlet allows you to gather information about an Exchange Server system so that it can be used for an analysis of the data with respect to best practices. This cmdlet does not provide you with a list of roles deployed in a specific server that hosts Exchange Server 2010.

    B. Incorrect: The *Set-ExchangeServer* cmdlet allows you to configure attributes within Active Directory for a particular server. This cmdlet does not provide you with a list of roles deployed in a specific server that hosts Exchange Server 2010.

    C. Correct: The *Get-ExchangeServer* cmdlet can be used to verify which roles have been deployed to a specific computer that has Exchange Server 2010 installed.

    D. Incorrect: The *Test-ServiceHealth* cmdlet allows you to verify that all Microsoft Windows services that Exchange Server 2010 depends on have started properly. This cmdlet does not provide you with a list of roles deployed in a specific server that hosts Exchange Server 2010.

6. **Correct Answer: C**

   A. **Incorrect:** Users delegated the Discovery Management role can perform searches of mailboxes. They are unable to install Mailbox servers in an existing Exchange Server 2010 organization.

   B. **Incorrect:** Users delegated the Recipient Management role are able to create or modify recipients. They are unable to install Mailbox servers in an existing Exchange Server 2010 organization.

   C. **Correct:** A user needs to be delegated the Organization Management role if Exchange Server 2010 Mailbox servers are to be installed in an Active Directory forest where Exchange Server 2010 has already been deployed.

   D. **Incorrect:** Users delegated the Public Folder Management role are able to manage public folders. They are unable to install Mailbox servers in an existing Exchange Server 2010 organization.

Chapter 1: Case Scenario Answers

Case Scenario 1: Preparing for the Deployment of Exchange 2010 at Contoso

1. You should run the command *Setup /PrepareSchema*. It is not necessary to run *Setup /PrepareLegacyExchangePermissions* at Contoso, as there is no Exchange Server 2003 organization.

2. You should install Exchange Server 2007 Service Pack 2 on the servers running Exchange Server 2007, as this is required for coexistence.

3. You should introduce an Exchange Server 2010 server with the Client Access role prior to installing other roles in the existing Exchange Server 2007 environment.

Case Scenario 2: Exchange Deployment at Fabrikam

1. The account used to run the *Setup /PrepareSchema* command must be a member of both the Schema Admins group and the Enterprise Admins group.

2. *Setup /PrepareSchema* must be run in the fabrikam.internal domain at the Melbourne site.

3. Laura's account must be a member of the Domain Admins group. Laura's account does not need to be a member of the Organization Administrators group, as the Victoria.fabrikam.internal domain existed prior to the decision to deploy Exchange Server 2010 being made. If the Victoria.fabrikam.internal domain was created after the *Setup /PrepareAD* command was run, it would be necessary for Laura's account to be a member of both the Organization Administrators group and the Domain Admins group.

Chapter 2: Lesson Review Answers

Lesson 1

1. **Correct Answer: C**
   - **A. Incorrect:** This command creates the database, and it is likely that you have already used it. It does not enable the database to be used to provision new mailboxes.
   - **B. Incorrect:** This command sets the database warning quota, and it is likely that you have already used it. It does not enable the database to be used to provision new mailboxes.
   - **C. Correct:** This command mounts the database. You need to mount the database to enable it to be used to provision new mailboxes.
   - **D. Incorrect:** This command dismounts the database. To enable the database to be used to provision new mailboxes, you need to mount it, not dismount it.

2. **Correct Answer: D**
   - **A. Incorrect:** You do not need to dismount a database before entering the command to move the path to its transaction logs. The *Move-DatabasePath* cmdlet automatically dismounts the database if it is mounted, moves the path, and then, if appropriate, mounts the database again.
   - **B. Incorrect:** You do not need to mount a database before moving its transaction log file path.
   - **C. Incorrect:** You can use the Set-MailboxDatabase cmdlet to configure most database properties but not to move file paths. You need to use the Move-Database Path cmdlet for this purpose.
   - **D. Correct:** This command moves the transaction logs to the required folder.

3. **Correct Answer: C**
   - **A. Incorrect:** You accomplish the required tasks by configuring a maintenance schedule. However, you cannot do this using the *Get-MailboxDatabase* cmdlet. Also, the times given in this answer are incorrect (10:15 to 11:45 AM).
   - **B. Incorrect:** This command schedules the exchange database maintenance tasks listed in the question to run each Saturday, not each Sunday.
   - **C. Correct:** This command schedules the exchange database maintenance tasks listed in the question to run each Sunday between 10:15 and 11:45 PM.
   - **D. Incorrect:** This command schedules the exchange database maintenance tasks listed in the question to run each Sunday between 10:15 and 11:45 AM.

4. **Correct Answer: D**
   - **A. Incorrect:** This command creates the public folder database. However, you have already done this. The *New-PublicFolderDatabase* cmdlet cannot be used to set an item retention period.
   - **B. Incorrect:** The *New-PublicFolderDatabase* cmdlet cannot be used to set an item retention period and does not support the ItemRetentionPeriod parameter.

C. **Incorrect:** The *Set-PublicFolderDatabase* cmdlet does not support the Server parameter and uses the Name parameter to change the name of a database. It requires that you identify the database using the Identity parameter.

D. **Correct:** This command sets the item retention period for the CompanyInformation public folder database.

Lesson 2

1. **Correct Answer: C**

   A. **Incorrect:** The location of the server that performs the OAB generation task is not considered to be an OAB property, and you cannot use the *Set-OfflineAddressBook* cmdlet to change it. The *Set-OfflineAddressBook* cmdlet does not support the Server parameter.

   B. **Incorrect:** The location of the server that performs the OAB generation task is not considered to be an OAB property, and you cannot use the *Set-OfflineAddressBook* cmdlet to change it. The *Set-OfflineAddressBook* cmdlet does not support the Server parameter.

   C. **Correct:** This command moves the generation task for the AdatumDenver OAB to the server DEN-EX2.

   D. **Incorrect:** The Server parameter of the *Move-OfflineAddressBook* cmdlet specifies the server to which you want to move the generation process. You do not need to specify the server on which the OAB is currently generated, and a syntax error is returned if you attempt to do so.

2. **Correct Answers: A and B**

   A. **Correct:** This command creates the address list ColoradoStaff as specified.

   B. **Correct:** This command creates the address list DenverStaff as a child of the ColoradoStaff address list.

   C. **Incorrect:** This command creates an address list named DenverStaff but not as a child of the ColoradoStaff address list.

   D. **Incorrect:** This command specifies the ColoradoStaff address list as a child of the DenverStaff address list when it should be the other way around.

3. **Correct Answer: B**

   A. **Incorrect:** This command creates an OAB that uses public folder distribution and is available to Outlook 2003 and other MAPI clients.

   B. **Correct:** This command creates an OAB named ColoradoOffline, based on the ColoradoStaff address list, generated on the server named DEN-EX1, and using web-based distribution. Because the OAB does not use public folder distribution, it is not available to Outlook 2003 and other MAPI clients.

   C. **Incorrect:** The *Set-OfflineAddressBook* cmdlet edits an existing OAB, and you cannot use it to create an OAB. The cmdlet does not support the Name parameter.

   D. **Incorrect:** The *Set-OfflineAddressBook* cmdlet edits an existing OAB, and you cannot use it to create an OAB. The cmdlet does not support the Name parameter.

4. **Correct Answer: D**

   A. **Incorrect:** The *Set-AddressList* cmdlet configures an existing address list. It does not create a new GAL.

   B. **Incorrect:** This command creates an address list called Blue Sky Airlines – All Employees. However, this address list is not a GAL.

   C. **Incorrect:** The *Set-GlobalAddressList* cmdlet configures an existing GAL. It does not create a new GAL.

   D. **Correct:** This command creates a GAL called Blue Sky Airlines – All Employees that includes all mailbox users employed by Blue Sky Airlines.

Chapter 2: Case Scenario Answers

Case Scenario 1: Creating a Mailbox Database

1. New-MailboxDatabase -Name Marketing –Server BSA-EX1 -EdbFilePath "C:\DatabaseFiles\ Marketing.edb" -LogFolderPath "D:\LogFiles\Marketing"

2. Set-MailboxDatabase –Identity Marketing –IssueWarningQuota 2GB –DeletedItemRetention 28

3. Mount-Database –Identity Marketing

Case Scenario 2: Creating an Address List and an OAB

1. New-AddressList –Name Sales-Coho-Vineyard-Addr –Container \ –IncludedRecipients MailboxUsers –ConditionalDepartment Sales –ConditionalCompany "Coho Vineyard"

2. Update-AddressList –Identity Sales-Coho-Vineyard-Addr

3. Don needs to use both the web-based distribution method and the public folder distribution method.

4. New-OfflineAddressBook –Name "Sales-Coho-Vineyard-Addr-OAB" –Server Coho-EX3 –AddressLists Sales-Coho-Vineyard-Addr –PublicFolderDistributionEnabled $true –VirtualDirectories "Coho-EX3 \OAB (Default Web Site)"

Chapter 3: Lesson Review Answers

Lesson 1

1. **Correct Answer: C**

   A. **Incorrect:** *Set-Mailbox* is used to configure mailbox properties but is not used to move mailboxes from one server to another.

B. **Incorrect:** *Move-Mailbox* is used to move mailboxes in previous versions of Exchange and is not used to move mailboxes in Exchange Server 2010.

C. **Correct:** The *New-MoveRequest* cmdlet is used to perform online mailbox moves from one Exchange Server 2010 Mailbox server to another Exchange Server 2010 Mailbox server.

D. **Incorrect:** *Get-Mailbox* is used to view the properties of a mailbox but is not used to move a mailbox.

2. **Correct Answer: C**

A. **Incorrect:** The *Add-MailboxPermission* command listed grants access to read the contents of a mailbox but not the Send As permission.

B. **Incorrect:** The *Add-MailboxPermission* command listed grants access to read the contents of a mailbox but not the Send As permission.

C. **Correct:** The *Add-ADPermission* command, run against Don Hall's mailbox and specifying Kim Akers as the user with the "Send As" extended right, grants Kim Akers Send As permission on Don Hall's mailbox.

D. **Incorrect:** This command would give Don Hall Send As permission on Kim Aker's mailbox rather than the other way around, as specified by the question.

3. **Correct Answer: D**

A. **Incorrect:** *New-Mailbox* can be used to create new mailboxes but cannot be used to connect disconnected mailboxes to Active Directory user accounts.

B. **Incorrect:** *Set-Mailbox* can be used to modify the properties of mailboxes but cannot be used to connect disconnected mailboxes to Active Directory user accounts.

C. **Incorrect:** *Enable-Mailbox* can be used to create new mailboxes for existing Active Directory user accounts but is not used to connect disconnected mailboxes to user accounts.

D. **Correct:** The *Connect-Mailbox* cmdlet is used to connect disconnected Exchange Mailboxes to Active Directory user accounts.

4. **Correct Answer: A**

A. **Correct:** This answer correctly specifies the MaxReceiveSize and MaxSendSize parameters, which are used to limit incoming and outgoing message sizes.

B. **Incorrect:** This answer incorrectly mentions the ProhibitSendQuota parameter, which is used in relation to mailbox quota but not outgoing or incoming message size restriction. This answer does limit send size to the correct value.

C. **Incorrect:** This answer incorrectly mentions the ProhibitSendQuota parameter, which is used in relation to mailbox quota but not outgoing or incoming message size restriction. This answer does limit receive size to the correct value.

D. **Incorrect:** This answer incorrectly mentions the IssueWarningQuota and ProhibitSendQuota parameters, which are used in relation to mailbox quota but not for incoming our outgoing message size restriction.

5. **Correct Answer: B**

   A. **Incorrect:** The SCLQuarantineEnabled and SCLQuarantineThreshold parameters relate to routing mail that exceeds a specific SCL threshold into quarantine. Quarantine allows administrator review to determine whether the messages have been correctly identified as unsolicited commercial email.

   B. **Correct:** The SCLJunkEnabled and SCLJunkThreshold parameters allow you to configure the threshold at which messages will be routed to the junk email folder.

   C. **Incorrect:** The SCLDeleteEnabled and SCLDeleteThreshold parameters relate to the threshold at which messages will be deleted rather than be moved to the junk email folder.

   D. **Incorrect:** The SCLRejectEnabled and SCLRejectThreshold parameters relate to the threshold at which messages are rejected rather than be moved into the junk email folder.

Lesson 2

1. **Correct Answer: B**

   A. **Incorrect:** The *New-Mailbox* cmdlet is used to create new mailboxes and cannot be used to modify the resource capacity of existing mailboxes.

   B. **Correct:** You would use the *Set-Mailbox* cmdlet with the –ResourceCapacity parameter to modify the resource capacity of an existing mailbox.

   C. **Incorrect:** The *Get-Mailbox* cmdlet is used to get information about existing mailboxes and cannot be used to modify the resource capacity of an existing mailbox.

   D. **Incorrect:** The *Enable-Mailbox* cmdlet is used to provision existing Active Directory user accounts with mailboxes. You cannot use this account to modify the resource capacity of an existing mailbox.

2. **Correct Answer: B**

   A. **Incorrect:** *Set-Mailbox SalesInfo –Type Room*

   B. **Correct:** *Set-Mailbox SalesInfo –Type Shared*

   C. **Incorrect:** *Set-Mailbox SalesInfo –Type Equipment*

   D. **Incorrect:** *Set-Mailbox SalesInfo –Type Regular*

3. **Correct Answer: C**

   A. **Incorrect:** Although the *Set-Mailbox* cmdlet allows you to configure the settings of mailboxes, the *Set-Mailbox* cmdlet does not allow you to delegate control of a room mailbox. This must be done with the *Set-CalendarProcessing* cmdlet.

   B. **Incorrect:** The *Set-CalendarNotification* cmdlet allows you to configure notifications for calendar events. It does not allow you to delegate control of a resource mailbox.

   C. **Correct:** The *Set-CalendarProcessing* cmdlet allows you to set a delegate on a resource mailbox. The delegate is able to control the scheduling options.

   D. **Incorrect:** The *Get-Mailbox* cmdlet allows you to get information about a mailbox. It does not allow you to delegate control of a room mailbox.

4. **Correct Answer: B**

   A. **Incorrect:** The *Set-Mailbox* cmdlet is used to configure the properties of a mailbox but cannot be used to specify delegates and booking windows for resource mailboxes.

   B. **Correct:** The *Set-CalendarProcessing* cmdlet can be used to specify delegates and booking windows for resource mailboxes.

   C. **Incorrect:** The *Set-LinkedUser* cmdlet is used to configure the properties of linked users, but cannot be used to specify delegates and booking windows for resource mailboxes.

   D. **Incorrect:** The *Set-Group* cmdlet allows you to modify group settings but cannot be used to specify delegates and booking windows for resource mailboxes.

Chapter 3: Case Scenario Answers

Case Scenario 1: Provision Mailboxes at Alpine Ski House

1. You can ensure that users cannot send or receive attachments that are greater than 10 MB in size by configuring send and receive quotas.

2. Use the EMS command to configure all mailboxes to reject messages with an SCL above 5 using the *Set-Mailbox* command with the –SCLDeleteEnabled and -SCLDeleteThreshold options. You should use these options, as these messages do not need to be placed in the junk folder or quarantined for review. Once this is done, you should then configure Don Hall's mailbox to accept messages by using the –AntispamBypassEnabled option of the *Set-Mailbox* command.

3. To allow Dan Park to send messages on behalf of Carol Phillips, you need to configure Dan Park with the Send On Behalf permission for Carol Phillips's mailbox.

Case Scenario 2: Fabrikam Resource Mailboxes

1. You would configure the resource capacity setting on each conference room mailbox so that guests could determine the size of each conference room.

2. Configure the booking policy so that repeating meetings cannot be scheduled and the maximum duration of a meeting is 120 minutes.

3. Configure the resource policy so that requests for the lecture theater require approval by a resource mailbox delegate. Configure Fabrikam staff as resource mailbox delegates.

Chapter 4: Lesson Review Answers

Lesson 1

1. **Correct Answer: C**

   A. **Incorrect:** The *Set-MailUser* cmdlet is used to modify the mail-related settings of an existing user. As Sam does not have an existing user account, you need to use the *New-MailUser* cmdlet to create a user account and associate it with an external email address.

B. Incorrect: The *New-MailContact* cmdlet allows you to create a new mail-enabled contact. Mail-enabled contacts represent external addresses in Exchange but do not confer local logon rights.

C. Correct: The *New-MailUser* cmdlet allows you to create a user account that allows for logon but also allows messages sent to Sam to be forwarded to an external messaging system.

D. Incorrect: The *Set-MailContact* cmdlet allows you to modify an existing mail-enabled contact. Mail-enabled contacts represent external addresses in Exchange but do not confer local logon rights.

2. **Correct Answer: D**

A. Incorrect: You cannot mail-enable a domain local group. Only universal groups can be mail-enabled. Under certain conditions, domain local groups can be converted to universal groups.

B. Incorrect: You cannot mail-enable a local group. Only universal groups can be mail-enabled.

C. Incorrect: You cannot mail-enable a global group. Only universal groups can be mail-enabled. Under certain conditions, global groups can be converted to universal groups.

D. Correct: You can mail-enable only security groups that have been configured with the universal scope.

3. **Correct Answer: C**

A. Incorrect: The *Set-Contact* cmdlet is used to configure the properties of a contact, not add proxy addresses to a distribution group.

B. Incorrect: The *Set-DistributionGroup* cmdlet cannot be used to set additional proxy addresses for a dynamic distribution group but can be used to set additional proxy addresses for a normal distribution group.

C. Correct: The *Set-DynamicDistributionGroup* cmdlet with the EmailAddresses parameter can used to set additional proxy addresses for a dynamic distribution group.

D. Incorrect: The *Set-Group* cmdlet is used to manage Active Directory groups rather than dynamic distribution groups. This cmdlet cannot be used to configure additional proxy addresses for a dynamic distribution group.

4. **Correct Answer: B**

A. Incorrect: Dynamic distribution group expansion occurs on Hub Transport rather than Mailbox servers.

B. Correct: Hub Transport servers are used for dynamic distribution group expansion. As the expansion of large dynamic distribution groups can be resource intensive, you should choose an underutilized Hub Transport server to expand dynamic distribution groups with an especially large number of recipients.

C. **Incorrect:** Dynamic distribution group expansion occurs on Hub Transport rather than Edge Transport servers.

D. **Incorrect:** Dynamic distribution group expansion occurs on Hub Transport rather than Client Access servers.

5. **Correct Answer: D**

A. **Incorrect:** The *Set-MailboxPermission* cmdlet is used to set permissions on mailboxes. It cannot be used to configure a distribution group so that it is hidden from Exchange address lists.

B. **Incorrect:** The *Set-DynamicDistributionGroup* cmdlet is used to manage dynamic distribution groups and not distribution groups. You can use the Set-DynamicDistributionGroup cmdlet to hide sensitive dynamic distribution groups using the HiddenFromAddressListsEnabled parameter.

C. **Incorrect:** The *Set-Group* cmdlet is used to manage active directory groups. It cannot be used to manage an exchange distribution group.

D. **Correct:** You can use the *Set-DistributionGroup* cmdlet with the HiddenFromAddressListsEnabled $true parameter and option to hide a sensitive distribution group from address lists.

Lesson 2

1. **Correct Answer: D**

A. **Incorrect:** You use the *New-PublicFolder* cmdlet to create new public folders. You cannot use this cmdlet to mail-enable an existing public folder.

B. **Incorrect:** You use the *Set-MailPublicFolder* cmdlet to configure the properties of a mail-enabled public folder. You cannot use this cmdlet to mail-enable an existing public folder.

C. **Incorrect:** You use the *Set-PublicFolder* cmdlet to configure the settings of public folders. You cannot use this cmdlet to mail-enable an existing public folder.

D. **Correct:** You use the *Enable-MailPublicFolder* cmdlet to mail-enable an existing public folder.

2. **Correct Answer: A**

A. **Correct:** You use the *Add-PublicFolderClientPermission* cmdlet to assign public folder client permissions such as PublishingEditor and PublishingAuthor roles.

B. **Incorrect:** You cannot use the *Set-PublicFolder* cmdlet to assign public folder client permission roles. This cmdlet is used to configure the settings of public folders, such as maximum item size.

C. **Incorrect:** You cannot use the *Set-MailPublicFolder* cmdlet to assign public folder client permission roles. This cmdlet is used to configure the settings of mail-enabled public folders, such as maximum size for received items.

D. **Incorrect:** You use the *Add-PublicFolderAdministrativePermission* cmdlet to assign explicit administrative permissions to public folders, but do not use this cmdlet to assign roles such as PublishingAuthor or PublishingEditor.

3. **Correct Answer: D**

A. **Incorrect:** The *New-PublicFolder* cmdlet is used to create public folders. It cannot be used to configure the item age limit settings on existing mail-enabled public folders.

B. **Incorrect:** The *Get-PublicFolder* cmdlet is used to display information about public folders but cannot be used to directly configure public folders.

C. **Incorrect:** You cannot use the *Set-MailPublicFolder* cmdlet to configure item age limit settings on mail-enabled public folders. You must use the Set-PublicFolder cmdlet to accomplish this task.

D. **Correct:** You use the *Set-PublicFolder* cmdlet to configure item age limit settings on both mail-enabled and non–mail-enabled public folders.

4. **Correct Answers: B and D**

A. **Incorrect:** You cannot configure maximum message size using the *Set-MailPublicFolder* cmdlet. You can do this directly only by using the *Set-PublicFolder* cmdlet for the folder or *Set-PublicFolderDatase* to configure these settings indirectly through the host database settings.

B. **Correct:** You can use the *Set-PublicFolder* cmdlet with the MaxItemSize parameters to configure maximum item size settings for a public folder.

C. **Incorrect:** You cannot use mailbox database settings to configure settings for public folders. Public folders are hosted in public folder databases.

D. **Correct:** You can use the *Set-PublicFolderDatabase* cmdlet to indirectly configure public folder maximum item size settings, as these settings are inherited by public folders hosted on the database.

Chapter 4: Case Scenario Answers

Case Scenario 1: Contacts and Distribution Groups at Contoso

1. You should create a distribution group, as it is not necessary to assign security permissions to the group and membership must be managed manually. If you created a dynamic distribution group, the group would be populated automatically through a defined recipient filter.

2. You should configure the filter to include only users with mailboxes that are associated with the Engineering Department.

3. Configure the distribution group's permissions so that only the group manager, in this case the executive assistant to the company president, can remove users from the group.

Case Scenario 2: Public Folders at Fabrikam

1. Mail-enable the public folders and publish the address externally.

2. Use the *Set-MailPublicFolder* cmdlet to configure the maximum receive size. You should not use the *Set-PublicFolder* cmdlet to configure maximum item size, as you want to treat items posted through email and items posted directly differently.

3. Use the *Set-PublicFolder* cmdlet to configure maximum item age.

Chapter 5: Lesson Review Answers

Lesson 1

1. **Correct Answer: C**

   A. **Incorrect:** The *Test-OwaConnectivity* cmdlet allows you to test that OWA is running as expected but does not allow you to verify that the Autodiscover service settings for Outlook 2007 and 2010 clients are configured correctly.

   B. **Incorrect:** The *Test-WebServicesConnectivity* cmdlet allows you to verify the functionality of Exchange Web Services but does not allow you to verify that the Autodiscover service settings for Outlook 2007 and 2010 clients are configured correctly.

   C. **Correct:** The *Test-OutlookWebServices* cmdlet allows you to verify that the Autodiscover service settings for Outlook 2007 and 2010 clients are configured correctly.

   D. **Incorrect:** The *Test-ActiveSyncConnectivity* cmdlet allows you to perform a test ActiveSync synchronization against a mailbox but does not allow you to verify that the Autodiscover service settings for Outlook 2007 and 2010 clients are configured correctly.

2. **Correct Answer: D**

   A. **Incorrect:** The *Test-WebServicesConnectivity* cmdlet allows you to verify the functionality of Exchange Web Services but does not allow you to verify that ActiveSync is functioning correctly for a specific user.

   B. **Incorrect:** The *Test-OutlookWebServices* cmdlet allows you to verify that the Autodiscover service settings for Outlook 2007 and 2010 clients are configured correctly but does not allow you to verify that ActiveSync is functioning correctly for a specific user.

   C. **Incorrect:** The *Test-OwaConnectivity* cmdlet allows you to test that OWA is running as expected but does not allow you to verify that ActiveSync is functioning correctly for a specific user.

   D. **Correct:** The *Test-ActiveSyncConnectivity* cmdlet allows you to verify that ActiveSync is functioning correctly for a specific user.

3. **Correct Answer: B**

   A. **Incorrect:** The *Get-ActiveSyncDeviceStatistics* cmdlet is used to retrieve a list of mobile phones that are configured to synchronize with a specific user's mailbox; this cmdlet cannot be used to delete all data from a mobile phone.

B. **Correct:** The *Clear-ActiveSyncDevice* cmdlet is used to delete all data from a mobile phone.

C. **Incorrect:** The *Remove-ActiveSyncDevice* cmdlet is used to remove a mobile phone partnership but cannot be used to delete all data from a mobile phone.

D. **Incorrect:** The *Get-ActiveSyncDevice* cmdlet allows you to view a list of devices that have existing ActiveSync partnerships; this cmdlet cannot be used to delete all data from a mobile phone.

4. **Correct Answer: A**

A. **Correct:** You use the *Set-ActiveSyncMailboxPolicy* cmdlet with the PasswordRecoveryEnabled parameter to enable password recovery for mobile devices.

B. **Incorrect:** You use the *Set-OwaMailboxPolicy* cmdlet to configure options for OWA mailboxes. You use the *Set-ActiveSyncMailboxPolicy* cmdlet to enable password recovery for mobile devices.

C. **Incorrect:** Although you can use the *Set-ActiveSyncVirtualDirectory* cmdlet to configure options such as whether basic authentication is enabled for Activesync, you use the *Set-ActiveSyncMailboxPolicy* cmdlet to enable password recovery for mobile devices.

D. **Incorrect:** The *Set-OwaVirtualDirectory* cmdlet is used to configure the properties of the OWA virtual directory. You use the *Set-ActiveSyncMailboxPolicy* cmdlet to enable password recovery for mobile devices.

5. **Correct Answer: B**

A. **Incorrect:** You use the *Set-OwaVirtualDirectory* cmdlet to configure the properties of OWA virtual directories. You use the *Set-ActiveSyncVirtualDirectory* cmdlet with the BasicAuthEnabled parameter to configure Exchange ActiveSync to use basic authentication.

B. **Correct:** You can use the *Set-ActiveSyncVirtualDirectory* cmdlet to configure Exchange ActiveSync to use basic authentication. You use the BasicAuthEnabled parameter to accomplish this goal.

C. **Incorrect:** You use the *Set-OawMailboxPolicy* cmdlet to configure the properties of OWA. You use the *Set-ActiveSyncVirtualDirectory* cmdlet with the BasicAuthEnabled parameter to configure Exchange ActiveSync to use basic authentication.

D. **Incorrect:** Although *Set-ActiveSyncMailboxPolicy* can be used to configure options such as minimum device password length; it cannot be used to configure ActiveSync to use basic authentication. You use the *Set-ActiveSyncVirtualDirectory* cmdlet with the BasicAuthEnabled parameter to configure Exchange ActiveSync to use basic authentication.

Lesson 2

1. **Correct Answer: B**

A. **Incorrect:** The *Test-WebServicesConnectivity* cmdlet allows you to test the functionality of Exchange Web Services but does not allow you to test outlook anywhere connectivity.

B. Correct: You use the *Test-OutlookConnectivity* cmdlet to test Outlook Anywhere connectivity.

C. Incorrect: The *Test-OutlookWebServices* cmdlet allows you to verify that the Autodiscover settings, rather than the Outlook Anywhere settings, are correctly configured.

D. Incorrect: The *Test-OwaConnectivity* cmdlet allows you to test that OWA is running as expected but does not allow you to test the Outlook Anywhere settings.

2. **Correct Answer: C**

   A. Incorrect: The *Set-ActiveSyncOrganizationSettings* cmdlet allows you to configure ActiveSync organization settings but does not allow you to specify the Outlook Anywhere external host name.

   B. Incorrect: The *Set-ActiveSyncVirtualDirectory* cmdlet allows you to configure the ActiveSync virtual directory settings but does not allow you to specify the Outlook Anywhere external host name.

   C. Correct: You use the *Set-OutlookAnywhere* cmdlet to configure the external host name for Outlook Anywhere, whether it uses a single Client Access server or a client access array.

   D. Incorrect: The *Set-OwaVirtualDirectory* cmdlet allows you to configure the Outlook Web App virtual directory but does not allow you to set the external host name for Outlook Anywhere.

3. **Correct Answer: B**

   A. Incorrect: While the *Set-ClientAccessServer* cmdlet can be used to configure properties on a specific Client Access server, it cannot be used to create a new client access array for a specific Active Directory site.

   B. Correct: The *New-ClientAccessArray* cmdlet is used to create a new client access array for a specific Active Directory site.

   C. Incorrect: The *Set-CASMailbox* cmdlet allows you to set attributes related to client access for a specific user, but this command cannot be used to create a new client access array for a specific Active Directory site.

   D. Incorrect: The *Set-RpcClientAccess* cmdlet manages settings for the Exchange RPC Client Access Service but cannot be used to create a new client access array for a specific Active Directory site.

4. **Correct Answer: D**

   A. Incorrect: You use the *Set-ClientAccessArray* cmdlet to configure a client access array; you use the *Set-OutlookAnywhere* cmdlet to configure Outlook Anywhere client authentication methods.

   B. Incorrect: You use *Set-ActiveSyncOrganizationSettings* to configure organizational ActiveSync settings; you use the *Set-OutlookAnywhere* cmdlet to configure Outlook Anywhere client authentication methods.

C. **Incorrect:** The *Set-OutlookProvider* cmdlet allows you to configure the Autodiscover service but does not allow you to configure Outlook Anywhere. You use the *Set-OutlookAnywhere* cmdlet to configure Outlook Anywhere client authentication methods.

D. **Correct:** You use the *Set-OutlookAnywhere* cmdlet to configure the client authentication method for Outlook Anywhere. The options available include Basic, Digest, NTML, forms-based authentication, Windows Integrated, and Certificate.

5. **Correct Answer: C**

A. **Incorrect:** The Message Queuing component provides message delivery between applications. Although this component has a name that sounds as though it is related to Exchange, it is unnecessary on a computer Windows Server 2008 R2, where you want to install the client access role with the Outlook Anywhere component.

B. **Incorrect:** The Peer Name Resolution Protocol is a name resolution protocol that allows clients to find computers on the network using a simplified addressing scheme. This component is not necessary to support the Client Access server role.

C. **Correct:** You must install the RPC over HTTP Proxy feature on a Windows Server 2008 R2 computer if that computer is going to support the Client Access server role with the Outlook Anywhere component.

D. **Incorrect:** Remote Differential Compression is a feature that assists in the transfers of files across a network but is not a component that is necessary to support the Exchange Client Access server role with the Outlook Anywhere component.

Lesson 3

1. **Correct Answers: A and B**

A. **Correct:** You can use the *Set-OwaMailboxPolicy* cmdlet to configure an OWA mailbox policy for a group of users so that those users are unable to change their passwords when connected to OWA.

B. **Correct:** You can use the *Set-OwaVirtualDirectory* cmdlet to block all users from changing their password when connected to OWA, but you must use OWA mailbox policies, applied to users, to block this functionality from only some users. When you need to configure a setting for all users, do it at the OWA virtual directory level, but if you want to configure different settings based on group or department membership, do this through OWA mailbox policies.

C. **Incorrect:** The *Get-OwaMailboxPolicy* cmdlet provides details of an OWA mailbox policy but cannot be used to configure policy settings.

D. **Incorrect:** The *Get-OwaVirtualDirectory* cmdlet allows you to view the properties of a virtual directory but does not allow you to alter settings applied to that virtual directory.

2. **Correct Answer: C**

A. **Incorrect:** The *Test-OutlookConnectivity* cmdlet allows you to verify that services that support Outlook, such as Outlook Anywhere, are functioning. This cmdlet does not allow you to test OWA functionality.

B. Incorrect: The *Test-ActiveSync* cmdlet allows you to verify that ActiveSync is functioning correctly.

C. Correct: The *Test-OwaConnectivity* cmdlet can be used to verify that OWA is functional.

D. Incorrect:. The *Test-PopConnectivity* cmdlet can be used to test POP3 functionality. This cmdlet does not allow you to test OWA functionality.

3. **Correct Answer: D**

   A. Incorrect: You need to obtain a certificate that supports SANs, as users need to access OWA using both the address https://owa.tailspintoys.com and the address https://owa.wingtiptoys.com.

   B. Incorrect: You need to obtain a certificate that supports SANs, as users need to access OWA using both the address https://owa.tailspintoys.com and the address https://owa.wingtiptoys.com.

   C. Incorrect: While you do need a certificate that supports SANs, you should not choose to obtain this certificate from an internal CA, as this will not minimize the effort required to configure the home computers of the users accessing OWA.

   D. Correct: You need to obtain a certificate that supports SANs, as you want to support the address https://owa.tailspintoys.com and the address https://owa.wingtiptoys.com. You need to obtain a certificate from a trusted third-party CA, as you want to minimize the effort required to configure the home computers of the users accessing OWA.

4. **Correct Answer: A**

   A. Correct: You can use the *Set-OwaMailboxPolicy* cmdlet to allow and block attachments on the basis of file type.

   B. Incorrect: Although you can enable and disable OWA for a user using the *Set-CASMailbox* cmdlet as well as specify an OWA mailbox policy, you cannot specifically allow or block attachment types using this cmdlet.

   C. Incorrect: The *Set-RpcClientAccess* cmdlet allows you to configure the RPC Client Access service but cannot be used to allow and block attachment types for OWA.

   D. Incorrect: The *Set-ActiveSyncMailboxPolicy* cmdlet allows you to configure synchronization between Exchange and mobile devices but does not allow you to configure which attachment types are blocked and allowed in OWA.

5. **Correct Answer: C**

   A. Incorrect: Although *Set-OwaMailboxPolicy* can be used to configure per-user OWA settings, you cannot use *Set-OwaMailboxPolicy* to configure the authentication method used by OWA.

   B. Incorrect: While the *Set-ClientAccessServer* cmdlet is used to configure some Client Access server properties, this cmdlet cannot be used to configure the authentication method used by OWA.

   C. Correct: You use the *Set-OwaVirtualDirectory* cmdlet to configure the authentication method used by OWA.

D. Incorrect: The *Set-OutlookAnywhere* cmdlet is used to configure the properties of Outlook Anywhere. You cannot use this cmdlet to configure the properties of OWA.

Chapter 5: Case Scenario Answers

Case Scenario 1: Fabrikam Client Access

1. Configure the IMAP4 service on CAS-1 so that it starts automatically.

2. You need to install the RPC over HTTP Proxy feature to support Outlook Anywhere.

3. You should obtain a certificate that supports SANs. The certificate should map to the names owa.fabrikam.com and owa.adatum.com.

Case Scenario 2: OWA at Tailspin Toys

1. You can use *Set-OwaVirtualDirectory* to block users from changing their password through OWA. It is also possible to block access to this feature through individual OWA mailbox policies, though the question stated that this should apply to all users regardless of policy, which is why you should apply it using the *Set-OwaVirtualDirectory* cmdlet.

2. Configure an OWA mailbox policy for members of the Accounting Department that blocks access to attachments in ZIP format but allows access to attachments in XLS format. Configure a separate OWA mailbox policy to ensure that users in other departments have access to attachments in ZIP format.

3. The *Test-OwaConnectivity* cmdlet can be used to test OWA connectivity.

Chapter 6: Lesson Review Answers

Lesson 1

1. **Correct Answer: C**

   A. Incorrect. The *New-ManagementScope* cmdlet creates a management scope. However, the HubTransport Scope management scope already exists.

   B. Incorrect. The *New-ManagementScope cmdlet* creates a management scope. However, the HubTransport Scope management scope already exists.

   C. Correct: This command configures the management scope to include Hub Transport servers Hub01, Hub02, Hub03, and Hub04.

   D. Incorrect: This command configures the management scope to include only Hub Transport server Hub04.

2. **Correct Answers: D and E**

   A. **Incorrect:** Jeff cannot configure settings that are unavailable in Outlook Web App options, such as mailbox size.

   B. **Incorrect:** Jeff cannot configure settings that are unavailable in Outlook Web App options, such as mailbox database configuration settings.

   C. **Incorrect:** Jeff can modify only the Outlook Web App options that the user himself or herself can modify. He cannot modify a user's display name when that user is not permitted to modify it.

   D. **Correct:** Jeff is a delegate and can manage membership of the role group.

   E. **Correct:** Jeff can view and modify the Microsoft Office Outlook Web App options of any user in the organization. These might include display name, address, phone number, and so on. Note that, by definition, a user can configure his or her own Microsoft Office Outlook Web App options. If a user cannot configure, for example, the display name, this is not a Microsoft Office Outlook Web App option for that user, and Jeff cannot modify it either.

3. **Correct Answers: B and E**

   A. **Incorrect:** You can use the *Add-ManagementRoleEntry* cmdlet to add management role entries to an existing management role. The question requires you to remove management role entries, not add them.

   B. **Correct:** The *Remove-ManagementRoleEntry* cmdlet removes a management role entry (or permission) from a management role. However, in order to use this cmdlet, you first need to obtain the permission you want to remove by using the *Get-ManagementRole* cmdlet with a filter (Where) condition.

   C. **Incorrect:** You can use the *New-ManagementRoleAssignment* cmdlet to assign a management role to a management role group, management role assignment policy, user, or universal security group. You cannot use it to remove a management role entry.

   D. **Incorrect:** You can use the *New-ManagementRole* cmdlet to create a custom management role. You cannot use it to remove a management role entry from an existing management role.

   E. **Correct:** Although the *Remove-ManagementRoleEntry* cmdlet removes a management role entry (or permission) from a management role, you first need to use the *Get-ManagementRole* cmdlet with a filter (Where) condition to obtain the entry you want to remove.

4. **Correct Answer: A**

   A. **Correct:** This command creates a new management role named MyManagementRole based on the Journaling management role.

   B. **Incorrect:** This command attempts to create a new management role named Journaling based on the management role MyManagementRole. This is not possible because a built-in management role called Journaling already exists.

C. **Incorrect**: The *New-ManagementRoleAssignment* cmdlet assigns a management role to a management role group, management role assignment policy, user, or universal security group. It does not create a new management role.

D. **Incorrect**: The *New-ManagementRoleAssignment* cmdlet assigns a management role to a management role group, management role assignment policy, user, or universal security group. It does not create a new management role.

5. **Correct Answers: A and E**

A. **Correct**: Membership of the Recipient Management role group enables Kim to create or modify recipients within the Exchange organization.

B. **Incorrect**: Membership of the Organization Management provides access to the entire Exchange Server 2010 organization. Kim would be able to carry out all the tasks listed but would have more administrative permissions than the question specifies.

C. **Incorrect**: Membership of the Public Folder Management role group permits Kim to manage public folders and databases on Exchange Server 2010 servers. It does not enable her to create or modify recipients within the Exchange organization and to configure compliance features.

D. **Incorrect**: Membership of the Server Management role group permits Kim to perform Exchange server configuration. It does not enable her to create or modify recipients within the Exchange organization and to configure compliance features.

E. **Correct**: Membership of the Records Management role group enables Kim to configure compliance features, including retention policy tags, message classifications, and transport rules.

Lesson 2

1. **Correct Answer: D**

A. **Incorrect**: Provided that an X.509 certificate is trusted by Windows Live Domain Services, it can be used to verify a federation trust, even if it is also being used for other purposes.

B. **Incorrect**: When you use the EMC to create a federation trust, that trust must be named Microsoft Federation Gateway. However, when you use the EMS, you can specify any name that is syntactically correct, including Microsoft Federation Gateway.

C. **Incorrect**: You can create a federation trust on a Client Access server. You cannot create it on a domain controller unless that domain controller is also an Exchange Server 2010 server (which would be bad practice).

D. **Correct**: You have chosen the thumbprint of a certificate that is not exportable and not trusted by Windows Live Domain. It is likely that you have chosen a self-signed certificate.

2. **Correct Answer: A**

A. **Correct**: Your network is isolated from any other network, which would include the Internet. An Internet connection is necessary to create a federation trust.

B. **Incorrect:** Certificates are frequently exported using removable media. Provided that the certificate is an X.509 certificate trusted by Windows Live Domain Services, it can be used to verify a federation trust.

C. **Incorrect:** You are testing Exchange Server 2010 configuration, and therefore the EMS is available on your network.

D. **Incorrect:** A trusted third-party CA is by definition trusted by everyone, including Windows Live Domain Services.

3. **Correct Answer: B**

A. **Incorrect:** You use *Get-Mailbox* to obtain the Marketing mailboxes and *Set-Mailbox* to apply the Adatum Marketing sharing policy. This answer has the cmdlets the wrong way around.

B. **Correct:** This command uses *Get-Mailbox* to obtain the Marketing mailboxes and *Set-Mailbox* to apply the Adatum Marketing sharing policy.

C. **Incorrect:** The Organization parameter is reserved for Microsoft use and does not in any event specify a department. Also, the cmdlets are the wrong way around.

D. **Incorrect:** The Organization parameter is reserved for Microsoft use and does not in any event specify a department.

4. **Correct Answer: D**

A. **Incorrect:** You use the *New-OrganizationRelationship* cmdlet to create a relationship with an external Microsoft Exchange Server 2010 organization. The cmdlet does not create an account namespace for your Exchange organization with the Federation Gateway and enable federation.

B. **Incorrect:** You use the *Get-FederatedOrganizationIdentifier* EMS cmdlet to retrieve your Microsoft Exchange Server 2010 organization's federated organization identifier and related details, such as federated domains, organization contact, and status. The cmdlet does not create an account namespace for your Exchange organization with the Federation Gateway and enable federation.

C. **Incorrect:** You use the *Set-OrganizationRelationship* cmdlet to modify a relationship with an external Microsoft Exchange Server 2010 organization for the purposes of, for example, accessing free or busy information. The cmdlet does not create an account namespace for your Exchange organization with the Federation Gateway and enable federation.

D. **Correct:** You can use the *Set-FederatedOrganizationIdentifier* EMS cmdlet to configure the federated organization identifier for your Exchange organization. You configure a federated organization identifier to create an account namespace for your Exchange organization with the Federation Gateway and enable federation.

5. **Correct Answers: B, C, and D**

A. **Incorrect:** The Blue Sky airlines organization cannot access the Consolidated Messenger organization until the sharing relationship has been verified and a token issued. No Consolidated Messenger servers are involved in the first three steps of this process.

B. **Correct:** The domain controller in the originating organization needs to verify the sharing relationship. This is the second step of the process.

C. **Correct:** When the sharing relationship is verified, a token is requested from the Federation Gateway. This permits access to the Consolidated Messenger organization. This is the third step of the process.

D. **Correct:** The message is sent from a Mailbox server to a Hub Transport server in the originating organization. This is the first step of the process.

E. **Incorrect:** The sending organization requests the token, and a Consolidated Messenger Hub Transport server cannot request a security token for the Blue Sky Airlines user. No Consolidated Messenger servers are involved in the first three steps of this process.

F. **Incorrect:** The message is initially sent internally to a Hub Transport server in the originating organization. No Consolidated Messenger servers are involved in the first three steps of this process.

Chapter 6: Case Scenario Answers

Case Scenario 1: Adding a Delegate to a Role Group

1. Kim stores the role group delegate list in a variable. For example, the following command stores the delegates in the Recipient Managers role group in the variable $RecManRoleGroup:

```
$RecManRoleGroup = Get-RoleGroup "Recipient Managers"
```

2. Kim adds Don to the role group stored in the variable by entering the following command:

```
$RecManRoleGroup.ManagedBy += (Get-User "Don Hall").Identity
```

3. Kim applies the revised delegate list variable to the role group. She enters the following command:

```
Set-RoleGroup "Recipient Managers" -ManagedBy $RecManRoleGroup.ManagedBy
```

4. To remove Don from the delegate list, Kim would use an almost identical procedure except that at the second step she would remove Don from the delegate list in the variable by entering the following command:

```
$RecManRoleGroup.ManagedBy -= (Get-User "Don Hall").Identity
```

Case Scenario 2: Replacing an X.509 Certificate in a Federation Trust

1. Jeff needs to obtain the certificate's thumbprint, which is a digest of all the information that the certificate contains. To do this, he uses the *Get-ExchangeCertificate* EMS cmdlet without parameters to list the thumbprints of all certificates installed in the Fabrikam organization.

2. Jeff uses the *Set-FederationTrust* EMS cmdlet and the certificate thumbprint to configure the certificate as the next certificate to be used to verify the federation trust. For example, if the certificate had the thumbprint AC00F12CBA8358253F412FD0984B5CCAF2AF4F27, he would enter the following command in the EMS:

```
Set-FederationTrust -Identity "Microsoft Federation Gateway" -Thumbprint
AC00F12CBA8358253F412FD0984B5CCAF2AF4F27
```

3. Don then needs to verify that the certificate is available on all Hub Transport and Client Access servers. On each of these servers, he enters the *Test-FederationTrust* EMS cmdlet without parameters. This checks that certificates, including the next certificate, are valid and can be used with the Federation Gateway.

4. Finally, Don configures the trust to use the next certificate as the current certificate. To do this, he enters the following command:

```
Set-FederationTrust -Identity "Microsoft Federation Gateway" -
PublishFederationCertificate
```

Chapter 7: Lesson Review Answers

Lesson 1

1. **Correct Answer: B**

   A. **Incorrect:** This creates a rule that adds Paul West to the recipients whenever an email message is sent to Don Hall, except when the either the message subject or the message body includes the word "holiday." The requirement is that the rule is not applied only when the message subject includes the word "holiday."

   B. **Correct:** This creates a rule that adds Paul West to the recipients whenever an email message is sent to Don Hall, except when the message subject includes the word "holiday."

   C. **Incorrect:** This creates a rule that adds Don Hall to the recipients whenever an email message is sent to Paul West, except when the message subject includes the word "holiday." This is not what is required.

   D. **Incorrect:** This creates a rule that adds Don Hall to the recipients whenever an email message is sent to Paul West, except when the message subject or the message body includes the word "holiday." This is not what is required.

2. **Correct Answer: C**

   A. **Incorrect:** The *Get-TransportRule* cmdlet returns details about a specified transport rule, but you cannot use it to amend the rule.

   B. **Incorrect:** The *New-TransportRule* cmdlet creates a new transport rule. You cannot use it to amend an existing transport rule.

C. **Correct:** You can use the *Set-TransportRule* cmdlet to amend the AddPaulWest transport rule.

D. **Incorrect:** You can use the *Get-TransportRulePredicate* cmdlet to retrieve a list of all available rule predicates that you can use with the transport rules agent on a Hub Transport server or an Edge Transport server. You cannot use it to amend an existing transport rule.

3. **Correct Answers: A, C, and E**

A. **Correct:** The first two metacharacters are nonnumeric digits (not numbers and not symbols), and A and B fit that specification. The next two metacharacters match any single character that is not a space, and C and A fit that specification. The next four metacharacters match any single numeric digit, and 1, 2, 2, and 1 fit that specification. The next three metacharacters match any single character (numeric, alphabetic, or symbol) that is not a space, and Y, Z, and z fit that specification. The final four metacharacters match any single numeric digit, and 3, 3, 3, and 3 fit that specification.

B. **Incorrect:** The first two metacharacters specify nonnumeric digits (not numbers and not symbols), and the second digit, 1, does not match this specification. There is no point in further analysis. The pattern does not fit the specification.

C. **Correct:** The first two metacharacters are nonnumeric digits (not numbers and not symbols), and A and B fit that specification. The next two metacharacters match any single character that is not a space, and 9 and 8 fit that specification. The next four metacharacters match any single numeric digit, and 6, 5, 5, and 6 fit that specification. The next three metacharacters match any single character (numeric, alphabetic, or symbol) that is not a space, and +, +, and + fit that specification. The final four metacharacters match any single numeric digit, and 9, 6, 8, and 8 fit that specification.

D. **Incorrect:** The first two metacharacters specify nonnumeric digits (not numbers and not symbols), and the first digit, 1, does not match this specification. There is no point in further analysis. The pattern does not fit the specification.

E. **Correct:** The first two metacharacters are nonnumeric digits (not numbers and not symbols), and G and o fit that specification. The next two metacharacters match any single character that is not a space, and o and d fit that specification. The next four metacharacters match any single numeric digit, and 4, 4, 4, and 4 fit that specification. The next three metacharacters match any single character (numeric, alphabetic, or symbol) that is not a space, and b, a, and d fit that specification. The final four metacharacters match any single numeric digit, and 2, 2, 2, and 2 fit that specification.

F. **Incorrect:** The first two metacharacters specify nonnumeric digits (not numbers and not symbols), and the first digit, 4, does not match this specification. There is no point in further analysis. The pattern does not fit the specification.

4. **Correct Answer: B**

A. **Incorrect:** You would select the Append Disclaimer Text And Fallback Action If Unable To Apply check box if you were configuring a disclaimer. You do not need to select that check box when configuring a transport protection rule that IRM-protects email traffic.

B. Correct: You IRM-protect email traffic by configuring a transport protection rule that applies an RMS template. Therefore, you need to select the Rights Protect Message With RMS Template check box.

C. Incorrect: You select the Add A Recipient In The To Field Address check box if you want to send specified email traffic to an additional user. You do not need to select that check box when configuring a transport protection rule that IRM-protects email traffic.

D. Incorrect: You select the Forward The Message To Addresses For Moderation check box if you are configuring moderation. You do not need to select that check box when configuring a transport protection rule that IRM-protects email traffic.

5. **Correct Answer: A**

A. Correct: This creates a transport rule that appends an HTML disclaimer as specified to all messages sent outside the organization Adatum.com. If, for any reason, this disclaimer cannot be appended to an email message, the message is rejected.

B. Incorrect: This creates a transport rule that appends an HTML disclaimer to all messages sent inside the organization Adatum.com.

C. Incorrect: This creates a transport rule that appends an HTML disclaimer as specified to all messages sent outside the organization Adatum.com. However, if this disclaimer cannot be appended to an email message, the requirement that the disclaimer should be appended is ignored, and the message is sent without the disclaimer.

D. Incorrect: This creates a transport rule that appends an HTML disclaimer as specified to all messages sent within the organization Adatum.com. Also, if this disclaimer cannot be appended to an email message, the requirement that the disclaimer should be appended is ignored, and the message is sent without the disclaimer.

Lesson 2

1. **Correct Answer: C**

A. Incorrect: The *Get-AdSite* cmdlet displays configuration information about one or more Active Directory sites. You cannot use it to designate a site as a hub site.

B. Incorrect: The *Get-AdSiteLink* cmdlet lets you view configuration information about an Active Directory IP site link. You cannot use it to designate a site as a hub site.

C. Correct: This command designates the Active Directory site MySite as a hub site.

D. Incorrect: You can use the *Set-AdSiteLink* cmdlet to assign an Exchange-specific cost to an Active Directory IP site link. You can also use this cmdlet to configure the maximum message size that can pass across an Active Directory IP site link. However, you cannot use it to designate a site as a hub site.

2. **Correct Answer: B**

A. Incorrect: Setting the Exchange cost of IP site link Site02-Site03 to 100 does not ensure that the total cost of the route from Site01 to Site03 via Site02 is greater than 300 for email traffic. This setting would not guarantee that traffic is routed through Site04 rather than Site02.

B. Correct: Setting the Exchange cost of IP site link Site02-Site03 to 400 ensures that the total cost of the route from Site01 to Site03 via Site02 is greater than 300 for email traffic. This setting guarantees that email traffic is routed through Site04 rather than Site02.

C. Incorrect: The *Set-ADSite* EMS cmdlet is used to reconfigure a site. For example, you could use it to configure a site as a hub site. You cannot use this cmdlet to configure the cost of a site link.

D. Incorrect: The *Set-ADSite* EMS cmdlet is used to reconfigure a site. For example, you could use it to configure a site as a hub site. You cannot use this cmdlet to configure the cost of a site link.

3. **Correct Answer: D**

   A. Incorrect: You would select the Custom usage type for a Send connector on an unsubscribed Edge Transport server that sends email to a Hub Transport server, for a cross-forest Send connector on a Hub Transport server that sends email to an Exchange Server 2010 or Exchange Server 2007 Hub Transport server, or for an Exchange Server 2003 bridgehead server in a second forest. To send email to a domain with which you have established MTLS authentication, you need to create a Send connector with the Partner usage type.

   B. Incorrect: You would select the Internal usage type for a Send connector on a subscribed Edge Transport server that sends email to a Hub Transport server or to an Exchange 2003 bridgehead server. To send email to a domain with which you have established MTLS authentication, you need to create a Send connector with the Partner usage type.

   C. Incorrect: You would select the Internet usage type for a Send connector on an Edge Transport server that sends email to the Internet. To send email to a domain with which you have established MTLS authentication, you need to create a Send connector with the Partner usage type.

   D. Correct: You would create a Send connector with the Partner usage type to send email to a domain with which you have established MTLS authentication.

4. **Correct Answer: A**

   A. Correct: This command reconfigures the ContosoSend Send connector so that it rejects any email message greater than 5 MB.

   B. Incorrect: You cannot reconfigure the usage type of a Send connector by using the *Set-SendConnector* EMS cmdlet. In any case, the Send connector is already configured to send email to the contoso.com domain and all its subdomains. and you require only to reconfigure the maximum message size.

   C. Incorrect: The Send connector is already configured to send email to the contoso.com domain and all its subdomains, and you require only to reconfigure the maximum message size. This command also reconfigures the address space so that the Send connector sends email only to the contoso.com and mail.contoso.com domains, which is not what is required.

- **D.** **Incorrect:** If you set the IsScopedConnector parameter to $true, the Send connector is available only to Hub Transport servers within your own Exchange organization. This is not what is required.

5. **Correct Answer: C**

- **A.** **Incorrect:** You use the *New-ReceiveConnector* EMS cmdlet—not *Set-ReceiveConnector*—to create a Receive connector.

- **B.** **Incorrect:** You use the *New-ReceiveConnector* EMS cmdlet—not *Set-ReceiveConnector*—to create a Receive connector. Also, the arguments for the Bindings and the RemoteIPRanges parameters are incorrect in this command.

- **C.** **Correct:** This command creates a Receive connector named MyRC with the Custom usage type. The connector listens for incoming SMTP connections on the IP address 10.10.123.123 and port 25. It accepts incoming SMTP connections only from the IP range 10.10.8.1 through 10.10.8.127. The authentication mechanism of this Receive connector is set to Integrated Windows authentication.

- **D.** **Incorrect:** The Bindings parameter defines the IP address and port on which the connector listens. This parameter should take the argument 10.10.123.123:25. The RemoteIPRanges parameter should take the argument 10.10.8.1-10.10.8.127. In this answer, these arguments are reversed.

Chapter 7: Case Scenario Answers

Case Scenario 1: Configuring Moderation

1. *Set-DistributionGroup –Identity Sales -ModerationEnabled $true -ModeratedBy "Kim Akers" -SendModerationNotifications Internal*

2. *Set-DistributionGroup –Identity Sales -ByPassModerationFromSendersOrMembers "Don Hall"*

3. *Set-DistributionGroup –Identity Sales –BypassNestedModerationEnabled $true*

Case Scenario 2: Setting Up MTLS-Protected Email Communication with a Partner Organization

1. *$Request = New-ExchangeCertificate -GenerateRequest -SubjectName "c=US,o=Adatum Corporation,cn=mail.adatum.com" -DomainName blueskyairlines.co.uk -PrivateKeyExportable $true*

   ```
   Set-Content -Path "C:\Requests\ TreyProjectRequest.req" -Value $Request
   ```

2. Both the Send and the Receive connector should have a usage type or partner because you are configuring MTLS-protected communication with a partner organization.

3. *New-SendConnector -Partner -Name TreySendConnector –AddressSpace *.treyresearch.com*

4. *New-ReceiveConnector -Name TreyReceiveConnector -Usage Partner -Bindings 192.168.20.6:25 -RemoteIPRanges 10.100.10.15-10.100.10.16 –MaxMessageSize 15MB*

Chapter 8: Lesson Review Answers

Lesson 1

1. **Correct Answer: D**
   - **A.** Incorrect: The *Set-ForeignConnector* cmdlet allows you to modify the properties of a foreign connector but does not allow you to modify the properties of an accepted domain.
   - **B.** Incorrect: The *Set-SendConnector* cmdlet allows you to modify a send connector but does not allow you to modify the properties of an accepted domain.
   - **C.** Incorrect: The *Set-AddressRewriteEntry* cmdlet is used to reconfigure an address rewrite entry but does not allow you to modify the properties of an accepted domain.
   - **D.** Correct: You can use the *Set-AcceptedDomain* cmdlet to convert an existing accepted domain from being an internal relay domain to one that is authoritative.

2. **Correct Answer: A**
   - **A.** Correct: You can configure whether out-of-office messages are sent to a particular external location by configuring a remote domain for that location using the *New-RemoteDomain* cmdlet.
   - **B.** Incorrect: The *new-ForeignConnector* cmdlet creates a new foreign connector. You cannot configure whether out-of-office settings for foreign connectors.
   - **C.** Incorrect: The *new-Sendconnector* cmdlet creates a send connector. You cannot configure out-of-office settings for send connectors.
   - **D.** Incorrect: The *New-AcceptedDomain* cmdlet is used to configure accepted domains, which involve incoming rather than outgoing messages.

3. **Correct Answer: B**
   - **A.** Incorrect: An internal relay domain is a domain for which your organization accepts messages but where those messages are forwarded to an internal messaging system other than Exchange.
   - **B.** Correct: Authoritative domains are domains for which your Exchange organization accepts email messages.
   - **C.** Incorrect: External relay domains are domains for which your organization will accept email but for which your organization hands off the messages to an external third party. You configure an authoritative domain when your organization accepts email messages for a specific domain.
   - **D.** Incorrect: Foreign connectors are connectors to external mail systems. You should configure an authoritative domain in this situation.

4. **Correct Answer: C**
   - **A.** Incorrect: Address rewrite entries are used to rewrite addresses as they are going out but do not configure email addresses for users. You use an email address policy to accomplish this goal.

B. Incorrect: You have already configured Wingtip Toys and Tailspin Toys as authoritative domains, so there is no need to use the *New-AcceptedDomain* cmdlet. You use an email address policy to accomplish this goal.

C. Correct: You use the *New-EmailAddress* policy to create a set of new email addresses for users. For example, you could create a policy that automatically populated email addresses based on the format. firstname.lastname@tailspintoys.com.

D. Incorrect: The *New-AddressList* cmdlet is used to create new address lists but is not used to create new email address formats.

5. **Correct Answer: C**

A. Incorrect: The *Set-TransportServer* cmdlet is used to configure options for a single transport server but is not used to configure transport dumpster properties, which are configured at the organization level.

B. Incorrect: The *Set-TransportAgent* command allows you to modify the settings of a transport agent but does not allow you to configure the settings of the transport dumpster.

C. Correct: The *Set-TransportConfig* cmdlet is used to configure transport dumpster properties on an organization's Hub Transport servers.

D. Incorrect: The *Set-SendConnector* cmdlet allows you to modify the settings of a send connector but does not allow you to configure transport dumpster properties.

Lesson 2

1. **Correct Answers: A and B**

A. Correct: You need to ensure that .NET Framework 3.5.1 or later, Active Directory Lightweight Directory Services, and the RSAT tools for Active Directory Directory Services are installed on a computer running Windows Server 2008 R2 before you can deploy the Edge Transport server role.

B. Correct: You need to ensure that .NET Framework 3.5.1 or later, Active Directory Lightweight Directory Services, and the RSAT tools for Active Directory Directory Services are installed on a computer running Windows Server 2008 R2 before you can deploy the Edge Transport server role.

C. Incorrect: The RPC over HTTP role is necessary if you are going to install the Client Access server role and support Outlook Anywhere, but it is not necessary to install this role to support the Edge Transport server role.

D. Incorrect: The Active Directory Directory Services role does not need to be installed on a server to support the Edge Transport server role. The RSAT tools to administer Active Directory Directory Services role are required, but these are separate from Active Directory Directory Services.

2. **Correct Answer: C**

A. Incorrect: TCP port 443 is used for Secure Sockets Layer transmissions. You must open TCP port 50636 to support EdgeSync synchronization.

B. Incorrect: TCP port 110 is used to support the POP3 protocol. You must open TCP port 50636 to support EdgeSync synchronization.

C. Correct: The EdgeSync synchronization process requires that TCP port 50636 be open on a firewall separating the screened network from the internal network that hosts your organization's Hub Transport servers.

D. Incorrect: Port 80 is used by the HTTP protocol. You must open TCP port 50636 to support EdgeSync synchronization.

3. **Correct Answers: A and B**

   A. Correct: You must export the configuration of server VAN-EX-A, which has the existing custom transport rules.

   B. Correct: You must import the configuration exported from VAN-EX-A onto server VAN-EX-B. This will transfer the existing custom transport rules from the original server to the new server.

   C. Incorrect: You should not import the configuration onto VAN-EX-A, as this server already has the custom transport rules.

   D. Incorrect: You should not export the configuration of server VAN-EX-B, as this server does not have any transport rules that you wish to copy to another location.

4. **Correct Answers: C and D**

   A. Incorrect: The *Start-EdgeSynchronization* cmdlet initiates synchronization when an existing subscription is present; it cannot be used to create a subscription.

   B. Incorrect: The *Start-EdgeSynchronization* cmdlet initiates synchronization when an existing subscription is present; it cannot be used to create a subscription.

   C. Correct: You can import a subscription file generated on an Edge Transport server using the *New-EdgeSubscription* cmdlet.

   D. Correct: You can create a subscription file on an Edge Transport server by using the *New-EdgeSubscription* cmdlet.

5. **Correct Answer: C**

   A. Incorrect: You should not set up a new send connector, as send connectors cannot be used to rewrite outbound email so that they use a consistent email address format.

   B. Incorrect: You should not use the *New-EmailAddressPolicy* cmdlet, as you want to keep existing internal addresses but rewrite the addresses associated with outbound messages.

   C. Correct: You can use the *New-AddressRewriteEntry* cmdlet to configure a new address rewrite entry so that all outbound email uses a consistent email address format.

   D. Incorrect: You should not set up a new remote domain, as remote domains cannot be used to rewrite outbound emails so that they use a consistent email address format.

Chapter 8: Case Scenario Answers

Case Scenario 1: Hub Transport Configuration at Coho Winery

1. Configure Cohovineyard.com as an accepted domain in the Coho Winery Exchange organization.

2. Configure an email address policy to ensure that the format firstname.middleinitial .lastname@cohowinery.com is the default email address.

3. You can ensure that email to a specific mail domain uses a specific character set by setting up a remote domain.

Case Scenario 2: Edge Transport Configuration at Tailspin Toys

1. Clone the configuration of the first Edge Transport server. Import that configuration on to the other two Edge Transport servers.

2. Configure DNS round-robin so that each Edge Transport server shares traffic. This is not as effective as network load balancing, but that is not an option as specified in the question text.

3. Configure an address rewrite policy to change @australia.tailspintoys.com and @newzealand. tailspintoys.com email addresses to @tailspintoys.com email addresses.

Chapter 9: Lesson Review Answers

Lesson 1

1. **Correct Answer: D**

    A. **Incorrect:** You identify the Mailbox server by using the Server parameter, not the Identity parameter. Also, you need to specify the Status parameter to view status information.

    B. **Incorrect:** You need to specify the Status parameter to view status information.

    C. **Incorrect:** You identify the Mailbox server by using the Server parameter, not the Identity parameter.

    D. **Correct:** This command enables you to view detailed information, including backup and mount status information, about the public folder database on the ContosoMail01 Mailbox server.

2. **Correct Answer: A**

    A. **Correct:** This command returns the status of the mailbox database MyMailboxDatabase and tells you how much free space is available in the database root.

B. **Incorrect**: To identify a specific mailbox database, you need to use the Identity parameter, not the Server parameter.

C. **Incorrect**: Specifying the DumpsterStatistics parameter lets you obtain statistics (if available) about the transport dumpster, such as dumpster deletes per second, dumpster inserts per second, and dumpster item count. This parameter does not return the status of the mailbox database and does not tell you how much free space is available in the database root.

D. **Incorrect**: To identify a specific mailbox database, you need to use the Identity parameter, not the Server parameter. Also, specifying the DumpsterStatistics parameter lets you obtain statistics (if available) about the transport dumpster, such as dumpster deletes per second, dumpster inserts per second, and dumpster item count. This parameter does not return the status of the mailbox database and does not tell you how much free space is available in the database root.

3. **Correct Answer: C**

A. **Incorrect**: You use the Identity parameter to specify a single mailbox when you are viewing mailbox statistics. You do not need to use the Server parameter.

B. **Incorrect**: You use the Identity parameter to specify a single mailbox when you are viewing mailbox statistics. You do not need to use the Database parameter.

C. **Correct**: If you attempt to obtain statistics for a mailbox that has not been accessed, you will get no statistical information but will instead receive a warning message that tells you the user has not logged on to the mailbox.

D. **Incorrect**: You can use the *Get-StoreUsageStatistics* EMS cmdlet to generate a report on the 25 accounts that are using the greatest amount of resources within a mailbox database. You can use this cmdlet to generate a report on a single user, but only if that user is in the top 25 resource users list. The command specified in the question is the correct command for obtaining mailbox statistics for a single mailbox.

4. **Correct Answer: A**

A. **Correct**: The DisconnectedAndResynchronizing status indicates that the mailbox database copy is no longer connected to the active database copy and that it was in the Resynchronizing state when the loss of connection occurred. This status represents the database copy's view of connectivity to its source database copy. It may be reported during DAG network failures between the source copy and the target database copy.

B. **Incorrect**: The ActivationSuspended status indicates that an administrator has manually blocked the mailbox database copy from activation. It does not indicate that the mailbox database copy is no longer connected to the active database copy and that it was in the Resynchronizing state when the loss of connection occurred.

C. **Incorrect**: The Seeding status indicates that the mailbox database copy is being seeded, the content index for the mailbox database copy is being seeded, or both. It does not indicate that the mailbox database copy is no longer connected to the active database copy and that it was in the Resynchronizing state when the loss of connection occurred.

D. Incorrect: The DisconnectedAndHealthy status indicates that the mailbox database copy is no longer connected to the active database copy and was in the Healthy state when the loss of connection occurred. It does not indicate that the mailbox database copy was in the Resynchronizing state when the loss of connection occurred.

5. **Correct Answer: B**

A. Incorrect: The *Get-MailboxStatistics* cmdlet enables you to view the statistics for all the mailboxes on a server, for all the mailboxes in a mailbox database, or for a single mailbox. It does not generate a report on the 25 accounts that are using the greatest amount of resources within a mailbox database.

B. Correct: The *Get-StoreUsageStatistics* cmdlet enables you to generate a report on the 25 accounts that are using the greatest amount of resources within a mailbox database.

C. Incorrect: The *Get-MailboxDatabase* cmdlet enables you to obtain general information about mailbox databases. It does not generate a report on the 25 accounts that are using the greatest amount of resources within a mailbox database.

D. Incorrect: The *Get-MailboxDatabaseCopyStatus* cmdlet enables you to view status information about mailbox database copies. It does not generate a report on the 25 accounts that are using the greatest amount of resources within a mailbox database.

Lesson 2

1. **Correct Answer: D**

A. Incorrect: You use the *Set-MailboxServer* cmdlet, not the *Set-TransportServer* cmdlet, to configure message tracking for the Mailbox server role.

B. Incorrect: This command disables message tracking on the Mailbox server AdatumMail02.

C. Incorrect: You use the *Set-MailboxServer* cmdlet, not the *Set-TransportServer* cmdlet, to configure message tracking for the Mailbox server role.

D. Correct: This command enables message tracking on the Mailbox server AdatumMail02

2. **Correct Answer: B**

A. Incorrect: The MessageTrackingLogMaxDirectorySize parameter sets the maximum size for the entire message tracking log directory, not the maximum size of each message tracking log file.

B. Correct: This command changes the maximum size of each message tracking log file on the Edge Transport server NY-Edge01 to 15 MB.

C. Incorrect: To change message tracking log message sizes on an Edge Transport server, you need to use the *Set-TransportServer* cmdlet, not the *Set-MailboxServer* cmdlet. Also, the MessageTrackingLogMaxDirectorySize parameter sets the maximum size for the entire message tracking log directory, not the maximum size of each message tracking log file.

D. Incorrect: To change message tracking log message sizes on an Edge Transport server, you need to use the *Set-TransportServer* cmdlet, not the *Set-MailboxServer* cmdlet.

3. **Correct Answer: A**

    A. **Correct**: This command lists the number of messages on the Edge Transport server on which it is entered that are bound for the BlueSkyAirlines.com domain as their next-hop destination.

    B. **Incorrect**: This command lists all the queues on the Hub Transport or Edge Transport server on which it is entered that that contain more than 50 messages. It does not take the next-hop destination into account.

    C. **Incorrect**: This command lists the number of messages on the Edge Transport server on which it is entered that are bound for the Adatum.com domain as their next-hop destination.

    D. **Incorrect**: This command lists all the queues on the Hub Transport or Edge Transport server on which it is entered that that contain more than 50 or more messages. It does not take the next-hop destination into account.

4. **Correct Answer: D**

    A. **Incorrect**: This command suspends all queues on the Hub Transport server on which it is entered that have a message count equal to or greater than 450 and have a status of Retry. However, the command does not work immediately and requires confirmation.

    B. **Incorrect**: This command suspends all queues on the Hub Transport server on which it is entered that have a message count greater than 450 and have a status of Retry. It would not suspend a queue that has a message count of exactly 450.

    C. **Incorrect**: This command suspends all queues on the Hub Transport server on which it is entered that have a message count equal to or greater than 450 and have a status of Active.

    D. **Correct**: This command suspends all queues on the Hub Transport server on which it is entered that have a message count equal to or greater than 450 and have a status of Retry. The command works immediately without requiring confirmation.

5. **Correct Answer: A**

    A. **Correct**: This command tests the message flow from the Mailbox server NY-EX1 to the Mailbox server NY-EX2.

    B. **Incorrect**: This command tests the message flow from the Mailbox server NY-E2 to the Mailbox server NY-EX1.

    C. **Incorrect**: You use the TargetMailboxServer parameter to specify the target Mailbox server. The TargetDatabase parameter specifies a target mailbox database.

    D. **Incorrect**: You use the TargetMailboxServer parameter to specify the target Mailbox server. The TangetEmailAddress parameter specifies a target email address.

Lesson 3

1. **Correct Answer: C**

    A. **Incorrect**: You need to specify a port on which you access the specified server. For SMTP and ESMTP, this is port 25.

B. Incorrect: This command tests that ESMTP is operating in the Fabrikam.com domain. It does not access the server Mailbox02.fabricam.com using SMTP and ESMTP.

C. Correct: This command accesses the server Mailbox02.fabricam.com using SMTP and ESMTP.

D. Incorrect: This optional command lets you view the characters as you type them. It does not access the server Mailbox02.fabricam.com using SMTP and ESMTP.

2. **Correct Answer: A**

A. Correct: You can use the *Get-NetworkConnectionInfo* cmdlet to view the network configuration information for all network adapters configured on a computer running Exchange Server 2010.

B. Incorrect: The *Test-WebServicesConnectivity* cmdlet tests the functionality of EWS and performs basic operations to verify the functionality of Outlook Anywhere. You cannot use this cmdlet to view the network configuration information for network adapters.

C. Incorrect: The *Test-OutlookWebServices* cmdlet enables you to verify the service information returned to an Outlook client from the Autodiscover service. You cannot use this cmdlet to view the network configuration information for network adapters.

D. Incorrect: The *Set-ActiveSyncVirtualDirectory* cmdlet enables you to configure the Exchange ActiveSync virtual directory. You cannot use this cmdlet to view the network configuration information for network adapters.

3. **Correct Answer: D**

A. Incorrect: You use the ClientAccessServer parameter, not the MailboxServer parameter, to specify a Client Access server. Also, the ConnectionType parameter in this answer is TLS. It should be SSL.

B. Incorrect: The ConnectionType parameter in this answer is TLS. It should be SSL.

C. Incorrect: You use the ClientAccessServer parameter, not the MailboxServer parameter, to specify a Client Access server.

D. Correct: This command tests POP3 connectivity over an SSL connection between the Client Access server VAN-CAS01 and all mailboxes in your Exchange organization.

4. **Correct Answer: A**

A. Correct: IMAP4 uses port 143 by default. SSL-protected IMAP4 uses port 993. For either port, you can use commands based on the *Test-ImapConnectivity* EMS cmdlet to verify that the IMAP4 service is working as expected.

B. Incorrect: POP3 uses port 110. SSL-protected POP3 uses port 995. Therefore, commands based on the *Test-PopConnectivity* EMS cmdlet verify that the POP3 service is working on these ports, not on port 143.

C. Incorrect: RPC uses port 135. MAPI negotiates a dynamic port with a port number greater than 1024. Therefore, the *Test-MapiConnectivity* cmdlet tests connectivity on these ports, not on port 143.

D. **Incorrect:** The *Test-WebServicesConnectivity* cmdlet tests the functionality of EWS and performs basic operations to verify the functionality of Outlook Anywhere. It does not test connectivity on port 143.

5. **Correct Answer: B**

   A. **Incorrect:** This command tests Web services continuity for the Getfolder operation. The test operates over a secure channel authenticated by any available SSL certificate. However, the command also tests continuity for the CreateItem, DeleteItem, and SyncFolderItems operations.

   B. **Correct:** This command tests Web services continuity for the Getfolder operation only. The test can operate over a secure channel authenticated by any available SSL certificate.

   C. **Incorrect:** This command tests Web services continuity for the Getfolder operation. However, the test can operate over an insecure channel but cannot operate over a secure channel authenticated by any available SSL certificate. Also, the command tests continuity for the CreateItem, DeleteItem, and SyncFolderItems operations in addition to the Getfolder operation.

   D. **Incorrect:** This command tests Web services continuity for the Getfolder operation. However, the test can operate over an insecure channel but cannot operate over a secure channel authenticated by any available SSL certificate.

Chapter 9: Case Scenario Answers

Case Scenario 1: Monitoring Mailboxes and Viewing the Continuous Replication Status of Mailbox Database Copies

1. Jeff enters the following command to obtain general information, including status information, about all the mailbox databases on the Mailbox server WWT-Mail01:

   ```
   Get-MailboxDatabase -Server WWT-Mail01 -Status | FL
   ```

2. Jeff enters the following command to obtain statistical information about all the mailboxes on all the databases, including recovery databases, on the Mailbox server WWT-Mail01:

   ```
   Get-MailboxStatistics -Server WWT-Mail01 | FL
   ```

3. The following EMS command returns a list of the 25 mailbox users that are consuming the most resource for the top 25 mailboxes on all the active databases on the Mailbox server WWT-Mail01:

   ```
   Get-StoreUsageStatistics -Server WWT-Mail01
   ```

4. Jeff enters the following command to test replication health on server WWT-Mail01 and view failure information:

   ```
   Test-ReplicationHealth -Identity WWT-Mail01 -OutputObjects | FL
   ```

Case Scenario 2: Managing Queues

1. Terry enters the following command to list all the queues on the Hub Transport server BSA-Hub02 that that contain more than 50 messages:

```
Get-Queue -Server BSA-Hub02 -Filter {MessageCount -gt 50}
```

2. Terry enters the following command to display the number of messages in queues on the Hub Transport server BSA-Hub02 where the next-hop destination is the Adatum.com domain:

```
Get-Queue -Server BSA-Hub02 -Filter {NextHopDomain -eq "adatum.com"
```

3. Terry enters the following command to resume all suspended queues on the Hub Transport server BSA-Hub02:

```
Resume-Queue -Server BSA-Hub02 -Filter {Status -eq "Suspended"}
```

Case Scenario 3: Testing Protocol Connectivity

1. To test connectivity between a Client Access server and user mailboxes on ports 110 and 995, you use the following EMS cmdlet:

```
Test-PopConnectivity
```

2. To test IMAP4 connectivity between a Client Access server and all mailboxes on the Mailbox server NY-EX1, you enter the following EMS cmdlet on the Client Access server:

```
Test-ImapConnectivity -MailboxServer:NY-EX1 | FL
```

3. You enter the following EMS command on a Client Access server to test MAPI connectivity between that server and the Kim Akers mailbox in the Contoso.com domain:

```
Test-MapiConnectivity -Identity "contoso\Kim Akers"
```

Chapter 10: Lesson Review Answers

Lesson Review 1

1. **Correct Answer: D**

   A. **Incorrect:** *Sort-Object* does not sort in descending order by default. You need to include the Descending switch parameter.

   B. **Incorrect:** *Sort-Object* sorts in the order defined by a statistic. You use *Select Object* to define the number of objects listed. In this answer, the cmdlets are the wrong way around.

   C. **Incorrect:** You use *Get-MailboxStatistics*, not *Get-Mailbox*, to return such statistics as item count.

   D. **Correct:** This command lists the top 10 mailboxes in the mailbox database Research in descending order of item count.

2. **Correct Answer: C**

   A. **Incorrect:** You can use System Center Operations Manager 2007 for server monitoring. The tool does not generate a health scan report.

   B. **Incorrect:** You use Exchange Server Mail Flow Analyzer to troubleshoot mail flow problems. The tool does not generate a health scan report.

   C. **Correct:** ExBPA can generate a health scan report.

   D. **Incorrect:** Although you can use EMS commands to obtain information that could indicate problems, the tool does not directly generate a health scan report.

3. **Correct Answer: A**

   A. **Correct:** This command outputs the logon statistics for the mailboxes in the Research database in table format. In a production system, you might want to capture the statistics in a CSV file or view only selected statistics, but neither of these facilities is required by the question.

   B. **Incorrect:** This command outputs the logon statistics for the mailboxes in the entire DEN-EX1 server in table format.

   C. **Incorrect:** This command outputs the logon statistics for the mailboxes in the Research database in list format.

   D. **Incorrect:** This command outputs the logon statistics for the mailboxes in the entire DEN-EX1 server in list format.

4. **Correct Answer: B**

   A. **Incorrect:** The *Get-MailboxStatistics* cmdlet returns statistics for one or more entire mailboxes. It does not return mailbox folder statistics.

   B. **Correct:** This command lists all folders in the Kim Akers mailbox in descending order of item count. It reports the result in list format and displays only the folder name and the number of items.

   C. **Incorrect:** The *Get-MailboxStatistics* cmdlet returns statistics for one or more entire mailboxes. It does not return mailbox folder statistics. Also, the *FT* cmdlet displays the results in table format, not list format.

   D. **Incorrect:** The *FT* cmdlet displays the results in table format, not list format.

5. **Correct Answer: B**

   A. **Incorrect:** The *Test-Message* cmdlet always sends test messages from a system mailbox. The Identity parameter identifies the server that holds the system mailbox.

   B. **Correct:** This command tests that the system mailbox on the Mailbox server DEN-EX1 can send email to the mailbox with the SMTP address KimAkers@adatum.com.

   C. **Incorrect:** You can use the *Get-Message* cmdlet to view the details of one or more messages in a queue on a computer that has the Hub Transport server role or the Edge Transport server role installed. You cannot use the cmdlet to send test messages.

D. **Incorrect:** The Identity parameter of the *Test-Mailflow* cmdlet should identify a server. The TargetEmailAddress parameter should identify the mailbox to which the test message is sent, in this case KimAkers@adatum.com.

Lesson 2

1. **Correct Answer: B**

   A. **Incorrect:** You need to disable subject logging on the tracking logs. This command enables it.

   B. **Correct:** This command disables subject logging on the tracking logs so that you cannot track messages by specifying message subject.

   C. **Incorrect:** You cannot run the *Set-MailboxServer* cmdlet on an Edge Transport server.

   D. **Incorrect:** You cannot run the *Set-MailboxServer* cmdlet on an Edge Transport server.

2. **Correct Answer: A**

   A. **Correct:** This command enables protocol logging for the intraorganization Send connector.

   B. **Incorrect:** This command disables protocol logging for the intraorganization Send connector.

   C. **Incorrect:** The intraorganization Send connector exists on Hub Transport servers. You cannot enable or disable it using commands based on the *Set-MailboxServer* cmdlet.

   D. **Incorrect:** The intraorganization Send connector exists on Hub Transport servers. You cannot enable or disable it using commands based on the *Set-MailboxServer* cmdlet.

3. **Correct Answer: D**

   A. **Incorrect:** Connectivity logs record the connection activity of the outgoing message delivery queues. They do not record all activity by anti-spam and antivirus agents.

   B. **Incorrect:** Protocol logs record SMTP activity between messaging servers as part of messaging delivery. They do not record all activity by anti-spam and antivirus agents.

   C. **Incorrect:** Message Tracking logs record all message activity on Hub Transport, Edge Transport, and Mailbox servers. They do not record all activity by anti-spam and antivirus agents.

   D. **Correct:** Agent logs record all activity by anti-spam and antivirus agents.

4. **Correct Answer: C**

   A. **Incorrect:** You need to changes the maximum age of the connectivity log files on the Hub Transport server DEN-EX2. You cannot use the *Set-MailboxServer* cmdlet to configure a Hub Transport server.

   B. **Incorrect:** You need to changes the maximum age of the connectivity log files on the Hub Transport server DEN-EX2. You cannot use the *Set-MailboxServer* cmdlet to configure a Hub Transport server.

c. **Correct:** This command changes the maximum age of the connectivity log files on the Hub Transport server DEN-EX2 to 30 days

D. **Incorrect:** The ConnectivityLogMaxAge parameter requires a time span argument, for example, 30.00:00:00.

5. **Correct Answer: B**

A. **Incorrect:** The maximum size of the routing table log directory is set on a per-server basis. The cmdlet uses the Identity parameter to specify the server. The Server parameter is used in commands where a per-server setting is optional.

B. **Correct:** This command sets the maximum size of the routing table log directory to 70 MB on the Edge Transport server DEN-EDGE01.

C. **Incorrect:** This command sets the maximum age of routing table log files to 14 days on the Edge Transport server DEN-EDGE01.

D. **Incorrect:** The server DEN-EDGE01 is an Edge Transport server. You cannot use the *Set-MailboxServer* cmdlet to set any properties associated with the Edge Transport server role.

Chapter 10: Case Scenario Answers

Case Scenario 1: Obtaining a Server Health Report and Detecting Suboptimal Settings

1. The ExBPA.

2. The EXPBA generates a list of issues, such as suboptimal configuration settings or unsupported or not-recommended options. You can also use it to report on the general health of a system.

3. No. You can run ExBPA against an entire deployment, against a specific server, or against a set of servers.

4. You can select a Health scan (with or without generating a Performance Baseline), a Permission Check scan, a Connectivity Test scan, or a Baseline scan.

5. You can view list reports, tree reports, and other reports.

Case Scenario 2: Auditing Protocol Log Configuration

1. You need to configure Administrator Audit logging to record changes to protocol log configuration on Receive connectors and Send connectors, including the intraorganization Send connector.

2. The following cmdlets are used to configure protocol log settings and need to be audited:

   ▪ *Set-TransportServer*

   ▪ *Set-ReceiveConnector*

   ▪ *Set-SendConnector*

3. The following parameters are changed when configuring protocol log settings and need to be audited:

   - IntraOrgConnectorProtocolLoggingLevel
   - ProtocolLoggingLevel
   - ReceiveProtocolLogPath
   - SendProtocolLogPath
   - ReceiveProtocolLogMaxFileSize
   - SendProtocolLogMaxFileSize
   - ReceiveProtocolLogMaxAge
   - SendProtocolLogMaxAge
   - ReceiveProtocolLogMaxDirectorySize
   - SendProtocolLogMaxDirectorySize

4. There is no uniquely correct answer to this question. The following commands are suggested:

   - *Set-AdminAuditLogConfig -AdminAuditLogCmdlets Set-TransportServer, Set-ReceiveConnector, SetSendConnector*
   - *Set-AdminAuditLogConfig -AdminAuditLogParameters *ProtocolLoggingLevel, *ProtocolLogPath, *ProtocolLogMaxFileSize, *ProtocolLogMaxAge, *ProtocolLogMaxDirectorySize*

Chapter 11: Lesson Review Answers

Lesson 1

1. Correct Answers: A, B, D, and F

   A. **Correct:** You can create RPTs for the Deleted Items, Drafts, Inbox, Junk E-mail, Outbox, Sent Items, RSS Feeds, Sync Issues, and Conversation History default folders.

   B. **Correct:** You can create RPTs for the Deleted Items, Drafts, Inbox, Junk E-mail, Outbox, Sent Items, RSS Feeds, Sync Issues, and Conversation History default folders.

   C. **Incorrect:** Exchange Server 2010 does not support the creation of RPTs for the Calendar, Contacts, Journal, Notes, and Tasks default folders.

   D. **Correct:** You can create RPTs for the Deleted Items, Drafts, Inbox, Junk E-mail, Outbox, Sent Items, RSS Feeds, Sync Issues, and Conversation History default folders.

   E. **Incorrect:** Exchange Server 2010 does not support the creation of RPTs for the Calendar, Contacts, Journal, Notes, and Tasks default folders.

   F. **Correct:** You can create RPTs for the Deleted Items, Drafts, Inbox, Junk E-mail, Outbox, Sent Items, RSS Feeds, Sync Issues, and Conversation History default folders.

2. **Correct Answer: C**

   A. **Incorrect:** The *New-RetentionPolicy* cmdlet creates a retention policy, which consists of logical grouping of retention tags that can be applied to user mailboxes. You cannot use the cmdlet to create a DPT.

   B. **Incorrect:** The *Set-RetentionPolicy* cmdlet reconfigures an existing retention policy. You cannot use the cmdlet to create a DPT.

   C. **Correct:** You use the *New-RetentionPolicyTag* cmdlet to create retention tags. These can include RPTs, DPTs, and personal tags.

   D. **Incorrect:** The *Set-RetentionPolicyTag* cmdlet reconfigures an existing retention policy tag. You cannot use the cmdlet to create a new retention policy tag, such as a DPT.

3. **Correct Answers: A and C**

   A. **Correct:** This applies the retention policy Accounting directly to the Don Hall mailbox.

   B. **Incorrect:** This creates a retention policy named Accounting and links it to an already existing retention policy tag named Tag-Don-Hall. It does not apply the retention policy Accounting to the Don Hall mailbox.

   C. **Correct:** This applies the retention policy Accounting to all members of the Accountants distribution group. Because Don Hall is a member of this group, the policy is applied to his mailbox.

   D. **Incorrect:** This creates a retention tag named Tag-Don-Hall. It does not apply the retention policy Accounting to the Don Hall mailbox.

4. **Correct Answer: D**

   A. **Incorrect:** This command creates the specified managed folder, but Outlook users are able to minimize the message.

   B. **Incorrect:** This command creates a default managed folder of type Calendar.

   C. **Incorrect**: You use the *Set-ManagedFolder* cmdlet to reconfigure an existing managed folder. You cannot use it to create a new one.

   D. **Correct:** This command creates the specified managed folder. Outlook users are unable to minimize the message.

5. **Correct Answer: A**

   A. **Correct:** This command applies the managed folder mailbox policy TechnicalSupportPolicy to the Kim Akers mailbox.

   B. **Incorrect:** You use the *New-ManagedFolder* EMS cmdlet to create a managed folder. You cannot use it to apply a managed folder mailbox policy to a user mailbox.

   C. **Incorrect:** This command applies a retention policy, not a managed mailbox policy. Also, it assumes that Kim Akers is a member of the TechnicalSupport distribution group, and this information is not given in the question.

   D. **Incorrect:** This command applies a retention policy, not a managed mailbox policy.

Lesson 2

1. **Correct Answer: D**

   A. **Incorrect:** This disables IRM for the default OWA mailbox policy. However, as this policy is not typically applied to all mailboxes in an Exchange organization, the command does not disable IRM features in OWA for the entire Exchange organization.

   B. **Incorrect:** This command disables IRM in OWA for the virtual directory MyVirtualDirectory on server VAN-EX2 but not for the entire Exchange organization.

   C. **Incorrect:** This command sets transport decryption to mandatory. Any message that cannot be decrypted is rejected, and an NDR is returned to the sender. The command does not disable IRM features in OWA for the entire Exchange organization.

   D. **Correct**: This command disables IRM features in OWA for the entire Exchange organization.

2. **Correct Answer: B**

   A. **Incorrect:** This command configures the Kim Akers mailbox as a journaling mailbox, not the KimAkers-Journaling mailbox.

   B. **Correct:** This command ensures that all mail sent to the KimAkers@adatum.com mailbox is also sent to the journaling mailbox KimAkers-Journaling for compliance purposes.

   C. **Incorrect:** This command creates the Outlook protection rule KimAkers-Journaling. This rule protects messages sent to the Kim Akers mailbox with the AD RMS template Protect-Confidential. The command does not configure a journaling mailbox.

   D. **Incorrect:** This command creates a MailTip. It does not configure a journaling mailbox.

3. **Correct Answer: C**

   A. **Incorrect:** To create a locale-specific version of an existing message classification, you need to create a new instance of the message classification. You use the *Set-MessageClassification* cmdlet to configure an existing message classification, not to create new instance.

   B. **Incorrect:** You use the *Get-MessageClassification* cmdlet to view an existing message classification instance. You cannot use this cmdlet use to create a locale-specific version of an existing message classification.

   C. **Correct:** To create a locale-specific version of an existing message classification, you need to create a new instance of the message classification. You can use the *New-MessageClassification* cmdlet to create new message classifications and new instances of existing message classifications.

   D. **Incorrect:** You use this procedure to modify the settings of a default message classification. You cannot use it to create a locale-specific version of an existing message classification.

4. **Correct Answer: A**

   A. **Correct:** This command configures the existing mailbox MyJournalingMailbox@adatum .com to hold NDRs if any journaling mailbox cannot accept messages and hence configures it as an alternate journaling mailbox.

   B. **Incorrect:** This command configures the mailbox MyJournalingMailbox to accept messages only from the Microsoft Exchange recipient and to accept messages only from authenticated senders. It does not configure it as an alternate journaling mailbox.

   C. **Incorrect:** This command configures the Prohibit Send And Receive At setting for the mailbox MyJournalingMailbox to 500MB. It does not configure the mailbox as an alternate journaling mailbox.

   D. **Incorrect:** This command creates the mailbox MyJournalingMailbox@adatum.com in the mailbox database MyMailboxDatabase. It applies the password held in the secure string $password. It does not configure the mailbox as an alternate journaling mailbox.

5. **Correct Answers: B and E**

   A. **Incorrect:** You can use the *Set-TransportConfig* EMS cmdlet to modify the transport configuration settings for the whole Microsoft Exchange Server 2010 organization. One significant use of this cmdlet is to configure an alternate journaling mailbox. You cannot use this cmdlet to create an ethical wall.

   B. **Correct:** You can create and configure an ethical wall by creating a transport rule using the New Transport Rule Wizard in the EMC.

   C. **Incorrect:** You can use the *Set-IRMConfiguration* EMS cmdlet to configure IRM features such as journal report decryption. You cannot use this cmdlet to create an ethical wall.

   D. **Incorrect:** You use the *New-OutlookProtectionRule* EMS cmdlet to create an Outlook protection rule. Typically, you might apply an AD RMS template to such a rule. You cannot use this cmdlet to create an ethical wall.

   E. **Correct:** You can create and configure an ethical wall by creating a transport rule using the *New-TransportRule* EMS cmdlet.

   F. **Incorrect:** You can use the New Mailbox Wizard in the EMC to create a user mailbox or a journaling mailbox. You cannot use this cmdlet to create an ethical wall.

Chapter 11: Case Scenario Answers

Case Scenario 1: Configuring Retention Tags

1. *New-RetentionPolicyTag "RPT-DeletedItems" -Type "DeletedItems" -Comment "Deleted Items purged after 62 days" -RetentionEnabled $true -AgeLimitForRetention 62 -RetentionAction PermanentlyDelete*

2. *New-RetentionPolicyTag "MT-Default" -Type All -Comment "Items without a retention tag are deleted after 270 days." -RetentionEnabled $true -AgeLimitForRetention 270 -RetentionAction MoveToDeletedItems*

3. New-RetentionPolicyTag "MT-PersonalArchive" -Type Personal -Comment "Tagged messages are moved to the archive after 1805 days." -RetentionEnabled $true -AgeLimitForRetention 180 -RetentionAction MoveToArchive

4. Set-RetentionPolicyTag "RPT-DeletedItems" –AgeLimitForRetention 60

Case Scenario 2: Configuring MailTips

1. Set-OrganizationConfig -MailTipsAllTipsEnabled $true

2. Set-OrganizationConfig -MailTipsLargeAudienceThreshold 30

3. Set-OrganizationConfig -MailTipsExternalRecipientsTipsEnabled $true

4. The external recipients MailTip relies on group metrics data. MailTips that rely on group metrics data are enabled by default, but in this case they have likely been disabled. You should enable them using the command *Set-OrganizationConfig -MailTipsGroupMetricsEnabled $true*.

5. Set-Mailbox -Identity "NWT-HelpDesk" -MailTip "A Technical Support representative will contact you within 2 hours."

Chapter 12: Lesson Review Answers

Lesson 1

1. Correct Answers: B and C

   A. **Incorrect:** You need to run the command as specified on the server on which the Internet Send connector is configured, in this case DEN-Edge1.

   B. **Correct:** This command enables domain security on the Send connector Internet on the Edge Transport server DEN-Edge1

   C. **Correct:** This command specifies the domain to which you want to send domain-secured email (in this case contoso.com). Because the changes that you make in outbound domain security are global, you need to run this command on an internal Exchange Server 2010 server (for example, Hub Transport server DEN-Hub1). The configuration changes you make are replicated to Edge Transport servers by using the EdgeSync service.

   D. **Incorrect:** Because the changes that you make in outbound domain security are global, you need to run this command on an internal Exchange Server 2010 server and not on the Edge Transport server DEN-Edge1.

   E. **Incorrect:** This command enables protocol logging. Also, you need to run it on the server that has the Internet Send connector configured.

   F. **Incorrect:** This command enables protocol logging on the Internet Send connector on DEN-Edge1. It does not enable domain security or specify the domain to which you want to send domain-secured email.

2. **Correct Answer: D**

   A. **Incorrect:** TLS can be configured only to encrypt messages or to authenticate only the receiving sender. It does not mandate the authentication of both the receiving and the sending servers.

   B. **Incorrect:** SSL is the HTTP implementation of TLS. It authenticates only the receiving sender.

   C. **Incorrect:** HTTP is used to send web-based traffic over the Internet. Unless combined with SSL to form HTTPS, it does not authenticate servers or encrypt messages.

   D. **Correct:** MTLS mandates the authentication of both the receiving and the sending server and encrypts email messages.

3. **Correct Answer: A**

   A. **Correct:** This command disables S/MIME on the OWA virtual directory in the default IIS website on the server on which it is entered.

   B. **Incorrect:** This command disables S/MIME on the OWA virtual directory in the default IIS website on the server on which it is entered, assuming that S/MIME has previously been disabled.

   C. **Incorrect.** This command removes the virtual directory. The question requires that S/MIME is disabled on the virtual directory, not that the virtual directory is removed altogether.

   D. **Incorrect:** The *Get-OwaVirtualDirectory* cmdlet retrieves and displays the configuration settings currently set on OWA virtual directories or on a specific OWA virtual directory. However, you cannot use it to change the configuration of a virtual directory.

4. **Correct Answer C**

   A. **Incorrect:** AD DS stores directory data and manages communication between users and domains, including user logon processes, authentication, and directory searches. It is involved in the process of deploying AD RMS with identity federation but does not specifically enable you to create an RMS Federation.

   B. **Incorrect:** AD CS provides customizable services for creating and managing public key certificates used in software security systems that employ public key technologies. Such certificates are utilized in the deployment of AD RMS with identity federation support (and for many other purposes). However, AD CS does not specifically enable you to create an RMS Federation.

   C. **Correct:** AD FS specifically enables you to create an RMS Federation.

   D. **Incorrect:** AD LDS is an LDAP directory service that provides flexible support for directory-enabled applications without the restrictions of AD DS. AD LDS does not specifically enable you to create an RMS Federation.

5. **Correct Answer: B**

   A. **Incorrect:** This command grants Kim Akers the permission to send email as Don Hall.

   B. **Correct:** This command specifically denies Kim Akers the permission to send email as Don Hall. A Deny Send As permission overrides any Send As permission that Kim might be granted because of group membership.

C. **Incorrect:** This command removes the permission granted to Kim Akers to send email as Don Hall. However, if Kim is granted Send As permission through group membership, she can still send email as Don Hall.

D. **Incorrect:** This command removes the Deny Send As permission that prevents Kim Akers from sending email as Don Hall. If Kim is subsequently granted this permission directly or through group membership, she can send email as Don Hall.

Lesson 2

1. **Correct Answer: C**

   A. **Incorrect:** This command removes the IP allow list provider contoso.com from connection filtering configuration.

   B. **Incorrect:** This command disables connection filtering using the IP block list.

   C. **Correct:** This command disables connection filtering using the IP allow list but does not affect connection filtering using other lists or list providers.

   D. **Incorrect:** This command disables connection filtering entirely.

2. **Correct Answer: B**

   A. **Incorrect:** You need to obtain an ID for an allow list entry before you can remove it using the *Remove-IPAllowListEntry* EMS cmdlet. You cannot specify an IP address directly using the Identity parameter.

   B. **Correct:** This command uses the *Get-IPAllowListEntry* EMS cmdlet to get the ID of the IP access list entry and then pipes this into the *Remove-IPAllowListEntry* cmdlet to remove it.

   C. **Incorrect:** You need to obtain an ID for an allow list entry before you can remove it using the *Remove-IPAllowListEntry* EMS cmdlet. You cannot specify an IP address directly using the IPAddress parameter.

   D. **Incorrect:** This removes an IP block list entry, not an IP allow list entry.

3. **Correct Answer: A**

   A. **Correct:** The email messages are received from KimAkers@contoso.com, so KimAkers@contoso.com is a sender. This command bypasses content filtering for that sender.

   B. **Incorrect:** KimAkers@contoso.com is a sender, not a recipient. This command would bypass content filtering for all email sent to KimAkers@contoso.com.

   C. **Incorrect:** This command bypasses content filtering for all email sent from any mailbox in the contoso.com domain. This is not what is required.

   D. **Incorrect:** KimAkers@contoso.com is a single mailbox, not a domain.

4. **Correct Answer: C**

   A. **Incorrect:** The value is set to Pass if the IP address and PRA passed the Sender ID verification check.

   B. **Incorrect:** The value is set to Fail if the IP address is not permitted; no PRA is found in the incoming mail, or the sending domain does not exist.

C. **Correct:** The value is set to None if no published SPF data exists in the sender's DNS.

D. **Incorrect:** The value is set to TempError if a temporary DNS failure occurred (for example, the DNS server was unavailable).

5. **Correct Answer: D**

A. **Incorrect:** A file name extension attachment filter entry should have a Type parameter set to FileType, not ContentType.

B. **Incorrect:** A file name extension attachment filter entry should have a Type parameter set to FileType, not ContentType. Also, you use the Name parameter, not the Identity parameter, to specify the name of a file name extension attachment filter entry.

C. **Incorrect:** You use the Name parameter, not the Identity parameter, to specify the name of a file name extension attachment filter entry.

D. **Correct:** This command filters all email attachments that have the file name extension .vba.

Chapter 12: Case Scenario Answers

Case Scenario 1: Configuring Domain Security

1. You would run the following commands:

```
$Data1 = New-ExchangeCertificate -GenerateRequest -FriendlyName "Internet certificate
for TST-EX2" -SubjectName "DC=com,DC=Tailsintoys,CN=TST-EX2.adatum.com" -DomainName
mail.tailspintoys.com

Set-Content -Path "C:\Certificates\TST-EX2-request.req" -Value $Data1
```

2. You would run the following command:

```
Import-ExchangeCertificate -FileData ([Byte[]]$(Get-Content -Path C:\Certificates\
TST-EX2-certificate.pfx -Encoding Byte -ReadCount 0)) | Enable-ExchangeCertificate
-Services SMTP
```

3. You would run the following command:

```
Set-TransportConfig -TLSSendDomainSecureList treyresearch.com
```

4. You would run the following command:

```
Set-SendConnector Internet -DomainSecureEnabled:$true
```

Case Scenario 2: Configuring Anti-Spam Settings

1. Sender reputation can be used on Edge Transport servers to block messages according to sender characteristics. For example, SMTP servers that repeatedly send messages with high SCL ratings, that fail sender open proxy or reverse DNS lookup tests, or that are identified

as likely spammers through HELO/EHLO analysis are given an SRL rating that identifies them as probable spam sources. Sender reputation can be automatically configured to block email messages from senders based on their SRL levels for configurable periods of time.

2. They can add the IP address of NorthWind Traders' SMTP servers to the IP allow list. Alternatively, when configuring content filtering, they can exclude the northwindtraders.com domain and its subdomains from content filtering so that commercial messages from those domains do not generate a high SCL rating.

3. They can use the *Add-ContentFilterPhrase* cmdlet to add the allowed word and the blocked phrases. This will result in a high SCL rating for messages whose subject contains the blocked phrases but not for those whose subject contains the allowed word. An example follows:

```
Add-ContentFilterPhrase -Phrase "bicycle" -Influence GoodWord

Add-ContentFilterPhrase -Phrase "earn extra cash" -Influence BadWord

Add-ContentFilterPhrase -Phrase "lose weight" -Influence BadWord
```

Chapter 13: Lesson Review Answers

Lesson 1

1. **Correct Answer: A**

   A. **Correct:** You can use the *Set-DatabaseAvailabilityGroup* cmdlet to configure an alternate witness server for an existing DAG.

   B. **Incorrect:** The *Add-DatabaseAvailabilityGroupServer* cmdlet is used to add servers to existing DAGs. This cmdlet cannot be used to configure an alternate witness server for an existing DAG.

   C. **Incorrect:** The *New-DatabaseAvailabilityGroup* cmdlet is used to create new DAGs. This cmdlet cannot be used to configure an alternate witness server for an existing DAG.

   D. **Incorrect:** The *Set-MailboxDatabaseCopy* cmdlet allows you to configure the properties of a database copy. This cmdlet cannot be used to configure an alternate witness server for an existing DAG.

2. **Correct Answer: C**

   A. **Correct:** Microsoft recommends that you host the DAG witness server on a computer running the Hub Transport server role. You should not place the DAG witness server on a server hosting the Mailbox server role, as this will preclude you from adding the Mailbox server to the DAG at some point in the future.

   B. **Incorrect:** Microsoft recommends that you host the DAG witness Server on a computer running the Hub Transport role rather than the Client Access server role.

C. **Correct:** You should plan to host the Witness server role on a Hub Transport server that does not host the Mailbox server role.

D. **Incorrect:** You should not plan to host the Witness server role on an Edge Transport server. Edge Transport servers should not be members of the same Active Directory domain or forest as the DAG member servers.

3. **Correct Answer: D**

   A. **Incorrect:** The *Set-MailboxDatabaseCopy* cmdlet configures the properties of an existing mailbox database copy. This cmdlet does not allow you to add copies of mailbox databases to servers within the DAG.

   B. **Incorrect:** The *Add-DatabaseAvailabilityGroupServer* cmdlet allows you to add a new Mailbox server to an existing DAG. This cmdlet does not allow you to add copies of mailbox databases to servers within the DAG.

   C. **Incorrect:** The *Set-DatabaseAvailabilityGroup* cmdlet allows you to configure the properties of a DAG but does not allow you to add copies of mailbox databases to servers within the DAG.

   D. **Correct:** The *Add-MailboxDatabaseCopy* cmdlet is used to create a new copy of an existing mailbox database that is hosted within a DAG.

4. **Correct Answer: B**

   A. **Incorrect:** The *Add-MailboxDatabaseCopy* cmdlet is used to add a new mailbox database copy. You cannot use this cmdlet to configure the replay lag time and activation preference for an existing mailbox database copy.

   B. **Correct:** The *Set-MailboxDatabaseCopy* cmdlet allows you to configure the replay lag time and activation preference for an existing mailbox database copy.

   C. **Incorrect:** The *Set-DatabaseAvailabilityGroup* cmdlet is used to configure a DAG's properties. You cannot use this cmdlet to configure the replay lag time and activation preference for an existing mailbox database copy.

   D. **Incorrect:** The *Resume-MailboxDatabaseCopy* cmdlet resumes a suspended mailbox database copy. You cannot use this cmdlet to configure the replay lag time and activation preference for an existing mailbox database copy.

5. **Correct Answer: C**

   A. **Incorrect:** The *Set-DatabaseAvailabilityGroup* cmdlet allows you to configure the properties of a DAG but does not allow you to configure the failover priority of mailbox database copies.

   B. **Incorrect:** The *Add-DatabaseAvailabilityGroupServer* cmdlet is used to add an existing Exchange Server 2010 Mailbox server to an existing DAG. You cannot use this cmdlet to configure the failover priority of mailbox database copies.

   C. **Correct:** Use the *Set-MailboxDatabase* copy cmdlet to configure the failover priority of a mailbox database copy. Failover priority is configured on a per-mailbox-database-copy basis and not on a per-DAG-member basis.

D. Incorrect: The *Set-DatabaseAvailabilityGroupNetwork* cmdlet allows you to configure the properties of a DAG network. This cmdlet does not allow you to configure failover priority for mailbox database copies.

Lesson 2

1. **Correct Answer: C**

   A. Incorrect: You use the *Get-PublicFolder* cmdlet to get information about public folders. You cannot use this cmdlet to configure an existing public folder to replicate to specific public folder databases.

   B. Incorrect: You use the *New-PublicFolder* cmdlet to create new public folders. You cannot use this cmdlet to configure an existing public folder to replicate to specific public folder databases.

   C. Correct: You use the *Set-PublicFolder* cmdlet to configure an existing public folder to replicate to specific public folder databases.

   D. Incorrect: The *Remove-PublicFolder* cmdlet removes a public folder. You cannot use this cmdlet to configure an existing public folder to replicate to specific public folder databases.

2. **Correct Answer: A**

   A. Correct: The *Set-PublicFolder* cmdlet allows you to specify which public folder databases host content replicas of specific public folders. You can modify which databases host content replicas by modifying the list of databases.

   B. Incorrect: The *Remove-PublicFolder* cmdlet allows you to remove a public folder. This cmdlet does not allow you to adjust the list of public folder databases that host a specific content replica.

   C. Incorrect: The *Set-MailPublicFolder* cmdlet allows you to configure the mail-related settings of mail-enabled public folders. This cmdlet does not allow you to adjust the list of public folder databases that host a specific content replica.

   D. Incorrect: The *Disable-MailPublicFolder* cmdlet allows you to disable mail settings for a mail-enabled public folder. This cmdlet does not allow you to adjust the list of public folder databases that host a specific content replica.

3. **Correct Answer: C**

   A. Incorrect: The *Update-PublicFolder* cmdlet allows you to update a public folder but does not allow you to configure public folder replication schedules.

   B. Incorrect: The *Update-PublicFolderHierarchy* allows you to force and update of the public folder hierarchy. This cmdlet does not allow you to configure the replication schedule for a public folder.

   C. Correct: The *Set-PublicFolder* cmdlet allows you to configure the replication schedule for that public folder.

D. Incorrect: The *Set-MailPublicFolder* cmdlet allows you to configure mail settings for public folders but does not allow you to configure replication schedule settings for public folders.

4. **Correct Answer: B**

    A. Incorrect: The *Set-PublicFolderDatabase* cmdlet allows you to configure the properties of a public folder database. It does not allow you to update the public folder hierarchy.

    B. Correct: The *Update-PublicFolderHierarchy* cmdlet allows you to update the list of folders.

    C. Incorrect: The *Get-PublicFolder* cmdlet allows you to get information about a public folder. It does not allow you to update the public folder hierarchy.

    D. Incorrect: The *Update-PublicFolder* cmdlet allows you to synchronize a public folder. It does not allow you to update the public folder hierarchy.

5. **Correct Answer: A**

    A. Correct: You can configure an existing public folder database so that it can be overwritten by a restore operation using the *Set-PublicFolderDatabase* cmdlet with the AllowFileRestore parameter.

    B. Incorrect: You cannot use the *Set-PublicFolder* cmdlet to configure the properties of a public folder database. You must use the *Set-PublicFolderDatabase* cmdlet with the AllowFileRestore parameter to configure an existing public folder database so that you can overwrite the database during a file restore.

    C. Incorrect: You cannot use the *New-PublicFolderDatabase* cmdlet to modify the properties of an existing public folder database. You also cannot use the *New-PublicFolderDatabase* cmdlet to configure a new public folder database in recovery mode, as public folder databases do not support recovery mode. You must use the *Set-PublicFolderDatabase* cmdlet with the AllowFileRestore parameter to configure an existing public folder database so that you can overwrite the database during a file restore.

    D. Incorrect: You cannot use the *New-PublicFolder* cmdlet to modify the properties of an existing public folder database. You must use the *Set-PublicFolderDatabase* cmdlet with the AllowFileRestore parameter to configure an existing public folder database so that you can overwrite the database during a file restore.

Lesson 3

1. **Correct Answer: D**

    A. Incorrect: Client access arrays cannot span sites. You are going to need to deploy a client access array in each site if you are going to meet the goal of ensuring that each Client Access server at the organization is a part of a client access array.

    B. Incorrect: Client access arrays cannot span sites. You are going to need to deploy a client access array in each site if you are going to meet the goal of ensuring that each Client Access server at the organization is a part of a client access array.

C. **Incorrect:** Client access arrays cannot span sites. You are going to need to deploy a client access array in each site if you are going to meet the goal of ensuring that each Client Access server at the organization is a part of a client access array.

D. **Correct:** Client access arrays cannot span sites. If there are five sites and two client access arrays in each site, you need to deploy five client access arrays.

2. **Correct Answer: C**

A. **Incorrect:** You need to configure one EdgeSync subscription per Edge Transport server.

B. **Incorrect:** You need to configure one EdgeSync subscription per Edge Transport server.

C. **Correct:** You need to configure one EdgeSync subscription per Edge Transport server. Subscribing and Edge Transport server to one Hub Transport server in a site will subscribe the Edge Transport server to all Hub Transport servers in the site.

D. **Incorrect:** You do not need to configure six subscriptions, as three subscriptions will be sufficient. It is necessary to subscribe each Edge Transport server to only a single Hub Transport server in a site. The subscription information will replicate to the other Hub Transport servers in that site.

3. **Correct Answers: A and B**

A. **Correct:** You can ensure that clients are able to access their mailboxes through OWA by deploying a Client Access server array at each site. This requires you to add an additional Client Access server at each site before joining both Client Access servers in an array.

B. **Correct:** You can ensure that clients are able to access their mailboxes through OWA by deploying a Client Access server array at each site. This requires you to add an additional Client Access server at each site before joining both Client Access servers in an array.

C. **Incorrect:** Client Access servers cannot leverage DAGs to ensure that the Client Access servers are highly available.

D. **Incorrect:** Adding an additional Hub Transport server at each site will not ensure that OWA is available in the event that a Client Access server fails.

4. **Correct Answer: C**

A. **Incorrect:** Hub transport servers cannot be members of a DAG. You can make Hub Transport servers highly available by ensuring that there is more than one Hub Transport server in each site.

B. **Incorrect:** Hub transport servers cannot be added to a Client Access server array. You can make Hub Transport servers highly available by ensuring that there is more than one Hub Transport server in each site.

C. **Correct:** To provide high availability for Hub Transport servers, add additional Hub Transport servers to each site. It is not necessary to configure NLB to make Hub Transport servers highly available.

D. **Incorrect:** You can make Hub Transport servers highly available by ensuring that there is more than one Hub Transport server in each site.

5. **Correct Answers: C and D**

   A. **Incorrect:** You cannot use DAGs to provide high availability to Edge Transport servers. You can use DNS round-robin and NLB to provide high availability to Edge Transport servers.

   B. **Incorrect:** You cannot use a Client Access server array to provide high availability to Edge Transport servers. You can use DNS round-robin and NLB to provide high availability to Edge Transport servers.

   C. **Correct:** You can use DNS round-robin and NLB to provide high availability to Edge Transport servers.

   D. **Correct:** You can use DNS round-robin and NLB to provide high availability to Edge Transport servers.

Chapter 13: Case Scenario Answers

Case Scenario 1: Database Availability Groups at ProseWare

1. *New-DatabaseAvailabilityGroup*
2. *Add-DatabaseAvailabilityGroupServer*
3. *Add-MailboxDatabaseCopy*

Case Scenario 2: High Availability at Contoso

1. Deploy an additional Edge Transport server in the perimeter network. Configure multiple MX records. Subscribe each Edge Transport server using EdgeSync.

2. Configure NLB prior to configuring a client access array.

3. Add additional public folder databases and configure replication between them.

Chapter 14: Lesson Review Answers

Lesson 1

1. **Correct Answer: A**

   A. **Correct:** This command merges the databases by exporting the data from the RDB RecoveryDB and importing it into the recovered database MyRecovery.

   B. **Incorrect:** To perform a merge, you use the *Get-Mailbox* command to select the recovered database and then pipe the result into the *Restore-Mailbox* command, identifying the RDB in the second command. In this answer, the commands are in the wrong order.

C. Incorrect: This command attempts to merge the contents of MyRecovery into RecoveryDB. This is not what is required.

D. Incorrect: In this command, both the databases and the EMS cmdlets are in the wrong order.

2. **Correct Answer: C**

A. Incorrect: The time period is in an incorrect format. The format is *dd.hh:mm:ss*.

B. Incorrect: The DeletedItemRetention parameter defines a period during which deleted items in mailboxes can be retrieved by the end user. It does not define the mailbox retention period. Also, the time period is in an incorrect format.

C. Correct: This command configures the mailbox retention period for all mailboxes in the mailbox database Research to be 24 days.

D. Incorrect: The DeletedItemRetention parameter defines a period during which deleted items in mailboxes can be retrieved by the end user. It does not define the mailbox retention period.

3. **Correct Answer: A**

A. Correct: You can use the Eseutil utility to defragment your Exchange databases offline, to check their integrity, and to repair a damaged or lost database. One use of this utility is to bring a mailbox database that is in a dirty shutdown state into a clean shutdown state.

B. Incorrect: You can use the Isinteg utility to run tests on the Information Store and to fix detected errors and problems in mailbox databases. You cannot use this utility to bring a mailbox database that is in a dirty shutdown state into a clean shutdown state.

C. Incorrect: You can use the *Get-MailboxDatabase* cmdlet to retrieve one or more mailbox database objects. You cannot use this cmdlet to bring a mailbox database that is in a dirty shutdown state into a clean shutdown state.

D. Incorrect: You cannot mount a database that is in a dirty shutdown state. You therefore cannot use this cmdlet to bring a mailbox database that is in a dirty shutdown state into a clean shutdown state.

4. **Correct Answers: B and D**

A. Incorrect: The database you want to restore is still online. You need to perform a dial tone recovery only if the database is offline and service to your end users has been interrupted.

B. Correct: When recovering a single database on a Mailbox server that holds multiple databases, you need to recover to another location and move the recovered data into an RDB.

C. Incorrect: If you recover to the original location, this recovers all databases on the server. You do not need (or want) to recover the unaffected databases.

D. Correct: When you want to recover only one database rather than all databases on the server, you recover to another location.

5. **Correct Answer: D**

   A. **Incorrect:** You want to obtain the user mailboxes in the database OldDatabase in order to move them into the database NewDatabase. The EMS cmdlet you use to do this is *Get-Mailbox*, not *Get-MailboxStatistics*.

   B. **Incorrect:** You need to use the *Get-Mailbox* EMS cmdlet to get the user mailboxes in the mailbox database OldDatabase and then the *Set-Mailbox* EMS cmdlet to put them in the mailbox database NewDatabase. In this answer, the two cmdlets are the wrong way around.

   C. **Incorrect:** You need to get the user mailboxes in the mailbox database OldDatabase and then put them in the mailbox database NewDatabase. In this answer, the two databases are the wrong way around.

   D. **Correct:** This command moves all the user mailboxes but not the system mailboxes from the database OldDatabase to the new database NewDatabase.

Lesson 2

1. **Correct Answer: C**

   A. **Incorrect:** The CloneConfigData parameter requires the full path to the XML configuration file as its argument, and the CloneConfigAnswer parameter requires the full path to the XML answer file. In this answer, the configuration and answer file paths are the wrong way around.

   B. **Incorrect:** In this answer, the configuration and answer file paths are the wrong way around. Also, the IsImport switch parameter needs to be set to $true to import configuration settings.

   C. **Correct:** This command imports the DEN-EDGE1 configuration settings on DEN-EDGE2.

   D. **Incorrect:** This command creates the XML answer file. The IsImport switch parameter needs to be set to $true to import configuration settings.

2. **Correct Answer: B**

   A. **Incorrect:** You need to run Setup in Recoverserver mode from the Exchange Server 2010 installation media. The operating system should already be installed.

   B. **Correct:** This procedure runs Setup in Recoverserver mode from the Exchange Server 2010 installation media and recovers the Hub Transport server role.

   C. **Incorrect:** The /RecoverCMS switch was used to recover a cloned Mailbox server in Exchange Server 2007. It is not used in Exchange Server 2010. Also, you recover a server role by running Setup on the Exchange installation media, not the operating system installation media.

   D. **Incorrect:** The /RecoverCMS switch was used to recover a cloned Mailbox server in Exchange Server 2007. It is not used in Exchange Server 2010.

3. **Correct Answer: A**

   A. **Correct:** This command reconfigure a mailbox database copy of the Research database and specifies the replay lag time and the truncation lag time with the same values that they had on the failed server.

B. Incorrect: The format for the lag times is incorrect. It should be *dd.hh:mm:ss*.

C. Incorrect: The format for the lag times is incorrect. It should be *dd.hh:mm:ss*.

D. Incorrect: This command specifies replay lag time of three days and a truncation lag time of two days instead of the other way around.

4. **Correct Answer: A**

   A. Correct: The Edge Transport server role is installed on a stand-alone server. Because the server is not in a domain, its configuration is not held in Active Directory and cannot be recovered by using the *Setup /m:RecoverServer* command.

   B. Incorrect: The Client Access server role is installed on a member server in a domain, and its configuration is held in Active Directory. You can restore a failed server running the Client Access server role to its initial default state by running Exchange Setup in Recoverserver mode.

   C. Incorrect: The Mailbox server role is installed on a member server in a domain, and its configuration is held in Active Directory. You can restore a failed server running the Mailbox server role by running Exchange Setup in Recoverserver mode. You then need to restore mailbox and public folder database information from backup.

   D. Incorrect: The Hub Transport server role is installed on a member server in a domain, andits configuration is held in Active Directory. You can restore a failed server running the client Hub Transport server role by running Exchange Setup in Recover server mode.

Chapter 14: Case Scenario Answers

Case Scenario 1: Recovering Mailbox Data

1. Because the mailbox is disconnected and the deleted mailbox retention period (typically 30 days) has not expired, you can reconnect the disconnected mailbox to the user account. You can use the EMC to find the disconnected mailbox, right-click it, and click Connect, or you can use an EMS command, such as the following:

```
Connect-Mailbox -Database "Marketing" -Identity "Don Hall" -User "Don Hall"
```

2. Create an empty database as a dial tone database that enables users to receive and send email. Carry out a dial tone restore, which places restored mailbox data in an RDB that you then merge with the dial tone database. Run transaction log files against the new database to ensure that information is restored to the point of failure.

Case Scenario 2: Restoring a Client Access Server

1. The changes you have made to HTTP virtual servers running on the Client Access server are not restored.

2. Changes to these virtual servers are stored in IIS configuration data.

3. You need to ensure you have a valid SSL certificate installed.

Index

Symbols and Numbers

.txt files, 479, 485

A

A records, 327–28, 716–17
Accept Client Certificates, ActiveSync properties, 187
Acceptance policies, 118
accepted domains, 334–36, 358–60, 371–72
access control, 456–57, 575, 580–81, 588–89
access control lists (ACLs). *See* Role-Based Access
    Control (RBAC)
AccessRights, 108, 631–32
AccessSystemSecurity, 632
account federation server (AFS), 640
account namespace, federated sharing, 241, 250
account organizations, 635
account partner cookies, 636
ActivationPreference, 702
ActivationSuspended, 401
Active Directory. *See also* routing
    dynamic distribution groups, 147–49
    EdgeSync, 370–71
    installation preparation
        coexistence and migration, 8–10
        domain preparation, 7–8
        more information, 8
        overview, 3, 6–7
        preparing for Exchange 2010, 3–8
    installing Exchange Server 2010, 21–27
    mail flow, 436–37, 484
    mailboxes, 96, 98–100, 111–13
    mail-enabled users, 142–43
    managed folders, 555, 557
    message routing, 314–21

Microsoft Exchange Best Practices Analyzer
    (ExBPA), 487–93
objects, permissions for, 631–34
OWA certificates, 620
practice, installation preparation, 34–36
recovery planning, 758
remote delivery queue, 420–21
replicating journal rules, 576
self-signed certificates, 623–24
share mailboxes, 124
site map, 321
transport rules, storage, 277, 282–83
Active Directory Application Mode (ADAM), 278, 656–57
Active Directory Certificate Services (AD CS), 623, 635, 642
Active Directory Domain Services (AD DS), 221,
    433–37, 634–35. *See also* Role-Based Access
    Control (RBAC)
Active Directory Domain Services Installation Wizard, 34
Active Directory Domains and Trusts, 3–4
Active Directory Federation Services (AD FS)
    authentication, 639–41
    business-to-business partnerships, 635–36
    certificates, 637
    claims, 636
    configuring, 638–39, 641–42
    cookies, 636
    IRM, applying, 292
    role services, 638
Active Directory Lightweight Directory Services
    (AD LDS), 278, 282–83, 484, 623–24, 674
Active Directory Replication Monitor, 5
Active Directory Rights Management Service (AD RMS)
    AD RMS rights policy templates, 291–92, 296,
        300–01, 569
    AD RMS server, compliance, 568–69
    ADRMSuperUsers distribution group, 293–94
    installing, 288–89

H

N

R

T

W

X

About the Authors

ORIN THOMAS, MCSE, MCTS, MCITP, MCT, MVP, is an author, trainer, and frequent public speaker who has authored more than a dozen books for Microsoft Press. He has contributed to and written several books on different versions of Exchange over the past decade. He holds the MCITP: Enterprise Messaging Administrator 2010 certification.

IAN MCLEAN, MCSE, MCTS, MCITP, MCT, has over 40 years' experience in industry, commerce, and education. He started his career as an electronics engineer before going into distance learning and then education as a university professor. Currently, he runs his own consultancy company. Ian has written over 20 books plus many papers and technical articles. He has been working with Microsoft Server operating systems since 1997 and with Microsoft Exchange Server since 1999.

Get Certified—Windows Server 2008

Resources for Microsoft Exchange Server and Forefront

**Microsoft®
Exchange Server 2010
Best Practices**

Siegfried Jagott and Joel Stidley
with the Microsoft Exchange
Server Team

ISBN 9780735627192

Apply real-world best practices, field-tested
solutions, and candid advice for administering
Exchange Server 2010 and SP1—and optimize
your operational efficiency and results.

**Microsoft Forefront®
Threat Management
Gateway (TMG)
Administrator's Companion**

Jim Harrison, Yuri Diogenes,
and Mohit Saxena from the
Microsoft Forefront TMG Team
with Dr. Tom Shinder

ISBN 9780735626386

Help protect your business from Web-based
threats with this essential administrator's reference
to planning, deploying, and managing Forefront
TMG—successor to Microsoft ISA Server.

**Microsoft
Exchange Server 2010
Inside Out**

Tony Redmond

ISBN 9780735640610

Pre-order now
This supremely organized reference packs all
the details you need to deploy and manage
your Exchange Server 2010–based system—
from the inside out. Covers SP1.

**Microsoft
Exchange Server 2010
Administrator's
Pocket Consultant**

William R. Stanek

ISBN 9780735627123

Portable and precise, this pocket-sized guide
delivers ready answers for the day-to-day
administration of Exchange Server 2010.

**Microsoft®
Press**

Windows Server 2008—
Resources for Administrators

Windows Server® 2008 Administrator's Companion

Charlie Russel and Sharon Crawford

ISBN 9780735625051

Your comprehensive, one-volume guide to deployment, administration, and support. Delve into core system capabilities and administration topics, including Active Directory®, security issues, disaster planning/recovery, interoperability, IIS 7.0, virtualization, clustering, and performance tuning.

Windows Server 2008 Administrator's Pocket Consultant, Second Edition

William R. Stanek

ISBN 9780735627116

Portable and precise—with the focused information you need for administering server roles, Active Directory, user/group accounts, rights and permissions, file-system management, TCP/IP, DHCP, DNS, printers, network performance, backup, and restoration.

Windows Server 2008 Resource Kit

Microsoft MVPs with Microsoft Windows Server Team

ISBN 9780735623613

Six volumes! Your definitive resource for deployment and operations—from the experts who know the technology best. Get in-depth technical information on Active Directory, Windows PowerShell® scripting, advanced administration, networking and network access protection, security administration, IIS, and more—plus an essential toolkit of resources on CD.

Internet Information Services (IIS) 7.0 Administrator's Pocket Consultant

William R. Stanek

ISBN 9780735623644

This pocket-sized guide delivers immediate answers for administering IIS 7.0. Topics include customizing installation; configuration and XML schema; application management; user access and security; Web sites, directories, and content; and performance, backup, and recovery.

Windows PowerShell 2.0 Administrator's Pocket Consultant

William R. Stanek

ISBN 9780735625952

The practical, portable guide to using *cmdlets* and scripts to automate everyday system administration—including configuring server roles, services, features, and security settings; managing TCP/IP networking; monitoring and tuning performance; and other essential tasks.

ALSO SEE

Windows PowerShell 2.0 Best Practices
ISBN 9780735626461

Windows® Administration Resource Kit: Productivity Solutions for IT Professionals
ISBN 9780735624313

Windows Server 2008 Hyper-V™ Resource Kit
ISBN 9780735625174

Windows Server 2008 Security Resource Kit
ISBN 9780735625044

microsoft.com/mspress

System Requirements

The exercises in this training kit require a minimum of four servers or virtual machines running Windows Server 2008 R2 Enterprise edition. Instructions for configuring all computers used for the practice labs are provided in the appendix. You need access to either the full or an evaluation version of Exchange Server 2010 to be able to perform the practice exercises in this book.

You can complete almost all practice exercises in this book using virtual machines rather than real hardware. The minimum and recommended hardware requirements for Exchange Server 2010 are listed below.

Hardware Requirements

Each separate server should have the following minimum hardware configuration:

- X64 architecture–based computer with either Intel 64 architecture or AMD processor that supports AMD64 platform
- 4 GB (though possible to perform labs on virtual machines that have each been assigned 2 GB RAM)
- 1.2 GB on the volume where Exchange is installed
- 800 × 600 pixels or higher

If you intend to implement all virtual machines on the same computer (recommended), a higher specification will enhance your user experience. In particular a computer with 8 GB RAM and 100 GB available disk space can host all the virtual machines specified for all the practice exercises in this book if each virtual machine is configured with 2 GB of RAM. No single lab exercise in this book requires more than three computers to be active at any one time.

Software Requirements

To use the companion CD, you need a computer running Windows 7, Windows Vista, or Windows XP. The computer must meet the following minimum requirements:

- 1 GHz 32-bit (x86) or 64-bit (x64) processor (depending on the minimum requirements of the operating system)
- 1 GB of system memory (depending on the minimum requirements of the operating system)
- A hard-disk partition with at least 700 MB of available space
- A monitor capable of at least 800 × 600 display resolution
- A keyboard

- A mouse or other pointing device
- An optical drive capable of reading CDs

The computer must also have the following software:

- A Web browser, such as Windows Internet Explorer
- An application that can display PDF files, such as Adobe Reader, which can be downloaded at *http://www.adobe.com/reader*

These requirements support your use of the companion CD. To perform the practice exercises in this training kit, you might require additional hardware or software. See the Introduction to the book for detailed hardware requirements.

What do you think of this book?

We want to hear from you!

To participate in a brief online survey, please visit:

microsoft.com/learning/booksurvey

Tell us how well this book meets your needs—what works effectively, and what we can do better. Your feedback will help us continually improve our books and learning resources for you.

Thank you in advance for your input!

Microsoft®
Press

Stay in touch!

To subscribe to the *Microsoft Press*® *Book Connection Newsletter*—for news on upcoming books, events, and special offers—please visit:

microsoft.com/learning/books/newsletter